MANAGERS VS. OWNERS

THE
RUFFIN SERIES IN BUSINESS ETHICS
R. Edward Freeman, *Editor*

Managers vs. Owners

The Struggle for Corporate Control in American Democracy

Allen Kaufman

Lawrence Zacharias

Marvin Karson

New York   Oxford
OXFORD UNIVERSITY PRESS   1995

Oxford University Press

Oxford   New York
Athens   Auckland   Bangkok   Bombay
Calcutta   Cape Town   Dar es Salaam   Delhi
Florence   Hong Kong   Istanbul   Karachi
Kuala Lumpur   Madras   Madrid   Melbourne
Mexico City   Nairobi   Paris   Singapore
Taipei   Tokyo   Toronto

and associated companies in
Berlin   Ibadan

Copyright © 1995 by Oxford University Press, Inc.

Published by Oxford University Press, Inc.
200 Madison Avenue, New York, New York 10016

Oxford is a registered trademark of Oxford University Press

Library of Congress Cataloging-in-Publication Data
Kaufman, Allen, 1947–
Managers vs. owners: the struggle for corporate control in
American democracy / Allen Kaufman, Lawrence Zacharias, Marvin Karson.
p.   cm.—(The Ruffin series in business management)
Includes bibliographical references and index.
ISBN 0-19-508817-4
1. Social responsibility of business—United States—History—20th century.
2. Business ethics—United States—History—20th century.
3. Management—Social aspects—United States—History—20th century.
4. Business and politics—United States—History—20th century.
5. Political action committees—United States—History—20th century.
I. Zacharias, Lawrence.
II. Karson, Marvin J. (Marvin Jay), 1937   .
III. Title.
IV. Series.
HD60.5.U5K38   1995
658.4'08—dc20   94-18603

1 3 7 9 8 6 4 2

Printed in the United States of America
on acid-free paper

FOREWORD

The theory and practice of business have developed along essentially antihistorical lines. Rare is the executive who looks to history for insight into how to manage in a changing world. And the disciplines of business, from economics to ethics, are mostly concerned with the latest technique and the most recent case study. The appetite for novelty seems unquenchable, be it business process engineering, excellence, total quality management, or becoming customer driven. Even though commerce is as ancient as humans themselves, there are no readily available lists of the great business thinkers of all times. Indeed the popular press is filled with books on what Lincoln, or Ghandi, or Lao Tzu would say about modern business. Allen Kaufman, Lawrence Zacharias, and Marvin Karson aim to take a small step in a new direction.

Working in the tradition of Alfred Chandler and other business historians, Kaufman, Zacharias, and Karson try to show how many of our current conceptual and practical problems are rooted in history. In particular they examine the history of the owner-manager relationship, and situate much of the current debate on corporate governance in this history. While there is a great deal of merit in their specific argument, there is also a practical value in their method. It is only by undertaking a serious investigation of what we can learn from those who came before us that we can ever hope to create a body of knowledge worthy of the attention of both scholars and executives.

The purpose of the Ruffin Series in Business Ethics is to publish the best thinking about the role of ethics in business. In a world in which there are daily reports of questionable business practices, from financial scandals to environmental disasters, we need to step back from the fray and understand the large issues of how business and ethics are, and ought to be, connected. The books in this series are aimed at three audiences: management scholars, ethicists, and business executives. There is a growing consensus among these groups that business and ethics must be integrated as a vital part of the teaching and practice of management.

Allen Kaufman, Lawrence Zacharias, and Marvin Karson have shown us that if this integration is to be meaningful, we must pay careful attention to the lessons and conceptual frames of the past. They have given us one more thread of this rich conversation—the thread of history.

R. Edward Freeman

PREFACE

Our aim in this book is to show how discussions about the "problem of the modern corporation" informed the construction of the regulatory state in twentieth-century America. By the turn of the century, citizens and policymakers were voicing three principal concerns: first, that corporate size would result in substantial market power or monopoly; second, that corporate deep pockets would corrupt democratic electoral and legislative processes; and third, that corporate managerial autonomy would lead to managerial opportunism, irresponsibility, and the erosion of traditional private property, or ownership, values. By unpacking the discussions about the corporation and its legitimate role in a democracy, we describe how constitutional values such as federalism, pluralism, and the separation of powers unfolded in response to perceptions about the large corporation's utility, or threat, as an economic and political institution.

A central part of our story is the organization of collective action in the corporation and its effect on corporate and government practices. The book traces the articulation of shared values among competing groups of corporate stakeholders, values that have eventually taken shape as broader-based or societywide political ideologies. Groups that are stakeholders in large corporations are continually in search of legitimacy—that is, coherent ideologies that enable them to organize and press their collective demands legitimately upon corporate boards, government officials (including judges), and elected policymakers.

We focus on the shared values and collective efforts of managers. We argue that corporate managers' shared interest in autonomy from political and financial controls gave rise to a professional ideology. On the one side, constitutional values surrounding private property reinforced corporate autonomy from government regulation of markets. On the other, political and economic justifications for the "separation of ownership from control" underscored managerial discretion in matters of corporate policy. The managerial ideology, in turn, served to organize corporate sector collective action on a broad variety of legal and regulatory issues. Beyond these central themes, this book also contributes to the literature in history and social science.

First, we provide an interpretive history of the debates that gave rise to the various political and regulatory strategies of interest groups with stakes in large, publicly held corporations—for example, managers, investors, bankers, unions, state governments, and federal regulators. Our book bridges and synthesizes the writing on the modern corporation in several disciplines, including law and legal history, economics, business and business history, philosophy and business ethics, and political science and theory.

Second, we account for the political position of management as a profession. In this respect we provide a framework for understanding the bases of managerial collective action and elaborate on the role of professional ideology in reconciling corporate power with constitutional democracy. We offer not only historical case studies of managerial collective action, but also statistical analyses of managerial political action to support our thesis.

Third, we contribute to an understanding of New Deal and postwar regulation. We argue, for instance, that the crystallization of the federal regulatory structure during FDR's "second New Deal" reflected the emergent managerial ideology. Generally speaking, accounts of the New Deal and the resulting postwar regulatory structures have emphasized party politics, geographic coalitions, and traditional economic interests, such as business and labor. More particularly, historians attribute the distinctive decentralized organization of postwar regulation to the fragmented, pluralistic nature of interest group politics that prevailed through the Great Depression and World War II. We offer an alternative, somewhat more cohesive perspective. Namely, the shape of federal regulation can, in large part, be understood through the legal and policy debates surrounding the modern corporation. Those debates gave rise to the observation that the managerial profession itself depended on two prerequisites, corporate autonomy and managerial control. In this respect, decentralized regulation preserved corporate autonomy and enhanced managerial control. Moreover, those prerequisites, in turn, became the central tenets of an emergent professional ideology that best explains broad-based regulatory strategies and collective political action on the part of large corporations during the postwar era.

Finally, we suggest how the postwar order has been changing in recent years, both through the erosion of the management profession's ideological bases and through practical changes in corporate management. In recent years, for instance, investors organized by financial institutions and financial entrepreneurs appear to have won concessions and redistributions from the earlier status quo. Meanwhile, attempts to organize communities, workers, and consumers have foundered, except to the extent that managers have been able to resist institutional financial control.

We conclude by examining recent developments in corporate restructuring and managerial practice, and ask what their implications may be for the managerial profession. Will investor collective action, facilitated by the growth of institutional investors and the rise of a new generation of investment bankers, undercut future managerial alliances to secure autonomy? And if so, are there coherent alternative value configurations—that is, ideologies—that may serve to guide the management profession in its practices and in mobilizing for constructive, democratic business-government relations? In viewing the debates and shifts historically, we offer fresh insights into the profoundest current economic and political policy questions.

Durham, N.H.   A. K.
Amherst, Mass.   L. Z.
December 1994   M. K.

ACKNOWLEDGMENTS

Long-term interdisciplinary projects depend on the encouragement and support of individuals and institutions. Our collaboration on this book began some ten years ago, quite accidently. Like so many others, Allen Kaufman and Larry Zacharias lived in commuting marriages. Allen's work was at the Whittemore School of Business and Economics at UNH in Durham, N.H.; his life as father and spouse was in Amherst, Mass. In New Hampshire, Allen began working with Marvin Karson on statistical analyses of corporate PAC donations; in Amherst, he took the occasion to pursue his historical and other interests. He met Larry in Bob Griffith's faculty seminar on corporatism at the UMass Institute for the Advanced Study of the Humanities in 1983–1984. Larry was then commuting between the UMass School of Management in Amherst and family life in Washington, D.C. The corporatism seminar led to further discussions. Bonducci's Cafe, which afforded Allen a conversational haven in Amherst when family responsibilities permitted, soon became the meeting place of choice where we initially floated and bandied about the questions that grew into this book. As discussions transformed into writing, our venue shifted to the Amherst College computer center.

Eventually, Allen's two sets of conversations, with Marvin on one hand and Larry on the other, blended together. Economists might say that the three saw a way to appropriate the benefits of our informal network; a social historian might argue that Allen was seeking to meld the two dialogues in which he found himself, to bridge his homes.

At any rate, the resulting project had to accommodate more than one way of talking about the corporation and so we tended to ignore the boundaries that generally identify studies of the modern corporation and American democracy by discipline. Our disrespect for disciplinary convention was rooted logically in our backgrounds: Allen had earned a doctorate in American intellectual history before he moved over to management; Larry had been trained and practiced as a lawyer before he pursued his interest in legal and business history; and Marvin had studied operations research before he became professor of statistics.

From the outset Marvin Karson played a senior role. He warned that without a disciplinary or ideological base the project would have to foster its own audience. We quickly appreciated Marvin's point when potential colleagues to our right and left began chiding us. Few of our readers were able to disassociate analytic forms from conventional empirical expectations. Public choice theorists congratulated us on appreciating their analytic contributions, but resisted our conclusions, for instance that managers acted collectively over long periods of time for consistent political gains or that industrial democracy could produce social utilities. Institutional and theoretical marxists resisted our theoretical approach, with its reliance on microeconomics and collective action theory, and so discounted our empirical results even though our conclusions about political rivalry and democracy's tilts coincided with theirs.

There were exceptions, however, and they became the audience who kept the project going. While studying management at MIT, Mel Horwitch, Harvey Sapolsky, and Gordon Walker encouraged Allen to continue on with the project. Edwin Epstein delighted in our provocations and encouraged us throughout. So too did Lee Preston, James Post, John Mahon, and Bill Frederick. These scholars introduced us to the Academy of Management Division on Social Issues Management (SIM), where we found others who shared our intellectual concerns. Alfred Marcus, Ian Maitland, and Barry Mitnick deserve particular thanks, but we also owe much to SIM's members who provided us with our first intellectual forum.

Historians also gave us their attention. Bob Griffith was supportive and other members of the corporatism seminar, notably Leonard Rapping and Jim Crotty, kept us engaged. Eventually, we found a larger receptive audience among historians affiliated with the Business History Conference. Throughout our project Bill Becker provided criticism that kept our manuscript focused. Richard Sylla, George Smity, James Livingston, and Paul Miranti offered useful commentaries and helped ease our way in this circle of business historians. So too did the *Business History Review,* which has published two articles drawn from the manuscript.

The Law and Society Association also provided a logical forum for interdisciplinary scholarship and over the years a number of lawyers and legal historians gave us support, through their instruction, interest, and feedback. Marc Linder has consistently afforded us the benefits of his wisdom. Morty Horwitz, whose seminar on the legal history of the corporation in 1982 provided Larry with a formal introduction to the literature, has been generous with his encouragement, guidance, and friendship. We are grateful also to Tom Hazen, Bill Bratton, Donald Ritchie, Maxwell Bloomfield, Bill Nelson, and Dave Millon for reading, commenting on, and encouraging at various times the work that grew out of this collaboration.

The continued opportunity to find our audiences would not have materialized without the support we received from colleagues and administrators in home institutions.

At UMass, the Institute for the Advanced Study of the Humanities, under the aegis of Jules Chametzky, invited us to join Bob Griffith's seminar and two years later enabled Larry to offer a faculty seminar on the intellectual history of the corporation. The Graduate Research Council also made available a Faculty Research Grant to examine the uses of unfairness in New Deal legislation. The University Library reference staff, whose morale has somehow withstood the siege of state budget cuts over the years, answered impossible questions and found unknown treasures. Among supportive colleagues, we have only space to mention the obvious. The late Leonard Rapping, always the iconoclast, set high standards for us and a wonderful example of how unorthodox methods may produce truly important results. Sid Sufrin remains a source of wisdom and good counsel, and he together with Linda Smircich and Marta Calas regularly spoke out on the importance of this research. Mark Kesselman also found time during his weekend stays in Amherst to talk with us about the manuscript. The deans of the School of Management, Harry Allan, George Spiro, and Tom O'Brien, not only helped smooth the way for us to do this work, but set a tone for the School that featured interdisciplinary and humanistic scholarship. Barbara Morgan's helpfulness was unflagging. Several students, including Andrew Brown, Greg Field, Chuck Horvath, Susan McKenna, Ali Mir, Glaudine MtShali, and Anshu Prasad, helped with the research or contributed in other ways.

The UNH's Whittemore School of Business and Economics continually gave us both moral and financial support. Dean Dwight Ladd and the late Robert Barlow established a pattern for the school's generosity. They insisted that WSBE students take a course on business ethics and they supported the research that went into shaping this course. The support continued when Lyndon Goodridge took over as dean. The faculty too watched our work closely. Jeff Sohl, Fred Kaen, and Jim Horrigan had much to do in shaping our thinking on corporate political action and on financial oversight. The University of New Hampshire Central University Fund regularly funded our research proposals and Faye Rubin did much to help us assemble our original data base.

   The National Science Foundation provided an early grant that
paired Allen Kaufman with Dan Clawson on a Corporate Pacs' project. In working with Dan, Allen gained insights into the basic issues
regarding corporate power and political corruption. Jerry Him-
melstein deserves a special thanks for sponsoring Allen as a fellow
at Amherst College where Allen worked with Larry to bring the
manuscript into form. Allen revised the manuscript as a research
fellow at the Kennedy School's Center for Business and Government
and he owes a special thanks to John Dunlop and John White, who
alternated as director of the Center during Allen's residency there.
While at the Center, Robert Glauber provided invaluable insider information on bank reform and offered criticisms that certainly improved the manuscript even if errors still remain.
   Lastly, we have some special debts. Ernie Englander played an especially important role. He commented on various drafts and actually contributed to the research for the chapter on Kohlberg, Kravis,
and Roberts. The manuscript itself could not have come to comple-
tion if Carol True had not devoted so much time and attention to
the project. Adele Wick read the entire manuscript and offered
guidelines for winnowing the manuscript into its current concise
format.
   As we noted, most of the writing took place in the Amherst College computer lab, a beautiful, congenial, and hospitable setting for
collaboration. We are grateful to Betty Steele (now Romer) for
allowing us to use the lab as guests. Lewis Bateman of the University
of North Carolina Press provided encouragement during the initial
stages of this project and an anonymous reviewer who carefully read
the manuscript for that press offered thoughtful suggestions. Our
thanks go to the editors at Oxford University Press, in particular
Herb Addison, who shepherded the project through its final stages.
Finally, special thanks go to Doris Sommer, who advised us on how
to shape the manuscript and provided moral support throughout
the project; in this latter regard, we also are indebted to Cathy
Shoen and Paula Karson for continuing to meet life's demands as
this project wound its irregular course toward conclusion.

CONTENTS

MANAGERS VS. OWNERS

I
THE RULES

1
Introduction

America's constitution rests on the liberal premises that voluntary association enhances liberty and that democracy and rule by law ensure a well-ordered society. Some see democracy as merely protecting liberty by holding public officials electorally accountable, whereas others believe it also cultivates liberty by developing enlightened citizens. Both sides, however, agree that public office should not be the primary site for exercising freedom, because of the public realm's monopoly on law enforcement and its potential for abuse.

From the start, American legal and political theorists viewed the market as both liberty's principal arena and an important supplement to democratic politics. By separating the private from the public sphere, the market created a space in which individuals were free from government interference. But the modern corporation of the late nineteenth century raised doubts about the market's service to politics. By concentrating wealth, the corporation ended the individual's direct ownership, or control, of productive property and created relationships of economic and political dependency in its stead. Both its scale and its complexity made investor oversight seem improbable, but trusting management to subordinate its selfish, narrowly defined interests to the firm's stakeholders seemed problematic as well. Even after World War II, when students of the large firm were praising its economic effectiveness and management's technical competence, similar concerns persisted because managers still lacked a coherent claim to legitimacy. These lingering doubts have informed much of the recent scholarly defense of the modern corporation.

Edward Mason formulated the problem for the post–World War II generation in his introduction to *The Corporation in Modern Society:* America is a "society of large corporations . . . [whose] management is in the hands of a few thousand men. Who selected these men, if

3

not to rule over us, at least to exercise vast authority, and to whom
are they responsible?"[1] Managerial authority, he continued, has two
components: dedication to scientific standards of efficiency that lead
to meritocratic career paths and bureaucratic hierarchies, and responsibility for social equity, since administrative hierarchies appear
to have displaced the market as society's basic distributive mechanism. In his judgment, a satisfying account of these components
would yield a definition of "professional" management that could
ease misgivings over the privilege of its position.

Since Mason wrote his essay, many scholars have studied the functional and technical dimensions of management. Through detailed
historical studies or theoretical considerations of economic determinants, they have concluded that firms come into being to reduce
transaction costs and take advantage of economies of scale and
scope. Accordingly, firms review management performance primarily by means of market criteria, and only the most effective and
trustworthy ostensibly receive promotions.

Meanwhile, the public dimension in Mason's definition, has received relatively short shrift, and so we propose to address this deficit by posing questions that are not just economic but also legal and
political in nature. How, for example, did the large firm, controlled
by a professional managerial staff, gain constitutional acceptance in
the eyes of public officials? How did legal doctrine reconcile the reality of the modern corporation with broad constitutional norms based
on individual persons and designed to balance minority and majority
interests, public and private spheres? On the other side, how did
managers join together to help fashion legal guidelines to define and
limit their own authority and privilege? In doing so, how did they
learn to resolve (or at least temporarily suppress) the economic competition that divided them and find solutions to the coordination
problems that complicate any form of voluntary collective action?

Teachers of management will find these questions familiar. Since
1967, accredited business schools have been expected to offer
courses that explore the complicated interactions among business,
government, and society.[2] These courses engage prospective managers in resolving problems concerning the large firm's role in a democratic society and management's professional duty to ensure compat-
ibility between the corporate sector's interests and those of
majoritarian rule. They also teach managers how to influence the
regulatory process through electoral campaigns, advocacy advertising, lobbying, judicial review, and so on.

But the questions also involve politics in a broader sense. How
should we define democratic processes? How should we balance de-

mands for liberty with those for equality? How do we determine a just distribution of social wealth? And inside the firm, how do we select competing "goods" among corporate financial goals and social objectives?

Although business, government, and society courses may cover similar topics, instructors approach the material from the perspectives they have developed during their training in a variety of fields, including economics, law, ethics and history. Because two of us share a discipline base in history, we approach these questions from this vantage point. We do so, however, in a way that differs from that of traditional business historians, who, influenced greatly by Alfred D. Chandler, customarily detail how managers developed firm-specific strategies and organizational structures for competing in the marketplace.[3] Other historians have extended Chandler's insights by studying firms as they interact with government, but they maintain his emphasis on the firm and treat these interactions in purely instrumental terms. The questions then become, first, how government regulations restrain managers and, second, how managers respond politically and economically to offset these constraints. Although these studies have contributed enormously to our understanding of the dynamics between business and government, in the main they have neglected the field of managerial collective action and have resolutely refused to discuss normative issues in any way whatsoever.

We accordingly began to look for supplements to research in the school or spirit of Chandler and found them largely in the tradition of "corporate liberalism."[4] Although writers in this tradition disagree on many issues, most contentiously over whether or not the large firm has detracted from democracy, they share a strong commitment to understanding the interactions between interests and norms, markets and rules of law. They tend to explore the contributions not only of Chandler but also of pluralists who focus on public-policy debates. In probing the democratic issues raised in regulatory struggles, they also treat intellectual discourse on law, administration, and economics as more than mere ideological ammunition. We share these presumptions.

Ellis Hawley's *The New Deal and the Problem of Monopoly* (1966) has, for years, been the exemplary text in corporate liberalism.[5] More recently, Martin Sklar's *The Corporate Reconstruction of American Capitalism* (1988) has been the standard for understanding how social movements responding to the rise of the modern corporation reshaped democratic life.[6] Sklar attends to the legal and political controversies that accompanied the shift from proprietary to corporate organization, and we sustain that attention.

But we have changed significantly the vocabulary that Sklar employs, from one that speaks of "classes" to one that speaks of "groups." In altering the terminology in this way, we do not intend to imply that "classes" no longer exist in America. On the contrary, we share the belief that class has always been at the center of American political discourse. Democracy's success appeared for a time to depend on avoiding the kind of class antagonisms that plagued Europe. One of us has even written about how the Civil War confronted "classist" slavery with free and independent labor.[7] And when the large corporaton appeared on the scene, it clearly challenged the Republican Party's promise of industrialization without a working class.

If the corporation shattered that myth, it offered a modern avenue for reconciling class with democratic rule. The corporation demanded a complicated network of new opportunities, a network that could include the dispossessed farmer and the de-skilled worker. For this reason, we assert that its rise has made anachronistic the concept of class that depends critically on the amassing of tangible assets that are then passed down from generation to generation. Huge fortunes assuredly still exist, and descendants still inherit them. But in the main, individual wealth now takes the form of paper assets. This change in portfolio, if you will, dilutes the associated economic power. Mutual funds and even equity holdings in single corporations trade in markets that are markedly "thick."

We also part company with the "class" of corporate liberalism in another sense: We move from concepts of "entity" to those of "process." Rather than assuming fixed and distinct forms, we study formation and simultaneity. This orientation we borrowed from the microeconomics of collective action, bargaining, and social choice.

"Group as entity" challenged the individual person's sociological relevance in the late nineteenth and early twentieth centuries and supported socialist and other collectivist arguments for radical political reform. Constitutional theorists have long addressed the challenge to "reduce as much as possible . . . the coercion of some by others," as Friedrich von Hayek so distinctively put it.[8] But as "class" yields to "group" and "group as entity" yields to "group as process," the social divisions that once seemed so threatening to democracy now appear as just one more form of competition that undercuts the more serious problem of monopoly coercion.

Our shift in vocabulary helps us not only emphasize the process of forming voluntary associations to pursue individual ends but also communicate successfully with students and teachers in business schools by adopting the analytic categories they favor. Narrative is rarely in their number; it is usually summarily dismissed as an anecdotal form at best inviting further study in accordance with more rigorous scientific methods. In this book, collective action theory helps us distill the themes of our research. Its microeconomics delineate the conditions necessary to solve problems of cooperation. But because the variables are multiple, with some effects counteracting others, economics often offers more mathematical indeterminancy of the "on the one hand, on the other" sort than concrete solutions. Assessing the relative weights of the variables requires historical studies of how different groups have in fact successfully or unsuccessfully sought to coordinate ther collective enterprise. We provide these studies as well.

The first part of our discussion concerns debates over broad constitutional issues involving the modern corporation and its effects on American democratic life. We examine how the regulatory state tried to reconcile the existence of large firms and their control groups with traditional views that a decentralized economy preserves liberty and that powerful minorities disrupt majority preferences. We also study how the emergence of large firms forced the federal government to create regulations with a national reach and how the law provided a vocabulary to describe management as a semipublic profession.The second part of our discussion continues the story from management's vantage point and considers how managers have responded to the system by forming a variety of associations to further their ambitions. In the rhetoric of collective-action theory, first we discuss the "rules" that persons or groups agree to follow in pursuing gain through interaction, and then we identify regulations that support managerial control as the "public good" that individual managers desire enough to band together to achieve.

Chapter by chapter, the book reads as follows: Chapter 2 begins our story with a review of the role of private property in the original vision of America's constitutional order, and Chapter 3 details the shift from instrumental to developmental concepts of property. Chapter 4 examines Adolf A. Berle and Gardiner Means's great work, *The Modern Corporation and Private Property*, which summarizes the new attitude toward corporate regulation by identifying the alternative approaches of "trust" and "contract."

With the groundwork now laid, Chapters 5 and 6 show how this classification of trust and contract led to opposing regulatory approaches in the postwar period, with a transition in rule making from government oversight of managerial discretion through social regulations to private-market regulation of the firm through contract. Chapter 7 reviews the debates on the potentially corrupting political powers of corporations and the postwar discussions of the benefits of pluralism and process in restraining them. The result was substantial deregulation justified by emphasizing the electorate's ability to make its own decisions as long as the flow of information was both free and abundant.

From Chapter 8 onward, the story shifts from the general rules that shaped managerial control to the processes by which managers took advantage of opportunities both inside and outside their own firms to secure their victory over rival candidates for this position. Chapter 8 observes the sense of professional identity that managers acquired. Together with Chapter 9, it looks at how managers' interactions and confrontations with both the state and their contractual stakeholders helped them develop corporationwide conventions, associations, and an ideology that claimed managers to be democracy's modern stewards. Chapter 9 also adds detail on how managers mobilized politically in the late 1970s and 1980s, allying with conservatives to ensure that public policy reinforced their discretion but still disagreeing on issues of tax policy and control.

Chapter 10 looks a bit to the future with a case study of the takeover firm of Kohlberg, Kravis, and Roberts (KKR). The depth of our investigation into the dealings of one particular firm distinguishes this chapter from the rest, and we justify the departure by suggesting that KKR has provided an innovative organizational alternative to the managerially controlled corporation. KKR has done so by creating an "investor association" that solves many of the collective-action and agency problems that have recently plagued large institutional investors in their dealings with corporate organization.

Chapter 11 gathers up the themes of the narrative into an economic model of managerial collective behavior. In elaborating the model, we summarize collective-action theory and discuss how concepts in this theory provided themes for our narrative. The model itself recognizes that the privileges that corporate control bestows on managers induce them to cooperate politically, but the model still discerns their fractious makeup and so their inability to control the polity. By testing the model with data from political action committees' (PAC) contributions from 1980 to 1986, we corroborate our assertion that corporations simultaneously fragment and cohere over political issues.

The brief afterword foresakes our neutral approach to corporate history to exhort the makers of corporate history (as well as its students and readers) to view their firms in a developmental way, with an emphasis on participation and a leaning toward equality. This, we believe, will advance both equity and efficiency as the twentieth century yields to the twenty-first.

2

Constitutional Acceptance of the Business Corporation: From State to Federal Regulation

To understand how regulatory contests over corporate control and participation in national government gave managers a collective, professional identity, we shall first review the constitutional themes that underlie these confrontations.

At the turn of the twentieth century, lawyers and policymakers engaged in a debate on the nature of the corporation by trying to define the "corporate (or group) personality." That "great" debate focused the national attention on the emergence of the large, modern corporation in American life and synthesized, for the first time, questions about the older values of liberal democracy through a different lens, namely, the place of the large corporation in constitutional law. In this regard, lawyers and policymakers reconsidered some fundamental aspects of the nation's constitution, including the meaning of private property, individual liberty and development, federalism, interstate commerce, and American destiny—all through the lens of intensified industrial concentration and rapid nationalization of the economy.

We take an interest in that debate because it initiated the ongoing discussion that is at the heart of this book. During the corporate personality debate, intellectuals and policymakers first began to address two features of American life simultaneously: the emergence of the managerial profession and the democratic ideals, economic as well as political, that founded and shaped the profession.

In this chapter, we begin by sketching how private property and federalism (territorial pluralism) established the physical conditions for an active free citizenry and set constitutional limits on national authority. Next we shall consider the business corporation's equivocal fit into this liberal paradigm and how the large firm exacerbated the legal quandaries concerning individual rights, private property, group formation, and popular sovereignty. Indeed, once the multistate corporation dominated the economy, regulation shifted from the state to the federal level, reducing liberalism's ambiguity regarding corporate property to a conundrum between individual rights and group solidarity, between liberty and popular sovereignty.

LIBERTY, PROPERTY, AND CONSTITUTIONAL RULE

During the state and federal constitutional conventions that followed the American Revolution, the founders struggled to extrapolate governmental principles from the rhetoric of independence, democratic ideals, and human rights. In this endeavor, they shared both political values and personal experience. As men who were economically independent, commercially minded, and successful in turning acres of America's wilderness into productive private holdings, they conditioned entry into social contracts on the gains that such associations offered, compared those available under the existing "state of nature."[1] By posing constitutional rule in this manner, the revolutionary generation reinterpreted the classical idea of liberty, making it an endowment that preceded association rather than an attribute dependent on a balanced government and a virtuous citizenry. In this vision, government came into existence to benefit its citizens by securing property, providing for the common defense, and establishing a legal framework for enhanced commercial activity. More government would threaten liberty itself; history had taught the founders that the state was more likely to oppress than to nurture. To limit public authority to its legitimate purposes, the founders therefore established a representative government to make public officials dependent on the citizenry; institutionalized conflicting centers of power by adopting a federal system and separating the executive, legislative, and judicial branches of government; and drew a sharp line between public authority and private rights by insisting on the right to property and due process.

Private property, then, safeguarded liberty. In establishing a basis for separating the private from the public sphere, property erected a barrier against governmental actions that diminished individual freedoms. This vocabulary of the "public" versus the "private" formed the essential elements for legal reasoning that would develop and endure over the next two centuries.

FEDERALISM AND TERRITORIAL PLURALISM

Incorporating this basic vocabulary into a written document, of course, proceeded with much raucous discord. Historians have recounted the conflicts between the Federalists, who favored more centralization, and the Antifederalists, who favored less. The Federalists carried the day and won more centralization than the Antifederalists wanted. Still, the framers of the Constitution conceived of the nation as a unity of sovereign states, each of which had jurisdiction over disputes concerning individual rights from which the national government was excluded. That is, the Constitution reserved powers for the state governments to provide for the morals, health, safety, and welfare of their citizens.

These "police powers," as they came to be known, permitted the state governments to act in certain ways without fear of federal intervention, and the union's diverse composition protected citizens against abusive state majorities. By "voting with their feet," citizens could migrate from less desirable states to those with political and economic packages more to their liking.[2] The federal government preserved the citizen's freedom to move, and in fact, as Congress opened up vast territories for settlement, the Supreme Court eventually inserted into the Constitution the right to travel.

INSTRUMENTAL VERSUS DEVELOPMENTAL PROPERTY RIGHTS

Another set of disagreements emerged after the Constitution was ratified when the nation recognized that property and its effects on personality, citizenship, and economic growth were open to interpretation. Although earlier historians of the period identified the quarreling camps by their leading advocates, Hamilton and Jefferson or as "libertarians" and "egalitarians," more recent writing in political philosophy recasts them abstractly as "instrumentalists" and "developmentalists."[3] This discord also has had ramifications for the legal status of corporations, a background condition or presumptive value that legal logicians have had to weave into (or hide within) their technical exercises. Periodically, we return to the elusive values of liberty and equality, but the reader should not anticipate the existence of any simple correspondence between value presumptions and technical, legal argumentation. Indeed, values and technical logic often combine in the most surprising ways.

The debates over property and democratic values began with a shared recognition of the stages in commercial development: In the early and rude stage, land was abundant relative to labor, but as the economy matured, land became relatively scarce. Jeffersonians believed the first stage to be more supportive of democratic values than the second. They prized the wide distribution of productive property which would mitigate economic and social differences and foster a civic sense of mutuality; they feared that as all the land was settled and the country industrialized, inequalities in resource ownership and access would destroy self-sufficiency and create conflicts between those with property and those without. In response, the Jeffersonians called for westward expansion and the opening of foreign markets to absorb the agricultural surplus, and they refrained from policies that encouraged manufacturing. In contrast, Hamilton and his associates looked forward to the advanced stage: They saw increased wealth as the instrument for resolving distributive conflicts and advocated both domestic policies and tariffs designed to stimulate manufacturing.

These contrary visions continued well into the late nineteenth and early twentieth centuries. Long after the United States had lost its youthfulness, heirs to the Jeffersonian vision replaced their agrarian and organic rhetoric with a language of "development" more suitable to the industrial age. Those who looked back to the Hamiltonian tradition treated property as an "instrument" for enhancing wealth and argued that government should protect liberty rather than substantive equality. But modern Jeffersonians now reminded their opponents that the virtues of property ownership were intimately linked to its oversight: Management shaped character, particularly in respect to prudence, foresight, and rationality. While conceding that property rights spurred economic development and that modern technology required large capital sums, they worried about massive industrial organizations that might provide labor with decent wages but also preclude them from developing responsible personality traits. Modern-day Jeffersonians asked whether or not such workers could form independent political judgments. If they could not, would the consequences not disable democracy?

Through questions like these, the traditional defenders of America's agrarian order moved intellectually into the modern machine age by becoming advocates of industrial democracy. They insisted that liberty was meaningless for the many persons whose limited property ownership also limited their life choices. These debates make up much of the next chapter's subject matter. Here our focus remains on the business corporation's uneasy relationship to individual liberty, private property, and federalism. As the large corporation forged a national economy, its contradictory constitutional position provoked a doctrinal crisis over sovereignty. Let us start with the technical legal reasoning about the large corporation: Was it to be understood as part of the natural order of individual endeavor, beyond the state government's reach, or as an artificial creation, dependent on the public will and subject to its authority?

THE CORPORATION: NATURAL OR ARTIFICIAL, PRIVATE OR PUBLIC?

Before independence, subjects successfully petitioned the Crown to grant corporate charters for a broad variety of social purposes, including economic development and colonial settlements like Connecticut and New York City. The states assumed this function after independence. Because it was implicitly condoned by the federal Constitution, especially through the Tenth Amendment,[4] corporate chartering power bolstered states' rights and American federalism from the very start.

The legal community, however, could not easily resolve questions about the chartering power itself. To what extent did citizens have innate rights to associate in the corporate form, and to what extent did state legislatures have the power to curb those associations or, once they had licensed them, to participate in revising corporate charters? As nineteenth-century constitutional thought evolved, the distinction between private and public spheres sharpened, relegating some activities to private life and others to public.[5] The corporation, however, defied ready classification. On the one hand, it seemed subject to public scrutiny because its officers derived charter powers from the state legislature's "implied and necessary" regulatory powers under the state constitution.[6] On the other hand, private citizens formed corporations through their right to associate and to hold private property; in this regard, constitutional thought tended to guard corporations against the reach of public officials.[7]

Over time the courts seemed to oscillate between the two views. Near the end of the nineteenth century, however, just at the time the modern interstate corporation was coming into view, the Supreme Court was primarily focused on keeping corporate development from state officials' control. In this context a new *economic* understanding of the corporation, as a relatively autonomous engine of industrialization and national growth, combined with constitutional or *political* ideas about private property, giving rise to the most privacy-favoring approach to the corporation—the "natural-entity" theory.[8]

The Shift from Specific to General Incorporation

Before midcentury, state legislatures kept close control over incorporation and awarded charters on an individual or special basis.[9] Although the states may have implicitly adopted policies of unrestricted incorporation early on, the charters themselves continued to reflect explicit exchanges of state resources, such as public lands or waters and powers of eminent domain, in return for private investments.[10] Many therefore feared legislative corruption and corporate privileging.[11] In drawing attention to economic disparity, such abuses of charter power moved critics to call for reforms in the name of democracy and individual liberty.[12]

Corporate leaders, of course, asserted that the benefits of their activities to society as a whole outweighed any alleged costs of increased inequality among individuals. They argued further that their prominent role in improving society materially suited them to look after the welfare of those who fell under the aegis of their power, above all, employees and communities.[13] Yet by midcentury, increasing industrial competition had begun to erode the sort of corporate paternalism under which special charters and privileges had earlier won political favor.[14] Although there were exceptions (corporations in fields that tended toward a natural monopoly, such as railroads and utilities, prompted special legislation to limit their economic power and to ensure their responsiveness to community and consumer demand), for the most part, potential competitors impressed on legislatures the advantages of freeing access to the corporate apparatus.[15] Changes in the polity that began with Jacksonianism, including extensions of suffrage and the maturing of party politics, aided these ascending capitalists in pressuring state legislatures to eliminate special privileges by enacting general incorporation laws. These laws succeeded because they tended to combine the instrumentalist arguments concerning the market's economic power with the developmentalist/egalitarian impulse to make corporate property widely accessible to the states' citizenry.

The Transition from State to Federal Regulation

A high point in the recognition of the states' power over corporations occurred around the time of Chief Justice Roger B. Taney's *Charles River Bridge* decision in 1837. Until then, constitutional chal-

lenges to state regulation of corporate powers had usually evoked
the "contract clause."[16] The Supreme Court's *Dartmouth College* decision in 1819 had initially read into the state's obligation to uphold
contracts an obligation not to impair its charter obligations to *private*
corporations.[17] Indeed, the *Dartmouth* case rendered the distinction
between private and public corporations salient for constitutional
purposes. Nevertheless, the Supreme Court did not press the distinction very far; for as Chief Justice John Marshall's opinion for the
Court in *Dartmouth* noted, corporations were themselves legal fictions
or creatures of the state, and the states, in giving life to a corporation, might well reserve the power to alter subsequently the corporation's powers in the original terms of its charter. By 1837, Marshall's successor, Taney, could hold that states implicitly reserved at
least a limited power to amend corporate charters retroactively in
all cases.

Over the next forty years, however, the idea that state legislatures
gave life to the artificial corporate creatures receded. State legislatures throughout the young nation moved from granting special
charters to selected groups to adopting general incorporation laws.
These laws not only cleared the way for all businessmen to use the
corporate machinery, but they also freed investors and promoters to
tinker with the corporate machinery itself, which in turn led to a
series of financial and managerial innovations.[18] In this way, the
states expected to promote competition both among industrial entrepreneurs, bankers, and investors as they formed corporate alliances
and among established corporations, by emphasizing the dynamic
nature of corporate governance and purpose. Initiated during the
acme of competitive individualism in America, these statutes ironically helped propel the nation into an era of association, consolidation, and bureaucratization.[19]

More than any constitutional provision, the statutes also tended to
compromise the legislatures' power to control corporate privilege.[20]
As technological change created economies of scale and widened
markets, corporate systems tended to ignore state boundaries and
become more national in scope, highlighting the inadequacies not
only of state charters but also of the Constitution itself with respect
to corporate issues. As long as corporations had been viewed as joint
public and private enterprises, haggling over powers and benefits
remained a matter of charter interpretation, and the states reserved
the right to the final word. However, the enactment of general incorporation statutes obscured the public's contribution and dissolved
the image of a corporation as a venture both public and private.
General incorporation also motivated businesses to claim new federal
constitutional privileges.

To remain sovereign over their territories, the states now had to discover alternative constitutional bases for regulating industry. After the Civil War they increasingly came to rely on "police powers." Although these reserved powers, as we noted earlier, inhered in the federal system, thereby protecting the state governments from federal intrusions,[21] their definition did not play a regular part in constitutional discourse until the latter part of the century.[22] Renewed interest followed ratification of the Fourteenth Amendment and a series of cases challenging the states' regulatory authority.[23]

Congress had ratified the Fourteenth Amendment in 1868 as part of federal efforts to bolster the social and political status of former slaves. Of the three Civil War amendments, it had the most enduring effect on the states' relationship to the federal system. By instituting national citizenship, ensuring that all citizens were guaranteed equal protection and due process regardless of state actions, the Fourteenth Amendment questioned the former application of the Bill of Rights only as a check against federal authority. Now lawyers argued with increasing success that the Fourteenth Amendment also worked to limit the states' authority in general and their police powers in particular.

The Court accordingly allowed the states to restrict individual and corporate freedoms and property rights only within "reason," a legal term with a great capacity to evolve over time.[24] It acknowledged, for example, the probity of regulating public utilities at a state level, for their creation in most instances depended on special charters or franchises granting monopoly.[25] The Court also legitimated police powers that conformed to the Court's perceptions of social norms, for instance, protective legislation seeking to preserve industrial employees' contracting rights by securing their incomes and regulating their working conditions.[26] As historian Melvin Urofsky concluded from his review of federal and state cases during the Progressive Era as a whole, the courts may have "delayed the acceptance of protective legislation, but they ultimately blocked very little of it."[27]

The *Munn v. Illinois* case, decided in 1877, set the stage for much of the ensuing debate over the legitimate reach of the states' police powers.[28] In *Munn* the Supreme Court held state price regulation to be legitimate. Speaking for the majority, Chief Justice Morrison R. Waite found business enterprise affected with a "public interest." So long as corporate charters did not expressly prohibit price controls, such regulation was accordingly an appropriate exercise of the states' regulatory powers.[29]

In his dissent, Justice Stephen J. Field countered that the lines between public power and private property must be defined more clearly, or else "the prices of everything, from a calico gown to a city

mansion, may be the subject of regulation."[30] Justice Joseph P. Bradley also dissented, writing an opinion with far-reaching implications.
In his view, the majority in *Munn* had interfered with the fundamental rights of choosing one's occupation, property, and liberty itself.[31]
Due process had previously addressed only matters of legal procedure; Bradley's new interpretation explicitly converted it to a substantive right that would allow the courts to void legislation that allegedly deprived a person of liberty or property.[32]

In general, late nineteenth-century judicial resort to interpreting
states' police powers under the Constitution helped resolve sticky
doctrinal issues still surrounding the business corporation. By replac-
ing reserved charter powers with independently conceived police
powers as the conceptual basis of the states' corporate regulations,
legislatures avoided the problem of the foreign corporation's peculiar place under state law.[33] As long as the states relied on chartering
powers to regulate home corporations, they perpetuated the idea
that corporate properties were mixed in nature, at once public and
private. But by resorting to their police powers, they distinguished
in effect between sovereign and subject, public and private, thus re-
linquishing the public's claim to corporate property in all but the
clearest instances of state grants like special franchises and monopolies. Increasingly, then, the law tended to treat large, multistate corporations as purely private undertakings.

The Supreme Court rendered its *Santa Clara* decision in just this
context of redefining state sovereignty in terms of confrontations
between private property and police powers, rather than as elaborations of the "public's interest" in corporate enterprise.[34] When the
Court took up the constitutional validity of a tax on railroads in this
case, it decided that corporate properties were subject to the equal
protection provisions of the Fourteenth Amendment and that the
states must therefore treat them just as they would the private property of ordinary "persons," including the associated owners of a business corporation. This decision, according to a leading historian of
nineteenth-century American corporation law, thus simply extended
the logic of the corporate fiction or "artificial entity" that had long
prevailed.[35] Moreover, by identifying the corporation with private
property instead of with public grants and state interests, *Santa Clara*
also came close to extinguishing whatever prior claims the public
may have made on corporate charters and properties. *Santa Clara*
insisted instead that judges treat challenges to the states' corporate
regulations under the rubric of their police powers to safeguard
property.

By extending to the corporation the due process and equal protection that the Constitution had originally intended for individual per-

sons, the Court moved a step toward converting due process to a substantive matter, much as Justice Bradley had suggested in *Munn v. Illinois*. By 1890, the Court actually took this position in a ruling against Minnesota's authority to establish railroad rates *(Chicago, Milwaukee & St. Paul Railway v. Minnesota)*. This finding gave the courts the power to review legislation on the basis of redistributive intent.[36]

Following *Santa Clara*, corporate promoters and their lawyers stimulated the "race for the bottom," as one state after another began to compete for corporate favor by lifting restrictions on corporate financing and management practices.[37] Before 1889, for example, states like Ohio typically prohibited holding companies, viewing them as leading to greater social costs from monopoly than benefits from economies of scale. However, in 1889, following a series of charter revocation suits, the New Jersey legislature modified its laws to allow the formation of holding companies in the corporate form.[38] Soon competitive pressure forced other large industrial states to follow suit by loosening up their own restrictions.[39]

The earlier form of territorial pluralism had respected majority rule in each state, tempering its harshness on individuals and minorities through guarantees of mobility.[40] By the 1890s, in contrast, legislatures in the industrial states were coming to be ruled by national (suprastate) minorities pursuing lower business costs and broader business freedoms.[41] Only the overarching authority of the federal government, with its powers under the "commerce clause," appeared able to frame and control what to citizens at the time must have appeared to be an impending, thoroughgoing disorder and fracturing of social life.[42]

The federal government during this period did become more active. The year after New Jersey deregulated holding companies, for example, Congress enacted an antitrust law to curb the pace of corporate consolidation. Initially, the Supreme Court thwarted antitrust enforcement against large industrial consolidations, but in a landmark 1904 decision that disbanded a holding company devised to consolidate formerly competing interstate railroads, the Supreme Court began to interpret Congress's "commerce clause" powers more broadly in matters relating to business corporations.[43] Moreover, although it had initially disarmed federal railroad regulation by restrictively interpreting a series of statutory amendments, the Court eventually acquiesced in Congress's broadening of the Interstate Commerce Commission's (ICC) powers after the turn of the century, first in the Hepburn Act of 1906 and later in the Mann–Elkins Act of 1910 and the Valuation Act of 1913.[44] Thus Congress and the

Court each contributed to the framing of federal control over the national economy.

Increasingly, federal agencies won the power to regulate economic matters independent of day-to-day legislative or judicial control. For example, the immigration case *U.S. v. Ju Toy* (1905) held rather broadly that courts should not second-guess federal administrative agencies with specific knowledge and expertise in their fields.[45] Congress passed new laws regulating bankruptcy, trade, and the manufacture of food and drugs—expanding the federal court system to handle the burgeoning caseloads that resulted. In so doing, legislators overcame specific objections raised by the states. They also promoted professional legal standards and economic expertise in such agencies as the ICC, the Justice Department, and the Bureau of Corporations that undercut the direct influence of interest-group politics on federal decisions.[46]

In conclusion, although the Progressive Era has long impressed historiographers as the transition from laissez-faire Court decisions like *Santa Clara* to a series of reform regulations,[47] we divide the era in two chronologically overlapping parts: the end of effective control by the states over their economies, and the start of federal sovereignty over the national economy. In this regard, the Supreme Court's work takes on a more generous spirit than that ordinarily accorded by progressive historians. In effect, the Court interposed itself to manage the transition from state to federal control. The constitutional limits it imposed on the states' sovereignty can be interpreted as a prerequisite leveling that would clear the way for the federal government's potential as an effective, alternative regulator. The search for regulatory legitimacy at this level included a deeper look at the corporate character, and to this examination we shall now turn.

BEHIND THE CENTRALIZATION OF REGULATION: THE SEARCH FOR A CORPORATE PERSONALITY

Without a clear national regulatory framework to centralize the federal system both economically and politically, writers near the turn of the century proposed various alternative approaches. On the practical side, economists debated the pros and cons of concentration.[48] Despite their contradictory political beliefs, the leading economists including John Bates Clark, Richard Ely, and Thorsten Veblen, tended to agree on the extent that profits represented efficiency and value and the extent that profits were merely redistributive and monopolistic. In the end, even the conservative Clark conceded a need for public oversight to regulate anticompetitive and "unfair" behaviors and the dislocations of price fluctuation and irregular employment.[49]

While the economists discussed practicalities, the lawyers moved a step further and debated the very nature of "group (or corporate) personality."[50] The modern corporation appeared simultaneously to decompose labor into skilled and unskilled specialization by function and to reconstitute these components through bureaucratic means into a collective enterprise, apparently acting with a single will. As economic machines on which many people were dependent for their livelihoods, the large, multistate corporation threatened older liberal notions of individualism, economic independence, and territorial pluralism.[51]

For Marxist and other socialist thinkers, this collectivist transformation appeared inevitable. It confirmed their critique of the public/private distinction as a fiction that protected capitalist interests from egalitarian, working-class redistributions. But even to less radical observers, traditional liberal assumptions about the individual's autonomy, including the capacity to own private property and contract freely, could no longer be taken for granted.

This challenge inspired a deeper look at the very nature of corporations, and the response first crystallized in the legal community in discussions about whether or not the corporation itself had a "personality." Ascriptions ranged broadly, from almost mystical, medieval accounts of communitarian commitments to functional assessments based on institutional studies and nineteenth-century insights into collective action.[52] But by the end of the century, lawyers no longer felt that they could design appropriate rules for the interests, rights, and activities of the corporation's individual members. Instead, they envisioned the corporate entity as irreducible, a thing of its own, warranting legal and constitutional recognition on its own terms.[53]

More recently, historians of the period have parsed the discussions about corporate personality into three relatively distinctive, though overlapping, positions.[54] The first position developed out of the earlier nineteenth-century case law which, as we have seen, regarded the corporation as an "artificial entity." Following the *Santa Clara* decision, questions emerged about the nature of the "corporate person": whether it had taken on something like a tangible unity—to wit, an institutionalized collectivity—or whether it was still nothing more than a fiction used to characterize the activities of individual persons associating in a business. Those who feared the destruction of the classical, liberal constitutional design—who persisted in be-

lieving, as Frederick Maitland put it, that "all that stands between
the State and the individual has but a derivative and precarious existence"—insisted that the business corporation itself could be nothing
more than an artifice and that its "personality" had to be tied inextricably to the individual private citizens who invested their properties
in the venture and continued to associate in its operations.[55]

In thus reducing the corporation to its voluntary or contractual
roots, artificial-entity theorists believed they were safeguarding the
state from capture by powerful minority influences. This strategy led
them to interpret corporate rules by analogy to partnerships, which
were defined in terms of the contracts connecting the partners as
principals and agents. But it became apparent during the two decades following *Santa Clara* that artificial-entity theory's reductionism
would not withstand technical legal counterarguments. And so theorists asked on what basis the corporation should be privileged as a
unity or entity independent of its members.

The second position, which emerged near the turn of the century,
combined the privacy features accorded to the business corporation
in the *Santa Clara* decision with the insight that corporations (along
with industrial concentration) were relatively autonomous and inevitable, or "natural," outgrowths of a modern economy. The constitutional justification for privileging corporations as natural entities or
virtual persons was somewhat obscure. Lawyers argued that the common law itself reflected a natural process and that the private corporation as an outgrowth of that process was vested with a certain
pretense to naturalness. In any case, the proponents of this
natural-entity position, including a majority of the justices on the
Supreme Court, were interested, above all, in immunizing this latest
human achievement in economic development (i.e., the modern corporation) from contamination by the political winds then current in
state legislatures. To insulate corporations by clothing them with the
character and rights of private individuals, the natural-entity theorists may have deliberately confused form and substance.[56]

The third, "real-entity," position mediated between the other two.
Supporters of this theory tended to be somewhat more pragmatic
than their contemporaries. They feared the advantages that corporations already enjoyed through legal privilege, but at the same time
they recognized the institutional character and technological unity of
corporate practice. Accordingly, they focused on the malleability of
group (including corporate) practices, through both internal and external means, and they set about designing rules that would take into
account and respond to the practical, behavioral concerns raised by
economists and sociologists at the time. In proposing rules, the realists also insisted that government—if not the states, then the still

nascent federal government—have the power to level particular
group advantages.

Indeed, once the Supreme Court had committed itself to throt-
tling the states' control of corporate behavior through natural-entity
theory, the real-entity theory presented itself as the more practical
alternative (to artificial-entity theory) for developing a federal regulatory apparatus. In effect, by curbing the states' powers to regulate
corporate property directly or through the charter mechanism, the
Supreme Court forced policymakers to seek more effective external,
or market, regulations. The federal government, meanwhile, had
the capacity to regulate corporations externally. And real-entity theory, in proceeding from the same premises regarding the corporation as natural-entity theory—namely, that the corporate unit should
be treated as a functioning whole—provided reformers with a constitutional position that would in time lend itself to developing the public arena as the Supreme Court's focus shifted from state to federal
regulation.

To reiterate briefly, discussions among proponents of the three
positions convinced the Supreme Court that groups could have personalities that were separate and distinct from the personalities of
their individual constituents and yet that also enshrined the values
of private liberty, much like individual persons in their relationship
to private property and to other citizens in the commonwealth. Accordingly, the Court replaced the artificial-entity conception, which
had prevailed in constitutional law throughout most of the 1800s,
with the natural-entity conception. In a series of cases around the
turn of the century, the Court used natural entity to erect constitutional barriers against state regulation of the corporation.[57] However, since applications of natural-entity theory were confined
largely to interpretations of state power, by World War I the more
pragmatic real-entity position became the organizing principle for
public (federal) policy discussions.

Although artificial-entity or contract theories of the firm lost support at the time, their proponents did make important contributions
to the constitutional debates over the corporation. Most significantly,
they raised concerns about the moral and political ramifications of
the corporation in constitutional law, in particular the problem of
preserving (or restoring) the classical liberal balance between sovereign and citizen. For instance, Victor Morawetz tried to reinstitute
the individualistic basis of corporate practice. Yet contemporaries
found his disaggregation of the firm unsettling, for by suggesting
that corporations were simply contractual arrangements, possibly beyond the reach of both state and federal government, he seemed to
promise chaos.[58]

Edmund Seymour, Jr., a supporter of Morawetz, developed a similarly unsettling prospect.[59] Although his arguments were discernibly circular and inconclusive, they expressed contemporary moral concerns about entity theory. For in emphasizing the temporal nature of both corporations and the laws that regulated them,[60] Seymour brought to the fore such important questions as whether there could be a moral center to a system of rules so dependent on the particular individuals who held the reins of power. The existence of a moral center seemed especially problematic under U.S. federalism, in which the bulk of regulation emanated from a competitive, atomistic framework of state-centered politics. In such a setting, could there be a reconciliation between those two competing sets of liberal ideals, one stressing instrumental, libertarian values and the other emphasizing developmental, egalitarian values?

Leon Duguit, a contemporary French political theorist on whose works Seymour relied, apparently thought not. He recommended realism and scientific objectivity as sources of faith. Seymour, in turn, hoped that judges and legislators, "guided by past experience and accumulated wisdom," would continue to modify the rules in favor of "minority shareholders" and "the public."[61] It would take federal officials some thirty years to come to grips with that task.

Without moral prescriptions, it was impossible to formulate a unified conception of the group or the state based on voluntary collective action. As we shall see, the long-standing differences between Hamiltonians and Jeffersonians, instrumentalists and developmentalists, made it difficult to form a moral consensus for regulatory discussions over corporate property. The ascendancy of a purely contractual legal conception of the firm would have to wait until World War II ended and the state was truly national. Theories about rational actors, social choices, and bargaining theory would then shape their judgments.

The truly promising route for the moment seemed to be the scientific/analytic one proposed by Duguit, among others, for it allegedly avoided value judgments.[62] Indeed, as increasingly subtle observations about the business firm's functional attributes became available,[63] lawyers exhausted the notion of corporate personality as a promising concept for comprehending the corporation (or regulating government). After 1910, lawyers gradually withdrew from formalistic explorations, giving up the supposition that an understanding of the corporate entity's "true" personality would conclusively determine the corporation's constitutional status—whether or not it was a public or private entity, subject to regulation.[64]

By the 1920s, legal scholars on both sides of the "entity" controversy instead agreed that they had to come to grips with the firm's functional aspects.[65] They conceded that the firm need not pose an ineradicable threat to an economically and politically balanced, constitutional democracy. Its legal conception should derive from an understanding of transaction and process. Problems of governance (rules, consent, leadership) seemed common to all associations, and the corporation appeared less like a rival with "personality" and more like a set of functional relationships that could help focus competing ideals.

Indeed, by World War I, even social democrats like Harold Laski were sanguine about the corporate entity. Considering government itself as a voluntary, though legally recognized, association,[66] Laski drew comfort from the possibility of state competition with, rather than intolerance of, other groups within itself. His recommendation to "test" the sovereign's uses of power through the legal recognition of groups helped move constitutional law conceptually from an emphasis on guaranteeing individual privacy and property rights (i.e., issues of "economic" or "substantive due process") to a focus on political and legal process rights. In a pluralistic society, when institutionalized groups rather than individual persons were viewed as the significant source of political pressure and activity, the important guarantees for effectively testing public authority became those of free association, free speech, group access to the elective process, and so on.

Buoyed by responsive and responsible behavior among leaders of national competing groups, political theorists gradually evolved ideas about the federal government's legitimate intrusions into what had once been sovereign state matters. This emergent group-based pluralist theory could accommodate the "corporate personality" along with the group personalities of labor unions, communities, and a wide range of politically effective coalitions.[67] National sovereignty could develop from the cooperation and the battles among diverse groups.

A new national conception of sovereignty, based on group association, emerged to cope with regulatory issues of the industrialized nation. As the ideals of individualism and territorial pluralism gradually yielded to the reality of large-scale organizations that spanned the several states, the functional, scientific approach to group formation and action slowly produced a liberal alternative in modern pluralism, which helped shape and legitimate the new state.[68] In contrast with an earlier, classical liberalism that had defined citizenship through individual people's active participation in the market and in local politics, the new pluralist liberalism defined citizenship through individual people's voluntary association in national groups.

Once pluralism advanced as a general political philosophy, along with the administrative state, it drove constitutional thought in two different directions.[69] First, national public policy achieved increasing legitimacy through political pluralism, in which conflicting associations inhibited stable national majoritarian coalitions. Associational pluralism thus replaced older states' rights defenses against the tyranny of a populist national majority. Second, the requirements of pluralist democracy gradually superseded appraisals of democracy premised on earlier forms of individualism. Guarantees of individual economic rights yielded to constitutional guarantees of process (including the freedom to associate and disassociate, to hear and be heard), since individual persons were now invested with political meaning through their association in groups. In short, freedom now meant the right to find one's political and economic allies in a process that respected alliances.[70]

Attention then turned to ensuring that this competition would be fair, and the courts decided that because deep pockets could corrupt both legislators and judges directly, regulation was appropriate here as well. Federal legislation proceeded to address corrupt practices. Nevertheless, courts and policymakers probably worried less about alliances between economic and political corrupting centers of power than about the broad-based political polarization that could develop.

Although political and legal equality had perhaps earlier worked to defuse class tensions, now it appeared to exacerbate them. Alliances could easily enable captains of industry to put one set of party leaders on a leash; the other party would then organize another set of economic interests in opposition. Given the rapidly growing capacity of the major parties to organize interests on a nationwide scale, politics without regulation threatened to turn into contests between party masters.[71] Policymakers in general and the Supreme Court in particular therefore preferred to discourage alliances between rich corporations and elected political representatives and so enacted laws that kept corporate financial clout out of the election process.

From a constitutional standpoint, the Supreme Court's apparent lack of concern for corporate personhood in the political domain might have appeared to contradict its radical protection of the natural entity from state economic regulations. But the legal mind practiced fine distinctions, and so just as the Court had delicately distinguished public powers from private rights near the turn of the century, it could now sharply separate political from economic undertakings, elections from contracting and property holding.[72] Although the Court conceded that the corporate entity merited recognition for its economic efficiency in the private realm of property and contract, it did not condone corporate success in matters politi-

cal. Formal or political equality broke down when constitutional prescriptions were applied to groups rather than persons. Corporations
had to be precluded from the voluntary, spontaneous realm of political elections, and symmetry required that political parties be kept
out of the profit-making sphere. Chapter 7 will continue this tale.

3

The Progressive Move
from Ideology to Functional
Administration

This chapter continues to explore how the concerns of expertly trained bureaucrats came to dominate debates over ethical issues that the corporation seemed once to have raised so enduringly. After administrative interests were given pride of place, discussions of general corporate function yielded to a focus on specific problems like the effect of corporate size, social costs, and control,[1] and new rules emerged to regulate the multistate corporation with the help of ample databases and advanced scientific techniques.[2]

This evolution from a moral to a scientific discourse occurred for the precise reasons that Seymour outlined in his 1903 article. That is, a moral consensus on political norms (ends) was lacking, and adminstrative rules (means) depended on scientific methods that facilitated discourse among groups with opposing—but not irreconcilable—interests.[3]

To illustrate the problem and the solution, we turn to the presidential election of 1912. Unrivaled as a three-party contest, this election featured Republican incumbent William Taft against not only the Democratic contender, Woodrow Wilson, but also the Republican breakaway candidate, Teddy Roosevelt. Roosevelt ran on the Progressive Party line, and both challengers ran as "progressive" candidates. The differences in their programs, especially with respect to the large firm, highlight just how broad the meaning of progessive had become. They also demonstrate how founding-father clashes between the Jeffersonians and the Hamiltonians had persisted and developed over the nation's first 150 years. Consider, then, two of the most articulate and influential proponents of turn-

of-the-century progressivism, Herbert Croly (who supported Teddy
Roosevelt) for the instrumentalists and Louis Brandeis (who supported Woodrow Wilson) for the developmentalists.

CROLY, BRANDEIS, AND THE ENDS OF PROGRESSIVISM

Herbert Croly emphasized individual liberty and utility as the principal ends of social reform, arguing that these twin aims could best be
realized by giving leaders the freedom to distinguish themselves and
to rule broadly over matters with which ordinary individuals were ill
prepared to deal. Criticizing reforms that he believed had been turning America into a democracy of conformists, he insisted that modern democracy could succeed only with the leadership of "selected
individuals who are obliged constantly to justify their selection."[4]
That leadership would free ordinary Americans to contribute to society at their own pace and through their "own special work with
ability, energy, disinterestedness, and excellence."[5]

On a more concrete and economic level, Croly called for an increased nationalization of laws that would break down state barriers
to commerce and facilitate the ongoing and inevitable nationalization
of the economy. Acknowledging some doubts about industrial concentration, he insisted that national control of commerce supplant
state regulation, especially for large corporations that were national
in scope. Praising the Interstate Commerce Commission, he also advocated more industry-specific forms of public supervision to check
potential abuses. But at the same time, Croly sought repeal of federal antitrust laws, which he claimed generally favored smaller over
larger firms; their repeal would enable more efficient firms to continue growing. While conceding the benefits of a graduated inheri-
tance tax and laws for collective bargaining to create a more level
playing field for enterprises and workers, Croly trumpeted market
efficiency as the surest means to increase wealth and expand the
opportunities of all U.S. citizens. This sustained voluntarism made
him an instrumentalist heir to the Hamiltonians.

Croly labeled as "Jeffersonian" the more egalitarian and decentralized progressives like Louis Brandeis. Although Croly emphasized
the "peculiar advantage" afforded by fifty years of industrial reorganization, Brandeis focused on the deterioration of industrial democracy that had accompanied individual liberty under a laissez-faire
regime. As relatively independent producers became relatively dependent employees, any salutary effect of consolidation on productivity was being undercut by the apathy and powerlessness of investors who had surrendered their control over corporate property to

its managers. Brandeis doubted the ability of ordinary voters to form opinions about candidates' political views or personal competence that were sufficiently accurate to elect or depose them intelligently. The more centralized the power was, the more distant the voter would be; distance, in turn, bred ignorance and apathy.

"Can any man be really free," asked Brandeis, "who is constantly in danger of becoming dependent upon somebody and something else than his own exertion and conduct?"[6] This dependency had adverse consequences for the polity as well as the individual. "While there are many contributing causes of unrest," Brandeis testified before Congress, "there is one cause which is fundamental. That is . . . the contrast between our political liberty and our industrial absolutism."[7]

In economics as in politics, Brandeis departed from Croly. Brandeis favored antitrust laws as a means to ensure competition; he also favored decentralized forms of regulation whenever possible. In the democratic sovereignty of the various states, he saw useful laboratories for legal- and public-policy experimentation. Pluralism could be a competitive process that engaged not only private sovereigns and their followers but a range of public authorities as well.

Brandeis also advocated a comprehensive social insurance system in order to make individuals less dependent on employers and to care for them during periods of sickness, unemployment, and retirement. Acknowledging that corporate consolidations under particular circumstances enhanced industrial efficiency, Brandeis also argued that corporate directors and managers were motivated by more than competition and efficiency: They also sought prestige and market and political power, enriching themselves at the expense of other corporate constituents. The ills of general industrial despotism called for strong medicine, requiring serious alteration of the corporation's internal governance. Labor could not regain its preindustrial independence until it participated in management. Unions had done good work, but mostly as adversaries. Industrial democracy would require sharing both profits and responsibilities in a more cooperative relationship between management and labor.[8]

Despite their differences, both Croly and Brandeis were "progressives." Each decried the selfishness he found in individuals; each also had faith that a democracy supported by market forces could channel individual self-interest to socially useful endeavors. Their differences were largely over the degree to which they believed political democracy could renew itself without industrial reforms that went beyond wealth-maximizing concerns.

Croly was Roosevelt's adviser; Brandeis was Wilson's. And it was Wilson who won the election. During his first administration, Con-

gress responded to competitive business pressures by establishing the
Federal Reserve System to stabilize banking; it also passed the Federal Trade Commission (FTC) and Clayton acts, which strengthened
the antitrust laws for regulating business and limited their application to labor unions. Later, when the United States joined World
War I, the federal government even took over operation of the national railroad system, so that by the end of the war, corporate regulation had moved even more firmly into the federal arena.[9] Both
federal fiscal powers and the court system expanded when the Six-
teenth Amendment was ratified in 1913 and litigants were invited to
develop the rules of corporate practice and governance under a
"federal common law."[10]

National powers under the Constitution therefore seemed adequate to control the large corporation. But the constitutional
grounds for accommodating the modern corporation remained
vague. Progressive reform still failed to provide any moral consensus
to guide regulatory policy, and the Supreme Court's construct, the
"natural entity," remained formalistic, strained, and ultimately unconvincing.

REALISM DISPLACES IDEALISM IN REGULATORY POLICY

Intellectual historians have characterized the 1920s and 1930s as an
era of ideological crises and mounting "realism," in both law and
social theory. Success in World War I provided a moment of optimism, but the world's leaders soon squandered their opportunity for
lasting peace, and in the following years normative discussions about
the ends of public policy became more polarized and less amenable
to theoretical resolution.

Lawyers and policymakers faced two major problems in constitutional thought. The first involved synthesizing geographic federalism
and group pluralism; the second, translating the realities of group
process and functional relationships into meaningful individual
rights. Without social agreement on democracy's precise ethical
ends, lawyers and administrators began paying more careful attention to the underlying "social facts" on which public policies rested;
they also relied on social scientific analyses to mitigate institutional
conflicts. This turn to policy and administrative science won even
more adherents after 1912, when the election indicated that the
ideological differences that separated progressive reformers were
more powerful than the similarities that united them. Furthermore,
social scientists increasingly found analytic overlaps and interdependencies in what had traditionally been labeled the public and the

private spheres. They responded by addressing all policy problems as part of the same fabric.[11]

The new consciousness exhibited a flexible attitude toward groups and optimism about multiple, competing sovereignties. Conservatives began to experiment politically, buoyed by the belief that courts would defend business interests against state sovereignty. At the same time, progressives hoped that the growth of national controls would lead to a predictable system of economic regulation. Although fears of class polarization persisted, the discussions gradually took into account the diverse kind of pluralism that had been transforming the nation's political and economic landscape. Constitutional practices would reshape themselves now around groups, be they corporations, political parties, trade associations, labor unions, universities, or churches. Attention therefore focused anew on the functional character of different organizations. Functionalism, in turn, served to limit, or "particularize," proposals for public intervention into private life and thus began eroding the older generation's adherence to rugged individualism, laissez-faire, and other precepts of a Darwinistic social norm.

Mary Parker Follett's *The New State,* published in 1918, provided both a cogent criticism of individualism and a coherent new constitutional ideology based on pluralism.[12] Drawing on William James's view that an individual person developed psychologically by drawing on a "pluralistic universe,"[13] Follett found group identity to be the proper grounding for both individual fulfillment and "true democracy."[14] She also distinguished the territorial associations characteristic of federalism (the "neighborhood groups") from other kinds of interest groupings that her contemporaries labeled pluralism (the "occupational groups"). Each in its own way contributed to the dynamics of the "unifying state."[15]

Follett's concept of fluid groupings, which led to a sort of blending, had inherently more optimistic political implications than did one-to-one group identification, which led to a state so compelled to "balance interests" that it would eventually breed irreconcilable antagonisms and the sort of ultimate domination by factions that James Madison had feared.[16] Blanket identification of businessmen with capitalistic enterprises and workers with socialistic endeavors denied or ignored the lessons of this new psychology and its pluralistic individualism, and the static conception of the state as a "machine" or a "collection of units" made citizenship appear passive in the extreme. Although Follett's support for legal rules that would nurture the group process and develop the individual person's role was certainly sympathetic to Brandeis's prescriptions for decentralized egalitarian democracy, it also lent itself to Croly's centralized utilitarian kind of nationalism through unifying functional inquiries into the group process.

Frank Kent followed Follett with *The Great Game of Politics* (1923), which provided a popular account of how the synthesis between group and government developed as a collective bargaining game. In a language anticipating the New Deal, he explained that the rules of the game mattered and that the state functioned as an impartial umpire who made occasional adjustments to keep the game fair.[17]

Between the world wars, Follett's global, unifying idealism disappeared in the main, and only recently have historians begun to mourn its loss. In the early 1920s, academic legal writing clearly reflected a convergence of social science, pragmatic jurisprudence, and group (as opposed to class) analysis. Although schools of realist or pragmatic legal thought continued to fragment in the law, academicians did not revert to the earlier formalism. The new focus on rules for "interest balancing" was evident in scholarly work both conventional and radical in nature.

The new realism's reach was extensive. Studies ranged from comparative assessments to empirical inquiries, supporting broad-based reform, especially in federal administration.[18] Proposals continued to reflect the earlier range of progressive values, from centralized and integrated forms of power to decentralized, parallel or competing forms of power.[19] But appealing to the facts of governmental processes helped move public policy from reflection to action.

John R. Commons and Karl N. Llewellyn were among the leading reform writers of the period. Commons's *The Legal Foundations of Capitalism* began with a polemic against the Supreme Court's rampant formalism as an uninformed economic interpretation of constitutional history. Having correctly anticipated economic regulation along the lines of market adjustment rather than redistribution, Commons carefully distinguished the two premises in constitutional doctrine. He also emphasized economic interdependencies. Because, for example, the legal institutions that governed transactions might themselves present significant market risks, actors might react by substituting cooperative group processes for the arm's-length bargaining and competition characteristic of the market. Unfortunately, Commons's writing was so elusive that many of his valid observations about the "going-concern" and corporate regulation generally went unheeded for over a generation.[20]

Around the same time, Karl Llewellyn was also taking an interest in the intersections of law and economics.[21] Although the "working rules" that grew out of market transactions were not laws in the formal sense, he observed that to the degree that they were limited and licensed by the state, they certainly had the same effect. Moreover, they were often of the "very [technical] type . . . which the official legal institutions [were] unable to construct."[22] By and large, the law could condone the working rules of "a lesser group, of more or less voluntary constitution" and so, too, arrangements of two or more such groups for particular ends.[23] Nevertheless, as they became the basis of social policy, these rules also created some problems for modern pluralist society, the most notable being disparities in bargaining power. Ongoing but specialized public-sector interventions were an appropriate counterforce. Unfortunately, these were the very sorts of actions that judges and legislatures were inadequately prepared to undertake, although "administrative law [had] in part stopped the gap."[24] Llewellyn accordingly recommended both designing administrative agencies with the requisite expertise to reform existing working rules and limiting the role of courts and legislatures to one of oversight and guidance. In many ways recalling Follett's "unifying state," his proposals prized the diversity of continually changing working rules, and they also leveled the older conceptual divisions between private and public law.

Gradually Llewellyn's concepts entered public-policy considerations. During the 1920s, federal regulators still relied on private actors to initiate working rules for administrators to reshape, but with the Great Depression and the first New Deal, Congress became more actively involved. In passing the National Industrial Recovery Act (NIRA), Congress empowered the National Recovery Administration (NRA) to persuade interest groups to work out rules of conduct in a wide range of industrial and commercial markets. When the Supreme Court later ruled the NIRA to be unconstitutional, Congress both decentralized and strengthened the authority of the public administrators in a series of laws that constituted the "Second New Deal."

REALISM, THE CORPORATION, AND PUBLIC POLICY

Actual public policy regarding large corporations evolved in a fashion somewhat parallel to the theoretical policy discussions. Realists critiqued existing rules empirically from a social science perspective, but explorations in the different areas of corporate regulation, such as antitrust and firm size, social cost, and contract diverged.

Antitrust and Firm Size

Following the enactment of the Clayton and Federal Trade Commission (FTC) acts in 1914, federal antitrust enforcement aimed in the main to restrict the growth of individual firms, their collaboration, and any unfair methods of competition.[25] At the turn of the century, economists as divergent politically as Thorstein Veblen and John Bates Clark had come to agree that firm size could give rise to economies of scale, not just market power. They continued to disagree, however, on the relative weights of the factors, with Clark on the whole being more sanguine about the market's ability to discipline prices.

Such discussions persisted throughout the decade, with the Supreme Court as well trying to balance considerations that minimized production costs with those that maximized competition. In the 1911 suit against the Standard Oil Trust, Chief Justice Edward D. White found the company to be in violation of the Sherman Act and ascribed a "rule of reason" to the act's prohibitions against monopolization and agreements in restraint of trade. For its part, Congress passed both the Clayton Act, whose Section 7 prohibited mergers that tended "to substantially lessen competition," and the FTC Act, whose Section 5 prohibited "unfair methods of competition."[26] Neither act specified standards for determining when businesses had illicitly enfeebled competition, by either undesirable levels of market concentration or particular market practices. Legal commentators continued therefore to speculate on which trusts were "good" and which trusts were "bad."[27]

The realist critique of judicial policy developed shortly after the *U.S. Steel* case of 1920, in which the Supreme Court upheld the legality of the steel trust, pursuant to the "rule of reason." In his 1922 article, "The Change in Trust Policy," Myron Watkins argued that the Supreme Court's establishment of a "rule of reason" under federal antitrust law was wholly without legal foundation.[28] Nevertheless, "[i]f there is an economic basis for the changed attitude toward business enterprise, we may very well overlook the lack of legal precedent and find satisfaction in the ease with which our legislative wants are recognized and filled by the courts."[29] To determine whether or not the courts' policy was "industrially sound," Watkins drew on then current economic literature and made a thorough analysis of the economic performance of several of the challenged trusts.[30] He concluded with alarm that the public had much more to lose than to gain from this kind of "reason."

Along with a Brandeisian preference for decentralized competition, Watkins's analysis led to the gradual weakening of antitrust "rule of reason" exceptions. Even so, larger monopolies, such as the Aluminum Company of America, persisted well into the 1930s, as did industrial consolidations of all but the very largest firms. Judges even invited market leaders to testify on the reasonableness of consolidation in their industries. In effect, the courts allowed merging firms to overcome the presumption that the consolidations were designed merely to restrain competition.

Increasingly sophisticated economic literature on industrial organization provided more support for business. These economic tools were honed throughout the 1920s and 1930s as the theory advanced. First Frank Knight described the large firm's structure and operation in economic terms. Then John Maurice Clark developed an analytic framework for how firms responded to different forms of regulation. Edward Chamberlin related market structures to firm strategies, and Edward Mason and Nicholas Kaldor developed the economics of industrial organization.[31]

During the same era, public regulation of utilities or natural monopolies generally moved from the federal to the state and local levels. Early in the century, progressive reformers had still been calling for the municipal ownership of utilities in order to ensure fair rates. But by the 1920s, "local socialism" had run its course, displaced by state public service commissions engaging in rate regulation. Like antitrust policy, rate regulation suffered from the Supreme Court's ambiguous reading of the legal requirement that commissions price corporate capital inputs "fairly" in setting rates.[32]

For two decades, commentators resorted to legal precedents and logic to ascertain the Court's meaning and apply it to particular cases. Beginning with Gerard Henderson's 1920 article on railway valuation and culminating in Donald Richberg's more generally applicable insights in 1922, they moved from ambiguous prescriptions to realistic economic appraisal.[33] Scattering references to economists throughout his article, Richberg exhorted lawyers and policymakers to "forget [the "fair value" doctrine] and its horrible brood of supporting opinions" and instead "put rate making on a reasonably scientific basis and stabilize public utility securities, all of which will benefit both the consumers and the investors."[34] In time, the economic literature provided analyses to secure cost-based rate ceilings, and by the end of the decade even skeptical economists like Richard Ely had grown confident that rate regulation would prove more effective than alternative means of control.[35] Federal regulators followed much the same pattern for national and interstate industries. They both relaxed control over consolidations and relied on cost-based rate regulation rather than more direct control mechanisms.[36]

Social Costs

Corporate operations increasingly affected people not involved in governing the firm. These groups included workers, customers, suppliers, and even the community at large. Just what should the corporation's responsibility to these affected parties be? State legislatures responded by exercising their "police powers," which the courts had reined in fairly tightly. By and large, the legislatures could draw on industrial labor rules, including compensation procedures, hours-of-work rules, injury compensation, and other norms reflected in collective-bargaining arrangements.[37] The courts tended to scrutinize legislation through a prescriptive constitutional lens. Thus, certain kinds of working rules took on a "public" character—insofar as they touched on norms of public health, welfare, or morals—and so warranted legislative concerns. Others were more private, concerning only the judgments of the independent individuals directly involved.

Social-cost regulation developed on two levels. First, it tried to establish an "industrial policy" of enhanced participation in company policymaking and better working conditions in general, at the same time mitigating such specific problems as unemployment, periodic layoffs, unsecured pensions and life insurance for the workers' survivors, health benefits, and workers' compensation. Publicity increasingly helped pressure and reward businesses, inform unions, and convince legislators. Especially notable in these efforts were John Commons and his associates at the University of Wisconsin on the academic level,[38] and "muckrakers" like Ida Tarbell on the popular front.[39]

Second, lawyers confronted judges with a more realistic understanding of what was at stake when working rules were elevated to the status of law. Supreme Court Justices Oliver Wendell Holmes and Louis Brandeis, in particular, responded by moving the Court's style of review from substantive to procedural judgments, eventually including assessments of the quality of the challengers' political and legal access.[40] Brandeis, for example, emphasized not just the facts underlying particular kinds of legislation but also those of the legal system itself, drawing attention to how the technical rules of governmental organization could help counter group and state fragmentation, thereby reducing administrative costs.[41] He played also an extremely important role in beginning to analyze legal institutions from the viewpoint of scarcity. One should not just reckon the value but also the cost of legal/judicial decisions; no free lunch existed in either the law or the marketplace. Llewellyn seconded this observation of limits. The problem of "how to apportion the available energy," he noted, was one of "ethics," a realm in which courts were hard pressed to demonstrate any superiority of judgment.[42]

Corporate Control

The third set of policy concerns centered on corporate control groups. The scale of modern technology, impersonal markets, and antitrust traditions helped create the corporate system and made the alternative of cartel arrangements inherently unworkable. Market size and impersonality inhibited cooperation among cartel participants: Each firm wanted to sell more, not less, despite the higher price the cartel made possible, and cartel enforcement was difficult when antitrust laws prevented formal arrangements to discipline cartel members. The families that had amassed huge fortunes sought mergers and incorporation as ways to sustain their wealth; the advantages of permanent organizations with limited liability outweighed in most cases the loss of direct control.[43] Now wealth worked through passive financial instruments that were easily traded in America's burgeoning financial markets. As ownership dispersed, public policy enshrined shareholders as the ultimate control group, even as they might practically be losing the power to influence corporate decisions; the rhetoric of private property and active citizenship seemed worth preserving. Was it not essential to democratic rule?

For the same reason, policymakers fretted over the two other control groups, the bankers and the managers. The former were particularly disturbing, as the great merger movement of the late nineteenth century had transformed the nation's economy into a modern industrial system with their considerable assistance. To protect the interests of their creditors, investment bankers joined client boards, creating an interlocking network that seemed to give them effective control.

Instead of a decentralized economy populated by family-controlled firms, America now appeared as a financially dominated industrial complex in which a few banking houses emerged as a ruling plutocracy. National debate over the transformation had begun in 1912 when a special House committee chaired by Arsene Pujo explored the accusations that money trusts controlled industry both directly and indirectly.[44] Although no formal legislation emerged from these investigations, many of the proposals put forth by the Pujo committee became law during the New Deal, and the concerns that motivated the hearings lasted well after the World War II era.

Even before the hearings got under way, however, industrial organization itself had weakened the bankers' ability to scrutinize and effectively impose their will on these giant firms. As managers used investor funds to build empires, their expertise and superior access to pertinent information substantially reduced the bankers' ability to act as an effective voice in corporate decision-making. Shareholder control seemed diminished as well. Here, the relative bargaining power of management improved not just because firms became too complicated for a hands-on approach from equity owners but also because legal reforms further increased their independence.

Investor dependency could be hazardous to more than the people directly involved. As we noted earlier, progressive reformers like Brandeis had already argued that public oversight or the restructuring of corporate governance was necessary to prevent socially irresponsible conduct and redistributions. While acknowledging that professional managers could run giant bureaucracies efficiently, he feared that "the permanent separation of ownership from control must prove fatal to the public interest. The responsibility of ownership is lacking."[45] Policy debates continued to evolve during the first three decades of the century. Insisting on the "private" nature of the corporation, promoters and insiders pressured state legislatures to loosen restrictions under general incorporation statutes so that operations could respond more ably to changing financial market conditions. At the same time, critics suggested that these "insiders" were simply relying on the states' jurisdictional vulnerabilities to manipulate and exploit an ever growing and relatively uninformed investing public, not to mention dependent workers and consumers.

It was in the context of this debate that John Dewey cut through the formal legal conceptions of corporate personality with unrestrained realism.[46] Concluding that the lawyers' resort to conceptualism allowed them to support just about any conclusion they desired, Dewey insisted that the time had come to engage in more straightforward practical debates, to "eliminat[e] the *idea* of personality until the concrete facts and relations involved have been faced and stated on their own account."[47]

Among the contemporaries who took into account "concrete facts and relations" were two Harvard Business School professors, Nathan Isaacs and Adolf A. Berle. In contrast with those whom Dewey scorned—writers like Edward H. Warren, who still felt compelled to draw on sixteenth-century legal precedents to justify twentieth-century corporate rules[48]—Isaacs and Berle focused entirely on modern practice, and they did so in ways still tied to both formal logic and the 1920s culture of relatively minimal public interventions.[49]

Isaacs tended to concentrate on "private working rules" that required legislative attention. In his view, lawyers and judges paid too little attention to accountants and engineers; this neglect was damaging not only in matters of corporate investment[50] but also in those of corporate promotion.[51] In the latter case, for example, judges had been establishing rights and obligations based on whether promoters were legally related to the corporation as contractors or officers. But since their work was usually accomplished before the corporation even came into legal existence, judges resorting to the logic of the law had trouble discovering any relationship at all.[52] Applying common sense and experience instead, Isaacs examined the actual practices of promoters to discover working rules that could then be used as the basis for more useful legislation.[53] He also found in the "trust" concept a useful supplement to the corporate form, especially when freed from the encrustations of judicial formalism.[54] Trust, Isaacs decided, had a role "[n]ext to contract, the universal tool, and incorporation, the standard instrument of organization . . . wherever the relations to be established are too delicate or too novel for these coarser devices."[55]

Berle took the concept of trust a step further: He wanted directors and "control" groups to be held accountable, as trustees or "fiduciaries," for a wide range of innovative financial practices. For example, when Berle studied the matter of nonvoting stock issued to investors so that bankers could continue to control corporate boards even as they held a diminishing fraction of the outstanding equity, he concluded that "[s]eparation of management from actual ownership is complete and permanent; the management shareholders appear bound to consider no interests but their own."[56] For recourse against mismanagement, the ordinary shareholder had no avenue but in equity, and this course was circuitous at best.[57]

Applying an empirical eye to decisions in courts of equity, Berle began to discover a pattern: Board policies were set aside when "a group in control was acting unconscionably towards persons who had no effective voice in, and had not assented to, the corporate result."[58] "Bankers' control" appeared to be a general problem for corporate action, and corporate law allowed minority control groups to breach their fiduciary duties in many different ways.[59]

As in the case of social-cost regulation, the policies governing corporate control remained decentralized, developed largely in private arrangements or by limited intervention on the part of state legislatures and courts. Throughout the 1920s, for example, the public stock exchanges elaborated working rules based on day-to-day technical experience. State legislatures modified their separate business and public securities ("blue sky") laws in line with corporate lawyers' designs and perhaps their more realistic perspective.[60]

By the end of the decade, however, the concept of managerial trusteeship had taken broad hold. As trustees of the corporation's assets, managers were now expected to be held liable to shareholders. When concerns about the large firm's economic performance became urgent with the onset of the Depression, trusteeship became the focus of attention, inextricably bound to broad deliberations about social policy.

4

Negotiating a New Deal: Problems of Corporate Control and Dependency

In this chapter, we continue to develop the distinctions between "trust" and "contract." Applying these alternative approaches to both stockholders and labor, we also advance our argument that they provide a better understanding of the complexities of FDR's new Deals than do the older perspective offered by "class." Once again, our mentor in these pursuits is Adolf Berle. We later review his text, *The Modern Corporation and Private Property,* which is so influential to both research and policy that it deserves the full treatment we provide, and more.

The chapter also supports our assertion that studying the history of the corporation in America is much more than an exercise in economic history. Because it forces reconsideration of such central issues as the proper role of private property, government, and free enterprise in working toward goals of both efficiency and equity, it provides a useful perspective on social and political history as well.

THE TRUST-VERSUS-CONTRACT DIVIDE IN THE 1930s

We introduced Adolf Berle in Chapter 3, as he helped shape discussions of corporate America along with Nathan Isaacs. He returns to our narrative in the *Harvard Law Review.* Now prodded by an able intellectual adversary, E. Merrick Dodd, he continues to develop his ideas about the proper role of the corporation in American life. Both these realists saw the firm as a set of socially adjustable transactions among identifiable groups rather than as an entity with a distinct personality protected under the Constitution. Their disagreements centered on accountability and its consequences. In asserting the control group's accountability to shareholders, Berle tried to preserve the private property incentives of the corporation, whereas Dodd insisted on public accountability and so threatened the traditional distinction of shareholders' from others' interests.

Berle opened the debate in 1931, arguing that corporate power was held in trust, with the shareholders as the principal beneficiaries in accordance with their "ratable interests."[1] Dodd responded that corporate powers were indeed held in trust but that managers had social as well as shareholder reponsibilities.[2] The modern corporation, in his view, was no longer strictly a proprietary enterprise. It was also a social institution. The law was already moving to reflect these new managerial mandates, and public opinion, not formal claims of ownership, was forcing the change.

Berle conceded that the scale of modern enterprise created problems. Technological dependence on large-scale production and financial concentration made corporate managers effective administrators of industrial government.[3] Functioning more "as princes and ministers than as promoters or merchants," they therefore had social as well as strictly corporate responsibility. But Dodd's argument involved "theory, not practice": No enforcement mechanism existed to support this broader responsibility, and in its absence, weakening managerial mandates to stockholders would serve only to make their authority "for all practical purposes absolute."[4] Although skeptical of lawyers who had "not given too good an account of themselves thus far, either in theory or administration," Berle still believed that they were the most promising candidates to entrust with the responsibility of redressing the balance.[5] Unlike social theorists or economists, lawyers were not free to experiment broadly. On the contrary, they "must meet a series of practical situations from day to day. . . . Legal technique does not contemplate intervening periods of chaos; it can only follow out new theories as they become established and accepted by the community at large."[6]

The legal system had already taken on this responsibility. As corporate law evolved in the nineteenth century, the courts had become the ultimate arbiters in disputes between corporate constituents and corporate control. However, as power shifted from the state to the federal arena, reformers advocated a transfer of power from the judiciary to expert administrative agencies empowered to set, among other things, explicitly distributive policies.[7]

Discussions during the 1920s had anticipated two widely divergent models for federal administration. The first centralized at least some part of the administrative processes, for example, planning, rule making, and enforcement; William F. Willoughby of the Brookings Institution was perhaps its leading advocate.[8] The second model supported decentralization in a number of ways: along lines of occupation or industry, function (planning, rule making, enforcement, adjudication, auditing, and evaluation), and jurisdiction (state and federal government, and the courts). Corporations had such important roles in either model that Berle, writing with Gardiner C. Means, could conclude *The Modern Corporation and Private Property* by observing: "The law of corporations . . . might well be considered as a potential constitutional law for the new economic state, while business practice is increasingly assuming the aspect of economic statesmanship."[9]

Berle's contributions in this now classic work merit close attention. Not only are they far more original and extensive than has often been assumed, but they also highlight many of the issues that the United States was forced to consider during and after the Great Depression.[10] Both Berle and the administrators and shapers of the Second New Deal proceeded pragmatically. Neither chose definitively between instrumental and developmental approaches to public policy or *ex ante* contract and *ex post* trust approaches to judicial intervention. Perhaps herein lie the sources of the misunderstanding and ambiguities that have plagued interpretations of both the book and the New Deal. A careful reading of Berle therefore offers a fresh look at government in the time of Franklin Roosevelt.

The Modern Corporation and Private Property

With Means's able quantitative analysis of industrial organization, the first part of Berle's argument asserted that corporate organization had taken over most fields of business practice, while concentration proceeded apace.[11] Because public markets now financed most of the necessary capitalization, stock ownership in individual firms had often become so dispersed that no significant interests within the firms remained capable of organizing and mobilizing a majority of the stock owners to assert control over corporate policies.[12] As a result, minority owners—often top management alone—had taken control of the board of directors,[13] and perhaps as few as two thousand men were therefore in charge of over half of the nation's corporate wealth.[14]

The four chapters (of Book 1) outlining this argument are perhaps more curious for their tone and what they do not say than for their demonstration of the separation of ownership from control. These chapters read as a technological thriller: Berle presents the corporate person as a machine whose growth and domination of the economy were inevitable.[15] Berle passed no judgment on corporations themselves; they appeared to have served the economy well.[16] Rather, he reserved his criticism for shareholders and control, one a crowd of passive bystanders caught up in modern society and technology and the other active manipulators not necessarily dedicated to the machine's best uses.[17] Because the separation of financial risk-bearing from operational management seemed an efficient division of function, Berle questioned only the legal policy of unregulated corporate control in a society no longer composed of the active, self-reliant individuals so esteemed by Jeffersonians and Hamiltonians alike.

Books 2 and 3 form the crux of the work. There Berle laid out the means for regulating the uneasy relationship between active and passive corporate constituents. Instead of pinpointing specific problems or prescribing solutions, he simply described the legal and market treatment of that connection. The relationship among shareholders, the corporation, and the state had once been governed by charter contracts. General incorporation laws had then begun to remove state government from the field of bargaining, so that managers were now calling most of the shots, leaving shareholders "virtually at the mercy of an adverse majority, and in some instances even of a minority which has control."[18]

Although the common law had "wrestled" with this problem "without conspicuous success," Berle was still able to derive three legal doctrines from his study of case-by-case responses.[19] First was the concept of "vested rights," which found little application in corporate regulation, except in restraining the state from nullifying the obligations that it had assumed expressly and without reservation. Second and third were contractual relationships based on market rules[20] and trust or fiduciary relationships based on the rules of equity or social norms.[21]

Under contract law, courts enforced arm's-length transactions and intervened only when the terms were too vague, the bargaining was insufficient, or one party had been unable to look after its own interests freely. Contract rules focused on the investor's expectations at the time the relationship began, and these, Berle assumed, included the conditions of corporate control. Effectively, contract law treated shareholders as just one of many specialized investors supplying capital at a price.[22] They differed from other creditors like bondholders and short-term lenders only with respect to the degree and nature of the risk they incurred and the statutory coverage of residual risk contracts.

Although shareholders on the whole cared little about participating in corporate governance, responsible investment required reliable information.[23] Policymakers could anticipate many market failures and thus correct them beforehand *("ex ante")* through disclosure requirements, independent verification of information, and adjustments to extreme disparities in bargaining (involving, say, "insiders" and other investors).[24] Relying extensively on the working rules of the New York Stock Exchange in insisting on realistic, transaction-by-transaction analysis, Berle suggested that a centralized agency parallel in function and expertise to the Federal Reserve Bank would prove more adept at rule making than the courts and state legislatures were.[25]

On the other hand, because trust doctrine evolved from considerations of "fairness" and social norms, those courts following this approach would intervene only later *("ex post")* to correct acts of "bad faith" and insufficient paternalism. And so they did: As corporate practice had gradually extinguished the shareholders' voice in the larger, publicly held firms, individual shareholders had appealed increasingly to state courts, and incrementally a trust doctrine had emerged from the precedents that followed. Nevertheless, as Berle observed, courts meddling in management created its own problems, in particular the demand for standards to resolve the conflicting claims on management by the firm's several classes of investors. In general, protection of each class of shareholders from property dilution, waste, misappropriation, and so forth served as a sufficient standard. Nevertheless, enforcement required such acute sensitivity to the problems of financial valuation that even following this line of thinking, Berle again favored enforcement by administrators who were experts in the field of finance.

Entitlement offered a more basic difficulty than the sorting out of competing shareholder claims. Why should only the otherwise passive and irresponsible owners of stock certificates be entitled to legal protection? Perhaps control's trust obligations should be extended to other corporate dependents as well. If courts privileged shareholders by regarding them as the sole beneficiaries of the corporate trust, then protective market rules would serve to privilege investors doubly, both beforehand and afterward.[26] Berle's resolution of this dilemma reflects the extent to which he had moved toward Dodd's position: He decided that corporate managers could respond to competing constituent interests like employees and consumers, giving shareholders a fair market return and keeping the remaining residuals as a reward for past efficiency and incentive for more of the same.[27] Corporate regulation in the "public interest" had to treat corporate constituents—"stakeholders," as students of management later called them—in a conceptually coherent manner, eschewing prescriptive legal concepts like "property" that corporate practice had changed substantially in meaning.

Both the formalism of earlier judicial analysis and the experience of the Great Depression persuaded Berle that neither legal institutions nor markets were entirely reliable. Rather than endorse either the *ex ante* contract approach or the *ex post* trust position, he disentangled the two and gave them more realistic foundations. Berle thus completed the task of the earlier realists. First, he destroyed the rather static concept of the corporation as a fixed mass of private property to which shareholders held title (i.e., an "entity" with "constitutional personality" run by its "controlled" agents). In its stead, he sketched out the framework for a dynamic model of a flexible set of labor, consumer, creditor, and investor transactions coordinated by managers and adjusted by public institutions in accordance with social norms and scientific insight into the various stakeholders' functions in generating the corporate system's wealth. Although other writers had suggested the pertinent stakeholder relationships before Berle did, he was perhaps the first lawyer to envision a legal framework that gave corporate regulation a coherent set of standards—efficiency tempered by equity. The concept of fairness would eventually work its way into the contract rules themselves, both through "unconscionability" doctrines under state law along with the principle that courts should not enforce contracts in contravention of "public policy," and through federal statutes outlawing unfair transactions of various kinds.

Thus *The Modern Corporation and Private Property* anticipated democratic pluralism in the postwar era. Its readers gained insight into postwar democracy, the specifics of that era's ambivalent ideological presumptions, and, above all, the central position of the corporation in defining the limits of postwar democracy and the functions of governance in this period.

Trust and Contract in Second New Deal Reforms

In 1933, the federal government attempted to codify working rules and oversee the corporate sector centrally through the National Recovery Administration (NRA).[28] As soon as Roosevelt realized that the NRA was doomed, however, he mobilized Congress to attempt a "Second New Deal," allocating rather than centralizing regulatory responsibilities and doing so among numerous independent agencies.

The Second New Deal secured revisions of stakeholder regulation and the formation or reform of the principal "stakeholder agencies":

the Federal Trade Commission (FTC) for consumers, the Securities Exchange Commission (SEC) for investors, and the National Labor Relations Board (NLRB) for workers. Each had relatively exclusive but narrowly defined jurisdiction over the relationship between particular stakeholder groups and corporate strategists, and each acted independently of other government agencies and pursued its mission, to use Follett's term, "particularistically."

Nevertheless, a variety of evidence suggests that Congress still intended to create a coherent regulatory framework. For example, in drafting the key stakeholder statutes between 1933 and 1938, legislators resorted consistently to such loaded legal terms as "unfair" and "fraudulent." In that same span, Congress empowered the SEC, the NLRB, and the FTC, respectively, to prevent insiders from making "unfair use of information," redress employers' "unfair labor practices," and enjoin acts and practices "unfair or deceptive" to consumers.[29] Moreover, although the regulatory policies of the stakeholder agencies were administratively separate, they cohered pragmatically and intellectually. Not only did they all focus on managerial practices in the modern corporation and the norms evolving around them, but they also came to depend on a common body of scientific insights into those practices.[30]

Berle influenced the New Deal substantially but indirectly. *The Modern Corporation and Private Property* anticipated much of FDR's legislation, and Berle associated closely with Roosevelt's "brain trust" and corresponded actively with those in direct control. Berle's conceptual and functional distinctions with respect to corporate power and its regulation appear in several statutes, albeit with arguably less clarity than his text provided. Provisions for statutory "fairness," for example, seemed to invite administrative adjudications designed to evaluate specific transactions or managerial conduct after the fact, to enforce standards of the day against aberrant business behavior and protect "passive" stakeholders. In contrast, statutory "deception" provisions led administrative rule making to design transactions to limit prospective market failures in advance. Judgments of the former kind might result in refunds or restitution for injuries, whereas the latter tended to require generally applicable information disclosures.

Perhaps this ambivalence between rules designed to liberate the stakeholders (contract) and the initiatives designed to shield or nurture them (trust) reflected a deeper set of tensions in public policy. Some policies emphasized the interests of "active" (or reasonably self-reliant) investors, workers, and consumers, who could be helped by broad-based prescriptive market adjustments. Another set focused on the interests of "passive" and less self-reliant stakeholders, whose fortunes had been or were likely to be compromised by their dependency and whose security seemed to require direct intervention.

Shareholder Reforms

To illustrate these regulatory principles, we begin with shareholders. Both *ex post*-versus-*ex ante* dualities and those of jurisdiction have sometimes clouded interpretations of the New Deal shareholder reform. By designing federal intervention to supplement, not supplant, state laws, Congress addressed primarily the role of shareholders as creditors.

The federal security and banking reforms had two objectives with respect to investors. First, the reforms sought to stabilize the financial system by such actions as keeping distinct the operations of investment and commercial banks and protecting individual investors from unfaithful or dissembling brokers, managers, and advisers.[31] Second, the reforms attempted to increase the system's efficiency by improving investors' capacity to appraise and liquidate all forms of capital investment. Policymakers looked for ways to standardize corporate procedures and information.[32] Under the 1933 Securities Act and the 1934 Securities Exchange Act, respectively, Congress required firms to register all new security issues and instituted standardized, more detailed, regular, and reliable reporting requirements for all publicly traded security issues of going concerns. Baseline public information enabled investors to make better comparisons of opportunities and weakened the informational advantage of insiders, investment bankers, underwriters, and brokers who had used private stock exchanges to shield their activities from public scrutiny and intervention.

In 1934, Congress passed the Securities Exchange Act, establishing the SEC to exercise government control over financial markets. Under James Landis's guiding hand, the new commission accomplished this task by 1937.[33] The SEC had power to regulate systematically two contracting processes, one between investors and their brokers and the other between investors and corporate insiders. The SEC could dissolve restraints on competition among brokers and lower transaction costs, such as brokerage fees, that locked investors into past commitments or discriminated between larger and smaller investors.

Deferring to the precedent of dual, state-federal authority over the corporation, however, Congress resisted considerable pressure to institute general incorporation laws and chose in the main to continue to delegate to the states the responsibility for supporting the

shareholders' ownership role. The states fulfilled this obligation by
enforcing trust standards in suits that alleged managerial misconduct. New Deal support of ownership roles at the federal level, on
the other hand, came largely through the contract route. The federal government established standards that regulated the content
and accuracy of proxy statements and required corporations to issue
both regular and extraordinary financial reports. Thus the New Deal
added duality to duality: State governments maintained their jurisdiction over matters of incorporation and governance with a "trust"
approach, whereas the federal government oversaw questions of interstate commerce in the form of national securities markets, using
the "contract" approach.

During the postwar era, the active shareholders' role had in effect come to be framed in terms of "exit" and "voice": The shareholders could pressure management (as market actors) with threats
of defection through equity sales, and at the same time they could
participate directly by vote or veto.[34] For passive shareholders the *ex
post* approach could ameliorate past injuries and discourage future
abuses through the perceived probability of court awards for
damages.

These judgments regarding the appropriateness of a contract or
trust approach toward corporate regulation had important implications for defining management as a semipublic profession. If no significantly dependent relationships could be established for an entire
class or classes of corporate stakeholders, then no justification existed for public action. Private contracting parties could negotiate
relatively freely, thereby maintaining a constitutional conception of
regulation that distinguished public control from private autonomy,
politics from economics. Consequently, this regulatory vision conceived of managers as private agents with no greater public responsibilities than any other citizens had, and those favoring a contractual
approach argued that managers had no social responsibility, no professional duty beyond that of technical competence. Public supervision became necessary when systemic disparities existed among the
bargaining parties and trustee standards were required to ensure
equitable outcomes. The trust approach demanded that managers
and legislators together decide on public norms and turn them into
working rules, thus blurring distinctions between private and public
authority.[35]

But even when the trustee position prevailed, the bargaining process (as well as group formation itself) remained outside direct government interference. The regulatory process established the working rules for negotiations. It did not establish the ends. Management
accordingly remained a private calling, even when vested with public

expectations. This peculiar status in turn ascribed another public function to managers: For both professional and self-interested reasons, they were expected to aggregate into an effective political voice opposing general government interference at the same time that many would continue to favor particular, self-serving rules. Thus, when the trustee position assigned management fiduciary responsibilities for corporate property, it simultaneously anticipated that managers would be the guardians of America's liberal polity (see Chapters 8 and 9 for a development of these ideas).

Generally, the dual treatment of shareholders under the law appeared reasonable as long as the underlying realities of the two shareholder functions—overseeing managers and supplying capital—lent themselves to distinct bodies of regulation. Insofar as the federal government restricted itself to market-enhancing rules and deferred to state regulation in matters of corporate managerial accountability, the language of "trust" tended to dominate managerial conduct. Over time, especially with the "business judgment rule," the state courts themselves increasingly deferred to the principal corporate trustees (the board of directors), but the added dependency that this latitude might create was offset by the broader avenues of escape opened up by the continuing maturation of securities markets. The rise of a national "market for corporate control" during the 1960s, however, caused state and federal roles in corporate regulation necessarily to converge, and their use of distinct enforcement standards—trust and contract—became increasingly problematic (see Chapters 4 and 10).

Banking Reforms

By adopting market-based rules to reinforce the shareholders' ability to monitor management, Congress signaled its continued bias against concentrated financial control. The Glass–Steagall Act of 1933 not only separated the commercial and investment banking functions into distinct industries but also prohibited commercial bank equity ownership in nonfinancial firms. The Senate Banking Committee hearings that immediately preceded this act retraced much of the Pujo inquiries of 1912/13, particularly in examining the possibility of financial control over corporate enterprise. In accepting the banking industry's investment functions as legitimate but denying its right to establish holding companies to control industrial undertakings, Congress asserted anew that decentralized ownership both promoted economic growth and guarded against the creation of a ruling class hostile to democratic government. The Investment Company Act of 1940, which prevented mutual funds from holding more than 5 percent of any single company, also expressed this conviction.[36]

Labor Reforms

Before the New Deal courts had by and large presumed that employees were basically independent, because they could either sell their services elsewhere or become self-employed. If workers could develop skills and experience that transferred readily across a broad range of alternative jobs, their mobility would protect them from exploitation and ensure that they would share in any gains from technological progress. With limited statutory modifications, courts continued to "imply" contracts in labor relations that imposed on workers many of the costs of industrialization, both those that were internal to the employment relationship, such as work-related accidents, and those that were external, such as the loss of earned income due to cyclical unemployment, disability, and old age.

Industrialization's increasingly high degree of organizational, technological, and geographic specialization, however, made job transfers quite costly, a fact that the courts tended simply to ignore.[37] Employees in large corporations tended to develop quite firm-specific skills. This specialization inhibited their mobility, because the value of their services would be sacrificed even in lateral moves. Indeed, the longer that workers remained on the job, the more closely their career expectations would become tied to the long-term performance of the firm and their personal treatment by the firm's managers.

Regulators could address these dependencies with either a trust or a contract approach. That is to say, they could give workers express claims against managers of the firm to ensure fair treatment of employee interests that grew out of commitments to the firm. Or they could strengthen workers' capacities to look after their own interests or, at least, preclude those kinds of contracts that appeared to exploit workers unreasonably. New Deal labor reforms reflect a mixture of contract approaches designed to minimize market disparities and promote negotiations between workers and managers.

On the one hand, labor reforms concerned with workers as individual contractors centered on making the employment contract more reasonable. Policies enhancing worker mobility served to curb exploitation. So the costs of changing jobs could be reduced, for instance, by disassociating disability pension, cyclical unemployment, and other benefits from particular employers or by making them transferable; and subsidies for retraining also facilitated worker mobility.[38] Tax incentive packages could help increase the range of contracts managers negotiated with groups of similar employees, giving individual workers a wider choice of wage and benefit packages.

On the other hand, regulations concerned with group vulnerability to management concentrated on giving employees bargaining power as units. Since both industry and trade unions had often insisted on standard contracts for groups of workers, regulators conceded their cost effectiveness.[39] Regulations could render whole groups of workers covered by such contracts less dependent on the good faith or fairness of their employers. They could, for example, neutralize the restrictive effect of monopsonistic labor markets by enabling unions to negotiate industrywide contract standards. Regulations could also place worker groups on relatively equal footing with their employers in negotiating over issues surrounding career control and job information by enforcing training, seniority, security, promotion, and other working-condition provisions of collectively bargained contracts. And although standardization seemed to make individual workers' loss of autonomy inevitable, regulations could give them process rights within their unions at the representation and contract ratification stages.[40]

Until the New Deal, courts had frequently overturned or narrowed the scope of protective labor legislation at both the federal and the state level. They had done so under their powers both to interpret statutes and review their constitutionality (under the guise of "due process," "private property" and "freedom of contract"). Yet the state legislatures had also enacted some modest "protective" statutes that provided generalized market rules and insurance programs to limit the hours of work, standardize workers' compensation, and regulate disability and life insurance or pension savings programs.[41] The federal government began entering the field on two fronts. First, it tempered judicial intervention in labor disputes, both to force employers to work out their differences with groups of workers directly and to preserve the integrity of state legislation protecting labor.[42] Second, it provided protections for workers in the federal government and in nationalized industries like railroads and navigation that eluded effective state regulation.[43]

The courts also tried to preserve employer and employee autonomy in labor relations and the preeminence of the individualized contract in labor regulation. Before the Norris–LaGuardia (1932) and Wagner (1935) acts, those resorting to "common-law" property and contract doctrine had regularly interceded on behalf of employers to thwart employees acting collectively to take advantage of their circumstances.[44] Firm-specific development of worker skills made not only employees but also their employers somewhat vulnerable.[45] Skilled labor could bargain effectively over the firm's quasi rents to which they had contributed, ultimately by threatening to withhold their labor collectively.[46] Up through 1930, the courts broadly encouraged employers to write contracts and assert property rights to avert such behavior; they also imposed financial penalties on collective and individual actions that undermined individual employment contract provisions and sent more aggressive and interfering labor leaders to jail. The Norris–LaGuardia Act, passed in the year before Franklin Roosevelt took office, restricted the use of federal court injunctions in labor disputes and so rebalanced the law's role in the collective bargaining process.

New Deal legislation went further to correct the bias against labor. The Social Security Act (SSA) in 1935 strengthened labor's mobility and therefore its bargaining power by allowing workers to change jobs without concern about their retirement. The National Labor Relations Act (NLRA) of 1935, in recognizing union organizing and collective bargaining rights, instructed business to stop resisting union expansion.[47] The latter in effect gave employees a collective choice. Workers could bargain individually and so take their chances on managerial good faith with respect to open–ended aspects of the employment relationship. In these cases, the government continued to intervene against sharp dealing and exploitation, but only in strictly limited ways. Or workers could bargain in organized groups under the aegis of the NLRA, at arm's length and for a variety of express contract concerns. In these cases, the NLRB ensured that workers could in fact organize themselves and bargain effectively.

Among its benefits, collective action enabled workers to seek outside representation by more effective and knowledgeable negotiators, institutionalize their access to contract information and market conditions, reconcile cooperatively before management could exploit differences, and increase their bargaining power by threatening to withhold their labor as a group. Among the costs of collective action, however, was its undercutting of individual liberties both economically and politically. Just as economically weak or naive investors came to depend on the trustworthiness of brokers and investment bankers, so too did workers increasingly rely on the good faith of their bargaining and organizing agents, the unions.[48]

By and large, New Deal regulation of managerial discretion over labor took the form of *ex ante* intervention in the writing of contracts. Only later did worker protection policies shift and then, but briefly, toward an *ex post* trust approach: Here we anticipate the various discrimination and equal employment opportunity regulations of the 1960s and 1970s along with certain policies embedded in employers' liability law as they emerged in tort doctrine and occupational safety and health regulation.[49]

Standardized contract limitations imposed responsibilities on management under the SSA, Fair Labor Standards Act (FLSA) and various state statutes, though not, strictly, in the sense of quasi-ownership claims that Berle or Dodd may have had in mind when they were debating stakeholder protection. During the years immediately following their enactment, these statutory limitations did induce the courts to adopt somewhat of a trust approach in labor regulations. The statutes imposed specific constraints on the kinds of contracts that employers could negotiate with all employees, whether or not they were unionized. By the time of FDR and the New Deal, the industrialized states had already enacted workers' compensation insurance programs designed to spread the cost of work-related accidents. The SSA supplemented these measures by encouraging state unemployment compensation insurance programs and by instituting federal retirement and disability income programs that spread social costs across the workforce as a whole. In 1938, Congress also passed the FLSA, which set minimum wages in most industries and restricted managerial discretion in requiring overtime work. Again, these reforms protected employees against exploitation somewhat paternalistically, but did so through generally applicable rules restricting specific terms in labor contracts.

Nevertheless, from 1935 to 1946, the rationale for labor law protection gradually broadened.[50] Under the "economic reality of dependency" doctrine, the New Deal courts extended organizing rights, social security, unemployment benefits, minimum wages, and maximum hours protection to workers who had little or no bargaining power. Firms often treated relatively unskilled and easily replaceable workers as "independent contractors," thus avoiding the reach of protective statutes that applied only to "employees." In response, the courts began to extend the coverage of these newly enacted federal protective labor laws to help this extra class of dependents. In effect, this action redrew the boundaries of the corporate entity. During this brief period, the corporation took on the personality of a "public trust" (at least with respect to labor markets), and this corporate personality, as opposed to the corporation's legal form, drove legal judgments and policy.

In 1947, however, Congress amended the Taft–Hartley Act to curb the courts' expansive reading of statutory labor protection. The emergent idea that a worker's dependence on managerial will was cause for him just as other employees was supplanted by the narrower conception of statutory entitlement that deferred to managerial designations of who was and was not an "employee." In this way, Taft-Hartley decisively foreclosed the brief opportunity for managerial "trusteeship" to take on a more public aspect.

Given the continued ambivalence of policymakers toward the corporation's personality and the extent to which wages and health insurance and pensions depended on employment status, unskilled workers not suprisingly continued the battle in the courts for protection as stakeholders. Throughout the 1960s and 1970s, workers deemed "independent contractors" by their employers still won recognition as "employees" in a number of cases (i.e., were found to be integrated into rather than independent of the firm). Moreover, in cases involving discrimination in hiring, would-be employees also won claims against firms for managerial violations of a quasi-public trust. By the 1980s, however, the renewed conservatism of judges and federal administrators ensured that employee status under the relevant statutes would be construed narrowly.[51]

The Court's Pluralist Realignment

By treating the multistate corporation as a "natural entity" immune to state police power, the Court forced the federal government to develop an administrative apparatus. In turn, as Congress mandated its administrative agents to manage corporate control's relationship to the firm's various stakeholders, legal and social science research challenged the Court to discard its formalism. It took time to meet this challenge.

Realism seemed important, at least in the context of the Great Depression, and the Court moved narrowly to accept state innovations in meeting economic crises. Yet even as late as the spring of 1935, the Court annulled a number of federal and state initiatives. These actions provoked a crisis in 1937 when FDR unsuccessfully attempted to "pack" the Court with justices sympathetic to the New Deal. Roosevelt eventually prevailed when the Court's most conservative justices retired. Between 1937 and 1941, he made eight new appointments, which brought about a doctrinal realignment that sustained the New Deal's basic legislation, including the Wagner Act, the Social Security Act, and the Fair Labor Standards Act.

Even after its reorientation, however, the Court ruled unanimously against the NIRA. Justice Brandeis, quoted in an appraisal of the Court's opinion, noted: "This is the end of this business of centralization . . . we're not going to let this government centralize everything."[52] In the Court's opinion, the NIRA had delegated legislative powers to the executive branch and extended public powers to private associations working out its plans. Subsequent New Deal legislation adhered to this finding, avoiding centralized administration in favor of decentralized, fragmented, and potentially competing administrative enactments.

In reorienting itself doctrinally to the nation's modern organizational realities, the Court disavowed substantive due process and in its place espoused a procedural due process consistent with an administrative state that was to manage, not merely police, the national economy. Under the doctrine of substantive due process, the Court had actively reviewed legislation to ensure liberty and impede redistribution. Now it relinquished its shadow legislative function, allowing Congress to enact laws freely, with one proviso: that parties affected directly by enforcement have an adequate opportunity to elaborate their objections.

The Court also refused to comment substantively on either the administrative rules or their adjudication, choosing instead simply to review the procedural process to guarantee adequate and fair representation. Congress itself subscribed to this revision in the due process interpretation when it enacted the Administrative Procedures Act (APA) of 1946. The sponsors of the bill intended to satisfy both defenders and opponents of the New Deal. Although the law recognized that each agency had separate mandates and was accountable to different constituencies, the APA nonetheless established general procedural guidelines for rule making and adjudication.[53] With these internal mechanisms to minimize administrative discretion, New Deal reformers also limited their own penchant for abuse. They not only preserved liberty but further strengthened equality, by demanding equal representation in legislative formulation and administration.

Because not just public utilities and railroads were now subject to federal regulation, it became important for corporate control groups in general to consider national politics as well as market conditions in formulating their strategy and structure. Senior management, as Berle prophesied, had truly became a matter of statesmanship.

CONCLUSION

Technically, it appeared that the new administrative order had resolved the corporation's constitutional status without fundamentally altering the premises of America's liberal heritage. Consciously or not, New Deal architects had fashioned a system that preserved America's division of governmental powers. The states retained authority over incorporation and corporate governance, and the federal government interfered in corporate matters only when they involved interstate commerce. New Deal reformers also respected the constitutional separation of powers. By acquiescing in the Court's *Schechter* decision that invalidated the NIRA, they abandoned central planning and reaffirmed the liberal distinction between public authority and private life. By employing a scientific, functional methodology, Roosevelt's administrators also claimed that they were merely neutral technocrats, outside the continuing value discussions about whether democracy's true ends were the preservation of liberty and the enhancement of social utility or the development of citizenship and self-rule.

This technical neutrality and expertise served democratic rule by reducing the probabilities of both corporate abuse and corporate centralization. Newly established public disclosures minimized mismanagement and misappropriation. Combined with antitrust laws and banking laws such as the Glass–Stegall Act separating investment and commercial banking, they also lessened the possibility of centralized corporate control, particularly by financial sources.

Yet the administrative response to the modern corporation was not so benign as its proponents suggested. By sanctioning a control group, typically management, the state had created a powerful collective body capable of creating majority coalitions. Moreover, particularly when trust doctrines were applied, the regulatory process broadened the discretionary powers of both management and public administrators. As we shall see, these concerns about the shift in power from the legislature to technocrats like corporate managers and public administrators came to inform postwar debates about democracy. In struggling for answers to the perennial question of how to demarcate free-market and government spheres, the regulatory state helped make and unmake corporate manangement as a semi-public profession. Read on.

5

From Trust to Contract: The Regulatory Making and Unmaking of a Profession and the Market in Corporate Control

With the alternatives of "trust" and "contract" perspectives on corporations and their control described through a discussion of *The Modern Corporation and Private Property,* we are now able to show how this divide played out in contradictory approaches to corporate regulation in the postwar period and beyond. We can discern a transition in rule making, partly in reaction to totalitarianism and collective values. The framework shifted from government oversight through trust to market regulation through contract. And as time passed, the market for corporate control through corporate takeover seemed an adequate, though perhaps a costly, method of disciplining managers who put their own ambitions egregiously ahead of those of their stockholders.

CONTEXT

As the postwar years yielded to the decade of the 1950s, social scientists were tenaciously trying to identify a unifying theme in regulatory actions. These attempts proved bootless. Instead of a government imbued with a central and vitalizing ideology, they found a broker state that lessened class conflict by narrowing issues to group disputes and facilitating group negotiations. Pragmatism had replaced ideology, and procedural norms ensured that each group, regardless of its political or economic clout, had access to political and administrative forums.[1]

Far from deploring this discovery, social scientists found it cause for celebration. The terrors of mass society and ideological manipulation just confronted abroad convinced both students and makers of policy to reject "moral absolutes" and to embrace "relativistic empiricism" and its complement, the value-neutral state.[2] The perseverance of democracy appeared to depend on resisting mass ideology—the sudden cohesion of values that characterized totalitarian regimes—and committing instead to pragmatic procedures for resolving social differences and dislocations. In developing a "liberal" state, political and intellectual leaders could coordinate the industrial economy without radically compressing social values.

Libertarian critics like Friedrich Hayek,[3] Frank Knight,[4] and other associates of the "Chicago school"[5] distinguished technocracy from democratic legislation by juxtaposing planning alongside market rules.[6] The market had great power to preserve, even nurture, individual freedoms. Its rules promised formal equality. They allowed people to solve problems as they saw them and according to their own tastes, instead of forcing everyone to accept collective definitions, priorities, and solutions. Moreover, because information was so diversified and so costly to centralize, individual problem solving was likely to be more efficient, even if planners could actually be induced to behave in the "public interest." How could one even begin to define the public weal? And how could incentives be set to follow it instead of election pressures and vested interests?[7] The answers were so resoundingly and immediately negative that skeptics found these questions merely rhetoric (see also Chapter 6).

The new political science of pluralist democracy borrowed "neutrality" and "efficiency" from economics to grasp the subtleties of group bargaining in politics and administration. Social-choice theory flourished in the 1950s through the writings of economic thinkers like Kenneth Arrow, Anthony Downs, Gordon Tullock, and James Buchanan and confirmed the stabilizing tendencies of a fragmented electorate and a two-party system of majority rule. Political science focused on theoretical and empirical studies of the conditions for democratic rule or polyarchy: elective processes that recognized majority rule and were bolstered by guarantees of individual and associational freedom.[8] As Daniel Bell put it: "In the Western world, there is today a rough consensus among intellectuals on political issues: the acceptance of a Welfare State; the desirability of decentralized power; a system of mixed economy and of political pluralism. In that sense, too, the ideological age has ended."

Optimism about the broker state, however, did not entirely allay special concerns about the corporation. Another criticism contrasted liberal democracy with bureaucratic corporatism.[9] James Burnham, for example, observed that although

> sovereignty may still be chiefly located in Congress (together with the Supreme Court) . . . , no one with eyes open during the past decade will believe its claims are undisputed. Most laws are not being made any longer by Congress, but by the NLRB, SEC, ICC, AAA, TVA, FTC, FCC, the Office of Production Management (what a revealing title!) and the other leading "executive agencies."[10]

The drift toward expedience appeared to increase the potential for dependent relationships and the corruption of politics by "Big Business" and, in some quarters, "Big Labor." Federal interventions that were intended to correct corporate abuses by protecting dependent stakeholders under the aegis of "trust" also threatened to reduce citizens to economic and political passivity. Paradoxically, they might thus reinforce the effects of federally unregulated corporations. In America's brave new world, how could one expect these dependents to participate autonomously and actively in electoral and legislative politics?

Totalitarianism might thus lurk ominously behind trust, and this threat loomed large in postwar writings on the modern corporation. Few could avoid comparing the concentrated power of large corporations and their "supporting" regulatory apparatus with that of various Soviet counterparts. This comparison was particularly disturbing in regulated industries like energy, communications, and transportation, in which the distinctions between private and public administration were far from clear. By solidifying managers as an interest group and motivating them to participate in the electoral/political process, the "regulated" might actually capture the regulatory regime, making the state itself a corporate dependent and obliterating the distinction between public and private authority.

CORPORATE CONTROL, DECENTRALIZATION, AND THE PLURALIST STATE

As Adolf Berle noted, analogies between the totalitarian and democratic systems in industrialized economies never went beyond perceived congruencies of industrial concentration and the potential for separating ownership from control to centralize industrial decisions among either state bureaucrats or financial institutions.[11] In

America, both characteristics arose spontaneously from the market, but constitutional traditions worked to preserve the corporation as a decentralized, private arrangement separate from its public administrative units and its sources of capital. In contrast, Soviet industrial organization had been institutionalized through statist directives that simultaneously concentrated industry into large aggregates and centralized authority over them.

Antitrust regulators, encouraged by congressional antitrust reforms, worked hard after the war to ensure that the few hundred largest firms in the United States were unable to increase their market power through mergers, acquisitions, or other monopolizing practices. In vigorously pursuing these policies, antitrust administrators tried to preserve both efficiency and pluralism.

Congress continued to scrutinize the efficiency of New Deal provisions prohibiting banker and mutual fund control over large firms. But the following brief history of banking regulation illustrates how hard it is to keep energetic people from continuing to advance their own interests; it is the story of how closing one loophole seems to open up another.

Banking Regulation

Between 1945 and 1980, Congress was fighting a two-front war. On the one side, Congress was making sure that managers would not get together to monopolize industrial production; on the other, Congress tried to keep increasingly larger financial institutions from getting together to monopolize industries through securities ownership. Detecting gaps in the Glass–Steagall Act that allowed bank holding companies to gain control of nonfinancial corporations, Congress passed the Bank Holding Company Act of 1956, specifically prohibiting them from owning 5 percent or more of the voting stock of a nonbank company.[12] Because the act applied only to firms with multiple banks, however, many of the nation's largest banks bypassed the law simply by establishing themselves as single banking companies, especially after 1966 when Congress simplified the act's merger standards.

In 1968, the Pateman Subcommittee again warned that banks were centralizing control, not only through the huge financial resources at their disposal, but also through their interrelationships with the nonbanking community.[13] The committee called for immediate antitrust action under the Clayton Act to alleviate the situation, and Congress established new regulations prohibiting the banks' trust departments from holding any more than 10 percent of any single corporation.[14]

In 1968, Congress instructed the Securities Exchange Commission (SEC) to determine how the "sale, purchase and holding of securities by institutional investors" affected fairness and stability in the securities market and whether the increasing number of shares concentrated among banks, pension funds, insurance companies, and mutual funds reflected inappropriately centralized economic power.[15] In 1971, the SEC reported that although savings were becoming concentrated among financial intermediaries that invested increasingly in corporate equity, institutional ownership had increased from only 24 to 26 percent between 1952 and 1968. Indeed, corporations themselves were becoming less dependent on new equity issues for capital expansion and more dependent on internal funds and commercial debt than ever before.[16] Institutional investors still held disproportionate positions among large firms, however, and these increased during the 1960s from approximately 31 to 40 percent among firms listed on the New York Stock Exchange.[17] Thus, the SEC was unable to rule out any long-term trend that might eventually place the nation's largest industrial firms under institutional investors' control.[18]

During the 1970s, congressional concern continued. Indeed, Congress began the decade by passing another Bank Holding Company Act to avoid the merger loophole in the Holding Act of 1956. In 1974, two subcommittees of the Government Operations Committee explored the adequacy of information about ownership[19] and control of publicly traded firms and developed uniform disclosure regulations,[20] and in 1976 two additional reports emerged from the Subcommittee on Reports, Accounting and Management. In 1975, in the midst of these inquiries, Congress passed the Securities Acts amendments, which required the SEC to gather information and issue public reports concerning the major institutional investors' discretionary holdings. In 1980, the Senate Committee on Governmental Affairs used these new data to examine the connections between the nation's major institutional investors, primarily commercial banks, and the nation's top one hundred nonfinancial corporations. The committee's report echoed concerns that America's major corporations were increasingly controlled by financial interests. Because the study was inconclusive on this matter, the report recommended that Congress establish an independent commission, similar to the Temporary National Economic Committee of the late 1930s, to explore the issue exhaustively.[21]

Having restrained the concentration of financial control by closing loophole after loophole and having adopted stringent antitrust measures and corporate stakeholder regulations to restrain managerial excess, Congress now accepted managerial stewardship as the surest means for reconciling the dictatorial needs of large-scale enterprises with democracy's commitment to self-government. "Stewardship" here echoed Berle's notion of trust and fiduciary responsibilities. Congress had constructed a public set of working rules to guide managers in their private transactions. Because managers shared an interest in preserving the authority to promote efficiency within their own firms, they could also be expected as a group to resist unnecessary financial intrusions into the firm and unnecessary public intrusions into the economy. Thus did Congress consider managers a helpful, even a necessary, force in preserving the liberal distinction between public and private.

Tender-Offer Regulation and the Intellectual Climate of Corporate Control, 1955–1968

Shareholder regulation in general and tender offer regulation in particular provide direct documentation of this widespread acceptance of the managerially controlled firm as an integral force in preserving the public/private distinction in modern industrial society.[22] Tender offers are the principal market means for dislodging a managerial control group, and until recently, managers have been considered fiduciaries in handling the transfer. Sounding some early Berlean themes, however, contractarians began to caution that the trustee position was sliding down a slippery slope in seeking public standards for private enterprise. They defended contract approaches instead because they plainly held the protection of private rights as the sole justification for governmental coercion. Legally and economically, the contract approach considered managers nothing more than contracting agents whose responsibilities and duties were no greater than those of any other citizen. Contractarians accordingly turned to the market for safeguards against managerial discretion. These, they believed, were not only more efficient than fiduciary standards but also more protective of liberty.

Writing in 1958, Berle defined control as the capacity to mobilize a majority of voting shares in favor of the controlling number (usually a majority) of corporate directors. In large, publicly held firms with a dispersion of equityholders, the capacity to mobilize votes was closely linked to influence over the proxy machinery. In most instances, this power was in the hands of management, but in some cases shareholders or shareholder groups with substantial minority positions were capable of exercising control, either by openly competing for proxies in elections for board seats or by threatening to compete and thereby gaining access to the proxy machinery with the cooperation of management in a form of joint control. Shareholders

with control, moreover, could generally sell their blocks of shares at a premium over market prices. This premium, Berle claimed, belonged to the corporation as a whole and therefore ought to be shared proportionately with the other shareholders or repaid to the corporation's treasury.[23]

Even though policy judgments had been inconsistent and even ambivalent, court opinions and regulations concerning the nature of corporate trusteeship had still drifted in the direction of Merrick Dodd's 1932 position favoring recognition of a broad range of corporate stakeholders instead of shareholders alone. In a series of emerging rules, the law had purified the process by which any group could exercise control. State law first prohibited the purchase of votes, deceptive claims designed to win votes, and side deals that compromised the autonomy of directors. Federal securities law then supplemented state law by standardizing disclosure requirements in proxy solicitations. These restrictions were quite similar to those the law had long placed on trustees in general: obligations to disclose transactions fully, treat beneficiaries fairly, conserve assets, eschew potential conflicts of interest, and exert cautiously the power to influence beneficiaries that came with the trustee's position.

The law also restricted the exercise of control, again with reference to trust standards. Departing directors and the shareholders who "conspired" with them were obligated to discover the intentions and trustworthiness of their proposed successors.[24] Controlling shareholders could neither exact nor retain a premium for their controlling interest.[25] Control, in sum, was a position of power within the corporation, rather than a property right, and there were fiduciary responsibilities in its exercise.

Why did trust seem such a useful concept for governing corporate control in 1958? Given their potential for exploiting the corporate system self-interestedly, why did policymakers assume that managers could be trustworthy? And if trust depended on shifting social norms, how could it be prevented from becoming the rationale for brute power and political manipulation? Answers came from analyses of the microfoundations and behavioral propensities of the managerially controlled firm.

No one elaborated the latter more completely than John Kenneth Galbraith. In his *The New Industrial State,* Galbraith claimed that the managerial "technocracy" dominated the market so thoroughly that the economy behaved as if it were administered or planned.[26] Shareholders no longer functioned to keep managers acting in the firm's best interests. They no longer even provided the economic function of supplying the firm with risk capital, which now came almost wholly from internal sources. Technocrats sought autonomy, which

depended on expanding corporate control over resources. Because growth under competitive markets required able asset management, managerially directed expansion served the cause of efficiency. It also satisfied not only shareholders but other stakeholders as well, especially those protected by public policy. With the industrial system meeting economic needs so admirably, Galbraith just hoped that once these needs were satisfied in some measure, society would assert other goals of a more noble sort.[27]

Robin Marris, perhaps the leading managerial economist of the period, reacted favorably to Galbraith's work but wondered why financial markets persisted if they no longer served a useful purpose.[28] Marris went so far (left) as to propose removing the firm from the shareholders' grasp, because the basic corporate objective should be job creation, not profit maximization. Less extreme leftists pushed the idea of corporate social responsibility along radical democratic lines, by questioning whether society could really trust management to conform to social norms. For these public-interest reformers of the late 1960s and 1970s, managerial trusteeship could be secured only through direct controls, and they proposed seats on the board of directors for otherwise unrepresented stakeholder groups. Public administrators should also be given stronger powers to enforce corporate compliance with norms of social responsibility.[29]

Critics of the managerial thesis on the right, most notably Henry Manne, favored a contractarian approach over one based on trust.[30] Although consistently acknowledging Berle's contributions, Manne objected to the notion that investor shareholders were passive. On the contrary, they played significant roles in regulating the conglomerate mergers just heating up in the 1960s.[31]

> Only the take-over scheme provides some assurance of competitive efficiency among corporate managers and thereby affords strong protection to the interests of vast numbers of small, non-controlling shareholders. Compared to this mechanism, the efforts of the SEC and the courts to protect shareholders through fiduciary duty and the shareholder's derivative suit seem small indeed.[32]

In general, Manne explained, the market for corporate control regulated managerial abuses by allowing outside managerial groups to compete in dislodging underachieving CEOs. In proxy contests, insiders enjoyed significant technical and resource advantages, so that the costs to an outsider of a risky campaign to win over the majority of shareholders often outweighed any potential gain.[33] In share purchases, the high cost of capitalization also frequently prohibited persons or syndicates from buying control.[34] In contrast,

mergers arranged by knowledgeable managers and effected through low-cost, tax-free stock swaps were relatively feasible.[35]

Accordingly, Manne both resisted antitrust policies that sought to restrict conglomerate mergers and, on the whole, favored deregulation of the market for corporate control, since competition among managers promised to reduce corporate mismanagement. Not only would a market for corporate control create standards for managerial performance that were reflected in stock prices, but it also would empower shareholders to play an active role, that is, to exercise their powers of voice and exit to favor or oppose a shift in corporate control.[36] Manne's market alternative to public administration also undercut the privileging of management as a justly empowered, semipublic profession, and it directly confronted the interest-group politics that led to increasing and even reckless delegations of power to public agents.[37]

Notwithstanding Manne's arguments, federal enforcement agencies continued to oppose mergers throughout the conglomerate wave of the 1960s. Since antitrust laws served only moderately to inhibit conglomeration, enforcement focused primarily on tender-offer regulations. Between 1953 and 1963, managers of large firms used stock tender offers as the principal means of taking over small profitable firms that promised future growth and diversification, but by 1965 they had come to rely on large-scale cash offers instead.[38] Opponents of conglomerate mergers therefore tried to make cash tender offers more restrictive.

By 1966, the leading advocates of tender-offer restrictions came from the managerial ranks of large publicly held firms, especially old-line firms in the steel, oil, banking, and insurance industries which had become the targets of hostile takeovers most frequently initiated by eleven rapacious "conglomerateurs."[39] This handful of firms accounted in 1968 for 92 percent of the value of acquisitions.[40]

The debates for regulating cash tender offers centered on two sets of relationships: that between shareholders and bidders and that between shareholders and managers. In both cases, reformers asked whether existing rules supported efficiency and responsible shareholder action. Federal legislators still presumed that when shareholders were forced to act as the control group, as in the case of a tender offer, they should be held accountable to management's standards of trust, and they remained rather skeptical of the power of competitive bidding in financial markets to safeguard dependent stakeholders from unscrupulous raiders. Concentrating on bidders' intentions and shareholders' responsibility to other stakeholders, the legislators apparently either trusted existing management or deferred to the states' jurisdiction to regulate managerial trusteeship.

   Whereas the states had responsibility for rules on corporate governance, federal lawmakers had jurisdiction over cash tender offers,
and the procedure raised two concerns. First, the shareholders were
vulnerable to managerial influence because they lacked their own
detailed information. Second, the target firm's management was susceptible to corruption by the offeror. Although the target's directors,
or management, had an obligation to review offers and pass along
good-faith recommendations to their shareholders, the promise of
side deals could tempt them to make better arrangements for themselves than for their shareholders.
   Cash tender offers thus threatened to dissolve the procedures for
ensuring trust. Bidders proposed to take both the shares and control
at once. They circumvented the firm's autonomous governance process and consequently dissolved any shareholder desire to judge the
firm's prospective management responsibly. Reformers therefore
heeded the warnings of target managements. Cash tender offers
would make well-run corporations vulnerable to unscrupulous and
incompetent management. Tender offers should be regulated in
ways that complemented trust objectives, proxy regulations, and corporate governance rulings.

The Williams Act, 1968 and Beyond

The Williams Act of 1968 responded to both financial market and
corporate governance concerns. Although the reform aimed to insulate target managements from hostile takeovers, its ultimate purpose
may have been to protect shareholders by making mandatory a variety of disclosures.[41] These provisions had been the most contentious
issue for advocates of trust and contract during the debates that led
up to the Williams Act. Its sponsor, Senator Harrison Williams, argued that they were necessary to safeguard proxy requirements and
the trust orientation of state corporate governance rules. The senator reasoned that shareholders acknowledged the responsibility of
the existing control group when they assumed an equity position in
the firm, and their continuing participation reflected a degree of
continuing faith. Although tender offers differed in key respects
from proxy solicitations (in particular by virtue of terminating the
shareholder's relationship to the corporation), Williams sought to
conform their requirements by making obligatory the disclosures
about bidders' qualifications and intentions. Like Berle, he viewed
shareholders confronted with a tender offer as a control group
obliged to act collectively as the corporation's trustees. Responsible
action required adequate information about the shareholders' choice
and justified the disclosure regulations.

Critics rejected as absurd the trusteeship argument and collective responsibility. Law professors Stanley Kaplan and Robert Mundheim favored the alternative approach of contract. Borrowing from Henry Manne, they found disclosures regarding the tender offeror's qualifications and intentions of minimal significance to shareholders on the verge of surrendering their stake and voting interests in the firm. Disclosures would only inhibit competition among potential tender offerors. Outsider premiums suggested that what should be questioned was not the bidders' intentions but the competence of current management.[42] Congress should simplify rather than obstruct cash tender offers. Requiring original bidders to publish their intentions, as Williams proposed, and thereby to share their insights into the target firm's profit potential, would in effect deprive them of the fruits of their labor and transfer the gains to passive shareholders and subsequent bidders. Disclosures would also constitute ill-gained information for the control group in power if the shareholders chose not to tender.

Continuing debate over the Williams Act discomfited most policymakers, in part because of the problem of defining a proper role for federal regulators. As we noted earlier, federal securities law had by and large limited itself to supplementing and coordinating state laws, concentrating on the issues surrounding financial market regulation and not on the procedures for internal corporate governance.[43] Introducing substantive trust concepts into federal regulation, as Williams proposed, intruded into the state's domain and also posed a general threat to modern federalism.

Among others, the SEC's chairman, Manuel Cohen, sought to mitigate the tension pragmatically. His congressional testimony acknowledged both the issue of intrusiveness and the persuasiveness of Kaplan's and Mundheim's arguments about the market for control.[44] Skirting the broad theoretical and ideological issues, however, he focused the debate on a series of hypothetical circumstances under which bidders' disclosures might be necessary for the shareholders' protection. For example, when tender offers involved 51 percent of the outstanding shares, shareholders' tenders might be only partially accepted, leaving them with ongoing stakes in their firms. In such cases, much like those of proxy battles, they deserved to be informed about a new control group's intentions.[45] Similarly, when some shareholders remained as participants, either by choice or by exclusion (tendering too late), they should be entitled to information about the prospective management of the firm in which they would continue as investors. Cases like these raised issues of contract, not trust.

While admitting that takeovers could benefit society by dislodging incompetent management, Cohen doubted that they all shared this motivation. Many were simply ways to acquire more cash or credit and involved so staggering an acquisition of debt that new management would be forced to auction off parts of the firm.[46] Cohen concluded that merger regulations should center on making investments efficient. Concentrating on contract could also help federal regulators retain the traditional division of federal and state authority. Be cause the states tended to view management–shareholder relationships as trusteeships, they would also implicitly reinforce fiduciary doctrines.

Persuasive as the other side sometimes appeared, Williams and his camp carried the day, and the Williams Act set up the following provisions: Bidders were now required to disclose pertinent information so that shareholders could evaluate their managerial qualifications and the financial implications of the offer, and offer forms were restricted to avoid coercion. The regulations also required disclosures by current (targeted) boards of directors, with specific note of their reasons for supporting or opposing a tender offer.[47]

Following passage of the Williams Act, falling stock prices ended the wave of conglomerate mergers. Much of the debate between market and trust advocates subsided for a decade, though it continued in discussions about "insider-trading" regulations.[48]

When corporate takeovers reemerged as a salient issue in the 1980s, however, a number of factors combined to continue weakening the trust approach to managerial responsibility. First, a decade of social activism and intense international competition had undermined public confidence in both the efficiency and the ethics of American management.[49] Second, innovations in takeover technology (such as the use of strip financing and high-yield, investment-grade, "junk" bonds), more sophisticated financial and legal advisers, and new capital from independently managed pension funds and foreign investors spurred ther development of a takeover market that put large, financially underperforming firms at greater risk than they had been in the 1960s.[50] Deregulation and weaker antitrust enforcement added to the impetus for takeovers.[51]

Armen Alchian and Harold Demsetz, among others, heeded Manne's clarion call to refine the microanalytic tools of corporation lawyers and developed a libertarian economic theory of property rights. Asserting that property rights were instruments of control, Alchian and Demsetz concluded that public policies should promote growth by conforming property rules to wealth-maximizing principles.[52] They modeled the firm as a nexus of contractual exchanges among various rational agents with specified bundles of rights. These agents derived utility from the exchanges, ably calculated their benefits and costs, and pursued their best opportunities with creative zeal.

Parallel developments occurred in financial-agency theory, which elaborated on the essentials of Berle's contractual model of the firm and rooted the separation of ownership from control in the benefits gained from better allowing people to specialize in monitoring, risk bearing, and operational management.[53] Both stockholders and managers had the incentive to monitor firm performance. In pursuit of good investments, the former constantly appraised the firm's present and future earnings as reflected in stock prices that provided comparison with competing firms. The latter monitored their own behavior to avoid the relatively low stock prices that might put their firms "into play." These self-imposed monitoring techniques included the board of directors, independent accountants, hierarchical review processes, and reward structures connected to firm performance.

As claimants on the firm's residual or surplus, shareholders bore much of the financial risk. But because they were able to reduce their overall risk by diversifying their portfolios, even strongly risk-averse shareholders might act as if they did not care about how chancy any one investment might be and demand that managers pursue high returns over safe ones. Managers, on the other hand, were tied to their jobs by constricted managerial labor markets and firm-specific investments. Unable to diversify their investments in human capital, they sought to reduce risk by retaining earnings rather than paying out excess corporate cash to shareholders. Cash reserves could then meet unanticipated commercial difficulties. They could also provide the capital to make corporate acquisitions, which could help managers both by reducing risk through diversification and by expanding managerial hierarchies and thus enhancing their career opportunities. Considerations like these made agency theorists concerned that although the managerially controlled firm offered significant benefits, it did so at a signficant cost.[54]

The managerially trained Oliver Williamson also asked what prompted firms to grow, to produce rather than purchase, but the explanations he pursued had less to do with managerial ambitions than with the transaction costs that Coase had originally highlighted in 1937. Williamson's microeconomic analysis identified the organizational arrangements or "alternative governance structures" that most efficiently economized on these transaction costs.[55] In buying from others, an entrepreneur's commitment was minor, but costs arose from specifying, monitoring, and policing the independent, self-interested agent-suppliers. These might be relatively minor in the face of competition, product fungibility, and transaction infrequency, but when exchanges involved repeated negotiation or were supported by transaction-specific investments, they might be substantial. The firm emerged as a way to overcome such market inconveniences.

Masahiko Aoki examined instead both the firm's nature as a unit of production and the managerial role. Describing the firm as a cooperative undertaking among workers and investors for mutual gain, Aoki posited that managers coordinated operations to obtain and preserve "organizational rents," using negotiations to mediate or arbitrate workers' and investors' respective claims to the rents.[56] As long as managers could keep workers and investors committed to cooperation, the firm as a unit could seize on differentiating strategies in production or distribution that would create organizational rents.

For Aoki, the stakeholder's commitment depended on perceptions that the firm fairly operated and distributed its rents. Differing preferences for risk critically influenced the outcome of negotiations and stakeholder perceptions. As in agency theory, investors were risk neutral with respect to any one firm. Their ability to diversify holdings gave them bargaining advantages, and they generally favored firms with high rates of growth or competitive pricing. Workers, in contrast, were risk averse, since they were relatively overinvested in (committed to) the firm; they preferred to restrict the firm's growth to keep marginal revenues higher and raise the average wages of existing workers rather than hiring more labor. Although workers were reluctant to sacrifice their jobs and regular income, they still had bargaining power: They could protect their claims to profits by threatening to withdraw their firm-specific skills.[57] A "core" of alternative cooperative solutions therefore existed. And even though the managerial function was entrepreneurial at first—to establish the firm by attracting the needed resources and arranging bargaining procedures to produce organizational rents[58]—the function later became "judicial"—to preserve the firm by renewing the stakeholders' commitments within the core of cooperative solutions.[59]

In ascribing cooperative features to the firm, commitments that could not be "cashed out" or readily disaggregated with respect to their contributing value, the Williamson and Aoki models differed markedly from those of property-rights and financial-agency theorists. Yet all shared contractual premises. Although trust won the day in the tender-offer legislation of 1968, economic writing in many quarters and with many different objectives—finance, antitrust, managerial economics—combined to develop the contract model that Coase had imagined some thirty years before and made it a more forceful challenger to trust.

Indeed, when the takeovers reemerged in the 1980s, this new economic thinking quickly entered legal discussions about corporate regulation. Enthusiasts included not only free-market idealists pursuing Manne's and others' prescriptions for laissez-faire but also managerialists ready to break with the no longer compelling logic of trust.[60] Nevertheless, the libertarians did differ from more conventional writers in regard to legal doctrine, particularly in their willingness to sacrifice traditional organizational boundaries to individualistic claims.[61]

University of Chicago law professors Frank H. Easterbrook and Daniel R. Fischel favored an active market in corporate control with low premiums. To avoid inhibiting takeover bids, they advocated rescinding Williams Act provisions that extended offer periods[62] and holding managers to a standard of passivity during such bids.[63] An active market for control would correct for deviations between share prices and underlying (bust-up or redeployment) values.[64] Investors on the whole would benefit because rules that enhanced the market's function as a low-cost corrective mechanism would also serve shareholders by providing an inexpensive way to oversee and discipline management.

John C. Coffee, the Adolf A. Berle Professor at Columbia Law School and a leading managerialist, adopted the Easterbrook–Fischel contractarian model of the firm, concurred with some of their proposals for reform, and agreed that the preferred regulatory regime should be market enhancing rather than fiduciary. In his view, managers of target firms created a significant source of "friction" (transaction costs) in the market that brought together outside bidders and target firms' shareholders, and this potential for managerial opportunism could justify market-enhancing regulations.[65]

But Coffee would not concede that an active market for corporate control automatically maximized shareholder wealth. To Easterbrook and Fischel, the benefits of frequent bidding and opportunities for managerial transition outweighed the longer-term advantages of managerial stability, including the development of organizational rents that might accompany investors' as well as other stakeholders' commitments. In contrast, Coffee preferred a market for corporate control characterized by infrequent bids and high premiums, one in which the shareholders of target firms would realize the maximum potential value of control. Regulations, he believed, should foster an auction market in which managers would trigger bidding contests among offerors.[66] He therefore approved of the

Williams Act for making the takeover process slower, the number of tender offers fewer, and the premiums paid higher than they would otherwise have been.[67] Rescinding the act to promote a more active market for corporate control would lead to organizational inefficiencies, managerial sloth, and demoralization due to "excessive" deterrence.[68] Too much bidding could disrupt the managers' mediating functions (as in Aoki's model) and continual negotiations with the firm's cooperating stakeholders. Battles for control could well erode the firm's continued production of organizational rents and so, too, shareholders' returns on investment. Michael Jensen and others in the more libertarian camp responded that taking a firm's stock out of play through closed shareholding and increased debt financing was a better way to resolve this tension.[69]

For all the disagreements on policy, this debate over tender-offer regulation reveals a narrowing of regulatory assumptions since the early 1960s. All of these writers shared in their contractual conception of the firm a skepticism about the validity of earlier dependency analyses and the presumption that investor-shareholders could actively and adequately determine their own destinies. Regulations should therefore enhance the market, facilitating negotiations among all the various constituent groups—not just shareholders but also managers, creditors, and employees.

Even Coffee, Berle's titular successor, no longer saw shareholders as both owners and investors. Few writers in the 1980s expected them to behave as anything more than traders in corporate shares. Most viewed shareholder property rights in terms of the market's proper functioning rather than in terms of equality and substantive fairness. Berle had argued that the premium paid for control had to be returned to the corporation or at least proportionately divided among all the shareholders; he rested his argument on the firm 's associational reality. But Coffee and others asserted instead that shareholders understood that in firms that were "tightly" controlled by others, these others, whether they constituted a majority or a substantial minority, could command the premium for control; the rest then could discount their own share values accordingly.

The fiduciary character of management also took on a meaning close to market and contractarian prescriptions. Although neither Coffee nor Easterbrook and Fischel openly challenged the states' corporate chartering powers or the states' trustee standards, both sides favored restricting management's fiduciary duties to the shareholders' interest in wealth maximization. In this new contractual and self-regulating vision, the firm acted like a market and simply ordered bargaining among independent groups. Control had a market value that each group could take into account, and managers had neither a semipublic responsibility to the firm's underrepresented stakeholders nor to the liberal values that distinguished private from public pursuits.[70] Rather managers had become merely contracting agents whose services were evaluated by the firm's internal monitoring devices and by the market for corporate control. In short, management was not a calling but a job, with technical competence and honesty the only criteria for success.

Despite their similarities, however, libertarians in the Manne mode did differ markedly from managerialists like Coffee who valued a degree of stability in corporate control. By reducing the firm to a "nexus of contracts" and managers to agents serving solely to maximize shareholder wealth, the former tended to dismiss the traditional view of the firm as a collaborative undertaking. In their view, the markets for shares and control served as the most effective checks on managerial discretion.[71] In contrast, managerialists noted that cooperation made resistance possible, so that managers had to act as interpretive agents in settling contests over reinvestment, distribution, and reserves.[72] Because the firm's organizational reality could exceed the terms of its contractual obligations, managerial discretion should be shaped to accommodate a broader set of stakeholder norms as well as product market competition.[73]

Chapter 10 carries these considerations a step further as it looks at the market for corporate control in the 1980s. The takeover firm of Kohlberg, Kravis & Roberts, in particular, created a new form of organization that promises the benefit of overcoming certain agency problems at the cost of increased financial concentration. This innovation could be the answer to increased global competition, particularly from Germany and Japan, to whose bank-centered conglomerates and *keiretsu* it bears more than a passing resemblance. But it would also require a loosening of financial regulations that reflect a distrust in financial control that dates back at least to the days of Glass–Steagall.

THE LEGISLATIVE DEBATES ON CORPORATE TAKEOVER REGULATION

This newly consistent vocabulary for the large managerial firm also shaped congressional considerations of corporate tender-offer regulation in the 1980s. In 1984, T. Boone Pickens's battle for Gulf Oil signaled that with the help of financial innovations like low-grade, high-yield, "junk" bonds, huge corporations were no longer beyond the takeover reach of small firms or even aggressive individuals.[74]

Leveraged buyouts converted publicly traded firms and/or their subsidiaries into private undertakings. Using the target firm's assets as collateral, the offeror purchased the target's shares with debt like junk bonds and then sold off subsidiaries or used earnings to retire the debt.[75] Debt-financed buyouts increased enormously in the 1980s. In 1979, there were 75 buyouts valued at $1.3 billion; by 1988 there were 214 transactions, exceeding $77 billion.[76] In 1981, leveraged buyouts accounted for only 4.6 percent of the completed mergers; the decade's peak was 22.7 percent of merger activity in 1986.[77] The nation's elite investment banks became actively involved in the market, even arranging debt for hostile takeovers of *Fortune* 500 companies. Their involvement also distinguished the older conglomerate merger wave from the new one, since investment bankers had rarely assisted the conglomerateurs of the 1960s in their raids.[78] Indeed, Michael Jensen and Carol Loomis suggested that the 1980s takeover binge represented an effort by finance capital to regain the control over the large firm that it had lost during the 1920s and 1930s.[79]

Tender-offer bids, meanwhile, made up only a small fraction of the total merger activity in the early and mid-1980s, and hostile takeovers were even less frequent. In 1984 and 1985, for example, when transactions totaled 6,000, there were only 263 tender offers, of which only 76 were hostile.[80] In 1979, Congress nonetheless had shown renewed interest in regulating this market when the Senate Committee on Banking, Housing, and Urban Affairs asked the SEC to review the adequacy of existing law in meeting the challenges of the new merger mania.[81]

Matters seemed more urgent in 1982 when the controversial Bendix–Martin Marietta takeover battle became the focus of much public attention, and a year later the House Subcommittee on Telecommunications, Consumer Protection, and Finance of the Committee on Energy and Commerce began deliberations on the topic.[82] For four years, it remained at the center of the legislative controversy. The regulatory rhetoric of the hearings disclosed much the same shift from trust to contract that we have noted in the scholarly debates, but less so in its theoretical gloss than in its detailed accounts of how shareholders, managers, and raiders functioned in market contests for corporate control.

As in the case of the Williams Act, the legislators began their investigation of bidder–shareholder relationships with the presumption that the shareholders had the dual role of investors and owners. During the early stages of the hearings, for example, Congressman Edward J. Markey accepted the trust idea that shareholders, when functioning as the control group, should put aside their short-term investor perspective and act as responsible owners.[83] To help them decide whether a tender offer truly promised long-term economic benefits or was merely a clever financial manipulation, the subcommittee recommended extending the twenty-day tender-offer period mandated by the Williams Act. However, as the hearings proceeded, it became evident that the shareholder was neither unduly susceptible to bidder manipulation nor particularly interested in the responsibilities of ownership.

Indeed, the idea of individual shareholding itself proved to be a thing of myth or anachronism. As John J. Phelan, Jr., chairman of the New York Stock Exchange, observed, vast numbers of shares had become concentrated in a few competing institutional investors, run by professional managers whose training in modern finance allowed for careful evaluation of tender-offer bids. By 1980, major institutional investors held approximately 35 percent of the shares listed on the New York Stock Exchange;[84] among the 912 corporations that *Business Week* listed on its Investment Outlook Scoreboard, the proportion of holdings rose to more than 50 percent.[85] The preponderance of this growth came from the institutional management of pension funds, which had increased from $3.5 billion in 1955 to $219 billion in 1980.[86] The Employment Retirement Income Security Act (ERISA) of 1974 had placed these funds under federal regulation which set fiduciary standards preempting all other state and federal laws,[87] and the testimony provided clear evidence that pension fund managers evaluated tender offers only as prudent investors, paying no attention to the effects on target firms or their various constituents. No one seriously doubted that the corporation's substantive character had been fundamentally altered since 1968, when Congress passed the Williams Act. Economic and legal developments had made unrealistic the concept of shareholders as responsible owners, and the increase in takeover activity had countered problems associated with their dependency on bad management. Overcoming the difficulties of organizing shareholders to act collectively on their own, the concentration of shareholding into large funds gave them an effective voice in public-policy debates and corporate governance, perhaps for the first time since the 1920s.

Although the issues of shareholder independence and function seemed settled, other questions remained. Were other corporate constituents similarly independent of management, and could they bargain effectively? If not, should they be encouraged to continue to regard managers as trustees for their interests and commitments to the firm?

The subcommittee responded indirectly by examining the charge that corporate restructuring had imposed excessive social costs on

employees and communities. It acknowledged that no one had systematically calculated these costs; no evidence existed to demonstrate
that corporate restructurings were unreasonable, particularly if reorganization improved America's competitiveness.[88] Only on the question of worker retraining did the subcommittee find justifications for
public intervention, and here it suggested that corporate dependency was a smaller problem than had been previously thought.[89]

However, by the 1980s, Congress's earlier faith in the role of trusteeship had waned. The House subcommittee attended as much (or
more) to managerial opportunism as it did to bidder abuses and by
1987 recommended harsh measures against managerial takeover defenses.[90]

The research showed unambiguously that managers typically acquired firms and fended off hostile takeovers in order to promote
their own careers.[91] The excess cash flow theory proved quite persuasive. Managers often financed internal investments with cash
flows that might otherwise have gone to dividend payments. Because
econometric analysis suggested that these internal investments often
yielded returns below the discounted cost of capital, the incentive to
retain control of cash flows had evidently led many managers to expand their firms beyond the size that maximized shareholder wealth,
making them ripe for takeover bids.[92]

Experts disagreed, however, on public policies to deal with this
managerial abuse. Financial-agency theorists vigorously opposed any
additional tender-offer regulation, since they believed that existing
laws were already onerous. To bolster their case, they cited evidence
that target shareholders had received large premiums and that by
releasing underused resources, the market for corporate control had
"created" new wealth, which was reflected in higher share prices.[93]
In contrast, industrial economists cautioned the subcommittee
against major reforms that in effect would create a zero-premium
market in corporate control.[94] Backed by studies of mergers in the
1960s and 1970s that found average declines in firm profitability and
market share, these economists warned that a permissive environment might not only correct earlier managerial abuses but also promote yet another round of self-serving managerial deals.[95] Listening
to both arguments, the House subcommittee chose to reemphasize
the desirability of a regulatory environment that treated bidders and
targets in a balanced fashion.[96]

Although the subcommittee's investigations illustrated just how
pervasive the contractual vision had become by the mid-1980s, the
doctrine of trusteeship still reigned at the state level. Between 1968
and 1980, at least thirty-five states passed tender-offer regulations,
most of which set up legal hurdles against hostile bids.[97] In 1983,

the Supreme Court invalidated an Illinois antitakeover statute, holding in *Edgar v. MITE Corp.*[98] that the statute interfered with interstate commerce.[99] This decision gave rise to a second generation of antitakeover state provisions. In contrast with the earlier statutes, which had been patterned largely on the Williams Act and regulated market transactions, the later statutes specified internal governance procedures and standards. The statutes took many forms. Some required the majority vote of shareholders to approve a transference of control; others required the board of directors to weigh all of the firm's stakeholder interests when evaluating a tender offer.[100]

In 1987, as we mentioned earlier, the Supreme Court upheld these antitakeover laws, noting that a contrary action would abrogate states' rights.[101] This decision seemed to ensure that the constitutional conflict between state and federal regulation would persist unless Congress took remedial legislative action, as, for example, by enacting a federal incorporation charter.[102] So long as Congress did not act, trusteeship remained the norm for managerial practices while the states reinforced trust standards and served as protectorates for managerial authority.

6

Dependencies, Externalities, and Corporate Social Responsibility

As the debate over tender-offer regulations has shown, the fiduciary conception of management had become quite appealing by the mid-1960s. This chapter examines how the turbulent 1960s and 1970s extended corporate responsibilities far beyond stockholder interests to other corporate constituency groups whose contracts with companies were at best implicit and at times nonexistent.

Civil rights, antiwar, and other public-interest groups charged that managers had in fact been untrustworthy, had ignored the needs of the unemployed and underemployed, had collaborated with the government in an unjust war, and had degraded the environment. At first, pressuring management through various protest movements, including proxy battles over the composition of the corporation's board of directors,[1] these groups soon put their trust instead in the reinvigorated democracy of participatory government, shifting to political efforts to regulate management.[2] They succeeded in bringing back issues of ideology and equity to the political agenda in general, and they also won specific redistributive and protective legislation for their own groups. Only with the Reagan administration and increased competitive pressures from abroad was this thicket of regulation pruned as policymakers embraced market solutions and contract approaches.

TRUST AND SOCIAL REGULATION

The insights of economic and political theory often guided postwar social activists and policymakers in drafting the social regulations that would define managerial stakeholder accountability. Many economic theorists thought optimistically at this time about the government's ability to assist the economy in resolving frictions that reduced economic efficiency. Economic theory, for example, supported government intervention in the case of "externalities," costs like pollution that were external to parties of private contracts. With only a few notable exceptions, they had faith that the government had both the capacity and the will to improve the situation, sometimes with market forces as its instrument.[3] Taxing pollution, for example, internalized the externality by raising the private costs of production to include its social cost. The polluters themselves could then decide whether and how to continue production. Postwar economists generally presumed that some degree of government regulation was better than either banning the activity or allowing it full, unfettered play. In some cases, however, they faced the humbling reality that not all difficulties could be made to disappear, that some "solutions" created more problems than they resolved.

Postwar economists also cited stakeholder dependency as a problem that called for regulatory relief owing to the "informational asymmetries" involved in the broader field of "transaction costs." Managers, in brief, could be expected to know more about their business than other stakeholders and to use this information to their own advantage.

Economists identified a number of remedies available to legislators. Policymakers could encourage the production of activities with positive externalities. For example, they could subsidize research because its benefits were likely to spill over into the community at large, not just reward scientist/creators privately and in full. And they could discourage the production of activities with negative externalities. For example, they could set production standards to reduce pollution by law, or they could tax the polluters to reduce pollution by private incentive. The former would be appropriate if the costs of negotiating among all the affected parties were significant, but the latter would allow more flexibility and would encourage alternative production processes.

Another option simply asked managers to act responsibly, to account for externalities and dependencies from a sense of moral suasion and trusteeship. Perhaps managers would then adopt on their own production processes that balanced profitability and social costs or would freely divulge information to minimize bargaining discrepancies. As a doctrine of corporate social responsibility, it asked managers to establish norms privately and to enforce them through persuasive, noncoercive means, and managers preferred this option.

'Managers claimed that they acted responsibly, but the evidence convinced few. Critics on the left soon noted that neither managers nor government officials were working to lower social costs. Industry persisted in degrading the environment; workers continued to find themselves at risk in the workplace; and minorities and women still found themselves relatively disadvantaged. Critics observed that the legal and normative logic of trust that empowered managers also entrusted government officials with society's general welfare. Indeed, during the 1930s, shortly after Berle and others first conceived of the trust approach as an equitable hedge against the virtually absolute powers of corporate control, James M. Landis, in his landmark series of lectures on the administrative process, suggested that public administrators also be trusted—that is, be freed of legal restraints that kept them from applying their expertise and experimenting with new regulatory techniques in the manner of managers.[4] Such reasoning assumed that government bureaucrats were not political appointees but professionals, armed with techniques to articulate the public interest objectively. By the 1960s, public administrators had used their expertise to win such broad discretion from courts that questions of "fair" treatment had been reduced to administrative procedural safeguards.[5]

Economic studies of the administrative process during the postwar period contributed to the perception that trust in government had been misplaced. Regulation had become largely a vehicle for rent seeking, in which groups sought not to create income but to redistribute it—to themselves.[6] According to some economists, industry regulation had become more like cartel management than consumer and labor protection.[7] Political scientists concurred. Broad legislative oversight of the public's interest, which the electoral process was supposed to preserve, had hardened into "iron triangles" with administrative bureaus, and congressional committees; these triangles merely served special-interest groups.[8] Long-term committee assignments tended to make legislators as narrowly focused and susceptible to "industry capture" as were the regulatory agencies that they ostensibly oversaw[9] (see also Chapter 8).

Although both Left and Right came together in criticizing the New Deal's regulatory architecture, their proposals for reform remained divided. The former observed that the poor, racial minorities, women, and others were underrepresented in political affairs.[10] Not only did they remain victims of corporate environmental policies and racial and ethnic discrimination, but their work as self-employed and part-time or other marginal workers was not protected under existing employment legislation.

Economic analysis had much to offer in accounting for this un-

derrepresentation. In his 1965 *The Logic of Collective Action,* Mancur
Olson argued that because groups were associations of rational
actors, collective activity was often suboptimal.[11] Once "public
goods" like national defense existed for anyone, they existed for everyone. Lighthouses, for example, guided all ships in the harbor,
whether or not the shipowners had contributed to their construction.
Economists tagged this inability to exclude noncontributers as the
"free rider" problem. Members of a group—a nation, a community,
a shipyard—found it in their self-interest not to participate actively,
with either time or money, hoping that the work would be done
anyway, to everyone's benefit.

Collective action therefore seemed probable only for small groups,
in which free riders stood to suffer serious consequences—when
their noncooperation was easier to detect and more likely to jeopar-
dize whole projects. Olson considered these groups to be "privileged." For large, "latent" groups like trade unions, the poor, and
environmentalists, on the other hand, collective action would be
probable only when selective incentives or legal coercion induced
membership. Olson was not surprised that industry groups, particularly oligopolistic ones, had secured substantial regulatory benefits,
whereas others, say those concerned with economic justice, had not.

Pluralist political scientists appreciated the rigor of Olson's economic approach but read him as directly challenging their contention that society spontaneously generated groups and balanced
interest-group politics. Critical appraisals attempted to revamp
Olson's analysis to account for the success of such latent groups as
the civil rights and environmental movements in securing at least
some remedial and protective public policies. If pluralists could re-
vise Olson, then they could also mollify pessimistic claims about
America's biases toward privileged groups.

James Q. Wilson offered perhaps the first full-length retort in his
Political Organizations (1973), arguing simply that noneconomic incentives motivated individual association and effective organizational
action.[12] In *The Politics of Regulation,* he then offered a taxonomy to
account for regulatory provisions, dividing regulatory politics according to whether the costs and benefits of a public good were concentrated or dispersed. For example, in industry regulation (e.g.,
publicly supervised cartels), the benefits were concentrated in publicly sanctioned rents, and the costs were dispersed over a large number of consumers; this situation encouraged collective industrial action. But cost-benefit calculations discouraged reform when benefits
were dispersed and costs concentrated, as in the case of environmental regulation or affirmative-action programs.[13] Wilson recognized,
therefore, that issues concerning the poor and the environment

would be underrepresented. But he argued that the disincentives could be overcome by political entrepreneurs who found ways to communicate among the groups' members and pressure public officials for the public good and their own personal satisfaction.

Despite Wilson's steps to incorporate economic analysis into a pluralist account of group formation and action, he fell short of creating a formal alternative to Olson. Others advanced more technical expositions of pluralist politics that respected the economic categories of public goods and collective action. One who did so was Terry Moe in his 1980 book *The Organization of Interests,* another was Russell Hardin in his 1982 book *Collective Action.*[14]

While political scientists were refining economic categories to account for interest-group formation and action, activists were learning how to campaign for public goods from the corporate sector. In coining the phrase "public-interest groups," these new political entrepreneurs claimed their activities to be correctives to America's imperfect pluralism. Citizen groups now demanded that policymakers, as well as corporate executives, acknowledge some degree of "public interest" in the private production of goods. Although pursuing a variety of political avenues to reach their objectives, all these reformers drew ideologically on the professional manager's own notion of practicing "corporate social responsibility."[15] Rather than rely on managerial good faith, however, they then advocated regulatory measures to enhance the political liberty of the underprivileged and underrepresented and to encourage the formation of new interest groups. These reformers sought to restructure corporate control within the confines of a reformed administrative state and to hold the control group accountable to "dependent stakeholders." In this respect, the social regulatory movement of the 1960s and 1970s continued to elaborate Merrick Dodd's legal and regulatory ideas about public opinion and managerial trusteeship.[16]

Despite criticism from libertarians, regulation became increasingly expansive and intrusive. Throughout the 1960s, reformers imposed pluralist principles on both the administrative and the legislative levels of government.[17] Suits by individual persons led to class actions; private litigation against firms led to administrative enforcement proceedings against entire industries; and public enforcement led to industrywide rule making. Managers quickly pointed out that the new regulatory environment was enhancing the powers of government bureaucrats at the firm's expense. If this shift continued, corporate defenders warned, a second managerial revolution would take place, in which public bureaucrats would seize control of the modern firm.[18]

Meanwhile, the courts resisted attempts to impose constitutional limits or statutory rules that would check the bureaucracy. Instead, they developed broad "standing" rules for allowing interest groups to contest agency decisions. These rules eventually led to "outreach" programs in which agencies actively helped organize interest groups. In the words of Richard Stewart, a leading professor of administrative law, "The function of administrative law was [no longer primarily] the protection of private autonomy, but the provision of a surrogate political process to ensure the fair representation of a wider range of affected interests."[19] In this manner, public administrators began to displace private managers from their role as corporate trustees.[20]

Consumer Protection

The "consumerism" movement of the 1960s, for example, sought to protect consumers from generic managerial social irresponsibility by requiring information disclosures, unbundling of products, and product safety features.[21] In its presumption that purchasers of corporate products were "dependent" on good faith and full disclosure, the concept of fairness to consumers conformed to the trust approach.

Poverty, illiteracy, and general gullibility made some consumers dependent because they were relatively incapable of looking after their own interests. Corporations could not be expected to perform competitively and at the same time protect these vulnerable groups. To be "responsible," the industry would have to regulate itself or be regulated from the outside. In light of antitrust curbs on "self-regulation," it seemed better to empower federal agencies like the Federal Trade Commission (FTC), Food and Drug Administration (FDA), Consumer Products Safety Commission (CPSC), and National Highway Transportation and Safety Administration (NHTSA) to serve as public trustees and set protective standards for the market. Early on, agencies developed their standards after the fact through prosecutions of individual firms' practices. By the 1970s, however, they anticipated inappropriate practices and began to promulgate generally applicable, *ex ante* rules, relying on industrywide rule-making proceedings to support the enactment of the more extensive standards.[22]

Dependency also referred to consumers' reliance on competent and reasonably priced service for costly durable goods. Oliver Williamson characterized the hazards of this kind of dependency in terms of *ex post* contractual opportunism—for instance, if manufacturers extracted monopoly rents on replacement parts or service knowledge once consumers had committed themselves to a big ticket, durable good. Consumer advocates insisted that firms in monopolized or oligopolistic markets owed their "dependent" customers a duty to act "fairly" by honoring a broad array of remedies. When individual consumers raised claims or when agencies like the FTC sued individual sellers, the claimants read obligations into contracts *ex post*. In time, the FTC began proposing to extend these responsibilities to whole industries through trade regulation rules.[23] At the peak of the consumer movement, Congress passed the FTC Improvements Act of 1975, which not only imposed protective standards like warranties but also delegated rule-making and other remedial powers explicitly to the FTC.[24]

Environmental Protection

Environmental regulations paralleled the expansion of consumer protection, even though the environmentalists' constituency generally had no direct ties to the firm, through neither contracts nor ownership.[25] Environmentalists initially made the legal claim to compensation for specific harms. These demands moved inexorably from redress to broad-scale proposals for protecting water, soil, and air.[26] Congress responded by creating the Environmental Protection Administration (EPA) in 1970. As Congress's surrogate or the public's trustee, the EPA identified appropriate standards based on technical studies that considered the risks inherent in various kinds of pollution and the available means of minimizing them.[27] During the early years of the EPA's work, policymakers assumed that practicable standards were a rather simple matter of promulgating, monitoring, and enforcing federal rules. However, the EPA soon became a battleground on which business tested the regulators' notion that they could fix norms based on corrective measures that were technically achievable without paying more attention to the costs and benefits of other, perhaps less perfect, solutions.[28]

Labor Protection

Only on the labor front did the congressional zeal abate. Except to blunt labor militancy and corruption in unions, lawmakers found little reason to tamper with industrial labor relations from 1947 to 1960.[29] Congress had already neutralized the judicial bias against workers' collective action and had established baseline standards for employment contracts. As we have already seen, federal administrators had treated the employer–employee relationship not as a trust but as a contract in which workers could choose to negotiate directly with managers or to unionize and bargain collectively. After 1960, however, the federal concern about socially underrepresented constituencies sharpened the issue of worker dependency.

Congress first addressed the problem of employment discrimination. Victims of discrimination, including people of color, women, gays, the elderly, and handicapped, were dependent in two ways. Employers had the power to exclude them from large portions of the market altogether, and even when employers did hire underrepresented workers, they could discriminate against them through promotion and other workplace policies.[30] Congress passed a variety of antidiscrimination laws during the 1960s, both to repair and to prevent damage. Though not initially premised on managerial abuses of trust, the employment reforms of the 1960s and early 1970s came to embody the requirements of social responsibility.[31] The period's first antidiscrimination law, the Equal Pay Act of 1963, prohibited sex-related differential wage scales for similar work.[32] The second law, Title VII of the Civil Rights Act of 1964, was considerably more intrusive.[33] It provided redress to victims of employer discrimination on the basis of race, sex, religion, national origin, and—through legislative amendments in 1967 and 1973—age, and physiological disadvantage.[34] Discrimination came to include unintended as well as deliberately discriminatory consequences of hiring and promotion decisions or policies. By enacting the law, Congress acknowledged that private organizing and contract bargaining rules were of no use so long as employers had the power not to bargain at all. The victims, like other beneficiaries of corporate trusteeship, required at least *ex post* protection from managerial power.

Congress established the Equal Employment Opportunity Commission (EEOC) to guard against discrimination, and this agency vigorously pressed claims.[35] Beyond negotiating affirmative action programs with "guilty" managers, it sought to establish guidelines meant to keep all managers out of trouble (i.e., *ex ante*).[36] Even firms that complied voluntarily with the EEOC's hiring and promotion procedures encountered difficulties, especially when they exposed themselves to charges of discrimination based on particular local circumstances that the guidelines failed to correct.[37] Discontinuity among procedures to ensure "fairness" and actual workforce outcomes resulted.

Antidiscrimination rules made managers vulnerable to the specific claims of several subclasses of labor, each empowered to seek intervention from either the courts or the EEOC and its state agency counterparts.[38] When the agencies began resorting to general rules that extended the restrictions on managerial discretion to firms that had not been found guilty of discrimination, the regulatory process effectively held the corporate sector responsible for the shortcomings of American society as a whole with regard to racial and gender equality. In addition to issues of invidious discrimination, Congress addressed a broad array of other social issues related to employment, such as poverty and structural unemployment, industrial accidents and disease, and corporate and union mismanagement of employee retirement funds. Regulatory enactments in these areas further curbed managerial discretion.[39]

On other work-related fronts, public-interest groups won occupational health and safety regulations that gradually tied the hands of all managers. The principal law, the Occupational Safety and Health Act of 1970 (OSHA), attempted to standardize working-condition provisions in labor contracts.[40] Unlike the earlier worker compensation statutes, this law aimed to prevent workplace accidents and occupational disease, not simply to compensate workers for injuries they had already suffered. Unlike the ground rules for compensation, insurance premiums, or payroll withholding, which were easily monitored and corrected, safety and health conditions depended on regular, intrusive monitoring, with substantial enforcement discretion. The regulation attempted both to level the ground on which employers competed, by the promotion of generally applicable health and safety standards, and to prevent all injuries by local supervision. Both aims came under attack. "Best guess" standards to protect all the employees in a given industry accordingly had the potential to do both too much and too little. Individual employers could claim that the general standards were inefficient and unfair because workplaces that were already safe still had to incur costs to comply with the standards, and unsafe ones might remain unsafe, their compliance with specific standards notwithstanding. At the same time, on-site monitoring, which forced local OSHA offices to confront individual employers as they adapted standards and compliance rulings to local conditions, faced charges of overzealousness, unequal or arbitrary treatment, and corruption.

The Employee Retirement Income Security Act (ERISA) of 1974 was the last in the series of worker-related laws that sought to ensure the fair treatment of employees.[41] The ERISA provisions differed, however, from earlier acts that grew out of broad normative assessments of hiring criteria and the conditions of employment. Congress drafted ERISA in response to employee pension plan failures and abuses. In some instances, employers simply mismanaged funds. In others, they set aside insufficient funds to cover payouts or dissolved the funds before employees could claim their due. Sometimes managers deliberately terminated employment before pension rights vested. Congress established requirements to eliminate these abuses and insure pensioners' incomes. Most significantly, ERISA imposed fiduciary duties on fund managers that in effect separated management of the pension plan from management of the corporation. Trusteeship on behalf of the plan's participants and beneficiaries meant that fund managers could not serve as corporation trustees without conflict of interest.[42] ERISA required employers to fund their plans according to proper actuarial calculations, with sufficient reserves and insurance against dissolution of the plan. Because of "participation" and "vesting" rights, they could no longer keep workers out of a plan on the basis of age, length of service, or termination of employment once they had qualified for retirement income or other benefits.

Unlike such earlier worker-related legislation as social security programs, ERISA insisted that pension plans be voluntary contracts between the firm and its employees. Employee participation, vesting, and insurance rights were simply restrictions on the form of the contract. Moreover, the law could not designate as a trustee for the beneficiaries the firm's management, a worker representative, or a public official. Rather, it had to be an independent private agent. In these respects, ERISA combined both contractarian and fiduciary approaches to corporate stakeholder regulation.

TRANSITIONS IN THE REGULATORY APPROACH

As social regulation displaced managerial trust, public-interest groups systematized their demands and proposed general reforms along pluralist political lines. In going beyond the narrowly functional regulatory language of trust and contract, they reencountered democracy's apparently unanswerable questions. How could society ensure equality without restricting liberty? How could government regulate the private use of property without making its citizens dependent on the state?

Through the late 1960s and 1970s, reformers continued to place the issue of corporate governance on the public agenda, invoking egalitarian and participatory values and advocating direct representation of the public's interests on corporate boards, usually in the form of public-interest group nominees.[43] Reform proposals ranged from amending the securities laws to drafting federal corporation or licensing laws that would govern the charters and practices of the large firms.[44] During the late 1970s, the Senate and House of Representatives actively considered a federal incorporation bill that would reconstitute boards of directors "to make [corporate managers] more accountable to their shareholders and the public."[45]

Advocates for this bill still viewed the corporation as an entity and argued that it was an instrument of public policy and not the spontaneous consequence of market negotiations.[46] They also moved beyond the trust doctrine in their belief that dependent stakeholders could protect their own interests only through rights to participate in corporate policymaking, that is, through a voice in the firm's internal code of ethics.[47] In this way, corporate regulations might avoid the citizenship paradox associated with regulations in the trust form, because participation would make stakeholders more politically knowledgeable and active and therefore more independent in broader political affairs.

Because the influence of large industrial corporations was ubiquitous, reformers contended that the public would best be served by adjusting the firm's governance structure to pluralist principles. All the firm's various stakeholder groups should be represented on the board of directors—union officials for workers, consumer specialists for consumers, fund managers for investors, experts in matters of public policy for environmentalists, and so on.[48] These reformers urged democratic participation in selecting and influencing the various representatives to the board, citing equitable political participation, not market efficiency, as their guiding principle.[49]

Perhaps no one did more to advance the egalitarian argument than John Rawls in *A Theory of Justice*.[50] Like his adversaries, Rawls reasoned from a contractarian point of view, but he also asked the reader to reason hypothetically, from behind a "veil of ignorance." From this vantage point, where one's social identity and privileges were unknown, a prudent social contract should promise economic redistributions to the least advantaged and guarantees of civil and political liberties to all economic classes. Despite the extraordinary range of Rawls's argument, he did not directly take up the problem of the modern corporation. This topic became the subject for another egalitarian, Robert Dahl.

Dahl went beyond the trust logic that many others maintained. Like them, he asked what kind of governing structure would ensure the large firm's accountability to democratic values, including individual self-government (liberty) and participation in the governing process (equality). But he also insisted that the reconciliation of liberty and equality not violate market principles (for more on Dahl, see Chapter 7).

According to Dahl, the large firm tended to concentrate and redistribute wealth unequally, to separate the traditional rights and responsibilities of property ownership, and to institute hierarchical, bureaucratic authority structures in management. These tendencies reflected the substantial political privilege of controlling minorities; they also undermined the countertendencies on which more egalitarian democratic norms depended. Concentration and redistribution of economic resources discouraged the organization of broader-based opposition to the interests of corporate control. The hierarchical authority structures discouraged enlightened understanding of the economy and fostered political dependencies. And the firm's capacity to resist reforms, such as economic intervention, gave managers a privileged voice in packaging political agendas and preempted the influence of others.

Because the large corporation was principally an economic machine, solutions to corporate governance had to reconcile demands of efficiency with demands for equality, and Dahl therefore elaborated an argument that attempted to stay within the framework of property rights.[51] Whereas the property rights school endorsed dispersed "ownership" and shareholder privilege as the best means for motivating management, Dahl recommended that ownership be concentrated among workers. Such a distribution, he believed, was better than traditional managerial control. It would give workers both economic performance standards and a voice in the firm's internal policy deliberations. In this worker cooperative, property would function both as a Hamiltonian instrument of wealth and in the venerable Jeffersonian tradition as a means of developing citizenship.

During the 1970s, Congress considered proposals to reform corporate governance that were less radical but that still included interest group representation on boards of large firms. However, the 1980 election of Ronald Reagan began a new regulatory era in which issues of corporate governance were to be worked out in the market for corporate control.

It is not altogether surprising that federal regulators finally abandoned the trust approach, which had led them to encumbered and contradictory systems of regulation. Perhaps more peculiar is that it persisted at all through an era of deep mistrust. Interventions for the sake of fairness had been considered out of the ordinary, because trustees were presumed to act for the most part in good faith. After Vietnam and Watergate, evidence of public and private malfeasance made "bad faith" seem ordinary. And even though the trust approach extended corporate policies to formerly neglected constituents, it failed to offer administrators or courts any formula for resolving differences, let alone determining "the public interest."[52] On the contrary, the regulatory process had increasingly become an arena for particularism and interest balancing.[53] In a society split along ideological positions like equality versus efficiency, perhaps the adroit manipulation of the process mattered more than God- or government-given rights. Seen in this light, public administration offered no better forum than the market, except perhaps with regard to the extremes of the income distribution.

Finally, giving voice contradicted the legal analysis of trust itself. The doctrine of equitable intervention had been founded on the beneficiaries' dependence and the trustees' control. As long as they merely served to signal unfairness to trustees and public authorities or to appeal trustees' dispositions to outside judges, voice rights were consistent with the concept of trust. But when they empowered corporate constituents to look after their own interests directly and rested, as in Dahl's configuration, on redistribution, they went far beyond what Berle and Dodd had understood by trust enforcement.

THE CONTRACTARIAN APPROACH TO SOCIAL REGULATION

America's continuing economic woes and inability to meet the challenges of foreign competition armed critics who argued that voice rights had indeed gone too far. As tender offers proceeded apace, the 1980s saw a shift from voice to exit in corporate governance issues. This market in corporate control seemed the best way to revitalize a lethargic managerial class (see Chapters 5 and 10).

Critics of government intrusion complained that trusteeship itself bred stakeholder dependencies and imposed unacceptable economic costs on both managers and government officials. At first inspired by libertarian ideals, they claimed that social regulation was paternalistic, turning citizens into children and regulatory agencies into their nannies. People should look after their own interests in the market, and they could express their preferences by entering or exiting stakeholder relationships.[54]

The technical side of the mounting counterattack on the social regulatory movement grew out of Ronald Coase's trenchant 1960 article, "The Problem of Social Cost."[55] Using the transaction-cost framework that he had first applied to his analysis of the firm, Coase challenged the reigning economic theory of externalities, which, in his opinion, gave license to unwarranted governmental interventions. Emphatically denying that the identification of an externality was a *prima facie* case for government regulation insofar as every corrective measure promised both oportunity costs and administrative costs, he insisted instead that the government demonstrate that the private solution was suboptimal and that intervention would make it better.

Coase made his argument by first analyzing a world with secure property rights and no transaction costs. In this frictionless state, private contracting in the market would maximize the overall or social value of output regardless of whether the producer was held liable for negative externalities. However, since transaction costs did in fact exist, Coase challenged analysts to devise ways to examine whether or not policy changes could improve on market conditions. In addition to insisting on a cost–benefit analysis of public as well as private actions, he asked economists and legal scholars to explore how legal and administrative alterations might reduce transaction costs, internalize externalities, and forestall the need for government interference.[56]

Instrumental and libertarian writers, inspired by the work of Frank Knight and Friedrich Hayek, questioned the idea that government interventions reflected the "public good" and protected the "innocent bystander." Conventional pluralist analyses of legislation had neglected the tendency of government to revolve around special-interest coalitions and trade-offs rather than broad moral principles.[57] Building on Hayek's observations about the failings of administrative (as opposed to market) priority setting and on Arrow's model of the voting paradox (see Chapter 7), a new generation of public-policy analysts demonstrated the tendencies of political-ordering mechanisms to generate social costs of their own.[58]

James Buchanan and Gordon Tullock examined the legislative process and pointed out that majoritarian decisions imposed externalities on dissenting minorities.[59] Since electoral politics encouraged incumbent legislators to "logroll"—that is, to promote rent-producing legislative coalitions—public-policy outcomes tended to be inefficient. To protect the minority from the majority and the majority from itself, Buchanan and Tullock recommended that the concept of externalities be used as a constitutional check, acting to restrain politicians in much the same way that a balanced budget amendment would make Congress consider total spending and taxes and not just the special programs that made individual legislators so popular with their constituents. The latter received theoretical backing from William Niskanen, who suggested that bureaucrats had incentives to overinvest in their budgets and create social inefficiencies.[60]

As scholars elaborated generally on technical details of property rights and transactional efficiency and Oliver Williamson examined specifically how transaction costs affected bargaining between management and the firm's stakeholders (see Chapter 5), contract gradually came to replace trust as the dominant regulatory model.[61] The normative *ex post* focus of rule making under the trust regime gave

way to a Coasian *ex ante* perspective,[62] and the burden of proof
turned against intervention, even for those of more liberal persua-
sion.[63] Charles Schultze's work *The Public Use of Private Interest* suc-
cinctly encapsulated the new consensus, and Alfred Kahn's *The Economics of Regulation* played a particularly important role in forging
an alliance that moved public policy from normative to economic
justification.[64]

Inside the executive branch of government, the commitment to
deregulation deepened independently of party. President Gerald
Ford required major policy and rule-making initiatives to file inflationary impact evaluations and submit them to the Council on Wage
and Price Stability.[65] President Jimmy Carter created the advisory
Regulatory Analysis and Review Group to consider more cost-effective alternatives to existing regulations, and President Reagan centralized the oversight of regulatory policies through the Office of
Management and Budget, explicitly shifting the burden of proof for
new initiatives from private-sector opponents to program advocates.[66] The Reagan administration also demanded that agencies use
cost–benefit analysis to justify their rules and to dismantle them
when they failed this test; the Ford and Carter regimes had demanded simply that agencies reach their goals in the most efficient
manner.[67] Congress also became more suspicious of direct government administration and more tolerant of market solutions. Even
though the 1976 election had little effect on its party composition,
the House of Representatives reversed voting patterns on prolabor
reforms, consumer protection laws, and environmental standards.[68]

Although some of Reagan's efforts met with resistance in both the
Congress and the courts, the polity came increasingly to insist on
well-considered and relatively unintrusive social-cost regulations.[69]
The new consensus looked to market-based instruments to correct
market deficiencies. Even some environmentalists conceded that
mandated standards for air quality were inferior to marketable per-
mits for polluting: The latter allowed for flexibility and provided
greater incentive for technological change and cost reduction.[70]

This consensus reduced government officials from command-
controlling to contract-monitoring roles, and managers were pleased
in the main to be liberated from the constraints of social regulation
on their firms. Yet in abandoning trust, professional managers un-
wittingly forfeited their adjudicating, semipublic function as corporate trustees. Managers would now have to bargain with rather than
decide on behalf of the corporate stakeholders.

7

Postwar Corporate Political Regulation: From Peddling Influence to Providing Information

Political reforms during the 1970s and 1980s also demonstrate the shift from trust to contract. In general, contractarians argued that reducing government interventions through deregulation and budget cuts would correspondingly reduce rent-seeking political activity on the part of powerful minority coalitions. Moreover, as concern grew about the citizenry's dependence on business and governmental leaders, reformers expressed renewed optimism about individual citizens' rationality and political self-reliance. Confidence in the citizenry increased as political scientists argued, much as economists did, that politically relevant information flowed rapidly and inexpensively. In this new information age of politics, utilitarian public-sector deals depended less on faithful or trustworthy leadership than on effective processes—such as referenda, compaigns, and challenges to legislative incumbents—that enabled individual voters to become at once more actively involved and more rationally informed.

As political reform proceeded, the question of corporate size and its effects on political participation became more acute once again. When only a few large companies constitute an industry, should they automatically be regulated under federal antitrust provisions? And by amassing so many resources, do corporate control groups threaten political freedoms by buying votes both directly and indirectly?

ANTITRUST AS A SAFEGUARD AGAINST
CORPORATE POLITICAL CORRUPTION

When policymakers spoke of majoritarian rule in the 1950s, they presumed that antitrust enforcement and "pure" elections kept the corporate sector from unduly exercising its considerable power. Conglomerate mergers, however, had for some time avoided antitrust regulation. By combining firms that shared only financial and accounting services, they did not appear to reduce competition, at least of the economic sort. But when conglomeration intensified in the earlier 1960s, federal administrators grew anxious about the political ramifications. Such concentrated wealth, it was feared, could be used to win political gains and turn them into economic rents.

Despite these concerns, two Supreme Court decisions during the early 1960s held that combinations by firms designed to win political gains were relatively immune from prosecution. The Court reasoned that the First Amendment privileged collective political action, such as speech and assembly, against government interference and, in that respect, preempted antitrust law.[1]

The new thinking saw little to fear in oligopolies as long as there were no artificial barriers to entry and much to doubt in the reigning structure–conduct–performance model for antitrust enforcement. This model presumed that when a few large firms constituted an industry (structure), the conditions for collusive behavior (conduct) were rife and monopoly rents (performance) more likely. Consequently, those who belonged to this school asked for antitrust enforcement based on industry structure, that is, to break up firms or to prevent mergers when an industry reached a threshold concentration level.

Lawyers like Robert Bork and Richard Posner and economists like George Stigler, Harold Demsetz, and Sam Peltzman challenged these premises in the early 1970s, arguing that conduct, not structure, should guide antitrust policy. According to their "new learning" on antitrust, managers hardly had the power to contain competition in all but the shortest of runs. Even oligopolists intent on acting like monopolies would fail to bar entry or enforce price and quantity standards without government help. Indeed, they argued, the most enduring examples of collusive, cartel-like behavior occurred under the aegis of federal and state regulatory agencies. Less-regulated oligopolists tended to price their products competitively. Perhaps such public agencies as the FCC, ICC, CAB, and state public utility and service commissions should be dismantled. Never mind how the legislation *read*. It *served* to bolster industrywide agreements that protected existing firms against new competitors and more vigorous competition.

The turning point for the "new learning" came during the Ford administration in 1974, with the Airlie House Conference on industrial concentration.[2] Those who had guided policies throughout the trust era continued to support measures to break up and prevent highly concentrated oligopolies.[3] But the challengers punctured the structure–conduct–performance model both logically and empirically. Attacking with ambiguities in the evidence,[4] they argued along Coasian lines that firms grew to an optimal size as they decided whether to make or buy components; hence market competition served consumers better than did government intervention. The latter was more likely than not to be ill informed from the start and to become ill intentioned over time. Research on concentration and regulation ceased to characterize the market as very strong or very weak and began to take a more moderate approach. Alfred Kahn, for example, elaborated on the microeconomic tools available to public administrators to deregulate public utilities or set their prices to achieve competitive results.[5]

At the same time, Oliver Williamson began to model the potential productive efficiencies of internal organization simply assumed by earlier writers.[6] The contracting of dominant firms or monopolists, he asserted, was different from that of competing oligopolists. Whereas monopolists could afford to respond after the fact to contract contingencies, conspiring oligopolists had to anticipate them. Nonprice competition ("conduct" in the structure–conduct–performance model) predictably grew out of their inability to achieve comprehensive coordination. The empirical evidence, also, suggested that they behaved opportunistically, taking advantage of information differences and thereby persistently cheating their coconspirators. Antitrust enforcement was thus likely to be worth its costs only in "highly concentrated industries producing homogeneous products, with non-trivial barriers to entry, and at a mature stage of development."[7]

Two significant changes in antitrust law followed the Airlie House Conference, and both centered on mergers. The Hart–Scott–Rodino Antitrust Improvements Act of 1976 supported the structure–performance tradition by setting premerger notification requirements. Although the act's immediate impact on mergers was apparently slight, especially after initial court interpretations resisted any substantive enlargement of the Clayton Act's limits on concentration by narrowing the act's scope to informational and procedural purposes, it undoubtedly increased the cost of mergers and subsidized law firms experienced in this line of work.

The second change reflected the new consensus, through a combination of practice and policy. Because of premerger notification procedures, the FTC and the Antitrust Division could negotiate with merging firms and give their approval or not prosecute on specific spin-offs and organizational or marketing adjustments. As the anti-trust agencies began in this process to consider the efficiencies of internal organization and nonstandard contracting, they reversed their presumption against mergers in concentrated industries. This practice of negotiation and adjustment then became explicit policy in the Antitrust Division's 1982 and 1984 merger guidelines.[8]

By the mid-1970s, antitrust regulation had lost much of its earlier appeal. In focusing on only the cost of monopoly behavior in raising prices and restricting output, regulators appeared to have unduly increased both the costs of production and the costs of compliance. Distribution effects aside, was not competition from abroad the cheapest antitrust tool of all? American automobile corporations, for example, might seem few in number and vast in size when only the American market was considered, but if trade were freed up, world competition would surely restrain their prices and force them to bring their technology up to speed.

And then there was the market for corporate control. It provided support for deregulating all mergers so that managers would be pressured to maximize corporate profits to resist contests for control.

CHALLENGING THE TRUST REGULATION OF CORPORATE POLITICAL ACTIVITY

What about the effect of corporations on politics? So many found troubling the possibility of monied groups' buying votes, not just di-rectly and illegally, but also indirectly and legally through the power of advertising, name recognition, and the mobilization of citizens. In 1907 Congress had originally responded to these concerns by pass-ing the Tillman Act, which made it illegal for a corporation or a national bank to make monetary contributions in federal elections; the states followed in kind. In 1910 and 1911, Congress passed addi-tional laws requiring House and Senate disclosures on political con-tributions and setting limits on campaign expenditures. It over-hauled the system in 1925 with the Federal Corrupt Practices Act and added refinements in the Hatch Act and subsequent amend-ments.

By the end of the 1960s, however, elections were still far from pure and loopholes were wide and many.[9] Corporations freely of-fered their goods and services to support electoral campaigns and to reimburse their employees' political contributions through compen-sation and expense account subterfuges. In contrast, labor unions faced tighter supervision under the Taft–Hartley and Landrum–

Griffin acts. Congress accordingly had to choose between closing the loopholes that favored corporations or lifting certain of the restrictions on labor unions. Congress chose deregulation, and so the Federal Election Campaign Act (FECA) of 1971 authorized controlled campaign donations for both corporations and labor unions.[10]

Throughout the postwar period, social scientists had argued that the elective process could benefit from corporate participation, regardless of the privileged and potentially undemocratic character of corporate control. Above all, keeping an elective process open required curtailing corruption and ensured the flow of reliable information. With a license to participate, policymakers reasoned, firms would no longer need to engage in political subterfuge or corruption, and they could benefit the citizenry by releasing important campaign information at low cost to the citizens.

The threat that corporate participation in elections would result in a few high-spending firms imposing their will on the majority struck social scientists as unlikely. Corporations generally competed with one another in politics and so guarded the system against the dominance of a few firms. Only with substantial coherence on any issue might they successfully throw the weight of their money against the political majority, but such a high degree of cohesiveness seemed improbable.

Economics again provided the support for this political view. Kenneth Arrow's "impossibility theorem" illustrated the difficulty of stabilizing majority outcomes in the absence of remarkably homogeneous political values and interests;[11] and when Robert Dahl applied this model to a large population with complex and varied preferences and frequent voting opportunities, he found majoritarian coalitional instability in both electoral and legislative processes.[12] By "vastly increas[ing] the size, number, and variety of minorities whose preferences must be reckoned in making policy choices," the U.S. political process was probably "not of majority rule or even of minority rule, but of *minorities* rule."[13]

Dahl concluded that American politics should be judged with respect to the relationships among minorities and the degree to which privileged minorities could "frustrate the ambitions of one another with the passive acquiescence or indifference of a majority of adults or voters."[14] Wealthy, well-educated citizens, with their access "to the organizational, financial, and propaganda resources that weigh so heavily in campaigns, elections, legislative, and executive decisions," had far more advantages than did poor and less-educated citizens, who were barred from political success "by their relatively greater inactivity, by their elatively limited access to resources, and by Madison's nicely contrived system of constitutional checks."[15] But Dahl

remained optimistic in the main, for he believed that America's political institutions were sufficiently robust to undo any dominant coalition, however privileged its members.

As early as 1959, Dahl began working out a procedure to determine whether or not one minority—in particular, the large business
corporation—could use its financial, organizational, and/or constitutional advantages to control the political process.[16] He reasoned that
to assert its will consistently in a functional polyarchy, a minority had
to engage in indirect or "latent" forms of coercion. It had either to
manipulate the legislative agenda or to ensure the election of an ap-
proving or beholden group of candidates.[17] At the very least, it had
to condition the public to respect the minority's advantages, and it
might even be able to threaten a polity that obstructed those advantages.[18] Dominance depended on strategic craft, a consensus on the
ends and means of political action, and its effective coordination.
Political homogeneity or cohesion within the minority group, in
other words, was a necessary, but not a sufficient, condition for its
control over the polity.

In addition to the analytic categories of "latent" control and minority "cohesion," Dahl added the descriptive concepts of the
"scope" and "magnitude" of control.[19] The former referred to the
range of public policies that a minority could influence, from narrowly framed issues like education, taxes and health care, to those
that encompassed the entire realm of policy. The latter characterized
the degree to which a minority could make policy outcomes diverge
from majoritarian preferences.

When Dahl applied these concepts to the New Haven, Connecticut, local government, he found that the actual linkages among these
apparently simple analytic categories were more difficult to specify
than his initial methodological inquiry had led him to believe.[20] Because the possibilities for control were numerous, one could interpret the data rather too freely for the standards of scientific rigor,
especially when minority domination hinged on indirect forms of
power such as the anticipated reactions of the ruled to the rulers.[21]
"[A]ll this," he concluded playfully, "presents me with a task of such
formidable proportions that from now on I shall hesitate to speak of
potential influence at all."[22] Others, however, quickly took on the
empirical hunt, and for the most part they found that the threat of
corporate political control had been greatly exaggerated.

The development of a collective-action theory approach to the
problem further assuaged fears. In his often cited *The Logic of Collective Action*, Mancur Olson applied individual cost–benefit calculations
to regulation as a public good and argued, as we saw in Chapter 6,
that problems of free riding made long-term corporate cohesion

quite unlikely. Possible distortions in public policy were still trouble-some, however, because smaller groups like industry and trade asso-ciations were more politically effective in the competition for public goods and policies than were the political interests of larger groups like taxpayers, consumers, and employees.

On the empirical front, Edwin M. Epstein demonstrated that the corporate sector mirrored the fractious tendencies of the population as a whole and contributed to the general political intensity and dy-namism of American pluralism.[23] Although he conceded the poten-tial for corporate political power, Epstein concluded that several out-side forces limited its realization.[24] Not only did other groups like labor unions, educators, and professionals share many of the same advantages as corporations and therefore neutralized them, but po-litical parties militated against the dominance of one minority inter-est group over others: The parties' very survival depended on pre-serving larger coalitions by mediating competing interests. The electorate itself was also sufficiently committed to democratic rule to thwart self-interested control of the political process through the corporate corruption of public officials.

Corporate political advantage had internal checks as well. The cor-porate sector divided along its own set of pluralist tendencies—both intrafirm rivalries growing out of the multiplicity of political interests and interfirm rivalries within and among industries. For example, employee and owner interests regularly diverged. As for intra-industry strife, consider how often the energy industry fragmented along fissures of size, fuel type, and domestic versus foreign markets, and heavy-energy consumers rallied against policies that supported prices above their free-market levels.

Managerial political pragmatism in Epstein's analysis, provided an-other important internal check on corporate-sector cohesion. Since markets and career ambitions drove managers to focus on their firms' financial success, they rarely acted as political ideologues. As self-defined technocrats and opportunists, they took a pragmatic view of politics. Seeking the best means for gaining access to and influence over politicians and public administrators, they tended to support electoral candidates with the best chance for success, regard-less of their party affiliation. In general, that meant backing incum-bents, a conservative and stabilizing strategy.

Thus did the corporate manager, in the Epsteinian mode, become a paragon of pluralist democracy: a pragmatist who abhorred ideol-ogy and saw politics as a means to achieve the stability and predict-ability necessary for economic growth. Although Epstein did note the rare alliances that frustrated common threats to autonomy and political power, in particular to thwart labor coalitions, he still so fully believed that managerial pragmatism and corporate-sector rivalries would mitigate any potential for harm that he endorsed the FECA's reforms to permit corporate political participation.

In addition to dispelling concerns about corporate cohesion, pluralist social scientists suggested that the "locus of control" in American government was too elusive or dispersed for control to be practicable. Political deliberations appeared to be so fragmented and multilayered that even powerful organized groups could impose little meaningful coherence over time. The pluralist paradigm of the American polity predicted that businesses would seek influence in special policy matters but that costs of information and organization would inhibit their participation in more general areas in which they had little interest and even less expertise.

One of the corporation's principal defenders, E. E. Schattschneider, remained a bit skeptical, however. He believed that there was more cohesion in both government and business than the pluralists generally admitted.[25] Policies might be formed and conflicts resolved in either a private or a public forum, and because control abated as the process moved from the private to the public domain, strong interests like Big Business would try to settle important matters of cohesion without public oversight. Business people would therefore resist the impulse to attack one another publicly or to take their disputes before public tribunals. They would support their own in conflicts with both the government and labor, and they would do so quietly.[26]

Yet despite appearances and possibilities to the contrary, Schattschneider found corporate-sector control sharply limited. Public officials and other minority groups could draw business into the public arena on matters of broad concern. Indeed, the very existence of corporate-sector political action indicated weakness as well as strength: It showed that business could not insulate its policies from the democratic process.[27] Political parties comprised the core of the process, and during contested elections, parties cared less about the demands of pressure groups traditionally in their fold than about attracting voters on the margin. When elections were close, uncommitted voters accordingly had more political clout than did either labor for the Democrats or Big Business for the Republicans.[28]

In the end, therefore, although Schattschneider acknowledged considerable business solidarity, he tended to deny the control hypothesis. Moreover, he concluded, the privileged position of Big Business served democracy by keeping in check the abuses of Big Government.[29]

In this, he found considerable confirmation from the sophisticated economic modeling of spatial theory. Anthony Downs, for example, began by assuming that both voters and candidates were rational. The former tried to maximize the return on their votes by selecting candidates favorable to their interests, and the latter tried to maximize votes in order to gain or remain in office. With additional simplifying assumptions that elections were single-issue affairs and that candidates knew their constituents' preferences and were free to adjust their positions to them, Downs's model showed that candidates would maximize their votes by adopting positions close to those of the median voter.[30]

The existence of interest groups, uncertainties about voter preferences, and high information costs could compromise this outcome. Interest groups sought to maximize the value of their investment in candidates, and candidates sought both the groups' low-cost information about voters' preferences (salient issues that would appeal to the median voter) and their contributions for campaigns to inform voters persuasively.[31] Unmotivated voters abstained from voting, since the expected benefit was less than the cost of making an informed vote, with the probability of affecting the outcome being negligible.

The spatial model predicted that a rational citizenry would choose to be politically ignorant. Most citizens and interest groups, would educate themselves only on those matters that promised gains sufficient to outweigh the costs of gathering information. Most would therefore rely on relatively costless forms of data like party affiliation, endorsements, polls and advertisements. Only those persons and groups with substantial benefits from their electoral investments would be adequately represented; for most, it would be rational not to vote at all. Economic producers were therefore likely to be overrepresented. Not only were their gains easier to estimate and greater in sum, but they also had more resources to invest in this activity.

The right to vote might be equally distributed, but the information and the incentive were not. Despite these obvious biases in the electoral system, Downs concluded, as Dahl did, that American electoral politics was sufficiently dynamic and responsive to frustrate over time the corrupting efforts of any privileged minority.

During the 1960s and 1970s, the earlier pluralist consensus came under persistent attack, especially by Charles Lindblom, Michael Useem, and Thomas Ferguson. To Lindblom, the difference between political control by totalitarian regimes and political control by the American corporate sector was only one of degree.[32] Useem affirmed this assertion by insisting that recent trends in corporate concentration and diversification, intercorporate ownership, and interlocking directorates had created an infrastructure through which a unified managerial class position could develop.[33] In Useem's opinion, high-level managers translated this "classwide rationality" into political strategies through their participation in elite business organizations such as the Business Roundtable and the Committee for Economic Development (see Chapter 8 for a discussion of these associations in the context of developing collective action among managers). Ferguson began with Downs's insight, that resource and information disparities favored the wealthy and well organized in the elective process and that Big Business, with its "old boy" networks, could parlay its privilege into effective control over electoral competition.[34] Because ill-informed voters were unlikely to discriminate adequately, candidates misrepresented themselves as friends of the people when in fact they functioned as agents of the rich, and privileged minorities used their superior resources to rig outcomes either by mobilizing sympathetic voters or by making strategic donations to candidates to limit voters' choices.

Political scientists found Ferguson's points valid in theory, but by no means convincing in practice: The causal links necessary to sustain his empirical argument, which covered nearly a century of ostensible political control, were too extraordinary in number to be persuasive.[35] Even Ferguson had ended with a qualification: Although corporations shared certain beliefs that served as a basis for collective action, their disagreements on other important matters helped support two-party competition. Critics also quickly pointed out the limitations of Lindblom's functional logic and the relatively inconsequential nature of Useem's findings. Data could be massaged in vague support of either outcome.

David Vogel reminded his readers that business was not the only powerful minority interest and that the state had substantial coercive means to bring a rebellious business community into line with majority interests.[36] Offering an extensive political history of corporate America over the last two decades, Vogel asserted that the relative cohesion of the Reagan years, particularly early on, was the exception rather than the rule, having emerged during a rare period when all businesses found themselves confronted with the recognizable, common foe of "excessive" social regulation. By the 1980s, foreign competition and technological innovation had weakened entrenched managerial hierarchies and had again unsettled the political solidarity of the preceding decade.

Robert Dahl added another voice to the optimists. Although the corporate sector tilted American social life away from democracy, the system, in his view, was still as dynamic and chaotic as it had appeared in the 1950s, when he first argued that control by any consistent grouping of interests, whether minority or majority, was unlikely.[37]

THE DRIFT TOWARD CONTRACTS IN POLITICAL REGULATION

The general irreverence with which Americans responded to authority in the 1960s made their responses to institutions ambivalent in all
facets, be they social, political, or economic. On the one hand, they
demanded more "voice" in the affairs of the institutions to which
they remained committed. On the other hand, they demanded easier
"exit" so that they could be disencumbered of undesirable commitments and freed up to join alternative groupings without restriction
or responsibility.

Party leaders responded with efforts to stabilize their domains and
improve their fortunes by conceding to diverse interests rights to
participate in setting agendas and selecting candidates. By capping
individual contributors' donations, they neutralized disparities in
economic power among the party's constituents and curbed somewhat the tendency to compete for sizable donations by selling political favors and influence.

Nevertheless, expensive media campaigns had become so effective
in the 1960s that some feared that candidates would become dependent on the rich and well organized to run successfully for office.
Incumbents, particularly Democrats, feared that they were at a substantial disadvantage to (Republican) opponents with broader access
to wealthy contributors. To maintain balance in the two-party system, Congress therefore sought restrictions on media spending for
all federal election campaigns.

Congress had been struggling for some time with the issue of campaign finances. Electoral reform had been a focus of much attention
during the 1960s, when President John F. Kennedy submitted five
draft bills to Congress. Although none passed, the increasing publicity about Congress's financial dependency later forced the Nixon administration to enforce the virtually dormant Federal Corrupt Practices Act and press charges against corporations that had violated
the act in the 1968 election.[38]

In 1971, Congress revised the laws, and organized contributions
from business and labor became legal.[39] The Federal Election Campaign Act (FECA) imposed limits on hoaaw much federal candidates
could spend on all forms of media and provided for comprehensive
and timely disclosures of their campaign revenues and expenditures.
It allowed corporations and unions to spend their own funds to establish, administer, and solicit contributions for segregated funds or
political action committees (PACs), but precluded them from contributing their funds directly to federal candidates' campaigns.

Thus corporations and labor unions had a more explicit and active
role in the electoral process. Acknowledging that earlier regulatory

bans had failed to keep business and labor outside politics, Congress now invited their limited participation. Still insisting that their contributions remain voluntary, if organized, it hoped that public scrutiny would keep them honest.

The Watergate scandal soon exposed the naïveté of this aspiration. Corporate money would clearly continue to find its way secretly into Republican political campaign coffers, the 1971 reforms notwithstanding.[40] Again Congress faced the problem of whether to police campaign expenditures more strictly or to loosen campaign spending restrictions in favor of disclosure rules.

The FECA amendments of 1974 pursued both avenues of reform. The revised law imposed ceilings on each candidate's total campaign expenditures in all of the elections leading up to office, primaries included;[41] and it further encouraged the formation of corporate and labor PACs by allowing each PAC to contribute up to $5000 directly to any candidate's election campaign.[42] Apprising the public fully about the political advantages that these interests sought would help keep corporate and labor PAC influences in check: for voters could discount the campaign promises of PAC-funded candidates rationally.

Advocates on both sides soon challenged the law, arguing that the limitations on campaign contributions and expenditures curbed contributors' as well as candidates' freedom of expression in the political marketplace. In 1976, the Supreme Court's *Buckley v. Valeo* decision upheld the ceilings on PAC contributions.[43] Such ceilings, it contended, restrained only slightly the opportunity for individual political expression through group association. Other forms of expression, like independent political advertising, could proceed apace. Groups could still publicly endorse candidates and provide important information to public deliberations surrounding the electoral process, and individual persons could join and contribute through more than one group. The negligible costs of ceilings, then, were amply exceeded by their benefits. By working to equalize competing groups' financial disparities and encouraging congressional candidates to seek funds from a greater number of sources, they lessened the potential for political corruption.[44]

The Court did, however, strike down the ceilings on total campaign expenditures. It held that candidates' First Amendment rights to freedom of expression (or expenditure) outweighed any legitimate government interest in maintaining financial resource parity among candidates. Expenditure limitations had the additional and unpleasant effect of arbitrarily lessening the flow of information available to the public.

Earlier expectations about groups characterized by centralized "control" and broad "dependency" were thus giving way to prescriptions for encouraging more self-reliant individual behavior in the political as well as the economic arena.[45] Corporations had the active and basically benign political function of supplying valuable and low-cost information to voters, who were now considered less gullible and more competent in evaluating sources.

The Supreme Court extended this analysis to the states' regulation of corporate political participation as well. In 1978, *First National Bank of Boston v. Bellotti* ruled against the Massachusetts regulations designed to foreclose corporate participation in referenda proposing a graduated income tax.[46] Although the Court had already acknowledged substantial state power to regulate corporate political activities, it had also begun to erase earlier distinctions between commercially motivated and politically motivated speech.[47]

Justice Byron R. White's dissenting opinion in *Bellotti* was based on the trust approach. He argued that managers who tried to shape public policies and reform laws that did not directly affect corporate interests were violating their responsibilities to stakeholders.[48] But Justice Lewis F. Powell, Jr.'s majority opinion basically disavowed the relevance of corporate entity theories to constitutional discussions, making light of concerns about the "corporate identity of the speaker" and emphasizing instead the importance of information to the electorate and the dangers of allowing public officials to restrict such information, regardless of the source. An earlier Court decision had found that "exit" options gave shareholders ample means to express their discontent.[49]

Not until 1990 did a case finally press the Supreme Court to acknowledge that there could be problems of managerial collectivity in addition to those of corporate privilege.[50] In *Austin v. Michigan Chamber of Commerce,* the Court upheld Michigan's prohibition of the state chamber of commerce's use of corporate funds contributed by managers to support a candidate in a partisan state election campaign. The ban aimed admirably, in its view, to correct "the corrosive and distorting effects of immense aggregations of wealth that are accumulated with the help of the corporate form and that have little or no correlation to the public's support for the corporation's political ideas."[51] The Court refrained, however, from challenging its 1976 decision regarding the consitutionality of the FECA: Corporate PACs, as voluntary associations, improved political life by adding to the nation's stock of political organizations in which individuals could aggregate resources to amplify their political voice.

This ascendancy of a market-oriented, contractual approach to corporate political regulation did not go unchallenged. Herbert Alexander, the leading authority on campaign finance policies, railed against "blue chip" corporations that had engaged in unprecedented political corruption between 1973 and 1975.[52] Other leading students of campaign finance contended that campaign financing should become less dependent on PACs in general and corporate PACs in particular. They also advocated limits on aggregate expenditures, *Buckley v. Valeo* notwithstanding.[53]

These objections, however, had little appreciable influence on Congress, as incumbents and well-organized interests settled into the *status quo*. During the deliberations leading up to the 1976 FECA reforms, advocates of political equality were powerless to override the Court's First Amendment edicts and had to settle instead for relatively modest amendments that further limited individual contribution ceilings. Of the measures they continued to advocate to make the electoral process more equitable, the most notable were proposals for public funding of congressional elections. Congress responded with the 1979 FECA reforms, which offered only modifications in the original legislation.[54]

Shifts in the approach to antitrust both supported deregulation and put an end to reform proposals seeking to reduce the concentration of wealth and associated imbalances in the distribution of political resources. Although many proposals in the 1970s attempted to restrict conglomerate mergers, none succeeded, despite testimony such as that of John Flynn.

Before the Senate Select Committee on Small Business in December 1975, during hearings that led to the 1976 Hart–Scott–Rodino Antitrust Improvements Act, Flynn urged legislators not to restrict their analysis simply to economic quantification.[55] They were responsible also for bringing "less quantifiable but very real social and political insights" to bear on public policy; they "must realize that *they are the trustees of our value system.*"[56] Congress should therefore consider restricting corporate size to "maximiz[e] individual potential even at some cost, real or imagined, to economic efficiency."[57] Big Business had a deleterious effect on the citizenry. "[L]arge institutions, seemingly of necessity, enforce conformity, circumscribe creativity and defend the status quo."[58] Recalling Brandeis's critique, Flynn continued, "individual responsibility becomes diffused and the standards for performance established for underlings in the bureaucracy of the big firm become artificial and mechanical." In skewing the distribution of wealth, large firms also demoralized the less advantaged and undermined democratic politics.[59]

In 1979, Senator Edward Kennedy echoed these themes by sponsoring a bill to limit mergers, including those of a conglomerate nature, on the basis of overall size alone.[60] As wealth became more concentrated, he explained, Congress was increasingly in danger of becoming indebted to a few. Edwin Epstein, one of the leading scholars in the field, was one of many who testified against the bill. Size and potential influence, he noted, had a somewhat inverse relationship, because corporate mergers consolidated PACs as well as economic assets. Reducing the number of PACs would also lower the legal ceiling on total corporate-sector contributions to individual election campaigns. The pluralist tendencies of individual donors within and across PACs would tend to destabilize attempts to coalesce, as perceptions of a unified political interest became harder to define and sustain. Congress responded by rejecting Kennedy's bill. It continued to review suggestions for election campaign finance reform, but proposals to restrict firm size generally languished during the 1980s.

In sum, the FECA reforms of 1971, 1974, and 1976 established a regulatory system of financial disclosures to inform the voting public on campaign contributions.[61] Although these reforms still barred both corporations and unions from drawing on their own treasuries to contribute directly to election campaigns, the new laws did enable them to fund and organize PACs, control PAC policies, and spend virtually unlimited aggregates of voluntary PAC contributions in a coordinated, strategic fashion. PAC activity soared in late 1970s.[62] Although critics continued to express fears about corporations' corrupting influences, the prevailing opinion held that as long as the electorate had access to accurate information, the electoral process itself could keep corporate power in bounds. Only in those few instances when managers seemed exceptionally heavy handed, did the courts permit federal and state enforcement agencies to intervene.

Although the new order rested on contractual arrangements that were less stable and more diverse than E. E. Schattschneider's countervailing powers of institutionalized Big Business and Big Government, this consensus still resembled the position he had outlined two decades before. Over the past two decades, then, the regulatory system consistently eroded the older trust relationships by facilitating bargaining relations between management and the firm's constituents and between management and the administrative state. But little has been done to ensure that the corporate PAC managers remain accountable to the donors, and many writers have suggested that this will become an important topic for reform in the coming decades.

The shift to a contract approach continues. Corporate law and constitutional ideals remain ambivalent. In response to the economic pressure of tender markets and the political pressure of government regulations, managers have been developing their own conventions and collective actions, and to these topics we now shall turn.

II
THE MANAGERS

8

The Regulatory State and the Professionalization of Management

This chapter examines how managers developed a sense of individual and collective professional identity. The narrative begins at the turn of the century and ends with the conclusion of World War II. On the way, we see professional standards evolve both in particular leaders' visions and in general, practical corporate responses to government regulation.

THE EARLY DEVELOPMENT OF MANAGERIAL DEFINITION AND INSTITUTIONAL FORM

In 1901, shortly after J. P. Morgan had established U.S. Steel as the nation's largest manufacturing concern, the chairman of the board, Elbert Gary, warned him that the government would not allow so large an amalgamation to survive, unless members of the board demonstrated to the public that their "intentions were good."[1] Quite in contrast with the financiers who ruled American industry near the turn of the century with attitudes that ranged from Commodore Vanderbilt's "the public be damned" to Morgan's noblesse oblige, Gary's early prototype for the professional corporate-sector manager showed a profound respect for public opinion and for the government responses it could evoke. And although he identified the corporation with the concerns of its investors, this recognition of a "public interest" in the firm's operations became increasingly important to management.

The legislative debate over the Federal Reserve Act of 1913 marked a turning point. As the historian James Livingston put it, the "language of reform used by both parties was the invention of a corporate business community that saw in the wreckage of the nineteenth century's 'self-regulating' competitive market the obligation and the opportunity to remake American banking in the image of the new corporate economy."[2] Over the next two decades, the once controlling banking establishment centered in New York City came largely under the power of that national corporate community, with managers assuming the reins of power; in the third decade, New Deal reforms completed this transition.

Managers were drawn from a wide variety of ranks active in corporate affairs, including financial analysis, law, cost accountancy, human resource and "scientific" management, production engineering, and conventional administration.[3] What they had in common was a sense of the urgency of striking deals among the corporate stakeholders and developing a moral climate that would legitimate their decisions to those stakeholders and so expedite the firm's operations. In part, the managers' ascendancy was a by-product of the large firm's increasing dominance and management's unchallenged technical authority. By the 1920s, this expertise, coupled with a capacity for bureaucratic innovation, had established the corporation as the central organization in the economy.[4]

A number of the leading firms, such as General Motors (GM) and Du Pont, had also instituted a decentralized structure in which autonomous profit centers, or "divisions," reported their earnings to central headquarters. These kinds of adjustments were managerial solutions to complicated coordination problems that grew out of having to face distinct labor, customer, geographic, and product markets.[5] Just as important, managerial accounting procedures and standards helped the modern corporation adapt to the private investment and commercial banking system and so reinforced the private nature of the economy.[6] In addition, they held managers accountable to a comparable standard so that they could evaluate one another's performance and develop a common sense of their responsibilities.

Innovative decentralized structures also separated daily operations from long-term planning and so permitted top managers to concentrate on strategic activities.[7] Corporate headquarters functioned like internal capital markets, reallocating the firm's resources among profit centers based on long-term expectations of growth. As a result, corporate managers performed functions that had once been in the domain of investment banking.[8] And as increased corporate profits were used to build up retained earnings, managers gained in bargaining power against their own investment bankers and even pressed them to compete with others. Still, managerial and banking authority did not split until the Great Depression, when financial control of the economy proved itself generally inadequate.

As managers' skills in handling their firms' long-term planning requirements improved, so too did their ability to coordinate activity within their industries. Industry associations and individual firms like GM gathered data that enabled them to make both microeconomic and macroeconomic forecasts so that they could make more informed production decisions.[9] These activities were also supported by government sponsored publications of useful statistics.[10] The federal government began collecting and publishing extensive price and wage data during World War I and had earlier made available even more data for particular industries such as railroads, shipping, and commodities subject to tariffs.[11]

One of the first institutional frameworks in which the managerial interest emerged was the War Industries Board (WIB), established during World War I to allocate and stabilize production.[12] A number of board administrators came from the managerial ranks, and under Bernard Baruch's able leadership, the WIB illustrated the benefits that could be gained through cooperation between business and government. Ironically, the bulk of power in the WIB rested in private hands, and the government's influence was due largely to Baruch's persuasiveness about the virtues of cooperation. Seeing themselves as the technical experts on regulating production, managers nevertheless valued the assistance of the WIB in making such regulation feasible. After the war, notwithstanding the liquidation of the WIB, managers continued to expect from government the sort of statesmanship that Baruch had personified.

The Federal Trade Commission (FTC), established in 1914, in part standardized enforceable methods of competition, and managers, small businesses, and labor all supported this aspect of the legislation. But the FTC failed to develop a clear sense of its own mission, and when it began to use its enforcement powers to support industry codes during the Hoover administration, the federal courts curbed the agency's authority.[13]

Nonetheless, increasing corporate political activity throughout the period continued to shape managerial interests. Large firms helped establish strong trade associations to promote their interests within the government.[14] From these activities the field of public relations burgeoned in the 1920s.[15] Corporate staffs eventually did more than provide information about public opinion, legislative activity, and regulatory actions that could be useful in securing the firm's political objectives. They also shaped public opinion itself.

In general, then, corporate managers slowly gained definition and institutional form during the first three decades of the century. Among other concerns, they had to adjust corporate activities to the demands of the bankers, who had the power both to disinvest the firm's capital and, in most instances, to replace one management team with another. Though more sanguine than financiers about the capacity of public administrators to construct codes of conduct and otherwise influence market regulations, managers followed the financial community's lead in entrusting industrial policy to the courts and to the "rules of reason" that the courts developed in scrutinizing other government agencies.

Just as important, however, managers had to adjust their operations to the needs of at least four different constituencies: their workers, their consumers, the small businesses that served as both suppliers and distributors and competed with them in certain geographical and product markets, and the local, state, and federal public officials who might respond to demands for legislation and regulation whenever the large corporations played cavalierly with any of the other interests.[16]

By the early 1920s the managerial function became sufficiently independent to be presented as a profession with both a meritocratic structure and a public purpose. No one developed these ideas more thoroughly than Owen Young, chairman of General Electric (GE) from 1922 to 1939 and 1942 to 1944. From his reading in the common-law and public utilities regulation,[17] Young believed that by aggregating capital, the modern corporation had invested private property with a public purpose that limited the rights of equity owners.[18] He also recognized that in separating control from ownership, the corporation had given management an unprecedented degree of autonomy.[19] Experience led Young to conclude that it was necessary to displace the traditional logic of corporate ownership, according to which investors could maintain rights over management, with a modified fiduciary doctrine, according to which managers were the public's trustees, authorized to balance the public's interest with those of investors and employees.[20] He observed that his own performance as the manager of GE varied significantly according to whether he was a trustee for an institution or a lawyer for investors.

In a 1927 address dedicating the Baker facilities at the Harvard Business School, Young urged professional business schools to educate their students in the standards of trusteeship.[21] Such standards would make management a profession, one that would be able to anticipate social needs before government regulation became necessary. Yet Young did not react sympathetically to earlier statist visions, such as those depicted by Teddy Roosevelt and Herbert Croly, in which managers were to be executives for a strong regulatory state. Instead, he viewed managers as the bulwarks of a modern liberal order. In mediating private negotiations among the firm's constituents, they participated in a spontaneous order that required only minimal public supervision. Sympathetic to Louis Brandeis's developmental vision of the corporation, Young also longed for the day when the large firm would be owned by the people who were giving their labor and their lives to these organizations. Worker-owned firms seemed the sensible way to overcome the problems of managerial opportunism that arose with the separation of ownership from control.

CREATING A MANAGERIAL COLLECTIVE INTEREST

When the country fell into the prolonged Depression that, among other things, signaled an end to the bankers' central role, managers had an opportunity to assert control not only over their individual firms, but over their industrial sector and the economy as a whole.[22] To do so, they needed shared aims and conventions. In its struggle for corporate control and experimentation with regulations, the New Deal helped provide both.

Federal policy deliberations centered corporate managers' attention collectively on establishing their control. They failed in some attempts, like trying to control macroeconomic policy through the National Recovery Act (NRA), but succeeded in others, like winning a central coordinating role in stakeholder regulation. More important, they emerged from World War II with a highly articulated sense of collective interest in the managerial prerogative and its role in a pluralistic constitutional democracy.

The battles of the New Deal spurred managers to seek means to enlighten one another and to coordinate their political activities—to develop, in other words, their conventions for collective action. *Fortune* magazine and the Committee for Economic Development (CED) emerged from this era as the central enlightening and coordinating agents; educational institutions like the Harvard Business School took the lead in refocusing succeeding generations of business leaders on the corporate managerial role; and leading lights began to take charge and strengthen their relationships with government.

Swope and the NIRA

GE's president, Gerard Swope, for example, offered a plan that would give managers effective control over the economy. Although

it exceeded anything in Young's previous thinking, exceptional times
called for exceptional daring, and Swope felt that nothing less than
a managerially coordinated, cartelized economy would bring the nation into recovery.[23]

Centralization would allow regulation of the economic cycles over
which individual managers of even the biggest corporations had little
control. It would do so with means that mirrored the administrative
procedures with which corporate executives had become both familiar and comfortable, namely, corporate boards, trade and industry
associations, and intracorporate negotiations with several classes of
interest, above all labor.

Hoover rejected Swope's plan in no uncertain terms, arguing that
it would subject the American people to the control of monopolies
bolstered by federal law.[24] When Franklin Roosevelt became president, however, Congress enacted a modified version of his plan in
passing the National Industrial Recovery Act (NIRA). The National
Recovery Administration (NRA) was empowered to write industry
codes of conduct on practices pertaining to competition, consumers,
and workers and to stabilize wages and prices within industries.[25]
Like its World War I predecessor, the WIB, the NRA drew a large
share of its administrators from business management.

Although this experiment had the initial blessings of Big Business
as well as Roosevelt's radical planners, it eventually gave way to the
factiousness of particular interests. The NRA tended to rubber-
stamp any codes of which industries approved; these tended to favor
larger businesses that could spread the cost of accommodating new
rules over a greater volume of sales and would benefit substantially
from a more consistent competitive environment. Smaller businesses
had little incentive to get involved. Since enforcement depended
mostly on voluntary compliance and the threat of consumer boycotts
(businesses upholding the codes were permitted to post "blue eagles"
as signals to consumers of compliance), the NRA's prospects for
long-term success were, at best, remote.

In any case, the U.S. Supreme Court questioned the delegation of
effective lawmaking power to private interests and quickly disposed
of major portions of the NIRA. The traditional liberal distinction
between public and private authority did more than protect private
business interests from being overrun by public officials. It also
served to protect the public domain from domination by more powerful economic interests. Managers began to understand more
clearly the extent of their autonomy within the firm and the interests
they shared with managers of other large firms. After so decisive a
defeat of their proposals to control production and price by extending corporate techniques to government, most chose to distance
themselves in the future from similar plans.[26]

In the years following the demise of the NRA, a series of alternative proposals managed to accomplish what the NIRA had not, namely, to stabilize labor and consumer markets, to safeguard individual workers and consumers from unfair business practices, and to shelter smaller businesses and communities from the consequences of recession.[27] By most accounts, corporate management had considerably less impact on this spate of legislation than during the earlier years when FDR's "brain trust" informed New Deal policies.[28] Their public image had been tarnished not just by the ineffectiveness and eventual collapse of the NRA but also by a series of studies, of which the most important was Berle and Means's *The Modern Corporation and Private Property,* which documented the increasing concentration of relatively unchecked economic power in the hands of corporate managers.[29]

Corporate managers, then, retreated in the latter part of the 1930s. They attempted to come to grips with the new era and react to the broad range of new laws, administrative rulings, and court decisions that they no longer shaped so prominently. By interacting as firm representatives with the two principal stakeholder agencies, the SEC and the NLRB, managers came to appreciate their possible collective interest. Federal laws that sought to restore investor confidence and to develop the securities markets by modifying and stabilizing industry practices generally benefited managers, and they welcomed investment regulation that liberated them from banker control while setting up accounting procedures that formally recognized the large firm as a "public" undertaking.

The Light Hand of the SEC

The SEC won broad cooperation in its efforts to stabilize the various security markets by recognizing the self-interest of the institutions it tried to regulate—the bankers, brokers, dealers, and investment specialists. Although retaining the power to license brokers and underwriting, it basically yielded two vehicles to protect investors, handing back market rules and corporate governance to the self-regulation of the New York and American Stock Exchanges (NYSE and ASE). By establishing corporate and underwriting disclosure requirements, the SEC relied on private, independent accounting firms to ensure disinterested professional auditing procedures and financial reporting standards. Since regulations and structural changes in the banking system already tended to safeguard average savings from speculative risk, SEC officials were relatively sanguine about keeping only a light hand on the affairs of those private investors eager for higher, though also riskier, returns. These officials worked to secure the public's general confidence in investment markets rather than to provide direct protection from dubious market practices.

The Heavier Hand of Labor Regulations

By contrast, developments in labor regulation during the New Deal and World War II threatened managerial autonomy. Managers found it necessary to reaffirm publicly the legitimacy of both corporate power and managerial roles, and they mounted their defense through the legal language of trusteeship.

Federal labor policies were of two kinds. First, Congress had sought to equalize the workers' bargaining power against large industrial firms.[30] The NLRA eased common-law property and contract prescriptions that had inhibited unions from organizing and bargaining collectively, and it placed those activities under the administrative jurisdiction of the National Labor Relations Board (NLRB). Second, Congress set standards for minimum wages and maximum hours to protect the majority of unorganized workers; the Fair Labor Standards Act (FLSA) designated the Department of Labor as the enforcer of those standards.

Nevertheless, much as in the case of consumer protection, federal statutes concerning labor unions contained enough ambiguities to sustain battle. From the passage of the National Labor Relations Act (NLRA) in 1935 to its amendment in the Taft–Hartley Act of 1947, corporate managers and labor leaders engaged in a vicious struggle for the soul of the NLRB. Its original version, the Wagner Act of 1935, had supported two broad conceptions of the structure of labor relations and the role of federal administrators in the workplace[31] (see also Chapter 4).

On the one hand, the trade union version saw labor as part of a large market in which groups of workers could organize themselves according to the particular skills they offered. Because unions served to match workers' skills with firms' demands, they could bargain with managers over the terms of employment. Generally, the unions gained their strength from monopolizing the supply of certain crafts, and corporate power derived from its role as monopsonist in certain areas. The Wagner Act empowered the NLRB in two ways: It balanced the weights that the courts had earlier placed on the side of management, and it guarded against managerial practices that coerced individual workers engaged in legitimate union activities.

On the other hand, the industrial union version of labor relations considered employees relatively captive to their firms. Proposals to make internal labor markets more equitable from the workers' point of view ranged from organized bargaining to appointing public bargaining agents or having workers select private agents to represent them in individual firms. Managers found these last proposals untenable, as they would pit managers against public officials, severely limit their initiatives to prevent unionization, and move the economy closer to socialism.

As the NLRB institutionalized the Wagner Act in union certification battles, managers often found themselves in a tacit alliance with the American Federal of Labor (AFL). Its craft union membership vigorously opposed the board's view that unions were simply bargaining agents that could be replaced more or less at will. The AFL claimed instead that it had in effect property rights over the skills that workers sold to employers and therefore a valid claim to represent them in negotiations. By 1939, the AFL pressured the Roosevelt administration to overhaul the Board and root out its radical elements.[32]

Meantime, managers bolstered their own rights and weakened the Wagner Act by an able resort to the courts but remained divided on the best means to address the threat of unionization in general.[33] Smaller and middle-size manufacturers, such as Republic Steel and National Steel, tended to band together in the National Association of Manufacturers (NAM), belligerently resisting all federal intervention on behalf of unions. Another group of large firms, including AT&T, Du Pont, and Standard Oil of New Jersey, were just as adamant as the NAM in stopping unionization and were even willing to use violence but preferred sophisticated techniques of personnel management designed to make unionization unattractive. A third set decided that unions were here to stay and mapped out a strategy to make the situation favorable for management. In this group, GM and Allis Chalmers eventually accepted unionization but held the line on management's prerogatives over strategic investment decisions and production and insisted that union leaders discipline workers who did not honor contracts. Finally, a small group of progressive firms, most notably U.S. Rubber and General Electric, put up no resistance whatsoever to unionization. Instead, they welcomed the unions and attempted to set up cooperative relations with them.[34] In the case of GE, this nonadversarial attitude grew out of Owen Young's vision of managerial trusteeship and Gerard Swope's recognition that the company's success depended on a stable and cooperative labor force.[35]

In spite of these divisions, after World War II, the business community coordinated a political assault against the NLRA. Differences in the business community on the labor question had narrowed, with both the NAM and progressive firms moving closer to the center. The former recognized unionization as an industrial fact of life, best approached realistically by tilting the rules governing labor relations in management's favor.[36] In the latter group, especially as a new generation came to power at GE, managers found that unionization had made their labor force quite radical, and they were willing, perhaps even eager, to support a business coalition led by the NAM to reform the NLRA.[37] The reform movement secured the Taft–Hartley Act in 1947. Reasserting its political clout had become particularly important to business as labor continued to endorse liberal reform.[38]

In entering the political debate, managers adopted the fiduciary doctrine outlined by Owen Young. Yet because they had to rebuff labor's radical demands for extending their rights and curtailing managerial discretion, they revised Young's ideas and expunged its social democratic implications. Although the firm was conceived as a set of ongoing negotiations among constituents, it had fiduciary responsibilities principally to its shareholders. Managers therefore acted in a socially responsible manner when they treated corporate property in purely instrumental terms by increasing wealth. Any demands for industrial democracy, they asserted, would undermine the hierarchical command structure that had made firms so productive. Technical necessity thus argued against democratic demands for worker participation and justified managers' absolute authority over the corporation. They alone had the requisite expertise to make competent economic decisions.

Stabilization and Growth Policies and the CED

World War II offered corporate managers the opportunity both to explore regulatory alternatives to keep state planners at bay and to develop an understanding of their own role as statesmen. Held in check by stakeholder regulation and by the emergent corporate norms of social responsibility, they responded by capitalizing on the pluralist vision and persuading the American public of the fundamentally democratic nature of the large corporation.[39]

Modern industrial regulation began with Franklin Roosevelt. During the 1930s and 1940s, Congress enacted regulations on an industry-by-industry basis. It placed communications, trucking, and airlines under the jurisdiction of the FCC, ICC, and CAB, where they were managed essentially like cartels. Industries vital to the national security, like transportation, aerospace, and computers, found support both from federal spending programs like the Highway Trust Fund and defense appropriations and from research contracts via the National Science Foundation.[40] A variety of other industries, from mining and energy to food and drugs, also obtained government support through subsidies or restrictive entry barriers

Two consistent patterns gradually emerged. First, the administrative process gained some coherence, particularly in the Administrative Procedure Act of 1946.[41] Second, in Roosevelt's seemingly haphazard array of rules, processes, agencies and bureaus, postwar political scientists began to see a series of "iron triangles" emerge to govern policy development and execution.[42] Congressional committee staffs in charge of drafting legislation, federal bureau or agency staffs vested with rule-making and enforcement powers, and industry or trade association staffs for political affairs comprised the three sides of each industrial polygon. In overseeing and administering programs, the first two appeared over time to equate public service with catering to their private constituencies,[43] and specific private interests also gained control over particular public-policy programs.[44]

The business community generally favored iron triangles as a political base for securing beneficial industrial policies and defeating New Deal radicalism.[45] Trade associations were usually the principal business actors in this policy environment, although regulated industries employed specialized personnel as well.

To be effective, however, the iron triangles required economic expansion, and growth no longer seemed to be a self-sustaining phenomenon. Careful macromanagement might be necessary instead, with Congress and the president monitoring the legislative and executive staffs' regulatory activities.

Unlike other industrialized countries, American business had no "peak" association that legitimately represented, let alone ruled, diverse corporate interests. The U.S. Chamber of Commerce, for example, included businesses both large and small, each end of the spectrum with its own sense of proper corporate-sector policy.[46] Its leaders came mainly from Big Business, and when they proposed new methods of business–government cooperation to stimulate growth, the majority responded negatively. Small businesses hated the New Deal's "radical" labor and social welfare policies, and the membership forced the chamber to break all ties with the Roosevelt administration. More moderate members of the corporate sector felt that dialogue, not confrontation, would constrain the New Deal's excesses and reform the federal government in line with their own interests, so in 1942 they broke away from the chamber to establish the Committee for Economic Development (CED).[47]

The CED brought together three kinds of groups. The first consisted of top managers recruited by the Business Advisory Council (BAC) from large industrial firms. Secretary of Commerce Daniel

Roper had initiated the BAC in 1933 as a semipublic body to provide
the New Deal administration with ongoing contacts to Big Business.[48] A second group came from progressive entrepreneurs who
seriously studied how government spending could help moderate
business cycles. Ralph Flanders, head of a medium-size machine
company, and Henry Dennison, head of a Boston-based family paper company, helped consolidate this group. Finally, the CED en-
listed the support of social scientists, mostly from the University of
Chicago, who were convinced that solutions to the problems of modern life required combining the insights of managers and academicians.

The CED quickly gained prominence among corporate leaders.
Owen Young, for example, looked approvingly on its formation but
did not become a member because he believed that the organization
would best serve the nation if it fostered a new generation of leaders.[49] Perhaps the most prominent of this new generation was Paul
Hoffman, a top executive at Studebaker. As chairman of the CED,
Hoffman did much to convince his corporate colleagues to cooperate
with the New Deal. Although opposed to the NRA, he consistently
collaborated with government officials in finding solutions to America's economic problems. Believing that these solutions should not
threaten liberty as the NRA had done, Hoffman joined ranks with
the more progressive corporate leaders of the period, sharing their
views on labor relations and management's fiduciary responsibilities.[50]

Hoffman also made contributions of his own. Reared in the mass
marketing techniques of the auto industry, Hoffman was acutely
aware of the importance of public opinion and how its manipulation
required scientific study to target appropriate markets. To help educate corporate executives in the workings of public policy, he elicited
the support of the University of Chicago, where he was a trustee.[51]
In addition, he turned to Henry Luce, the inspired founder of *Time*
magazine, to help disseminate the CED's contributions among the
nation's top executives. Luce's new venture, *Fortune* magazine, held
out great promise in this regard.[52]

Those who came together under the aegis of the CED gradually
came to support more liberal macroeconomic policies, which they
coupled with the stabilizing industry regulations of iron triangles as
central to securing stable national economic growth.[53] The CED offered a number of policy proposals in statements issued in 1944,
1945, and 1948, urging that the government use appropriate fiscal
and monetary tools while denying the effectiveness of the NRA's
price controls and other proposals to direct investments and redistribute incomes.

The CED first gained broad recognition within business circles when it helped coordinate the economic transition as the United States entered World War II, by establishing regional offices that produced detailed reports on local business plans.[54] But after considerable discussion, the CED decided that efforts to become a mass organization were impractical and might be incompatible with the nation's democratic traditions. Abandoning these ambitions, it chose instead to be a conduit for corporate executives to participate with government officials and academics in broad public-policy discussions. Coordinated managerial political action remained narrowly confined to general macroeconomic concerns and policy formulation, leaving its implementation to politicians and public administrators. But the iron triangles that created a web of industrial policies still required managers to engage in industrywide political actions, where they gained some skill in lobbying and electoral politics. This activity was particularly important to the regulated industries.

EDUCATION THROUGH *FORTUNE* AND MBA PROGRAMS

During its founding years, *Fortune* magazine helped fashion a cultural climate conducive to the CED's formation and to the wide acceptance of its managerial vision.[55] As *Fortune* recognized early on, few of the two thousand executives who controlled the economy shared a common business education. Because only a handful had graduated from the nation's professional business schools, the corporate community had little of the academic training that Owen Young had believed so vital to enlightened business practice.[56] In founding *Fortune*, Henry Luce hoped to correct this situation by highlighting both exemplary corporate behavior[57] and areas that could benefit from reform, particularly in the area of business–government relations.[58] As the CED became a viable group, *Fortune* championed the organization, even reissuing a CED statement for "mass consumption."[59] *Fortune*'s 1951 special issue entitled "The Permanent Revolution," which detailed more thoroughly than even the CED did a vision of the modern economy, its workings, and its contributions to democracy, best illustrates *Fortune*'s educative and partisan function.[60]

At the center of this new order, *Fortune* saw an enlightened management imbued with a fiduciary code and dedicated to the norms of efficiency and economic liberty. While drawing on Young's original formulation of management's fiduciary duties and accepting modern management–labor relations, *Fortune* did not share Young's enthusiasm for converting modern corporations to worker cooperatives. In-

stead, the editors held fast to the notion of the supremacy of shareholders, to the sanctity of private property and to the instrumental
vision of the corporation's social utility. They also believed that as an
organized private group with a common interest in subduing public
interventions in the corporate sector, management had become the
single most important check on the government's intrusive nature.
Not only did these articles serve as educational material for the corporate executives who read them, but they also provided liberal academicians and policy analysts with the basic understanding of the
new managerial "class."[61] This understanding encouraged the corporate liberal alliance that characterized the postwar period, at least
until the Johnson administration.[62]

The Leading Role of Harvard

The formal education of corporate managers also changed apace.
The Harvard Business School (HBS), which had gained a reputation
as the premier training ground for managers of large corporations
after World War I, refocused its educational aims during and after
World War II.[63] More than any other business school, Harvard had
identified itself with the federal government and the war effort. The
school operated continuously from 1941 through 1945 at full capacity and even overenrollment to train federal administrators and military personnel to deal with the massive war-mobilization efforts. At
the end of the war, the school's chief administrators decided that
they would not simply return to business as usual. Instead, they
elected to retool education at HBS in a plan that Dean David envi-
soned as "almost a complete break with [the] past."[64]

The plan aimed to shift the school's teaching focus from cases that
emphasized functional areas and analytic skills to a perspective that
emphasized professional management: HBS should aim to be "an
important center where men are helped to acquire or develop the
technical confidence, the personal qualities, the vision, the instinctive
acceptance of responsibility, and the insight into the nature of the
administrative process, which characterize *great administrators*."[65] The
Educational Policy Committee's "MBA Report of February 1945" revised the curriculum to reflect a new focus on "getting action
through human beings, tasks and duties of operating executives,
[and] public responsibilities of enterprise."[66] It sought to pull together the first-year curriculum by developing a professional perspective on the material, "to foster an overall 'administrative point
of view,' and to minimize any undue influence exercised by strong
functional area faculty groups."[67] Unlike its antecedent second-year
Business Policy course, a new offering, Administrative Policy, would
integrate the MBA student's experience from the start. The revised

curriculum would also include for the first time courses such as Communication and Social, Economic, and Political Considerations. Other business schools did not begin comparable efforts to integrate the curriculum until the 1960s.[68]

Harvard's leadership in developing the modern corporation's postwar managerial ethic occurred in numbers as well as in words. From 1908 to 1945, HBS awarded a cumulative total of 7,757 degrees. In 1945 alone, over 6,000 correspondents indicated an interest in enrolling, and 2,700 applied for admission. The entering class expanded from 550 to 900.[69] As the number of graduates grew, individual faculty members continued their active involvement in public-policy deliberations about the postwar economy, striving to show that "private enterprise . . . could meet the postwar challenge of avoiding a disastrous relapse into depression."[70] Through the classroom, an active faculty shared its experience and interest in public policy with the next generation of managers. By the mid-1950s, Dean Donald K. David could say with justifiable pride that the HBS had advanced significantly on the lines envisioned by Dean Wallace B. Donham and Owen D. Young. The school had developed a curriculum that inculcated professional ethics to temper business practices and form a managerial elite dedicated to preserving America's social and political order.[71]

CONCLUSION

We have seen how the CED came to be accepted as the premier corporate-sector association. On the public-policy front, even the Employment Act of 1946 reflected the CED's ideas to a gratifying degree.[72] During the Eisenhower and Kennedy administrations, interest groups and elite macroeconomic policymakers were at the center of a public–private partnership that helped establish political and economic values.[73] By the early part of the 1960s, management had emerged as a distinctive professional group.[74]

Yet, political conflict within big business persisted. For the most part, disagreements surrounded policy details and specific claims to government largesse, rather than ground rules for the new political order, and through most of the 1960s, economic growth tended to confirm the wisdom of pragmatic and fragmented corporate politics.[75] In this economic climate, the business community found it unnecessary to gather ideological and partisan support for congressional and presidential contestants. With its own voice seemingly so powerful in working out the details of the postwar administrative state, management took few steps toward reforming government intervention in the economy.[76]

9

Managerial Solidarity in a Pluralist Polity

In Chapter 8, we began to shift from the story of how lawyers, politicians, and professors formulated corporate regulations to a narrative of the gathering together of managers not only to operate optimally within these rules as given but to shape them as well. This chapter continues to study the development of managerial collective action, first through the CED's macroeconomic policy recommendations to deal with problems of inflation and declining productivity and second through the Business Roundtable. The battles for tax reform and corporate control illustrate the pattern of simultaneous cohesion and fragmentation in corporate political action, a pattern formally consistent with America's "polyarchical" political order.

THE MACROECONOMIC BACKGROUND

Business leaders first ascribed inflation in the late 1960s to President Lyndon B. Johnson's fiscal irresponsibility or cowardly failure to raise sufficient taxes for the wars against poverty and Vietnam.[1] Increased government spending spiraled because of an undeclared foreign war and also the multiplying domestic interest-group demands when postwar pluralism encouraged government agencies to listen to all readily definable groups. Business had been the principal beneficiary of the federal government's liberal orientation toward process rights, and the federal bureaucracy dealt largely with matters of industrial stabilization and growth. Accordingly, when new groups won political recognition and "social regulations" from Congress (see Chapter 6), corporate managers initially had limited moral ground to object to the new social regulations.[2] But all these demands on Congress were emptying the public trough.[3]

When President Richard M. Nixon took office, business leaders expected more responsible fiscal policies to bring the rise in prices under control. But inflation went up instead of down, and in defiance of the Phillips curve, so did unemployment. Even more worrisome, perhaps, were declines in productivity and investment relative to both America's current competitors and its own past. "Demand-driven" inflation now seemed to shift into a "cost-driven" process, and business leaders responded by turning their attention away from federal expenditures and toward trade unions, which they accused of increasing wages more than productivity, thus causing both inflation and the deficit in the balance of trade. Like many other organizations, the CED advised President Nixon to impose temporary wage and price controls to break the wage–price spiral.[4] Although reluctant at first, he agreed to do so in August 1971, when he also abandoned the gold standard to gain a freer hand in dealing with the trade deficit.[5]

When wage–price controls were lifted, those market forces that had been repressed instead of eliminated caused a jump in the price level; inflation was further fueled by the Arab oil embargo. Finally, the 1980–1982 global recession lowered energy prices in the 1980s and broke labor's ability to win inflationary wage demands. But the problem of lagging productivity remained.

The CED's Plan

Shortly after wage–price controls failed, the CED undertook a lengthy study to formulate a strategy for reversing the economy's decline.[6] Although Europe seemed to be moving in a corporatist direction, the CED recommended that the United States retain the flexible decentralization of postwar liberal pluralism while improving the coordination of fiscal and monetary policy and constraining interest-group politics by means of economic "logic."[7] The CED adamantly opposed industrial policies that would enable the federal government to shift investments from falling to rising industries.[8]

The CED saw declining productivity as the nation's central problem. Between 1945 and 1965, labor productivity increased some 3.2 percent a year, a rate that fell to between 2.0 and 2.5 percent a year during the slowdown of 1966–1972 and then to less than 1 percent before reaching a near standstill by the end of the 1970s.[9] The CED cited inadequate capital investment as the principal cause for the economy's lackluster performance. By the end of the decade, although gross investment had remained relatively stable since 1945, net investment had dropped dramatically from 64 percent to 49 percent in the 1970s.[10] Low productivity not only contributed to inflation but, in so doing, gave managers pause in their commitments of capital to new undertakings. Especially when it was repressed or hard to predict, inflation disrupted capital markets, increased interest rates, and undermined the value of equities, forcing managers to concentrate on short-term projects that would meet debt obligations and maintain price–earnings ratios.

When inflation created a substantial wedge between "nominal" and "real" prices, all manner of distortions appeared. Throughout the period, real corporate tax payments to the federal government increased, with only nominally surging profits. Standard accounting statements failed to reflect true replacement costs for capital and inventories. Financial managers diverted their attention from productive investment to tax-saving schemes.[11] Thus did inflation and decreasing productivity become mutually reinforcing phenomena.

To break this spiral, the CED insisted on reforming macroeconomic policy. Ever since the CED's original support for modified Keynesian policies in the 1940s, it had supported fiscal, not monetary, initiatives to steer the economy. With the stagflation of the 1970s, the CED reasserted its support for fiscal policy and objected to the Federal Reserve Board's erratic handling of the money supply, in particular Chairman Arthur Burns's abrupt shift from expansive monetary policies in 1971/1972 to severely restrictive actions in 1973/1974. The consequent recession prompted politicians to respond with expansionary/inflationary fiscal policies to mobilize the economy. As interest rates rose, foreign capital would flow into the United States, push up the dollar's value, and cause even more unemployment as exports fell in response to this relative price change. Monetary policy should instead serve fiscal policy by avoiding extremes of expansion and contraction and concentrating on sustaining an efficient capital market.[12]

Since the mid-1960s, the CED continued, the federal government had been competing with industry for private savings and had forced up interest rates in the process. To make matters worse, it invested in an unsound manner, through unchecked federal loan guarantee programs. The enormous expansion of social welfare spending after 1964 functioned as an alternative to the market for distributing wealth. The congressional budget process encouraged excess by simply adding up separate budget proposals instead of limiting to total spending consistently with economic trends. This imprudence allegedly arose from the social excess that stymied individual freedom and economic efficiency.[13] Federal officials had disrupted the postwar pluralist design of business–government relations, along with its balance of public and private power.

To redress the situation, the CED advocated budgetary reforms to enhance changes already instituted in 1974. It also reviewed federal programs to ensure their conformance to strict market principles.[14] Conflicting policy demands should be reconciled on the basis of market efficiency alone. Though insufficient on its own to satisfy the demands for greater substantive equality, environmental protection, and improved public health, a prosperous economy remained a necessary first step.[15]

The CED's agenda for restructuring government's role in the economy also included tax reform. Reducing the effective tax rate on income generated from capital would shift tax burdens from producers to consumers in general.[16] Not only should capital be depreciated rapidly for tax purposes, but special tax breaks should yield to an across-the-board reduction of the corporate tax rate. This would improve the market and contribute to sustained growth, as profits would depend once more on economic rather than political considerations.[17]

Finally, the CED sought regulatory reform. Hoping to improve productivity, it advocated a review of economic regulation that had long protected certain industries from market competition. Social regulation interfered with the managerial prerogative and sound economic decisions.[18] Market incentives and cost–benefit analysis should be incorporated into all regulatory designs, and they would most certainly cause an end to oil price controls.[19]

As well as courting power and gaining impressive connections to high government officials and influential policy analysts, the CED proclaimed its legitimate statesmanship with sophisticated policy statements like its 1971 publication, *Social Responsibilities of Business Corporations,* its first formal profession of faith in the ideal of managerial trusteeship.[20] The theme restated what had originally been formulated by Owen Young and propagated by *Fortune,* although with less emphasis on employee rights. The document also testified to the growing importance of public-interest groups, especially in drawing out the administrative implications of the managerial trustee doctrine through social regulation. Painfully aware of its limited influence, the CED encouraged its member firms to establish public-affairs offices to anticipate social issues they both favored and opposed. Through these firm-specific organizations, perhaps the corporate sector would regain its influence in legislative and regulatory matters.

This appeal to corporate executives to make public affairs an integral part of their operations found a receptive audience. Before 1970, even firms with active public-policy programs had small public-affairs offices with narrow responsibilities. Trade associations had evolved to take up the slack, and together with peak associations, they still constituted the focal points of corporate-sector political activity. After 1970, however, large firms became increasingly active politically, to ward off challenges by "public-interest" reformers and to gain flexibility in an era of deteriorating public–private commitments. By the early 1980s, a large and diverse proportion of *Fortune* 500 firms had integrated substantial public affairs offices into their daily and strategic operations.[21] They also subcontracted projects to Washington consultants when the cost savings were substantial or the issues were highly symbolic.[22]

At the firm level, the transformation was pervasive. Trade associations had lost their leadership roles in formulating political strategies, particularly for those industries hard hit by social regulation or economic decline. In industries in which the firms were large, many lobbying costs had been internalized and integrated into strategic policies; big firms preferred to formulate independent strategies rather than support industry lobbyists that duplicated efforts or sustained competitors' political interests.[23] By setting up Washington offices and retaining lobbyists, they began to erode the trade associations' leadership in Washington's corporate community. The business proportion of Washington-based representatives had remained stable since the 1950s at about 55 percent, but hired consultants, law offices, and the like rose from 57 percent of the total in 1960 to 72 percent in 1980, mostly in response to the increased participation of large firms.[24]

Corporate campaign contributions to federal elections also signaled the growing political presence of large firms in Washington. In 1974, approximately ninety PACs registered with the Federal Election Commission (FEC); by 1988 this number had soared to two thousand.[25] Expenditures increased during the same period from $6.3 million to $56.2 million, and labor's contributions in 1988 totaled $35.5 million.

But corporations never took full advantage of their latent power, for they failed to establish a central mechanism for coordinating corporate campaign donations. Each corporate PAC functioned separately, with no central recommendations. This procedure contrasted markedly with the labor union PACs, which drafted a coordinated preference list.[26]

Corporate PACs did operate within an informational network that lowered the costs of assessing political opportunities during an election cycle.[27] As we shall see in Chapter 11, between 1980 and 1986, they also appeared to share a reward-and-punish donation strategy (see Chapter 11 for an empirical analysis of the PACs' strategy). But the corporate sector still lacked both a coherent voice inside Congress's chambers and the direct access to congressional representatives that individual firm donations could secure. Top managers therefore tried to enhance their individual firms' political power by forming an organization to lobby for the corporate sector. Because the CED's avowed purpose was to provide impartial policy statements, it could not take over this particular function, and so the Business Roundtable was formed in 1972 to fill the void.

The Business Roundtable and Managerial Solidarity

This new organization resulted from the merger of three smaller business associations: the Construction Users Anti-Inflation Roundtable, which was composed of big and medium-size construction companies that were trying to bring down rising construction costs; the March Group, which was an association of big firms that were hoping to promote a better image of business in the media and in government; and the Labor Law Study Committee, which served as a business counterweight to labor's political influence. From the start, the Roundtable differentiated itself from other groups by restricting its membership to the CEOs of the nation's largest firms. It quickly became corporate America's political vanguard.

Among the most active early leaders of the Business Roundtable were men like Thomas Murphy of GM, Reginald Jones of GE, John D. Harper of ALCOA,[28] and Irving Shapiro of Du Pont. They belonged to a generation of business leaders whose careers had begun during World War II and who had been educated in the managerial practices and ideals that emerged from that period. Perhaps more than anyone else, Irving Shapiro testified to the public, fiduciary sensibility that permeated this leadership.

According to *Fortune* in the 1930s, Owen Young's leadership at GE symbolized the democratic pluralism of American society in which competing groups bargained with one another for mutual advantage; at Du Pont, in contrast, the eponymous founders held fast to a class-based, paternalistic society.[29] As leaders of the business reaction to Franklin Roosevelt and the broker state that his administration was constructing, the Du Ponts became the symbol of recalcitrant proprietary interests.[30]

Shapiro's appointment in 1973 as chairman of Du Pont's board of directors and executive committee stunned the business community, for it ended Du Pont's 171-year-old tradition of the family-controlled firm.[31] Moreover, whereas in the past, the top executives had generally had scientific backgrounds, Shapiro served as company lawyer who had spent about a third of his career in Washington with the Justice Department. His training and experience, however, made him well suited for Du Pont's most pressing issues.

Energy and environmental regulations had constrained Du Pont, contributing in important ways to its poor performance in the years preceding Shapiro's promotion,[32] and the company also had to negotiate a host of other public-policy issues, from antitrust and fair-employment practices to patent laws.

During his reign at Du Pont, Shapiro devoted nearly 30 percent of his time to matters outside the company. As chairman of the Business Roundtable, he participated in discussions on how to overcome the membership's rational biases against collective action. The rewards seemed plain enough. A united managerial front might effectively ward off new government interventions and reform misguided existing intrusions. Such an effort could supplement the already dense interactions among corporate executives through the sector's complicated system of interlocking directorships and prestigious business associations like the CED and the Business Council.[33]

Membership in the Business Roundtable signified standing in the corporate community and provided vital information and contacts. By 1977, the organization had about fifteen task forces, each a small committee devoted to a single important issue. Because its staff were only ten to fifteen in number, members were expected to be full participants in the task forces and to use their own employees for research and writing. Among the issues they tackled were problems of antitrust, consumer interests, corporate organization, government regulation, and environmental affairs; and their composition tended to reflect the differential impact of these topics. The task forces directed their work to the forty-member Policy Committee, which met several times a year to work out the Roundtable's general strategy. Before a policy decision was made, the Roundtable generally sponsored several conferences with both members and outside experts and then issued a white paper for the membership's consideration and commentary.

This participatory structure proved quite efficient in ensuring frequent contact among the Roundtable's membership and easy access to information on salient issues. The Roundtable was surprisingly successful in mounting seamless business campaigns to defeat pro-consumer and labor reform in the late 1970s, and critics feared they would endanger democratic rule. However, in pointing to these and other recent examples of corporate solidarity, they tended to overlook the competitive dimension of corporate political action.

As a membership organization, the Business Roundtable has relied on individual firms for political muscle to reform government. Like the CED, it has consistently shied away from centralizing proposals, thus seriously undercutting Big Business's organizational capacity to act as a "class." The Business Roundtable has only the power of moral suasion to impose political discipline on its members; it has no resources of its own to carry out independent courses of action. The strategies it advocates have been decentralized efforts to promote macroeconomic and industrial reform through *ad hoc* coalitions.[34]

Nevertheless, business's multiple representation through firm-level activities, trade associations, peak associations, and a host of single-issue organizations has leveraged its relative power.[35] Even though these multiple forms of representation create some fragmentation, the corporate sector has achieved enough unity, particularly in opposition to labor and its allies, to have played an important role in the recent bipartisan conservative shift in public policy.[36] Politicians have become aware that large corporations are potentially more important sources of campaign funds than labor is, and candidates have found that support for market principles increases their probability of gaining access to these funds.[37]

Because the American economy has remained decentralized and the regulatory system has sanctioned only a fractured solidarity, cohesion and fragmentation remain the norm for corporate political behavior. Indeed, managers could incorporate their electoral participation as part of their stewardship for preserving democratic rule. As corporate trustees, managers claim that they preserve decentralized private bargaining arrangements even within concentrated industries. In this respect, managerially controlled firms help recreate the public–private distinction essential to a liberal polity. Thus, managers could claim (as Schattschneider suggested) that they coalesce electorally around public challenges to their private coordinating role, thereby limiting government intrusions. At the same time, managers could calm fears about their power to undermine majoritarian rule. Market competition, managers could argue, incessantly splinters them on specific economic questions, and management's professional responsibilities enforce a pragmatic rather than a partisan approach to politics. Chapter 11 backs up these assertions with some empirical discussion of PACs. For the moment, however, consider the following two policy issues as more anecdotal illustration. The first story involves tax reform; the second, the battle for corporate control.

Tax Reform

In 1975 the Business Roundtable helped forge an *ad hoc* coalition on tax reform by meeting regularly with other business associations for breakfast discussions at the Sheraton-Carlton Hotel in Washington, D.C.[38] The Carlton Group was highly—and surprisingly—inclusive in character.[39] It joined together such diverse interests as representatives of big business; the heads of small and medium-size firms in the National Association of Manufacturers, U.S. Chamber of Commerce, and National Federation of Businesses;[40] members from the American Council of Capital Formation, which represented mature, smokestack industries; and people from the American Business Conference, which participated on behalf of the one hundred fastest-growing companies in America.

In 1978, congressional debates on reducing the capital gains tax rate resulted in a bipartisan consensus that the nation needed a tax policy that would stimulate investment.[41] When Congressmen James R. Jones and Barber B. Conable of the all-important Ways and Means Committee addressed the Carlton Group, they insisted that change would not occur until the business community spelled out and then supported appropriate reforms in the tax code.

The Carlton Group responded with a rallying call of "10–5–3," a formula for rapid depreciation that would write off investments in buildings over ten years, equipment and machinery over five years, and vehicles over three years.[42] Such an approach would benefit all of the Carlton Group's diverse membership, although capital-intensive firms involved in major new undertakings stood to reap the most substantial gains.

The group actively promoted 10–5–3 over the next few years, and the formula entered Ronald Reagan's platform when Charls Walker, the head of the American Council of Capital Formation, became the tax adviser for his 1980 presidential campaign.[43] A supply sider by instinct, Reagan had already committed himself to a personal income tax reform program promising a 10 percent reduction in marginal rates annually for the next three years. Walker easily persuaded Reagan to add 10–5–3 to this 10–10–10 program, and he and other Republican candidates then gained quick support from the corporate community. Not only was the ultraconservative Reagan elected president, but the Republicans also captured a majority in the Senate and won thirty-two new seats in the House.[44]

When Reagan entered office, he moved swiftly to make his tax slogans law through the Economic Recovery Tax Act of 1981 (ERTA).[45] The new legislation was purported to be revenue neutral at any given level of GNP, by simultaneously broadening the base (eliminating deductions and loopholes) and lowering the rates, even as it encouraged growth by reducing distortions.

Throughout the ensuing legislative debate, the corporate sector continued to display a remarkable degree of cohesion, forcefully lobbying for reform[46] and arguing with the support of experts that the existing system discouraged investment and rewarded the government for inflation.[47] In the end, its rewards included a modified 10–5–3 depreciation schedule, a reduction in the capital gains tax from 28 percent to 20 percent, and an investment tax incentive.

In 1982, despite the supply-side kick of lower marginal tax rates and handsome investment credits, the country fell into what became the worst recession since the Great Depression. Coupled with Reagan's substantial rate cuts and commitments to defense spending, this recession pushed the government into a peacetime deficit of unprecedented magnitude that remains with us today.

In the remaining years of Reagan's first term, budgetary constraints forced Congress to consider cutting spending and raising taxes. The business community found at least a rhetorical common ground for arguing that any tampering with the ERTA would hamper economic recovery.[48] According to most business associations, spending cuts offered the best way to contain the government's red ink. Because it fostered inflationary expectations and discouraged private investment by increasing real interest rates, the deficit in their view now threatened long-term economic growth.[49]

In 1982, the Business Roundtable advocated the spending cuts that business favored in general and also substantially higher taxes. These would take the form of federal excise taxes and user fees and, more controversially, a delay in some of the 10 percent in individual tax cuts for 1983 outlined in the ERTA.[50] Any new business taxes, like corporate minimums, would interfere with investment.

Not only did the Roundtable proposals fail to gain consistent membership support, but the possibility of increased corporate taxes gained favor as Reagan steadfastly refused to consider increasing personal income tax rates. Corporate contributions to government had steadily declined for decades. The tax *breaks* won in 1981 actually exceeded the tax *totals* paid by corporations in 1982 and 1983, despite upward revisions in the corporate tax code in 1982.[51] Although some businesses had paid higher taxes, the general gains were striking. Of 250 large and profitable firms, 128 paid no taxes at least once between 1981 and 1983, and 17 paid no taxes during all three years.[52]

These circumstances put corporate political solidarity to an unsuccessful test. Perhaps those firms whose tax burdens were heavy and those that paid little or nothing at all were the most deeply divided. Treasury's schism reflected the differential effect of the ERTA, which benefited industries that were capital intensive more than those that employed relatively more labor.

With its own house divided, the business community lost clout with powerful congressional committees. In 1982, Republican Robert

Dole, chairman of the Senate Finance Committee, helped formulate a bill that would become the nation's largest peacetime tax increase, with half the new revenue coming from business. Dole contended that additional corporate taxation was equitable because it closed loopholes in the tax code. With this argument, he attempted to appropriate the issue of "fairness" from the Democrats and set the symbolical terms for tax reform over the next four years.[53]

Senator Bill Bradley responded with a revenue package that combined the Democratic concern for equitable distribution with the Republican concern for growth. Tax revisions would close unfair loopholes for wealthy individuals as well as corporations, and reductions in tax rates would decrease the number of disincentives. Democratic presidential candidate Walter Mondale reviewed the proposal and rejected it in favor of new taxes.

Winning a second term, President Reagan asked the Treasury Department to come up with a plan to create a simpler, fairer, and revenue-neutral tax system. Its response involved variations of the two strategies in Bradley's proposal: increasing the tax base by eliminating loopholes and then offsetting the effect on revenue by decreasing personal and corporate tax rates.[54] Reagan found bipartisan support for this approach because representatives feared the electoral consequences of opposing it. But many of the president's business allies, including the Carlton Group, withheld their approval.[55]

In the Roundtable's view, the Treasury proposal both demanded too much from business and diverted attention from the budget deficit. The consequent high interest rates and overvalued dollar posed the most serious threats to economic growth.[56] Some provisions in the plan would aggravate this situation by further curtailing investment and weakening America's competitive position abroad. For example, the proposed increase in corporate taxes (primarily from revisions in the ERTA's accelerated depreciation schedules) would cost the corporate sector an estimated $160 billion in additional taxes, thus increasing the user cost of capital and discouraging investment.[57] The nation would be better served if the administration would retreat, instead of advance, on the issue of tax reform.

Most pundits predicted that reform would succumb to these powerful interests.[58] Business representatives from industries like oil, gas, banking, and insurance and firms like Ford Motors, Dow Chemical, and Texas Instruments swarmed the principal tax-writing committees, the House Ways and Means Committee, and the Senate Finance Committee.[59] Not just the Business Roundtable but the U.S. Chamber of Commerce and other traditional business associations initially condemned the reform effort because it would weaken or

even eliminate many of the incentives provided by the 1981 tax measure. In particular, they opposed repeal of the 1981 investment tax
credit and revisions in accelerated write-offs. By promising to decrease corporate tax rates in exchange for eliminating or reducing
these and other tax breaks, the reformers appealed to a large number of labor-intensive and fast-growing firms that had not fully benefited from the 1981 provisions. These firms, and in some cases their
trade associations as well, joined to form two *ad hoc* groups, the Tax
Reform Action Coalition and the CEO Tax Group, to lobby for
change.[60] This split in the business community allowed members of
Congress to come up with a bill that would cost them neither revenue nor reelection.

When reform seemed inevitable, many in the opposition came
around in hopes of influencing final refinements. The Business
Roundtable endorsed the Senate bill as less detrimental than the
House version but was unable to spell out its position on the bill's
many provisions because its membership was deeply divided over the
revenue-balancing requirements.[61] Instead, the Roundtable advised
each member "to pursue its own areas of interest and encourage a
successful conclusion to the tax reform effort."[62] Its final assessment
tried to cast the reform in a positive public light by arguing that it
would undo implicit industrial biases that had misdirected investments[63] and by drawing attention to the $120 billion in new business
tax revenues that made it revenue neutral.[64] These increases came
from eliminating the investment tax credit, moderating the accelerated depreciation schedule, and closing special tax breaks like deductions for business meals and entertainment expenses and write-offs
for bad-debt bank reserves.

In summary, the corporate sector came together in common concern about the declining performance they attributed to excessive
government interference. But theirs was a fragile solidarity, and it
gave way once political circumstances shifted, forcing the administration and Congress to reassert their authority and pursue tax reform
for partisan, electoral advantage. After 1982, both branches of government offered positions different from that of the Business
Roundtable and its allies. Firms dissatisfied with ERTA's distribu-
tional consequences could therefore seek other alliances. The corporate sector, in brief, achieved sufficient cohesion to advise the public
on the government's excesses and how to reform them, but corporate collectivity proved too weak to get its first-choice policies from
elected officials ever conscious of their own and their party's standing in the polls. In all, the electoral system functions much as E. E.
Schattsneider had described, pulling together the corporate sector
but limiting its ability to control outcomes.

The Legislative Debate over Takeovers

Mondale's defeat by Reagan in 1984 put an abrupt end to the debate over a national industrial policy. Under his stewardship, the Democratic Party had promised to institute such a policy if it won the election, and it had made this decision after meetings with trade unions and a few business leaders close to the Democratic Party, most notably Michael Blumenthal of Burroughs and Irving Shapiro.[65]

By keeping out of industrial reorganization, the government invited the financial markets to play an increasingly important role. In 1984 the nation witnessed another merger wave, one distinguished from its predecessors by the size of the deals and by the importance of leveraged buyouts (LBOs), which rose from approximately 4 percent of all merger activity in 1981 to over 20 percent by 1986.[66] Although most occurred with the approval of management, corporate raiders had management on the defensive. Chapter 10 deals with LBOs in more depth, but we advance the themes of this chapter by making some summary observations of management's economic and political responses.

On an economic front, managers responded through massive corporate restructuring to make their companies less attractive to takeovers. While they divested underperforming businesses and sold them directly to shareholders, they also acquired new ventures with excess cash, repurchased stock, swapped debt for equity, liquidated overfunded pension funds, and arranged their own buyouts.[67] The net effect of these maneuvers on nonfinancial corporate debt was an increase of $300 billion from 1984 to 1986.[68]

On the political front, managers sought regulatory protections at both the federal and the state levels. Managers had considerable political capital, as they rallied with employees, unions, and other community groups that also felt threatened by the wave of takeovers.[69] As before, the Business Roundtable spearheaded the political offensive. This time the Roundtable successfully built and sustained a corporate-sector consensus against the corporate raiders, since they uniformly threatened managerial control.

The Roundtable built a coalition of business, union, and academic interests to pressure Congress to close gaps in the Williams Act. Its specific ambitions were to lower the threshold point at which outsiders' stock purchases must be publicly disclosed, shorten the disclosure period, and lengthen the tender-offer period. The Roundtable urged its members to lobby the Senate Banking Committee and the House Committee on Energy and Commerce, which were actively considering revisions of the Williams Act, and to encourage local unions to join the Committee for Williams Act Reform and become active members themselves.

To justify these reforms, the Business Roundtable issued position statements documenting the adverse effects of corporate raids. Brewster Atwater, Jr., chairman of the Business Roundtable Task Force on Corporate Responsibility and chairman and CEO of General Mills, went on the attack and argued that financial manipulators were misusing the securities market to make speculative gains at the expense of the corporation.[70] Although the raiders might be few in number, they had devastating effects. These self-styled "industrial renovators" and their investment bank allies were in fact nothing more than financial swindlers. Instead of purchasing stock to wrench control away from an incompetent management team, raiders typically bought stock to profit from the mere threat of a takeover. Once a raider acquired a significant block of shares, the price of the target company's stock would most likely rise in anticipation of a buyout. The raider could then sell his shares, at substantial personal gain, to any of three groups: the target company as it restructured to fend off the threat of a takeover battle (the strategy of "greenmail"), a friendly company ("the white knight"), or a third party lured into the bidding.

According to Atwater, these raids hurt target firms, which in effect paid extortion, and a lively takeover market also prompted other firms to restructure in order to ward off hostile bids. Management had to act defensively to live up to its fiduciary duty to both its shareholders and other stakeholders. Only in this way could the firm be preserved as an ongoing enterprise. The alternative allowed financial manipulators to take over the firm for short-term gains that would impose higher costs on its constituents. In developing this argument, Atwater drew on the Business Roundtable's earlier position paper which recognized management's social responsibility not only to the firm's shareholders but to other prominent stakeholders as well.[71] He basically asked Congress to trust managers as they tried to maximize profits in an environment constrained by competition in all markets but those for corporate control.

Atwater and the Roundtable coalition confronted a formidable counterforce of two basic groups: investment bankers and corporate raiders who had taken advantage of the decade-long surge in deregulation and theorists who in increasing number believed that the takeover market helped lower managerial agency costs. In place of fiduciary responsibilities and public oversight, the proponents for an active market in corporate control advocated a return to proprietary relations. Making managers also owners would solve the problem of aligning managerial and shareholder interests. The result would be a more efficient economy in which all could benefit.

Michael Jensen, a leading financial-agency theorist, played an important advocacy role during these hearings. He concluded that if the leveraged buyouts were arranged by firms that specialized in this activity and worked in conjunction with management, they could restore responsible financial ownership.[72] Not since J. P. Morgan and his associates presided over the corporate sector had there been such an active financial interest overseeing management. But financial control had reappeared in a new package. By assuming a substantial equity position in their corporations, the principal management teams would have stockholder interests of their own, and the motivation to promote efficiency would be immediate. Removing corporate ownership from the public stock markets would therefore revitalize the American economy by once again making the corporate sector a proprietary endeavor.

The Senate Banking Committee and the House Subcommittee on Telecommunications, Consumer Protection and Finance of the Committee on Energy and Commerce was responsible for deciding whether or not these corporate restructurings enhanced America's competitiveness internationally, and if so, whether or not they were appropriately supported by corporate raiders.[73] By 1987, they offered proposals. Although they agreed on many issues, like the need to restrict the use of greenmail and to extend the time that tender offers would remain open, the two bills differed in their judgment of whether corporate raiders or managers needed more constraint.[74] The Senate committee came down hard against the former, and the House committee found the latter more at fault.

Neither bill came to a vote in the appropriate chambers. Highly visible and easily scrutinized, they pitted powerful forces against one another and made members of Congress quite vulnerable. To the inherent complexity of the matter, they were forced to add the volatile issue of federalism, since tender-offer reform inevitably demanded an assessment of whether the federal government or the states should have regulatory responsibility for corporate governance.[75]

The question of political principle ended in a legislative impasse when the 1987 Supreme Court found constitutional an Indiana law giving shareholders the power to approve a transference in corporate control.[76] The decision confirmed earlier rulings permitting state antitakeover laws as long as they neither interfered in interstate commerce nor preempted the Williams Act. The Business Roundtable could now redirect its efforts to the state governments, reducing the pressure for congressional action.[77] Any such action seemed problematic to managers, who feared it would enhance the possibility of the SEC's gaining authority to develop uniform takeover procedures. The stock market crash in October 1987 was therefore not an unmitigated disaster for some managers. By putting a temporary halt to the merger mania, it reduced the pressure for legislative reform.[78]

Because their influence had not waned in those state legislatures that offered regulatory protection and political legitimacy, managers still had an opportunity to set up regulatory barriers against hostile bidders.[79] And on the state level, they could concentrate on the local effects of corporate takeovers without worrying about the national implications. They could also find willing allies among workers and community groups. Yet management's local victories were Pyrrhic in a larger sense. With self-interest in fact dominating programs designed to maintain professional standards, they demonstrated to Congress the emptiness of fiduciary rhetoric. The Business Roundtable's strategy thus backfired. Complaining about actions only when they were committed by others, managers lost credibility in Congress.

Nor did their victory, at least temporarily, over the raiders testify to the Business Roundtable's increasing political clout. Success came as much from its convenient alliance with labor and the peculiarities of American federalism as it did from the Business Roundtable's skill in coordinating managerial collective action. Moreover, the very issue of corporate takeovers underscored the fragility of managerial solidarity in a society that valued decentralization. Hostile takeover bids brought members together in a defensive posture. But since they were free to arrange their own leveraged buyouts, they could defect from the Business Roundtable's fiduciary doctrine and ally with advocates of a privatized economy. Fortunately for the Roundtable market circumstances stalled the movement to transfer corporate control to closed groups of private investors and funds. Management buyouts then ceased to be a vital, and potentially divisive, issue.

CONCLUSION: CORPORATE COHESION, CORPORATE FRAGMENTATION

The formation of the Business Roundtable as the corporate sector's peak political association and the integration of the public-affairs function into the strategic planning process gave operationally spe-

cific meaning in an unforeseen fashion to Adolf Berle and Gardiner
Means's 1932 claim that good management was in fact good statesmanship.[80] The consequent business mobilization, along with the
far-ranging policy recommendations of both the CED and the Business Roundtable, caused some to conclude that corporate collective
action was not only possible but present.[81] Others highlighted instead the fractious consequences of decentralized corporate political
power. Studies covering a wide range of cross-industry public-policy
issues, including deregulation, industrial policy, and environmental
regulation,[82] lent support to earlier pluralist assessments that corporate solidarity was highly unlikely.[83]

The truth, as usual, lay somewhere in the middle, between the
work of E. E. Schattschneider and Robert Dahl. Both could agree
that the nation's regulatory environment brought managers together
to protect their general interest in controlling the large firm. But
the market for products and votes fragmented managers and forced
politicians to pacify "marginal" voters. These latter tendencies limited managers' power to dominate the polity. However, as Dahl
noted, even if America's political rules prevented a group as privileged as management from controlling the state, the rules overseeing
corporate governance would not promote a democratic culture.

10

Kohlberg Kravis Roberts & Co. and the Investor Challenge to Managerial Capitalism

This chapter reviews the decade-long contest for corporate control by focusing on one notable protagonist: the merchant-banking firm of Kohlberg Kravis Roberts & Co. (KKR). By scrutinizing their experience in transferring control from managers to investors, we can evaluate the claim that the market in corporate control offers the best opportunity to redeem American capitalism. Our concern here lies less in understanding whether or not hostile raids per se efficiently constrain managers than in examining the novel reorganizations and governance configurations that KKR initiated.

KKR developed an investor-controlled structure of governance, the Leveraged Buyout Association, which reduces collective-action problems that have inhibited institutional investors, particularly public pension funds, from acting as a unified group. It also reduces agency costs that have plagued the large firm since the separation of ownership from control in the early part of this century. In both cases, KKR's solution lies in aligning managerial and property interests through common ownership.

KKR's organizational entrepreneurship seriously challenges the managerial firm's saliency and offers the alternative model of an investor-controlled firm. This model not only addresses collective-action and agency problems, as just mentioned, but it also takes note of the trend in shareholder ownership toward concentrations of pension funds. Given the implications of these reforms, KKR's actions may represent the Schumpeterian "creative destruction" of corporate organizational forms rather than more traditional product markets.

145

HISTORY OF THE FIRM

KKR was originally formed as a partnership among Jerome Kohlberg and cousins Henry Kravis and George Roberts. In the early
1970s, they all had worked together at Bear Stearns, where Kohlberg, the senior of the three, had already identified a specialized
market in "bootstrap deals," the early moniker for leveraged buyouts (LBOs).

Two types of sellers operated in this market: entrepreneurs with
family businesses and managers of large conglomerates. In the mid-
1960s, a generation of the former were nearing retirement. These
commercial patriarchs wanted to pass on their successful firms to
their heirs in a way that would reduce estate taxes and retain family
control. At that time, only the tax reduction ambition was possible
and could be realized by going public or selling out to a larger company. Kohlberg came up with another option that could retain family control: the leveraged buyout. In this scenario, the firm sold off
most, but not all, of its equity to a group of investors, who purchased
the firm with borrowed funds but allowed the family to remain as
co-owners and to run the business. If the family, under the pressure
of a greater debt burden succeeded in improving the firm's cash flow
and paying off the debt, the investor group could sell its shares for
a substantial profit,[1] leaving the family with a controlling interest in
a firm that had become more valuable than before.[2] KKR's buyouts
of family firms included Norris Industries (1981), Fred Meyer
(1981), Dillingham Corporation (1983), and Cole National (1985).

Kohlberg also found promising clients in the second type of seller,
conglomerate managers. By the early 1970s, the stock market no
longer favored their companies, and so they began to search for
ways to sell off underperforming divisions, many of which had performed better before their acquisition.[3] Starting in 1970, the number of conglomerate divestitures increased dramatically, accounting
for 53 percent of all transactions by 1977.[4] Kohlberg entered this
area as well, targeting stable industrial firms that generated the cash
flows necessary to service the heavy debt payments that LBOs incurred. He also restricted himself to only those buyouts with the
initial approval of inside management, who had the knowledge and
power to identify and actualize the firm's potential value, and he
ensured their continued cooperation in each phase of the buyout by
distributing lucrative stock incentives to make them owners of the
firms they once had only superintended.[5]

Kohlberg educated his junior colleagues Kravis and Roberts in
these techniques, and the three soon carved out a niche for themselves at Bear Stearns. When top management disagreed with their

appraisal that it was sufficiently promising to become a separate business unit, the team formed their own partnership in 1976.

KKR was a specialized investment banking firm from the very start. It focused on leveraged buyouts within the broader field of mergers and acquisitions but also acted somewhat like a merchant bank by taking equity positions in its deals. The experience of integrating ownership and control had been most positive. When the partners put their own capital at risk, investors had good reason to trust them as both financial advisers and fiduciaries. Signaling to investors that they would have little reason to act opportunistically reduced the monitoring costs of their investments.

Large institutional investors found KKR's approach appealing. The traditional method of simply selling off (exiting) equity positions in underperforming firms became more costly in the 1970s and 1980s, when their investments were too important a part of the market to dump without affecting the price. At first they responded by seeking a greater voice on the boards of directors of companies in which they held substantial positions. Public pension funds even formed an association, the Council of Institutional Investors, to promote this effort.[6] But because institutional representation remained essesntially latent, KKR's approach to agency problems seemed especially attractive.

To leverage its buyout funds, KKR relied on large commercial banks for senior bank debt secured by the firm's assets. Insurance companies supplemented these funds by supplying subordinated debt. Until the mid-1980s, the absence of significant competition allowed insurance companies to impose strict conditions on subordinated debt. By the mid-1980s, however, the developing market in high-yield, or "junk," bonds undercut this power.[7]

True to its principle that ownership matters, KKR has developed LBO associations, the three parts of which all are designed to coordinate principal investors and management.[8] The general partners (KKR) sponsor LBO transactions and monitor their performance; the limited partners provide capital; and the top managers hold substantial equity stakes in the company and continue to control it. Because KKR assumes a stake in each of its investment funds, it has holdings in numerous and unrelated businesses. In April 1991, for example, KKR's fifteen companies included heating and cooling, lumber, department stores, food/supermarkets, and commercial banking; with combined revenues of $40 billion.

In this respect, KKR resembles a conglomerate. However, unlike a conglomerate, each partnership controls stand-alone enterprises that do not divert cash from one to another, as is typical of multidivisional undertakings. Nonetheless, these partnerships are tied together through KKR's equity participation in each of its sponsored deals and by the fact that many of KKR's investors participate in multiple partnerships. KKR's obligation to sit on the each firm's board of directors reinforces this interdependence. Each firm therefore has an interest in the others' well-being: Profitable business connections benefit the investors' commonwealth in addition to the two firms in the transaction.

If the LBO is successful and its debt is paid off, KKR may sell the firm to another bidder or take it public again so that investors can cash out at a premium. Indeed, it is not unusual for limited LBO partnerships to last only a decade, a period so brief that it raises questions about the concern for long-term growth. Buyers, however, presumably decide the price they are willing to pay today by discounting earnings past the immediate future, so artists of the LBO would sell themselves short by being myopic.[9]

Some KKR actions show an explicit interest in the longer-run health of their companies. For example, when Safeway went public again in April 1991, KKR sold 11.5 million shares of common stock, or 10 percent of the company's equity, at $11.25 a share; but it used the proceeds of this fourfold increase in initial investment to fund part of a $3.2 billion capital-expenditure program for 1990–1994 to improve Safeway's competitive position.[10] When the junk-bond market collapsed in 1989, KKR also recapitalized RJR Nabisco. The company went public, and KKR provided $1.7 billion to help pay down debt by increasing equity holdings from 58 to 68 percent fully diluted. With RJR's balance sheet much improved, management could return to long-term strategies for improving the firm's competitive position instead of scrambling for short-term cash.[11] Both companies are still so tightly held, however, that they remain under investor rather than managerial control.

These two case histories also soften another criticism typically raised against LBOs: that taking firms private removes the investors' best source of information on management performance, the daily stock price.[12] Maybe so. But by taking Safeway and RJR public, KKR not only regained this information on managerial effectiveness in short order but also affirmed that the firms were more valuable under its umbrella.[13]

To acknowledge KKR's innovative building of investors' commonwealth, we find it more appropriate to describe the organization as an "investor" rather an "LBO association." KKR's interlocking governance structure reinforces this concept. KKR serves as an informational clearinghouse, making it difficult for a company to misrepresent itself and allowing for early intervention when a firm is experiencing financial distress.[14] Accurate information promotes trust, which is reinforced by the aforementioned equity connections that KKR maintains. It also supports implicit contracts among KKR partners that are more flexible and less costly than the contract writing of more typical market relationships.[15] Yet because each firm is a stand-alone unit, it need not enter into a business relationship with any other KKR-controlled business. Market prices, not administrative command, still link supplier/buyer connections within KKR's investor association, providing KKR member companies with a mechanism for evaluating the benefits and costs of their internal cooperation.[16] The market, in other words, still provides its own sources of verifiable information.

KKR has linked its economic returns to its agency, merchant- and investment-banking functions. As an agent for investors, it typically receives a 1.5 percent management fee for the money committed to a KKR investment fund, a retainer fee for monitoring performance, and a fee for serving on boards of directors. As a merchant banker, it earns returns on its equity investment, and as an investment banker, it receives a 1 percent fee after the deals are completed.[17]

KKR's first four investment funds grew from $24 million in 1978 to $1 billion in 1984.[18] In 1979, it arranged the first leveraged buyout of a large publicly held company, Houdaille Industries, Inc., for $370 million; and in 1984 it arranged the first $1 billion LBO, Wometco Enterprises, and the first tender-offer LBO of a publicly held company, Malone & Hyde.[19]

Whereas the 1979 and 1980 funds had relied heavily on wealthy individual persons, in 1982 KKR approached commercial banks, which had previously participated in the deals only as creditors.[20] The timing was again excellent, as corporate lending was floundering. Corporations had become more sophisticated financially, and domestic banks now faced international competition.[21] The market for consumer loans also became tougher from the lender's perspective. Auto companies, for example, offered attractive financing programs, and credit-card issuers proliferated. In this context, the returns on KKR's first two funds, which eventually averaged about 30 percent a year, seemed especially attractive. Being on an inside track to supply the credit that KKR would need in arranging buyouts in the future might provide even more handsome returns.[22] Commercial banks responded by providing about 30 percent of the equity capital in KKR's 1982, 1984, 1986, and 1987 funds.[23]

But KKR needed even more capital to become the dominant firm in the leveraged buyout market. It found this source in pension funds. Both public and private pension funds had grown enormously since the 1970s, and they invested heavily in corporate equity and debt. In 1984, for example, private pension funds had approximately $981 billion in assets, and state and local government pension funds held $357 billion in equity alone.[24] KKR realized that if it could serve a small portion of these pension funds as an agent executing leveraged buyouts, it could profit handsomely.

The entrepreneurial opportunity came unintentionally in the early 1980s when public officials revised public pension fund fiduciary standards. For some time, government policies at both the state and the federal level had encouraged the formation of pension funds to supplement social security benefits for retired employees. States deferred taxes on employee contributions until benefits were paid, and the Employee Retirement Income Security Act (ERISA) allowed sponsors to deduct contributions from income. Both set strict fiduciary standards for fund managers.[25] For our purposes, the most notable standards prohibited equity investments, a paternalistic form of protection against the volatility of stocks, especially in imprudent hands. When pension funds began to earn below-market rates of return, they lacked sufficient income to meet their obligations. State legislators were therefore forced to review investment policies, and in many cases legislators permitted pension fund managers to invest in equity.

Oregon led the states in revising pension fund guidelines.[26] In 1981 its fund contributed $178 million to the $420 million KKR-sponsored leveraged buyout of Fred Meyer, an Oregon-based retail chain. The returns exceeded 50 percent through most of decade. Such success did not go unnoticed. Washington's state pension fund managers followed Oregon's lead with a cautious $10 million investment with KKR in 1982. When the returns matched KKR's previous performance, it then leaped in with a $150 million contribution to KKR's 1984 fund of $1 billion.[27] Because this fund also substantially outperformed the market, KKR could increase its 1986 fund to an unprecedented $1.6 billion. Public pension fund participants rose from three to eleven in number.[28] KKR had secured their trust and, with their contributions, became the acknowledged kingpin of leveraged buyouts.

KKR's competitive position also lay in becoming part of an extensive credit network, the most important element of which was its working relationship with the investment house of Drexel Burnham Lambert, the innovating force in high-yield (junk) bonds. This association gave KKR access to new sources of subordinated debt and freed the firm from its former reliance on insurance companies.[29]

Drexel's junk-bond network put even the largest firms at risk from hostile takeovers, as became evident when T. Boone Pickens tried to acquire Gulf Oil with his small Mesa Oil Company and $2 billion of

Drexel junk bonds.[30] With Drexel Burnham Lambert assisting the equity capital could be leveraged by a factor of ten. No firm was now too large for a KKR takeover, not even Beatrice Foods, which KKR took over by raising $2.5 billion of junk bonds arranged by Drexel. (One new source did not dry up another, however: KKR then raised $5.6 billion for its 1987 investment fund, 53 percent of which came from eleven public pension funds.[31])

In forsaking its founding principle that leveraged buyouts should be cooperative ventures between management teams and investors, KKR won Beatrice but lost Kohlberg. He left the company in 1987 to start a new firm more consistent with its original purpose.[32]

In 1986, KKR earned on the Beatrice deal $45 million in fees alone, and KKR projected returns to be $2.4 billion.[33] Investment bankers responded to these extraordinary profits as good economists would have expected: They rushed into the hostile takeover arena.[34] As their banks took equity positions in LBOs, merchant-banking activities grew dramatically, from only 13 percent of the value of merger and acquisition activity in 1986 to 25 percent in 1988.[35] The acme of this period of buyouts was KKR's hostile takeover of RJR Nabisco in 1988. KKR led a syndicate of Morgan Stanley and Merrill Lynch as well as Drexel Burnham in a bidding war against such well-armed opponents as the alliance of RJR management with Shearson and Salomon Brothers. Competition became so stiff that the final purchase price was $25 billion.[36]

Now that size alone was no guarantee of protection against corporate raiders, management responded with swift and, at first, defensive actions to make their firms less attractive to them (see Chapter 9). In these efforts, they often acted like an internal variety of raider themselves, as, for example, when selling off units that were net cash drains to buyers who could make them more profitable. Divestitures increased from less than one thousand in 1980 to almost two thousand in 1986.[37] In a counterstrategy, managers also recapitalized their companies, paid out superdividends to shareholders, and then assumed more debt, draining off in its service the excess cash flows that attracted raiders. At least the recapitalization gave them more control, but at the price of more risk.[38] Perspectives were probably shortened as managers scrambled to meet the demand for extra cash. The quantity of debt assumed in the 1980s was enormous, especially in the stable industries that raiders favored. Between 1980 and 1990, for example, the debt-to-service ratio of stable industries rose from 0.15 to 0.20, and that of cyclical industries increased from about 0.10 to 0.15.[39]

To this array of economic defenses, managers added both internal corporate governance protection and external regulatory barriers. They devised charter amendments like "supermajority" and "fair price" provisions, "dual capitalization," and "poison pills" and, as we saw earlier, acted collectively to lobby for legislative relief at both the state and the federal levels.[40] Although KKR's approach to politics remained rather quiet, it did coordinate political contributions among both its partners and its businesses and hired Washington firms to ensure access to the political process in general and to members of the Senate Finance Committee and the House Banking, Housing and Urban Affairs Committee in particular.[41]

CREATING AN INVESTOR-CONTROLLED INDUSTRIAL ASSOCIATION

The probity of regulatory reform to protect managers and sometimes employees from the dismemberment of their firms has never been clear-cut. Theoretical arguments that the country as a whole was better off when management had to compete and meet interests other than their own countered vivid but anecdotal stories of rapacious greed and short-term bonanzas. But the pressure for reform abated perhaps less due to the cogency of economic modeling than to the incontrovertible fact that investors began from self-interest to withdraw from the market for corporate control, especially in 1989 when the junk bond market crashed. Not only did the number of defaults increase, but new offerings seemed lower in quality from the very start.[42] The secondary market receded as well, sending Drexel Burnham into bankruptcy in February 1990. When financing for the buyout of United Airlines failed, the LBO craze came to a symbolic end.

KKR responded by recasting its business strategy for an era of financial retrenchment and by focusing on the reorganization of distressed industries.[43] KKR has considerable experience in industrial development. Although the firm often acted in the 1980s as a financial auctioneer, buying and selling firms for short-term gains, it still owns ten of the thirteen buyouts it arranged in the last six years and has fashioned them into industry blocs like lumber and wood products, industrial machinery and equipment, commercial printing and publishing, and consumer food products and supermarkets. Deciding to assist only those industries that complement its existing business strengths, the firm has also committed its investor association to competition on a global scale by targeting the printing and publications and the commercial banking industries. The rest of our story will focus on the latter.

KKR AS AN INVESTMENT AND COMMERCIAL BANKER?

Commercial bank failures increased dramatically in the 1980s. In 1988, 221 banks failed, whereas between 1943 and 1981, at most 17 had failed in any one year.[44] As inflation abated and no longer helped reduce nominal debt, borrowers, especially in the agricultural and energy sectors, found it difficult to repay their loans. Many became insolvent and took their banks along with them.[45] Not all bank failures during this period occurred because of macroeconomic events, however. A substantial number came from the competitive pressures and the moral hazard problems that the regulatory system itself provoked.

Recent studies attribute the extraordinary rise in commercial bank failures to two managerial practices. The first is negligence and self-dealing. Having careless collection policies, making loans in excess of legal limits, misusing brokered funds, forging notes, and making improper loans to officers and directors have been generally attributed to a culture that emphasizes wealth over ethics and to the rapid pace of deregulation that overwhelmed government supervision. But these failures are dwarfed in magnitude by the second class of failures arising from strategic responses to the rapidly changing competitive environment. In general, banks that departed abruptly from past philosophies and practices to enter new markets, speculated, instituted aggressive liability management practices, and substituted individual judgment for an internal monitoring system were more likely to fail than were banks that continued to emphasize prudent portfolio management.[46]

In our earlier discussion of banking regulation, we observed how closing one loophole inspires discovery of another. Regulations designed to respond to one problem have unexpected side effects. Congress and the Federal Deposit Insurance Corporation (FDIC) attempted to undo inflation's adverse effects on the banking industry. Inflation had made nominal ceilings on interest rates and deposits too low in real terms, and so banks could no longer compete for funds. Accordingly, Congress eliminated interest rate ceilings on deposits, and the FDIC increased its insurance for deposits to $100,000. But when both ceilings were lifted, undisciplined competition ensued, ultimately causing the banking crisis of the 1980s. Insuring accounts for $100,000 each basically eliminated management's fears of bank failure. The new regulation automatically covered people with modest means, and wealthier individuals could spread out their savings among different accounts and institutions so as to stay within the insurance limits. They would suffer inconvenience but not the ultimate loss of their funds. Bank managers then began to buy and sell these accounts to make seductive returns on extra loan portfolios, especially in the booming market for real estate.

As the banking crisis mounted, KKR sought out bargains in what was fast becoming a capital-poor industry. By 1991 KKR announced in its prospectus that banking would be a top priority, and KKR succeeded in securing $1.5 billion from investors who had soured on LBOs.[47] KKR's first full-scale foray into the industry came in 1989 when it bid in the FDIC auction of the economically defunct Texas bank, Mcorp.[48] To make its bid legally viable, KKR had worked with the Federal Reserve Board for three and a half years to develop guidelines that would conform to existing regulations prohibiting nonbanks from owning more than 25 percent of any one bank. This plan left existing management essentially intact and limited both KKR's total stake in the bank and its authority to control the nomination process for board directors. Despite this agreement and an offer price well above its nearest rival, the FDIC awarded Mcorp to Banc One Corp. A majority of the FDIC's board of directors, in particular the comptroller of the currency, Robert Clarke, opposed KKR because of its reputation as a leveraged buyout firm, interested only in short-term profits. From this unhappy experience, KKR recognized that entering into an alliance with a commercial banking firm would be quite helpful, as under such circumstances, regulators could hardly raise objections to KKR's time horizon.[49]

As KKR was laying out its plans to become an active investor in Mcorp, a passive investment opportunity came its way. In the winter of 1989/1990, First Interstate Bancorp of California, the nation's eighth-largest commercial bank, approached the firm for assistance in raising much needed capital, and KKR agreed to purchase up to 40 percent of an 8.6 million share offering, but no more for at least two years. With a bloc of 9.9 percent of First Interstate's outstanding shares, KKR could still ally with other investors and pressure management to change its policies or personnel; it could also sit still and wait for a potential bidder. With $55 billion in assets and a coveted branch network in the lucrative California market and fourteen other states, First Interstate loooked like a handsome takeover candidate for such dynamic California-based banks as Wells Fargo and Security Pacific; even more "suitors" were likely once California's ban on interstate banking ended in 1991.[50]

These two experiences prepared KKR to join with Fleet/Norstar in an acquisition of the defunct Bank of New England Corp. (BNEC). Once the fifteenth-largest commercial bank in the United States, BNEC had been too aggressive in its efforts to diversify. Abandoning its traditional local banking policies in 1985 for more regional ambitions, BNEC had expanded through both mergers and acquisitions and new ventures in commercial real estate lending, with the result that in three years its assets had increased from $7.5 to $33.1 billion. Its commercial real estate loans grew from 16.9 to 27.9 percent of BNEC's total loans in the same period.[51]

BNEC had achieved its goal of becoming a major regional bank, but only briefly. Management had ignored basic internal procedures for reviewing loans and paid little attention to consolidating offices and processing capabilities. As a result, the quality of BNEC's assets declined and its costs rose. When the New England economy faltered in the late 1980s, BNEC was unprepared to cover its loan losses in commercial real estate and accordingly went into receivership on January 6, 1991.[52]

Like BNEC, Fleet/Norstar had also grown through acquisitions. In 1988, after Rhode Island dismantled interstate barriers to banks outside New England, Fleet Financial Group (headquartered in Providence, Rhode Island) had merged with Norstar Bancorp (based in Albany, New York).[53] The new corporation was less dependent on New England than were its regional competitors and also had more diversified product lines, with more than one-quarter of its earnings coming from nonbanking financial services by 1989. It also developed exacting internal procedures to ensure the quality of its assets and to take full advantage of the cost savings inherent in their consolidation.[54]

Fleet/Norstar needed KKR for the capital to qualify for the bidding on BNEC, and KKR needed Fleet/Norstar for the bank regulators' approval for joining the industry; the two decided to join forces four days before the deadline. When the FDIC awarded them the bank, over competing bids from Bank of Boston and BankAmerica, John Dingell responded with equal celerity. The chair of the powerful House Committee on Energy and Commerce sent a letter to the regulators questioning whether or not their bid violated existing laws. The Bank Holding Company Act had restricted mergers between banks and nonbanks. The latter could hold no more than 25 percent of any class of the bank's voting securities and could in no way control the selection of the bank's directors. The Federal Reserve Board had to make certain that the company neither directly nor indirectly influenced the bank's management. Its guidelines also forbade partnership sponsors that invested in insured depository institutions from managing the investment partnership.[55] Nor could they have representatives on the board from either the partnership or the acquired company. As long as they retained their investment status, advising and soliciting the partnership were banned as well.

Drawing on its previous experiences in the Mcorp negotiations, KKR had anticipated these objections and had already worked them out with the Federal Reserve Board. When the deal was finally completed, KKR held a passive position in Fleet, as it did in First Interstate. Fleet paid a $125 million premium to the FDIC and gave $500 million of capital to BNEC's three subsidiaries. To finance the purchase, Fleet/Norstar would raise $708 million, of which $283 million would come from KKR and its investors. In exchange, KKR received both preferred stock, which carried no coupon and was convertible after three years at $17.65, and warrants to buy 6.5 million shares of Fleet/Norstar common stock, again at $17.65. The two combined would give KKR a 16.5 percent equity stake in Fleet/Norstar, well below the 25 percent limit prescribed by the Bank Holding Act, and none of the shares came with voting rights. Neither KKR nor its partnerships would have directors on Fleet's board, acquire shares in Fleet beyond 24.9 percent, exercise or attempt to exercise a controlling influence over Fleet's management, propose a director or slate of directors for Fleet's board, solicit or participate in any shareholder proxy battles, become party to any new banking or nonbanking transactions with Fleet, increase the extent of any current banking and nonbanking activities with Fleet, or advise the limited partners in the partnership on handling its shares in Fleet.[56]

In awarding BNEC to Fleet, the FDIC rejected a bid by Bank-America that was worth $112 million more on paper. In a written memo, the FDIC detailed its technical reasoning for evaluating Bank-America's offer as only superficially more valuable.[57] For most analysts, however, the reasons for the FDIC's decision lay instead in its belief that Fleet/Norstar was more likely than BankAmerica to take full advantage of the economies of scale that consolidation would bring, the political pressures exerted by New England representatives to block BankAmerica's entry into the region, and the Bush administration's commitment to attract new capital into the industry.[58] T. Timothy Ryan, Jr., director of the Office of Thrift Supervision and a member of the FDIC's board, made this last point clear when he heralded KKR's involvement as marking the entry of sophisticated investors into the consolidation of the banking system. Robert L. Clark, the comptroller of the currency who only two years earlier had staunchly opposed KKR's attempt to acquire Mcorp, now noted that KKR was "really performing an investment banker function" that would attract institutional investment funds into the troubled industry.[59] The stock market reacted to the deal by increasing the price of Fleet/Norstar's stock from $17 to $25 a share. Based on its conversion price of $17.65, KKR earned a 40 percent paper profit in three weeks.

KKR poised itself to become an investor-controlled industrial association, the kind of commercial and financial service holding company recommended by the Bush Treasury.[60] Success in bringing securities to market depends on investment bankers' knowledge of both their clients' creditworthiness and the macroeconomic conditions that so significantly influence the proper timing and pricing of a distribution. Assembling a syndicate of other financial institutions, including commercial banks, can reduce these risks, but the banks must draw on the same skills for assessing the prospectus that informed the investment bankers in preparing it.

These skills also aid commercial bankers when they service their corporate clients with commercial and industrial loans. When they act as lead lenders for these loans, they need additional "investment banker" organizational talents to coordinate the syndicates. Not only can a merger therefore represent additional business for each financial institution, but it also offers the promise of enhanced efficiency by taking advantage of economies of scope.[61]

By owning a commercial bank, KKR may realize another possible economy in the transaction costs of doing a deal. The information for both making and monitoring an investment might be sufficiently less costly than those of the normal contractual arrangements to justify "preferential" terms for loans to a KKR acquisition or a KKR-controlled firm. Moreover, if a KKR bank could provide other KKR affiliates with commercial credit and other financial services at competitive rates, then an intricate financial network could emerge among KKR-controlled firms. This network would complement and strengthen the proprietary and governance bonds that give KKR's investor association its commonwealth identity, and it would come to resemble not only the industrial empire that J. P. Morgan created at the turn of the century but also the *keiretsu* of today's Japan and the bank-centered conglomerates of modern Germany.[62]

Financial deregulation would first be necessary, however, and this would require persuading Congress to abandon its historical opposition to financial control of commercial enterprises and also playing hardball with threatened vested interests as powerful and varied as banking, manufacturing, insurance, and securities. KKR would then be a leading force in transforming American managerial capitalism into a banker/investor-dominated economy. Until then, its full Schumpeterian power to destroy the old with innovative and better ways of doing business will remain latent. Still, KKR has used the pension funds' concentration of shares to provide an alternative to the managerially controlled firm, an alternative that recasts investors as owners.

III
THE MODEL

11

The Games That Managers Play: Themes for a Story, a Model, and a Test

Our narrative may appear to have wandered rather widely, but it really is divided into two parts. First, we discussed the framework or rules that politicians, legislators, judges, and theorists developed to contain as well as bolster the economic and political development of the modern corporation. With this framework in place, we then turned to an analysis of how corporate managers both worked within these rules and continued to modify them in an effort to consolidate and strengthen their position of control.

We arrived at this structure from recent developments in economics, namely, that people both simultaneously accept rules, optimizing their behavior subject to these given constraints, and work to change them and expand their opportunities. Economists have borrowed from game theory the language to describe this control, and in this chapter, we use this language intentionally. We use models to gather up the various themes of our narrative, and in so doing we indicate how the preceding histories of corporate regulation and managerial collective action can help clarify economic theory. Historical and economic approaches have much to teach and contribute to each other in studying the modern corporation and its place in a democratic polity.

The chapter proceeds as follows: First we review the literature on game theory and collective action in constructing a model of managerial collective action in America's democratic polity. The issue involves several questions. First, how are we to define a general corporate interest both broad enough to overcome the competitive rivalries that separate corporate entities and narrow enough to be

161

compatible with American values regarding the large firm's place in a democratic order? Second, how does the corporate sector's general interest assert itself against the tendency toward self-interested corporate fragmentation? Third, how does this general interest or structure grow out of firm-specific strategies yet still allow individual corporations to diverge and even compete in a broad range of political contests? Without this competitive fragmentation, corporate-sector solidarity would appear so vital as to endanger polyarchical political arrangements.

Next we study the research on corporate PACs in particular, since social scientists have used these data to determine whether corporate-sector cohesion appears so enduring as to signal a minority danger to majoritarian rule. After introducing the data, we finally test our assertion that corporations simultaneously cohere and fragment over efforts to change public policy (rules). We carry out this test by analyzing corporate PAC activity in recent elections, and our results corroborate our hypothesis.

A REVIEW OF THE THEORY

Think of the corporate sector as engaged in a game played simultaneously on two fields: an internal one in which negotiations occur among the corporate control group and the firm's constituent stakeholders, primarily investors and labor; and an external one, in which the teams assembled by the corporate control group compete. Each of the firm's stakeholders has an interest in influencing the oversight board or commission that determines not only the rules that govern their behavior in both fields but also the very identity of the teams themselves.

Game theory provides some incisive observations about the conditions under which managers, in particular, attempt to shape the rules governing the firm and its competition with other firms. Insights from this work have contributed significantly to the development of collective-action theory, yet the models are so abstract and so determinedly in pursuit of equilibrium solutions that they often seem far removed from the historian's interest in events, particularities, and ceaseless change. Their exercises in comparative statics beg historical questions, for the problems they address and the solutions they seek all are played out in real time. Nevertheless, both game theory and collective-action theory clarify and distill themes that historical investigations (as illustrated in the preceding chapters) may then use to structure their various narratives.

Both theories, for example, raise questions about the problems that corporate interests pose for constitutional democracy. According to game theorists John Von Neumann and Oskar Morgenstern, a society's constitution may be described as the rules of a game that develop as independent and rational individuals interact over time.[1] America's constitution, for example, forms an established order whose norms foster democratic or, perhaps more precisely, polyarchial rules of behavior. Although not all persons share all the same views about citizens' rights and responsibilities, they agree to sort out their differences according to general principles and procedures—guarantees of basic political and economic rights through majority rule and market exchange.[2]

Individual persons and groups of persons prefer some forms of established order and constitutive norms over others. They compete to win approval of their own interests and visions from the polity, associate, and agree to act collectively. Institutionalized and tacit agreements among people therefore create their own effective "constitutions." A multidimensional constitutional order develops over time, and the corporate sector functions in one of these dimensions.

Collective-action models suggest that individual citizens form minority groupings like corporations; that these groups form a larger, yet still cohesive minority like the corporate sector; and that all citizens, individually and as minorities, create the broad constitutional norms that define the democracy. At each of these three levels, the theory points to the kinds of laws and private agreements that develop to encourage or discourage group behavior. By reviewing the basic "games," we can construct the patterns of managerial collective action.

Cooperation and/or Privilege: Between the Prisoner's Dilemma and Playing Chicken

In a "one-shot, two-person Prisoner's Dilemma," two persons, who are prevented from communicating and are therefore bargaining, are simultaneously confronted with choosing either to cooperate in or defect from a two-person project. Each has the same order of preferences: It is best to defect, provided the other one tries to cooperate; second best for both to cooperate; third best for both to defect; and worst to cooperate while the other defects. If they cannot communicate, both will choose to defect.

Take another noncooperative game, the game of "chicken," which Michael Taylor has illustrated as follows:[3] Two neighboring cultivators rely on a dike for flood control. Each can maintain it alone but prefers to free-ride on the other's efforts. The consequences of the work's not getting done are so disastrous, however, that each would be willing to do the work himself rather than have it go undone. Unlike the "Prisoner's Dilemma," each therefore finds cooperating to be a better response to the other's failure to oblige, but each also delays in hopes that the other will move first. Although the game has an effective group of one, the presence of a second player leaves the outcome unclear.

The Coordination Problem: Convention and History

Theorists tend to distinguish coordination problems like the Prisoner's Dilemma from those of "cooperative games," in which communication and bargaining are possible. In this set of games, the actors recognize that it is in their self-interest to coordinate their strategies, but they differ in their preferences on how to cooperate.[4] The problem of coordination often therefore involves agreeing on one among many competing sets of strategies.[5]

Coordination requires implicit understandings or conventions of behavior among players. As von Neumann and Morgenstern suggested, experience facilitates coordination. Or as Russell Hardin put it, "convention is honored because, once it exists, it is in our interest to conform to it."[6] The probability of coordination is increased significantly by the possibility of playing the game more than once.

"Iterated" n-person Prisoner's Dilemma games provide this insight more formally.[7] Repetition and communication can transform self-defeating selfish actions into cooperative behavior if the players discount the value of future paybacks at sufficiently low rates.[8] In the amended setup, the consequences of failing to cooperate are sufficiently suboptimal that players learn to signal their strategies to opponents by playing in recognizable patterns. For example, a player can gradually induce cooperation by indicating her intentions to reward and punish an opponent based on the latter's cooperation or selfishness ("tit for tat"). Because the game is extended indefinitely, each player can calculate over time whether it is better to cooperate or defect. A subgroup of players may consistently choose to cooperate, even though others defect with equal regularity. Their strategy may be either conditional, in which each move depends on preceding moves or patterns, or unconditional, in which moves are set by predetermined rules; similar discount rates for future paybacks substantially reinforce each strategy. But internal pressures are likely to be extreme because members have incentives to play chicken in the expectation that the others will continue to play cooperatively.

Games of "assurance" resemble those of chicken except in the new assumption that neither player can secure the public good unilaterally. Assume now that the two cultivators of our earlier example can no longer maintain the dike alone. Each will prefer either to cooperate or to defect simultaneously. Failing to cooperate is so potentially disastrous that neither will expect the other to defect; cooperation is thus the positive outcome.

Unfortunately, as the number of players expands beyond the minimum effective group and their tastes begin to differ, elements of chicken reemerge as individual players begin to push for differentiated contributions.[9] Indeed, relaxing the simplifying assumptions and beginning to add what we are happy to call historical detail, has the following effect on cooperation in cooperative games. Coordination is more likely if

1. The games can be played more than once.
2. The payback structure readily invites cooperation or threatens catastrophic consequences for noncooperation.[10]
3. The discount rates of the players continually and mutually emphasize future payback.[11]
4. Interactions, communications, and bargaining among players are direct and frequent.[12]
5. The internal structure of the group tends to reduce transaction costs or other barriers to organization.[13]
6. The players are altruistic, socially enlightened, or otherwise socially and economically self-selected.[14]
7. The group includes powerful players capable of levying sanctions against noncooperating players.
8. Institutions external to the group are able to facilitate the group's behavior.[15]

Coordination, in other words, develops through understanding and agreement and ultimately through conventions of behavior. Theory can elucidate the conditions for group association and cooperation. But it alone cannot predict or explain the details; it requires assistance from history.

STRUCTURING CORPORATE-SECTOR COLLECTIVE ACTION

The corporation exemplifies an ongoing cooperative game that depends on both mutually beneficial outcomes for the players—investors, workers, control, and, loosely speaking, consumers—and effective means of coordination. Technical advantages of administration have historically led participants to prefer collective corporate action to alternative, more decentralized forms of production and distribution. Over time, these coordinating factors have created similarities in the organization of all large-scale corporations, and these have been reenforced through the rule-governed setting of general incorporation laws and securities, labor, and consumer regulations.

Since Russell Hardin's work, collective-action theorists have elaborated conditions both conducive amd resistant to coordinated action.[16] If, for example, corporate-sector firms share an interest in public goods of an enduring and "pure" nature (i.e., the benefits do not diminish as the group's size increases), they or an effective subgroup can develop conventions that move their strategies toward a cooperative solution. In order to secure benefits or redistributions in the long run, however, corporations must also appear legitimate in the public eye, not just in the sense of obeying laws, but in the stronger sense of serving the public will. They must therefore meet challenges on two broad fronts: from stakeholders with a special agenda within the firm and from a democracy threatened by corporate size and power.

Collective action also recognizes that for large groups the effect of any one firm's contribution will be minimal, encouraging firms to free-ride. Thus, small groups that seek public goods with concentrated benefits have a higher propensity for collective action than do large groups for which the benefits are either widely dispersed or diminish with group size. For this reason, analysts such as Mancur Olson believe that industries or strategic groups within industries tend to associate voluntarily while the corporate sector itself remains poorly organized.[17] These two tendencies—to cohere and to fragment—actually structure corporate collective action and provide the basis for management's claims that its control over these concentrated resources is conducive to democratic rule.

Inside the Corporation's "Blackbox"

We have already explored—albeit with a slightly different vocabulary and orientation—how the rules governing the corporation's principal stakeholders determine which group will control the corporation and represent it in the public domain. The interpretation of the firm as a cooperative game can now provide some general conclusions about the internal "constitution" or design of corporate entities that encourages corporationwide collective action.

Firms require coordinators who seek to maximize organizational rents through the attraction and subsequent development of firm-specific resources. The coordinators encourage cooperative trade-offs to minimize risk, establish a broad range of forms in which labor can participate in the production process, limit investors' functions to considerations of risk and return, and retain broad discretion in devising alternative cooperative solutions and day-to-day resource allocations. We have previously given these "coordinators" the appellation "control."

As a group, coordinators/control will also try to establish legal rules that support and legitimate their authoritative position in the firm; thus they will share an underlying interest in collective action. Although many groups have competed to lay claim to this privileged position—entrepreneurial families, bankers, managers, workers, and public officials among them—the unambiguous winners over time have been the managers. In the preceding history, we chronicled this contest for control and how the regulatory state emerged from it and helped oversee the contest. The regulatory state itself sanctioned managerial control, but in doing so it institutionalized a powerful public agency that could undo or limit managerial discretion. This threat encouraged corporate voluntary associations and an enlightened ideology that has sustained managerial collective action.

Enlightened managers focused the public's attention on their corporate executive responsibilities for garnering "rents" to sustain the firm's internal coalition. In this role, managers reasoned that they privately negotiate contracts among the firm's stakeholders, resisting public interference and preserving the public–private distinction vital to liberty. Here, managers share a common function, and when they band together to preserve this interest, their collective actions protect liberty. Yet this mutual interest to serve as corporate coordinators forces managers to compete with one another in the marketplace, thereby reducing the possibilities for broad collective action over industrial policies or the polity more generally.

A REVIEW OF THE LITERATURE ON PACS AND OUR CONTRIBUTION

As we documented in Chapter 7, social scientists have consistently debated whether corporate concentrations threatened American democratic life. As these debates wore on, scholars developed procedures for "testing" corporate political control. The most recent efforts in assessing the potential for corporate political mischief have concentrated on corporate PAC donations, so that this field of research offers an attractive setting for testing our basic model.

The literature offers several models of corporate PAC behavior, and the political investor approach is especially useful for our purposes. This model, which owes much to the work of Anthony Downs, considers corporate PAC allocations as investments made by political entrepreneurs and expected to bring returns to the firm.[18]

The investment model gives little weight to ideological motives.

Rather, PACS are assumed to respond strategically to the volative political market, embarking on new cost–benefit analyses for each electoral cycle. This model thus considers corporate PACs to be rational in the same sense that collective-action theorists apply the term to individuals and organizations.

Studies of corporate PAC spending usually begin at the firm level. Although labor union PACs have a centralized procedure for assembling an official prounion candidate list, corporate PACs have no authoritative means for coordinating their donation strategies, even though business associations like the U.S. Chamber of Commerce and the Business Industry PAC do formulate probusiness electoral donation strategies. Given this starting point, Theodore Eismeier and Phillip Pollock concluded that corporate PAC contributory patterns are "the products of many thousands of spending choices that differ significantly from industry to industry and from PAC to PAC."[19] Differences range from the individual firm's initial decision whether or not to form a corporate PAC to differences among PACs about how and when to allocate their resources.[20]

But similarities in individual spending patterns still suggest underlying corporate PAC political strategies. All PACs must choose to spend on either incumbents or challengers, in contested or uncontested elections, early or late in the campaign, and on candidates from a single party or candidates from several parties.

In order to simplify the data analysis, the literature focuses primarily on the first of these spending decisions.[21] When PACs favor incumbents, corporate funds also tend to flow disproportionately to contested races. Researchers have therefore observed that when corporate PACs favor candidates who are out of power, their strategy coincides with ideological PACs that target challengers and contested races as part of their effort to influence Congress's ideological makeup.[22] Thus, the literature identifies two generic contribution patterns: an ideological strategy, in which a disproportionate amount of dollars flows to challengers, and a pragmatic strategy that favors incumbents and appears designed to maximize a firm's access to Congress.

Most researchers agree that in any given election year, some corporate PACs gave pragmatically and others gave ideologically, but they diverge sharply in their interpretation. To some, for example, the existence of an ideological strategy is *prima facie* evidence of corporate control over the legislature. But what perplexes these scholars is that the corporate sector also fragments along two strategic lines, undermining the case for cohesion and control. To other researchers, these differences do not suggest real political competition, because firms rarely confront one another by supporting opposing candidates.[23] Still others argue that the PACs cohere more than they fragment.[24]

Thomas Edsall took yet another approach, suggesting that the divisions between pragmatic and ideological PACs make strategic sense when the patterns are aggregated over time. Corporate PAC figures totaled through 1982 led Edsall to conclude that corporate PACs pursue a two-dimensional strategy in which pragmatic and ideological giving work together to advance business's political interests. Corporate PACs give pragmatically to incumbent Democrats (particularly in the House, where the Democrats remain firmly entrenched) as a way to influence their votes on important economic issues, and they give ideologically to Republican challengers and open-seat contestants in hopes of shifting Congress's partisan makeup.[25] This two-pronged strategy appears to be the product of conscious coordination, a political response to recent social regulatory intrusions by the government. Coordination is facilitated by a variety of business associations, particularly the Business-Industry PAC, that provide the information on congressional campaigns necessary for corporate PACs to act as enlightened corporate citizens.[26]

Without engaging in the controversy over corporate minority privilege, Jacobson's studies of American congressional elections between 1974 and 1984 offer similar evidence regarding the corporate sector's reward-and-punishment strategy.[27] Business's increasing importance to the Democratic Party represents for Jacobson the most striking feature in recent PAC contribution trends. Before the PAC explosion in the 1970s, labor provided more than three times as much money to the Democrats as did business-oriented groups.[28] But between 1980 and 1984, Democrats running in House elections received about the same amount of funding from corporate, trade, and professional organizations as they did from labor PACs. Corporate and trade association PACs rarely gave to Democratic challengers, however. Instead, business funds to unseat incumbents overwhelmingly found their way into Republican coffers.[29] Thus, business's increasing financial participation in electoral politics has contributed to a Republican advantage in bringing well-funded challengers onto the scene. For Jacobson, this threat, coupled with the business community's willingness to support sympathetic incumbents, regardless of party affiliation, has afforded ample incentives for Democratic incumbents to adopt conservative, probusiness positions.[30] Like Edsall, Jacobson suggests that corporate PACs have engaged in a reward-and-punishment strategy, and in his opinion, this corporate strategy helps explain why, without political realignment, the Democrats have recently shifted to the right on economic matters.[31]

In contrast with both Jacobson's and Edsall's assessments that the probability of corporate PAC collective action is reasonably strong, Keim and Zardkoohi remain skeptical.[32] They ask whether corporate PAC investments can be economically justified, if they are "profitable" only when these organizations act in unison to influence congressional voting records. Keim and Zardkoohi consider congressional campaigns as part of a market in political power, in which the sellers are congressional representatives and the buyers are PACs. There is relatively more power on the congressional side of the transaction. Legislators find it easier to act collectively because they are fewer in number, and although they can acquire campaign funds from a large number of sources, the PACs face an effective "monopoly" over powerful congressional positions, there being only one chair of the House Ways and Means Committee. Powerful political bosses thus effectively "coerce" corporations into forming PACs to pay "extortion."[33]

Keim and Zardkoohi further argue that the large number and diverse interests of corporate PACs disadvantage them not just compared with politicians but also compared with labor PACs. Labor faces fewer obstacles in coordinating PAC donations.[34] Its alleged leverage over incumbents suggests that unions will be far more willing to support challengers than corporate PACs will. After subjecting these propositions to statistical analyses, Keim and Zardkoohi come to their final assessment about corporate investments in administering PACs: They are "uneconomical" and should be curtailed. Their analysis, then, complements arguments about the impossibility of broad corporate-sector political action and attempts to recast the debate concerning minority political privilege by directing attention from the corporate sector to the labor unions and to an elite coterie of political representatives.

A similar conclusion comes from Eismeier and Pollock.[35] Whereas Keim and Zardkoohi rely on public-choice theory to posit strong generalizations about the character and possibilities of corporate PAC behavior, Eismeier and Pollock raise methodological doubts and instead sift through the details of corporate PAC giving between 1980 and 1984 before offering any generalizations.[36] Despite their attention to firm-specific factors, they finally agree with Edsall that a singular pattern emerges in corporate PAC donations over a series of election cycles, but they seriously doubt that this coincidence occurred through central administration and explore the alternative of firm-specific decisions spontaneously adding up to a collective strategy. By attempting to analyze the interactions between firm-specific decisions and corporationwide political action, their study considers the possibility that corporate political cohesion and fragmentation are simultaneous and mutually reenforcing rather than discrete and oppositional.

From their election-year analyses, Eismeier and Pollock devised three distinct contributory strategies.[37] They relabeled the pragmatic strategy "accommodationist" and divided the ideological approach into "adversarial" and "partisan" categories. Adversarial PACs contribute to candidates in a way that strongly resembles the aggressive challenger-oriented strategy of conservative ideological PACs, but partisan PACs follow a donation strategy that more closely mimics the cautionary politics of the Republican party.

A number of factors account for this fragmented political environment. The size of a corporate PAC's treasury and whether it is located inside or outside the Beltway significantly affect the firm's strategic orientation.[38] Small PACs outside Washington tend to be both less pragmatic and more national in scope than large, Washington-based PACs. As a PAC becomes more complicated and professionally managed, it tends to become more accommodating to the *status quo*. Recent battles over social regulation are another factor that influences strategic orientation. Firms involved in these contests are more likely to adopt an adversarial strategy than other corporations are, especially those in regulated industries like transportation, communications, and financial services.[39]

In short, Eismeier and Pollock contend that differences in each corporate PAC's organization and resources, as well as its parent organization's interactions with government, fragment the business community into competing strategic groupings. Viewed in terms of a single cycle, they find a variegated and contentious corporate political "community." But when the perspective is extended and aggregate corporate PAC donations are examined from 1980 to 1986, a contrary conclusion emerges: Corporate PAC contributions do indeed add up to a reflexive and unified political strategy. In 1980, the corporate sector rallied to support Republican challengers. Corporate PAC partisanship persisted in 1982 but became defensive as corporate PAC money flowed heavily to protect Republican incumbents made vulnerable by the economy's poor performance. The Republican misfortunes of 1982 discouraged strong Republican challengers from running for office in 1984 and persuaded corporate PACs that a moderate partisanship was the more businesslike posture.[40]

Unlike Edsall, Eismeier and Pollock do not presume that this discernible coincidence of corporate PAC activity unveils either a conscious coordination or a potential threat to the political system's integrity.[41] Instead, they argue that this pattern is created by a network of firm-specific decisions in which firms communicate and share information. Contrary to Edsall's contention, political forces and circumstances alone shape corporate PAC actions.

To support this argument, the authors offer four conceptually distinct ways in which corporate PAC giving may be related in the aggregate. First, corporate PACs formulate strategies from their reading of the political situation, and their assessments are likely to be similar. Second, the information that these readings require flows through formal and informal networks that link PACs to one another and to other political organizations. Third, corporate PAC managers as a group rely on candidates and political party organizations not only because of their expert knowledge on how an election is evolving but also because of their coercive powers. (In a manner reminiscent of Keim and Zardkoohi, they remind us that incumbents are usually not in dire need of money, so donations to these candidates may be more like tribute than bribery.) Finally, corporate PAC managers may end up acting in the same way simply because imitation is rational. In other words, they behave contingently.[42]

Corporate PACs are therefore dependent, reactive participants in the electoral system, and this dependency persuades Eismeier and Pollock to discount claims that cohesion (whether intended or unintended) in itself attests to corporate political control. Nor do they see any organized corporate intent to secure such broad political influence. If they had such designs, corporate PACs would give more heavily in primaries and earlier in the general elections. The partisan bias that Eismeier and Pollock do acknowledge appears to respond to opportunities, not to create them. Corporate PACs are basically content to give to incumbents of both parties, as in 1984 and 1986. For this reason, Eismeier and Pollock agree with standard pluralist analyses that portray the corporate sector as a pragmatic, bipartisan entity that tends to stabilize the *status quo* in Congress.[43] However, even if we accept this pluralist rendering of the corporate sector's tendency to cohere, the fact that corporate PACs cohere as they also fragment remains puzzling. Here we make our contribution to the literature on corporate political action, by reconciling Eismeier and Pollock's finding that a corporationwide interest apparently exists over time with their observation that in any given election the corporate sector competes pragmatically for local political advantage.

To review, we contend that corporations politically cohere and fragment. Cohesion centers on political issues that are at the heart of corporate political legitimacy and managerial autonomy, and fragmentation centers on issues that threaten neither the corporation's existence as an independent construct nor managerial control. Corporate-sector firms have shared characteristics, the most important being management's control over the firm's investment/distribution decisions and its internal governance. To maintain their collective hold over the firms, managers require regulatory policies that sanction them as the firm's arbitrator among its various stakeholders and that promote a macroeconomic policy conducive to economy growth and decentralized decision making. Managerial solidarity arises from these issues.

Yet for managers to become part of "an inner circle," they must prove themselves in the marketplace. They must demonstrate their abilities to move up a firm's corporate hierarchy, and in so doing, managers enhance their financial well-being. Thus, even when top managers come together to consider broad issues that affect management's professional position, they are drawn apart because of their firm-specific responsibilities. Market pressures prohibit management from coalescing around public-policy issues that seriously affect the competitive position of a firm, an industry, or a strategic group. For this reason, managers tend to fragment as they coalesce.

We therefore offer the following propositions about corporate PAC behavior:

1. Corporate PAC decisions display patterns of fragmentation and cohesion simultaneously. Although donations form discernible strategic groupings, a corporationwide strategy exists to protect corporate-sector interests, particularly managerial control. We assume that this cohesive pattern occurs through an aggregation of individual PAC donations in which communication takes place without systematic coordination.

2. The corporationwide strategy employs a "threat-and-reward" tactic—that is, corporate managers oppose or withdraw support from incumbents who have been disregarding corporate managerial interests, and they support candidates promising to make those interests central.

We expect corporate PACs to target candidates in contested races and/or candidates with probusiness voting records, adjusting their spending from offensive to defensive as electoral conditions warrant. By spending heavily in contested races, corporate PACs behave like ideological PACs, even though these two PAC types differ in the relative proportions they give to incumbents and challengers.

3. Corporate PAC cohesion usually forms in opposition to those attempting to constrain managerial control. In particular, corporate PACs oppose labor's electoral donation strategy, since labor most seriously challenges management and supports public interventions.

DATA, METHODOLOGY, AND STATISTICAL ANALYSIS

Thanks to the Federal Election Campaign Act of 1974, we now have access to the data necessary to perform a statistical analysis of PACs and their spending patterns in a series of House of Representative election years. These analyses allow us to test two of the generalizations we made during our narrative: that corporate political action displayed the fragmented solidarity anticipated by America's pluralist regulatory regime, and that corporate managers entered a political alliance with conservatives in the 1980s to bring about a shift in economic policy.

Because we wanted to study "professionally" managed PACs and the literature suggests a relationship between PAC size and its level of professionalization, we excluded those PACs that donated less than $25,000 to House of Representatives and/or Senate elections in a given year; we also restricted the data to House candidates who received at least a $1.00 contribution in the general election from the corporate PACs in our study.

Studying House elections has many empirical advantages. They provide a larger homogeneous database than do Senate elections. They also give large, professionally run firms an opportunity for simultaneous political action. Corporate PACs have historically preferred giving to House races over Senate races,[44] perhaps because the House's complicated committee and subcommittee system puts its members in bargaining situations in which they are able to broker legislation beneficial to their constituents.[45] The members of this "cradle of democracy" legislate for the nation as a whole yet are drawn from the broadest range of local interests visible in the official realm of national politics.

Tables 1 and 2 provide some descriptive information about the corporate PACs and candidates in our study.

We presume that a strategic pattern can be discerned by tracking and comparing corporate PAC contributions ("dollars") to individual candidates. Thus, for any election year, corporate PAC contributions

Table 1. A Summary of Corporate PACs and Candidates by Election Year

Year	Number of PACs	Number of Candidates	Mean Corp. PAC Contribution/Cand	% of Total Corp. PAC Contribution
1980	206	591	$14,217	70
1982	320	634	23,657	88
1984	400	582	31,007	79
1986	426	592	36,976	83

Table 2. Frequencies of Candidates by Status and Party by Election Year

	1980			1982			1984			1986[a]		
Status[b]	I	C	O	I	C	O	I	C	O	I	C	O
Democrat	241	19	33	212	67	42	255	30	21	232	50	39
Republican	139	122	37	166	98	49	153	100	23	159	72	39

[a] One candidate in 1986 was in a third party.
[b] I is incumbent.
C is challenger.
O is open.

form a matrix in which every entry is the dollar contribution from each PAC to each candidate. For example, in 1984 this matrix has 400 rows (PACs) and 582 columns (candidates), for a total of 232,800 entries.

To avoid biasing the data toward or away from the "control" hypothesis in our efforts to make sense of multidimensional contribution patterns, we rely on multivariate statistical methods.[46] And because of the magnitude of these dimensions, we analyze the data with a two-stage procedure of principal components and cluster analysis. For each of the 1980, 1982, 1984, and 1986 elections, we group candidates by similarities in dimensions like their campaign receipts and electoral returns and then group the corporate PACs by similarities in how they gave to the candidate groups.[47]

Candidates

Our original profile of individual candidates is composed of seven variables, six based on campaign dollars received from various sources and one based on the votes received in the election. These quantitative variables distinguish our study from others that rely solely on qualitative characteristics like incumbency or party affiliation.

Based on the FEC data, the variables are as follows:

1. Corporate PAC contributions, in dollars (CORP$).
2. Labor union PAC contributions, in dollars (LAB$).
3. Health/membership/but mostly trade PAC contributions, in dollars (TRAD$).
4. Nonconnected (parentless) PAC contributions, in dollars (NONCON$).
5. Contributions from all other sources, including money donated by parties and individuals, in dollars (OTHER$).
6. The percentage of corporate PAC contributions to all candidates in the race received by the candidate (CORP%).

7. The percentage of the vote received by the candidate in the election (VOTE%).

Because these variables provide no indication of the importance of ideology to a particular candidate's success, we augment them with an independent rating of each candidate. The published ratings from organizations like the U.S. Chamber of Commerce and the National Conservative Political Action Committee are based in general on congressional voting records and therefore describe only incumbents. Ratings also say nothing about an incumbent's electoral prospects and the strategic importance of his or her electoral contest to organizations hoping to shape Congress ideologically. Such a rating system is, however, implicit in the contributions that nonconnected ideological PACs gave during an election cycle. In general, these PACs are known for their aggressive and calculated use of dollars to influence election outcomes in an ideologically correct way; their contributions can accordingly serve as a measure of a candidate's or a race's strategic importance. Ideally, such a measure would draw on conservative and liberal PAC contributions. But in 1980 so few liberal unconnected PACs took part in the House elections that we were forced to use a political rating system based on thirteen conservative nonconnected PACs, and we used the same system in 1982.[48]

Denoted as CONRAT,[49] this value represents the number of identified conservative PACs from which an individual candidate received donations minus the number from which his or her opponent received donations.[50] Positive values reflect conservative PAC support; negative values reflect their opposition; and zeros reflect their indifference.

By 1984, a considerable number of liberal PACs were donating to the House elections. After 1984, therefore, instead of continuing to use our CONRAT rating system to assess political ideology, we relied on total contributions from twelve conservative and twelve liberal PACs, (CON$) and (LIB$), to augment the candidate profiles.[51] Because we also separated out party PAC contributions (PARTY$) from the earlier, more inclusive category of OTHER$, the 1984 and 1986 analyses include three extra candidate profile variables.

In the sense that they always contributed to many more winners than losers, the corporate PACs in our study were clearly careful in selecting their contestants. Because preliminary statistical analyses show that the winning and losing candidates in each year came from two significantly different populations, we separated the candidates into winners and losers for candidate data analyses. Table 3 lists this breakdown.

Table 3. Number of Winners and Losers by Study Year

	1980	1982	1984	1986
Winners	418	430	435	437
Losers	173	204	147	155

For each election, we performed a principal components analysis on the collection of candidate variables, which numbered eight in 1980 and 1982 and ten in 1984 and 1986. The principal components of each election's candidate provide independent bases for comparing candidates with one another. Based on the candidates' similarities in a reduced space of principal-component dimensions, we derived a clustering of candidates that we defined as a "strategic candidate grouping."

Table 4 lists the dimensions for winners and losers in each election year. Because the candidate variables for 1980 and 1982 differ slightly from those in 1984 and 1986, the two election sets are not easily compared and so we discuss each set separately.

In both 1980 and 1982, the first dimension for winners measures a candidate's margin of victory in terms of votes and dollars received (excluding labor PAC dollars). On average, this dimension, which accounts for 40 percent of the variation in the eight candidate variables in 1980 and 34 percent in 1982, corroborates the findings of Jacobson and others: Funds flow to contested races. In the language of the table, as the candidate's margin of victory nears zero, his or her campaign receipts increase. Exceptions include Dan Rostenkowski's ability to attract substantial dollars as the chairman of the powerful House Ways and Means Committee despite his commanding lead in the race for reelection.

This first dimension contradicts the earlier pluralist literature. This particular economic interest group did not pursue pragmatic policies for political access in 1980 and 1982. Instead, they acted like ideological and partisan political PACs. With the exception of labor PACS, they all followed a competitive strategy. Labor support alone seems to have reflected their economic interest-group status.[52]

The second dimension for winners, accounting for 25 and 31 percent of the variation in 1980 and 1982, respectively, indicates that business and labor PACs tend to oppose each other. In 1980, corporate PACs alone took up business's cause, so we speak of the "corporate/labor donation ratio." In 1982, they were joined by trade associations, and the relevant dimension is the "business/labor donation ratio."

For losing candidates in 1980 and 1982, the first dimension (viability) tells us which candidates received considerable amounts of

Table 4. Important Dimensions of Candidate Variables by Election
Year Dimensions

	1980	1982	1984	1986
Winners	1. Contestability of race	1. Contestability of race	1. Contestability of race	1. Contestability of race
	2. Corporate/labor donation ratio (CLDR)[a]	2. Business/labor donation ratio (BLDR)	2. Business and conservative/labor and liberal donation ratio (BCLLDR)	2. BCLLDR
				3. EIPDR
			3. Economic interest group/partisan donation ratio (EIPDR)	
Losers	1. Viability of candidate	1. Viability of candidate	1. Viability of candidate	1. Viability of candidate
	2. CLDR	2. Labor support	2. Labor and liberal/ conservative support donation ratio (LLCDR)	2. Labor and liberal support

[a] These abbreviations also appear in the text and Tables 5, 6, 7, and 8.

money and votes, and the second tells us the extent to which they
received labor PACs' financial backing. In 1980, this information
takes the form of a ratio between corporate support and labor PAC
giving, and in 1982, the dimension provides an absolute measure of
a candidate's labor PAC receipts.

The candidates' CONRAT values provide a third dimension for
our candidate cluster analysis in years when liberal PACS were few
and far between. As we shall show, this dimension reveals that conservative and corporate PAC support tended to coincide in 1980
and 1982.

The first dimension for winners in 1984 and 1986 again measures
a race's contestability. Corporate PAC money (CORP$) contributed
significantly in 1980 and 1982, but not in 1984 and 1986. Corporate
PACs must have altered their contribution criteria from giving heavily to ideologically "correct" candidates in contested elections to helping preferred candidates regardless of their electoral circumstances.
They ceased donating in ways that broadly resembled ideological
and partisan PACs, which target candidates in closely contested
races.

The second dimension also resembles its 1980 and 1982 counter-
part. The contest between labor and capital continued in 1984 and
1986. The dimension now includes the new candidate variables, conservative and liberal PAC contributions (CON$ and LIB$), however,
and we can further see that in each election the conservative PACs
lined up with business and the liberal PACs allied with labor—hence

the label, "business and conservative/labor and liberal donation ratio." For 1984 and 1986, a third dimension appears, one that tempers the ideological rift found in the second dimension. Contrasting partisan (ideological and party) PAC donations and interest-group (business and labor) PAC donations, it tells us that a candidate's shares of partisan dollars and interest-group dollars tend to move in opposite directions. We label this dimension the "economic interest group/partisan donation ratio." Whereas partisan PACs tend to contribute to candidates in contested races, interest groups tend to donate to powerful incumbents to help ensure access regardless of their partisan colors, party labels, or need for campaign support.

Tables 5 through 8 report the results of clustering candidates into strategic groupings. In general, we use the candidate dimension labels for each election year to describe these groupings and develop a 5–point ordinal classification of "very high," "high," "average or medium," "low," and "very low." For example, in 1980, there were 7 winning and 5 losing candidate groups. Within the winning candidate grouping, group 7 includes 29 candidates who on average were in highly contested races and obtained "high" support from conservatives and relatively equal support from corporations and labor unions. Another example is group 1 in 1980; which includes 110 candidates who were in uncontested races (low contestability) with relatively equal corporate and labor support and with medium conservative support.

Corporate PACs

Each year, a profile of an individual corporate PAC was constructed from the percentages of its total campaign contributions to each strategic candidate group. To account for the different corporate PAC parent groups, we studied five economic variables for each firm: market orientation, import penetration ratio, industrial sector, geographic location, and regulatory status.[53]

Principal components analysis of the percentages of total contributions that a corporate PAC gave to the strategic candidate groups for each year first created a corporate donation profile. Cluster analysis of the dimensions that emerged from the first step then produced the corporate PAC taxonomy presented in Table 9. The results confirmed our basic contentions about corporate political behavior, in particular our predictions of corporate fragmentation and cohesion.

The 1980 principal components analysis of the corporate donation profiles yielded three dimensions. The first, accounting for 42 percent of the total variation in the percentages of contributions, tells

Table 5. Strategic Candidate Grouping for 1980

Group	Winners	Number of Candidates[a]	Group	Losers	Number of Candidates
1	Uncontested races (low contestability); relatively equal corporate and labor support (average CLDR);[b] conservative indifference (average CONRAT)	110	8	Nonviable candidates (low viability); relatively equal corporate and labor support; conservative indifference	60
2	Average contested races; relatively equal corporate and labor support; conservative indifference	84	9	Average viable candidates; relatively equal corporate and labor support; conservative indifference	41
3	Average contested races; relatively equal corporate and labor support; low conservative support	75	10	Average viable candidates; high labor support relative to corporate support; high "liberal" support	58
4	Average contested races; relatively equal corporate and labor support; high conservative support	67	11	Average viable candidates; relatively equal corporate and labor support; very high conservative support	9

Cluster	Description				
5	Average contested races; high labor support relative to corporate support (low CLDR); high "liberal" support[c]	23	12	Highly viable candidates; very high labor support relative to corporate support; very high "liberal" support	5
6	Average contested races; very high labor support relative to corporate support; high "liberal" support	22			5
7	Highly contested races; relatively equal corporate and labor support; high conservative support	29			

[a] A total of eight candidates did not cluster.
[b] See Table 4 for abbreviations.
[c] "Liberal" support implies the mean CONRAT score was negative.

Table 6. Strategic Candidate Grouping for 1982

Group	Winners	Number of Candidates	Group	Losers	Number of Candidates
1	Highly uncontested races; high labor support relative to business support (low BLDR);[a] conservative indifference	133	9	Nonviable candidates; medium labor support; conservative indifference	54
2	Uncontested races; high business support relative to labor support (high BLDR); conservative indifference	82	10	Nonviable candidates; low labor support; conservative indifference	76
3	Uncontested races; high business support relative to labor support; high conservative support	18	11	Highly viable candidates; low labor support; very high conservative support	36
4	Average contested races; high business support relative to labor support; high conservative support	25	12	Very highly viable candidates; low labor support; very high conservative support	15

5	Average contested races; high business support relative to labor support; very high conservative support	17	Highly viable candidates; medium labor support; high conservative support	13	14
6	Highly contested races; high business support relative to labor support; high conservative support	40	Average viable candidates; high labor support; very high "liberal" support	14	9
7	Average contested races; high labor support relative to business support; high "liberal" support	91			
8	Highly contested races; high labor support relative to business support; high "liberal" support	24			

[a]See Table 4 for abbreviations.

Table 7. Strategic Candidate Grouping for 1984

Group	Winners	Number of Candidates[a]	Group	Losers	Number of Candidates
1	Average contested races; high business/conservative support relative to labor/liberal support (high BCLLDR);[b] relatively equal economic interest-group and partisan support (average EIPDR)	118	8	Nonviable candidates; relatively equal labor/liberal and conservative support (average (LLCDR)	62
2	Uncontested races; relatively equal business/conservative and labor/liberal support; relatively equal economic interest-group and partisan support	192	9	Highly viable candidates; high conservative relative to labor/liberal support (low LLCDR)	25
3	Average contested races; high labor/liberal support relative to business/conservative (low BCLLDR) support; relatively equal economic interest-group and partisan support	38	10	Nonviable candidates; high labor/liberal relative to conservative support	15
4	Highly contested races; high business/conservative support relative to labor/liberal support; high partisan support relative to economic interest-group support	35	11	Average viable candidates; relatively equal labor/liberal and conservative support	29

5	Very highly contested races; high labor/liberal support relative to business/conservative support; relatively equal economic interest-group and partisan support	18	
6	Highly contested races; high business/conservative support relative to labor/liberal support; relatively equal economic interest-group and partisan support	13	
7	Average contested races; relatively equal business/conservative and labor/liberal support; high economic interest-group support relative to partisan support	19	12
	Average viable candidates; very high conservative relative to labor/liberal support		16

[a] Two candidates did not cluster.
[b] See Table 4 for abbreviations.

Table 8. Strategic Candidate Grouping for 1986

Group	Winners	Number of Candidates	Group	Losers	Number of Candidates
1	Uncontested races; high labor/liberal support relative to business/conservative support; relatively equal economic interest-group and partisan support	140	8	Highly nonviable candidates; low labor/liberal support	66
2	Average contested races; relatively equal business/conservative and labor/liberal support; relatively equal economic interest-group and partisan support	119	9	Average viable candidates; average labor/liberal support	35
3	Average contested races; high labor/liberal support relative to business/conservative support; high economic interest-group relative to partisan support	36	10	Very highly viable candidates; very low labor/liberal support	21
4	Highly contested races; very high business/conservative support relative to labor/liberal; partisan relative to economic interest-group support	25	11	Nonviable candidates; high labor/liberal support	23

				10
				Highly viable candidates; very high labor/liberal support
5	57	Average contested races; high business/conservative support relative to labor/liberal support; very high economic interest-group relative to partisan support	12	
6	39	Highly contested races; relatively equal business/conservative and labor/liberal support; very high partisan relative to economic interest-group support		
7	21	Very highly contested races; very high labor/liberal support relative to business/conservative support; relatively equal economic interest group and partisan support		

Table 9. Corporate PAC Strategic Groupings by Year

1980		1982		1984		1986	
Strategic Groups	Number of Corporate PACs	Strategic Groups	Number of Corporate PACs	Strategic Groups	Number of Corporate PACs	Strategic Groups	Number of Corporate PACs
Ideological/conservative strategy	93	Pragmatic business/conservative strategy	125	Pragmatic business/conservative strategy	143	Pragmatic business/conservative strategy	264
Pragmatic strategy	47						
Mixed strategy	66	Pragmatic labor/ liberal strategy	56	Ideological; business/conservative strategy	93	Ideological; business/conservative strategy	87
		Ideological/conservative strategy	139	Mixed business/ conservative strategy	164	Mixed business/ conservative strategy	75

us that corporate PAC managers contributed to two sets of candidate groups. One set consists of candidate groups 1, 2 and 3, whose elections were relatively uncontested. Candidates received relatively equal support from corporate and labor PACs and were strategically unimportant to conservative PACs. The second set consists of two clusters, 4 and 7. The races here were relatively contested, and the candidates attracted equal support from corporate and labor PACs and strong support from conservatives. Corporate PACs cohered by following a strategy that refused to give to candidate groups favored by labor PACs and "liberals"; they also fragmented by disagreeing over the support that each of these two candidate sets merited.

The second dimension, accounting for 15 percent of the variation in contributions, differentiates corporate PACs by the type of conservative clusters to which they contributed. Some corporate PACs favored candidate group 4, which had "high" conservative support, and others preferred candidate clusters 7 and 11. Cluster 11 is a small group of losers who received very high conservative support.

The third dimension, accounting for 11 percent of the variation in contributions, indicates that corporate PACs supported in varying degrees three winning groups (2, 4, 7) and two losing ones (8, 9). This dimension tells us how well PAC managers spent their marginal dollars.

Based on these three dimensions, we clustered the corporate PACs and identified three groups, as presented in Table 9. Approximately 42 percent of the corporate PACs pursued an ideological/conservative strategy, targeting strongly contested races overlapping conservative interests. Twenty-one percent were pragmatic: They favored candidates who ran in relatively uncontested races and to whom the conservative PACs were indifferent. The third group followed a mixed strategy by donating equally to candidates in both ideological/ conservative and nonideological groups.

Corporate PACs again cohered and divided. They agreed to withhold funds from labor/liberal candidate groups but disagreed on how best to allocate their funds among the acceptable candidate groups. As Table 9 indicates, some followed ideological/conservative strategies, and others were more pragmatic.

In 1982, corporate PAC donation profiles had four significant dimensions. The first, accounting for 34 percent of the total variation in contributions, shows that corporate PACs decided to favor either three winning candidate groups (1, 2, 7) or one losing group (11). The candidates in group 1 and 2 won uncontested races and received little if any support from conservatives, whereas the candidates in group 7 won contested races and received "liberal" support.

In contrast, the candidates in group 11 lost their races despite very strong conservative support.

The second dimension describes a trade-off between groups 2 and 6 and group 7. Corporate PAC managers in the main gave to a set of candidates favored either by business or conservatives or labor and "liberals." The other two dimensions describe similar sorts of decisions.

Table 9 shows distinct strategies for three corporate groups. The first is pragmatic (winner oriented) and supports business and conservative-leaning candidate clusters; the second is pragmatic and supports labor and liberal-leaning candidate clusters; and the third is ideological (loser oriented) and supports conservative candidate clusters.

At first blush, these contribution patterns suggest a wide divergence in corporate PAC strategies. But 57 percent of the PACs did pursue pragmatic (winner-oriented) strategies, albeit in support of different clusters, and the percentage of corporate PACs "ideologically" allied with conservatives remained relatively constant from 1980 to 1982. Moreover, regardless of strategy, the PACs consistently supported candidate group 2, almost all incumbents in uncontested races. Fifty-nine percent of these candidates were Republican, and they had relatively high U.S. Chamber of Commerce political ratings but received little conservative support. A kind of corporate PAC solidarity therefore did emerge in 1982, as PACs rallied to group 2's support in an election year when adverse economic circumstances worked against probusiness candidates.

The three dimensions of corporate PAC donation profiles in 1984 account for 48 percent, 18 percent, and 11 percent of the variation in contributions. Corporate PACs targeted four candidate groups (1, 2, 4 and 9), not one of which had strong support from labor or liberal PACs. As in 1980, they cohered by refusing to give to candidate groups that were of strategic importance to labor and liberal PACs.

But they still disagreed on the best way to allocate funds to sympathetic candidate groups. The first dimension tells us that they tended to give either to candidates in group 1 and 2, who were in relatively easy races, or to candidates in group 4 and 9, who were not. Conservatives' support was strong for both the winners in group 4 and the losers in group 7. PACs supporting groups 1 and 2 acted pragmatically, funneling funds to candidates in relatively easy elections. In support of group 1, they also acted conservatively, giving to candidates with strong business and conservative backing. In contrast, PACs who favored groups 4 and 9 behaved ideologically, targeting candidate groups in contested elections.

The second dimension captures another decision over which managers disagreed: the allocation of funds between groups 1 and 2. Unlike the first two dimensions, the third does not have contrasting components but simply ranks the four candidate groups by the amounts of corporate PAC contributions received. As expected, candidates in contested races received more money, producing the ordering of 4, 9, 2, and 1.

A cluster analysis of the corporate PACs along these three dimensions produced three corporate PAC strategic groups. In general, the PACs were divided in varying degrees between an ideological business/conservative strategy and a pragmatic business/conservative one. Table 9 indicates that 143, or 36 percent, of the corporate PACs pursued a pragmatic strategy and that 93, or 23 percent, pursued an ideological one. The remaining 41 percent fell somewhere in between, following a mixed business/conservative strategy. When compared with the numbers in 1980 and 1982, these percentages show a pragmatic reorientation of corporate PAC giving.

There are three meaningful dimensions for 1986, and they account for 39 percent, 28 percent, and 11 percent of the variation in corporate PAC contributions. Just as in 1980, 1982, and 1984, corporate PACs declined to fund candidate groups that secured labor and liberal PAC financing. Once more, they acted collectively in rejecting campaign solicitations from labor/liberal candidate groups. But this solidarity again had its limitations: They continued to split along pragmatic and ideological business/conservative lines.

The first dimension pits candidate groups 2 and 5 against 4 and 10. The first two were winning groups, with group 5 receiving substantial business and conservative support. The second set received considerable business/conservative support. Candidates who ran in highly contested races comprise group 4, and well-funded losing candidates, group 10. The second dimension captures a contest between groups 2 and 5, and the third dimension indexes the two candidate groups, 4 and 5, that received the corporate PACs' marginal funds.

Table 9 indicates that when the corporate PACs were clustered along these three dimensions, three corporate PAC strategic groups emerged. Much as in 1984, two were at either extreme of the pragmatic/ideological continuum, and one was in the middle. But in 1984, although there was a distinct shift from the ideological giving in 1980 and 1982 toward pragmatism, a considerable number of PACs still pursued a middle course. By 1986, corporate PACs appeared to have disavowed an ideological orientation.[54] Fully 62 percent pursued a pragmatic business/conservative strategy.

For each election year, we also analyzed the corporate PAC strate-

Table 10. Important Economic Factors for a Strategic Grouping

Election Year	Important Factors
1980	Industrial sector/market orientation
1982	Industrial sector/market orientation/geographic location
1984	Industrial sector/market orientation
1986	Industrial sector/market orientation/geographic location

gic groups by using the five qualitative economic variables introduced at the beginning of this section. Table 10 indicates that in a given election year, firms congregate in groups according to their economic characteristics, some of which are more important than others.

For example, in the 1980 corporate PAC strategic grouping, multinational energy companies congregated in the ideological/conservative strategic group, whereas defense-related, high-technology firms showed a clear preference for the pragmatic strategic group. Firm-specific donation patterns apparently add up to economically comprehensible strategies for political advantage.

CONCLUSIONS

The statistical analyses confirmed our prediction of corporate cohesion and fragmentation. In the 1980, 1984, and 1986 election years, which boded well for conservatives, corporate PACs adopted a sectorwide strategy to join conservative PACs against labor unions and liberals. However, in the recession year 1982, when conservative candidates were on the defensive, a substantial number pursued a pragmatic strategy that favored candidate groups heavily backed by labor PACs and liberals. The defection is striking because other corporate PAC strategic groups in this unpromising election acted as good corporate citizens by holding fast to the conservative alliance.

Despite this discord, a coherent strategy did emerge in 1982. The corporate PACs rallied to support and reward a group of probusiness candidates whom the conservative PACs ignored financially. In coming to aid of this group, they showed that sectorwide cooperation was possible even in an adverse election year.

On the other hand, cooperation failed to suppress factious self-interest. Even in 1980, 1984, and 1986, disagreements arose over how vigorously to honor the alliance with conservatives. Some corporate PACs pursued an ideological donation strategy that roughly mimicked conservatives by targeting candidates in closely contested races. The second group donated pragmatically by supporting candidates in safe elections, and the third followed a mixed strategy. In 1982, those corporate PACs that adhered to the conservative strategy split into ideological and pragmatic groupings over targeting contested or uncontested races; the corporate sector was doubly divided in this election year.

The analyses also show that the corporate political strategic groups were made up of firms that shared similar economic characteristics. The most important predictors were industrial sector and multinational character.

Corporate-sector cohesion grows out of an antagonism with labor. There is a definite relationship between campaign chests and electoral approval. Another dimension speaks directly, if softly, to our proposition that "class struggle" promotes corporate solidarity: Labor union PAC money and corporation and trade association funds are inversely related. A parallel antagonism exists between conservative and liberal PAC donations, and the different interests of business and conservatives compared with labor and liberals provides a compelling reason for corporate PACs to cohere. Nevertheless, even though corporate PACs held to business principles in 1980, 1984, and 1986, a substantial number broke from the ranks in 1982 by following a donation strategy that embraced labor/liberal candidates.

The analyses also offered insight into the corporate PACs' reward/punishment disbursement policy. PACs tended to oppose or withdraw support from incumbents who paid too little attention to their interests and to support candidates who promised to make those interests central. Thus, in 1980, 1984, and 1986, when conservatism had substantial opportunities, corporate PACs allied with conservative PACs to support them. In 1982, when conservatives were clearly on the defensive and cottoning to other interests, a number adopted a prolabor/liberal contribution strategy. Their collective self-interest was better served by defensively targeting probusiness candidates who were of little interest to conservative PACs as a whole. During the first two elections, corporate PAC dollars also flowed to vulnerable incumbents, or promising challengers in close elections were targeted to aid friends and punish foes.

But in 1984, corporate PACs, on average, ignored partisanship and acted practically by giving disproportionately to friends and powerful incumbents. The data offer little insight into this shift from ideology to pragmatism. Perhaps the legislative victories of Reagan's first administration sated their political appetite. Perhaps the Democrats' resurgence in 1982 and their new responsiveness to corporate-sector proposals on economic matters persuaded corporate PAC managers that efforts for a political realignment were both irrelevant and politically precarious. Or perhaps corporate managers' "enlightened self-interest" made them sensitive to the limits of their political activism. All of these factors would indicate the inherent pragmatism in the corporate sector's political collectivity and so can be analyzed with the cost–benefit framework of collective action. There is more work ahead of us.

12

Afterword

In our opening pages, we described our teacherly interest in introducing MBA students to the ongoing discussions of management's professional responsibilities in America's democratic order. Our method of presentation has been historical, but many of our themes have come from collective-action theory and continue to constitute the analytic core in a number of standard MBA courses. The prospective practitioner, who will be making history and not chronicling it, may find our story a bit wanting, for it offers no rules for action. Without presuming to offer guides for action or predictions about the future, in this afterword we tender some comments for managers and policymakers to consider as working propositions when they evaluate private and public rules to reconcile the market's demands for efficiency with the polity's demands for self-government.

We left the 1980s with the managerial firm under serious public scrutiny. Management's stewardship has proved itself neither in the political alliances that were to help promulgate policies conducive to long-term economic growth nor in its role as the corporation's mediator among its basic constituencies. We find the notion of managerial stewardship to be anachronistic. The interpretation of contract offered by libertarians and agency theorists also falls short. They fail to understand either the firm's cooperative nature or management's role in motivating employees and committed shareholders to collaborate in differentiating and improving the firm's product. We subscribe instead to the form of contract that treats management as primarily communicative and democracy principally as participatory. The firm then emerges as a potentially self-governing, developmental organization. Although rooted in the literature of historians and political scientists, this approach has also been given a modern boost by recent applications of game theory to microeconomics. Ideally, managers would be impartial arbitrators who appraised stakeholder proposals for setting the enterprise's basic strategies and distributive policies and who reconciled differences to bring about bargaining solutions that satisfied all parties. In fact, disparities in power may force agreements or discourage certain parties from participating fully, so managers must continually review the conditions that lie behind current problems. In these circumstances, operational as well as financial know-how must be at work. Moreover, managers simply cannot avoid considering issues of fairness within the firm or asking broad questions about how the nation's institutional arrangements affect relative bargaining power.

To act as effective arbitrators, managers must rely on the governance structure as the basic forum in which the firm's constituents voice their opinions. Yet as late as 1990, managers demonstrated hardly any interest in drawing either shareholders or employees into the corporation's governing process. Quite the contrary. They resolutely opposed such participation, continuing to establish boards that limited major shareholder influence, proposing reforms that would reduce the number of outside board members, and lobbying for state antitakeover legislation that would prevent interested shareholders from using the market to dislodge them.

But autocratic, as opposed to "democratic," management no longer works. First a flourishing market in corporate control gave shareholders a way to discipline managers. Takeover markets may have become economically and politically less tenable by the late 1980s, but large institutional investors have found an admirable substitute. Because concentrated ownership has reduced the cost of coordinated shareholder action, in good pluralist fashion, they have formed shareholder groups to monitor management actively. It is now costeffective, for example, to organize shareholders' advisory committees to perform business audits that evaluate a firm's strategy over both a long period of time and a vector of variables including market position, innovation, productivity, human resource management, and financial performance.

A disgruntled committee may bring pressure to bear through the board's nominating procedures or by initiating a proxy battle at a shareholders' meeting. Avon's top managers regularly meet with outside directors and its major investors to review the firm's strategic plan. The California Public Employees Retirement System, the New York State Common Retirement Fund, and the Connecticut State Treasurer's Office have jointly pressured several dozen firms to put a majority of outside directors on their boards' nominating committees.[1] In our view, professional managers should welcome these actions and promote their development, for they facilitate the kind of dialogue necessary for solidifying the firm as a cooperative undertaking.

In the future, major shareholders will include employees as well as institutional investors. Employee stock ownership plans (ESOPs) have become increasingly popular because they provide patient (long-term) and flexible corporate financing. Corporate financial officers use these plans to buy back stock, issue new shares, spinoff new business units, restructure the firm's capital base, and assist in bankruptcies. ESOPs also dispense relatively inexpensive employee benefits that are directly tied to the firm's performance.[2] By linking remuneration to performance, ESOPs radically depart from traditional union negotiation patterns that historically sought industrywide fixed-wage increases and provided employee benefits by engaging in adversarial negotiations that paid little attention to the firm's needs.[3] Managers themselves have instituted a large number of ESOP plans; in fact, more workers now "belong" to firms with greater than 4 percent employee ownership than there are workers in private-sector unions.[4]

ESOPs ask employees to take additional risks by essentially putting their savings and their careers in the same basket. As Carnegie would have it, they then watch that basket! The extra risk increases their incentive to become active shareholders, and like institutional investors, they are insisting on more participation in the firm's governance.

Rather than seeing this new demand as an irksome challenge to their authority, as in years past, perhaps managers should welcome it as a way to effect the reorganization necessary to compete in global markets. The success of operational techniques like "just in time" and "total quality management" requires worker participation at the plant level;[5] the advanced manufacturing technology that combines computer science and engineering does so as well.[6] When these operational and technological innovations take place in companies with effective and far-reaching employee representation programs, the productivity gains can be significant.[7]

MIT's Industrial Productivity Center has already plotted changes in American manufacturing's productivity growth starting around 1987.[8] Although no studies have systematically accounted for these improvements, preliminary evidence suggests that managers' commitment to improving their product's quality and delivery by instituting total quality management and just in time has been making a difference.[9] So too do efforts, initiated by the large original equipment manufacturers (OEMs), to rely more heavily than before on suppliers to improve on products and processes that go into the making of a final product such as a computer or an automobile.[10] These changes too demand that managers become less dictatorial and that they rely more on horizontal and collaborative organizational arrangements.[11]

In addition to all these novelties, however, in our view unionization remains an additional valuable tool. Sometimes the threat itself suffices to encourage managers to adopt "progressive" human resource management programs. Workers could also gain bargaining power by instituting laws requiring companies over a certain size to establish nonunion employee participation committees.[12] These committees could represent employee interests on issues such as dismissals, plant closings, technological innovation, and the formation and oversight of an ESOP. Managers have historically resisted any legal devices for easing unionization and initiating nonmanagement-sponsored employee involvement programs,[13] but we suggest that such opposition has become self-defeating. Without union pressure or mandatory employee participatory programs, managers will be slow to adopt participatory management techniques and so will miss opportunities for enhancing their firms' competitive capabilities.

Increasing participation will force internal redistributions within the firm, narrowing the income differentials between management and production workers and bringing compensation at the top to levels more like what we see in other nations.[14] If managers continue to institute ESOPs and to accept employee representation, we may even witness a general restructuring in corporate ownership, one that induces managers to shift their allegiance from the wealthy to the less advantaged: Pension funds and other institutional investors already account for approximately 40 percent of the shares traded, with 10 percent of the nation's households commanding most of the rest.[15]

A management dedicated to developmental and egalitarian ends may seem foreign to America's managerial culture. Nevertheless, as the ideas of global management rapidly turn into everyday practices, the demand for a global managerial ethics will become increasingly urgent. American managers will have to compete not only on the basis of technique but of democratic values as well. Why should nations around the world tolerate the presence of American-run firms in their political economies, unless these firms are as self-conscious about their role in developing their host nations as are their Asian and European counterparts?

Still, developmental and egalitarian values have a long tradition in American history, with advocates as admirable and widely acknowledged as Louis Brandeis and Robert Dahl. Not so long ago, managers like Owen Young and Gerard Swope also pressed their own ranks to develop a professional ethic and collective identity to align the large corporation with America's democratic heritage. American managers and business educators must now recapture these values.

NOTES

Chapter 1

1. Edward S. Mason, "Introduction," in *The Corporation in Modern Society*, ed. Edward S. Mason (New York: Atheneum, 1974), p. 5.

2. Lee E. Preston, *Social Issues and Public Policy in Business and Management: Retrospect and Prospect,* Center for Business and Public Policy, University of Maryland, August 1986.

3. See, for example, Alfred D. Chandler, Jr., *The Visible Hand: The Managerial Revolution in American Business* (Cambridge, MA.: Belknap Press, 1977).

4. For a review of this literature, see Louis Galambos, "The Emerging Organizational Synthesis in Modern American History," *Business History Review* 44 (1970): 279–290, and "Technology, Political Economy, and Professionalization: Central Themes of the organizational Synthesis," *Business History Review* 57 (1983): 471–493; as well as Ellis Hawley, "The Discovery and Study of a 'Corporate Liberalism,'" *Business History Review* 52 (1978): 309–320.

5. Ellis W. Hawley, *The New Deal and the Problem of Monopoly: A Study in Economic Ambivalence* (Princeton, NJ: Princeton University Press, 1966).

6. Martin J. Sklar, *The Corporate Reconstruction of American Capitalism, 1890–1916: The Market, the Law, and Politics* (Cambridge: Cambridge University Press, 1988).

7. Allen Kaufman, *Capitalism, Slavery and Republican Values: Antebellum Political Economists, 1815–1848* (Austin: University of Texas Press, 1982).

8. Friedrich A. von Hayek, *The Constitution of Liberty* (Chicago: University of Chicago Press, 1960), p. 11.

Chapter 2

1. The broad line of agreement described here has emerged despite contentions on the importance of the Scottish Enlightenment, Locke, Calvinism, and republican theory on the founders' motivations. For a recent review of this literature, one conforming to the outline presented here, see Thomas L. Pangle, *The Spirit of Modern Republicanism: The Moral Vision of the American Founders and the Philosophy of Locke* (Chicago: University of Chicago Press, 1988). John P. Diggins, *The Lost Soul of American Politics: Virtue, Self-Interest, and the Foundation of Liberalism* (New York: Basic Books, 1984), offers similar

conclusions on the issue of property rights and constitutional norms, even though he stressed American Protestant impulses. J. G. A. Pocock provides the standard interpretation of the American Revolution as a continuing part of the classic republican tradition, in his *The Machiavellian Moment: Florentine Republican Thought and the Atlantic Republican Tradition* (Princeton, NJ: Princeton University Press, 1975). For a general review of the literature tracing classical republican thought on the founders, see Robert E. Shalhope, "Republicanism and Early American Historiography," *William and Mary Quarterly* 39 (1982): 335–356. For a discussion of how economic ideas and political ideals interacted in the early republic and later into the antebellum period, see Drew R. McCoy, *The Elusive Republic: Political Economy in Jeffersonian America* (Chapel Hill: University of North Carolina Press, 1980); and Allen Kaufman, *Capitalism, Slavery and Republican Values: Antebellum Political Economists, 1815–1848* (Austin: University of Texas Press, 1982).

2. William E. Nelson, *The Roots of American Bureaucracy, 1830–1900* (Cambridge, MA: Harvard University Press, 1982), pp. 15–16.

3. In particular, see Alan Ryan, *Property and Political Theory* (Oxford: Basil Blackwell, 1984).

4. See, for example, *The Federalist* no. 45 (Madison), on the states' retention of powers. In general, the colonies and then states during the late eighteenth century granted charters regularly to nonprofit enterprises in the corporate form, including towns, religious societies, and educational institutions. See Ronald E. Seavoy, *The Origins of the American Business Corporation, 1784–1855: Broadening the Concept of Public Service During Industrialization* (Westport, CT: Greenwood Press, 1982), pp. 3–38. Apparently, debates surrounding the Constitution raised few questions about these state powers. Land companies, the principal eighteenth-century precursors of the business corporation, did provoke constitutional discussion—see *The Federalist* no. 7 (Hamilton)—but largely on issues of territorial sovereignty, not powers of incorporation. Alexander Hamilton's "Report on a National Bank," *History of Congress,* Dec. 14, 1790 (Appendix), pp. 2032–2060, raises constitutional issues surrounding federal incorporation powers. On the status of the business corporation around the time of independence, see Shaw Livermore, *Early American Land Companies: Their Influence on Corporate Development,* ed. Julius Goebel, Jr. (Cambridge, MA: Harvard University Press, 1939), pp. vii–xxvi, and 61–69; and Joseph S. Davis, *Essays in the Earlier History of American Corporations,* 2 vols. (Cambridge, MA: Harvard University Press, 1917), vol. 1, pp. 3–29 and vol. 2, pp. 3–33.

5. See Hendrick Hartog, *Public Property and Private Power: The Corporation of the City of New York in American Law, 1730–1870* (Chapel Hill: University of North Carolina Press, 1983), pp. 179–258; Gerald E. Frug, "The City as a Legal Concept," *Harvard Law Review* 93 (1980): 1099–1120; and William Joseph Novak, "*Salus Populi:* The Roots of Regulation in America, 1787–1873" (Ph.D. diss., Harvard University, 1992), pp. 1–106.

6. In formal terms, the license to incorporate was subject to control by the legislature's reserved powers. This idea had become a part of doctrine through Chief Justice Taney's decision in *Charles River Bridge v. Warren Bridge,* 11 *Peters* 420 (1837). For a discussion, see Stanley I. Kutler, *Privilege*

and Creative Destruction: The Charles River Bridge Case (Philadelphia: Lippincott, 1971), pp. 133–171.

7. This, according to Morton J. Horwitz, "*Santa Clara* Revisited: The Development of Corporate Theory," *West Virginia Law Review* 88 (1985): 173–224, was the doctrine essentially reflected in the Supreme Court's decision in *Santa Clara County v. Southern Pacific Railroad,* 118 *U.S.* 394 (1886).

8. The conventional, post–New Deal view was spelled out in Howard J. Graham, "An Innocent Abroad: The Constitutional Corporate 'Person'," *U.C.L.A. Law Review* 2 (1955): 155–211: "The very corporations spawned by and waxing fat on public subsidies, for example soon were fighting public regulation. . . . Legislatures generally had issued the charters and often rendered aid in the first instance; state and federal courts took over increasingly thereafter. Because cupidity has a broad solid base, and because nineteenth century legislators and corporate promoters, whatever their limitations, certainly were representative in this, the judiciary from the first had a great deal to do. . . . What it eventually did, of course, in dealing with corporate rights and status, was to hold that corporations were artificial "persons" *in the constitutional sense,* under the Fourteenth and the Fifth Amendments. . . . States were thus forbidden to deprive any (corporate) person of property without due process of law (or to deny any (corporate) person the equal protection of the laws" (pp. 158–160, italics in original). Although more recent historiography—most important, Horwitz, "*Santa Clara*"—has shaded the edges of Graham's factual premises, it does not contradict his conclusion that the courts eventually sided with the private view of the business corporation. James Willard Hurst, *The Legitimacy of the Business Corporation in the Law of the United States, 1780–1970* (Charlottesville: University of Virginia Press, 1970).

9. This is the standard take—see Hurst, *The Legitimacy,* pp. 13–46. For concurring elaborations, see Lawrence M. Friedman, *A History of American Law,* 2nd ed. (New York: Simon & Schuster, 1985), pp. 188–201; Davis, *Essays,* vol. 2, pp. 3–329; Seavoy, *The Origins,* pp. 53–104, 177–190; and E. Merrick Dodd, *American Business Corporations Until 1860, with Special Reference to Massachusetts* (Cambridge, MA: Harvard University Press, 1954).

10. Louis Hartz, *Economic Policy and Democratic Thought* (Cambridge, MA: Harvard University Press, 1948), pp. 37–42; Edwin Merrick Dodd, Jr., "The First Half Century of Statutory Regulation of Business Corporations in Massachusetts," in *Harvard Legal Essays in Honor of Joseph Henry Beale and Samuel Williston* (Cambridge, MA: Harvard University Press, 1934), pp. 66–68; and Oscar Handlin and Mary Handlin, *Commonwealth: A Study of the Role of Government in the American Economy—Massachusetts, 1774–1861* (Cambridge, MA: Belknap Press, 1969), pp. 161–181. Indeed, during the earlier part of the century, many corporations, both municipal and business, were explicitly "mixed." See Hartog, *Public Property,* pp. 44–175; and Hartz, *Economic Policy,* pp. 82–128.

11. Hartz, *Economic Policy,* pp. 37–42, 69–81; Handlin and Handlin, *Commonwealth,* pp. 203–228.

The corporate charters of railroads. for example, empowered promoters to take private lands by means of eminent domain, to raise funds by enforcing subscriptions, to operate roads without fencing or other safety precautions warranted at the time by the common law governing private conduct, and eventually to escape liability for a variety of activities. See Seavoy, *The Origins*, pp. 199–216; George R. Taylor, *The Transportation Revolution 1815–1860* (Armonk, N.Y.: M.E. Sharpe, 1951), pp. 86–103; and Morton J. Horwitz, *The Transformation of American Law 1780–1860* (Cambridge, MA: Harvard University Press, 1977), pp. 69–71, 135–139.

12. See Hurst, *The Legitimacy*, pp. 30–57; Friedman, *A History*, pp. 511–521.

13. See John F. Kasson, *Civilizing the Machine: Technology and Republican Values in America, 1776–1900* (New York: Grossman Publishers, 1976), pp. 68–86; and Christopher L. Tomlins, "A Mysterious Power: Industrial Accidents and the Legal Construction of Employment Relations in Massachusetts, 1800–1850," *Law and History Review* 6(1988):375–438. For pamphlets of the period advocating corporate enlightenment, see Michael B. Folsom and Steven D. Lubar, eds., *The Philosophy of Manufactures: Early Debates over Industrialization of the United States* (Cambridge, MA: MIT Press, 1982), pp. 241–345.

14. Kasson, *Civilizing*, pp. 86–106; Tomlins, "A Mysterious Power."

15. Handlin and Handlin, *Commonwealth*, pp. 174–181; Carter Goodrich, ed., *The Government and the Economy, 1783–1861* (Indianapolis: Bobbs-Merrill, 1967), pp. 377–405.

16. On the both the earlier and the later significance of the "contract clause" in American constitutional law, see C. Peter Magrath, *Yazoo: Law and Politics in the New Republic: The Case of Fletcher v. Peck* (Providence: Brown University Press, 1966), pp. 101–117. Kutler, *Privilege and Creative Destruction*, pp. 133–171, also elaborated on the doctrinal impact and constitutional significance of the case.

17. *Dartmouth College v. Woodward*, 4 Wheaton 518, 636 (1819). Marshall continued as follows: "Being the mere creature of law it possesses only those properties which the charter of its creation confers upon it, either expressly or as incidental to its very existence. These are such as are supposed best calculated to effect the object for which it was created. Among the most important are immortality and, if the expression may be allowed, individuality; properties by which a perpetual succession of many persons are considered as the same and may act as a single individual."

18. See Alfred D. Chandler, Jr., *The Visible Hand: The Managerial Revolution in American Business* (Cambaridge, MA: Belknap Press, 1977), pp. 145–187, for a description of managerial innovations in the relatively more closely regulated railroad industry, innovations that then carried over into the management of other industries capable of taking advantage of general incorporation laws. The latter soon outstripped the former, in part because they were not as restricted (see pp. 209–286). To what extent the railroads were in fact restricted from innovating managerially by the nature of their franchises, or special grants, is not clear. See the contrasting views, for example, of Gabriel Kolko, *Railroads and Regulation 1877–1916* (Princeton, NJ: Princeton University Press, 1965); and Albro Martin, *Enterprise Denied: Origins of the Decline of American Railroads, 1897–1917* (New York: Columbia University Press, 1971).

19. On the direct effects, see Robert H. Wiebe, *Businessmen and Reform: A Study of the Progressive Movement* (Cambridge, MA: Harvard University Press, 1962), and, more recently, Martin J. Sklar, *The Corporate Reconstruction of American Capitalism, 1890–1916: The Market, the Law, and Politics* (Cambridge: Cambridge University Press, 1988). On the broader influence of incorporation on American society, see Robert H. Wiebe, *The Search for Order 1877–1920* (New York: Hill & Wang, 1967). See also the more general and more remote, yet still relevant, Alan Trachtenberg, *The Incorporation of America: Culture and Society in the Gilded Age* (New York: Hill & Wang, 1982); and Peter D. Hall, *The Organization of American Culture, 1700–1900: Private Institutions, Elites, and the Origins of American Nationality* (New York: NYU Press, 1984).

20. Nelson, *The Roots of American Bureaucracy*, pp. 10–16, noted that grants came to replace regulation early in the nineteenth century as a tool of government, in part because lawmakers could achieve majoritarian consensus by conferring benefits widely, whereas restrictive legislation promoted disagreement.

21. In 1762, for instance, Adam Smith noted that the principal function of government is "to maintain justice," in other words, to prevent individuals from seizing what does not belong to them. When this end is secured, he continued, "the government will next be desirous of promoting the opulence of the state. This produces what we call police." Regulations effecting commerce and manufacturing belong to the state's police powers. Adam Smith, *Lectures on Jurisprudence,* ed. R. L. Meek, D. D. Raphael, and P. G. Stein (Oxford: Clarendon Press, 1978), p. 5. On Smith's elaboration of the police powers, see pp. 331–394, 486–541.

22. The leading cases in this regard involved the federal commerce clause powers, specifically the degree to which they preempted state action, and the retention of parallel state police powers over such matters as immigration and harbor navigation, in *New York v. Miln,* 11 *Peters* 102 (1837), and *Cooley v. Board of Wardens,* 12 *Howard* 299 (1852), respectively. For a discussion, see Maurice G. Baxter, *The Steamboat Monopoly: Gibbons v. Ogden, 1824* (New York: Knopf, 1972), pp. 69–133.

23. On the adoption of the Fourteenth Amendment and its aftermath, see William E. Nelson, *The Fourteenth Amendment: From Political Principle to Judicial Doctrine* (Cambridge, MA: Harvard University Press, 1988).

24. The court applied varing forms of "rules of reason" to federal regulations as well; they led increasingly to bothsensitivity to social conditions and attentiveness to the observations of institutional, as well as theoretical, social scientists.

References to a "rule of reason" tended to be associated with the doctrinal development of the Sherman Act—see, for example, William Letwin, *Law and Economic Policy in America: The Evolution of the Sherman Antitrust Act* (New York: Random House, 1966), pp. 167–181, 253–270—in which the Court eventually reinterpreted Congress's prohibition on "contracts in restraint of trade" as contracts that unreasonably restrained trade. Yet the Court's inference of reasonable means and ends, both in legislative interpretation and in judging the constitutional legitimacy of regulation, was a growing business, not limited merely to antitrust. In coming to grips with what was reasonable, the Court gradually moved from hunches, presuppositions, and precedents about norm to facts, empirical studies and social scientific inquiry—see John Hart Ely, *Democracy and Distrust* (Cambridge, MA: Harvard University Press, 1980), pp. 200–236; and Paul L. Rosen, *The Supreme Court and Social Science* (Urbana: University of Illinois Press, 1972). On the perception of norm during the earlier era, see Michael L. Benedict, "Laissez-Faire and Liberty: A Re-Evaluation of the Meaning and Origins of Laissez-Faire Consitutional-ism," *Law and History Review* 3 (1985): 293–331.

25. Much of the doctrine grew out of the Delphic rule in *Smyth v. Ames,* p. 169 *U.S.* 466 (1898), which held essentially that the states could regulate rates so long as they did not, in effect, expropriate the "fair value" of the corporation's capital—that is, use price controls to transfer wealth, taking from the owners or creditors and giving to the consumers.

26. John R. Commons and John B. Andrews, *Principles of Labor Legislation* (New York: Harper & Row, 1920 [1916]), provided an appraisal of constitutionality in general (pp. 5–34, 458–465) and of the particular kinds of protective labor legislation (pp. 216–220 [minimum wage] and pp. 262–271 [maximum hours]). See also Margaret Anna Schaffner, "The Labor Contract from Individual to Collective Bargaining," *Bulletin of the University of Wisconsin, Economics and Political Science Series,* 2 (1907): 1–14.

27. Kermit L. Hall, *The Magic Mirror: Law in American History* (New York: Oxford University Press, 1989), p. 369, summarizing Melvin I. Urofsky, "State Courts."

28. See Edward S. Corwin, "The Supreme Court and the Fourteenth Amendment," reprinted in Corwin, *American Constitutional History* (New York: Harper & Row, 1964). The Munn case is reported at 94 *U.S.* 113.

29. See C. Peter Magrath, "The Case of the Unscrupulous Warehouseman," in *Quarrels That Have Shaped the Constitution,* ed. John A. Garraty (New York: Harper & Row, 1962); and Carl B. Swisher, *Stephen J. Field: Craftsman of the Law* (Chicago: University of Chicago Pess, 1969), pp. 362–395.

30. Quoted in Magrath, "The Case," p. 124.

31. Thomas Cooley, *General Principles of Constitutional Law in the United States* (Boston: Little, Brown, 1880), pp. 227–236. Cooley quoted at length the Supreme Court's decision in *Veazie v. Moor,* 14 *Howard* 568, 574 (18[73]) to describe the states' implied powers, which he did not immediately label "police powers" (p. 67). Earlier American treatises refer to the states' reserved powers under the Tenth Amendment in more general terms. See, for example, Theophilus Parsons, *Political, Personal and Property Rights of a Citizen of the United States* (Cincinnati: National Publishing Co., 1875). Edwin Cannan's edition of Smith's lectures on the police powers was apparently first published in 1896. See in that book, note 78, the editors' "Introduction," p. 5, by which time the Supreme Court was beginning to invoke "police powers" regularly as a way of defining state authority.

32. See William M. Wiecek, *Liberty under Law* (Baltimore: Johns Hopkins University Press, 1988), p. 116.

33. This strategy, on the other hand, had the practical effect of pressing the Supreme Court to deny states the power to regulate virtually all corpora-

tions, domestic as well as foreign. See, for example, *Allgeyer v. Louisiana,* 165 *U.S.* 578 (1897). The Court's earlier resolution of the foreign corporation dilemma was in *Bank of Augusta v. Earle,* 38 *U.S.* 519 (1839). The problem of the foreign corporation persisted into the next century. See Horwitz, "Santa Clara," pp. 216–222; and Charles W. McCurdy, "The Knight Sugar Decision of 1895 and the Modernization of American Corporation Law, 1869–1903," *Business History Review* 53(1979): 304–342.

34. *Santa Clara County v. Southern Pacific Railroad,* 118 *U.S.* 394 (1886).

35. Horwitz, "*Santa Clara,*" pp. 176–179. Unlike constitutional historians in the progressive tradition of Charles Beard and John R. Commons, who saw this case as a glaring symbol of Court subservence to Big Business and laissez-faire attitude, Horwitz argued that it was not inconsistent with earlier constitutional conceptions of the corporation. He insisted that such proponents of freeing corporate enterprise as John Norton Pomeroy, who defended the corporation in the *Santa Clara* case, claimed only that the voluntary, spontaneous association of individuals to do business was an extension of private property rights and personal freedoms guaranteed under the federal Constitution and in that respect was impervious to state control. Only in the following decade did this concept of the corporate person became distorted, when discussions of group personality convinced legal scholars of the corporation's irreducibility.

36. See Wiecek, *Liberty and Law,* p. 118.

37. Charles F. Bostwick, *Legislative Competition for Corporate Capital* ((Nw York: Charles Bostwick, 1899). For a more recent appraisal of the "race for the bottom," see Horwitz, "Santa Clara," pp. 190–197. But compare, for instance, the interpretation of Frank Easterbrook and Daniel Fischel, *The Economic Structure of Corporate Law* (Cambridge, MA: Harvard University Press, 1991), that such legislative competition represents a "race for the top," reflecting the political majority's (economic) aspirations rather than a political minority's (i.e., the corporate interests') corruptions.

38. Edward Q. Keasbey, "New Jersey and the Great Corporations," *Harvard Law Review* 13 (1899): 198–212, 264–278.

39. Ibid., pp. 193–197; and McCurdy, "The Knight Sugar Decision." James Bonbright and Gardiner Means, *The Holding Company* (New York: McGraw-Hill, 1932) describe the growth of the device and ensuing enactments.

40. See Nelson, *The Roots of American Bureaucracy,* pp. 15–16. Chief Justice Taney's decision in *Dred Scott v. Sandford,* 60 *U.S.* 393 (1857) was, of course, the most egregious exception to the rule favoring the mobility of oppressed minorities.

41. See Harold Stoke, "Economic Influences upon the Corporation Laws of New Jersey," *Journal of Political Economy* 38 (1930): 551–579; and McCurdy, "The Knight Sugar Decision."

42. See Horwitz, "*Santa Clara*"; and McCurdy, "The Knight Sugar Decision."

43. President Teddy Roosevelt initiated *Northern Securities Co. v. U.S.* (1904), which challenged J. P. Morgan, J. J. Hill, and Edward Harriman's attempt to consolidate competing Chicago-bound transcontinental rail lines

into one holding company. The Court held that the commerce clause empowered the federal government to regulate not only interstate traffic but also the underlying securities transactions and incorporation that had resulted in a monopoly of that trade. See Letwin, *Law and Economic Policy in America*, pp. 100–270.

44. Kolko, *Railroads and Regulation*, pp. 45–176.

45. See Adolf A. Berle, Jr., "The Expansion of American Administrative Law," *Harvard Law Review* 30 (1917): 430–448, p. 445.

46. See Nelson, *The Roots of American Bureaucracy;* and Stephen Skowronek, *Building a New American State* (Cambridge [Cambridgeshire]; New York: Cambridge University Press, 1982).

47. See Samuel P. Hays, *The Response to Industrialism: 1885–1914* (Chicago: University of Chicago Press, 1957); and Richard Hofstadter, *The Age of Reform: From Bryan to F.D.R.* (New York: Knopf, 1955).

48. Ibid.

49. See John B. Clark, *Control of Trusts* (New York: Macmillan, 1900). Mergers certainly continued apace: Between 1895 and 1904, more than 1,800 firms disappeared in the process of at least 150 significant consolidations. See Lamoreaux, *The Great Merger Movement* (Cambridge [Cambridgeshire]; New York: Cambridge University Press, 1985), pp. 1–6.

50. Horwitz, "*Santa Clara.*"

51. Thus, John P. Davis's citizen "discovers, in fine, that citizenship in his country has been largely metamorphosed into membership in corporations and patriotism into fidelity to them." John P. Davis, *Corporations: A Study of the Origin and Development of Great Business Combinations and of Their Relation to the Authority of the State* (New York: Capricorn Books, 1961), p. 281.

52. The literature was set forth in part by Horwitz, "*Santa Clara*"; Charles Jesse Bullock, "Trust Literature; a Survey and a Criticism," *The Quarterly Journal of Economics* 15 (February 1901); John Dewey, "The Historical Background of Corporate Legal Personality," *Yale Law Journal* 35 (1926): 655–673; and Max Radin, "The Endless Problem of Corporate Personality," *Columbia Law Review* 32 (1932): 643–667. Otto Gierke's *Political Theories of the Middle Age*, trans. and ed. F. W. Maitland (Cambridge: Cambridge University Press, 1900), pp. vii–xlv and "Translator's Introduction" were among the more influential uses of medieval history to provide nineteenth-century legal writers with the origins of the corporation's artificial and natural qualities. Davis, *Corporations*, provided an important American account.

53. Horwitz, "*Santa Clara*," pp. 216–224.

54. The first two groupings we owe to Horwitz; the third is our own.

55. Fredrick W. Maitland, "Moral Personality and Legal Personality," in his *Collected Papers*, ed. H. A. L. Fisher (Cambridge: University Press, 1911), vol. 3, p. 310. Progressive historians and legal scholars, pursuing the alternative path of Maitland's fork, gave public characteristics to the artificial-entity theory of the corporation, in contrast with the private version advocated near the end of the nineteenth century. In other words, the corporation was an artificial entity that owed its existence to the state (as opposed to its individual members) and should therefore be regarded as an instrument of state policy or at least subject to changing state policies. Before Horwitz's reexam-

ination of the *Santa Clara* case, artificial-entity theory was conventionally associated with the public version in legal discussions. See *Bank of Boston v. Bellotti*, 435 *U.S.* 765, 810 (1978) (J. White dissenting).

56. The Court's "confusion" was, no doubt, nurtured in part by concepts of the "evolution" of the common or judge-made law in the "social Darwinism" that enjoyed currency near the turn of the century. See James C. Carter, *Provinces of the Written and Unwritten Law* (New York and Albany: Banks & Braothers, 1889) and *The Ideal and the Actual in Law* (Philadelphia:; Dendo Printing and Publishing Co., 1890). In any event, one case, *Donnell v. Herring*, 208 *U.S.* 267 (1908), served to illustrate the approach. In *Herring*, a corporation promised another not to compete. The contract was ratified by the principal shareholders, who subsequently dissolved the corporation in question and established a new one in its place. The new corporation began competing, and the promisee sued for breach of contract. The lower court, in *Hall's Safe Co. v. Herring et al.*, 146 *F.* 37 (6th Cir, 1906), held that the contract of the original corporation in no way bound either the shareholders individually or the new corporation. The Supreme Court affirmed.

57. Horwitz, "*Santa Clara*," pp. 182, 189.

58. And so his views were discredited by citing such emerging corporate practices as the supplanting of a unanimity requirement by a simply majority rule in certain actions by the board of directors. Horwitz, "*Santa Clara*," pp. 199–203.

59. Edmund Bayly Seymour, Jr., "The Historical Development of the Common-Law Conception of a Corporation," *American Law Register (University of Pennsylvania Law Review)* 42 (1903): 529–551.

60. Ibid.

61. Ibid. p. 551.

62. See Dorothy Ross, *The Origins of American Social Science* (Baltimore: Johns Hopkins University Press, 1992).

63. Horwitz, for instance, cited Dewey, "Historical Background," on pp. 669–670, and Felix Cohen, "Transcendental Nonsense and the Functional Approach," *Columbia Law Review* 35 (1935): 809–849. But see, for instance, Morris R. Cohen's review in 1922 of Harold Laski's and Leon Duguit's work on the state, "On Three Political Scientists," in his *Law and the Social Order* (New York: Harcourt Brace, 1933), p. 325: "I think the limitations of both Mr. Laski's and M. Duguit's books are due to an unavowed craving for absolute distinctions, which is apt to be strongest in those not devoted to technical philosophy. The public demands it of those engaged in political discussion."

64. One puzzle that historians more recently have sought to decipher was the intensity with which lawyers suddenly took up the debate over the corporation's personality and the almost as sudden revelation some twenty years later that those debates would lead them nowhere. Horwitz, for instance, noted the breakdown of the several states' regulatory authority as a logical cause for concern about the virtually unregulatable multistate corporations. In this context, the quest to discover whether or in what ways the corporation's essential nature was self-regulating or conformed to the principles of liberal government seemed quite understandable. Entity theory was simply the framework in which those discussions then unfolded.

Horwitz does not, however, offer a similarly compelling explanation for the later abandonment of those corporate personality discussions. Why did the legal conception of the corporation, to use Horwitz's words, which tilted toward the natural-entity theory around the turn of the century, revert to a less determinate position during the 1920s? We offer a tentative answer here. Between 1900 and 1930, while the states' sovereignty was breaking down, an alternative regulatory framework was just emerging. Throughout much of the Progressive Era, lawyers could see the nationalization of government coming, but they remained uncertain about the forms it would take or the constitutional values that would underpin, or legitimate, the sovereignty of those forms. The circular debates around corporate personality finally came to an end once lawyers and policymakers recognized that judgments about the corporation and its regulation would depend on the constitutional framework for regulation by national forms of government and so would therefore have to await the materialization of the national administrative state. The latter did not in fact emerge until the 1930s.

65. Horwitz, for instance, cites Dewey, "The Historical Background of Corporate Legal Personality," pp. 655–673, on pp. 669–670; and Cohen, "Transcendental Nonsense."

66. See Harold J. Laski, "The Personality of Associations," *Harvard Law Review* 29 (1916): 404–426, reprinted in Harold Laski, *The Foundations of Sovereignty and Other Essays* (Freeport, NY: Books for Libraries Press, 1921), pp. 139–170.

67. On the emergence of some of these ideas, see R. M. MacIver, "Social Pressures," vol. 12; Francis W. Coker, "Pluralism," vol. 12; Edward Sapir, "Groups," vol. 7; and Morris Ginsberg, "Association," vol. 2, in *Encyclopedia of the Social Sciences,* ed. Edwin R. A. Seligman (New York: Macmillan, 1930–34). Curiously, to the extent that the authors mentioned Arthur F. Bentley's *The Process of Government* (Cambridge: Belknap Press of Harvard University Press, 1967) which Dahl, *A Preface* (Chicago: University of Chicago Press, 1952) among others, had credited as the starting point for modern pluralist theory, they are largely critical. See MacIver, "Social Pressures, p. 347. Bentley's analysis tended to be realistic and in that respect antagonistic to much of the idealism that flavored his contemporaries' writings. See Grant McConnell, *Private Power and American Democracy* (New York: Knopf, 1975), pp. 158–159, 353, on Bentley's lack of influence.

68. Nelson, *The Roots of American Bureaucracy,* pp. 160–161. The transition was not smooth, and worries over the conflict between individual and group freedoms tended to become circular. For example, those worried about empowering groups at the expense of individual persons tried to insist that group activity reflect only the voluntary submission of its members. Carried to its extreme, this individualist view would preclude the existence of government, with its binding rules.

Consider in this contexta 1905 ruling by the Supreme Court that held in effect that spontaneous voluntary corporate associations, "natural entities" in its view, had to be privileged against the artificial intrusions of that ultimate group, the state, because the corporation, like the ordinary person, was a constitutional person, whole, private, and impervious to public scrutiny. (Still, when it used these terms, the Supreme Court was speaking primarily of the public powers exercised by the several state legislatures, not by some ideal state or the federal government.)

69. Horwitz, "*Santa Clara.*"

70. See Nelson, *The Roots of American Bureaucracy,* on the transformation from a state system of governmental process to a pluralist system under federal control.

71. On the constitutional bias toward a nationalized party system, see, for example, Mark Tushnet, "The Constitution and the Nationalization of American Politics," in *A Workable Government: The Constitution After 200 Years,* ed. Burke Marshall (New York: Norton, 1987), pp. 144–169. For contemporary observations on the nationalization and control of parties, along with the attendant dangers, see Moisei Ostrogorski, *Democracy* (New York: Haskell House Publishers, 1970); Jesse Macy, *Party Organization and Machinery* (New York: The Century Co., 1918); Andrew McLaughlin, *The Courts, the Constitution, and Parties: Studies in Constitutional History and Politics* (Chicago: University of Chicago Press, 1912); and Herbert Croly, *Progressive Democracy* (New York: Macmillan, 1914).

72. See also Morton J. Horwitz, "The History of the Public/Private Distinction," *University of Pennsylvania Law Review* 130 (1982): 1423–1428.

Chapter 3

1. As early as 1908, Arthur F. Bentley outlined the implications of this evolution in his *The Process of Government.*

2. In this respect, both intellectual and constitutional historians have underestimated the overarching presence not just of organization but also of corporate organization in American thought between the wars. For instance, Edward Purcell, the leading intellectual historian of the New Deal, tends to neglect the modern corporation as a subplot. See Edward A. Purcell, Jr., *The Crisis of Democratic Theory: Scientific Naturalism and the Problem of Value* (Lexington: University of Kentucky Press, 1973). Similarly, see Cass Sunstein's description of the economy in constitutional change during the New Deal, "Constitutionalism After the New Deal," *Harvard Law Review* 101 (1987): 421–510.

3. See, for example, Mary O. Furner, *Advocacy and Objectivity: A Crisis in the Professionalization of American Social Science, 1865–1905* (Lexington: University of Kentucky Press, 1975); and Dorothy Ross, *The Origins of American Social Science* (Cambridge: Cambridge University Press, 1991).

4. Herbert Croly, *The Promise of American Life* (Indianapolis: Bobbs-Merrill, 1965 [originally published in 1909]), p. 412. This is our source for the following discussion and will be referenced only for specific quotations.

5. Ibid., p. 431.

6. Louis D. Brandeis, "The Road to Social Efficiency," in *Business—A Profession* (Boston: Small, Maynard, 1914), p. 59.

7. Testimony before the U.S. Commission on Industrial Relations, January 23, 1915, reprinted in Louis D. Brandeis, *The Curse of Bigness: Miscellaneous Papers* ed. O. Fraenkel, (New York: Viking Press, 1934), p. 72.

8. See L. S. Zacharias, "Repaving the Brandeis Way: The Decline of Developmental Property," *Northwestern University Law Review* 82(1988): 596–645.

9. Robert D. Cuff, *The War Industries Board: Business–Government Relations During World War I* (Baltimore: Johns Hopkins University Press, 1973).

10. See Kermit L. Hall, *The Magic Mirror: Law in American History* (New York: Oxford University Press, 1989), pp. 233–246. See also Tony A. Freyer, *Harmony and Dissonance: The Swift and Erie Cases in American Federalism* (New York: New York University Press, 1981).

11. The American legal realist movement in general and Karl Llewellyn's work in particular exemplified these tendencies.

12. Although considered seminal around the time of publication, Follett's work was largely ignored after the New Deal. See Mary Parker Follett, *The New State, Group Organization: The Solution of Popular Government* (New York: Longmans, Green, 1919).

13. The concept of a whole or centered personality is highly misleading in this world because each of the many tendencies that comprise the mind is capable of a variety of cultural and material associations.

14. Follett, *The New State*, pp. 73–84.

15. Ibid., pp. 189–330.

16. Ibid., pp. 22, 307–308. Madison expressed his fear, of course, in the tenth of the *Federalist Papers*.

17. Frank R. Kent, *The Great Game of Politics: The Ordeal of Self-Government in America* (New York: Arno Press, 1974: [1923]). For an interpretation of Kent's work see Bernard Crick, *The American Science of Politics: Its Origins and Conditions* (Berkeley and Los Angeles: University of California Press, 1964), p. 87.

18. Purcell, *The Crisis of Democratic Theory*, pp. 95–113.

19. Compare, for example, Lloyd Milton Short, *The Development of National Administrative Organization in the United States* (Baltimore: Johns Hopkins University Press, 1923), with Ernst Freund, *Administrative Powers over Persons and Property: A Comparative Survey* (Chicago: University of Chicago Press, 1928), pp. 579–585, and John Dickinson, *Administrative Justice and he Supremacy of Law in the United States* (Cambridge, MA: Harvard University Press, 1927).

20. Oliver Williamson, *Markets and Hierarchies: Analysis and Antitrust Implications: A Study in the Economics of Internal Organization* (New York: Free Press, 1975), p. 3, was among the first of the leading industrial organization economists to credit Commons with his insights into transactional analysis and its implications for a theory of the firm. For the most lucid attempt to found corporate regulation in the 1920s, see John M. Clark, *Social Control of Business* (Chicago: University of Chicago Press, 1926).

21. Karl N. Llewellyn, "The Effect of Legal Institutions upon Economics," *American Economic Review* 15 (1925): 665–683.

22. Ibid., p. 672.

23. Ibid., p. 673.

24. Ibid., pp. 670–671.

25. The exceptions occurred generally in cases of natural monopoly, in which either the states regulated rates or the federal government asserted industrywide controls—as in the case of the railroads, war-related industries, and, after 1929, agricultural commodities. The 1914 antitrust reforms, moreover, had exempted from prosecution the labor unions' collective bargaining that courts had prohibited earlier in the Sherman Act and in their common-law restraint of trade suits.

26. U.S. Federal Trade Commission, *Statutes and Decisions Pertaining to the Federal Trade Commission, 1914–1929* (Washington, DC: U.S. Government Printing Office, 1930), pp. 5, 17.

27. Albert M. Kales, "Good and Bad Trusts," *Harvard Law Review* 30 (1917): 830–872.

28. Myron W. Watkins, "The Change in Trust Policy," *Harvard Law Review* 35 (1922): 815–837, 926–949, esp. pp. 833–837.

29. Ibid., p. 926.

30. Ibid., pp. 926–949.

31. Frank H. Knight, *Risk, Uncertainty and Profit* (Chicago: University of Chicago Press, 1921); John M. Clark, *The Social Control of Business* (New York: McGraw-Hill, 1926); Edward H. Chamberlin, *The Theory of Monopolistic Competition* (Cambridge, MA: Harvard University Press, 1933). For a survey of the field of industrial organization, see Frederick M. Scherer, *Market Structure and Industrial Concentration,* 2nd ed. (Chicago: Rand McNally, 1980).

32. Under the Court's interpretation, in *Smyth v. Ames,* 169 *U.S.* 466 (1898), the Constitution's Fifth Amendment protected utility companies' private property from expropriation through redistributive rate setting. Public-service commissions were accordingly required to pay tribute to the "fair value" of the company's property (or capital) in setting rates.

33. See Gerard Henderson, "Railway Valuation and the Courts," *Harvard Law Review* 33 (1920): 902–928, 1031–1057; Robert L. Hale, "The 'Physical Value' Fallacy in Rate Cases," *Yale Law Journal* 30 (1921): 710–731; and Donald R. Richberg, "A Permanent Basis for Rate Regulation," *Yale Law Journal* 31 (1922): 263–282.

34. Richberg, " A Permanent Basis," p. 267.

35. Richard T. Ely, *Ground Under Our Feet* (New York: The Macmillan Co., 1938), pp. 252–265.

36. This was Teddy Roosevelt's policy of regulating the monopolies. Walter Lippmann's *Drift and Mastery: An Attempt to Diagnose the Current Unrest* (Englewood Cliffs, NJ: Prentice-Hall, 1961 [originally published 1914]) was the leading popularizer of that policy. See also Thomas K. McCraw, *Prophets of Regulation* (Cambridge, MA: Belknap Press of Harvard University Press, 1984), pp. 139–141. Regulated industries included transportation, energy, communications, banking, and public utilities.

37. See, for example, John R. Commons and John B. Andrews, *Principles of Labor Legislation* (New York,: Harper & Row, 1920).

38. See John R. Commons, *Industrial Goodwill* (New York: McGraw-Hill, 1919) and *Industrial Government* (New York: Macmillan, 1921).

39. See Ida M. Tarbell, *New Ideals in Business: An Account of Their Practice and Their Effects upon Men and Profits* (New York: D. Appleton, 1916).

40. See, for example, G. Edward White, *The American Judicial Tradition: Profiles of Leading American Judges* (New York: Oxford University Press, 1976), pp. 146–177.

41. L. S. Zacharias, "Repaving the Brandeis Way: The Decline of Developmental Property," *Northwestern University Law Review* 82 (1988): 596–645.

42. Llewellyn, "The Effect of Legal Institutions," p. 666.

43. See Martin J. Sklar, *The Corporate Reconstruction of American Capitalism, 1890–1916: The Market, the Law, and Politics* (Cambridge: Cambridge University Press, 1988), pp. 164–165.

44. See Richard M. Abrams, "Brandeis and the Ascendancy of Corporate Capitalism," introduction to Louis D. Brandeis, *Other People's Money and How the Bankers Use It* (New York: Harper & Row, [1914] 1967), pp. xii–xliv.

45. Louis D. Brandeis, "The Regulation of Competition against the Regulation of Monopoly," in Brandeis, *The Curse of Bigness*, p. 110.

46. John Dewey, "The Historic Background of Corporate Legal Personality," *Yale Law Journal* 35 (1926): 655–673.

47. Ibid., p. 673 (italics added).

48. See Edward H. Warren, "Safeguarding the Creditors of Corporations," *Harvard Law Review* 36 (1923): 509–547.

49. William O. Douglas adapted a realistic and functional approach to the corporation: He compared partnership, trust, and corporate rules along several practical lines, including organizational "control," to show how functional analysis was better than existing rules based on the formal logic of person and state. See William O. Douglas, "A Functional Approach to the Law of Business Associations," *Illinois Law Review* 23 (1929): 673–682.

50. Nathan Isaacs, "Business Security and Legal Security," *Harvard Law Review* 34 (1923): 201–213.

51. Nathan Isaacs, "The Promoter: A Legislative Problem," *Harvard Law Review* 38 (1925): 887–902.

52. Ibid., pp. 898–900.

53. Ibid., pp. 900–902.

54. Nathan Isaacs, "Trusteeship in Modern Business," *Harvard Law Review* 42 (1929): 1048–1061.

55. Ibid., pp. 1060–1061.

56. Adolf A. Berle, "Non-Voting Stock and 'Bankers' Control,'" *Harvard Law Review* 39 (1926): 675.

57. Ibid., p. 677.

58. Ibid., p. 681.

59. Ibid., pp. 681–692.

60. Charles E. Clark and William O. Douglas, "Law and Legal Institutions," in President's Research Committee on Social Trends, *Recent Social Trends in the United States: Report of the President's Research Committee on Social Trends* (New York: McGraw-Hill, 1933), vol. 2, pp. 1430–1488, esp. pp. 1435–1436; and E. Merrick Dodd, Jr., "Statutory Developments in Business Corporation Law, 1886–1936," *Harvard Law Review* 50 (1936): 27–59.

Chapter 4

1. Adolf A. Berle, Jr., "Corporate Powers as Powers in Trust," *Harvard Law Review* 44 (1931): 1049–1074.

2. E. Merrick Dodd, "For Whom Are the Corporate Managers Trustees," *Harvard Law Review* 45 (1932): 1145–1163.

3. Adolf A. Berle, Jr., "For Whom Corporate Managers *Are* Trustees: A Note," *Harvard Law Review* 45 (1932): 1365–1372.

4. Ibid, p. 1367.

5. Ibid., p. 1371.

6. Ibid. "The shareholder who now has a primary property right over residual income after expenses are met, may ultimately be conceived of as having an equal participation with a number of other claimants. Or he may emerge, still with a primary property right over residual income, but subordinated to a number of claims by labor, by customers and patrons, by the community and the like, which cut down that residue. It would, as Professor Dodd points out, be unfortunate to leave the law in such shape that these developments could not be recognized as a matter of constitutional or corporate law. But it is one thing to say that the law must allow for such developments. It is quite another to grant uncontrolled power to corporate managers in the hope that they will produce that development." Ibid., pp. 1371–1372.

7. Karl Llewellyn was a leading advocate of this perspective, in many ways the distinctive contribution of the "American legal realists" to the law.

8. See, for example W. F. Willoughby, *The Reorganization of the Administrative Branch of the National Government* (Baltimore: Johns Hopkins University Press, 1923).

9. Adolf A. Berle, Jr. and Gardiner C. Means, *The Modern Corporation and Private Property*, 2nd ed. (New York: Harcourt Brace & World, 1968), p. 313. Because Means's collaboration appears confined in the main to the statistics, we shall speak only of Berle when discussing the book's contribution to theory.

10. See George J. Stigler and Claire Friedland, "The Literature of Economics: The Case of Berle and Means," *Journal of Law & Economics* 26 (1983): 237–268, for the limited interpretation of ownership having been separated from control. Lawyers of both practicing and professorial bent, on the other hand, have tended to confine Berle's contribution to the area of "trust." See Carlos L. Israels, "Are Corporate Powers Still Held In Trust?" *Columbia law Review* 64: 1446–1457. Intellectual historians have cited the book as a leading example of interdisciplinary legal realism; see Edward A. Purcell, Jr., *The Crisis of Democratic Theory: Scientific Naturalism and the Problem of Value* (Lexington: University of Kentucky Press, 1973), p. 8. even though, in our opinion, the genius of the book lies in its conceptual, not empirical work.

11. The two hundred largest firms in the United States controlled roughly 50 percent of the nation's corporate wealth and 22 percent of its wealth entire. Berle and Means, *The Modern Corporation*, p. 33.

12. Ibid., pp. 64–67.

13. Among the two hundred largest firms, managers had come to control 44 percent of the firms and 58 percent of the wealth; in an additional 21 percent of the firms (22 percent by wealth), a substantial minority interest was exercising control, with at least 20 percent of the outstanding voting shares. Ibid., p. 109.

14. Ibid., p. 46.

15. Ibid., pp. 3–10.

16. Ibid., p. 17.

17. Ibid., pp. 3–10, 64–65, 110–116.

18. Ibid., p. 138.

19. Ibid.

20. Ibid., pp. 255–290.

21. Ibid., pp. 196–252. For a succinct distinction between "contract" and "trust," see the work of Austin W. Scott, the leading writer on trusts between the wars, especially his "The Trustee's Duty of Loyalty," *Harvard Law Review* 49 (1936) 521–565.

22. Berle and Means, *The Modern Corporation,* pp. 262–263, 300–302.

23. Ibid., pp. 276–277.

24. Berle reviews charter rights in ibid., pp. 141–195; he specifies potential market failures on pp. 152, 155, 181, 255–263, and corrective measures on pp. 264–290.

25. Ibid., p. 290.

26. Ibid., p. 301.

27. Ibid., pp., 301–302, 305–308.

28. See, for example, Bernard Bellush, *The Failure of the NRA* (New York: Norton, 1975); and John K. Ohl, *Hugh S. Johnson and the New Deal* (Dekalb: Northern Illinois University Press, 1985).

29. See *United States Code,* Title 15, Section 78p(b) (Securities Exchange Act of 1934); *United States Code,* Title 29, Section 158(a) (National Labor Relations Act); *United States Code,* Title 15, Section 45(a)(1) (Wheeler–Lea amendments to the FTC Act).

30. See L. S. Zacharias, "Unfairness, Advertising Regulation and Corporate Legitimacy," University of Massachusetts at Amherst, School of Management, working paper series, 1985/1986.

31. Thomas K. McCraw, *Prophets of Regulation* (Cambridge, MA: Belknap Press of Harvard University Press, 1984), pp. 169–181, sketched out the various pieces of New Deal securities and banking legislation together with their intended effects. Vincent Carosso, *Investment Banking in America: A History* (Cambridge, MA: Harvard University Press, 1970), described the banking reforms in context.

32. By widening both investment opportunites and the range of associated risk, some deregulations also gave shareholders more leeway to bargain with corporate managers over corporate policy.

33. See Donald A. Ritchie, *James M. Landis, Dean of the Regulators* (Cambridge, MA: Harvard University Press, 1980).

34. See Albert O. Hirschman, *Exit, Voice and Loyalty* (Princeton, NJ: Princeton University Press, 1970).

35. See James M. Landis, *The Administrative Process* (New Haven, CT: Yale University Press, 1938), chaps. 4 and 16.

36. The same bias against financial control flavored the Bank Holding Act of 1956, which brought prohibitions against equity investments for bank holding companies similar to those that the Glass–Steagall Act had provided for single standing commercial banks.

37. The literature on labor markets, including the distinction between entry-level job seeking and the large firm's internal labor markets, gradually elaborated on skill acquisition and benefit plans that vested the laborer in the firm. See Sanford Jacoby, "The Development of Internal Labor Markets in American Manufacturing Firms," in *Internal Labor Markets*, ed. P. Osterman (Cambridge, MA: MIT Press, 1984), pp. 23–69. See also Paul C. Weiler, *Governing the Workplace: The Future of Labor and Employment Law* (Cambridge, MA: Harvard University Press, 1990), esp. pp. 56–78; and Marc Linder and Larry Zacharias, "Opening Coase's Other Black Box: Why Workers Submit to Vertical Integration into Firms," *The Journal of Corporation Law* 18 (1993): 371–424.

38. For example, the social security system enabled workers to transfer from one private employer to another without losing all retirement benefits. Of course, state and federal workers were often locked in to somewhat narrower job markets. In contrast, many European health systems or insurers have provided universal coverage.

39. See David Montgomery, *The Fall of the House of Labor: The Workplace, the State and Labor Activism, 1865–1925* (Cambridge: Cambridge University Press, 1987), pp. 214–256.

40. The U.S. Supreme Court imposed on union officials a duty of "fair representation" under both the Railway Labor Act and the National Labor Relations Act. See *Steele v. Louisville & Nashville Railroad*, 323 *U.S.* 192 (1944), and *Syres v. Oil Workers*, Local 23, 350 *U.S.* 892 (1955).

41. John R. Commons and John B. Andrews, *Principles of Labor Legislation* (New York: Harper & Row, 1920), pp. 182–500.

42. Congress enacted Sections 6 and 20 of the Clayton Act in 1914, 15 *USC* Section 17 and 29 *USC* Section 52, to narrow application of the earlier Sherman Antitrust Act in cases involving union activities. In 1932 Congress also passed the Norris–LaGuardia Act, 29 *USC* Sections 101–115, to narrow further the intrusion of federal courts in labor disputes. On court interventions before the New Deal, see Felix Frankfurter and Nathan Greene, *The Labor Injunction* (New York: Macmillan, 1930); and Charles O. Gregory, *Labor and the Law* (New York: Norton, 1949).

43. The relevant acts are the Federal Employee Liability Act of 1908, revised in 1916; the Federal Seamen's Act of 1915; the Railway Labor Act of 1926, and the 45 *United States Code*, Sections 151–188. See, for example, Kermit L. Hall, *The Magic Mirror: Law in American History* (New York: Oxford University Press, 1989), pp. 208–209; and Commons and Andrews, *Principles of Labor Legislation*, pp. 373–374. Additional federal supports, like the federal Bureau of Mines, were mostly supplementary to state legislation. See Commons and Andrews, *Principles of Labor Legislation*, pp. 370–371.

44. On the history of the courts' enforcement of labor contracts under the common law, see Gregory, *Labor and the Law.*

45. For practical examples of this phenomenon in history, see Montgomery, *Fall of the House of Labor,* pp. 112–170. See also Jacoby, "The Development of Internal Labor Markets." For a theoretical analysis in contract bargaining, *ex post,* see Oliver Williamson, *Markets and Hierarchies: Analysis and Antitrust Implications* (New York: Free Press, 1975), p. 64.

46. On the implications of this phenomenon with regard to bargaining and the development of internal labor markets, see ibid., pp. 64–81; and Oliver Williamson, *The Economic Institutions of Capitalism* (New York: Free Press, 1985), pp. 242–263.

47. See Gregory, *Labor and the Law,* pp. 223–224.

48. See Howard Dickman, *Industrial Democracy in America: Ideological Origins of National Labor Relations* (LaSalle, IL: Open Court, 1987), pp. 267–268.

49. See Thomas A. Kochan, Harry C. Katz, and Robert B. McKersie, *The Transformation of American Industrial Relations* (New York: Basic Books, 1989), pp. 47–80. For a contrast of the American contractual obsession with alternative models of industrial labor policy, see Marc Linder, "Towards Universal Worker Coverage Under the National Labor Relations Act: Making Room for Uncontrolled Employees, Dependent Contractors, and Employee-Like Persons," *University of Detroit Law Review* 66 (1989): 555–602, esp. pp. 599–601.

50. Marc Linder makes this argument in *The Employment Relationship in Anglo-American Law: A Historical Perspective* (Westport, CT: Greenwood Press, 1989), pp. 185–241, and in "Paternalistic State Intervention: the Contradictions of the Legal Empowerment of Vulnerable Workers," *University of California, Davis Law Review* 23 (1990): 733–772.

51. Linder, "Towards Universal Worker Coverage," pp. 574–592.

52. In Arthur M. Schlesinger, Jr., *The Politics of Upheaval 1935–1936* (Boston: Houghton, Mifflin, 1960), p. 280.

53. In many ways, the act followed the writing of James Landis, whose 1937 volume, *The Administrative Process,* distilled the experience of the SEC during its formative years into generally applicable insights.

Chapter 5

1. Edward Pendleton Herring, *Public Administration and the Public Interest* (New York: McGraw-Hill, 1936).

2. See Hannah Arendt, *The Origins of Totalitarianism,* rev. ed. (Cleveland: Meridian Books, 1959); Richard H. Pells, *The Liberal Mind in a Conservative Age: American Intellectual in the 1940s and 1950s* (New York Harper & Row, 1985), pp. 47–51; and George Kateb, *Hannah Arendt: Politics, Conscience, Evil* (Totowa, NJ: Rowman & Allanheld, 1984).

3. Friedrich A. Hayek, *The Road to Serfdom* (Chicago: University of Chicago Press, 1944), and *The Constitution of Liberty* (Chicago: University of Chicago Press, 1960).

4. Frank Knight, *The Ethics of Competition and Other Essays* (Chicago: Uni-

versity of Chicago Press, 1935), and *Freedom and Reform: Essays in Economic and Social Philosophy* (Washington: Kennikat Press, 1947).

5. See Edmund W. Kitch, ed., "The Fire of Truth: A Remembrance of Law and Economics at Chicago, 1932–1970," *Journal of Law and Economics* 26 (1983): 163–234. See also Edward A. Purcell, Jr., *The Crisis of Democratic Theory: Scientific Naturalism and the Problem of Value* (Lexington: University of Kentucky Press, 1973), pp. 3–12.

6. For a response, see Gerhard Colm, "Is Economic Planning Compatible with Democracy?" in *Political and Economic Democracy*, ed. Max Ascoli & Fritz Lehmann (New York: Norton, 1937), pp. 21–41.

7. This has been an ongoing theme in American politics. In nineteenth-century manifestations, for instance, antagonism to planning took the form of anticodification sentiment among legislators and lawyers. In the twentieth century, it took the form of Brandeisian market-enhancing initiatives rather than hands-on regulation along with administrative centralization. See Ellis W. Hawley's discussion in *The New Deal and the Problem of Monopoly: A Study in Economic Ambivalence* (Princeton, NJ: Princeton University Press, 1966), pp. 383–403, 456–494 of the battle between New Dealers who favored strong antitrust measure and New Dealers who favored planning.

8. The conclusions of this research were brought together in 1957, when the Social Science Research Council called together a committee of prominent scholars to codify the growing scholarly consensus on democracy in a series of reports. See Suzanne Berger, "Introduction," in *Organizing Interests in Western Europe: Pluralism, Corporatism and the Transformation of Politics*, ed. Suzanne Berger (Cambridge: Cambridge University Press, 1982), pp. 1–9.

Interests groups arise spontaneously in civil society. Cross-cutting cleavages, overlapping group memberships, and social mobility inhibit the homogenizing and unifying of citizen preferences. Indeed, they both constrain and reconfigure the majority (even when elites have certain advantages in formulating group policies). The state is useful both in facilitating political negotiations among the interests and in setting rules and resolving impasses in the contest over distribution. It tends to resist ideology as long as political parties serve largely to house coalitions that agree on both political aims and, once in power, the distribution of political spoils. Only when parties exceed their coordinating role and intervene in the "natural" formation and representation of interests, does ideology replace pragmatism and autonomous groups become subordinate to the needs of the state. See also Robert Dahl, *Democracy and Its Critics* (New Haven, CT: Yale University Press, 1989), pp. 213–224.

9. See Douglas B. Copland, "The State and the Entrepreneur," in Harvard Tercentenary Publications, *Authority and the Individual* (Cambridge, MA: Harvard University Press, 1937), pp. 43–73. Along these lines, Joseph A. Schumpeter's *Capitalism, Socialism and Democracy* (New York: Harper & Row, 1942), offered contemporaries the most insightful analysis.

10. James Burnham, *The Managerial Revolution: What Is Happening in the World* (New York: John Day, 1941), p. 147.

11. Adolf A. Berle, Jr., *Power Without Property: A New Development in American Political Economy* (New York: Harcourt Brace, 1959).

12. Mark J. Roe, "Political and Legal Restraints on Ownership and Control of Public Companies," *Journal of Financial Economics* 27 (1990): 7–41, esp. pp. 10, 12.

13. House Committee on Banking and Currency, *Commercial Banks and Their Trust Activities: Emerging Influence on the American Economy. Volume 1 and Volume 2: Staff Report for the Subcommittee on Domestic Finance,* 90th Cong., 2nd. sess., Subcommittee Print, July 8, 1968. Commercial banks, the committee noted, held approximately $600 billion of the $1 trillion in assets controlled by all institutional investors. Forty-nine commercial banks accounted for more than half of these holdings and had 786 interlocking directorships with 286 of the nation's largest industrial firms.

14. Ibid., pp. 9–10. See also "Banking Concentration," *Congressional Quarterly Almanac* (Washington, D.C.: Congressional Quarterly Press, 1968), p. 262.

15. Securities and Exchange Commission, *Institutional Investor Study Report of the Securities and Exchange Commission, Volume 1,* 92nd Cong., 1st sess., March 10, 1971, H. Doc. 92–64, pt. 1, p. v.

16. Securities and Exchange Commission, *Institutional Investor Study, Summary,* pt. 8, pp. 65–124.

17. Securities and Exchange Commission, *Institutional Investor Study,* pt. 8, p. ix.

18. Ibid. For a more detailed analysis, see Securities and Exchange Commission, *Institutional Investor Study,* pt. 5, pp. 2549–2561.

19. Senate Committee on Government Operations, *Corporate Disclosure: Hearings Before the Subcommittee on Budgeting, Management, and Expenditures and the Subcommittee on Intergovernmental Relations, Part 1,* 93rd Cong., 2nd sess., March 21, 26, and 28, 1974; and Senate Committee on Government Operations, *Corporate Disclosure, Part 2,* April 23, 24, and May 20, 21, 1974.

20. Senate Committee on Government Operations, *Corporate Ownership and Control: Prepared by the Subcommittee on Reports, Accounting and Management,* November 1975, Committee Print, pp. 1–2.

21. Senate Committee on Governmental Affairs, *Structure of Corporate Concentration: Institutional Shareholders and Interlocking Directorates Among Major U.S. Corporations,* Committee Print 96th Congress, 2nd Session, 1980, p. 28.

22. William W. Bratton, Jr., "The New Economic Theory of the Firm: Critical Perspectives from History," *Standard Law Review* 41 (1989): 1471–1527; John C. Coates, IV, "Note—State Takeover Statues and Corporate Theory: The Revival of an Old Debate," *New York University Law Review* 64 (1989): 806–876; and Lucian Arye Bebchuk, "Foreword: The Debate on Contractual Freedom in Corporate Law," *Columbia University Law Review* 89 (1989): 1395–1415.

23. Adolf A. Berle, Jr., " 'Control' in Corporate Law," *Columbia Law Review* 58 (1958): 1212–1225. The distinction between direct pro rata payments and payments into the corporation's treasury was not insignificant, for only the latter instance validated the capital claims of such other stakeholders as workers, customers, and the community.

24. Ibid., pp. 1219–1220.

25. Ibid., p. 1221.

26. John Kenneth Galbraith, *The New Industrial State* (Boston: Houghton Mifflin, 1967).

27. "We have seen wherein the chance for salvation lies. The industrial system, in contrast with its economic antecedents, is intellectually demanding. It brings into existence, to serve its intellectual and scientific needs, the community that, hopefully, will reject its monopoly of social purpose" (ibid., p. 383).

28. Robin Marris, "Galbraith, Solow, and the Truth About Corporations," *The Public Interest* 11 (1968): 37–46.

29. See the collection of essays assembled by Ralph Nader and Mark J. Green, eds., *Corporate Power in America* (New York: Norton, 1973), particularly Robert A. Dahl, "Governing the Giant Corporation," pp. 10–24; Mark J. Green, "The Corporation and the Community," pp. 42–64; and Ralph Nader, "The Case for Federal Chartering," pp. 67–93. David Vogel, *Lobbying the Corporation: Citizen Challenges to Business Authority* (New York: Basic Books, 1978), provides a useful history of the public-interest movement and corporate social regulation.

30. Henry G. Manne, "The 'Higher Criticism' of the Modern Corporation," *Columbia Law Review* 62 (1962): 401–432.

31. Henry G. Manne, "Mergers and the Market for Corporate Control," *Journal of Political Economy* 73 (1965): 110–120.

32. Ibid., p. 113.

33. Ibid., pp. 114–115.

34. Ibid., pp. 116–117.

35. Ibid., p. 118. For a more general discussion, see Kenneth M. Davidson, *Megamergers: Corporate America's Billion Dollar Takeovers* (Cambridge, MA: Ballinger, 1985), pp. 137–142.

36. Manne, "Mergers," pp. 112–113.

37. Manne, "The 'Higher' Criticism," pp. 413–416, 423–430.

38. From 1960 to 1965, cash offers rose from $186 million, or 40 percent of the total number of tender offers, to $450 million and 70 percent. Samuel L. Hayes, III, and Russell A. Taussig, "Tactics of Cash Takeover Bids— For Bidders, Incumbent Managements, and Shareholders," in U.S. Senate Committee on Banking and Currency, *Full Disclosure of Corporate Equity Ownership and in Corporate Takeover Bids: Hearings Before the Subcommittee on Securities*, 90th Cong., lst sess., 1967, pp. 224–225.

39. House Committee on the Judiciary, *Investigation of Conglomerate Corporations: Report by the Staff of the Antitrust Subcommittee*, U.S. Congress, House Committee on the Judiciary, 91st Congress, 1st Session, 1971, pp. 24–25.

40. The eleven firms were Gulf and Western, Ling-Temco-Vought, International Telephone and Telegraph, Teledyne, General Telephone and Electronics, Litton Industries, General American Transportation, Textron, PMC, White Consolidated, and Colt Industries. U.S. Senate Committee on the Judiciary, *Economic Concentration: Hearings Before the Subcommittee on Antitrust and Monopoly, Part 8A, Staff Report of the Federal Trade Commission, Economic Report on Corporate Mergers*, 91st Cong., 1st sess., 1969, pp. 268–269.

41. David L. Ratner, *Securities Regulation in a Nutshell*, 3rd ed. (St. Paul: West Publishing, 1988), p. 106.

42. See Stanley A. Kaplan, "Testimony," in Senate Committee on Banking and Currency, *Full Disclosure,* pp. 132–136; and Robert H. Mundheim, "Testimony," in ibid., pp. 136–139.

43. At the time of the Williams Act, only one state had laws regulating tender offers. For the most part, the legislators looked to create a uniform set of rules that would serve the national market, favoring neither bidder nor seller, raider nor manager. After the Williams Act was passed, the states quickly passed a series of tender-offer regulations that decidedly favored management in defending against unwanted purchase offers. For an overview of these laws and the intent of the Williams Act, see U.S. Senate Committee on Banking, Housing and Urban Affairs, *Securities and Exchange Commission Report on Tender Offer Laws,* 96th Cong., 2d sess., 1980, Committee Print, pp. 12–13, 75–78.

44. See Manuel F. Cohen, "Testimony," Senate Committee on Banking and Currency, *Full Disclosure,* pp. 32–41.

45. Cohen, "Testimony," Senate Committee on Banking and Currency, *Full Disclosure,* pp. 180–181.

46. Ibid., pp. 179–180.

47. See Davidson's summary of the disclosure rules in his *Megamergers,* pp. 49–53.

48. Henry G. Manne's *Insider Trading and the Stock Market* (New York: Free Press, 1966) provided the seminal arguments for subsequent reform discussions, and research on financial markets provided the empirical basis for subsequent law-reform proposals. For a summary and references to the legal discussions, see William A. Klein and John C. Coffee, Jr. *Business Organization and Finance: Legal and Economic Principles* (Mineola, NY: Foundation Press, 1990), pp. 149–152.

49. For an assessment of the social activism of the 1970s, see David Vogel, "The 'New' Social Regulation in Historical and Comparative Perspective," in *Regulation in Perspective: Historical Essays,* ed. Thomas K. McCraw (Cambridge, MA: Harvard University Press, 1981), pp. 155–186. On America's slipping economic position, see Bruce R. Scott and George C. Lodge, *U.S. Competitiveness in the World Economy* (Boston: Harvard Business School Press, 1985); and Michael L. Dertouzos, Richard K. Lester, and Robert M. Solow, *Made in America: Regaining the Productive Edge* (Cambridge MA: MIT Press, 1989).

50. See Michael Jensen, "The Takeover Controversy: Analysis and Evidence," in John C. Coffee, Jr., Louis Lowenstein, and Susan Rose-Ackerman, *Knights, Raiders and Targets: The Impact of the Hostile Takeover,* (Oxford: Oxford University Press, 1988), pp. 314–354; and Gailen Hite and James Owers, "The Restructuring of Corporate America: A Review of the Evidence," in *The Revolution in Corporate Finance,* ed. Joel M. Stern and Donald H. Chew, Jr. (Oxford: Basil Blackwell, 1986), pp. 418–427.

51. See Jensen, "The Takeover Controversy," pp. 316–317; and Davidson, *Megamergers,* pp. 117–138, 247–280.

52. Armen A. Alchian and Harold Demsetz, "Production, Information Costs, and Economic Organization, *American Economic Review* 62 (1972): 777–795. For a review of the relevant property-rights literature, see Erik G.

Furubotn and Svetozar Pejovich, "Property Rights and Economic Theory: A Survey of Recent Literature," *Journal of Economic Literature* 10 (1972): 1137–1162.

53. Financial-agency theory grew out of post–World War II developments in corporate finance that used economic tools to assess various capital structures. These models allowed scholars not only to devise financial instruments to help shareholders invest optimally but also to discuss the probable effects of taxes on managerial decisions. The important works in agency theory include Stephen Ross, "The Economic Theory of Agency: The Principal's Problem," *American Economic Review* 63 (1973): 134–139; Michael C. Jensen and William H. Meckling, "Theory of the Firm: Managerial Behavior, Agency Costs and Ownership Structure," *Journal of Financial Economics* 3 (1976): 305–360; Eugene F. Fama, "Agency Problems and the Theory of the Firm," *Journal of Political Economy* 88 (1980): 288–307; Eugene F. Fama and Michael C. Jensen, "Agency Problems and Residual Claims," *Journal of Law and Economics* 26 (1983): 327–349; and Eugene F. Fama and Michael C. Jensen, "Separation of Ownership from Control," *Journal of Law and Economics* 26 (1983): 301–325. James O. Horrigan, "The Ethics of the New Finance,' " *Journal of Business Ethics* 6 (1987): 97–110, provides a critical assessment of agency theory while examining its connections to modern financial theory.

54. Eugene E. Fama and Michael C. Jensen, "Separation of Ownership from Control," *Journal of Law and Economics* 26 (1983): 301–325.

55. Oliver Williamson, *The Economic Institutions: Firms, Markets, Relational Contracting* (New York: Free Press, 1985), pp. 15–22, 72–79.

56. Masahiko Aoki, *The Co-operative Game Theory of the Firm* (Oxford: Oxford University Press, 1984).

57. Ibid., pp. 14–17, 61–69.

58. Ibid., pp. 11–12.

59. Ibid., 172–180.

60. See, for example, Harvey Goldschmid, H. Michael Mann, and J. Fred Weston, *Industrial Concentration: The New Learning* (Boston: Little, Brown, 1974).

61. See Frank H. Easterbrook and Daniel R. Fischel, "The Proper Role of a Target's Management in Responding to a Tender Offer," *Harvard Law Review* 94 (1981): 161–1204, "Corporate Control Transactions," *Yale Law Journal* (1982): 698–737, and "Auctions and Sunk Costs in Tender Offers," *Stanford Law Review* 35 (1982): 1–21.

62. Easterbrook and Fischel, "The Proper Role," p. 1162.

63. Ibid., p. 1164.

64. Ibid., pp. 1175–1176. Easterbrook and Fischel's arguments appear on pp. 1174–1180. For an economic treatment of this general thesis, see Gregg A. Jarrell and Michael Bradley, "The Economic Effects of Federal and State Regulations of Cash Tender Offers," *Journal Law and Economics* 23 (1980): 371–407.

65. John C. Coffee, Jr., "Regulating the Market for Corporate Control: A Critical Assessment of the Tender Offer's Role in Corporate Governance," *Columbia Law Review* 84 (1984): 1163–1164.

66. Ibid., pp. 1176–1183. Coffee explained that their disagreement arose from different assessments of the elasticity of the shareholders' demand function for tender offers, with Easterbrook and Fischel finding it far more elastic than he did.

67. Ibid., pp. 1204–1205. Coffee believed that shareholders had implicitly endorsed the Williams Act by developing similar techniques, like "fair price" provisions, to protect shareholders from bidders' efforts to stampede them into selling.

68. Ibid., pp. 1221–1243.

69. See Michael C. Jensen, "The Eclipse of the Public Corporation," *Harvard Business Review*, September–October 1989, pp. 61–74; and Alfred Rappaport, "The Staying Power of the Public Corporation," *Harvard Business Review*, January–February 1990, pp. 96–104.

70. For a similar assessment, one that also recognized the differences between the current managerial position and neoclassicism, see William W. Bratton, "The New Economic Theory of the Firm: Critical Perspectives from History," *Stanford Law Review* 41 (1989): 1471–1527.

71. See, for example, William Meckling and Michael Jensen, "Reflections on the Corporation as a Social Invention," *Midland Corporate Finance Journal* 1 (1983): 6–14.

72. For a discussion of the differences that separated agency theory and the broader, managerial approach, see Oliver E. Williamson, "Corporate Finance and Corporate Governance," *Journal of Finance* 43 (1988): 567–591.

73. Aoki, *The Co-operative Game Theory*, pp. 119–196, explores alternative corporate governance structures to facilitate cooperative behavior, and R. Edward Freeman, *Strategic Management: A Stakeholder Approach* (Boston: Pittman, 1984), examines the importance of norms in corporate strategy. For managerial assessments of recent hostile takeovers, see Malcolm S. Slater and Wolf A. Weinhold, "Corporate Takeovers: Financial Boom or Organizational Bust?" in Coffee et al., *Knights*, pp. 135–149; and William Lazonick, "Statement," in House Subcommittee on Economic Stabilization of the Committee on Banking, Finance and Urban Affairs, *Oversight Hearing on Mergers and Acquisitions, Hearing*, 100th Cong., 1st sess., May 12, 1987, pp. 98–107.

74. Davidson, *Megamergers*, pp. 143–145. For a discussion of Pickens's takeover attempt of Gulf, see John C. Coffee, Jr., "Shareholder Versus Managers," *Michigan Law Review* 85 (October, 1986): 116, n. 2. For an introduction to the financial impetus for corporate restructuring, see Hite and Owers, "The Restructuring of Corporate America."

75. For an excellent discussion of junk-bond financing, see Congressional Research Service, House Committee on Energy and Commerce, *The Role of High Yield Bonds [Junk Bonds] in Capital Markets and Corporate Takeovers: Public Policy Implications. A Report Prepared for the House Committee on Energy and Commerce*, Committee Print 99–W, 99th Cong., 1st sess., 1985.

76. Jensen, "Eclipse of the Public Corporation," pp. 62–63.

77. See Congressional Research Service, *Pensions and Leveraged Buyouts: A Report Prepared for the House Subcommittee on Labor–Management Relations of the Committee on Education and Labor*, Committee Print 101–B, February 1989, pp. 3–6.

78. Davidson, *Megamergers,* p. 143.

79. Jensen, "Eclipse of the Public Corporation," pp. 65–66; and Carol J. Loomis, "The New J. P. Morgans," *Fortune,* February 29, 1988, pp. 44–53. For a summary of this ongoing struggle, see Edward S. Herman, *Corporate Control, Corporate Power* (Cambridge: Cambridge University Press, 1981), pp. 65–68; and Beth Mintz and Michael Schwartz, *The Power Structure of American Business* (Chicago: University of Chicago Press, 1985), pp. 17–44.

80. House Committee on Energy and Commerce, *Corporate Takeovers: Public Policy,* p. 28.

81. Securities and Exchange Commission, *Report on Tender Offer Laws: A Re-examination of Rules Relating to Shareholder Communications, Shareholder Participation in the Corporate Electoral Process and Corporate Governance Generally. Printed for the Use of the Senate Committee on Banking, Housing and Urban Affairs,* 99th Cong., 2nd sess., Committee Print, 1980, pp. 1–6. In 1983, the SEC issued an advisory committee report with fifty proposals for reforming corporate takeovers. See Ronald Brownstein, "Merger Wars—Congress, SEC Take Aim at Hostile Corporate Takeover Moves," *National Journal,* July 23, 1987, pp. 1538–1540.

82. Brownstein, "Merger Wars," pp. 1538–1541.

83. House Committee on Energy and Commerce, *Corporate Takeovers (Part 1): Hearings Before the Subcommittee on Telecommunications, Consumer Protection, and Finance,* 99th Cong., 1st sess., February 27, March 12, April 23, and May 22, 1985, pp. 8–9.

84. Ibid., pp. 538–539, 571.

85. Ibid., p. 247. The figures came from Frederick Scherer's testimony.

86. Ibid., p. 571. Total pension-fund assets tripled during the 1980s, from $0.8 trillion in 1979 to an estimated $2.6 trillion by 1989. See Larry Light, "The Power of the Pension Funds: Everyone Is Battling over Their $2.6 Trillion Stash," *Business Week,* November 6, 1989, p. 154.

87. Ibid., p. 684.

88. In fact, the subcommittee's 1987 bill dropped an earlier provision that had asked raiders to calculate the social costs of their bids. House Committee on Energy and Commerce, *Corporate Takeovers: Public Policy,* p. 4.

89. Ibid., pp. 48–52.

90. Requirements included (1) that shareholders approve certain corporate defensive measures against takeovers, in accordance with SEC rules; (2) there be a one-share, one-vote standard for firms traded on national markets; and (3) that management list on corporate proxy statements the slate of nominees for the board of directors proposed by any shareholder with more than 3 percent of the shares or a holding of $500,000. See Paul Starobin, "Dingell, Markey Propose Takeover Measure," *Congressional Quarterly Weekly Report,* May 2, 1987, p. 836.

91. For a summary of the economic literature on the topic, see House Committee on Energy and Commerce, *Corporate Takeovers: Public Policy,* pp. 30–48; and Richard E. Caves, "Mergers, Takeovers, And Economic Efficiency: Foresight vs. Hindsight," *International Journal of International Industrial Organization* 7 (1989): 151–174. See also Michael C. Jensen and Richard

S. Ruback, "The Market for Corporate Control: The Scientific Evidence," *Journal of Financial Economics* 11 (1983): 5–50; Gregg A. Jarrell, James A. Brickley, and Jeffrey M. Netter, "The Market for Corporate Control: The Empirical Evidence Since 1980," *Journal of Economic Perspectives* 2 (1988): 49–68; and F. M Scherer, "Corporate Takeovers: The Efficiency Arguments," *Journal of Economic Perspectives* 2 (1988): 69–82.

92. See, for example, David J. Ravenscraft and F. M. Scherer, "Mergers and Managerial Performance," and F. M. Scherer, "Testimony," in House Committee on Energy and Commerce, *Corporate Takeovers (Part l)*, p. 242–255.

93. Michael C. Jensen, "Testimony," House Committee on Energy and Commerce, *Corporate Takeovers (Part 2)*, pp. 242–255.

94. House Committee on Energy and Commerce, *Corporate Takeovers: Public Policy*, pp. 32–33.

95. In summarizing this evidence, the House subcommittee cited a study by Douglas H. Ginsburg, assistant attorney general, and John F. Robinson of the Office of Management and Budget. The authors noted that even though takeovers were equally likely to cause both economic good and economic harm, it was virtually impossible to determine the outcome in advance. See Douglas H. Ginsbuarg and John F. Robinson, "The Case Against Federal Intervention in the Market for Corporate Control," *Brookings Review*, Winter–Spring 1986, cited in House Committee on Energy and Commerce, *Corporate Takeovers: Public Policy*, p. 47.

96. House Committee on Energy and Commerce, *Corporate Takeovers: Public Policy*, pp. 47–48.

97. Securities and Exchange Commission, *Report on Tender Offer Laws*, pp. 74–77.

98. 457 *U.S.* 624 (1982).

99. See House Committee on Energy and Commerce, *Corporate Takeovers: Public Policy*, pp. 90–9l; and Robert B. Thompson, "Tender Offer Regulation and the Federalization of State Corporate Law," in *Public Policy Toward Corporate Takeovers*, ed. Murray L. Weidenbaum and Kenneth W. Chilton (New Brunswick, NJ: Transactions Books, 1988), pp. 81–83.

100. House Committee on Energy and Commerce, *Corporate Takeovers: Public Policy*, pp. 90–91; and Thompson, "Tender Offer Regulation," pp. 85–89.

101. Elder Witt, "State Anti-Takeover Laws Upheld: Court Upholds Death Penalty Against Last Major Challenge," *Congressional Quarterly Weekly Report*, April 25, 1987, p. 781.

102. Thompson, "Tender Offer Regulation," pp. 92–104, summarized the conflicting trends in the Court's decisions regarding the federal government's authority to regulate the market for corporate control. The Court's decision in *CTS Corp. v. Dynamics Corp. of America*, 481 *U.S.* 69 (1987) upheld Indiana's antitakeover statutes, notwithstanding the concurrent, and allegedly preemptive effect of, federal legislation (i.e., the Williams Act). See, for example, John C. Coates, IV, "State Takeover Statues and Corporate Theory: The Revival of an Old Debate," *New York University Law Review* 64 (1989): 806–876, esp. pp. 860–864.

Chapter 6

1. David Vogel's *Lobbying the Corporation: Citizen Challenges to Business Authority* (New York: Basic Books, 1978) offered a useful introduction to this history.

2. See, for example, David Vogel, "The 'New' Social Regulation," in *Regulation in Perspective: Historical Essays,* ed. Thomas K. McCraw (Cambridge, MA: Harvard University Press, 1981), pp. 155–186; Stephen Breyer, *Regulation and Its Reform* (Cambridge, MA: Harvard University Press, 1982), though ahistorical, brings a coherent perspective to the broad range of regulations that had evolved by the end of the 1970s. Richard Stewart, "The Reformation of American Administrative Law," *Harvard Law Review* 88 (1975): 1667–1683, provides an overview of the administrative changes that accompanied the expansion of regulation and the pressures that these change imposed on the courts and administrative agencies.

3. One of these exceptions was Friedrich Hayek; see his "The Use of Knowledge in Society," *American Economic Review* 35 (1945): 519–530. Hayek's more fully articulated positions in *Law, Legislation and Liberty,* 3 vols. (Chicago: University of Chicago Press, 1973–1975), continued to stress the advantages of private-sector resolutions because individuals knew far more than central planners, though he still acknowledged occasions when government intervention to secure essential public goods or overcome externalities would be appropriate. Contrast this with Kenneth J. Arrow's "Social Responsibility and Economic Efficiency," *Public Policy* 21 (1973): 303–317, and his more pragmatic notion of moral codification.

4. James M. Landis, *The Administrative Process* (New Haven, CT: Yale University Press, 1938), pp. 111–122.

5. New Deal critics complained that the administrative state had illegitimately procured legislative power. In 1946 Congress passed a compromise bill, the Federal Administrative Procedure Act, that constrained the administrative state by setting up procedural norms susceptible to judicial review. Yet the bill did not satisfy skeptics for it still gave administrators discretionary powers in interpreting legislative intent. See, for example, Kenneth Culp Davis, *Discretionary Justice: A Preliminary Inquiry* (Westport, CT: Greenwood Press, [1969] 1980); Paul W. MacAvoy, *The Crisis of the Regulatory Commissions* (New York: Norton, 1970); Richard B. Stewart, "The Reformation of American Administrative Law," *Harvard Law Review* 88 (1975): 1667–1813; and James O. Freedman, *Crisis and Legitimacy: The Administrative Process and American Government* (Cambridge: Cambridge University Press, 1978).

6. Grant McConnell, *Private Power and American Democracy* (New York: Knopf, 1966), pp. 246–297; and Charles K. Rowley, Robert D. Tollison, and Gordon Tullock, eds., *The Political Economy of Rent-Seeking* (Boston: Kluwer Academic Publishers, 1988).

7. See, for example, George J. Stigler, "The Theory of Economic Regulation," in George J. Stigler, *The Citizen and the State: Essays on Regulation* (Chicago: University of Chicago Press, 1975), pp. 114–141, and "The Process of Economic Regulation," *The Anti Trust Bulletin* 17 (1972): 207–235. For a detailed review of the consensus among historians about industry regulations'

adverse economic effects, see Thomas K. McCraw, "Regulation in America: A Review Article," *Business History Review* 49 (1975): 162–183, pp. 171–175.

8. See, for example, McConnell, *Private Power,* pp. 294–295; and Theodore J. Lowi and Benjamin Ginsberg, *American Power: Freedom and Power* (New York: Norton, 1990), pp. 306–310, 551–557.

9. See J. Leiper Freeman, *The Political Process* (New York: Doubleday, 1955).

10. See Theodore J. Lowi, *The End of Liberalism: The Second Republic of the United States,* 2nd ed. (New York: Norton, 1979).

11. Mancur Olson, *The Logic of Collective Action: Public Goods and the Theory of Groups* (Cambridge, MA: Harvard University Press, 1965), pp. 9–16; and Mancur Olson, *The Rise and Decline of Nations: Economic Growth, Stagflation and Social Rigidities* (New Haven, CT: Yale University Press, 1982), chap. 2.

12. James Q. Wilson, *Political Organizations* (New York: Basic Books, 1973).

13. James Q. Wilson, "The Politics of Regulation," in *Politics of Regulation,* ed. James Q. Wilson (New York: Basic Books, 1980), pp. 357–394.

14. Terry Moe, *The Organization of Interests: Incentives and the Internal Dynamics of Political Interest Groups* (Chicago: University of Chicago Press, 1980); and Russel Hardin, *Collective Action* (Baltimore: Johns Hopkins University Press, 1982).

15. See David Finn, *The Corporate Oligarch* (New York: Simon & Schuster, 1969); and Eli Goldston, Herbert C. Morton, and G. Neal Ryland, eds., *The American Business Corporation: New Perspectives on Profit and Purpose* (Cambridge, MA: Harvard University Press, 1972).

16. See, for example, J. A. C. Hetherington, "Fact and Legal Theory: Shareholders, Managers, and Corporate Social Responsibility," *Stanford Law Review* 21 (1969): 248–292. For an elegant review of the various corporate responsibility positions, see Henry Mintzberg, "Who Should Control the Corporation," *California Management Review* 27 (1984): 90–115.

17. During the 1960s and early 1970s, public-interest, as opposed to private-interest groups (i.e., those advocating protection for the propertyless rather than the propertied) had the upper hand, perhaps in part because the logic of their demands—for restrictions on corporate control—fit the equitable logic of the trust approach then in place. Congress and the courts responded by revising election, judicial, and administrative procedures to invite broader and better represented interest-group participation and by establishing new federal agencies to hear and remedy complaints that had not won sufficient managerial attention.

18. Murray L. Weidenbaum, *Business, Government and the Public* (Englewood Cliffs, NJ: Prentice-Hall, 1975).

19. Stewart, "The Reformation," p. 1670.

20. Writers on the more general theory of corporate regulation and administrative law rarely resorted to the language of trust, though commentators on individual federal agencies (like the FTC) or on narrow bodies of regulation (like health) did view the public administrator's mission in those terms. By and large, the leading doctrinal writers on administration, such as Walter Gellhorn, Kenneth Culp Davis, and Louis L. Jaffe, were so absorbed

by neutrality that they avoided giving any substantive slant to administrative law. Those whose focus was on characterizing the work of the proliferating number of agencies used terms like "watchdogs" and "ombudsmen." See, for example, Louis M. Kohlmeier, Jr., *The Regulators: Watchdog Agencies and the Public Interest* (New York: Harper & Row, 1969).

21. See, for example, Robert N. Mayer, *The Consumer Movement: Guardians of the Marketplace* (Boston: Twayne, 1969), pp. 25–33, 59–85; Alan Stone, *Economic Regulation and the Public Interest: The Federal Trade Commission in Theory and Practice* (Ithaca, NY: Cornell University Press, 1977), pp. 232–253; and Mark V. Nadel, *The Politics of Consumer Protection* (Indianapolis: Bobbs-Merrill, 1971).

22. See Colin S. Diver, "Policymaking Paradigms in Administrative Law," *Harvard Law Review* 95 (1981): 393–434; and Gary C. Bryner, *Bureaucratic Discretion: Law and Policy in Federal Regulatory Agencies* (New York: Pergamon Press, 1987), pp. 19–29, 91–191.

23. See Kenneth W. Clarkson and Timothy J. Muris, *The Federal Trade Commission since 1970; Economic Regulation and Bureaucratic Behavior* (Cambridge: Cambridge University Press, 1981), pp. 161–203.

24. Ibid., pp. 246–275.

25. The parallels were made clear in Richard A. Harris and Sidney M. Miklis, *The Politics of Regulatory Change: A Tale of Two Agencies* (Oxford: Oxford University Press, 1989); Mayer, *The Consumer Movement*, pp. 38–40, sketched the conflicts as well as the mutual sympathies of the two movements. See also David Vogel, *National Styles of Regulation: Environmental Policy in Great Britain and the United States* (Ithaca, NY: Cornell University Press, 1986); Richard A. Liroff, *A National Policy for the Environment: NEPA and Its Aftermath* (Bloomington: Indiana University Press, 1976); and Walter A. Rosenbaum, *The Politics of Environmental Concern* (New York: Praeger, 1977).

26. See Liroff, *A National Policy;* and Joseph F. DiMento, *Environmental Law and American Business: Dilemmas of Compliance* (New York: Plenum, 1986). For standing to sue on behalf of the environment, see Christopher D. Stone, "Should Trees Have Standing? Toward Legal Rights for Natural Objects," *Southern California Law Review* 45 (1972): 450–501.

27. For a comprehensive and illuminating comparative view of the federal government's environmental laws, see Eckard Rehbinder and Richard Stewart, *Environmental Protection Policy*, vol. 2 of *Integration Through Law: Europe and the American Federal Experience*, ed. Mauro Cappelletti, Monica Seccombe, Joseph Weiler (Berlin: DeGruyter, 1985), pp. 43–56, 109–136, 177–220.

28. The literature on this point is voluminous. On specific policy reforms, see Charles Bullock and Harell R. Rodgers, *Coercion to Compliance* (Lexington, MA: Lexington Books, 1976). On the larger political and legal context for such reform in the United States, see Rehbinder and Stewart, *Environmental Protection Policy*, p. 191.

29. The earlier postwar legislation was largely limited to the Labor Management Relations Act of 1947 (Taft–Hartley Act) and the Labor–Management Reporting and Disclosure Act of 1959 (Landrum–Griffin Act). For a description of their provisions and legislative histories, see Charles J. Morris,

The Developing Labor Law: The Board, the Courts, and the National Labor Relations Act, 2nd ed. (Washington, DC: Bureau of National Affairs, 1983), pp. 35–67.

30. See, for example, Marc Linder, "Towards Universal Worker Coverage Under the National labor Relations Act: Making Room for Uncontrolled Employees, Dependent Contractors, and Employee-Like Persons," *University of Detroit Law Review* 66 (1989): 555–602, on the evolution of the "economic reality of dependency" doctrine in labor regulation.

31. On the parallels between the civil rights movement of the 1950s and 1960s and the labor movement of the 1930s, see Francis Fox Piven and Richard A. Cloward, *Poor People's Movements and Why They Failed* (New York: Pantheon Books, 1977). For an overview of federal civil rights legislation and policies during the 1960s and 1970s, see Barbara L. Schlei and Paul Grossman, *Employment Discrimination Law,* 2nd ed. (Washington, DC: Bureau of National Affairs, 1987).

32. See Schlei and Grossman, *Employment Discrimination Law,* pp. 436–481.

33. Ibid., pp. 1–12. See also Henry G. Manne, "The 'Higher Criticism' of the Modern Corporation," *Columbia Law Review* 62 (1962): 401–432, esp. pp. 423–424.

34. See Schlei and Grossman, *Employment Discrimination Law,* pp. 206–435, 482–532.

35. See Sar Levitan, Peter E. Carlson, and Isaac Shapiro, *Protecting American Workers: An Assessment of Government Programs* (Washington, DC: Bureau of National Affairs, 1986), pp. 57–58.

36. See Schlei and Grossman, *Employment Discrimination Law,* p. 870.

37. See James C. Sharf, "Personnel Testing and the Law," in *Personnel Management,* ed. Kendrith M. Rowland and Gerald R. Ferris (Boston: Allyn and Bacon, 1982), pp. 156–182.

38. See Charles Heckscher, *New Unionism: Employee Involvement in the Changing Corporation* (New York: Basic Books, 1988), pp. 62–81.

39. On the range of proposals concerning unorganized workers that had emerged by the 1970s, see David W. Ewing, *"Do It My Way or You're Fired!" Employee Rights and the Changing Role of Management Prerogatives* (New York: Wiley, 1982); and Alan F. Westin and Stephan Salisbury, eds., *Individual Rights in the Corporation* (New York: Pantheon Books, 1980).

40. The enabling legislation clearly stated Congress's intent that management should act as society's "fiduciary" in seeing to it that all American workers, regardless of their skills or income, would work in a safe and healthy environment.

41. Levitan et al., *Protecting American Workers,* pp. 197–221.

42. See Betty Linn Krikorian, *Fiduciary Standards in Pension and Trust Fund Management* (Stoneham: Butterworth Legal Publishers, 1989), pp. 11–12.

43. For a discussion of earlier proposals along these lines, see Manne, "Higher Criticism," pp. 418–430. Ralph Nader's 1971 Conference on Corporate Accountability, reported in Ralph Nader and Mark J. Green, eds., *Corporate Power in America* (New York: Grossman, 1973), organized the later call for governance reforms, including "Campaign GM," federal chartering of the corporation, and corporate disclosures. See Vogel, *Lobbying the Corpo-*

ration, pp. 71–125; and Rogene A. Buchholz, *Business Environment and Public Policy: Implications for Management and Strategy Formulation,* 3rd ed. (Englewood Cliffs, NJ: Prentice-Hall, 1989), pp. 263–276.

44. See Nader and Green, *Corporate Power;* Christopher Stone, *Where the Law Ends* (New York: Harper & Row, 1975); and Senate Committee on Banking and Urban Affairs, *Staff Report on Corporate Accountability: A Reexamination of Rules Relating to Shareholder Communications, Shareholder Participation in the Corporate Governance Process and Corporate Governance Generally,* Division of Corporation Finance, Securities and Exchange Commission, 96th Cong., 2nd sess., September 4, 1980, p. 712.

45. Senate Banking, Housing, and Urban Affairs Committee, *Protection of Shareholders' Rights Act of 1980: Hearing Before the Subcommittee on Securities,* 96th Cong., 2nd sess., November 19, 1980, p. 4.

46. See Mark Green, "Case for Corporate Democracy: On the Corporate Democracy Act," *Regulation Magazine,* May–June 1980, in ibid., pp. 354–359. For a contractarian view, see Henry G. Manne, "Testimony," in Senate Commerce, Science and Transportation Committee, *Corporate Rights and Responsibilities,* 94th Cong., 2nd sess., June 15–17, 21–23, 1976, pp. 225–241.

47. See the testimony and submitted documents of Lewis Gilbert, Ralph Nader, and Mark Green, in Senate Banking, Housing and Urban Affairs Committee, *Protection,* pp. 209–397; and Philip Blumberg, *Industrial Democracy: The Sociology of Participation* (New York: Schocken Books, 1969).

48. See, for example, Alfred F. Conard, *Corporations in Perspective* (Mineola, NY: Foundation Press, 1976), pp. 365–366.

49. Ibid., pp. 366–378.

50. John Rawls, *A Theory of Justice* (Cambridge, MA: Belknap Press, 1971).

51. See, Robert A. Dahl, *After the Revolution: Authority in a Good Society* (New Haven, CT: Yale University Press, 1970), esp. pp. 115–140; Robert A. Dahl, "Governing the Giant Corporation," in Nader and Green, eds., *Corporate Power,* pp. 10–24; Robert A. Dahl, *Dilemmas of Pluralist Democracy: Autonomy vs. Control* (New Haven: Yale University Press, 1982), pp. 81–205; and Robert A. Dahl, *A Preface to Economic Democracy* (Chicago: University of Chicago Press, 1952), pp. 111–160.

52. Stewart, "The Reformation," p. 1683.

53. Consider Follett's ideas about particularistic versus unifying administrative decisions, in Mary P. Follett, *The New State, Group Organization: The Solution of Popular Government* (New York: Longmans, Green, 1918); James Buchanan and Gordon Tullock's ideas about logrolling in *The Calculus of Consent: Logical Foundations of Constitutional Democracy* (Ann Arbor: University of Michigan Press, 1962); and Lester C. Thurow's discussion of a zero-sum game in *The Zero-Sum Society: Distribution and the Possibilities for Economic Change* (New York: Basic Books, 1980).

54. See Stigler, *The Citizen;* and Murray L. Weidenbaum, *The Costs of Government Regulation of Business* (Washington, DC: U.S. Government Printing Office, 1978).

55. Ronald H. Coase, "The Problem of Social Cost," *Journal of Law and Economics* 3 (1960): This article has apparently been more widely cited than any other in the field of economics.

56. Guido Calabresi, "Some Thoughts on Risk Distribution and the Law of Torts," *Yale Law Journal* 70 (1961): 499–553, made similar and cotemporaneous observations about transaction costs and the distribution of legal rights.

57. Milton Friedman believed that the government so little represented the public will that he insisted that students refer to the "government sector" instead of the "public sector." Adele Wick, classnotes, University of Chicago, Fall, 1974.

58. As Albert Hirschman noted, "What is a public good for some—say, a plentiful suply of police dogs and atomic bombs—may well be judged a public evil by others in the same community. The disginguishing characteristic of these goods is not only that they *can* be consumed by everyone, but that there is *no escape* from consuming them unless one were to leave the community by which they are provided." Hirschman, *Exit, Voice and Loyalty: Responses to Decline in Firms, Organizations, and States* (Cambridge, MA: Harvard University Press, 1970), p. 101 (emphasis in the original).

59. Buchanan and Tullock, *The Calculus of Consent.*

60. William A. Niskanen, *Bureaucracy and Representative Government* (Chicago: Aldine, Atherton, 1971), and *Bureaucracy: Servant or Master?* (London: Institute of Economic Affairs, 1973).

61. For a summary of this literature, see Steven E. Rhoads, *The Economist's View of the World: Government, Markets, and Public Policy* (Cambridge: Cambraidge University Press, 1985), pp. 67–75.

62. Coase described his approach as consonant with nineteenth-century industrial common law. For a discussion of his influence on twentieth-century legal thinking, see Bruce A. Ackerman, *Reconstructing American Law* (Cambridge, MA: Harvard University Press, 1984), pp. 46–71.

63. For example, Charles Schultze, a leading writer on fiscal policy at the Brookings Institution and chairman of President Carter's Council of Economic Advisers, urged forsaking conservative and liberal prejudices about government regulation and instead realistically assessing the complexities and costs of regulatory policy. Although he articulated a "rebuttable presumption" that basically rephrased Coase's basic argument in favor of market-based rules except in special circumstances, he also believed that political debate itself functioned to enlighten citizens to the public interest, which extended far beyond the economist's analytic reach. Charles L. Schultze, *The Public Use of Private Interest* (Washington, DC: Brookings Institution, 1977).

64. Ibid.; Alfred Kahn, *The Economics of Regulation: Principles and Institutions* (New York: Wiley, 1970).

65. Alfred A. Marcus, *The Adversary Economy: Business Responses to Changing Government Requirements* (Westport, CT: Greenwood Press, 1984), p. 177.

66. Ibid., pp. 178–179.

67. Charles Noble, *Liberalism at Work: The Rise and Fall of OSHA* (Philadelphia: Temple University Press, 1986), pp. 108–109, 158.

68. See David Vogel, *Fluctuating Fortunes: the Political Pwer of Business in America* (New York: Basic Books, 1978), pp. 148–150. Labor lost its campaign to pass legislation legalizing common situs picketing; consumer

groups failed to obtain legislation establishing a consumer protection agency; and environmentalists failed to stop auto manufacturers from weakening the 1970 Clean Air Act amendments.

69. For example, Congress battled to a statemate with the administration over environmental deregulation; and the courts did not always follow Reagan's lead. See its working out of Reagan's challenge to OSHA in a cotton dust standard case, in Noble, *Liberalism at Work*, pp. 168–170, n. 207; and John D. Aram, *Managing Business and Public Policy: Concepts, Issues and Cases*, 2nd ed. (Marshfield, MA: Pitman, 1986), pp. 239–249.

70. For more specific examples and across-the-board analyses of using market instruments to help improve market outcomes, see Vogel, *Fluctuating Fortunes;* Susan Tolchin and Martin Tolchin, *Dismantling America: The Rush to Deregulate* (Boston: Houghton Mifflin, 1983), and George C. Eads and Michael Fix, eds., *The Reagan Regulatory Strategy: An Assessment* (Washington, DC: Urban Institute Press, 1984). For an analysis of trade regulation, see Clarkson and Muris, eds., *The Federal Trade Commission Since 1970* (Cambridge: Cambridge University Press, 1981); for labor law changes, see Labor Law Exchange, *The Dotson Board's Decisions 1983–1985*, (Washington, DC: AFL–CIO Lawyers Coordinating Committee, 1985); and Labor Law Exchange, *Occupational Safety and Health* (Washington, DC: AFL–CIO Lawyers Coordinating Committee, 1985). For general discussions and conclusions about the growing importance of market-based incentives in the EPA, see Marcus, *Adversary Economy*, pp. 180–181; and Harris and Milkis, *The Politics of Regulatory Change*, pp. 246–250.

Chapter 7

1. *Eastern Railroad Presidents Conference v. Noerr*, 365 *U.S.* 127 (1961) and *United Mine Workers v. Pennington*, 381 *U.S.* 657 (1965). For the broader political and economic significance of these cases, see Robert Bork, *The Antitrust Paradox: A Policy at War with Itself* (New York: Basic Books, 1978), pp. 347–364.

By the late 1960s, the Justice Department was sufficiently suspicious that IT&T had corrupted the public process for corporate gain that it brought a public suit against its conglomerate acquisitions on economic grounds that were only nominal. The federal circuit court of appeals dismissed the suit, and the government withdrew from other similar ventures. See *United States v. International Telephone and Telegraph Corporation* (IT&T), 324 *F. Supp.* 19 (D. Conn. 1970).

2. See Kenneth M. Davidson, *Megamergers: Corporate America's Billion-Dollar Takeovers* (Cambridge, MA: Ballinger, 1985), pp. 119–120; and Harvey Goldschmid, H. Michael Mann, and J. Fred Weston, eds., *Industrial Concentration: The New Learning* (Boston: Little, Brown, 1974), p. 2.

3. See F. M. Scherer, *Industrial Market Structure and Economic Performance*, 2nd ed. (Chicago: Rand McNally, 1980).

4. They argued, for example, that instead of being collusive, advertising strategies might actually bolster competition by providing information about

alternative supplies and better prices. See Goldschmid et al., *Industrial Concentration;* and Bork, *Antitrust Paradox,* pp. 163–197.

5. See Alfred Kahn, *The Economics of Regulation: Principles and Institutions,* 2 vols. (Cambridge, MA: MIT Press, 1971).

6. Oliver Williamson, *Markets and Hierarchies: Analysis and Antitrust Implications* (New York: Free Press, 1975).

7. Ibid., p. 246.

8. See Oliver Williamson, *The Economic Institutions of Capitalism: Firms, Markets, Relational Contracting* (New York: Free Press, 1985), pp. 100–102.

9. See, for example, Congressional Quarterly, *Dollar Politics* (Washington, DC: Congresional Quarterly Press, 1982), pp. 1–8, and Alexander Heard, *The Costs of Democracy: Financing American Political Campaigns* (Garden City, NY: Doubleday, 1962), pp. 92–104; and Archibald Cox, "Constitutional Issues in the Regulation of the Financing of Election Campaigns," *Cleveland State Law Review* 31 (1982): 395–418, esp. pp. 396–398.

10. Congressional Quarterly, *Dollar Politics,* pp. 8–10.

11. For Arrow's discussion, see his *Social Choice and Individual Values,* 2nd ed. (New Haven, CT: Yale University Press, 1963).

12. Robert A. Dahl, *A Preface to Democratic Theory* (Chicago: University of Chicago Press, 1952).

13. Ibid., pp. 132, 128 (italics in original).

14. Ibid., p. 133.

15. Ibid., p. 81.

16. Robert A. Dahl, "Business and Politics: A Critical Appraisal of Political Science," in *Social Science Reserach on Business: Product and Potential,* ed. Robert A. Dahl, Mason Haire, and Paul Lazarsfeld (New York: Columbia University Press, 1959), pp. 3–44.

17. For more recent work on agenda manipulation, see William H. Riker, *Liberalism Against Populism: A Confrontation Between the Theory of Democracy and the Theory of Social Choice* (San Francisco: Freeman, 1982), p. 200.

18. Ibid., pp. 24–31. The classic work is by E. E. Schattschneider, *Politics, Pressures and the Tariff: A Study of Free Private Enterprise in Pressure Politics as Shown in the 1929–1930 Revision of the Tariff* (New York: Prentice-Hall, 1935), a study behind the scenes of the Smoot–Hawley Act.

19. Ibid., pp. 34–38.

20. Robert A. Dahl, *Who Governs? Democracy and Power in an American City* (New Haven, CT: Yale University Press, 1961).

21. Ibid., pp. 271–275.

22. Ibid., p. 273.

23. Edwin M. Epstein, *The Corporation in American Politics* (Englewood Cliffs, NJ: Prentice-Hall, 1969). See Raymond A. Bauer, Ithiel de Sola Pool, and Lewis A. Dexter, *American Business and Public Policy* (New York: Atherton Press, 1964), for another extensive empirical analysis of corporate political action and influence.

24. Epstein, *Corporation in American Politics,* pp. 1–7, 191, 212, 216, 240–242. The theoretical advantages included (1) organization, (2) riches, (3) access (to those in authority), (4) patronage (the dependency of others on busi-

nessperson's private decisions), (5) surrogateship (the performance of public tasks); (6) influence on the mass media, and (7) a backlog of political success.

25. E. E. Schattschneider, *The Semi-sovereign People: A Realist's View of Democracy in America* (New York: Holt, Rinehart and Winston, 1960). See also Peter Bachrach and Morton S. Baratz, "Two Faces of Power," *American Political Science Review* 56 (1962): 947–952; and Matthew A. Crenson, *The Unpolitics of Politics: A Study of Non-Decision Making in the Cities* (Baltimore, Johns Hopkins University Press, 1971).

26. Schattschneider, *The Semi-sovereign People,* p. 42.

27. Ibid., pp. 42–43.

28. "The relation of business and the Republican party is much like that of organized labor and the Democratic party. Republican critics of the Democratic party like to portray the Democratic party as the slave of organized labor. Actually, labor usually has no place else to go. As long as it thinks that elections are important, it *must* support the Democratic party, generally. The fact of political life are that neither business nor labor is able to win elections by itself" (ibid., p. 57, italics in original).

29. Ibid., pp. 118–128.

30. Anthony Downs, *An Economic Theory of Democracy* (New York: Harper, 1957). Even when more complex assumptions were brought to play, such as multiissue campaigns and imperfect information, the model offered analytic support for claiming popular control over elected officials. See Peter C. Ordeshook, *Game Theory and Political Theory* (Cambridge: Cambridge University Press, 1986), pp. 166–174, for refinements.

31. Downs, *An Economic Theory,* pp. 89–92. Donations did more than pay for advertisements and other campaign expenditures. They also attracted other endorsements which in turn served to inform voters and ensure sufficient voter interest in the election to go to the polls.

32. Charles E. Lindblom, *Politics and Markets: The World's Political–Economic Systems* (New York: Basic Books, 1977).

33. Michael Useem, *The Inner Circle: Large Corporations and the Rise of Business Political Activity in the U.S. and U.K.* (Oxford: Oxford University Press, 1984).

34. Thomas Ferguson, "Party Realignment and American Industrial Structure: The Investment Theory of Political Parties in Historical Perspective," in *Research in Political Economy,* vol. 6, ed. Paul Zarembka (Greenwich, CT: JAI Press, 1983), pp. 1–82; and Thomas Ferguson and Joel Rogers, *Right Turn: The Decline of the Democrats and the Future of American Politics* (New York: Hill & Wang, 1986), pp. 44–46.

35. See Richard D. McKelvey and Peter C. Ordeshook, "Information, Electoral Equilibrium and the Democratic Ideal," *Journal of Politics* 48 (1986): 909–937.

36. David Vogel, "Why Businessmen Distrust Their State: The Political Consciousness of American Corporate Executives," *British Journal of Political Science* 8 (1978): 45–78.

37. Robert A. Dahl, *Dilemmas of Pluralist Democracy: Autonomy vs. Control* (New Haven, CT: Yale University Press, 1982), pp. 166–205.

38. See Congressional Quarterly, *Dollar Politics,* pp. 6–8.

39. The inspiration for this change came from organized labor. The Justice Department had indicted the officers of a local pipefitters' union for allegedly coercing union members to contribute to the union's "voluntary" political action committee. With legal issues both complicated and novel, the case appeared likely to reach the U.S. Supreme Court. To preempt an unfavorable ruling, the unions pushed hard for electoral reforms that would safeguard their political voice. Anticipating corporate opposition, they also included provisions favorable to business, which then remained uncharacteristically aloof to the reform process.

40. Congressional Quarterly, *Dollar Politics*, pp. 10–11. The Senate Select Committee on Presidential Campaign Activity reported that during the 1972 presidential election, at least thirteen corporations used corporate funds to make donations in excess of $780,000, of which $749,000 ended up in Nixon's reelection campaign. As a result of the Watergate scandal, the SEC investigated whether or not corporate managers were misappropriating shareholder funds by diverting them into political campaigns. The study revealed massive illegal payments to political campaigns, but most of these funds were relatively small and evenly distributed among candidates of opposing views. See Graham Wilson, *Interest Group in the United States* (Oxford: Clarendon Press, 1981), pp. 63, 69.

41. Congressional Quarterly, *Dollar Politics*, p. 13.

42. The limit on individual donations was $1,000; the FECA supplemented private campaign donations with public financing in presidential election campaigns.

43. *Buckley v. Valeo*, 424 *U.S.* 1 (1976).

44. The Court applied a similar logic in upholding the $1,000 limit on individual contributions.

45. Downs, *Economic Theory of Democracy*, had pointed out that reducing the voter's cost of acquiring information would lead to a better informed citizenry, one that could then vote more readily in accordance with its interests. As long as citizens could identify representations about candidates' platforms and the sources of those representations, based on their own political identifications, they could then either support or oppose recognizable interests in elections. While still recognizing the possibility that "moneyed interests" might dominate the flow of information and thereby keep the citizenry from becoming informed about poorly financed positions of more central interest, students of the political process found that voters were both resourceful in gathering information of personal import and capable of discounting large quantities of one-sided information by referring to its sources of support, such as corporate contributions or spokespersons. For instance, although Ralph Charles Lindblom's *Politics and Markets* sought to demonstrate the evils of firm size, the consensus among political scientists tended to support the insights of people like Edwin Epstein, who believed that as long as the electorate had access to nonpartisan polls and was informed about a candidate's sources of support, individual voters would sort out campaign information adequately enough to protect their own interests.

46. 435 *U.S.* 765 (1978).

47. In sustaining the provisions that capped contributions, *Buckley v. Valeo* reflected substantial government discretion in regulating elections to ensure equality or fairness. But much corporate speech that was commercially motivated under its political gloss was still protected, for the Court had begun immunizing even ordinary commercial advertising against governmental restrictions. See *Virginia State Board of Pharmacy v. Virginia Citizens Consumer Council,* 425 *U.S.* 748 (1976). On the broader constitutional implications, see Laurence H. Tribe, *Constitutional Choices* (Cambridge, MA: Harvard University Press, 1985), pp. 188–220, esp. pp. 210–218.

48. Tribe, *Constitutional Choices,* pp. 802–823.

49. See *Cort v. Ash,* 422 *U.S.* 66 (1975).

50. *Austin v. Michigan Chamber of Commerce,* 58 LW 4373 (1990).

51. Ibid.

52. David Vogel, *Fluctuating Fortunes: The Political Power of Business in America* (New York: Basic Books, 1978), pp. 117, quoting Herbert Alexander, *Financing Elections* (Washington, DC: Congressional Quarterly Press, 1976), p. 112.

53. See Theodore J. Eismeier and Phillip H. Pollock, III, *Business, Money and the Rise of Corporate PACS in American Elections* (New York: Quorum Books, 1988), pp. 98–100.

54. See Congressional Quarterly, *Dollar Politics,* pp. 23–24. In 1979 the House of Representatives passed the Obey–Railsback bill, which would have reduced from $10,000 to $6,000 the amount that a PAC could contribute to a candidate during the primary and general election and limited House candidates to no more than $70,000 in contributions from PACs during a two-year election cycle. But this bill died in the Senate. See Eismeier and Pollack, *Business, Money,* p. 98.

55. Even though the antitrust hearings did lead to one set of reforms, requiring premerger notification for firms with assets over $10 million, the Hart–Scott–Rodino Act did little to inhibit the pace of mergers or make relevant information more widely available.

56. John J. Flynn, "The Social Political and Economic Consequences of Corporate Size," *Law of Contemporary Law* 163 (1976): 165 (italics added).

57. Ibid., p. 184.

58. Ibid., p. 171.

59. Ibid., p. 174.

60. As quoted in Kenneth M. Davidson, *Megamergers: Corporate America's Billion Dollar Takeovers* (Cambridge, MA: Ballinger, 1985), p. 348.

61. See Congressional Quarterly, *Dollar Politics,* pp. 8–17. The 1976 FECA amendments also worked out a compromise between labor and business over a controversial 1975 FEC decision that allowed corporate PACs to solicit contributions from all of the corporation's employees, including union members. Labor unions found this decision particularly troubling because the law continued to confine their PAC solicitations to union members. Under the revised statute, however, both union and corporate PACs were permitted to solicit contributions by mail from all employees twice each year (p. 16).

62. Ibid., pp. 41–42. See also Edwin M. Epstein, "The PAC Phenomenon: An Overview," *Arizona Law Review* 22 (1980): 355–372.

Chapter 8

1. Ida M. Tarbell, *The Life of Elbert H. Gary: The Story of Steel* (New York: D. Appleton, 1925), p. 137.

2. James Livingston, *Origins of the Federal Reserve System: Money, Class, and Corporate Capitalism, 1890–1913* (Ithaca, NY: Cornell University Press, 1986), p. 215.

3. See Alfred D. Chandler, Jr., *The Visible Hand: The Managerial Revolution in American Business* (Cambridge, MA: Belknap Press, 1977), pp. 464–468.

4. John Desmond Glover, *The Revolutionary Corporations: Engines of Plenty, Engines of Growth, Engines of Change* (Homewood, IL: Dow Jones–Irwin, 1980), pp. 35–41.

5. See Alfred D. Chandler, Jr., *Strategy and Structure: Chapters in the History of the Industrial Enterprise* (Cambridge, MA: MIT Press, 1962), pp. 7–17.

6. H. Thomas Johnson and Robert S. Kaplan provide an excellent historical treatment of the accounting profession in their *Relevance Lost: The Rise and Fall Management Accounting* (Boston: Harvard Business School Press, 1987); see also David F. Hawkins, "The Development of Modern Financial Reporting Practices Among American Manufacturing Corporations," *Business History Review* 37 (1963): 135–168.

7. Chandler, *Strategy and Structure*, pp. 290–298.

8. Oliver Williamson, *The Economic Institutions of Capitalism: Firms, Markets, Relational Contracting* (New York: Free Press, 1985), pp. 287–288.

9. Louis Galambos and Joseph Pratt, *The Rise of the Corporate Commonwealth: U.S. Business and Public Policy in the Twentieth Century* (New York: Basic Books, 1988), pp. 92–99.

10. William J. Barber, *From New Era to New Deal: Herbert Hoover, the Economists and American Economic Policy, 1921–1933* (Cambridge: Cambridge University Press, 1985), pp. 8–13; and Ellis Hawley, *The New Deal and the Problem of Monopoly: A Study in Economic Ambivalence* (Princeton, NJ: Princeton University Press, 1966), pp. 7–13.

11. U.S. Department of Commerce, *Historical Statistics of the United States: Colonial Times to 1970* (Washington, DC: U.S. Government Printing Office, 1975), p. 284; and Daniel Horowitz, *The Morality of Spending: Attitudes Toward the Consumer Society 1875–1940* (Baltimore: Johns Hopkins University Press, 1985), pp. 120–123.

12. For a thorough discussion of this topic, see Robert D. Cuff, *The War Industries Board: Business–Government Relations During World War I* (Baltimore: Johns Hopkins University Press, 1973).

13. For the principal histories of the period, see G. Cullom Davis, "The Transformation of the Federal Trade Commission," *Mississippi Valley Historical Review* 49 (1962): 437–455; Carl McFarland, *Judicial Control of the Federal Trade Commission and Interstate Commerce Commission, 1920–1930: A Comparative Study in the Relations of Courts to Administrative Commissions* (Cambridge,

MA: Harvard University Press, 1933); and Thomas C. Blaisdell, *The Federal Trade Commission: An Experiment in the Control of Business* (New York: Columbia University Press, 1932). For an interpretive assessment, see Lawrence S. Zacharias, "Unfairness, Advertising Regulation and Corporate Legitimacy," School of Management Working Paper Series, University of Massachusetts at Amherst, 1986.

14. Galambos and Pratt, *Rise of the Corporate Commonwealth*, pp. 92–99.

15. Richard S. Tedlow, *Keeping the Corporate Image: Public Relations and Business, 1900–1950* (Greenwich, CT: JAI Press, 1979), pp. 31–48.

16. Thomas C. Cochran, *Business in American Life: A History* (New York: McGraw-Hill, 1972), pp. 305–312.

17. Young was an accomplished public utilities attorney.

18. Josephine Case and Everett Case, *Owen D. Young and American Enterprise: A Biography* (Boston: David R. Godine, 1982), pp. 143–144.

19. Ibid., pp. 252–253.

20. Ibid.

21. Case and Case, *Owen D. Young*, pp. 370–376; and Owen D. Young, "Dedication Address," *Harvard Business Review* 5 (1927): 385–394.

22. Vincent Carosso, *Investment Banking in America: A History* (Cambridge, MA: Harvard University Press, 1970), chaps. 15–19.

23. See David Loth's account in his *Swope of G.E.* (New York: Simon & Schuster, 1958).

24. Barber, *From New Era to New Deal*, pp. 190–192.

25. For a detailed look at the codes in such industries as coal, oil, autos, textiles and lumber, see John K. Ohl, *Hugh S. Johnson and the New Deal* (Dekalb: Northern Illinois University Press, 1985), pp. 190–192. Johnson was appointed head of the NRA.

26. Robert Collins, *The Business Response to Keynes, 1929–1964* (New York: Columbia University Press, 1981), pp. 31–42; and Thomas C. Cochran, *The American Business System: A Historical Perspective, 1900–1955* (Cambridge, MA: Harvard University Press, 1957), pp. 316–321.

27. William E. Leuchtenberg, *Franklin D. Roosevelt and the New Deal, 1932–1940* (New York: Harper & Row, 1963), pp. 146–166; and Arthur M. Schlesinger, Jr., *The Age of Roosevelt: The Politics of Upheaval, 1935–1936* (Boston: Houghton Mifflin, 1960), pp. 316–321.

28. Schlesinger, *The Age of Roosevelt*, pp. 291–342, 385–423.

29. Jordan A. Schwarz, *Liberal: Adolf A. Berle and the Vision of an American Era* (New York: Free Press, 1987), pp. 50–68.

30. Christopher L. Tomlins, *The State and the Unions: Labor Relations, Law and the Organized Labor Movement in America, 1880–1960* (Cambridge: Cambridge University Press, 1985), pp. 100–138; and Howell John Harris, *The Right to Manage: Industrial Relations Policies of American Business in the 1940s* (Madison: University of Wisconsin Press, 1982), pp. 20–23.

31. Tomlins, *The State and the Unions*, pp. 132–138.

32. Ibid., pp. 172–195, 216–239; and Bert Cochran, *Labor and Communism: The Conflict That Shaped American Unions* (Princeton, NJ: Princeton University Press, 1977), pp. 148–246.

33. Tomlins, *The State and the Unions*, pp. 237–241.

34. These four groupings come from Harris, *The Right to Manage*, pp. 23–37.

35. Schatz, *The Electrical Workers: A History of Labor at General Electric and Westinghouse, 1923–1960* (Urbana: University of Illinois Press, 1963), pp. 17–19, 37–38, and 53–76.

36. Harris, *The Right to Manage*, pp. 118–125.

37. Ibid., pp. 123, 152; and Schatz, *The Electrical Workers*, pp. 167–186.

38. Tomlins, *The State and the Unions*, pp. 247–248.

39. Robert Griffith, "Dwight D. Eisenhower and the Corporate Commonwealth," *American Historical Review* 87 (1982): 87–122.

40. Galambos and Pratt, *The Rise of the Corporate Commonwealth*, pp. 131–154, 211–213.

41. Ernest Gellhorn and Barr B. Boyer, *Administrative Law in a Nutshell*, 2nd ed. (St. Paul: West Publishing, 1981).

42. Richard B. Stewart, "Regulation in a Liberal State: The Role of Non-Commodity Values," *Yale Law Journal* 92 (1983): 1537–1590; J. Ronald Fox, *Managing Business–Government Relations: Cases and Notes on Business–Government Problems* (Homewood, IL: Irwin, 1982), pp. 137–138; Grant McConnell, *Private Power and American Democracy* (New York: Knopf, 1966), pp. 338–352. See also our own Chapter 6.

43. J. Leiper Freeman, *The Political Process: Executive Bureau–Legislative Committee Relations* (New York: Doubleday, 1955), pp. 6–14; and Thomas L. Gais, Mark A. Peterson, and Jack L. Walker, "Interest Groups, Iron Triangles and Representative Institutions in American National Government," *British Journal of Political Science* 14 (1984): 161–163.

44. Theodore J. Lowi, *The End of Liberalism: The Second Republic of the United States*, 2nd ed. (New York: Norton, 1979), pp. 50–63.

45. Robert Griffith, "Forging America's Postwar Order: Politics and Political Economy in the Age of Truman," unpublished manuscript, 1984. The oil industry, for example, allied with bureaucrats in the Department of the Interior to forestall the interior secretary's designs to develop a national oil company, and the utility industry blocked the government's entry into the lucrative power distribution business.

46. Collins, *The Business Response to Keynes*, pp. 43–52.

47. Ibid., chaps. 3, 4.

48. Ibid., pp. 57–62. For a discussion of the Business Council's current function, see Edward Herman, *Corporate Control, Corporate Power* (Cambridge: Cambridge University Press, 1981), p. 213.

49. Case and Case, *Owen D. Young*, p. 755.

50. Alan R. Raucher, *Paul G. Hoffman: Architect of Foreign Aid* (Lexington: University of Kentucky Press, 1985), pp. 22–27, 42–47.

51. Ibid., pp. 50–51.

52. Ibid., pp. 17–18.

53. John K. Galbraith summarized these ideas in *American Capitalism: The Concept of Countervailing Power*, 2nd ed. (Boston: Houghton Mifflin, 1956), and *The New Industrial State* (Boston: Houghton Mifflin, 1956).

54. Editorial, "Management in the Transition," *Fortune*, July 1944, pp. 132–33; and Collins, *The Business Response to Keynes*.

55. Henry Luce believed that business's inability to comprehend the dignity and the beauty of the new corporate order created a splendid publishing opportunity. In 1940 he targeted thirty thousand executives as the corporate executive community and hoped that *Fortune* would help them draw the line between responsible and irresponsible business practices. See Robert T. Elson, *Time Inc.: The Intimate History of a Publishing Enterprise 1923–1941* (New York: Atheneum, 1968), pp. 128–130.

56. For example, as late as 1950, Mable Newcomer found that out of a sample of 428 top executives, only 4 percent had graduate degrees in business administration (and nearly all of these were from Harvard). See Mabel Newcomer, *The Big Business Executive* (New York: Columbia University Press, 1955), pp. 68–69.

57. *Fortune* offered its readers feature stories on many notable managers. See, for example, "Life of Owen D. Young," *Fortune*, January, February, March 1931; "Oil Aboard," Ibid., March 1931; and "A Panel of General Motors Executives," Ibid., April 1930.

58. For example, see "American Workingman," August 1931, p. 54, and "Business-and-Government: Business, Faced with an Overwhelming Political Fact, Should Favor a More Socialized State," June 1938, pp. 51–52.

59. *Fortune* first published an article by William B. Benton, vice-chairman, Board of Trustees, Committee for Economic Development, entitled "The Economics of a Free Society: A Declaration of American Economic Policy," October 1944, pp. 162–165. *Fortune* reissued the article as a pamphlet in its December 1944 issue.

60. "U.S.A.: The Permanent Revolution," February 1951. Also see John Knox Jessup, "A Political Role for the Corporation," *Fortune*, August 1952, pp. 112–113; and "The Moral History of U.S. Business," *Fortune* December 1940, pp. 143–146. Adolf A. Berle, Jr., also weighed in with a similar discussions in his *The 20th Century Capitalist Revolution* (New York: Harcourt Brace & World, 1954).

61. Francis X. Sutton et al., *The American Business Creed* (New York: Schocken Books, 1962).

62. Allen J. Matusow, *The Unraveling of America: A History of Liberalism in the 1960s* (New York: Harper & Row, 1984), chap 2.

63. For accounts of the school's earlier history, see Melvin T. Copeland, *And Mark an Era: the Story of the Harvard Business School* (Boston: Little Brown, 1958); and Jeffrey L. Cruikshank, *A Delicate Experiment: The Harvard Business School, 1908–1945* (Boston: Harvard Business School Press 1987). Although other business schools were changing as well, none was so central to the development of a professional managerial ideology. For a parallel account of developments after World War II at the Wharton School, see Steven A. Sass, *The Pragmatic Imagination: A History of the Wharton School, 1881–1981* (Philadelphia: University of Pennsylvania Press, 1982), pp. 233–291.

64. Quoted in Cruikshank, *A Delicate Experiment,* pp. 263–277.

65. Quoting from a 1944 Educational Policy Committee report, Ibid., p. 264 (emphasis added).

66. Ibid., p. 270.

67. Ibid., p. 272.

68. These changes followed two critical reports on American business education published in 1959: Robert Aaron Gordon and James Edwin Howell, *Higher Education for Business* (New York: Columbia University Press, 1959); and Frank C. Pierson, *The Education of American Businessmen* (New York: McGraw-Hill, 1959). For an evaluation of how business schools have fared since the 1960s, see Lyman W. Porter and Lawrence E. McKibbin, *Management Education and Development: Drift or Thrust into the 21st Century?* (New York: McGraw-Hill, 1988).

69. Cruikshank, *A Delicate Experiment,* p. 273. He qualifies the increase, however, because substantial numbers of students used to drop out after their first year.

Business education as a whole expanded after the war. In 1949, business schools graduated 65,000 students, five times the prewar number of 13,000. Of these, 3,900 were graduate degrees. See Peter F. Drucker, "The Graduate Business School," *Fortune,* August 1950, pp. 92–94. By 1983, 227,000 bachelor of business administration degrees and 65,000 master's degrees were awarded. See Porter and McKibbin, *Management Education,* p. 93.

70. Cruikshank, *A Delicate Experiment,* p. 276.

71. Duncan Norton-Taylor, "The Business Schools: Pass or Flunk?" *Fortune,* June 1954, pp. 112–114 +.

72. Herbert Stein, *Presidential Economics: The Making of Economic Policy from Roosevelt to Reagan and Beyond* (New York: Simon & Schuster, 1984), chap. 3; Griffith, "Dwight D. Eisenhower," pp. 96–100; and Collins, *The Business Response to Keynes,* chaps. 6, 7.

73. See, for example, Collins, *The Business Response to Keynes;* Galbraith, *American Capitalism;* Robert Lekachman, *The Age of Keynes* (New York: Random House, 1966); McConnell, *Private Power and American Democracy;* and Galambos and Pratt, *The Rise of the Corporate Commonwealth,* pp. 119–154.

74. Harold C. Livesay, "The Profession of Management in the United States," in *The Professions in American History,* ed. Nathan O. Hatch (Notre Dame, IN: University of Notre Dame Press, 1988), pp. 199–220.

75. Allen J. Matusow, *The Unraveling of America: A History of Liberalism in the 1960s* (New York: Harper & Row, 1984), pp. 32–59.

76. See Edwin M. Epstein, *The Corporation in American Politics* (Englewood Cliffs, NJ: Prentice-Hall, 1969), chaps. 4, 5.

Chapter 9

1. Allen J. Matusow, *The Unraveling of America: A History of Liberalism in the 1960s* (New York: Harper & Row, 1984), chap. 6.

2. For an account of these developments see Hugh Heclo, "Issue Networks and the Executive Establishment," in *The New American Political System,* ed. Anthony King (Washington, DC: American Enterprise Institute for Public Policy Research, 1978); and Thomas L. Gais, Mark A. Peterson, and Jack L. Walker, "Interest Groups, Iron Triangles and Representative Institutions in American National Government," *British Journal of Political Science* 14

(1984): 164–185. For a useful introduction to public-interest groups, see Andrew S. McFarland, *Public Interest Lobbies: Decision-Making on Energy* (Washington, DC: American Enterprise Institute, 1976). See also Mark V. Nadel, *The Politics of Consumer Protection* (Indianapolis: Bobbs-Merrill, 1971); Jeffrey M. Berry, *Lobbying for the People: The Political Behavior of Public Interest Groups* (Princeton, NJ: Princeton University Press, 1977); and Simon Lazarus, *The Genteel Populists* (New York: Holt, Rinehart and Winston, 1974).

3. Mancur Olson, *The Rise and Decline of Nations: Economic Growth, Stagflation and Social Rigidities* (New Haven, CT: Yale University Press, 1982), pp. 69–73; Samuel P. Huntington, "The United States," in Michel J. Crozier, Samuel P. Huntington, and Joji Watanuki, *The Crisis of Democracy: Report on the Governability of Democracies to the Trilateral Commission* (New York: New York University Press, 1975), pp. 59–118; and Committee for Economic Development, *Redefining Government's Role in the Market System* (New York: Committee for Economic Development, 1979), pp. 13–15.

4. Frank V. Fowlkes, "Washington Pressures: CED's Impact on Federal Policies Enhanced by Close Ties to Executive Branch," *National Journal*, June 27, 1987, pp. 1015–1024; Hugh Rockoff, *Drastic Measures: A History of Wage and Price Controls in the United States* (Cambridge: Cambridge University Press, 1984), chap. 7; and Neil de Marchi, "The First Nixon Administration: Prelude to Controls," in *Exhortation and Controls: The Search for a Wage–Price Policy, 1945–1971*, ed. Craufurd D. Goodwin (Washington, DC: Brookings Institution, 1975), pp. 295–352.

5. Robert Gilpin, *The Political Economy of International Relations* (Princeton, NJ: Princeton University Press, 1987), pp. 134–142; David P. Calleo, *The Imperious Economy* (Cambridge, MA: Harvard University Press, 1982), chap. 4; Herbert Stein, *Presidential Economics: The Making of Economic Policy from Roosevelt to Reagan and Beyond* (New York: Simon & Schuster, 1984), pp. 155–180; and Fred L. Block, *The Origins of International Economic Disorder: A Study of U.S. International Monetary Policy from World War II to the Present* (Berkeley and Los Angeles: University of California Press, 1977), chaps. 6, 7.

6. Alfred C. Neal, *Business Power and Public Policy: Experiences of the Committee for Economic Development* (New York: Praeger, 1981), pp. 3–5.

7. See Suzanne Berger, "Introduction," in *Organizing Interests in Western Europe*, ed. Suzanne Berger (Cambridge: Cambridge University Press, 1981), pp. 1–26.

8. For a general introduction to the industrial-policy debate, see Charles Schultze, "Industrial Policy: A Solution in Search of a Problem," *California Management Review* 25 (1983): 5–26; and R. D. Norton, "Industrial Policy and American Renewal," *Journal of Economic Literature* 24(1986): 1–40.

9. Committee for Economic Development, *Productivity Policy: Key to the Nation's Economic Future: A Statement* (New York: Committee for Economic Development), p. 12.

10. Neal, *Business Power and Public Policy*, pp. 63–64.

11. On management's misinvestments, see Neal, *Business Power and Public Policy*, p. 67; for a discussion about the relationship between declining productivity and inflation, see Committee for Economic Development, *Produc-*

tivity Policy, p. 26. For a more scholarly account, see William J. Baumol and Kenneth McLennan, eds., *Productivity Growth and U.S. Competitiveness: A Supplementary Paper of the Committee for Economic Development* (New York: Oxford University Press, 1985); and Douglas Hibbs, Jr., *The American Political Economy: Macroeconomics and Electoral Politics* (Cambridge, MA: Harvard University Press, 1987), pp. 101–105.

12. These arguments were laid out in Committee for Economic Development, *Fighting Inflation and Promoting Growth: A Statement on National Policy* (New York: Committee for Economic Development, 1976); Committee for Economic Development, *Fighting Inflation and Rebuilding a Sound Economy* (New York: Committee for Economic Development, 1980); also see Neal, *Business Power and Public Policy,* chap. 3.

13. Committee for Economic Development, *Redefining Government's Role in the Market System,* pp. 13–14, 29–31, 41–44.

14. Ibid., pp. 86–90, chaps. 6, 7.

15. Ibid., pp. 18–19.

16. Neal, *Business Power and Public Policy,* pp. 69–76.

17. Committee for Economic Development, *Productivity Policy,* pp. 54–57; and Committee for Economic Development, *Strategy for U.S. Industrial Competitiveness* (New York: Committee for Economic Development, 1984), pp. 36–37.

18. Committee for Economic Development, *Fighting Inflation and Promoting Growth,* pp. 57–59: Committee for Economic Development, *Redefining Government's Role,* pp. 56–78; and Committee for Economic Development, *Productivity Policy,* pp. 65–68.

19. Committee for Economic Development, *Achieving Energy Independence* (New York: Committee for Economic Development, 1974); Committee for Economic Development, *Key Elements of a National Energy Strategy: A Statement on National Policy* (Washington, DC: Committee for Economic Development, 1977); and Committee for Economic Development, *Helping Ensure Our Energy Future: A Program for Developing Synthetic Fuel Plants Now* (Washington, DC: Committee for Economic Development, 1979).

20. Committee for Economic Development, *Social Responsibilities of Business Corporations* (Washington, DC: Committee for Economic Development, 1971).

21. Alfred Marcus and Allen Kaufman, "The Continued Expansion of the Corporate Public Affairs Function" *Business Horizons* 31 (1988): 58–62.

22. See B. Solomon, "Clout Merchants," *National Journal,* March 21, 1967, pp. 662–666. For a transaction-cost approach to determining whether a firm should internalize or contract out for public-affairs services, see Allen Kaufman, Ernest Englander, and Alfred Marcus, "Structure and Implementation in Issues Management: Transaction Costs and Agency Theory," *Research in Corporate Social Performance and Policy* 11 (1989): 257–271.

23. Kay Lehman Scholzman and John T. Tierney described the declining importance of the trade association for the business community in Washington in their *Organized Interests & American Democracy* (New York: Harper & Row, 1986), pp. 81–82. Robert H. Miles described the formation of the public affairs office in the tobacco industry in his *Coffin Nails and Corporate Strate-*

gies (Englewood Cliffs, NJ: Prentice-Hall, 1982) and offered a general theory in *Managing the Corporate Social Environment: A Grounded Theory* (Englewood Cliffs, NJ: Prentice-Hall, 1987). For other studies that explore the interactions between the firm and trade association, see John F. Mahon and James E. Post, "The Evolution of Political Strategies During the 1980 Superfund Debate," in Alfred Marcus, Allen Kaufman and David Bean, *Business Strategy and Public Policy: Perspectives from Industry and Academia* (Westport: Quorum Press, 1987), pp. 61–80; Martha Derthick and Paul J. Quirk, *The Politics of Deregulation* (Washington, DC: Brookings Institution, 1985), pp. 157–159; and Allen Kaufman, "Synthetic Fuels and Public Policy: Challenges for Business Solidarity," in *Research in Corporate Social Performance and Policy*, ed. Lee Preston (Greenwich, ACT: JAI Press, 1984), pp. 187–212.

24. Schlozman and Tierney, *Organized Interests*, p. 77.

25. "FEC Finds Slow Growth of PAC Activity During 1988 Election Cycle," Federal Election Commission press release, April 9, 1989, p. 3.

26. Richard Hurd and Jeffrey Sohl, "Strategic Diversity in Labor PAC Contribution Patterns," *Social Science Journal* 29 (1992): 65–86.

27. See Theodore J. Eismeier and Philip H. Pollock, III, *Business, Money, and the Rise of Corporate PACs in American Politics* (New York: Quorum Books, 1986), pp. 80–83.

28. For a discussion of John Harper's role in promoting social and political activism within the corporate sector, see George David Smith, *From Monopoly to Competition: The Transformations of Alcoa, 1888–1986* (Cambridge: Cambridge University Press, 1988), pp. 349–363. Harper's work during the war in labor relations helped him develop his appreciation for public relations.

29. See "Du Pont, Part I: The Family," *Fortune*, November 1934, pp. 65–75; "Du Pont, Part II: An Industrial Empire," *Fortune*, December 1934, 81–85; and "Du Pont, Part II: A Management and Its Philosophy," *Fortune*, December 1934, pp. 86–89.

30. For an account of Du Pont's resistance to the New Deal after the NRA's demise, see Robert T. Burk, *The Corporate State and the Broker State: The Du Ponts and American National Politics, 1925–1940* (Cambridge, MA: Harvard University Press, 1990).

31. Peter Vanderwicken, "Irving Shapiro Takes Charge at Du Pont," *Fortune*, January 1974, pp. 78–81.

32. "Pattern Breaker," *Forbes*, July 24, 1975, pp. 24–25.

33. See Beth Mintz and Michael Schwartz, *The Power Structure of American Business* (Chicago: University of Chicago Press, 1985); and Mark Mizruchi, *The American Corporate Network: 1904–1974* (Beverly Hills, CA: Sage, 1982).

34. For the Business Roundtable's and the CED's views on industrial policy, see Business Roundtable, "Analysis of the Issues in the National Industrial Policy Debate: Working Papers," January 11, 1984; Business Roundtable, *Strategy for a Vital U.S. Economy: Views on U.S. Economic Policy. U.S. Industrial Competitiveness and Legislative Proposals for a National Industrial Policy*, May 1984; and Committee for Economic Development, *Strategy for U.S. Industrial Competitiveness* (New York: Committee for Economic Development, 1984).

35. Schlozman and Tierney, *Organized Interests,* pp. 71–73.

36. Ibid.

37. Thomas Byrne Edsall, *The New Politics of Inequality* (New York: Norton, 1984), pp. 128–140; and Eismeier and Pollock, *Business, Money, and the Rise of Corporate PACs,* chap. 5.

38. Jeffrey H. Birnbaum and Alan S. Murray, *Showdown at Gucci Gulch: Lawmakers, Lobbyists, and the Unlikely Triumph of Tax Reform* (New York: Vintage Books, 1988), pp. 16–18; and Richard E. Cohen, "The Business Lobby Discovers That in Unity There Is Strength," *National Journal,* June 28, 1980, p. 1053.

39. William J. Lanouette, "Business Lobbyists Hope Their Unity on the Tax Bill Wasn't Just a Fluke," *National Journal,* October 24, 1981, pp. 1896–1897.

40. Sara A. Levitan and Martha R. Cooper, *Business Lobbies: The Public Good and the Bottom Line* (Baltimore: Johns Hopkins University Press, 1984), pp. 56–61; and Cohen, "The Business Lobby," pp. 1053–1055.

41. Lanouette, "Business Lobbyists," p. 1897.

42. Lanouette, "Business Lobbyists," p. 1897; and Business Roundtable, "Summary Statement of Richard D. Hill, Chairman of the Board of First National Bank of Boston on Behalf of the Business Roundtable. Submitted to the Subcommittee on Taxation and Debt Management of the Senate Committee of Finance," October 22, 1979.

43. Birnbaum and Murray, *Showdown,* p. 17.

44. Walter Dean Burnham, "The 1980 Earthquake: Realignment, Reaction of What?" in *The Hidden Election: Politics and Economics in the 1980 Presidential Campaign,* ed. Thomas Ferguson and Joel Rogers (New York: Pantheon Books, 1981), pp. 98–140. See also Austin Ranney, *The American Elections of 1980* (Washington, DC: American Enterprise Institute, 1981); Gerald Pomper, with colleagues, *The Election of 1980: Reports and Interpretations* (Chatham, NJ: Chatham House, 1981); and Ellis Sandoz and Cecil V. Crabb, Jr., eds., *A Tide of Discontent: The 1980 Elections and Their Meaning* (Washington, DC: Congressional Quarterly Press, 1981).

45. Pamela Fessler, "Reagan Tax Plan Ready for Economic Test," *Congressional Quarterly Weekly Report,* August 8, 1981, pp. 1431–1435.

46. Cohen, "The Business Lobby," pp. 1054–1055; Lanouette, "Business Lobbyists," p. 1896; Business Roundtable, "Summary Statement of Richard D. Hill"; Business Roundtable, "Statement of Robert H. B. Baldwin, President, Morgan Stanley and Co., Inc. on behalf of the Business Roundtable Before the Committee on Ways and Means," January 30, 1980; Business Roundtable, "Statement of Theodore F. Brophy, Chairman and Chief Executive Officer, General Telephone and Electronics Corporation of the Business Roundtable Submitted to the Committee of Finance, Senate of the United States," May 20, 1981.

47. With progressive, nominal income tax rates, "bracket creep" increases revenues more than inflation.

48. Timothy B. Clark, "Cracks Appear in Business' United Front in Opposition to Tax Boosts," *National Journal,* July 16, 1983. pp. 1493–1496.

49. Business Roundtable, "Memo," from Theodore F. Brophy, Chairman Taxation Task Force, March, 12, 1982.

50. Business Roundtable, "Statement of Theodore F. Brophy, Chairman and Chief Executive Officer, General Telephone and Electronics Corporation on Behalf of the Business Roundtable, Submitted to the Committee of Finance, Senate of the United States," March 19, 1982.

51. Robert S. McIntyre and David Wilhelm, *Money for Nothing: The Failure of Corporate Tax Incentives 1981–1984* (Washington, DC: Citizens for Tax Justice, 1986), pp. 1–2, 17–22; Timothy B. Clark, "Dole Hopes Tax Increase Bill Gives the GOP an Election-Year Advantage," *National Journal,* July 31, 1982, p. 1337.

52. Birnbaum and Murray, *Showdown,* pp. 11-12.

53. Clark, "Dole Hopes," p 1337–1338.

54. Timothy B. Clark, "Retreating to Tax Reform," *National Journal* June 1, 1985, pp. 1267, 1298– 1299.

55. Birnbaum and Murray, *Showdown,* p. 48.

56. Business Roundtable, "Statement on Tax Reform," November 13, 1985; and Business Roundtable, "Supplementary Statement on Tax Reform," November 13, 1985.

57. Business Roundtable, "Supplementary Statement."

58. Timothy J. Conlan, David R. Beam, and Margaret T. Wrightson, "Tax Reform Legislation and the New Politics of Reform." Paper delivered at the 1988 Annual Meeting of the American Political Association: Washington, DC, September 1–4, 1988, pp. 1–15.

59. Birnbaum and Murray, *Showdown,* pp. 3–5.

60. Ibid., p. 161; and Jeffrey H. Birnbaum, "Business's Schism over Tax Overhaul Reflects the Divide-and-Conquer Strategy of Proponents," *Wall Street Journal,* December 5, 1985, p. 64.

61. Business Roundtable, "Statement on Tax Reform," June 3, 1986.

62. Business Roundtable, "Memo: to the Members of the Policy Committee from Roger B. Smith, Chairman, Policy Committee," July 18, 1986.

63. Business Roundtable, *American Excellence in a World Economy: A Report of the Business Roundtable on International Competitiveness,* June 15, 1987, p. 36.

64. Business Roundtable, "News Release," October 22, 1986.

65. Thomas Ferguson and Joel Rogers, *Right Turn: The Decline of the Democrats and the Future of American Politics* (New York: Hill & Wang, 1986), p. 156. On pp. 154–165, Ferguson and Rogers examine the role of the industrial policy issue in Mondale's presidential bid.

66. Joint Committee on Taxation, *Federal Income Tax Aspects of Corporate Financial Structures, Scheduled for Hearings Before the Senate Committee on Finance on January 24–26, 1989 and the House Committee on Ways and Means on January 31 and February 1–2, 1989,* Joint Committee Print (Washington, DC: U.S. Government Printing Office, 1989), p. 11.

67. Alfred Rappaport, *Creating Shareholder Value: The New Standard for Business Performance* (New York: Free Press, 1986) p. 10; Walter Kiechel, III, "Corporate Strategy for the 1990s," *Fortune,* February 29, 1988, pp. 34–42; House Subcommittee on Telecommunications, *Corporate Takeovers: Public*

Policy Implications for the Economy and Corporate Governance: A Report, 99th Cong. 2nd sess., 1986, pp. 53–54, and Michael Jensen, "The Eclipse of the Public Corporation," *Harvard Business Review,* September–October, 1989, pp. 61–64.

68. House Committee on Energy and Commerce, *Corporate Takeovers (Part 2): Hearings Before the Subcommittee on Telecommunications, Consumer Protection and Finance of the Committee,* 99th Cong., 1st sess., May 23, June 12, and October 24, 1985, p. 54.

69. H. Brewster Atwater, Jr., chairman, Business Roundtable Corporate Responsibility Task Force, to Business Roundtable Member Company CEOs, March 13, 1987.

In addition, see Business Roundtable, "Statement of Principles on Hostile Takeover Abuses," May 9, 1985. Andrew C. Sigler, Chairman, Business Roundtable's Corporate Responsibility Task Force, "Testimony," House Committee on Energy and Commerce, *Corporate Takeovers (Part 2),* pp. 195–211; and Business Roundtable, "Corporate Takeover: A Search for the Public Interest," *Roundtable Report,* February 1989.

For a statement expressing labor's opposition to the market in corporate control, see Thomas R. Donahue, secretary-treasurer, AFL-CIO, "Testimony," Senate Committee on Banking, Housing, and Urban Affairs, *Hostile Takeovers: Hearings,* 100th Cong., 1st sess., January 28, March 4, and April 8, 1987, pp. 261–270. John C. Coffee, Jr., "Shareholder Versus Managers: The Strain in the Corporate Web," in John C. Coffee, Louis Lowenstein, and Susan Rose-Ackerman, eds., *Knights, Raiders, and Targets: The Impact of the Hostile Takeover* (Oxford: Oxford University Press, 1988), pp. 103–115, provided an excellent analysis of the interests that allied management and labor in a united front against corporate raids.

Also see A. A. Sommer, Jr.'s testimony in Senate Committee on Banking, *Hostile Takeovers,* pp. 94–104, for a very effective defense of managerial prerogative. Sommer, a Washington attorney and former member of the SEC, told the Senate committee he was testifying as a private citizen. However, his firm represented the Business Roundtable and the Coalition to Stop the Raid on America, two organizations actively involved in lobbying for anti-takeover legislation. See John Cranford, "Senate Banking Approves Anti-Takeover Bill," *Congressional Quarterly Weekly Report,* October 3, 1987, p. 2401.

70. H. B. Atwater, Jr., "Statement Before the House Subcommittee on Telecommunications and Finance on Williams Act Reform," June 11, 1987.

71. Business Roundtable, *Statement on Corporate Responsibility,* October 1981.

72. House Committee on Energy and Commerce, *Management and Leveraged Buyouts,* 100th Congress, 1989, pp. 81–91. For a fuller treatment, see Jensen's "Eclipse of the Public Corporation." For a rebuttal, see Alfred Rappaport, "The Staying Power of the Public Corporation," *Harvard Business Review,* January–February 1990, pp. 96–104.

73. House Committee on Energy and Commerce, *Corporate Takeovers: Public Policy,* p. 3.

74. Paul Starobin, "Takeover Debate Centers on States' Power," *Congressional Quarterly Weekly Report,* July 25, 1987, p. 1663.

75. House Committee on Energy and Commerce, *Corporate Takeover: Public Policy,* pp. 89–112, reviews the many nuances in this sensitive issue.

76. CTS Corporation v. Dynamics Corporation, 481 U.S. 69 (1987).

77. Starobin, "Takeover Debate," pp. 1663–1664. Dingell himself saw circumstances easing pressures for legislative action. See Rochelle L. Stanfield, "Plotting Every Move," *National Journal,* March 26, 1988, p. 796.

78. Once the market recovered, so did takeovers—until the slump in October 1989. See Sarah Bartlett, "Much Fuss, over What?" *New York Times,* October, 17, 1989, p. A1; Anise C. Wallace, "A Tumultuous Year for 'Junk Bonds'," *New York Times,* January 2, 1990, p. D1; and Judith H. Dobrzynski, "Leveraged Buyouts Fall to Earth," *Business Week,* February 12, 1990, pp. 62–65.

79. The Supreme Court had reaffirmed in its 1977 *Santa Fe Industries, Inc. v. Green* decision the reigning division of power between the state and federal governments over corporate governance. The Court rejected efforts to broaden the federal securities laws' antifraud provisions to include shareholder complaints against managerial misconduct. In reasserting that the federal government's authority could not exceed market standards, the Court refused to federalize state corporation law that specified the content of management's trusteeship. See Robert B. Thompson, "Tender Offer Regulation and the Federalization of State Corporate Law," in *Public Policy Toward Corporate Takeovers,* ed. Murray L. Weidenbaum and Kenneth W. Chilton (New Brunswick, NJ: Transaction Books, 1988), pp. 78, 99–100.

80. Adolf A. Berle, Jr., and Gardiner C. Means, *The Modern Corporation and Private Property* (New York: Macmillian, 1968 [1932]), pp. 356–357.

81. See Edsall, *The New Politics of Inequality;* Levitan and Cooper, *Business Lobbies;* Michael Useem, *The Inner Circle: Large Corporations and the Rise of Business Political Activity in the U.S. and U.K.* (Oxford: Oxford University Press, 1984); and Thomas Ferguson and Joel Rogers, "The Reagan Victory: Corporate Coalitions in the 1980 Campaign," in *The Hidden Election: Politics and Economics in the 1980 Presidential Campaign,* ed. Joel Rogers and Thomas Ferguson (New York: Pantheon Books, 1981), pp. 3–64; and Dan Clawson, Alan Neustadtl, and James Bearden, "The Logic of Business Unity: Corporate Contributions to the 1980 Congressional Elections," *American Sociological Review* 51 (1986): 797–811.

82. Martha Derthick and Paul J. Quirk, *The Politics of Deregulation* (Washington, D.C: The Brookings Institution); John Mahon and James Post, *Business Strategy and Public Policy: Perspectives from Industry and Academia* (New York: Quorum Books, 1987); and Alfred Marcus and Allen Kaufman, "Why It Is Difficult to Implement Industrial Policies: Lessons from the Synfuels Experience," *California Management Review* 28 (1986): 98–114.

83. Ian Maitland, "Self-Defeating Lobbying: How More Is Buying Less in Washington," *Journal of Business Strategy* 7 (1986): 67–74; Ian Maitland, "Collective Versus Individual Lobbying: How Business Ends up the Loser," in Marcus, *Business Strategy and Public Policy,* pp. 95–104; and Eismeier and Pollock, *Business, Money.*

Chapter 10

We are indebted to Ernest Englander who allowed us to draw material from his article coauthored with Allen Kaufman, "Kohlberg Kravis Roberts & Co. and the Restructuring of American Capitalism," *Business History Review* 67 (1993): 52–97.

1. For a detailed discussion of how LBOs are arranged, see Congressional Research Service, *Pensions and Leveraged Buyouts Prepared for the Subcommittee on Labor–Management Relations of the House Committee on Education and Labor,* Committee Print, February 1989, pp. 36–39; and Patrick A. Gaughan, *Mergers and Acquisitions* (New York: HarperCollins, 1991), pp. 269–299.

2. Bryan Burrough and John Helyar, *Barbarians at the Gate: The Fall of RJR Nabisco* (New York: Harper & Row, 1990), pp. 133–134. Kohlberg put together his first deal in 1965, when he found a group of investors to acquire a seventy-two-year-old founder's dental company, Stern Metals, for $9.5 million of other people's money. The new owners left the family with a substantial equity holding and let them run the business. When the investors sold their $500,000 investment to the public four years later, the family garnered an additional $4 million.

3. Scott C. Linn and Michael S. Rozeff, "The Corporate Sell-Off," in *The Revolution in Corporate Finance,* ed. Joel M. Stern and Donald H. Chew, Jr. (Oxford: Basil Blackwell, 1986), pp. 428–436.

4. Gaughan, *Mergers and Acquisitions,* p. 461.

5. Burrough and Helyar, *Barbarians at the Gate,* p. 134.

6. Robert A. G. Monks and Neil Minow, *Power and Accountability* (New York: HarperBusiness, 1991), p. 214.

7. Ibid, p. 169; and Gaughan, *Mergers and Acquisitions,* pp. 283–288.

8. This description relies heavily on Michael C. Jensen, "Eclipse of the Public Corporation," *Harvard Business Review,* September–October 1989, pp. 68–70.

9. And as Alfred Rappaport noted, it is also possible to cash out of the investments without taking the firm public again: LBOs can distribute profits to investors by recapitalizing with new borrowings, a process that can continue indefinitely and make the LBO a permanent organization. See Alfred Rappaport, "The Staying Power of the Public Corporation," *Harvard Business Review,* January–February, 1990, p. 98.

10. United States General Accounting Office, *Leveraged Buyouts: Case Studies of Leveraged Buyouts* (Washington, DC: General Accounting Office, September 1991), pp. 47–73.

11. Judith H. Dobrzynski, "RJR Gives Itself Some Running Room," *Business Week,* July 30, 1990; and Michael C. Jensen, "Corporate Control and the Politics of Finance," *Journal of Applied Corporate Finance* 4 (1991): 14, claimed that this new refinancing increased RJR's value as the new total stock value rose from $2 billion in March and April 1991 to $2.8 billion on July 15, 1991. The original equity owners saw their holdings increase in two years from $3.2 billion to $7.3 billion.

12. General Accounting Office, *Leveraged Buyouts,* p. 97.

13. Rappaport also developed financial techniques for multidivisional firms to determine whether divisions that are not listed on a public market

are worth more inside the firm or in the hands of a rival. For a summary of these techniques, see ibid., pp. 100–101; for a more detailed discussion, see Alfred Rappaport, *Creating Shareholder Value: The New Standard for Business Performance* (New York: Free Press, 1986), pp. 100–119.

14. For a discussion of how LBOs may lessen the cost of bankruptcy, see Jensen, "Eclipse of the Public Corporation," pp. 61–74, and "The Ebb Tide," *The Economist*, April 27, 1991, pp. 23–27. W. Carl Kester, *Japanese Takeovers: The Global Contest for Corporate Control* (Boston, MA: Harvard Business School Press, 1991), pp. 69–75 describes how debt and interlocking directorates provided incentive and mechanisms for Japanese banks to monitor firms' financial situation carefully and to resolve difficulties promptly.

15. For a discussion of the relative advantages of implicit as opposed to explicit contracts, see Paul Milgrom and John Roberts, *Economics, Organization & Management* (Englewood Cliffs, NJ: Prentice-Hall, 1992), pp. 132–133, 332–333. Oliver Williamson provided a similar framework in his analysis of transaction costs. See, in particular, his *The Economic Institutions of Capitalism* (New York: Free Press, 1985), pp. 68–84. For a game theoretic approach on the cost saving advantages of trust, see Robert T. Frank, *Passions with Reason: The Strategic Role of the Emotions* (New York: Norton, 1988).

16. Internal pricing has been a consistent problem for a vertically integrated firm; see H. Thomas Johnson and Robert S. Kaplan, *Relevance Lost: The Rise and Fall of Management Accounting* (Boston: Harvard Business School Press, 1987), pp. 125–146. Some vertically integrated firms have explored ways of creating internal markets to resolve this cost-accounting problem, which LBO associations presumably ameliorate. Cypress Semiconductor provides an extreme case. See Richard Brandt, "The Bad Boy of Silicon Valley," *Business Week*, December 9, 1991, pp. 64–70.

17. For a discussion of KKR's revenue sources, see George Anders, *Merchants of Debt: KKR and the Mortgaging of America* (New York: Basic Book, 1992).

18. Allan Sloan, "Luring Banks Overboard," *Forbes* 133 (1983): 39–42.

19. "Presentation of Leveraged Buy-Outs, by Kohlberg Kravis Roberts & Co.: Updated 1991" (mimeo), p. 1–1.

20. Sloan, "Luring Banks Overboard," pp. 39–42.

21. Samuel L. Hayes, III, and Philip M. Hubbard, *Investment Banking: A Tale of Three Cities* (Boston: Harvard Business School Press, 1990), pp. 108–110; and Richard Whitley, "The Transformation of Business Finance into Financial Economics: The Roles of Academic Expansion and Changes in U.S. Capital Markets," *Accounting Organizations and Society* 3 (1986): 171–192, pp. 180–183.

22. Sarah Bartlett, *The Money Machine: How KKR Manaufacturered Power and Profits* (New York: Warner Books, 1991), p. 228; and Sloan, "Luring Banks Overboard," pp. 39–42.

23. For a list of the holdings of the top ten banks in 1988 and their effect on the firm's financial vulnerability, see Gaughan, *Mergers and Acquisitions*, p. 319, and for a general discussion of the commercial bank role in placing highly leveraged debt, see pp. 318–320.

24. Congressional Research Service, *Pensions and Leveraged Buyouts*, p. 23. By 1989, private pension funds held $666.7 billion in equity, and state and

local government funds held more than $290 billion in equity. See Monks and Minow, *Power and Accountability*, p. 183. Peter Drucker reported that pension funds held 40 percent of "the medium-term and long-term debt of the country's bigger companies." See Peter F. Drucker, "Reckoning with the Pension Fund Revolution," *Harvard Business Review*, March–April 1991, p. 106.

25. For a discussion of state tax incentives, see Betty Linn Krikorian, *Fiduciary Standards in Pension and Trust Management* (Stoneham: Butterworth Legal Publishers, 1989), p. 38. For a discussion of the fiduciary standard in the law and its applicability to state investment funds, see pp. 1–11. The ERISA left the administration of nonfederal public pension funds to the states but brought private pension funds under federal jurisdiction. For a discussion of its tax advantages and fiduciary standards, see Krikorian, *Fiduciary Standards*, pp. 38, 11–34. The ERISA also protects employees through the Pension Benefit Guaranty Corporation, which insures defined benefit pension plans, in which the sponsor promises to pay the beneficiaries a certain income (see pp. 46–49).

26. Our discussion summarizes Bartlett, *The Money Machine*, pp. 99–134.

27. Ibid., p. 123. Washington eventually became the top state investor in KKR's investment funds.

28. These included Oregon, Washington, New York, Wisconsin, Illinois, Iowa, Massachusetts, Montana, Michigan, Minnesota, and Utah. Ibid., p. 130.

29. High-yield bonds include issues of debtlike corporate bonds, municipal bonds, and preferred stocks that either are not rated by the leading bond-rating firms or are listed below Moody's Baa investment grade. See Congressional Research Service, *The Role of High Yield Bonds [Junk Bonds] in Capital Markets and Corporate Takeovers: Public Policy Implications: A Report Prepared by the Congressional Research Committee for the Use of the Subcommittee on Telecommunications, Consumer Protection and Finance of the Committee on Energy and Commerce, U.S. House of Representatives*, Committee print, December 1985, p. 4.

30. The reward for his failure was $800 million when Gulf sold out to its white knight, Chevron Oil. See John C. Coffee, Jr., "Shareholders Versus Managers: The Strain in the Corporate Web," in *Knights, Raiders and Targets: The Impact of the Hostile Takeover*, ed. John C. Coffee, Jr., Louis Lowenstein, and Susan Rose-Ackerman (New York: Oxford University Press, 1988), p. 116, n. 2.

31. Bartlett, *The Money Machine*, p. 130.

32. For a discussion of this fallout, see Burrough and Helyar, *Barbarians at the Gate*, pp. 141–145; and Anders, *Merchants of Debt*, pp. 133–135.

33. For a full analysis of the Beatrice acquisition, see George P. Baker, "Beatrice: A Study in the Creation and Destruction of Value," *Journal of Finance* 47 (1992): 1081–1119.

34. Carol J. Loomis, "The New J. P. Morgans," *Fortune*, February 29, 1988, pp. 44–53; Hayes and Hubbard, *Investment Banking*, pp. 129–133; Robert A. Miller and Lawrence Fox, "Are Bankers Too Eager to Arrange LBOs?" *Journal of Commercial Bank Lending*, February 1987, pp. 19–26, and

Burrough and Heylar, *Barbarians at the Gate,* pp. 156–157, 216–219. Do note, however, that after an initial round of successful divestitures, KKR found it hard to unload Beatrice's remaining pieces because of unforseen legal liabilities, and at least at one point, the deal was only around the break-even point (ibid., p. 152). See also Carol J. Loomis, "Has the Beatrice LBO Gone PFFT?" *Fortune,* July 31, 1989, pp. 113–118; and Lois Therrien, "Beatrice Investors Will Just Have to Sit Tight," *Business Week,* March 12, 1990, p. 104. Eventually, KKR cashed out of Beatrice on favorable terms, with a 50 percent annual return on its original 1986 investment. See Leah J. Nathans, "KKR Is Doing Just Fine—Without LBOs," *Business Week,* July 30, 1990, p. 56.

35. Christopher J. Arts and George C. Lodge, "Senator Riegle and U.S. Corporate Restructuring," *Harvard Business School Case* N9-390-031, October 12, 1989, pp. 8–9.

36. The drama of this struggle to control RJR was skillfully told by Burrough and Helyar in *Barbarians at the Gate.* For a summary of the rivalry between KKR and Shearson Lehman Hutton, see Peter Finch, "And in This Corner Wearing White Trunks," *Business Week,* November 14, 1988, pp. 130–131.

37. Gaughan, *Mergers and Acquisitions,* pp. 462, 464.

38. Ibid., pp. 195–196. Management can either issue shares of stock to an employee stock ownership plan or create stock options that enhance their voting power. For a discussion on how stock ownership can enhance management's position, see Joseph Raphael Blasi and Douglas Lynn Kruse, *The New Owners: The Mass Emergence of Employee Ownership in Public Companies and What It Means to American Business* (New York: Harper Business, 1991), pp. 38, 45–46.

39. Jensen, "Ebb Tide," p. 17. The debt-to-service ratio climbed sharply in both kinds of industries at the end of the 1970s, but the cyclical industry ratio declined precipitously in 1982, and the stable industry ratio continued to increase.

40. "Supermajority" provisions require a majority greater than 50 percent to approve mergers; "fair-price" provisions modify the corporate charter to require the buyer to pay minority shareholders a fair market price for their shares; "dual capitalization" restructures the corporation's equity into two classes with different voting rights, and "poison pills" are securities issued by a target firm that give the shareholders the right to purchase at a discount the stock of an acquiring firm. For a general discussion of these takeover tactics, see Gaughan, *Mergers and Acquisitions,* pp.,154–219; and Richard Ruback, "An Overview of Takeover Defenses," in *Mergers,* ed. Alan J. Auerbach (Chicago: University of Chicago Press, 1988), pp. 49–67. For summary evaluations, see Gregg A. Jarrell, James A. Brickley, and Jeffrey M. Netter, "The Market for Corporate Control: The Empirical Evidence Since 1980," *Journal of Economic Perspectives* 2 (1988): 58–66.

41. For a general discussion of KKR's congressional strategy during these years, see Bartlett, *The Money Machine,* pp. 257–270.

42. Alison Leigh Cowan, "When Buyout Boutiques Find Little to Leverage," *New York Times,* December 11, 1991, p. D7. Campeau Corporation, a

leading takeover firm in the retail industry, made an offer for $1.5 billion worth of junk bonds in 1989, only to find few takers. To sell its wares, Campeau had to ask for fewer funds at higher interest rates. Even these additional funds were insufficient to save Campeau from financial ruin. Gaughan, *Mergers and Acquisitions,* pp. 390–391.

43. Nathans, "KKR Is Doing Just Fine," pp. 56–57.

44. "Financial Regulation," in *Congress and the Nation: A Review of Government and Politics* 6 (1981–84): 83–86 (Washington, DC: Congressional Quarterly, 1985).

45. U.S. Department of the Treasury, *Modernizing the Financial System: Recommendations for Safer, More Competitive Banks,* Washington, D.C. February, 1991, pp. I-23–24.

46. Duane B. Graddy and Austin H. Spencer, *Managing Commercial Banks: Community, Regional, and Global* (Englewood Cliffs, NJ: Prentice-Hall), pp. 606–607. See also General Accounting Office, *Bank Supervision.*

47. George Anders, "KKR Boosts Takeover War Chest by an Additional $1.5 Billion," *Wall Street Journal,* May 1, 1991, p. C1.

48. Actually, KKR considered in 1983 a joint bid with the Washington state pension fund for SeaFirst Corp. of Seattle, which BankAmerica eventually purchased. See Ron Suskind and Kenneth H. Bacon, "Fleet/Norstar Aided by KKR, Wins Bidding Battle for Bank of New England," *Wall Street Journal,* April 23, 1991, p. 1.

49. Robert J. McCartney, "KKR Bets Its Money on the Banks," *Washington Post,* April 24, 1991, pp. B1, 10.

50. Kathleen Kerwin, "First Interstate: A Big Test of KKR's Patience," *Business Week,* July 30, 1990, p. 61.

51. General Accounting Office, *Bank Supervision,* pp. 8–9.

52. For a general account of BNEC's demise, see House Committee on Banking, Finance, and Urban Affairs, *Failure of the Bank of New England: Hearing,* 102nd Cong., 1st sess., January 9, 1991; Laura Jereski, "A Stomach Ache for the Bank That Ate New England," *Business Week,* February 5, 1990, pp. 68–69; and John W. Milligan, "The Grim Countdown at Bank of New England," *Institutional Investor,* October 1990, pp. 187–191. For a discussion of how the regulatory system failed in preventing BNEC's excesses, see General Accounting Office, *Bank Supervision.*

53. Linda M. Watkins, "Fleet, Norstar Agree to Merger for $1.3 Billion," *Wall Street Journal,* March 19, 1987, p. A2.

54. James P. Meagher, "Fleet/Norstar Financial Group Inc." *Barron's/Investment News and Views,* September 9, 1989, pp. 58–59.

55. "Required Reading: Warning from Dingell About Fleet/KKR Bid," *American Banker,* April 24, 1991, p. 10.

56. Jennifer J. Johnson, association secretary of the Board of Governors of the Federal Reserve System, letter to Lee Meyerson, Esq., "Passivity Commitments," Appendix, July 12, 1991.

57. Barbara A. Rehm, "FDIC Details How It Discounted BankAmerica Corp.'s Bid for BNE," *American Banker,* May 23, 1991, p. 1.

58. For a discussion of Fleet/Norstar's consolidation plans, see Matt Bar-

thel, "Fleet's Tech Whiz Put to the Test," *American Banker,* July 10, 1991, p. 1.

59. See Ron Suskind, Kenneth H. Bacon, and George Anders, "Fleet/ Norstar, Aided by KKR, Wins Bidding Battle for Bank of New England," *Wall Street Journal,* April 23, 1991, p. A1; John W. Milligan, "KKR, Member FDIC," *Institutional Investor,* June 1991, pp. 59–60; and Fred Vogelstein, "Will KKR Stake Be a Guidepost for Investors?" *American Banker,* May 8, 1991, p. 1.

60. U.S. Department of the Treasury, *Modernizing the Financial System.*

61. Ibid., pp. xviii-13–16. Federal Reserve interpretations in 1987 and 1989 of Section 20 of the Glass–Steagall Act have allowed bank holding companies to set up nonbank subsidiaries that receive up to 10 percent of their revenue from investment-bank activities formerly excluded from commercial banks. Among these activities are "the underwriting of and dealing in commercial paper . . . , mortgage backed securities . . . , municipal revenue bonds . . . , securitized assets, and corporate bonds and equities" (p. xviii-15. Already, about thirty bank holding companies have established such subsidiaries, the most notable being J. P. Morgan (p. xviii-16). For a discussion of J. P. Morgan's extraordinary venture into investment banking and its near transformation into a European styled-European bank, see John Meehan, "Mighty Morgan," *Business Week,* December 23, 1991, pp. 64–69; and Fred R. Bleakley, "J. P. Morgan Expands Role in Underwriting, Irking Securities Firms," *Wall Street Journal,* November 13, 1991, p. A1. For an example of how investment-banking and commercial-banking functions overlap in the placement of a firm's securities, see Robert G. Eccles and Dwight B. Crane's discussion of Union Carbide's financial restructuring in 1986, in *Doing Deals* (Boston, MA: Harvard Business School Press, 1988), chap. 1, esp. p. 24. For an account of the RJR financing, see Gaughan, *Mergers and Acquisitions,* pp. 428–430.

62. See J. Bradford De Long, "The Great American Universal Banking Experiment," *The International Economy,* January–February 1991, pp. 68–79.

Chapter 11

1. John von Neumann and Oskar Morgenstern, *Theory of Games and Economic Behavior* (Princeton, NJ: Princeton University Press, 1953).

2. For an analysis of game theory's influence on contractual political theory, see Brian Barry, *A Treatise on Social Justice, Volume 1: Theories of Justice* (Berkeley and Los Angeles: University of California Press, 1989), pp. 56–57; and Jonathan R. Macey, "Competing Economic Views of the Constitution," *George Washington University Law Review* 56 (1987): 50–80, and "Transaction Costs and the Normative Elements of the Public Choice Model: An Application to Constitutional Theory," *Virginia Law Review* 74 (1988): 471–518.

3. Michael Taylor, *The Possibility of Cooperation* (Cambridge: Cambridge University Press, 1984), pp. 36–37.

4. Barry, *Theories of Justice*, pp. 9–24. R. Duncan Luce and Howard Raiffa, *Games and Decisions: An Introduction and Critical Survey* (New York: Wiley, 1957), provide the standard introduction to cooperation in game theory. For a review of the research, see Martin Shubik, *Game Theory in the Social Sciences: Concepts and Solutions* (Cambridge, MA: MIT Press, 1982), chaps. 6, 7, 11; and Peter Ordeshook, *Game Theory and Political Theory: An Introduction* (New York: Cambridge University Press, 1986), chaps. 7–9.

5. Russell Hardin, *Collective Action* (Baltimore: Johns Hopkins University Press, 1982), pp. 167–169, used the example of a stag hunt to illustrate the problem. Hunters can choose either to cooperate universally in the chase for a stag or to shoot hare on an individual basis. A coordination problem arises because the hunters prefer stag to hare yet will not commit themselves to hunt stag unless their fellow hunters remain true to the group chase. If a hunter expects that even one fellow hunter will go after rabbits, he will do the same, because all the deer are then likely to run for heavy cover, and one hare in the bag is better than several stags in the bush.

6. Hardin, *Collective Action*, p. 175. For his analysis of conventions, Hardin relied on David K. Lewis, *Convention* (Cambridge, MA: Harvard University Press, 1969).

7. See Taylor, *Possibility of Cooperation*.

8. This "discount rate" is also called "time preference."

9. See Iain McLean, *Public Choice: An Introduction* (Oxford: Basil Blackwell, 1987), pp. 125–148.

10. Robert M. Axelrod, *The Evolution of Cooperation* (New York: Basic Books, 1984), pp. 133–136.

11. Ibid., pp. 127–128.

12. Ibid., pp. 129–132; see also Hardin, *Collective Action*, pp. 174–187.

13. Hardin, *Collective Action*, pp. 174–187.

14. Ibid., pp. 103–117; see also Axelrod, *Evolution of Cooperation*, pp. 134–139.

15. Taylor, *Possibility of Cooperation*, p. 23.

16. Hardin, *Collective Action*.

17. Mancur Olson, *The Logic of Collective Action: Public Goods and the Theory of Groups* (Cambridge, MA: Harvard University Press, 1965).

18. Anthony Downs, *An Economic Theory of Democracy* (New York: Harper, 1957).

19. Theodore J. Eismeir and Phillip H. Pollock, III, *Business, Money and the Rise of Corporate PACs in American Politics* (New York: Quorum Books, 1988), p. 79.

20. Mike H. Ryan, Carl L. Swanson, and Rogene A. Buchholz, *Corporate Strategy, Public Policy and the Fortune 500: How America's Major Corporations Influence Government* (Oxford: Basil Blackwell, 1987), chap. 7, took up these questions systematically.

21. Kay Lehman Scholzman and John T. Tierney, *Organized Interests and American Democracy* (New York: Harper & Row, 1986), pp. 206–208, provided an excellent summary of this approach. Also, see Edward Handler and John R. Mulkern, *Business in Politics: Strategies of Corporate Political Action*

Committees (Lexington: Lexington Books, 1982), pp. 15–18; Michael J. Malbin, "Campaign Financing and Special Interests," *Public Interest* 56 (1979): 29–32; and Ian Maitland, "Interest Group Politics and Economic Growth Rate," *Journal of Politics* 44 (1985): 47–48.

22. For a general discussion of nonconnected/ideological PACs' contributory behavior, see Margaret Ann Latus, "Assessing Ideological PACs: From Outrage to Understanding," in *Money and Politics in the United States: Financing Elections in the 1980s,* ed. Michael J. Malbin (Chatham, NJ: Chatham Press, 1984), pp. 142–171.

23. Dan Clawson, Alan Neustadtl, and James Bearden, "The Logic of Business Unity: Corporate Contributions to the 1980 Congressional Elections," *American Sociological Review* 51 (1986): 797–811; and Dan Clawson and Tie-ting Su, "Was 1980 Special? A Comparison of 1980 and 1986 Corporate PAC Contributions," *Sociological Quarterly* 31 (1990): 371–381.

24. For other examples of arguments on corporate political cohesion, see Mark S. Mizruchi, "Similarity of Political Behavior Among Large American Corporations," *American Journal of Sociology* 95 (1989): 401–424; Mark S. Mizruchi and Thomas Koenig, "Economic Sources of Corporate Political Consensus: An Examination of Interindustry Relations," *American Sociological Review* 51 (1986): 482–491; and Val Burris, "The Political Partisanship of American Business: A Study of Corporate Political Action Committees," *American Sociological Review* 52 (1987): 732–744.

25. Thomas Byrne Edsall, *The New Politics of Inequality* (New York: Norton, 1984), pp. 128–136. James F. Herndon, "Access, Record and Competition as Influences on Interest Group Contributions to Congressional Campaigns," *Journal of Politics* 44 (1982): 998–1019, and Clawson and Su, "Was 1980 Special," pp. 383–384 offered evidence that conforms to Edsall's conclusion.

26. Edsall, *The New Politics,* pp. 105–128, 136–138.

27. See Gary C. Jacobson, *The Politics of Congressional Elections* (Boston: Little, Brown and Company, 1987).

28. Gary C. Jacobson, "The Republican Advantage in Campaign Finance," in *The New Direction in American Politics,* ed. John E. Chubb and Paul E. Peterson (Washington, DC: The Brookings Institution, 1985), pp. 166–167.

29. Ibid.; and Jacobson, *The Politics of Congressional Elections,* pp. 65–67.

30. Jacobson, "The Republican Advantage," pp. 162–168.

31. Ibid. Also see Gary Jacobson, "Money in the 1980 and 1982 Congressional Elections," in *Money and Politics in the United States: Financing Elections in the 1980s,* ed. Michael J. Malbin (Chatham, NJ: Chatham House, 1984), pp. 42–45; and Jacobson, *The Politics of Congressional Elections,* p. 65.

For evaluations similar to Jacobson's, see Douglas A. Hibbs, Jr., *The American Political Economy: Macroeconomics and Electoral Politics in the United States* (Cambridge, MA: Harvard University Press, 1987), pp. 208–210; and Thomas Ferguson and Joel Rogers, *Right Turn: The Decline of the Democrats and the Future of American Politics* (New York: Hill & Wang, 1986), pp. 11–36.

When Reagan won the presidency in 1980 and the Republican Party captured the Senate and won thirty-three seats in the House that same year, political scientists wondered whether or not these were the signs of a party realignment. Since then, most observers have agreed that the year 1980 forced a policy shift on Congress but that the election itself did not signal a major party realignment. For an introduction to the literature on party realignment and changes in congressional policy, see Richard J. Trilling and Bruce A. Campbell, "Toward a Theory of Realignment: An Introduction," in *Realignment in American Politics: Toward a Theory* (Austin: University of Texas Press, 1980), pp. 3–21; and David W. Brady, "Electoral Realignments in the U.S. House of Representatives," in *Congress and Policy Change*, ed. Gerald C. Wright, Jr., Leroy N. Rieselbach, and Lawrence C. Dodd (New York: Agathon Press, 1986), pp. 47–70. John E. Chubb and Paul E. Peterson, "Realignment and Institutionalization," in *The New Direction in American Politics*, ed. John. E. Chubb and Paul E. Peterson (Washington, D. C.: Brookings Institution, 1985), pp. 1–33, provided a summary of the discussion on party realignment during the Reagan administration.

32. Gerard Keim and Ashgar Zardkoohi, "Looking for Leverage in PAC Markets: Corporate and Labor Contributions Considered," *Public Interest* 59 (1988): 21–34.

33. Anecdotal evidence supporting Keim and Zardkoohi's characterization can be found in the testimony of corporate managers before the Ervin Senate Committee investigating the Watergate scandal. See Graham K. Wilson, *Interest Groups in the United States* (Oxford: Clarendon Press, 1981), pp. 69–70.

34. For supporting evidence on labor's political coherence, see Richard Hurd and Jeffrey Sohl, "Strategic Diversity in Labor PAC Contribution Patterns," *Social Science Journal* 92 (1992): 65–86.

35. Eismeier and Pollock, *Business, Money and the Rise of Corporate PACs.*

36. Ibid., pp. 2–3.

37. Eismeier and Pollock, *Business, Money*, pp. 27–30; and Mike H. Ryan, Carl L. Swanson, and Rogene A. Buchholz, *Corporate Strategy, Public Policy and the Fortune 500: How America's Major Corporations Influence Government* (Oxford: Basil Blackwell, 1987), pp. 155–156, also offered a slightly modified form of the pragmatic/ideological corporate PAC typology.

38. Eismeier and Pollock, *Business, Money*, pp. 17–18 and chap. 4.

39. Ibid., chap. 3.

40. Ibid., pp. 84–92.

41. Ibid., p. 79.

42. Ibid., pp. 80–83.

43. Ibid.

44. Ann Matasar, *Corporate PACs and Federal Campaign Financing Laws: Use or Abuse of Power?* (New York: Quorum Books, 1986), p. 54; and Eismeier and Pollock *Business, Money*, pp. 92–93.

45. Jacobson, in *The Politics of Congressional Elections*, pp. 35–36, summarized the benefits from donating heavily to House races as follows: "Positive-sum distributive politics, represented by the pork barrel and the Christmas Tree bill (one with separate little 'gifts' for a variety of special interest groups) is much more prevalent than zero-sum competition for scarce re-

sources. Members defer to each other's requests for particular benefits for their states or districts in return for deference to their own."

46. See Marvin Karson, *Multivariate Statistical Methods* (Ames: Iowa State University Press, 1982).

47. For an explanation of these techniques, see P. J. Huber, "Projection Pursuit," *Annals of Statistics* 13 (1985): 435–474; and D. M. Hawkins, M. W. Muller and T. A. ten Krooden, "Cluster Analysis," in *Topics in Applied Multivariate Analysis,* ed. Douglas M. Hawkins, (Cambridge: Cambridge University Press, 1982), pp. 301–350.

48. We draw on information from the Free Congress Research and Education Foundation, a conservative think tank. See Stuart Rothberg, *Campaign Regulation and Public Policy: PACs, Ideology and the FEC* (Washington, DC: Free Congress Research and Education Foundation, 1982).

49. Clawson et al., "The Logic of Business Unity," p. 800. David Gopian, "What Makes PACs Tick? An Analysis of the Allocation Patterns of Economic Interest Groups," *American Journal of Political Science* 28 (1984): 266, used a similar measure.

50. For example, if candidate A received donations from ten of the thirteen conservative PACs, and opponent B received a donation from only one, then A would have a CONRAT value of 9 (10 minus 1) and B would have a value of -9 (1 minus 10).

51. The liberal PACs include National Committee for an Effective Congress, National Abortion Rights Action League, National Organization of Women PAC, League of Conservation Voters, Voters for Choice, Americans for Democratic Action PAC, Sierra Club Committee on Political Education, Independent Action, Fund for a Democratic Majority, Friends of Earth PAC, SANE PAC, and National Council of Senior Citizens PAC.

52. We qualify this statement because our figures include only PAC contributions to candidates. Data are not available on expenditures made on educational, voter registration, and get-out-the-vote campaigns. The literature tells us that labor unions spent heavily on these activities relative to other organized groupings. Thus it may be that labor unions contribute in a defensive manner to Democratic incumbents, and that they try to mobilize votes in campaigns with strong Democratic challengers.

53. To define market orientation, we divide foreign sales by total sales; firms with less than 10 percent foreign sales are classified as domestic-oriented, and firms with more than 10 percent as multinationals. The Department of Commerce's *Industrial Outlook* provides us with an import penetration ratio for each election year. Firms are classified into the following industrial sectors: (1) energy, (2) high technology, (3) regulated and service, (4) old line, and (5) miscellaneous. These categories come from "America's Restructured Economy," *Business Week,* June 1, 1981, pp. 55–100. Firms are classified geographically by using locations of sunbelt and frostbelt headquarters. Finally, the corporations are placed into unregulated, economically regulated, and socially regulated categories.

54. In part, this shift occurred as corporate attention moved from the House to the Senate. The Republicans had twenty-two senators up for re-

election, and the Democrats had only twelve. The year 1986 was the first contest for the Republican victors of 1980, most of whom had won by narrow margins and so were vulnerable. To protect these gains, corporate PACs increased their contributions to Senate races by $8 million, giving approximately half to Republican incumbents. See Eismeier and Pollack, *Business, Money,* pp. 92–93.

Chapter 12

1. See John Pound, "Beyond Takeovers: Politics Comes to Corporate Control," *Harvard Business Review,* March–April, 1992, pp. 83–93.

2. ESOPs allow companies replace stock with wages, thereby increasing short-term cash flow. ESOPs are also less expensive than defined-benefit pension funds and may be used to finance retirement plans. Much of their flexibility comes from government regulations that allow them to circumvent the Employee Retirement Security Insurance Act's 10 percent limit on a pension fund's ownership position. For a full discussion, see Joseph Raphael Blasi and Douglas Lynn Kruse, *The New Owners: The Mass Emergence of Employee Ownership in Public Companies and What It Means to American Business* (New York: Harper Business, 1991).

3. See Paul C. Weiler, *Governing the Workplace: The Future of Labor and Employment Law* (Cambridge, MA: Harvard University Press, 1990), pp. 30–31. Unions historically abandoned employee participation programs in favoring of wage settlements. See ibid., pp. 30–31; and D. Quinn Mills and Malcolm Lovell, Jr., "Enhancing Competitiveness: The Contribution of Employee Relations," in *U.S. Competitiveness in the World Economy,* ed. Bruce R. Scott and George C. Lodge (Boston: Harvard Business School Press, 1985), pp. 455–478.

4. Blasi and Kruse, *The New Owners,* p. 13.

5. See Robert W. Hall, *Attaining Manufacturing Excellence: Just in Time, Total Quality, Total People Involvement* (Homewood, IL: Dow Jones–Irwin, 1987).

6. The technology combines computer-aided design, engineering, process planning, and manufacturing as well. See Office of Technology Assessment, *Computerized Manufacturing Automation: Employment, Education, and Work Place* (Washington, D.C.: U.S. Government Printing Office, 1984); and James W. Dean, Jr., Se Joon Yoon, and Gerald I. Susman, "Advanced Manufacturing Technology and Organization Structure: Empowerment or Subordination," *Organization Science* 3 (1990): 203–229; and L. Nye Stevens, *Valve Engineering: Usefulness Well Established When Applied,* Testimony before the Subcommittee on Legislation and National Security, Committee on Government Operations, House of Representatives (Washington, DC: United States Government Accounting Office, 1992).

7. See Blasi and Kruse, *The New Owners,* pp. 250–252.

8. Christopher Heye, "Five Years After: A Preliminary Assessment of U. S. Industrial Performance Since *Made In America*," MIT Industrial Performance Center (IPC) Working Paper 93-009WP, September 1993.

9. W. Edwards Deeming, *Out of the Crisis* (Cambridge, MA: Center for Advanced Engineering Study, MIT, 1986); and Lee Krajewski, Barry King, Larry Ritzman, and Danny Wong, "Kanban, MRP, and Shaping the Manufacturing Environment," *Management Science* 33 (1987): 39–57; James Welch, Laddie Cook, and Joseph Blackburn, "The Bridge to Competitiveness, Building Supplier Customer Linkages," *Target* (November/December, 1992): 17–29.

10. Gordon Walker and Laura Poppo, "Profit Centers, Single-Source Suppliers, and Transaction Costs," *Administrative Science Quarterly* 36 (1991): 66–87; Michael Smitka, *Competitive Ties: Subcontracting in the Japanese Automotive Industry* (New York: Columbia University Press, 1991); Allen Kaufman and Michael Merenda, "Corporate Downsizing and the Rise of Problem-Solving Suppliers: The Case of Hadco Corporation," University of New Hampshire Center for Enterprise Networking Paper, April 1994.

11. Peter M. Senge, *The Fifth Dimension: The Art and Practice of the Learning Organization* (New York: Doubleday, 1990); Ray Stata, "Organizational Learning—The Key to Management Innovation," *Sloan Management Review* (Spring, 1989): 63–74; and Thomas K. Kochan and Michael Useem, eds., *Transforming Organizations* (New York: Oxford University Press, 1992).

12. Ibid., pp. 282–295.

13. See Howell John Harris, *The Right to Manage: Industrial Relations Policies of American Business in the 1940s* (Madison: University of Wisconsin Press, 1982); and Terry M. Moe, "Interests, Institutions, and Positive Theory: The Politics of the NLRB," *Studies in American Political Development: An Annual* 2 (1987): 236–302.

14. See Graef S. Crystal, *In Search of Excess: The Overcompensation of American Executives* (New York: Norton, 1991).

15. Blasi and Kruse, *The New Owners,* pp. 253–254.

Preface

Writing this book over the last five years has been both a pleasure and a struggle. I have tried to bring sociologists' and economists' views of labor markets, statistical methods of analyzing national data, job evaluation techniques, legal opinions, feminist theory, and political philosophy into a dialogue with each other around the topic of comparable worth.

To do this, I had to learn things from many fields and find ways to translate between them. I could not have done this without the informal conversations I had with several good friends. The many hours I spent in discussion with them were a crucial, if indirect, contribution to this book. I especially acknowledge five colleagues at the University of Texas—Dallas, where I worked between 1975 and 1989. Nancy Tuana, a philosopher, and Karen Prager, a psychologist, profoundly influenced my thinking/feeling through our monthly feminist reading group. George Farkas helped me integrate recent developments from labor economics and sociology as we hammered out several manuscripts together. Debates with Peter Lewin and Ted Harpham deepened my understanding of the legacies of the classical liberal tradition in economic and political philosophy.

Others provided comments on earlier drafts of chapters. Economists Mark Killingsworth (Rutgers) and Kevin Lang (Boston University) sent constructive criticism of my uses of labor economics. (Kevin may often have wished I had never discovered bitnet!) Peter Kuhn (Economics, McMaster) saved me from error on one point. My understanding of Title VII case law was enhanced by comments from Paul Weiler (Harvard Law School), Douglas Laycock (University of Texas Law School), Robert Nelson (American Bar Association), and Michael Evan Gold (Cornell). My thinking about feminist and Marxist theory was enriched by comments from Beth Anne Shelton (Sociology, SUNY—Buffalo), Ben Agger (Sociology, SUNY—Buffalo), and Nancy Folbre (Economics, University of Massachusetts). Ronnie Steinberg (Sociology, Temple University), Helen Remick (EEO Office, University of Washington), and Richard

Arvey (Industrial Relations, University of Minnesota) shared their academic and practical knowledge of job evaluation with me.

Parts of this research were funded by grants from the National Science Foundation Sociology Program, the Rockefeller Foundation, the Texas Applied Research Program, and the University of Texas—Arlington Women and Minorities Research Center. Betty Demoney and Barbara McIntosh provided word processing through the long series of revisions I undertook, impressing me with their accuracy and good cheer.

Constructing the dataset, "doing the runs" for Chapter 3, and other editorial functions were carried out by the long line of skilled and fastidious research assistants that I have been blessed with at the University of Texas—Dallas and the University of Arizona. I especially thank Melissa Herbert, Irene Browne, Barbara Kilbourne, Lori McCreary-Megdal, Lori Reid, and Jim Emopolos, among whom I understand that I have a reputation for delegating everything that can possibly be delegated. Randy Filer, Randy Hodson, Toby Parcel, and Donald Treiman were kind enough to provide machine-readable data files.

To all those mentioned above, I am grateful. Without their help, the book would easily have taken a decade to research and write.

I dedicate this book to my parents, Bea England and Bill England, both of whose lives have conveyed the message that efforts toward long-term goals yield rich rewards.

Paula England
Tucson, Arizona

1

Segregation and the Pay Gap

I. Introduction

The terms *comparable worth* and *pay equity* refer to a form of sex discrimination that went virtually unrecognized until about 15 years ago. The issue is still little understood. Indeed, its status as a type of discrimination is controversial. Yet evidence abounds that jobs filled mostly by women have pay levels that are lower than they would be if the jobs were filled mostly by men. This is seen as sex discrimination by advocates of the principle of comparable worth.

At first glance, the issue sounds very much like the more familiar issue of "equal pay for equal work," which refers to men and women in the *same* job, with the same seniority, performing the same work equally well, but being paid differently. Comparable worth is a different issue. It is distinct because it refers to comparisons between the pay in *different* jobs, jobs that differ in that they entail at least some distinct tasks. The comparisons are between one job that is largely male and one that is largely female. (Throughout this book, for brevity, I will use the terms *male job* and *female job* to describe jobs that are *disproportionately* or *predominantly*, but generally not entirely, performed by persons of one sex.) The allegation of discrimination is the claim that the difference between the pay of the two jobs results from gender bias in wage setting rather than from other job characteristics. Needless to say, a thorny issue is how one decides when two distinct jobs are nonetheless comparable in the sense that we would expect them to pay the same in the absence of sex discrimination.

The wage discrimination at issue in comparable worth is also distinct from discrimination in hiring, initial job placement, and promotion (all of which, for brevity, I will refer to as *hiring discrimination*). Hiring discrimination against women seeking to enter traditionally male jobs is one (although not the only) reason for occupational sex segregation. Without segregation of jobs, female jobs could not be given a discriminatory pay level. This is obvious, since, without segregation, there would be no predominantly male and predominantly female jobs! Yet, in my view, engaging in discrimination on the basis of sex in setting the pay levels assigned to male and female jobs is analytically distinct from engaging in hiring discrimination on the basis of sex.

Some examples may help the reader to visualize the sorts of comparisons at issue in comparable worth. In the state of Washington, where female state employees sued over pay equity, the job of legal secretary, a female job, was found by an evaluation study to be comparable in worth to the job of heavy equipment operator, a job filled mostly by men. However, in 1972, heavy equipment operators made about $400 more per month. Stockroom attendants, mostly men, made much more than dental hygienists, who were mostly women. (The above examples are from Remick 1980, pp. 416–417, as cited in Steinberg 1990.) In 1975, nurses in Denver sued the city claiming that their jobs paid less than male jobs such as tree trimmer and sign painter (Blum 1991, p. 49). It would be hard to argue that the latter two jobs require as much skill or are as demanding as nursing. Women workers for the city of San Jose discovered in the mid-1970s that secretaries were generally earning less than workers in male jobs that required no more than an eighth grade education, including, for example, men who washed cars for the city (Blum 1991, p. 60). Eventually, women in San Jose succeeded in getting the city to do a job evaluation study. It showed, to choose some examples, that nurses earned $9120 per year less than fire truck mechanics and that legal secretaries made $7288 less than equipment mechanics (Blum 1991, pp. 82–83). In 1985, the California School Employees Association complained that school librarians and teaching assistants (female jobs) were paid less than custodians and groundskeepers (male jobs) (Steinberg 1990). To take yet another example, in recent years the city of Philadelphia was paying practical nurses (mostly women) less than gardeners (mostly men) (Steinberg 1990). These are not atypical examples. In addition, one is hard-pressed to come up with a single example of a male job paying less than a female job that reasonable people would find comparable in skill, effort, or difficult working conditions. Nor are these differences in pay a result of men averaging more years of experience than women, since in the above comparisons of employers' policies regarding pay levels in the various jobs, a constant level of experience was assumed. (For example, this can be done by comparing starting salaries.)

Recently, the concept of comparable worth or pay equity has been applied to issues of discrimination on the basis of race or ethnicity as well as gender. If a job in a particular organization is filled largely with African Americans or Hispanics, does the pay level tend to be lower than is commensurate with the job's skill level and other demands? We can examine whether the racial or ethnic composition of a job has an effect on its pay level just as we can examine whether its sex composition has this effect. In academic theorizing, as well as in legislation and litigation about *hiring* discrimination, issues of racial discrimination were raised first. They were later extended to sex discrimination. Where comparable worth is concerned, things have happened in the reverse order: The issue was first raised with respect to sex discrimination and has more recently been examined with respect to racial discrimination. In this book, I focus exclusively on comparable worth as an issue of gender discrimination. However, the reader should bear in mind that analogous questions can be raised with respect to race and ethnicity. (See Jacobs and Steinberg 1990a, note 12, on studies that have assessed effects of minority composition on wages. See also National Committee on Pay Equity 1987.)

This book is an interdisciplinary examination of the issue of comparable worth. This chapter sets the stage for the discussion by providing a sketch of the situation of men and women in paid employment in the United States. Twentieth-century trends and contemporary patterns in women's and men's employment, occupations, and pay are described, drawing from research by sociologists, economists, and psychologists. Chapter 2 compares various theories of labor markets from economics and sociology, with attention to how each view explains gender inequality in jobs and earnings, and how it treats the issue of comparable worth. Chapter 3 presents an empirical analysis of aggregate occupational data from the 1980 census that demonstrates the tendency of predominantly female occupations to pay less than predominantly male occupations, even after numerous measures of skill demands, working conditions, and market conditions are statistically controlled. It also demonstrates the penalty for doing nurturant work, a finding I interpret as evidence of indirect gender bias in wage setting. Chapter 4 examines methods of and findings from job evaluation, a technique used to evaluate jobs and assess comparable worth within a single organization. Chapter 5 explains the current legal status of comparable worth in the federal courts. Chapter 6 examines normative debates about gender inequality and comparable worth, drawing on social, political, and economic philosophies, including feminist theories. Finally, Chapter 7 takes the reader through the policy debates surrounding comparable worth, and presents my own view on these controversial issues.

Views of comparable worth hinge, in part, on empirical evidence. Yet such evidence is interpreted differently through the "lenses" of different theoretical models. Views of comparable worth are also affected by normative positions, by values. Although I am a sociologist by training, in this book I also draw upon the disciplines of economics, psychology, law, and philosophy, as well as on interdisciplinary feminist perspectives. Thus, I hope to present a view of the complex and controversial issue of comparable worth that is informed by debates over evidence, theories, and values.

The remainder of this chapter sets the stage for examining comparable worth by summarizing research findings on the situation of women and men in paid employment. For the most part, I will draw upon research from the United States. The situation is similar in other industrial countries, albeit with some variations (Rosenfeld and Kalleberg 1990; Brinton 1988; Blau and Ferber 1986; Roos 1985). This chapter discusses the increases in women's employment in recent decades, the tendency of women to be clustered into a limited number of occupations, changes in the degree of occupational sex segregation, and changes in the sex gap in pay.

II. Increasing Employment Among Women

Some women have always worked outside the home for pay in addition to working within the home. One often sees the term *working women* used to differentiate women who work for pay from full-time homemakers. This is misleading, of course, since homemakers work as well. To avoid this misleading juxtaposition, I will use the term *employment* or *labor force participation* to refer to paid work typically done outside the home.

A. Which Women Are Employed?

Women are more likely to be employed if they are single, have fewer children, are black, have considerable education and other job skills, have high potential earnings, or have a husband with low earnings (Killingsworth and Heckman 1986; Desai and Waite 1991; O'Neill 1981). These are each "net" effects, that is, differences that are observed when other things are "held constant" via statistical controls. Yet, since some of these factors are negatively correlated with each other, real women often experience conflicting pulls. For example, consider a woman with a college education, three children, and a husband who is a well-paid manager. The fact that she is married, has children, and has a husband with relatively high earnings all mitigate against her employment. However, her college education increases the earnings she could make in a job, as well as her nondomestic interests, and thus makes it more likely that she will be employed. Marital homogamy, the tendency to marry persons from a similar class and educational background, means that women whose high education and potential earnings mitigate in favor of employment typically have husbands with relatively high earnings, a factor mitigating against employment.

Today, many women remain employed during pregnancy and return to their jobs immediately or within a few weeks or months of birth. Relatively continuous employment around a birth is more common among women who are well educated, are in more skilled jobs, and have higher wages, perhaps because the financial loss from leaving their jobs would be greater for such women (Desai and Waite 1991). However, continuous participation around a birth is also more common among women with more economic need—single mothers or women whose husbands have low earnings (Desai and Waite 1991). Continuous participation is also aided by the availability of a more flexible work schedule or by working in an occupation containing more women with young children (Desai and Waite 1991).

B. Trends in Women's Employment

It was traditionally believed that many women entered and left the labor force numerous times during their lives. Recent research that traces the employment histories of birth cohorts has challenged this view. (A birth cohort is a group of people born in the same year.) This research shows that, while many women left employment at the time of marriage or a first birth, after marriage, every birth cohort in this century has had continuous increases across time in the proportion of women employed (Goldin 1990, p. 22). This implies that while many women spent some years out of the labor force, if they stayed employed or reentered employment after marriage, they generally stayed employed fairly continuously. The reentries were typically after a period of childrearing. What has been changing most is how many women enter the labor force at all and how early those who leave for childrearing reenter to stay (Goldin 1990).

The proportion of U.S. women who are employed has increased steadily since the early 1800s (Goldin 1990). More and more women have moved from working exclusively in the home to working both in their homes and for pay. As Table 1.1 shows, 19% of women were in the labor force (i.e., either employed or looking for a job) in 1890. By 1950 this figure was up to 30%. It was 35% in 1960, 42% in 1970, 51% by 1980, and 56% by 1987. The only time in this century that a decline in the proportion of women employed has ever occurred was right after World War II.

Table 1.1. shows increases in the proportion employed for both white and black women since 1950. However, the black and white trends differ in that black women did not increase their employment rate between 1890 and 1950; it was already very high (40%) in 1890. As Table 1.1 shows, black women have had higher employment rates than white women during every period, although white women had nearly caught up by 1987.

Married women with small children are still the group with the lowest employment rates. Yet this group has shown the fastest rate of increase, and now has participation rates only slightly lower than women's over-all average. Consider, for example, married women who have at least one child under the age of 3. Table 1.1 shows that in 1960, only 15% of such women were in the labor force, compared to 35% of women over-all. In 1975, 33% of such women were in the labor force, compared to

Table 1.1. Labor Force Participation[1] of Women by Marital Status, Presence of Youngest Child, and Race, 1890–1987

| | All Women | | | White | | Black[2] | | |
| | | Married[4] | | | | | | Hispanic[3] |
	Total	Total	With child under 3	Total	Married[4]	Total	Married[4]	Total
1890	18.9	4.6	NA	16.3	2.5	39.7	22.5	NA
1950	29.5	23.8	NA	28.5	20.7	37.8	31.8	NA
1960	35.1	30.5	15.3	34.2	29.8	42.7	40.5	NA
1970	41.6	40.8	25.8	40.9	38.5	47.3	50.0	NA
1975	46.3	44.4	32.7	45.9	43.5	48.8	54.0	43.0
1980	51.1	50.2	41.1	50.9	49.3	53.1	59.3	47.4
1985	54.5	54.2	50.5	54.1	53.0	56.5	62.4	49.3
1987	56.0	55.8	54.2	55.7	55.1	58.0	65.1	52.0

Sources: Goldin 1990 (Table 2.1); U.S. Department of Labor 1987b (Tables 1 and 3), 1988, 1989 (Table 6); Lueck, Orr, and O'Connell 1982 (Table A-2); Taeuber 1991 (Table B1–5).
Notes:
[1] Numbers given are percentage of women in the labor force. The labor force consists of those who are employed and those looking for a job. Those out of the labor force include homemakers, students, the retired, and discouraged workers (those who want a job but have given up looking). NA, data not available.
[2] Data for 1890 through 1970 are for all nonwhites rather than for blacks.
[3] Includes all Hispanics, regardless of race. "Hispanic" is a diverse category, including persons whose ancestry is Mexican, Central American, Cuban, and Puerto Rican, and including citizens and noncitizens. Hispanics are also included in "white" and "black" categories according to their race. Figures for Hispanics by marital status not available in government documents.
[4] "Married" includes only married women with husband present.

46% of women overall. However, by 1987, the figure for women with children under 3 was up to 54%, only slightly less than the 56% of all women who were in the labor force.

One might wonder whether the dramatic increase in employment among mothers of young children is mainly an influx into part-time jobs. For the most part, this is not the case. To be sure, mothers are more likely than other women to be employed part-time. For example, in 1988 about one third of women with children had part-time jobs, while only about one fifth of all employed women worked part-time (Barrett 1991). Yet much of the increase in the employment of mothers has been in full-time jobs. This can be inferred from the fact that the proportion of employed women whose jobs are part-time has been relatively constant at around 20% since the early 1960s (Barrett 1991), even while the proportion of employed women who have small children has gone up dramatically.

Perhaps it is surprising, but very few women use part-time employment as a transition between full-time homemaking and full-time employment. It is much more common to move from homemaking to a full-time job (Blank 1989). For some, part-time work is an occasional alternative to full-time employment; for a few it occasionally punctuates nonemployment (Blank 1989). Few women use part-time employment as a transition because part-time jobs are largely dead-end; employers seldom structure jobs to facilitate smooth transitions from part-time jobs to attractive full-time jobs.

C. *Explanations of Increases in Women's Employment*

What explains the dramatic increase in women's employment since World War II? To examine this, let us separate various specific explanations into two broad claims: (1) those asserting women's increased economic need to be employed, and (2) those asserting their increased opportunities for jobs and higher wages.

Increased Economic Need. Do more women than ever have an economic need to be employed? Yes. This is true in that a growing proportion of women are single or divorced, and more of these women than ever have children. Especially since 1970, the divorce rate has increased, the average age at marriage has gone up, and the proportion of out-of-wedlock births has increased for both white women and women of color (England and Farkas 1986). If we look at families that include children, the proportion of families with no adult male stayed fairly near 10% from 1940 through 1970, but thereafter it began to increase, reaching 16% by 1982 (Norwood 1982). These facts explain some of the increase in women's employment in terms of economic need. However, they cannot explain the increase among *married* women with husbands present, except to the extent that more married women than previously are aware of the risk of divorce and invest in job experience as a form of insurance (Burkhauser and Duncan 1989).

Can the increase in employment among *married* women be explained by increased economic need for two incomes? The answer depends, in part, upon what we mean by "need." The question of what income a family needs is, at least in part, subjective. However, assuming *any constant* definition of need, only if the real (i.e., inflation-adjusted) incomes of men have gone down over time can the economic need for a second paycheck be said to have gone up. Table 1.2 presents data on men's income. "Income" includes interest, dividends, and government transfer payments, rather than just earnings from employment. The figures also include all men, not only those employed full-time year-round. Since these figures include men who had spells of unemployment, they will show men's incomes going down if annual earnings go down because more men are unemployed part of the year or because the average duration of unemployment goes up, as well as if wage rates go down. Table 1.2 shows that, on average, men's incomes were going up throughout the 1950s, 1960s, and early 1970s. Since 1973, however, men's incomes have gone down. They have rebounded since the early 1980s, but by 1988 had only returned to their late 1960s levels. These trends apply to both white and black men, though in any given year black men's earnings have been lower than those of white men. (For discussion of trends in men's earnings, see Levy 1987, 1988; Burtless 1990.) If decreasing male income causes increasing need for wives' employment, one cannot argue that such need was increasing in the 1950s, 1960s, early 1970s, or since 1983, but only between 1973 and 1983.

The reader might question whether increases in the percentage of earnings paid in taxes would alter this conclusion. Based on data presented elsewhere (Steurle and Wilson 1987; Steurle forthcoming) regarding families at the median income, I have calculated that the percentage of income paid in federal income tax plus Social Security tax (excluding the portion paid by the employer) was 7.6% in 1955, 10.8% in 1960, 14.2% in 1970, 17.5% in 1980, and 17.1% in 1990. The increases in federal taxes in the 1950s and 1960s were not more than increases in male earnings, and federal taxes have not increased in the 1980s. Thus, the conclusion that men's incomes have been going up continuously except between about 1973 and 1983 holds even when federal taxes are considered.

Since 1950, women's employment has gone up continuously, while men's income went down only between about 1973 to 1983. In sum,

Table 1.2. Median Income of Men by Race: 1950–1988[1]

Year	Total	White	Black[2]	Hispanic[3]
1950	12,615	13,298	7,221	NA
1955	14,823	15,644	8,232	NA
1960	16,306	17,169	9,032	NA
1964	17,734	18,836	10,678	NA
1965	18,864	19,867	10,692	NA
1970	20,337	21,376	12,675	NA
1971	20,164	21,139	12,607	NA
1972	21,085	22,115	13,395	NA
1973	21,465	22,522	13,623	NA
1974	20,281	21,246	13,164	15,461
1975	19,467	20,450	12,226	14,902
1976	19,597	20,660	12,439	14,658
1977	19,762	20,699	12,283	15,221
1978	19,841	20,781	12,449	15,205
1979	19,194	20,051	12,412	14,455
1980	17,989	19,135	11,498	13,867
1981	17,534	18,605	11,063	13,278
1982	17,101	18,080	10,835	12,836
1983	17,414	18,320	10,714	12,893
1984	17,762	18,749	10,757	12,640
1985	18,473	19,494	11,681	12,571
1986	18,473	19,494	11,681	12,447
1987	18,522	19,687	11,679	12,736
1988	18,908	19,959	12,044	13,030

Source: Hensen 1990.
Notes:
[1] All income is in constant 1988 dollars. Thus, these figures are adjusted for changes in the cost of living (as measured by the Consumer Price Index) such that they reflect real trends in pretax purchasing power. NA, data not available.
[2] This category includes black males for 1970–1988. Before 1970, the category includes all nonwhite males.
[3] Includes all Hispanics, regardless of race. Hispanics are also included in "white" and "black" categories according to their race.

while the decade after 1973 saw increases in economic need for a second paycheck, such increases in need have *not* been a *consistent* trend for married women. Thus they cannot be the main explanation of the *consistent* increases in women's employment.

Yet most people I talk to have a clear perception that, in some meaningful way that is missed in the above figures, since the mid-1970s couples have needed two paychecks more than they did in times past.

There is a way to reconcile the kernel of truth in this perception with the figures presented above. My reconciliation hinges on an assumption about how people perceive well-being that comes from research in behavioral economics and social psychology to be discussed in Chapter 2. There is an asymmetry between how gains and losses are perceived. As a result, a decrease in one's income of $5000 reduces one's sense of well-being more than an increase in income over the same income range increases the sense of well-being.

To illustrate, consider the situation of a couple with a nonemployed wife whose husband earns $30,000 a year, but suffers a loss in income of $10,000 due to conditions in the economy at large. Perhaps he worked in an auto plant that closed and the best job he can now find is a non-unionized job paying $20,000. In response to this loss, the wife finds a job that pays exactly the $10,000 that was lost, after expenses such as day care. Later, suppose that the man gets an offer of a better job that will restore him to his original earnings of $30,000 (in inflation-adjusted dollars). The couple had previously felt that this was an adequate income—perhaps not as much as they would like, but high enough to make them decide the wife would stay home and care for their young children. Based on this we would predict that the wife will quit her job when the husband begins his new job. But the data in Tables 1.1 and 1.2 have shown us that when men's incomes rebound after a loss, women's employment does not decrease as the "economic need" thesis would predict. So our task is to understand why our hypothetical wife does not quit even when her husband's earnings had returned to their former level. This could be because she has grown to like her job, but that is not the point I want to emphasize here. If she quits the job, their family income will be exactly where it was before she joined the labor force. However, the asymmetry in how losses and gains affect perceived well-being implies that the original loss of $10,000 lowered well-being more than the rebound of $10,000 increased well-being. Thus, the sense of well-being still dictates the wife's employment. If losses are perceived as larger than gains of the same amount, then permanent increases in women's employment will be spawned in periods when men have even temporary decreases in earnings.

Similarly, the asymmetry in the perception of losses and gains suggests that permanent increases in women's employment will result when earnings inequality among men goes up, even in the absence of declines in men's average earnings. Increased inequality in men's earnings can result from earnings of men in the lower portion of the distribution going down while the earnings of men toward the top of the distribution go up. The asymmetry principle above predicts increased employment among women from this trend. That is, the *losses* in male earnings in the families at the lower end of the distribution will do more to increase their wives' employment than the *gains* in male earnings in the families at the higher end of the distribution will do to lower their wives' employment. Since men's earnings have become substantially more unequal in the last two decades (Levy 1987; Burtless 1990), this may explain some of the increase in women's employment.

Finally, this principle regarding an asymmetry in how gains and losses are perceived helps explain how in recent decades the increases in wives' employment before childbearing make it likely that more wives will continue employment after childbearing than would have been the case in the absence of the prechild employment. Today, unlike in the 1950s and 1960s, most women are employed for several years, if not more, between marriage and the birth of the couple's first child. Consider the example of a woman whose potential wage is $20,000 per year. If she has been employed before having children, she experiences non-employment after childbirth as a loss of $20,000 per year. Had she not been employed before the birth, employment after the birth would be perceived as a gain of $20,000 per year. Since the loss is felt more saliently than the gain of the same amount, women who are employed before childrearing are more likely to be employed afterward than are women who were not employed before the birth, even when the two groups have the same potential postbirth earnings and the same husbands' earnings. Thus, the trend to later childbearing creates an increase in women's employment after childbearing over and above its effect via the higher potential wage of women with more experience.

Increased Opportunities. What about the second explanation of increases in women's employment? Is there evidence that women's employment has increased because of increased opportunities for jobs and higher wages? Since World War II, jobs that had long been sex-typed as "women's work" showed greater increases in labor demand than did jobs overall (Oppenheimer 1970). This growth resulted from a restructuring of the economy that produced declining employment shares in agriculture and manufacturing and increases in service industries (such as retail sales, health, banking, and restaurants) and in service occupations (such as secretary) (Glass, Tienda, and Smith 1988). This has provided women with increased opportunities for employment.

At the same time, real (i.e., inflation-adjusted) wage increases have made the rewards of employment greater. To put it another way, using economist's terminology, the opportunity cost of (i.e., what is forgone by) being a homemaker has increased. Table 1.3 shows that among full-time workers, women's real (i.e., inflation-adjusted) earnings were increasing in the 1950s, 1960s, and early 1970s. This was true for both white and black women, although in any given year black women

Table 1.3. Median Annual Earnings of Women and Men Employed Full-Time, Year-Round, by Race and Hispanic Origin, 1955–1987[1]

	White			Black			Hispanic[2]		
	Women	*Men*	*Ratio*[3]	*Women*	*Men*	*Ratio*	*Women*	*Men*	*Ratio*
1955	12,110	21,431	0.565	6,220	11,292	0.551	NA[4]	NA	NA
1960	12,988	21,431	0.606	8,804	14,165	0.622	NA	NA	NA
1965	14,155	24,468	0.579	9,612	15,367	0.625	NA	NA	NA
1970	16,187	27,623	0.586	13,637	19,409	0.703	NA	NA	NA
1975	16,323	27,918	0.585	16,030	21,416	0.748	NA	NA	NA
1976	16,719	28,487	0.587	15,737	20,914	0.752	NA	NA	NA
1977	16,642	28,852	0.577	15,848	20,707	0.765	NA	NA	NA
1978	16,955	28,502	0.595	15,855	22,549	0.703	NA	NA	NA
1979	16,624	28,144	0.591	15,454	21,218	0.728	NA	NA	NA
1980	16,142	27,200	0.593	15,055	19,138	0.787	13,637	19,021	0.717
1981	15,381	26,473	0.581	14,298	18,730	0.763	13,646	18,726	0.729
1982	16,310	26,186	0.623	14,577	18,598	0.784	13,384	18,362	0.729
1983	16,741	26,348	0.635	14,860	18,786	0.791	13,578	18,246	0.744
1984	17,040	27,162	0.627	15,357	18,537	0.828	14,253	18,790	0.759
1985	17,404	27,131	0.641	15,407	18,977	0.812	14,279	18,315	0.780
1986	17,721	27,582	0.642	15,507	19,447	0.797	14,706	17,625	0.834
1987	17,775	27,468	0.647	16,211	19,385	0.836	14,893	17,872	0.833

Source: Figart, Hartmann, Hoytt, and Outtz 1989 (Tables 3 and 4).
Notes:
[1] Earnings are in constant 1987 dollars. Thus, these figures are adjusted for changes in the cost of living (as measured by the Consumer Price Index) such that they reflect real trends in before-tax purchasing power. NA, data not available.
[2] Includes all Hispanics, regardless of race. Hispanics are also included in "white" or "black" categories according to their race.
[3] Ratio of women's annual earnings to men's annual earnings.

earned less than white women. These wage increases for women were fueled by general growth in the economy that provided increases to men as well. During these periods, the rewards of employment went up for women, and this brought into or kept in the labor force an increasing proportion of white and black women (Butz and Ward 1979).

III. The Sex Segregation of Jobs

In the United States, as in most societies, men and women generally hold different jobs. If we use the approximately 500 detailed occupational categories used by the U.S. Census Bureau as a benchmark, approximately 60% of men or women would have to change occupations in order to achieve integration (Blau 1988). "Integration" here refers to a situation in which each occupation has the same sex mix as the labor force as a whole. If we were to use a more detailed classification of job titles and look within firms, we would see segregation to be even more pervasive than these figures indicate (Bielby and Baron 1984). This is partly because some occupations are filled exclusively by men in some firms but exclusively by women in others. For example, many restaurants have either all males or all females waiting tables. Thus, for this occupation, the level of integration implied by national data is misleading as an indicator of how often men and women really work together in the same job within a restaurant. More segregation is seen within firms than in national occupational data for a second reason as well. Organizations often employ more detailed categories than the census categories. Take, for example, a census occupation like physician. The 1980 census shows this to be 14% female. But if we were to use most any clinic's or hospital's more detailed classification by department, we would see that certain specialties, such as pediatrics and psychiatry, contain more than 14% females, while others, such as surgeons, contain fewer (American Medical Association 1986).

Another type of segregation is by industry or firm. The industry one works in is defined by the good or service sold by the firm one works for. For example, one can work in the auto industry or the restaurant industry. Workers in all occupations are included within the industry. Thus, managers, secretaries, production workers, and janitors who work for General Motors are all classified as in the auto industry. Women are more likely than men to work in small firms and in industries with labor-intensive production and relatively low levels of unionization and profit. Yet sex segregation by firms and industries is nowhere near as pervasive as segregation by occupation. After all, most firms and certainly most industries have both male and female workers. In contrast, some occupations (e.g., nursing, secretarial work, plumbing) are filled almost exclusively by one sex or the other.

Segregation means that few jobs are substantially integrated by sex. If sex had no relation to the job one were in, we would expect the sex ratio of each job to approximate the sex ratio of the labor force as a whole, which was slightly over 40% female in 1980. Thus, one way to look at integrated jobs would be to look at what occupations are between, say, 30 and 50% female. According to the 1980 census, out of 503 occupations, this included only 87 occupations. Examples of these integrated occupations are personnel managers, accountants, buyers, physicians' assistants, authors, artists, shoe salespersons, door-to-door salespersons, bartenders, book binders, short-order cooks, ushers, and tailors.

A. What Kinds of Jobs Do Men and Women Hold?

Occupations filled mainly with women include maids, assembly line workers in the electronics industry, clerks in retail stores, secretaries and other clerical workers, teachers (at the grade school through high school level), nurses, real estate agents, social workers, and librarians. Men predominate in the highest status professions (such as doctor and lawyer), in higher levels of management, in blue-collar crafts (such as plumber, carpenter, and electrician), in assembly line jobs in durable manufacturing (such as autos, steel, and tires), and in jobs involving outdoor labor. One can see from these lists that women's jobs are not usually *less* skilled than men's, but women's and men's jobs generally require *different kinds* of skills. There are both male and female jobs at both low and high levels of education. For example, hairdressers (mostly women) and bus drivers (mostly men) each average 13 years of schooling. Examples of male and female jobs at higher levels of education include electrical engineers and librarians, each averaging 17 years of education. (These examples are taken from the 1980 census data used in Chapter 3.)

Although women's and men's jobs require approximately equal average amounts of formal education received prior to entering the job, women's jobs typically provide less on-the-job training (Corcoran and Duncan 1979; Barron, Black, and Loewenstein 1990). Thus, as the seniority of workers increases, women's jobs may *become* less skilled relative to men's.

Female jobs are also attached to shorter mobility ladders than male jobs, thus reducing women's possibilities for promotion (C. Smith 1979; Rosenbaum 1980; Bielby and Baron 1984; DiPrete and Soule 1988). Related to this is the fact that very few female jobs involve supervision of other workers (Jaffee 1989; Wolf and Fligstein 1979; Hill 1980; Ward and Mueller 1985), especially male workers (Bergmann 1986).

How compatible are women's jobs with family responsibilities? One might think that women would choose jobs most compatible with such responsibilities. To a limited extent this is true. For example, more men than women are concentrated in jobs requiring out-of-town travel, working evenings, or unusually long hours. However, even here there are exceptions. For example, nurses are often required to work evenings, nights, and weekends. Overall, on other dimensions, it does not appear that women's jobs are any more compatible with family responsibilities than men's. Indeed, one national survey (Glass 1990) found more men than women reporting flexibility of schedules, more unsupervised break time, and more paid sick leave and vacation, all of which would be helpful for a parent.

Black women, like white women, generally work in predominantly female occupations. Race discrimination and poverty have limited black women's options even more than those of white women. Thus, more black than white women fill jobs such as maid and nurse's aide. However, much of the convergence between black and white women's earnings during the 1960s and 1970s (seen in Table 1.3) came from black women moving into secretarial work as well as the professions of teaching, nursing, and social work. These jobs had previously been dominated by white women. However, black women in these jobs are more likely than white women to work for the government (local, state, or federal), making their jobs particularly vulnerable to budgetary cuts in this era of fiscal austerity (Higginbotham 1987).

B. Trends in Segregation

If we use the census detailed occupational categories for calculation, the extent of occupational sex segregation among nonfarm occupations declined very slowly and unevenly throughout the century until about 1970 (England 1981; Jacobs 1989a). Starting about 1970, a much faster decline has occurred (Beller 1984; Jacobs 1989a; Blau 1988). Most of the decline since 1970 came from women entering male jobs, rather than men entering female jobs.

The 1970s saw an increasing number of women becoming accountants, bank officers, financial managers, and janitors. These changes contributed heavily to the decline in segregation. Other male occupations that increased their representation of women by at least 10 percentage points during the 1970s include computer programmers, personnel and labor relations professionals, pharmacists, draftspersons, radio operators, public relations professionals, office managers, buyers and purchasing agents, insurance agents, real estate agents, postal clerks, stock clerks, ticket agents, typesetters, bus drivers, animal caretakers, and bartenders (Beller 1984). The decline in segregation was much greater among younger than among older cohorts. The decline was greater in professional occupations than in blue-collar occupations. The overall decline in occupational sex segregation in the 1970s was as great for African Americans as for whites (Beller 1984).

The decline in occupational segregation by sex continued in the 1980s, though at a pace somewhat slower than in the 1970s (Blau 1988). In general, the same jobs that saw large influxes of women in the 1970s did so in the 1980s as well. Examples are computer operators, insurance adjusters, animal caretakers, typesetters, personnel workers, vocational counselors, and public relations workers. There was little integration of women into the skilled blue-collar crafts such as plumbing or carpentry, or into durable goods manufacturing jobs (e.g., auto or steel workers), just as there had been little entry of women into these fields in the 1970s. These facts provide a hint about the reasons for the slowing of desegregation. First, occupations that, for whatever reasons, were the easiest targets for women's entry desegregated first, leaving the "hard cases" to move more slowly later. Second, since the influx of women continues to be largest in those occupations where it began, some initially male jobs have now "tipped" and become disproportionately female. Thus, further increases in the proportion of women in these jobs increase rather than decrease segregation. Examples of such occupations are public relations professionals, personnel and labor relations professionals, and real estate agents.

Thus far the discussion of trends in segregation has been based on research using the detailed occupational categories employed by the Census Bureau. We can think of jobs as specific occupations within a specific establishment (and hence, a specific industry). Such jobs would be the most meaningful categories across which to compute a measure of occupational sex segregation. Unfortunately, such data are not available for the economy as a whole for even one year, much less a number of years. However, as discussed above, we know that national occupational data understate the full extent of job segregation, since men and women in mixed-sex occupations often work in different industries and firms or in different subspecialties within the occupation. But what about *trends* in the sex segregation of these more detailed categories of jobs? Unfortunately, we have little information on this.

One cautionary note to the conclusion that *job* segregation declined in the 1970s comes from case studies of formerly male occupations into which there has been a large influx of women since 1970. In some cases there has been occupational desegregation but not job desegregation. That is, women and men in a newly integrated occupation may often work for different establishments, sometimes in different industries (Reskin and Roos 1990). For example, bus driving has also become integrated, but most of the women work for school districts while men still retain most of the better-paid jobs as city bus drivers. To take another example, the occupation bakers has become integrated as grocery stores have started hiring women for newly created in-store jobs using automated processes to make cakes and cookies. Yet men still dominate the less automated and more highly paid tasks of making bread in nonstore settings. Women are also becoming systems analysts. Yet in this occupation women often work in hospitals, banking, and insurance, while men are more likely to work in manufacturing industries. In each of these cases, women have gone into a formerly male occupation, but into a less desirable subpart of it, at least in terms of pay. Thus, even though an occupation has been integrated, when we use more detailed and industry-specific categories, we see that a new female "ghetto" has been created.

In summary, what can we conclude regarding trends in segregation? Occupational classifications measure the function or task people perform. Occupational segregation increased and decreased sporadically throughout the century, with a very modest net decline between 1900 and 1970. There was a faster pace of decline during the 1970s, and there has been a continued though slowed decline in segregation since 1980. We do not have data on whether segregation in jobs (defined by cross-classifying more detailed job titles and firms) has also decreased since 1970. Doubts about this are fueled by evidence that some of the occupational integration has led to new patterns of segregation within occupations. My conjecture is that some desegregation in jobs *is* occurring, particularly at the managerial and professional level, and will continue, but that the pace of desegregation of jobs is slower than that of occupations.

C. *Explanations of Levels and Trends in Segregation*

Why are some jobs filled by women, some by men, and few integrated by sex? What explains why levels of segregation change over time? As a way to organize research on these questions, I will divide the factors affecting segregation into those involving *choices* on the part of those entering jobs, and those involving *constraints* faced by job entrants. In making this distinction, we must remember that today's choices may be affected by past constraints, and vice versa. For example, parents or teachers may encourage different job choices for young women and men. This sex-differentiated reinforcement is a constraint that may lead to different job *choices* at the point one declares a college major or applies for a job. The emphasis in this chapter is not on which theory each factor is compatible with. Often a single factor plays a part in several theories, and theories are not my concern in this chapter. (For discussion of how this research forms evidence for particular theories, see Chapter 2.)

Choices. Segregation results, in part, because men and women choose different jobs. But why are these choices different? Some researchers argue that the choices are rational responses to the division of labor by sex in the family. In this view, women choose jobs compatible with their family responsibilities. I see this as playing a relatively minor role in job choices, since, as discussed above, the jobs women hold are generally not more accommodating to parenting than are men's jobs.

A variant of this argument sees the division of labor by sex in the family to cause women's employment to be intermittent, which leads women to choose jobs that maximize lifetime earnings, *conditional* on this intermittent employment. If jobs that provide much on-the-job training have steeper wage trajectories (i.e., higher rates of return to seniority) but lower starting wages, women may avoid such jobs because the gains from steeper wage gains do not outweigh the losses from the lower starting wages. Research on this question is discussed in Chapter 2 as it bears on the ability of human capital theory to explain segregation. In my view, this view is largely incorrect. Consistent with the view, women *are* concentrated in jobs that provide relatively low amounts of on-the-job training (Corcoran and Duncan 1979; Barron et al. 1990), and female jobs do have lower returns to seniority than male jobs (Rosenbaum 1980; Filer 1983). However, no research has ever demonstrated the higher starting wages that are the purported advantage of jobs offering less training. Given this, it is hard to see how women's efforts to maximize lifetime earnings would lead them to choose female jobs.[1]

Thus, if the job choices of men and women differ, I believe these differences are sustained by lifelong socialization that leads men and women to find different jobs interesting, respectable, of value, or consistent with their gendered identities. This is consistent with the view I develop in this book—that it is much more accurate to see men and women in jobs with *different skills*, than with *different amounts* of skill. Preferences for certain kinds of work entail preferences for exercising certain kinds of skills. The socialization that forms these proclivities begins in childhood and continues throughout adulthood. It operates through reinforcement patterns, role models, cognitive learning, sex-segregated networks of peers, and other processes.

These differences in interests can be seen early in life. Even preschool and elementary school children express sex-typed occupational goals (Marini and Brinton 1984). However, the occupational aspirations of boys are more highly sex typed than those of girls (Marini and Greenberger 1978).

Are these differences in job interests a reflection of broader differences in values? Some evidence supports this. Studies decades ago found that males claimed to place more value on money in choosing a job. Studies attempting to assess changes in the job dimensions valued by young adults have found surprisingly little convergence between the sexes (Lueptow 1980; Herzog 1982; Peng et al. 1981; Tittle 1981). Lueptow (1980) compared the occupational values of graduating seniors in 1961 and 1975 and found that in both years men claimed to place more value than did women on status, money, freedom from supervision, and potential for leadership. In both years, the study found that women placed more value on working with people, helping others, using their abilities, and being creative. Other surveys have shown that men place a greater value on autonomy, authority, and promotion possibilities than do women (Brenner and Tomkiewicz 1979; Murray and Atkinson 1981; Peng, Fetters, and Kolstad 1981; Herzog 1982), and these job dimensions have been found to affect men's job satisfactions to a greater extent than women's (Glenn and Weaver 1982; Crane and Hodson 1984; Murray and Atkinson 1981). There is also some evidence that men value taking risks more than women (Walker, Tausky, and Oliver 1982; Subich, Barrett, Donerspike, and Alexander 1989).

Yet we must be cautious in inferring from these studies that sex differences in occupational values explain segregation. Some of the studies surveyed adults already holding jobs. Thus, it is possible that jobs affected values as much as values affected the job chosen. The studies also show some conflicting findings. For example, while a number of surveys find that men claim to value pay more than women, one study found no such difference (Walker et al. 1982), and some studies have found pay to have a greater influence on women's job satisfaction than on men's (Crane and Hodson 1984).

It is also important not to assume that these sex differences show men to be more career or achievement oriented than women. Women may be equally career oriented but focused on different skills or values. One example of such bias in interpretation appears in an article by Brenner and Tomkiewicz (1979), who asked college students to rate job characteristics in terms of their importance to them. Men were found to place more value on income, opportunity to take risks, and supervisory authority. Women placed more value on good relations with coworkers, opportunity to develop knowledge and skills on the job, and intellectual stimulation. The authors conclude from these findings that women give less importance to careers than men. This is certainly not an obvious conclusion from the findings; one might regard an orientation toward continued learning of knowledge and skills, on which *women* placed more emphasis, as the best indicator in the survey of the sort of careerism we would expect employers to care about.

A preference for a sex-typical job does not always reflect values, tastes, or dispositions toward the kind of work in these jobs. It may rather reflect a preference for working with members of one's own sex or for doing work labeled male or female regardless of the content of the work. There is evidence of this sort of preference, especially among males. One experiment (Heilman 1979) divided high school students into two groups that received different information on the projected sex composition of the occupations of lawyer and architect. Students ran-

domly assigned to the first group were told that these jobs were projected to have a high percentage of males in them in coming years, while
those randomly assigned to the second group were told the jobs were
projected to contain a much higher percentage of females. The boys told
that the jobs were projected to have more women in them reported less
interest in going into those jobs. The opposite effect occurred for girls,
although the effect was stronger for the boys.

In my view, gender role socialization and sex-typed choices of jobs
clearly have some role in segregation. But what is their role in the desegregation observed since about 1970? There is evidence that occupational
preferences have shifted substantially among high school students (Marini and Brinton 1984). A decline in sex differences in college majors
occurred during this period as well (Beller 1984; Jacobs 1985, 1989b). Of
course, some of these shifts could be *responses* to changed constraints.
This is suggested by the evidence reviewed above that specific occupational choices shifted more than underlying occupational values. Yet
preferences were undoubtedly shifting for other reasons as well. However, these changes in preferences are probably *not* explained by changing patterns of childhood socialization, since the women who started
these changes in the 1970s were young children in the very traditional
1950s. Thus, to say that socialization is a factor in segregation does *not*
imply that changing patterns of childhood socialization is the only way
for desegregation to occur.

*Constraints Posed by Employers, Male Workers, and Institutional Prac-
tices.*   One sort of constraint faced by those seeking jobs is discrimination by employers. Our concern here is not with theories of discrimination, which are reviewed in Chapter 2, but with evidence about whether
hiring discrimination exists. Discrimination in hiring, placement, and
promotion is suggested by experimental studies that present randomly
assigned groups of managers or prospective managers with resumes
that differ only in the male or female names on them. Such studies often
find that men are preferred in typically male jobs (Rosen and Jerdee
1974, 1978; Levinson 1975; Rosen 1982). Sociologists Bielby and Baron
(1986) also found substantial evidence of discrimination in the statements of California manufacturers about their hiring practices.
Milkman's (1987) historical study showed that although many women
went into previously male jobs during World War II, this shifted rather
than eradicated boundaries between men and women's work; employers redivided jobs such that each job was done only by women or
only by men. Women were laid off after the war. As new hires were
made, employers refused to rehire women in the traditionally male jobs
they had held during the war, even when this violated union seniority

rules, and even when the women had more training in the job than the men newly returned from the war.

Employers may discriminate because of beliefs about sex differences in skills, because of values about the roles men and women should play, to create antagonisms that minimize workers' solidarity, or to avoid the disruption that occurs when male workers are faced with a woman entering "their" jobs.

Some women anticipate discrimination and alter their "choices" accordingly. Discrepancies between young women's aspirations and their expectations about future jobs are evidence that women anticipate a constraint. Marini and Greenberger (1978) found that girls expected to end up in occupations that averaged 75% female, but aspired to occupations that averaged 66% female. In contrast they found no difference between the average percentage female of the occupations high school boys said they expected to work in and those to which they aspired. Another survey of high school students showed that 34% of girls but only 22% of boys believed that their sex would prevent them from getting the kind of work they would like to have (Bachman, Johnston, and O'Malley 1980). This is evidence that young women anticipate constraints and this affects their plans.

One constraint women face is the way they are treated by male workers if they enter a male job. In one survey of female blue-collar workers, almost one third of the women reported that male coworkers gave them a hard time and that male coworkers disapproved of women doing craft work (O'Farrell and Harlan 1982). Schroedel's (1985) in-depth interviews with women who entered male-dominated blue-collar craft jobs revealed that many women felt unwelcome as a result of men's derogatory comments, men's attempts to sexualize the relationships (such as touching women while working next to them), and men's unwillingness to teach women the skills they would ordinarily teach a new male coworker. Case studies of occupations that many women entered in the 1970s show that men often tried to keep women out, either for fear that it would lower their wages or because they saw it as a threat to their sense of masculinity (Reskin and Roos 1990). Unionized men have been more successful than others at keeping women out (Reskin and Roos 1990; Hartmann 1976). There are several ways that unions have helped men to keep women out of "their" jobs. Some unionized jobs can only be entered through apprenticeships and one has to be selected by a union member to be an apprentice. Also, prior to the passage of the 1964 Civil Rights Act, which rendered such laws illegal, unions lobbied for laws that prohibited hiring women in particular jobs or for particular shifts.

Institutional inertia plays a role in perpetuating discriminatory constraints. Milkman (1987) examined historical data on a number of man-

ufacturing firms across the century and found that if an industry hires
one sex in a certain job at its origin, the sex label generally "sticks" for
decades because it gains the weight of tradition.

Institutional inertia perpetuates segregation in yet another way. Many
firms have structured mobility ladders, sometimes called internal labor
markets. While some jobs are a "dead end" from which one cannot be
promoted, others lead to a sequence of jobs through which promotions
are common. The jobs at the bottom of these mobility ladders are filled
from outside the firm; they may be thought of as ports of entry. Once
segregation has occurred in jobs that are ports of entry—for any of the
reasons discussed above—the existence of structured mobility ladders
will perpetuate segregation up the ladders and through the life cycle of
each cohort of workers without a need for further overt discrimination.

Another set of institutional practices that create constraints falls into a
category similar to the legal notion of "disparate impact," discussed in
more detail in Chapter 5. Job requirements that have a disparate and
adverse impact on women are those that, given prior sex differences in
experiences, make it more difficult for women to qualify for or remain in
the job. These constraints are distinct from direct sex discrimination
in hiring. That is, sex is not explicitly being used as a criterion for letting
people into the job. Yet other criteria are being used that tend to screen
out women. Examples of such criteria that have an adverse impact on
women include upper age limits for entering apprenticeships (which
disadvantage homemakers returning to the labor force), veterans' preferences (since more men than women have been veterans), limited public advertising of jobs (since more men than women are likely to talk to
men who work in the jobs and thus have access to the information), the
use of machinery designed for typical male height and strength, and
departmental rather than plantwide seniority being credited toward promotions (Roos and Reskin 1984).

It is hard to know how much discriminatory barriers of either an overt
or disparate impact variety have changed. My rough sense is that there
has been a substantial decline in hiring discrimination, but that a substantial amount remains. Antidiscrimination legislation has had some
effects on employers' hiring practices (Beller 1979, 1982a, 1982b; Leonard
1984; U.S. Department of Labor 1984; Burstein 1985; Gunderson 1989).
In this sense, the lessening of constraints has been an important factor in
desegregation. After legal requirements, Equal Employment Opportunity (EEO) was institutionalized as part of personnel departments in
most large firms, thus giving it some inertial force even in the absence of
governmental enforcement. The Republican administrations in office
since 1980 have been much less aggressive than prior Republican or
Democratic administrations about using the Equal Employment Oppor-

tunity Commission (EEOC) or the Office of Federal Contract Compliance Program (OFCCP) to sue or fine employers who discriminate against women or people of color.

Women have been helped by changes in some job requirements, whether these changes occurred because of successful lawsuits involving disparate impact (Burstein and Pitchford 1990) or for other reasons. To take an example of the latter, the development of real estate courses at community colleges around 1970 provided a way for women to circumvent apprenticeship systems that had required current brokers (mostly men) to sponsor new real estate agents (Reskin and Roos 1990).

The fact that resistance by male workers to women's entrance into jobs is a factor in discrimination suggests some conditions under which desegregation might proceed. Reskin and Roos (1990) show that women are more likely to enter male-dominated occupations when they are undergoing deskilling, losing autonomy, or their earnings relative to all jobs is going down. Women are more able to enter jobs at such times because men are less concerned with keeping women out when their jobs are losing desirability; in such times men themselves want to leave the jobs. Unfortunately for women, this means it will be easiest to enter those male jobs with declining advantages in terms of earnings, mobility prospects, or autonomy.

Desegregation has also been more likely to occur when there is an expansion in demand in a male occupation and women are found to be cheaper than men (Oppenheimer 1970; Richardson and Hatcher 1983; Cohn 1985).

IV. The Sex Gap in Pay

A. Trends in the Sex Gap in Pay

In the United States, as in most nations, women earn substantially less than men. For manufacturing workers, the female/male earnings ratio moved from 0.35 in 1820, to 0.50 in 1850, to 0.58 in 1930 (Goldin 1990). For all workers, the ratio rose from 0.45 to 0.60 between 1890 and 1930 (Goldin 1990). Table 1.3 shows little change between 1955 and 1980 for whites. During most of this period the ratio was about 0.59. Among blacks, Table 1.3 shows that the sex gap in pay narrowed considerably between 1955 and 1980, with women's relative earnings moving from 0.55 to 0.79. Thus, when it comes to women's pay relative to that of men, there have been eras of progress and eras of stagnation, and the timing of such change has differed by race.

Since 1980, white, black, and Hispanic women have made progress relative to men of their own racial or ethnic group, and relative to white men. As Table 1.3 shows, the sex ratio for whites moved from 0.59 to 0.65 between 1980 and 1987. For blacks the sex ratio moved from 0.79 to 0.84, and for Hispanics from 0.72 to 0.83. For the most part, women made these relative gains because their earnings showed slight (inflation-adjusted) absolute gains during the 1980s, while white and black men's wages were relatively stagnant and Hispanic men's wages declined.

The figures referred to so far (in Table 1.3) are based on annual earnings of full-time workers. Another way to look at trends in the pay gap is

Table 1.4. Female-Male Ratios of Median Usual Weekly Earnings among Full-Time Wage and Salary Workers, by Race, 1967–1989

Year[3]	Unadjusted for Hours Worked[1]		Adjusted for Hours Worked[2]	
	White	Black	White	Black
1967	0.608	0.700	0.676	0.732
1971	0.607	0.707	0.669	0.747
1973	0.606	0.718	0.669	0.756
1974	0.598	0.731	0.659	0.768
1975	0.613	0.751	0.672	0.789
1976	0.615	0.738	0.676	0.781
1977	0.606	0.731	0.669	0.775
1978	0.599	0.732	0.660	0.773
1979	0.611	0.747	0.673	0.790
1981	0.635	0.775	0.694	0.817
1982	0.639	0.794	0.698	0.838
1983	0.646	0.790	0.703	0.832
1984	0.670	0.798	0.731	0.842
1985	0.674	0.829	0.736	0.874
1986	0.679	0.827	0.742	0.866
1987	0.682	0.844	0.745	0.890
1988	0.684	0.830	0.746	0.877
1989	0.693	0.865	0.758	0.914

Source: U.S. Department of Labor 1967–1989.
Notes:
[1] Includes only full-time workers, i.e., those working at least 35 hours per week.
[2] Includes only full-time workers, i.e., those working at least 35 hours per week, and adjusts for sex differences in average hours worked among these workers.
[3] Data for 1967–1978 are for the month of May only.

to examine usual weekly earnings of full-time, year-round workers. Figures in the left two columns of Table 1.4 show these trends for black and
white men and women. For some reason the female/male ratios are
slightly higher in such data, but they show the same basic trends in the
sex gap in pay—steady decreases among blacks and decreases among
whites since 1980.

One limitation of the statistics in Table 1.3 and in the left two columns of
Table 1.4 is that all workers who work at least 35 hours a week are
considered full-time. Yet among these full-time workers, men average
slightly more hours per week than women. Thus, when figures on the sex
gap in pay are adjusted for differences in hours worked within full-time
workers, the ratios are several percentage points higher, although the
trends in sex gaps are similar, as the right two columns of Table 1.4 show.

One set of statistics that can mislead as an indicator of women's progress is comparisons between the sex gap in pay for different age groups.
Table 1.5 gives female/male earnings ratios separately by age group, for

Table 1.5. Adjusted[1] Female-Male Ratios of Median
Usual Weekly Earnings among Full-Time Wage
and Salary Workers, by Age, 1973–1988

Age	1973	1978	1983	1988
Total, 16 years and older	0.68	0.67	0.72	0.77
16–19	0.86	0.91	0.96	0.93
20–24	0.83	0.80	0.89	0.96
25–34	0.72	0.73	0.80	0.85
35–44	0.61	0.59	0.66	0.75
45–54	0.62	0.59	0.63	0.67

Sources: Figures for 1973 to 1983 from Table 3, O'Neill,
June. "The Trends in the Male–Female Wage Gap in the
United States." *Journal of Labor Economics* Vol. 3, No. 1, pp.
S91–S116. Copyright © 1985. Reprinted with permission.
Figures for 1988 from U.S. Department of Labor 1989a (Table
33) and 1989b (Table 41).
Notes:
[1] Adjusted for sex differences in hours worked among workers classified as full-time (i.e., 35 hours/week or more). For
1988 figures only, data on hours used for the adjustments
come from a slightly different age group than was used for
the figures on earnings because of unavailability of data on
narrow age groups in published sources. For 1988, hours for
those 25–44 were used to adjust earnings ratios of those 25–
34 and 35–44, and hours of those 45–64 were used to adjust
earnings ratios of those 45–54.

1973, 1978, 1983, and 1988. The table shows that, in each year, the gap is much smaller among younger workers. For example, in 1988, the female/male earnings ratio among those 20–24 was 0.96, whereas it was 0.85 among those 25–34, and 0.75 among those 35–44. Some interpret this to mean that the sex gap in pay is disappearing. This optimistic interpretation hinges on assuming that the differences in a given year across age groups result entirely from a cohort effect and not at all from a life cycle effect. Another way to put this assumption is to say that each cohort (i.e. people born in a given year) will retain the same sex ratio of pay it currently has as it ages. If this is true, as the older cohorts with the larger sex gap retire, the overall sex gap in pay will decrease. If, on the other hand, we interpret the age differences as entirely a life cycle effect, experienced by every cohort, the figures have no implications as to the future of the sex gap in pay. They simply reveal that the sex gap in pay increases with age. This results in part because the sex gap in experience increases as women go through the childbearing years, and in part because even those women who are employed continuously usually work in jobs low on prospects for mobility and raises. For both these reasons, women's earnings fall further and further behind men's across the life cycle. Further complicating matters is the possibility of period effects. Period effects refer to changes over time, for example, decreases in discrimination, that affect all employed cohorts and age groups approximately equally.

In reality, all three effects (cohort, life cycle, and period) are probably operative, as suggested by Table 1.5 (and by Bianchi and Spain 1986). In each of the years shown, younger workers have a higher female/male ratio of earnings. We can also follow one cohort across the years. To take one example, consider those who were aged 25–34 in 1973, with women earning 0.72 of men's earnings. Ten years later, in 1983, when this same cohort was aged 35–44, the women were earning only 0.66 what men earned. For this cohort, women's relative losses across the life cycle were great enough to override any period gains between 1973 and 1983. But, if we look at the cohort 25–34 in 1978, women earned 0.73 of men's earnings in 1978, but had decreased the sex gap slightly to a ratio of 0.75 by 1988 when the cohort was 35–44. Here the period progress accruing to the cohort appears to have been large enough to override any relative losses of women across the life cycle. This suggests that favorable change in women's relative pay is occurring via both period and cohort effects. However, net of these changes, women's relative position deteriorates across the life cycle. Thus, the progress is not as fast as would be indicated by interpreting all of the age differences in sex ratio for any given year as cohort effects.

B. Explanations of the Sex Gap in Pay

What factors explain the sex gap in pay? Here I will consider evidence for the role of a number of factors, leaving questions of what theories this evidence supports for Chapter 2. Some of these factors have their effects on the sex gap in pay via their effects on segregation.

Sex Differences in Productivity or Effort?   Are women less productive than men? We seldom have measures of productivity, so there is little direct evidence on this. Yet there is much speculation and some indirect evidence. Becker (1985) speculates that, because of their domestic responsibilities, women exert less intense effort on the job, saving energy for domestic pursuits. The fact that women who are employed do more household work than their husbands is well documented (Berk and Berk 1979; Ross 1987; Hochschild 1989). But despite this, tests of differences in effort have, if anything, suggested that women expend *more* effort than men in their paid jobs. Bielby and Bielby (1988) analyzed data from a national survey that asked respondents how "hard" their jobs require them to work, how much "effort, either physical or mental" their jobs require, and how much "effort" they put into their jobs "beyond what is required." Women reported slightly *more* effort than men. One might wonder whether this finding simply results from women "bragging" more than men about their effort level. This is doubtful, since social psychologists' experiments show that men generally overestimate and women underestimate their own performance (Colwill 1982). Evidence on time allocation also suggests that women's effort is higher than men's; national survey data show that women report less time than men in coffee breaks, lunch breaks, and other regularly scheduled work breaks (Stafford and Duncan 1980; Quinn and Staines 1979). Thus, research indicates that sex differences in effort explain none of the sex gap in pay.

Industries and Firms.   While the most obvious form of segregation is at the occupational level, there is some segregation by industry and firm as well, and this contributes to the sex gap in pay. Unlike occupations, many of which are nearly all male or female, almost all firms (and thus industries, since they are a collection of firms all selling the same product) employ both men and women. Yet, although sex segregation by firm and industry is not nearly as extreme as by occupation, there are, nonetheless, systematic tendencies for women to be employed in those firms and industries with low average wages (Blau 1977; Beck, Horan, and Tolbert 1980; Hodson and England 1986; Aldrich and Buchele 1989; Coverdill 1988; Ferber and Spaeth 1984). For example, Blau (1977) examined cases where men and women in the same very detailed occupation (like accounting clerk, payroll clerk, or computer programmer) had different wages, and found that this was usually a matter of women working in a lower-wage firm. Often the entire industry the lower-paying firms were in had lower average wage scales.

However, even when women move to higher-wage firms and industries, their wages do not go up as much as men's do. The wage premium associated with being in a high-wage firm or industry goes disproportionately to male jobs (Aldrich and Buchele 1989).

Amount of Human Capital Investment and Expected Human Capital Investment.   Are women in jobs requiring less skill, and, if so, does this affect the sex gap in pay? Here, let us confine our attention to *amount* of skills or training rather than *types* of skill. Amount of schooling, one type of human capital, explains virtually none of the sex gap in pay, since men and women in the labor force have virtually the same median years of formal education, as Table 1.6 shows. Among whites, women had 1.3 years more education than men in the labor force in 1952, and men did not close this gap until 1969. By 1979, white men's median was a trivial 0.1 year more education than white women's. For blacks the trends are somewhat different, but black women have had slightly more education than black men in all years since 1952, as Table 1.6 shows, although by 1983 this female advantage in median education had declined to a relatively trivial 0.2 year.

There *is* a sex difference in another sort of human capital: years of job experience. Because many women spend some years rearing children and keeping house full-time, the average woman in the labor force has fewer years of experience than the average man. Early studies had

Table 1.6.   Median Years of School Completed by Men and Women in the Labor Force, by Race, 1952–1983

	White			Black		
	Men	*Women*	*Difference*	*Men*	*Women*	*Difference*
1952	10.8	12.1	−1.3	7.2	8.1	−0.9
1959	11.8	12.2	−0.4	8.1	9.4	−1.3
1969	12.4	12.4	0.0	10.8	11.9	−1.1
1979	12.7	12.6	0.1	12.2	12.4	−0.2
1983	12.8	12.7	0.1	12.4	12.6	−0.2

Source: From: O'Neill, J. "The Trends in The Male–Female Wage Gap in the United States." *Journal of Labor Economics* Vol. 3, No. 1, pp. S91–S116. Copyright © 1985. Reprinted with permission.

shown that this difference explains between one quarter and one half of the sex gap in pay (Polachek 1975; Mincer and Polachek 1974, 1978; Sandell and Shapiro 1978).

A 1979 study by Corcoran and Duncan will be discussed in some detail since it is the best available for assessing the effects of various types of human capital on the sex gap in pay. They used a standard method of regression decomposition in which the amount that any variable contributes to the sex gap in pay is a function of (1) the rate of return of the variable (how much an additional increment contributes to earnings for both men and women) and (2) the size of the difference between men and women's average on this variable. They found that the regression coefficients or slopes—the rates of return—to different types of human capital were not terribly different for men and women. Their results do show that the *overall* rate of return to experience is higher for white males than other groups. (Hoffman 1981 also found this.) But when experience is divided into subcomponents according to whether the experience was with one's current employer (called "tenure") and whether it involved on-the-job training, rates of return for the subcomponents did not differ much by race or sex. This implies that the overall group differences in rates of return to experience came from groups spending different proportions of their employed years in different types of experience, which in turn offer varying rates of return. For example, white men are likely to have a higher portion of their experience in a job that provides on-the-job training, and years of tenure during which training was provided have a higher rate of return than other years of tenure in one's current firm or than years of experience in prior firms.

Since coefficients did not vary significantly between groups for most variables, Corcoran and Duncan used white male slopes for the decomposition, and my discussion that follows uses these results. Calculations from Corcoran and Duncan's study (1979) are presented in Tables 1.7 and 1.8. (They include decompositions using other groups' slopes.)

A striking implication of Table 1.7 is the amount of the sex gap in pay among whites that comes from men having more tenure (seniority with one's firm), including periods during which the employer was providing training. The training portion of tenure explains 11% of the gap between white men and white women. Although Table 1.7 shows that this same factor explains 8% of the gap between white men and black women, and 15% of the gap between black men and white men, Table 1.8 shows that on-the-job training is a relatively minor factor in the sex gap in pay between black men and women, explaining only 2%. It is also a trivial part of the pay gap between black women and white women (1%). Whether or not differences between groups in time spent in jobs with

Table 1.7.   Percentage of 1975 Wage Gap between White Men and Other Groups
Accounted for by Indicators of Human Capital

	Black Men		White Women		Black Women	
Years out of labor force since completing school	0	(0)	6	(5)	3	(−3)
Years of work experience before present employer	2	(6)	3	(1)	1	(−1)
Years with current employer prior to current position	5	(4)	12	(11)	7	(5)
Years of training completed on current job	15	(22)	11	(17)	8	(14)
Years of posttraining tenure on current job	−4	(−5)	−1	(−1)	−1	(1)
Proportion of total working years that were full-time	0	(−1)	8	(7)	4	(2)
Hours of work missed due to illness of others in 1975	−1	(1)	−1	(0)	−2	(−1)
Hours of work missed due to own illness in 1975	−1	(−1)	0	(0)	−1	(0)
Placed limits on job hours or location	0	(1)	2	(1)	1	(−1)
Plans to stop work for nontraining reasons	−1	(−1)	2	(1)	1	(2)
Formal education (in years)	38	(43)	2	(2)	11	(15)
Percentage of total gap explained by human capital	53	(71)	44	(45)	32	(32)
Percentage of total gap unexplained by human capital	47	(29)	56	(55)	68	(68)

Note: The decomposition calculates what percentage of the total gap in the natural log of hourly earnings between white men and each other group arises because of group differences in means on the independent variables, assuming the white male slopes. The calculation is the difference between the two groups' means times the slope. This is then divided by the total log-dollar gap and the quotient multiplied by 100 to convert to a percentage. (The percentages in parentheses are alternative estimates arrived at by using the lower-earning group's slopes.) The total gap is adjusted for whether individuals live in the South and the size of the largest city they live near. Adapted and computed from Corcoran and Duncan (1979, Table 1).

training are themselves explained by discrimination in job assignments or by job choices is a separate question that Corcoran and Duncan's analysis cannot answer.

White women also earn less if they have been out of the labor force. (See also Mincer and Ofek 1982.) This is shown by the net effects on wages of (1) years of work experience before present employer and (2) years with current employer prior to current position. The first of

Table 1.8. Percentage of 1975 Wage Gap between Black Men and Women and between Black and White Women Explained by Indicators of Human Capital

	Black Women and Black Men		Black Women and White Women	
Years out of labor force since completing school	10	(−7)	−8	(14)
Years of work experience before present employer	0	(−3)	−3	(3)
Years with current employer prior to current position	7	(6)	−12	(−12)
Years of training completed on current job	2	(2)	1	(2)
Years of posttraining tenure on current job	2	(−2)	−4	(3)
Proportion of total working years that were full-time	16	(4)	−10	(−6)
Hours of work missed due to illness of others in 1975	2	(−1)	3	(−5)
Hours of work missed due to own illness in 1975	0	(0)	3	(−2)
Placed limits on job hours or location	−3	(1)	−3	(−6)
Plans to stop work for nontraining reasons	3	(5)	−1	(7)
Formal education (in years)	−16	(−20)	76	(97)
Percentage of total gap explained by human capital	25	(−15)	43	(95)
Percentage of total gap unexplained by human capital	75	(115)	57	(5)

Note: The decomposition calculates what percentage of the total gap in the natural log of hourly earnings between the two groups arises because of group differences in means on the independent variables, assuming the slopes of the higher-earning groups, black men in column 1 and white women in column 2. (The percentages in parentheses are alternative estimates arrived at by using the lower-earning group's slopes.) The total gap is adjusted for whether individuals live in the South and the size of the largest city they live near. Computed from Corcoran and Duncan (1979, Table 1).

these two factors explains 3% of the gap between white men and white women (Table 1.7) but has no effect on the sex gap among blacks (Table 1.8). The second factor explains 12% of the sex gap among whites (Table 1.7), and 7% (Table 1.8) of the sex gap among blacks. The proximate cause of these portions of the sex gap in pay is women's lesser employment experience. However, discriminatory job and wage differentials may be behind some proportion of these sex differences in years of employment experience, since women have less motivation to stay employed if they are paid less. It is interesting that none of the measures of experience contribute to the pay gap between white and black women; black women have more experience but lower earnings.

Overall, Table 1.7 shows that Corcoran and Duncan (1979) found human capital (broadly construed to include all measures of education, employment continuity, and labor force attachment) to explain 44% of the pay gap between white men and women and 32% of the gap between white men and black women.

Tables 1.7 and 1.8, taken together, also reveal some facts about the interaction of race and gender. Overall, a much smaller proportion of the sex gap in pay between black women and black men is explained by human capital than is explained for either the gap between black and white women or between black women and white men. In particular, black women's higher average education than black men's makes a large *negative* contribution to the sex gap for blacks. That is, black women have higher education than black men, but lower earnings. In contrast, education makes significant contributions to the pay gap between black and white women (76%), between black women and white men (11%), and between black and white men (38%).

Let us now turn our attention to the question of whether women's *intentions* or *expectations* for less employment continuity at the time they first enter employment might explain some of the subsequent sex gap in pay. To the extent that job experience provides skill accumulation, this can be seen as relevant to the amount of human capital one accumulates. There are two versions of how expectations about continuity of experience might affect earnings. One posits that, if there is a trade-off between starting wages and steep wage trajectories (i.e., high returns to experience and/or tenure), women who plan intermittent employment will be more apt to choose jobs with relatively high starting wages than will either men or women planning continuous employment. This could possibly create an average sex gap in pay, despite the fact that it would produce higher lifetime earnings for women than if they chose jobs similar to men. However, as mentioned above, no study to date has found higher average starting wages for women or in women's jobs, even when other factors are controlled (England 1984; England, Farkas, Kilbourne, and Dou 1988). A milder version of this thesis might say that women will be more motivated to choose jobs with steep upward wage trajectories the longer they plan to be employed. I find this a more plausible claim, although we lack research on how much this has affected women's choices.

A second way that women's plans for intermittent employment may affect the sex gap in pay is via employers' statistical discrimination. (Definitions and theoretical discussion of statistical discrimination appear in Chapter 2.) If women have higher turnover rates, and employers know this, then based on this sex difference in turnover they may engage in what economists call statistical discrimination. That is, employers will be reluctant to hire women in jobs where turnover is especially expensive, particularly jobs that provide much on-the-job training. What evidence is there for this as a factor in the sex gap in pay? First, let us look at the evidence about sex differences in turnover. It is equivocal (Price 1977, p. 40). Several studies based on recent national probability samples of young workers (mostly in their twenties) found no sex differences in turnover, even when wage was not controlled (Waite and Berryman 1985; Donohue 1987; Lynch 1991). At first glance this seems extremely counterintuitive since we know that women leave the labor force for childrearing more often than men. The seeming anomaly is explained by the fact that men change firms more often than women (Barnes and Jones 1974). Other studies find gross differences, with women having higher turnover rates, but after statistically adjusting for wages or wage-related job characteristics, these differences disappear or reverse (Viscusi 1980; Blau and Kahn 1981; Haber, Lamas, and Green 1983; Shorey 1983). In general, workers of any sex or race are more likely to quit a job when it is low paying or has low opportunity for advancement (C. Smith 1979; Osterman 1982; Haber et al. 1983; Shorey 1983; Grounau 1988; Kahn and Griesinger 1989; Light and Ureta 1989). Thus, if women are placed in less desirable jobs through discrimination, this could explain part of their higher turnover in studies that do find gross sex differences in turnover. If this is true, then women's disadvantageous job placements may explain their higher turnover rather than vice versa. However, if the job placements result from statistical discrimination based on real exogenous turnover differences, then statistical controls for job characteristics are inappropriate in studies designed to assess exogenous sex differences in turnover propensity. Thus, the "chicken and egg" question of which is exogenous, the higher turnover or the discrimination, is virtually impossible to assess statistically. My best guess is that, except in the most recent cohorts (to which Waite and Berryman's 1985, Donohue's 1987, and Lynch's 1991 analyses were confined), exogenous sex differences in turnover existed but were very small and not present in all workplaces or occupations. However, it is important to note that among young cohorts in the recent period, turnover differences disappeared. Thus, if employers continue favoring men for jobs providing much training, it cannot be explained rationally via statistical discrimination but must reflect erroneous perceptions or other discriminatory motivations.

Thus far I have discussed how much of the sex gap in pay can be explained by human capital or anticipated human capital at any one point in time. But what of the trends in the sex gap in pay? Can these be explained by trends in human capital? Let us look at this question first in terms of the post–World War II period up until about 1980, a period during which the sex gap in pay was relatively unchanging. Were there trends in human capital that we would expect to have reduced the sex gap in pay? Several studies suggest not. For example, women's education relative to men's has not increased in the last 50 years (Goldin 1990; Smith and Ward 1984). Thus, based on education trends, we would not expect the sex gap in pay to change. Of course, during all this time, both men's and women's levels of education were increasing, and women had as much or more education than men (Jacobs 1989b). Thus, the point is not that at any one time education can explain the sex gap in pay, but rather that trends in the sex gap in education were not changing favorably to women, so we would not expect a change in the sex gap in pay on the basis of trends in education alone.

Similarly, prior to 1980, women's experience did not increase relative to men's (Smith and Ward 1984; Goldin 1990). At first this seems counterintuitive. One might think that as the percentage of women who are employed increases, this would lessen the sex gap in experience. But, in fact, the upward surge in women's employment affects the average experience of employed women in two conflicting ways: (1) On the one hand, the fact that fewer currently employed women have left the labor force (at all or for as long a time) increases the average experience of employed women. (2) On the other hand, the entrance of new female workers with little experience depresses the average years of experience of employed women. Thus, whether the average experience of employed women goes up, down, or stays the same as women's employment increases depends upon the relative strength of these two conflicting forces. Recent research (Smith and Ward 1984; Goldin 1990) suggests that they canceled each other out, so that women's average experience did not rise, and the sex gap in experience did not begin to close, until about 1980. Since 1980, however, women's relative experience has increased, and this is one factor in the declining sex gap in pay (Smith and Ward 1984; Goldin 1990; O'Neill 1985). However, this does not mean that experience completely "explains" the sex gap in pay. As we have seen, experience explains less than one half the sex gap in pay at any particular point in time.

Values and Preferences.   Do women's values and preferences help explain the sex gap in pay? In one sense, I have already considered this question above. I argued that gender-specific socialization orients both men and women toward kinds of jobs and skills typical for their gender. Insofar as women's jobs then pay less, values have played a part in the sex gap in pay. In a formal analysis of this type, Filer (1983) uses a large number of measures of tastes and personality characteristics to predict earnings and finds that they explain some of the sex difference in pay.

Much of this, I would argue, is an indirect effect. Values are affecting occupational choice and occupations are affecting earnings, but Filer's (1983) study does not make clear the mechanism through which occupational characteristics affect earnings. One such mechanism is the sort of wage discrimination against female jobs at issue in comparable worth, to be discussed below.

A thesis claiming a more direct causal line from values to earnings posits that men simply place a higher value on earnings when they decide which occupation to select, while women trade these off for other job characteristics. A number of studies have asked people what they value in jobs, and find that men rank earnings more highly than women (Brenner and Tomkiewicz 1979; Lueptow 1980; Peng et al. 1981; Herzog 1982; Major and Konar 1984). However, one study by Walker et al. (1982) found no such difference. Moreover, research on job satisfaction has found that women's satisfaction is *more* affected than is men's by the pay in their job (Glenn and Weaver 1982; Crane and Hodson 1984). In addition, studies of turnover find that the extent to which wage increases affect whether women will quit a job is as large or larger for women than for men (Shorey 1983; Kahn and Griesinger 1989; Light and Ureta 1989). Thus, if we look at responses to job characteristics, it appears that women may place more importance than men on earnings. In short, existing evidence provides no clear answer to the question of whether or not there is a sex difference in the value placed on money contributing to the sex gap in pay.

Sex Composition Effects. The call for comparable worth is based on the finding that a job's sex composition affects its wage level. This is a very consistent finding coming from a wide range of studies. Here I review this research, dividing studies into three types: those taking occupations as units of analysis and using national data, those taking individuals as units of analysis and (generally) using national data, and those taking jobs as units of analysis using data from a single organization or employer.

One type of study has taken U.S. Census detailed occupational categories as units of analysis and used national data. Such studies have controlled for occupational characteristics such as average requirements for education, and an array of occupational demands, with measures typically taken from the Dictionary of Occupational Titles (DOT). In general, such studies have found that, net of these measures, both men and women earn less if they work in a predominantly female occupation. This has been found for 1940, 1950, and 1960 with controls for education (Treiman and Terrell 1975b), for 1970 with controls for education, DOT skill measures, and other variables (England and McLaughlin

Table 1.9. Summary of Studies Examining the Effect of Occupational Sex Composition on Earnings and the Sex Gap in Pay

Study	Data Source[1]	Measure of Earnings	Pay Ratio (Female/Male)	Estimated Coefficients of Sex Composition[2]		Percentage of Sex Gap Explained by Sex Composition[3]: Coefficients			Unit of Analysis[4]	Control Variables[5] Included in Regressions
				Female Equation	Male Equation	Female	Male	Average		
Ferber and Lowry (1976)	1970 census	Median annual		−1438	−5008				Weighted occup. (n = 260)	1, 2
Snyder and Hudis (1976)	1970 census	Median annual		−2070	−3900				Unweighted occup. (n = 212)	1, 2, 7, 11, 27
Treiman and Hartmann (1981)	1970 census	Median annualized[6]		−1630	−2960				Unweighted occup. (n = 499)	1
England, et al. (1982)	1970 census	Median annual for full-time year-round	0.54	−1682	−3005	21	38	30	Weighted occup. (n = 387)	1, 26, 27, 29, 30, 31, 32
Aldrich and Buchele (1986)	1980 NLS	Hourly	0.64	−0.586	−0.686	9	11	10	Weighted occup. (n = 192)	1, 2, 4, 5, 6, 7, 12, 13, 14, 26, 27, 33
O'Neill (1983)	1980 CPS	Log hourly	0.68	−0.158 (0.049)	−0.148 (0.049)	12	11	11	Weighted occup. (n = 306)	1, 2, 6, 7, 11, 18, 27, 28, 36, 37, 38, 39
Johnson and Solon (1984)	1978 CPS	Log hourly	0.66	−0.090 (0.014)	−0.168 (0.015)	11	21	16	Individual n_f = 19,412 n_m = 24,056	1, 2, 3, 6, 7, 8, 9, 10, 12, 13, 15, 26, 27, 28, 36
U.S. Bureau of Census (1987)	1984 SIPP	Log hourly for full-time workers	0.70 nhs[7] — hs	−0.340 (0.067) — −0.211 (0.033)	−0.241 (0.060) — −0.225 (0.026)	43 — 28	30 — 30	37 — 29	Individual n_f = 5,555 n_m = 8,167	1, 4, 5, 7, 8, 9, 10, 12, 13, 16, 17, 18, 19, 20, 21, 22, 23, 24,

Sorensen (1989b)	1984	PSID	Log hourly	0.65	col	−0.417 (0.061) −0.230 (0.033)	−0.189 (0.056) −0.239 (0.040)	38	17	28	23	24	23	Individual $n_f = 2,411$ $n_m = 2,616$	25, 34	1, 2, 4, 5, 6, 7, 8, 9, 10, 12, 13, 15, 19, 23, 24, 26, 27, 28, 35

Source: Adapted from Sorensen 1989b (Table 4.1).

Notes:

[1] Abbreviations: NLS = National Longitudinal Survey, Center for Human Resource Research, Ohio State University. CPS = Current Population Survey, U.S. Government. SIPP = Survey of Income and Program Participation, U.S. Government; PSID = Panel Study of Income Dynamics, Institute for Survey Research, University of Michigan.

[2] All measured as the proportion of workers in an occupation who are female except Aldrich and Buchele, which is percentage female. Standard errors are in parentheses when available.

[3] Blanks exist because data were unavailable to calculate these figures or unweighted occupations were used as the unit of analysis and thus individual inferences could not be made. The percentage of the pay gap accounted for by the sex composition of an occupation using the male coefficient was calculated as follows: $b_m(X_m - X_f)/w_m - w_f)$. X_m and X_f are the sample means of the proportion of women in an occupation for men and women, respectively. w_m and w_f are the sample means of earnings for men and women. b_m is the male regression coefficient for the proportion of women in an occupation. To derive the figure using the female coefficient b_m is replaced by b_f.

[4] Weighted occup.: each observation is an occupation weighted by the proportion of the female or male work force in the occupation; unweighted occup.: each occupation counts equally; individual: each observation is an individual worker; n = number of observations; n_f = the number of women; n_m = the number of men.

[5] Independent variables included were (1) sex composition of an occupation, (2) education, (3) potential work experience, (4) actual work experience, (5) tenure (job and/or employer tenure), (6) region, (7) urban, (8) race, (9) marital status, (10) children (number and/or presence), (11) hours of work, (12) union status (membership and/or coverage), (13) government employment, (14) industry dummies for core/periphery distinction, (15) two-digit SIC code industrial categories, (16) firm size, (17) involuntarily left last job, (18) turnover, (19) health/disability, (20) blue-collar occupation, (21) high school curriculum, (22) attended private high school, (23) obtained advanced degree, (24) obtained college degree, (25) various fields of study in college, (26) general education development (DOT), (27) specific vocational preparation (DOT), (28) DOT measures of working conditions, (29) DOT measures of cognitive skills, (30) DOT measures of perceptual skills, (31) DOT measures of manual skills, (32) DOT measures of social skills, (33) race composition of an occupation, (34) usually work full-time, (35) part-time last year, (36) part-time this year, (37) employed five years earlier, (38) license or certification required, and (39) self-employed. DOT refers to measures from the Dictionary of Occupational Titles.

[6] Median annualized earnings = (median annual earnings · 2080)/mean annual hours.

[7] nhs: not a high school graduate; hs: high school graduate; col: college graduate. Separate analyses done by educational level.

1979; England, Chassie, and McCormick 1982), and for 1980 with similar controls (Parcel 1989). The one study that does not find this net negative effect of occupational percentage female (Filer 1989) used a very extensive list of controls. I will argue in Chapter 3, in conjunction with my analysis of this genre using 1980 census data, that Filer may have included inappropriate variables and "overpartialed" the effect. To foreshadow, my analysis in Chapter 3 finds a negative effect on wages of the percentage female in an occupation, under more rigorous controls than most previous studies have used for skill demands as well as characteristics of the firms and industry people in given occupations typically work in.

A second type of study takes individuals as units of analysis, and examines the effects of occupational sex composition by mapping this contextual variable onto each individual's record according to the occupation s/he holds. Controls for various other occupational characteristics are mapped on in the same way as contextual variables. Such studies find a net negative effect on both men's and women's wages of being in an occupation that is predominantly female (Johnson and Solon 1986). One advantage of such studies is that they employ controls for individuals' human capital. One study (England et al. 1988) found this negative effect of occupational percentage female using longitudinal data and a "fixed-effects" model to control for any unmeasured differences between unchanging pay-relevant attributes of those individuals in predominantly female and male occupations.

Sorensen (1989b) has assembled most of the published studies investigating the net effect of occupations' percentage female. (She includes studies using either census occupations or individuals as units of analysis.) These findings are summarized in Table 1.9. In general, these studies find that moving from an all-male to a comparable all-female occupation is associated with a wage penalty equivalent to between 10 and 30% of the sex gap in pay.

A third type of study employs data from one organization or employer. These studies show similar findings. One advantage of these studies is that they often employ more detailed job categories than do national studies. A second advantage is that they allow us to see the potential effects of comparable worth at the level at which they would occur in the version of the reform generally advocated—within a single employer or organization. A disadvantage of such studies is that they are limited to the public sector, where data on pay are more readily available. A number of states have done job evaluation studies for comparable worth purposes in the last ten years. Invariably, these studies have found that, net of measures of job skill or worth, female jobs pay less (Remick 1984; Rothchild 1984; Steinberg, Haignere, Possin, Chertos, and Treiman 1986; Acker 1989; Orazem and Matilla 1989). The job evaluation techniques used in such studies are discussed in more detail in Chapter 4.

Another study of public sector employment examined pay in the California state civil service. Baron and Newman (1989; forthcoming) found "smoking gun" evidence of discrimination in pay setting. A 1934 memo (Becker 1934) said that pay in jobs is set, among other things, according to the "age, sex, and standard of living of employees normally recruited for the given job." Baron and Newman's (1989; forthcoming) analysis of the California civil service data found higher pay levels in predominantly male jobs, even when controlling for the broader occupational category into which each more detailed job falls, and for the education and experience required of persons entering the job. Their study did not have the sort of measures of skill demands common to job evaluations. However, the validity of their conclusions is further buttressed by the fact that changes in the sex composition of jobs between 1979 and 1985 were associated with changes in a job's pay level such that a job's becoming more female depressed wages and becoming more male increased wages (Baron and Newman 1989). If we assume that any changes in jobs' skill demands were uncorrelated with changes in sex composition, then their findings about change effectively "hold constant" any unmeasured skill demands of the jobs.

Other studies that have also analyzed how change over time in jobs' sex composition affects change in their pay find that when a job changes its sex composition, the wage for both men and women goes up if more males come into the job, and the wage for both men and women goes down if more women come into the job (Ferber and Lowry 1976, p. 384; Pfeffer and Davis-Blake 1987). We cannot be sure if the changing sex composition affected the wages, as these authors suggest, if the change in wage affects sex composition (as suggested by Reskin and Roos 1990), or if both effects are operative.

Types of Skills and Working Conditions in Jobs: Indirect Gender Bias. Another factor affecting the sex gap in pay is the kind, rather than amount, of skills and working conditions jobs require. Some view this as a part of the comparable worth issue. The studies above implicitly do not. That is, they take as given the returns to different job characteristics, and, controlling for these factors, estimate the adverse effect on wages of being in a predominantly female occupation.

However, the types of skills common in women's jobs may have lower returns than the types of skills common in men's jobs *because* of gender discrimination. That is, if a type of skill or working condition has traditionally been associated with women's work in either the household or paid employment, it may come to be devalued via stigma that gets institutionalized into wage systems, so that this skill or working condition comes eventually to carry a low rate of reward, or a penalty, whether it appears in a male or female occupation. However, since such skills and working conditions are more common to female occupations, this devaluation has a disparate and adverse impact on women's wages. Many view this as a part of the discrimination at issue in comparable worth, as will be discussed in Chapter 4 as an issue in job evaluation studies, in Chapter 5 as an issue in legal proofs of discrimination, and in Chapter 6 as an issue of feminist theory. There is substantial evidence that women's concentration in jobs with different kinds of skills affects the sex gap in pay. Daymont and Andrisani (1984) show that one's college major has an important effect on pay, and women are in the majors associated with lower pay. Women are more often than men in jobs involving nurturant social skills, and these not only have lower returns than other skills, but actually have net negative returns (Kilbourne, England, Farkas, and Beron 1990; Steinberg et al. 1986; Jacobs and Steinberg 1990a; Steinberg 1990). The fixed-effects model used by Kilbourne et al. (1990) allows an assessment of the effect of doing nurturant work on earnings while controlling for all unchanging, unmeasured differences between individuals in nurturant and other jobs. Even under these stringent individual controls, as well as controls for factors computed from DOT measures and occupational sex composition, the penalty for nurturance is found. My analysis in Chapter 3 will show this penalty for doing nurturant work as well. The adverse working conditions typical in some women's jobs (such as interpersonal stress, exposure to death and suffering, or exposure to blood, urine, and feces) are often given fewer points in job evaluations used to set pay than are the kinds of adverse working conditions (such as exposure to dirt and the out-of-doors) more typical in men's jobs (Steinberg 1990). Even those adverse working conditions typical to male jobs seldom have a large effect on earnings, however.

Overall, I conclude that the *kinds* of skills traditionally exercised by women are valued less in wage determination than are traditionally male skills. This more indirect form of gender bias is seen by many advocates as part of the discrimination to be redressed by comparable worth.

C. Consequences of the Sex Gap in Pay

What are the consequences of the sex gap in pay? A person doubting the importance of the issue might argue that if marriage is nearly universal and husbands and wives pool their income, the sex gap in pay has little consequence for the economic well-being of either women or children. This would be a mistaken conclusion, however. The sex gap in pay has important consequences within marriage as well as for those women who are not married.

Not all women marry, and some women divorce. Many never-married and divorced women have children. Indeed, rates of both divorce and out-of-wedlock births have increased dramatically. About half of the cohort born in the early 1950s (Cherlin 1981; Preston and McDonald 1979), and two thirds of those marrying today (Martin and Bumpass 1989) are projected to experience divorce. Many divorced women have children. Out-of-wedlock births rose from 5% of all births in 1960 to 18% in 1980 (Preston 1984). Unmarried women with children—whether divorced or never married—typically have custody of their children and must support them on some combination of their own earnings, any child support they receive from the children's fathers, and government subsidies. Child support awards are typically small. For example, awards to divorced women averaged $2500 per year per family in 1981, and less than half the mothers received the full amount awarded (U.S. Bureau of Census 1983b). While it is true that many divorced women remarry, both age and the presence of children inhibit women's remarriage probabilities (Mott and Moore 1983), so a significant minority of women with children do not remarry (Preston 1984). Thus, the sex gap in pay, in combination with the fact that divorced and never-married women generally have financial responsibility for their children after divorce, is a crucial part of why such a high proportion of female-headed families is in poverty (McLanahan, Sorensen, and Watson 1989, p. 120).

There is a paradox here. To some extent the increase in divorce is probably itself a result of women's increased economic independence (England and Farkas 1986, pp. 64–65). The fact that more women than previously have jobs means that more can afford to leave marriages they consider unhappy and at least minimally support themselves and their children. Yet, because of the continued sex gap in pay and men's failure to support their children after divorce, the economic consequences of divorce for women and children are still grave (Preston 1984).

But what of marriages that remain intact? For married women, does the sex gap in pay have adverse consequences? Yes. A long line of research on marital power (reviewed in England and Kilbourne 1990c) has shown that women's employment and the relative earnings of husbands and wives affect the balance of power in marriages. When women's earnings are lower, even when they are making valuable contributions in the form of home management and child rearing, their bargaining power vis-à-vis their husbands is substantially lower than that of women with higher earnings. The fact that women's economic fate is more adversely affected by divorce than men's is part of why men can retain disproportionate bargaining power within marriages. The ability to leave a relationship with relatively few losses implies the power to hold out for a better bargain without risk of a big loss. Thus, the sex gap in pay has profound consequences for the degree of informal democracy in marriages. It adversely affects women's ability to negotiate for what they want in marriage on a wide range of issues, including intimacy, purchasing decisions, the sharing of household work, and geographical moves. The sex gap in pay is a part of what prevents equality in husbands' and wives' bargaining power over all these issues.

V. Conclusion

This chapter has presented an overview of women's and men's positions in paid employment. The chapter began by exploring explanations for the unabated increase in women's employment. One factor is the increasing proportion of women who are single, many with children. These women need jobs because, whether they are divorced or never married, they usually have the major responsibility for the support of themselves and any children they have. Among married women, increased potential wages have drawn more women into employment, as has a restructuring of the economy that brought disproportionate increases in labor demands in fields already labeled "female." I argued that couples today may perceive a greater need for two earners than previously despite the fact that, on average, male earnings have greater buying power today than in the 1950s or early 1960s. I speculated that this increase in perceived need can be reconciled with trends in men's earnings if a decrease in income is perceived as larger than a gain of the same amount over the same income range. The last 20 years have seen fluctuations in men's earnings because of recessions and recoveries, and increasing wage inequality among men. The asymmetry in the perceptions of losses and gains of the same size may explain why women who enter paid labor to buffer reductions in men's earnings often stay even after their husband's earnings have rebounded. Also, as the norm becomes for women to be employed before childbearing, couples get used to two incomes and want to avoid the loss that would occur if women did not return to their jobs shortly after childbearing.

The unabated increase in women's employment makes the issue of comparable worth more important: As employment becomes the norm for most women most of the time, the consequences of facing discriminatory wage penalties increase. The importance of comparable worth also results from occupational sex segregation. If there were no disproportionately female or male jobs, there would be no problem of comparable worth, at least as an issue of gender inequality. There might still be concerns about whether the pay levels of jobs were set in a consistent manner, or about whether the racial or ethnic composition of jobs had discriminatory effects. But without the sex segregation of jobs, comparable worth would not be the important women's issue it is today.

Occupational sex segregation has declined since about 1970, although it is still substantial. Yet even as national data show a decline in segregation, we also see sex segregation of subfields within occupations women have recently entered, and some occupations show desegregation and then resegregation, as they move from being mostly male to integrated, and then "tip" and become segregated female enclaves.

Occupational sex segregation is partly explained by social forces operating upon women's and men's choice of jobs. These social forces include influences of parents, educational institutions, peer groups, and other social networks. Discrimination by employers in hiring is also a factor, as is the resistance of male workers to women's entrance into their occupations. Finally, historical and institutional factors also contribute to segregation; if a job starts out as female or male, considerable inertia develops around that initial label. Also, if entry level jobs are of one sex or the other, this segregation will be perpetuated over time and up the mobility ladders that comprise internal labor markets.

Segregation more often takes the form of women and men exercising *different kinds* of skills than of women's concentration into less skilled jobs. This is precisely why the issue of comparable worth is so poignant; women are often being paid less for equally demanding, though different jobs. This fact also makes it more comprehensible that women's own choices could be one factor in job choices. When we focus upon the low wages and low mobility prospects of typically women's jobs, it appears that no rational woman would choose such jobs. But when we see that often equally high levels but different kinds of skills are exercised in female jobs, it is more plausible that reasonable people would find such work interesting and meaningful. This, however, does not imply that women want or agree with the low pay accorded their jobs.

This chapter also examined research on the sex gap in pay. Education and effort, the two "all-American" routes to economic success, do have payoffs for both men and women. Yet neither is particularly relevant to the sex gap in pay since women have as many years of education as men, and studies show women expend as much or more effort as men on their jobs. Women's fewer years of seniority and overall employment experience, and the intermittency of such experience, explains some proportion (between one quarter and one half) of the sex gap in pay.

Much of the sex gap in pay results from segregation itself. Some of this segregation is interfirm, with women concentrated in lower-paying firms and industries. This aspect of the sex gap in pay would not be touched by comparable worth reforms unless we envisioned a national wage setting board whose authority spanned the entire economy, something no American advocates of comparable worth have suggested.

A large component of the sex gap in pay comes about because women are segregated into lower-paying occupations within every firm. Proponents of pay equity reforms allege that at least some portion of the pay differences between male and female jobs arise *because* the jobs are filled by women or entail skills that are traditionally female. Evidence abounds that, controlling for a number of measures of skill and other occupational requirements, jobs with more women in them offer lower wages to both men and women than do jobs containing more men. I refer to this as direct gender bias in wage setting. There is also evidence that, net of this direct effect of jobs' sex composition, kinds of skills traditionally done by women, such as nurturant social skills, have lower (sometimes even negative) returns than other kinds of skills (such as cognitive skills). I refer to this as indirect gender bias in wage setting. Comparable worth is about both of these types of gender bias in wage setting: direct gender bias based on the sex composition of the job, and indirect gender bias in which the returns to jobs' requirements for various types of skill and working conditions differ according to whether the job characteristic is traditionally associated with women's or men's spheres.

This chapter has focused on empirical regularities rather than how these are interpreted by theories or help us to evaluate theories. The next chapter will focus on scientific theorizing, examining how a number of bodies of theory view labor markets, gender inequality, and, most specifically, comparable worth.

Note

1.   The evidence is mixed on whether women with more traditional family plans are more likely to choose female occupations. Waite and Berryman (1985) find that young women who aspire to have more children and less continuous employment are more apt to choose female occupations. In contrast, Lehrer and Stokes (1985) find that young women's plans to be employed at age 35 and expected family size affected the skill level of the occupation aspired to, but *not* its sex composition. Even if Waite and Berryman's finding is correct, this does not demonstrate that female occupations lead to higher lifetime earnings than male occupations for those who have intermittent employment. It may simply mean that the wage disadvantages of female occupations are taken into account more in occupational choices of women who plan more continuous employment.

2

Theories of Labor Markets

I. Introduction

This chapter considers competing theories of how labor markets work, and their implications for gender inequality and comparable worth. The theories to be discussed include orthodox neoclassical economics, a new neoclassical institutionalism, and framing models from behavioral economics that blend well with findings from experimental social psychology. I also consider Marxist views in sociology and economics, as well as other sociological and institutionalist perspectives. Finally, I propose an interdisciplinary view that draws selectively upon the theories reviewed.

I give a disproportionate amount of space to the neoclassical view for two reasons: First, the internal coherence of the neoclassical view makes it possible to spell out its implications clearly. Second, the neoclassical "market wage" argument has come to dominate arguments against comparable worth policies. I find some merit in neoclassical theories. Yet, in contrast to the view of most neoclassical economists, I believe that comparable worth policies could have salutary effects on women and address a very real form of discrimination. It is important to my argument to explain why I hold this view despite its tension with neoclassical thinking.

This chapter focuses on theories about how labor markets operate to produce wage differences between women and men, and between female and male jobs. In contrast, Chapter 6 focuses on *normative* theoretical questions about how rewards, including wages, *should* be allocated to men and women and across jobs. Of course, these positive and normative questions are never entirely separate, though some bodies of theory emphasize one aspect over the other. Both positive and normative issues underlie policy debates over comparable worth, to be discussed in the concluding Chapter 7.

II.   The Orthodox Neoclassical View

A.   Basic Neoclassical Concepts

The starting point of neoclassical economics is a vision of rational individuals who *optimize* or *maximize*, i.e., who make choices that yield the greatest amount of utility, given their constraints. *Utility* refers to happiness, satisfaction, or well-being, subjectively construed. The assumption of rationality is usually seen to have two components: First, preferences are transitive. This means that if I prefer A to B and prefer B to C, I will also prefer A to C. Second, individuals are assumed to make accurate calculations about the outcomes that can be expected to result from their actions, subject to the availability of information that is needed for the calculations. Economists traditionally have made the simplifying assumption that people have perfect and costless information with which to make calculations, and some economic models still assume this, even though no one really believes it to be true. Recently, however, economists have emphasized the importance of the costs of gathering and disseminating information. The notion of optimization now includes calculating what resources it is worthwhile to spend on information. These developments are referred to as the "new information economics." (See Stigler 1961, 1962; Arrow 1974; Lippman and Mc-Call 1976; Diamond and Rothschild 1989.)

In economic models, *endowments* and *tastes* are both typically assumed to be exogenous inputs. That is, they are assumed to be explained by something causally prior to economic processes, rather than by economic models. Endowments are the resources one acquires from biology, from one's family of origin, or from other gifts (Becker 1976, 1981, pp. ix–x). An individual's *tastes* (sometimes called preferences) determine the amount of utility provided by different combinations of leisure, job conditions, consumer goods, household arrangements, and other factors. These tastes determine one's *utility function*. Economists do not generally attempt to explain the origin of these tastes, nor do they believe that tastes change. However, to say that tastes do not change does not deny that a person will make different consumption choices as his or her income changes. For example, the optimal house to buy when one earns $30,000 a year is different than the optimal choice when one earns $60,000, even if one's tastes do not change. Stigler and Becker (1977) have argued that whether tastes are exogenous is moot, since there is little variation in tastes across persons or time. Thus they argue that most behavior can be explained by endowments or by variations in the economic constraints of prices.

We often think that economics deals with behavior directed toward gains that are pecuniary (i.e., relating to money), whereas sociology deals with behavior in which nonpecuniary tastes for things such as social approval are prominent. This is not true in principle, even if it is somewhat true in the practice of the two disciplines. Economists recognize that individuals often trade pecuniary compensation for the nonpecuniary rewards of interesting work or leisure. This is embodied in the notion of compensating differentials in labor markets (Flanagan, Smith, and Ehrenberg 1984, pp. 179–196), to be discussed later in this chapter, and in the contention that individuals maximize utility or "full income," not merely money income (Schultz 1981, Chapter 4). More fundamentally, the importance of nonpecuniary rewards is clear from the fact that, to economists, money is merely a medium of exchange used to buy goods or services that are enjoyed for the subjective utility one experiences from them. Since the ultimate goal of money is utility, forgoing a gain of money in order to experience utility directly from a nonpecuniary benefit is fully consistent with the paradigm.

Yet, despite their formal recognition of both pecuniary and nonpecuniary goals, economists seeking empirical predictions from their theory *sometimes* add the auxiliary assumption that actors maximize only money. This avoids the sticky problem of measuring utility and allows more determinate predictions.

Economics is concerned with relations of exchange within markets. When we apply the rationality assumption to exchange, we conclude that an individual will undertake an exchange when the anticipated outcome is preferred to that from any other *available* option. Of course, the social class into which one is born affects one's endowments, and thus the amount of resources available to one to use in exchange. Since economists recognize endowments as exogenous inputs to their models, they implicitly recognize these effects of social class background.

The results of an exchange are defined as *Pareto-superior* to the preexchange situation if at least one party's utility increases from the exchange while neither party to the exchange thereby loses utility. When all possible Pareto-superior moves have been made in a market, a Pareto-optimal equilibrium has been reached. Economists do not analyze which of the two parties "got more" from an exchange because of their assumption that interpersonal utility comparisons are impossible (Hirshleifer 1984, pp. 476–477; Gibbard 1986). Thus, Pareto-optimality, rather than equity or equality, is the type of efficiency that is generally taken by economists to be the yardstick for outcomes.

Economists make no use of the notion of coercion within market relations. For them, coercion involves appropriating something owned by someone else without compensation agreed to by both parties

48 Theories of Labor Markets

(Hirschleifer 1984, p. 12). Theft is an example. But capitalist property rights do not qualify as an example of coercion, no matter what the political or social consequences of such rights, and no matter how great the resulting inequality. For economists, market relations are never coercive; rather, coercion and power result from barriers to free market competition. Some of the actions of democratically elected governments in taxing and regulating the economy are viewed as non-Pareto-optimal. When economists do advocate such policies, they are defended on the basis of equity or of "market failures" that are seen as exceptions to the general rule that markets produce Pareto-optimal results (Thurow 1983; Averitt 1988).

Because individuals enter exchanges whenever it will make them better off, market systems generate constant pressure toward equilibrium via price adjustments to changes in supply or demand, discussed below.

B. Supply and Demand in Labor Markets

The concepts of supply and demand can be applied to wage determination in competitive labor markets, and thus are relevant to discussions of comparable worth. Labor markets are seen as competitive as long as there are many potential employers that might be interested in each employee and vice versa. Neoclassical theory has clear implications for why some jobs pay more than others. What labor will be paid in a given job (i.e., what a particular skill type of labor will be paid) hinges on the intersection of supply and demand curves, as seen in Figure 2.1.

An employer's demand curve for a particular job (skill type of labor) is a bivariate relationship between the wage rate and the person-hours of labor the employer will choose to employ. Demand is a curve or line, *not* a single number. This is because the quantity of labor an employer is willing to hire depends upon the price of labor. Demand curves generally slope downward because the more an employer has to pay for each unit of labor, the less s/he will hire. In competitive labor markets, the demand curve is the same as the marginal revenue product (MRP) curve.[1] Any one employer's demand curve reveals how much the employer is willing to pay per unit of labor for any given quantity or, looking at the same bivariate relationship the other way, how many workers will be hired at any given market wage. An employer hires labor at the going rate until a number of workers is employed that, through diminishing marginal returns, causes MRP to fall to equal the wage. At that point no more labor is hired.

A profit-maximizing employer will pay no *more* than the market clearing wage because there is no need to do so and no gain from doing so.

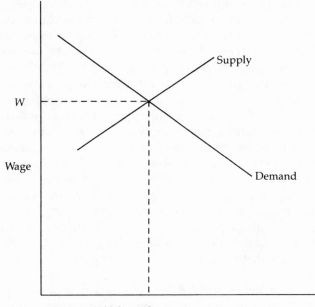

Quantity of labor   Q

Figure 2.1. The supply and demand for labor. The horizontal axis gives the
quantity of labor supplied for the supply curve, the quantity of labor demanded for the demand curve, and the quantity of labor supplied, demanded, and employed at the point of intersection. With these supply and
demand curves, the wage will be W and the quantity of labor employed will
be Q in equilibrium.

(We will see that this notion gets modified in the efficiency wage models
of the new institutionalism, discussed below.) Competition with other
employers for the same workers forces the employer to pay no *less* than
the market wage. Thus, neoclassical theorists argue that each employer
is a "price taker," paying the market wage.

The marketwide demand curve for a particular job (or skill-type of
labor) is the aggregation of all relevant employers' demand curves.
When there is discrimination against women, the aggregate market demand curve for women of a given skill type is below that for men, even
when MRP is the same for male and female labor. This reflects the fact
that employers are unwilling to pay as much for females as for equally
qualified male labor. However, for reasons discussed below, most economists view the persistence of discrimination in competitive labor markets as an anomaly for neoclassical theory.

The other half of the economic model is supply. Like demand, supply is a curve or line, not a single number. The marketwide supply curve for a job (or skill type of labor) is a bivariate relationship between the wage rate and the number of person-hours of labor that will be offered in the job. In general, the higher the wage in a job, the more people willing to work in this job, although at some point a high wage may lead individuals to choose fewer hours of work. The location of the supply curve for a particular job will be affected by opportunities outside this job for people with the same skills (e.g., wages of alternative jobs), by how much investment in training the job requires, and by whether the marginal worker finds doing the work in the job a "disamenity"— an unpleasantness—or an amenity. The theory of human capital implies that jobs requiring more investment will have to pay more, or workers will not be motivated to make such investments. The notion of compensating differentials posits that jobs the marginal worker finds unpleasant will have to pay more to be filled. If they do not, workers will choose other jobs with the same pay but more pleasant working conditions.

Above I said that neoclassical theorists believe employers pay the market wage. Having discussed both demand and supply curves, we are now in a position to discuss how they believe this market wage is determined. The supply-demand model implies that the market wage (read off the vertical axis in Figure 2.1) and the quantity of labor employed (read off the horizontal axis in Figure 2.1) are determined by the point at which the marketwide supply and demand curves intersect. This intersection point defines the only wage at which the quantity demanded (a single number on the demand curve) equals the quantity supplied (a single number on the supply curve). In this sense, markets move toward equilibrium (equating the quantity of labor supplied with the quantity demanded) via wage adjustments. Prices (wages) are the mechanism of equilibration.

Once equilibrium is achieved, further changes in prices will occur only if there is an exogenous shift in either the supply or demand curve. For example, a fall in prices for one industry's product would cause a downward shift in the MRP and labor demand curves for occupations over-represented in that industry. This would cause movement down the unchanging supply curve to a new lower price and lower quantity employed, defined by the intersection of the new demand curve with the unchanged supply curve.

Summarizing Figure 2.1, the neoclassical model says that a job will pay more if it has either a higher demand curve or a higher supply curve on the vertical dimension.[2]

C. Human Capital Theory

In this section I explain the theory of human capital and review research flowing from this theory that seeks to explain occupational sex segregation and the sex gap in pay. A later section applies human capital theory more specifically to comparable worth.

The neoclassical theory of human capital posits that individuals invest in their stock of skills by paying and/or forgoing something in the present for the sake of some future gain. For example, schooling is often undertaken to increase one's future wages. Schooling involves the direct cost of tuition, and the opportunity cost of forgone wages and forgone opportunities to use one's time in homemaking or leisure. Human capital investment could also include learning how to cook so one will be a better homemaker, or getting a doctorate in English so as to find a more satisfying job. In principle, the scope of the theory of human capital is not limited to investments that yield later *earnings,* although this is by far the most common application.

In neoclassical theory, whether one will undertake an investment (in human capital or anything else) depends in part upon one's "discount rate," the way in which present compared to future utility is valued. One's discount rate is part of one's tastes. The lower a person's discount rate, the more one defers gratification, and the less present-oriented one is. Whether one invests also depends upon the rate of return one can expect from the investment. This rate of return could, in principle, include nonpecuniary returns, though most research has focused on pecuniary returns.

Three kinds of investments relevant to earnings are emphasized by human capital theorists: One is education (schooling). A second is that subset of on-the-job training, formal or informal, that produces knowledge not only applicable to this firm, but that makes one potentially more productive in many other firms as well. Learning a common computer program on the job would be an example of this. Both of these kinds of investments are called general, rather than firm specific. This is because the investments should increase productivity and hence earnings in either one's current firm or working for another employer. A third type of human capital investment is the on-the-job training (formal or informal) that teaches firm-specific knowledge, i.e., things that are unique to this firm. This is called firm-specific human capital investment. Most on-the-job training is a mixture of the second and third type. Where on-the-job training is offered, human capital theorists presume that employees will pay for at least a part of its costs by accepting lower starting wages (Hashimoto 1981).

Human capital theory has been used to explain occupational sex seg-regation and the sex gap in pay, as explained below. These explanations have not focused on formal education because men and women in the U.S. labor force scarcely differ in their average years of educational attainment, as discussed in Chapter 1.

Human Capital and Occupational Sex Segregation. Uses of human cap-ital to explain occupational sex segregation have not focused upon the simple fact that employed women average substantially fewer years of employment experience than men. At first glance, one might think that the absence of women in male jobs requiring many years of experi-ence reflects the unavailability of women with sufficient years of experi-ence to enter these jobs. This may indeed explain a part of the absence of women from jobs at the top of lengthy promotion ladders that had plenty of women in the jobs from which the promotions usually occur. Yet this cannot be a *major* factor in segregation since entry-level positions themselves are very segregated by sex, despite the fact that, at entry level, men and women are equal in lacking any experience.

Applications of human capital theory to occupational sex segregation have focused on how differences in men's and women's initial *plans* for job experience will lead to different investments and job choices. Pol-achek (1979, 1981, 1984) suggests that women who plan breaks from employment for homemaking will choose jobs that have low deprecia-tion of human capital during years of homemaking. Since many more women than men plan years of homemaking, he sees these supply-side choices as generating segregation. "Depreciation" refers to the atrophy or obsolescence of job skills occurring during periods of homemaking that leads one to have a lower real wage upon returning to employment than one had prior to leaving a job. Most tests of this hypothesis have not supported it (Corcoran, Duncan, and Ponza 1984; England 1982, 1984; Abowd and Killingsworth 1983; England et al. 1988). (See Polachek 1984 for a counterargument.) Research shows that women do not experi-ence any more wage depreciation while out of the labor force if they are in male jobs than if they are in traditionally female jobs. Thus, those who plan spells of homemaking do not have the economic incentive to avoid male jobs that Polachek suggested.

Human capital theorists also argue that women who plan noncon-tinuous employment will choose jobs with relatively high starting wages but flat experience-earnings curves over jobs with lower starting wages but steeper wage increases with experience (Zellner 1975). Recalling the neoclassical view that low initial wages are an investment in the human capital received from on-the-job training, economists see the choices of jobs with higher starting wages and flatter trajectories as a choice to invest less in human capital formation. Such a choice would make sense for women who do not plan to be employed long enough for steep wage increases to make up for initially lower wages. However, studies show that this is *not* a cause of segregation. This is shown by the fact that women are not in jobs with higher starting wages than men's jobs requiring comparable education and skill. Indeed, women are in jobs with *lower* starting wages (Greenberger and Steinberg 1983; England 1984; England et al. 1988). Thus, women's jobs do not have the benefit of higher starting wages that human capital theorists see as motivating women's choice of these jobs.[3] In sum, the evidence does not support the explanations of segregation from human capital theory.

Human Capital and the Sex Gap in Pay. Chapter 1 reviewed trends in the sex gap in pay, a gap that is still significant. Findings from Corcoran and Duncan's (1979) study of the contribution of human capital to the sex gap in pay were also reviewed in Chapter 1. Here I consider the question of how the findings support or cast doubt on the ability of human capital theory to explain the sex gap in pay.

Corcoran and Duncan found that the number of years of education explains virtually none of the sex gap in pay among whites, and "negatively" explains the sex gap in pay among blacks. This is because, although education has a positive rate of return for all groups, black women average a fraction more of a year of education than black men, and white men and women have virtually the same average level of education.

A novel feature of Corcoran and Duncan's (1979) analysis lies in their use of measures of the subcomponent of one's total employment experience that was with one's current employer, and the subcomponent of this experience with the current employer that involved training. Length of on-the-job training was measured by asking individuals how long they think it takes a person in their job to be fully trained after hire. A major finding of the study is that experience with one's current employer, including the training portion, explains more of the sex gap in pay than prior experience. Clearly, the breaks women take for homemaking lower their seniority with their employers and this explains some of the sex gap in pay. Overall, however, less than half of the sex gap in pay was explained by human capital and other indicators of labor force attachment.

Explanations of the sex gap in pay in terms of human capital are often juxtaposed to explanations in terms of discrimination. While both forces may be present at any one time, they are separate forces in the sense that a given share of the sex gap in pay explained by one force at any one time is thereby not explained by the other. However, if we take a more dynamic view, it is important to recall that if women are discriminated against, they will have less incentive to invest in human capital. For example, if they receive lower wages, this gives them less incentive to stay in the labor force, and job experience is one form of human capital. Thus, some of the share of the gap explained by current sex differences in seniority or experience may actually be explained by past discrimination that led women to gain less seniority. This brings up the question of the theoretical status of discrimination within economic theory, to which I now turn.

D. Discrimination

Chapter 1 reviewed substantial evidence of discrimination against women in hiring and pay. Although the long-term persistence of discrimination by employers in competitive markets is an anomaly for neoclassical theory, economists have developed a number of models of discrimination. Models of discrimination are reviewed below, followed by an explanation of why theorists believe that discriminatory employers will gradually disappear from competitive markets. The discussion is summarized in Table 2.1.

Taste Discrimination.   Neoclassical discussions of discrimination generally begin with Becker's (1957) taste model, which posits that employers, workers, or customers may have a taste for discrimination. Such a taste refers to a preference in favor of or against hiring, working with, or buying from a group such as women. (His discussion generally referred to race discrimination, but the model can be applied to sex discrimination as well.) To economists, whether one is willing to pay an extra amount of money for something is indicative of whether one has a taste for it. Thus, a taste for discrimination implies that discriminators are willing to pay more to hire the group that is preferred than they are willing to pay for equally productive members of the disfavored group. Becker (1957) saw tastes for discrimination as explained by premarket factors, following the usual neoclassical assumption that tastes are exogenous to economic models.

An employer with a taste for discrimination against women is unwilling to hire women *unless* they offer themselves at a wage enough below the wage paid to men that it completely offsets the distaste they experience by employing women. How low this wage must be will depend upon the extent of the employer's taste for discrimination. Thus, to economists, there is an inextricable link between discrimination in wages and hiring; they are not distinct types of discrimination.

Table 2.1. Types of Discrimination

Type	Motivation	*Creates Group Differences in Earnings?*	*Erodes by "Arbitrage"?*
		Characteristics of the Type According to Neoclassical Theory	
Taste	Nonpecuniary individual gain in utility	Yes, unless based upon employee tastes, in which case leads to segregated firms but not segregated occupations and not group differences in earnings	Yes, unless altruism in employer's tastes leads to paying the favored group above MRP,[1] or unless discrimination is based upon customer tastes (but this should only affect jobs involving customer–employee interaction)
Statistical	Pecuniary individual gain through saving screening costs and obtaining more productive employees for the wage		No
	Subtype of statistical discrimination—based on group differences in:		
	Mean productivity	Not in excess of average productivity differences	No
	Variance in productivity	If employers risk averse	No
	Reliability of screening devices	If employers risk averse or via effects on groups' human capital investments	No
Error	Perceived (but at least partially illusory) pecuniary individual gain through saving screening costs and obtaining more productive employees for the wage	Yes	Yes
Monopoly	Pecuniary group gain through "dividing and conquering" of workers	Yes	Yes, unless ways of enforcing monopoly against free riders is successful

Note:
[1] MRP, marginal revenue product.

Some employers discriminate, not because of their own tastes, but as a response to their customers' tastes. Yet we would not expect customer discrimination throughout the economy; rather it should occur only in service firms (e.g., stores) where employees meet customers. In manufacturing and extractive firms, and even in many service firms, customers do not know the race or sex of workers, so customer-induced taste discrimination should not be pervasive.

Employers may also discriminate in response to their workers' tastes. For example, male workers may object to working with women (Bergmann and Darity 1981), requiring a higher wage to do so.

Statistical Discrimination. Models of statistical discrimination are a part of the new information economics, the key insight of which is that it is costly to gather information relevant to decisions. These models focus on the fact that employers make decisions about hiring in the absence of full information about each applicant's productivity. This is because it would be too expensive and perhaps impossible to get full information on each individual. There are several models of statistical discrimination. I will discuss models based on average differences between women and men on productivity, those based on differences in the variances of men's and women's productivity, and those based on differences between women and men in how reliably or accurately screening instruments (such as tests) predict their productivity.

Let us consider the model of statistical discrimination in which hiring decisions are made on the basis of race or sex group *averages* on ability to be productive in the job (Arrow 1972, pp. 96–97; Phelps 1972, p. 60; Lloyd and Niemi 1979, p. 11). These models assume that it is too expensive for the employer to measure each individual's ability, but that group differences in *average* productivity are correctly known. Thus, members of the group with a higher average productivity are preferred.

Since men and women have overlapping distributions on virtually all characteristics, using a group's average to estimate characteristics of individuals who are members of the group results in mistaken predictions about individuals who are qualified in a way unusual for their sex. However, since sex can be observed almost costlessly, in the absence of other cheap screening criteria, it may improve the average productivity of an employer's work force to choose all workers from the sex group with the higher average. This model does not imply that sex group differences are innate; it simply implies that they were not created by the employer who is engaging in the statistical discrimination.

Thurow (1975, p. 172) confuses the issue when he says that statistical discrimination "occurs whenever an individual is judged on the basis of the average characteristics of the group or groups to which he or she belongs rather than upon his or her own characteristics." Thurow is correct that the use of group averages is one of the defining charac- teristics of this model of statistical discrimination. However, Thurow's implication that nondiscriminators use "individual characteristics" rather than "group averages" makes no sense unless we are to consider virtually all hiring decisions discriminatory. All individual characteristics (e.g., test scores, education) define groups (e.g., the group with SAT scores over 1100, the group of college graduates). Thus, there is no operational difference between basing decisions on individual charac- teristics or on group means. Productivity is always estimated from indi- vidual characteristics of applicants that define groups, whether these groups are defined by achieved characteristics, such as education, or characteristics ascribed at birth, such as sex. The only exception to this is the case where the relevant individual characteristic *is* a direct measure of productivity on the job. But on-the-job productivity is virtually never measured before hire. It is the fact that *group averages* are used that makes us call a screening process *statistical* (whether an ascribed criteri- on such as sex or an achieved criterion such as education defines the group). It is the fact that *ascribed* criteria such as sex or race define the groups for which averages are compared that makes us label the process *discrimination*.

Is there evidence that supports the model of statistical discrimination based on sex differences in averages as an explanation of gender dis- crimination in hiring? The mean sex difference most often invoked by economists in discussions of statistical discrimination is women's al- legedly higher turnover rates. (For examples, see Landes 1977; Bulow and Summers 1986; Barron et al. 1990; Kuhn 1991.) Such discrimination should be particularly likely in jobs offering on-the-job training. If wom- en stay less long, then the cost of the initial training per year of em- ployment is greater for women, on average. Thus, after these larger per year training costs are subtracted from their productivity (assuming that before the subtraction it is equal to men's), the net productivity per year of women workers is less as a result of the higher probability of turn- over. Yet, as reviewed in Chapter 1, overall, studies do not provide unequivocal support for the idea that women have a higher propensity to quit jobs that is exogenous to their treatment by employers. The evidence can be read as either rejecting or supporting exogenous sex differences in turnover, since whether one should control for variables such as one's wage depends upon one's theoretical assumptions.

Less discussed in the literature, but probably more realistic, is the possibility of mean sex differences in specific kinds of learned abilities that are relevant to specific jobs but costly to measure. An example might be men's greater knowledge of auto mechanics or women's greater knowledge of how to operate sewing machines. Statistical discrimination might help explain the preference for one sex in such jobs where sex differences in averages exist on job-relevant skills.[4]

But can the model of statistical discrimination based on average difference in productivity-related characteristics explain discriminatory wage differentials disadvantaging women as a group? Aigner and Cain (1977) argue that it cannot, claiming that statistical discrimination based on averages does *not* reduce the *average* earnings of the race or sex group with the lower average productivity. They point out that since group means on productivity are the basis of hiring and pay decisions, groups will receive an average level of pay commensurate with their average productivity. For example, if women are 10% less productive at some jobs, employers will be unwilling to hire any women in such jobs unless they will work for 10% less than is paid to men. The "error" involved in statistical discrimination is that individuals who are atypical for their group will be paid more or less than their individual productivity, although, on average the group will be paid commensurately with its productivity. For example, the woman who, compared to the average woman, knows an unusually large amount about auto repair will not find a job as a mechanic or she will have to settle for a lower wage than she would in the absence of statistical discrimination. This is because all women will be treated like the average woman, and all men will be treated like the average man (holding constant observed indicators of productivity such as schooling). In sum, absent other forms of discrimination, statistical discrimination based on group averages might lead to occupational segregation, but it should not lead to group differences in *average* earnings in excess of average productivity differences (Aigner and Cain 1977).

A second type of statistical discrimination hinges on race or sex group differences in *variances* rather than averages (Phelps 1972; Aigner and Cain 1977). Suppose that women have the same average as men on a productivity-relevant characteristic, but the women's distribution has a larger variance, indicating more women than men at both extremely high and extremely low scores. If the cost of finding a better indicator of productivity and using it to screen each individual applicant is prohibitively high, will it pay employers to prefer the group with the smaller variance? The answer to this question depends upon whether employers are risk averse (Aigner and Cain 1977). If they are not risk averse, the expected value of productivity for women and men will be determined by the respective means of the two groups, and if they are the same, it is not rational to engage in statistical discrimination. However, if the employer is risk averse, the group with the smaller variance will be preferred even when group means are equal.

The relevance of risk aversion to preferring a group with a smaller variance can be seen by making an analogy to how people decide what stock investment to make. Suppose you have two investment possibilities, and each has an expected payoff of 9% in the next year. Your generally accurate broker tells you that investment A has an expected return of 9%, and the return is unlikely to fall outside the range of 8–10%. She estimates that investment B also has an expected return of 9%, but sees a reasonable chance of either losing all your money or making a huge return on B. The more risk averse you are, the more likely you are to pick investment A over B, although they have the same "average" (i.e., expected) return. Likewise, in hiring, the risk-averse employer is more likely to engage in discrimination against a more internally variable group because there is more risk of hiring an especially bad worker from this group. Unlike statistical discrimination based on means, if employers are risk averse, statistical discrimination based on variances *can* produce sex differences in average earnings that are in excess of sex differences in average productivity.

Is there any evidence that the realities of sex discrimination fit this model of statistical discrimination based on variances? I know of no evidence that women's distribution on unobserved productivity indicators is generally more variable than men's. There may be greater heterogeneity among women than men in turnover rates, and this might explain some statistical discrimination by risk-averse employers even if women's average turnover is not lower. However, this is a speculation; I know of no research documenting that this is the source of discrimination.

A third model of statistical discrimination posits race or sex differences in the degree of accuracy with which ability is measured by tests or other selection devices (Phelps 1972; Aigner and Cain 1977; Borjas and Goldberg 1978; Lang 1988; Lundberg and Startz 1983). For one group, the "error term" in a regression predicting productivity from the selection device is larger, and the R^2 (explained variance) is smaller. Thus the selection device has lower reliability for the group with the larger error term. This does *not* mean that productivity is systematically underestimated for the group for whom the screening device is less reliable. Most models assume that men and women with any given score on the selection device have the same average productivity, but there is more variability or dispersion around the regression line for women. And there is no assumption of *any* difference in the male and female distributions on productivity; both means and variances may be equal between the sexes. If the cost of finding and using a more reliable indicator of productivity is prohibitively high, will it pay employers to prefer the group for whom the available indicator has greater predictive power? As with models of statistical discrimination based on differences in variances in productivity, risk-averse employers will discriminate. (Even in the absence of risk aversion among employers, it is possible for this sort of discrimination to create discriminatory wage differences through creating incentives for groups for whom selection devices are worse predictors to invest less in unobservable forms or more in observable forms of human capital or other "signals" of productivity. See Lundberg and Startz 1983; Lang 1988.)

Is there evidence that the model of statistical discrimination based on differential reliability of selection devices for men and women explains a significant amount of sex differences in occupational placement or pay? I know of no evidence about sex differences in predictive validity of selection instruments, so the application of the model to gender differences remains speculative.

Error Discrimination. Error discrimination is a term I use to describe the situation where employers underestimate the relative average productivity of a group and, based upon this mistaken belief, are unwilling to hire group members or will hire them only for a lower wage. The error about group averages may entail believing that men and women differ in productivity for some job when in fact no group difference exists. Alternatively, it may entail an exaggeration of the size of an actually existing difference. Error discrimination has in common with statistical discrimination that the employer has no nonpecuniary distaste for employing women in the job, but rather is discriminating in an effort to hire a more productive work force. Error discrimination differs from statistical discrimination based on means in that the former involves erroneous estimates of group averages whereas the latter involves correct estimates of group averages (although even statistical discrimination causes erroneous predictions for individuals who are atypical for their group). Most economists ignore the possibility of error discrimination because they presume that such errors would eventually be corrected as employers accumulated experience. Some authors (Lloyd 1975, p. 17; Blau and Jusenius 1976, Note 33; Blau 1984; Bielby and Baron 1986) include what I am calling error discrimination in their definition of statistical discrimination. I prefer to distinguish the two because, as discussed above, statistical discrimination based on mean differences should not produce discriminatory group differences in average pay, whereas error discrimination will.

Monopoly Models of Discrimination. Monopoly or monopsony models of discrimination involve members of a group formally or informally colluding, acting collectively rather than as competing individuals. Monopsony is defined as a situation where there is only one buyer, in this case one employer buying female labor. (Monopoly is defined as a market with only one seller; but often the term *monopoly* is used to refer to either monopsony or monopoly.) Madden's (1973) monopsony model and Hartmann's (1976) and Strober's (1984) theories of patriarchy all posit that women are kept out of good jobs by collusion among men, as husbands, employers, legislators, and workers. It is clear that such a "cartel" or "gentlemen's agreement" benefits men *as a group* at the expense of women as a group. Indeed, members of any group will make relative gains if they can exclude nonmembers from opportunities.

Madden's monopsony model takes as an unexplained fact that men have substantial power over women's decisions to accept jobs. For example, women's options were limited in the past by laws barring them from some jobs. Even today they are limited by patriarchal customs in which husbands have the right to dictate in which city a couple will live. This creates a monopsonylike power for employers who hire women. The real situation is not so extreme that all women face a single employer, but the model's insight is to work out the implications of a situation where, because of various forms of male power, women are closer to being in a situation of having only one potential employer than are men. Monopsonistic employers can pay lower wages to women than they would be able to if they were in competition for female labor. The classic example of monopsony power is the labor market for nurses in small towns that only have one hospital.

Seen through neoclassical lenses, the Marxist notion of "divide and conquer" is also a monopoly model. This conception holds that employers discriminate to create divisions or hostilities between groups of workers. The purpose of discrimination is to prevent workers from organizing cohesively enough to threaten profit levels by raising wages through unionization, strikes, or more radical political action (Gordon 1972, pp. 71–78; Edwards, Reich, and Gordon 1975, pp. xiii–xiv; Bonacich 1976; Bowles and Gintis 1976, p. 174; Humphries 1976; Roemer 1979; Reich 1981; Stevenson 1988). Every employer has a material interest in preventing such solidarity of workers. Yet, in a neoclassical view, one employer cannot get away with limiting women to worse jobs unless other employers do too; otherwise women would leave the discriminating firm for other firms. Thus, the strategy of divide and conquer via gender discrimination works only if employers collude. It is the fact that employers *collude* to keep women's opportunities worse than men's, making the situation to some extent as if there were only *one* employer, which places the divide-and-conquer model of discrimination into the broader category of monopoly models when looked at through a neoclassical lens.

The Demise of Discrimination in Competitive Markets. Most neoclassical economists believe that discrimination sows the seeds of its own destruction because it costs money. Becker (1957) realized that this was a tension in his discrimination theory (Arrow 1973). The erosion of many types of discrimination should happen as long as labor markets are "competitive," by which economists mean that there are a number of possible buyers of labor for each seller of a particular type of labor and vice versa. Product markets need not be competitive for the conclusion to hold. Let us examine the process by which economists believe discrimination should eventually disappear.

Suppose that the discrimination is based on employers' tastes, but employers differ in the strength of their discriminatory tastes. Some employers' tastes not to hire women will be so strong that they will hire no women, regardless of how cheaply women offer to work. At the other extreme are employers we will call "nondiscriminators": They are indifferent between men and women, so they are open to hiring either men or women, or both, and paying them equal wages. Employers with an intermediate level of discriminatory tastes are willing to hire some women, but only if the women will work for a lower wage than they are willing to pay men. How much lower the wage would have to be to make them indifferent between men and women is a measure of the severity of their discriminatory taste.

How does this relate to supply and demand? Suppose, for simplicity, that we are dealing with a job that has average requirements for qualifications, and with equivalently qualified men and women. The labor demand curve for any type of labor is the sum of the labor demand curves of all the employers in the market. Since at least some employers are taking sex into consideration, we need to think of two different marketwide demand curves, one for men and one for women. The more discriminators there are in the market, and the greater the wage differential that discriminators require to make them indifferent between hiring men and women, the farther the labor demand curve for women will lie below the labor demand curve for men. Thus, if men had a supply curve identical to that of women, the market wage for men and women would differ because the two identical supply curves would intersect the lower female demand curve at a lower wage. This will yield a single marketwide wage for women and one for men (in the particular occupation in question). Neoclassical notions of supply and demand imply that any single employer can hire as many women (men) as s/he wants at the female (male) market wage, but cannot hire any at a lower wage. (The recognition of search costs modifies this to allow for some dispersion of wages because of information costs, but the basic principles of the model remain.)

In such a setting, what will the nondiscriminators who are indifferent between men and women do? Since women are available at a lower wage than men despite equivalent productivity, they will choose to hire the cheaper women. Employers will hire all men if their tastes for discrimination are so extreme that they are unwilling to hire women no matter how low the price. Employers whose tastes for discrimination are intermediate will hire women if the difference between the female and male market wage is great enough to offset their distaste, but will hire men if it is not. Employers whose taste (by coincidence) requires exactly the same wage differential to make them indifferent between men and women as the difference between the female and male market wage may hire some of each sex. These employers will pay men the male market wage and women the female market wage.

In this scenario, nondiscriminators are taking advantage of the exploited status of women, paying them a lower wage than men are making at other firms. Thus, in one sense, we might not want to call them nondiscriminators. Economists, however, label them nondiscriminators because, if other employers' discriminatory tastes had not provided them with cheapened labor, they would have been willing to pay men and women the same wage. Further, these nondiscriminators who hire women cheaply are not the source of women's discriminatory low wage; indeed, they are part of the mechanism of the erosion of discrimination. Such employers are like arbitrageurs in stock markets who buy up stocks that others are undervaluing.

Such nondiscriminators contribute to the demise of discrimination because their relatively low labor costs give them an advantage in competitive product and capital markets. Because they can sell their products for a lower price and/or offer higher returns on investments in the firm, such firms should come to sell an increasing share of the product market and hire an increasing share of the labor market in their industry. Because of their higher labor costs, employers with more taste for discrimination may go bankrupt. Alternatively they will be bought out by employers with less or no taste for discrimination. Eventually, the theory predicts, only the least-discriminatory employers will be left. By this point, the expansion of employment in the least-discriminating firms should have bid up the job opportunities and wages of women, leading women's wage and job distributions to converge toward men's. At this point, the wage at which women must offer to work to get hired is only as low as consistent with the tastes of the least-discriminatory employer. Through this process, competition is said to bring about the demise of taste discrimination in the long run. Of course, the length of the "long run" is an empirical question that theory cannot specify.

This economic reasoning implies that the *eventual average* amount of discrimination in the economy depends not on the *average initial* level of discriminatory tastes, but upon the amount of discriminatory taste held by the *least*-discriminatory employers. This latter amount will be the *eventual average* level of discrimination after the "arbitrage" has occurred.

As long as there are some employers with *no* discrimination in their tastes, arbitrage will erode all discrimination.

The description above of the demise of discrimination applies generally if the discriminatory tastes belong to employers. It will not occur in the case of customer tastes causing discrimination since customers do not go out of business for paying to indulge their tastes. However, the sex of those who work in a job is generally not visible to customers. So the neoclassical model would predict noneroding taste discrimination based on customers' tastes only in service jobs where customers interact with workers. In the case of discrimination based on workers' tastes, the erosion process should lead to enduring sex segregation by firm. However, this segregation by firm should not generate occupational segregation within firms or wage differences between men and women.

Analogous logic explains how the erosion of error discrimination would occur via market forces. Nondiscriminating employers who do not have erroneous estimates of women's abilities for particular jobs will get labor at a bargain price and can thus come to represent a larger share of their markets. Error discrimination should be even less likely than taste discrimination to persist since employers might correct their erroneous perceptions through observation. But even if no employers change their erroneous perceptions, the fact that there is some dispersion in the degree of employers' error about women's productivity implies that discrimination should eventually diminish to be consistent with the proclivities of the least-discriminatory employers. Eventually employers whose judgments are the least clouded by error should employ the whole work force.

From within the neoclassical camp, Goldberg (1982) has pointed out an important exception to the notion that taste discrimination will necessarily erode in competitive labor markets. (His discussion refers to race discrimination; I have adapted it to sex discrimination.) The argument hinges on the distinction between two types of taste discrimination: antifemale discrimination in which women are paid less than MRP while men are paid MRP, and promale discrimination, in which men are paid more than MRP while women are paid MRP. The distinction is depicted in Figure 2.2. Promale discrimination involves selective altruism toward men because the employer finds employing them rewarding in a nonpecuniary sense. Goldberg (1982) argues that antifemale discrimination will eventually erode in competitive markets (to the level of the least-discriminatory employer) by the process described above. However, his point is to show that the discrimination I call altruistic promale discrimination need not erode in competitive markets. The argument is that employers engaging in altruistic promale discrimination can survive in the long run if the nonpecuniary utility they get from altruistically pay-

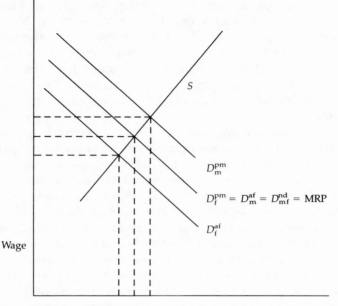

Figure 2.2. The demand for labor by nondiscriminators, antifemale discriminators, and promale discriminators. Key: D_f, demand for females; D_m, demand for males; D_{mf}, demand for males or females (where no distinction is made between them), af by antifemale discriminator, pm by promale discriminator, nd by nondiscriminating employer; MRP, marginal revenue product; S, supply of labor, assumed the same for males and females.

ing men more than MRP makes them willing to take a lower-than-market profit rate. This nonpecuniary gain leads them to reject buy-out bids from owners who are less (or non-) discriminatory, and thus could run the business more profitably. In contrast, if one is engaging in antifemale discrimination, the same buy-out offer from a less (or non-) discriminatory employer *will* be compelling because there is no offsetting nonpecuniary utility to be derived from keeping the firm.

The two models of taste discrimination, antifemale and altruistic promale, are similar in several senses, but crucially different in their ability to survive in competitive markets. Both types of discriminators are willing to take less profit than the maximum possible in order to indulge their taste for discrimination. That is, both antifemale and promale models of taste discrimination take the notion of nonpecuniary motives seriously and thus assume that firm owners may maximize utility (money profit plus nonpecuniary reward), not merely money profit. Both models feature employers that are willing to sell or buy a firm for the discounted present value of the expected stream of future utility from owning the firm. The critical difference between the two models is that in the altruistic promale model, the value of the firm is greater to one with more rather than less (or non-) discriminatory tastes, so nondiscriminators cannot buy out discriminators. In the antifemale model, the pecuniary gain that a nondiscriminator can make (at least temporarily) from hiring women at their cheapened wage makes it possible that the firm is more valuable to the nondiscriminator than the discriminator. This is because, if women are hired at their market price, the two employers have the same profit level but the antifemale discriminator suffers nonpecuniary disutility due to the antifemale taste. The nondiscriminator does not suffer this nonpecuniary disutility. Goldberg (1982) points out that Becker (1957) incorrectly assumed that the two types of taste discrimination, antifemale and promale, are identical with respect to their tendency to erode in competitive markets.

The concept of statistical discrimination has had great appeal to economists because it seems more capable than other models of discrimination of explaining the anomaly of the persistence of discrimination in competitive markets. Unlike taste or error discrimination, it is pecuniarily rational for employers to engage in statistical discrimination if the costs of the error it creates in predicting individuals' productivity are less than the expense of developing and administering screening instruments with greater predictive power. The latter costs exist because of limitations in the "technology" of personnel administration. They are examples of what economists call information or search costs. Because of these costs, there is no pecuniary advantage to ceasing statistical discrimination, as there is for taste or error discrimination. Why would an employer want to abandon a cheap method of estimating productivities when it is expensive to develop screening devices that allow one to find those individuals whose productivities are above the average of their sex? If employers are already using the most effective screening technology that is cost-effective, statistical discrimination will endure in competitive markets because it does not cost money. Thus, statistical discrimination is distinct from the other types of discrimination in that it cannot erode entirely through the pure market forces of arbitrage as the others can. However, it is important to remember that only those models of statistical discrimination involving variances or the reliability of screening instruments can produce group wage differentials in excess of productivity differentials. Models of statistical discrimination based on different group means will not produce such differentials. No compelling evidence of gender differences in variances or reliabilities of screening devices exists in the literature, so it is not clear that this is a factor in gender differences in pay.

What of the monopoly models of discrimination? How do economists think that discrimination involving the noncompetitive feature of group monopolies can disappear, since the very competition through which market forces work is suspended by the monopolistic collusion? As long as the restrictions against hiring a group, such as women, are successfully enforced by law, informal sanctions, or group loyalty, economists concede that the discrimination will not diminish. But economists focus on the difficulties of enforcement. The instability of such monopolies inheres in the pecuniary incentive each *individual* employer has to be a "free rider" on the colluding group. For example, a free rider would hire cheap female labor while the rest of the group continued to collude in the monopoly that is refusing to hire women and is thus providing the free rider with the cheapened female labor. Similarly, each individual consumer has a pecuniary incentive to buy from a firm that has hired cheaper female labor because of the lower prices of goods sold by such firms. Male workers do not have such an incentive to free ride on the monopoly, but individual employers and consumers have a pecuniary incentive to sabotage workers' efforts to enforce the monopolistic restrictions. Thus monopolies are unstable because they give many members of the dominant group an individual incentive not to follow the restrictions that benefit the group as a whole. As a result, monopolistic discrimination should erode unless the collectivity finds sufficient motivation and effective methods of enforcement against free riders.

One might try to counter this argument for the instability of monopolies by positing that employers and consumers in the dominant group have a group loyalty (e.g., to their fellow males) strong enough to make them cooperate with the restriction despite the pecuniary loss this decision entails. Undoubtedly this is often true. But such a group loyalty can be seen as a *taste* that one is willing to risk having to pay for. Thus, if the monopolistic restrictions are adhered to by all group members *only* out of loyalty, we really have a special case of taste discrimination, and the arguments above about how and whether taste discrimination can persist apply.

To summarize, most forms of discrimination, whether based on tastes, error, or group monopolies, tend to self-destruct in competitive labor markets in the long run, according to orthodox neoclassical reasoning. Taste discrimination should erode from arbitragelike markets forces alone unless it is altruistic promale discrimination that entails paying men above MRP. Error discrimination should erode from arbitrage as well as from updated information. Discrimination based on a group monopoly should erode from free riding, unless means of enforcement are found to avoid this. Statistical discrimination based on variances or differential reliability of screening devices will not erode through arbitragelike market forces alone. These theoretical deductions explain why neoclassical economists respond in stylized ways to evidence of persistent job and wage differentials by race and sex that cannot be explained by available measures of human capital or compensating differentials. Some see persistent discrimination as an anomaly for their theories, for which they do not yet have an explanation (Arrow 1973). Others concede only statistical discrimination, the persistence of which is viewed as least anomalous (Fuchs 1988). The discrimination described by the promale altruism model, while as likely to persist as statistical discrimination, is nonetheless less popular among economists because they generally do not presume altruism in market relations. Others deny that any significant amount of market discrimination still exists, positing supply-side explanations that hinge upon unmeasured group differences in preferences or human capital. Some of those who deny discrimination will concede that premarket (i.e., familial or societal) discrimination or past market discrimination may explain these supply-side differentials (Polachek 1984). Others see supply-side choices hinging on biological differences between men and women in comparative advantage in childrearing (Becker 1981).

E.   Comparable Worth and the Neoclassical View

Are wage differentials between predominantly male and female jobs discriminatory, as proponents of comparable worth claim? What are the likely effects of comparable worth policies? Here I consider how these two questions are approached from within a neoclassical view.

Neoclassical theory is couched in terms of the constraints faced and decisions made by individuals and firms, not in terms of aggregates such as jobs. Yet implications of neoclassical theory for wage differences between jobs can be teased out, as I suggest below. To move toward job-level conclusions, let us first consider how neoclassical theory implies that the work to be done in a firm is divided into distinct jobs. If firms seek to maximize profits, firm owners will adopt a division of labor that is most efficient *for profitability*. That is, they will choose the division of labor that gets the greatest output for the least costs of labor and other inputs. Efficiency, in this sense, does not deal merely with technical issues of production, but could also include organizing work in such a way that workers are less able to organize a union or other collective action.

Human Capital.   Human capital theory has clear implications about the wages offered in various jobs. Employers can fill jobs requiring substantial prior investments in training only if they pay high enough wages to induce workers to make these investments. This is a fact about the supply side of labor markets. The relevant fact about the demand side of labor markets is that better-trained workers will be hired only in some jobs, even if they are more productive in all jobs. Employers will not spend the extra money required to hire more highly trained workers except in those jobs where they calculate that the benefits exceed the costs of the higher wages they must pay (Lang and Dickens 1988). Thus, although human capital theory is often described as a supply-side theory, it has a demand side as well.

Suppose we take the skill level of a job to be a rough measure of how much productivity in that job is increased by investment in schooling or other training. In this case, human capital theory predicts that jobs with higher skill levels will pay more. Applying the theoretical reasoning above, this is true for two reasons: First, on the demand side, employers are willing to pay more because of the greater effects on profits of using better-trained workers in these jobs compared to other jobs. Second, because of supply-side constraints, employers must pay more to attract persons who have invested in obtaining the relevant skills.

Thus, before concluding that pay differentials between male and female jobs are discriminatory, a neoclassical economist wants to be sure that differences between the jobs in human capital requirements do not explain these wage differences. Since there are many types of human capital that are not well measured in available data, economists often suspect that *unmeasured* aspects of human capital actually explain group differentials.

Compensating Differentials. Suppose that male and female occupations with equal human capital requirements differ in pay, even after temporary disequilibria from shortages or gluts are remedied. Such differences are sometimes explained by the notion of compensating differentials. Other things equal, jobs that workers find more onerous have to offer higher wages in order to be filled. Equivalently, jobs that workers find more desirable because they are interesting, safe, pleasant, or otherwise satisfying can be filled for lower wages than if they were more onerous.

However, a wage premium will be unnecessary if a sufficient number of workers are indifferent to or even prefer the putatively onerous job characteristics in question. That is, compensating differentials depend on the tastes for nonpecuniary amenities and disamenities of the *marginal* rather than the *average* worker (R. Smith 1979). An example illustrates the point. Most of us think that collecting garbage would be awful because of the associated smells. Thus, many of us would have to be paid more to agree to collect garbage than to take a less onerous job requiring an equal investment in human capital. We might expect, then, that garbage collecting carries a compensating wage differential and pays more than other jobs at similar skill levels. However, suppose that the economy needed less than 1% of workers to be garbage collectors, and that 5% of workers were indifferent to the smells of garbage. In this case, because the *marginal* worker found no disamenity to the job, it would not carry a compensating differential, even though the *average* worker found the job distasteful. The marginal worker is the "last" worker hired. However, the theory does not construe "last" in a temporal but rather a metaphorical sense. To see this, imagine that workers are lined up in the order of their disutility for garbage, with those liking to collect garbage the most at the head of the line. Hiring will start at the head of the line. As we move down the line, we come to workers who require a higher wage to collect garbage. It is in this metaphorical sense that neoclassical theory sees the tastes of the "last" or marginal worker hired determining the wage paid to all workers in the job.

An interesting aspect of the theory of compensating differentials is that it shows us the inappropriateness of a sharp dichotomy between work and leisure, or of a definition of work as an activity undertaken only for pecuniary reward. If a job is enjoyable, one is willing to do it for less money. If we define leisure as activities we will undertake without pecuniary motivation, then enjoyable work can be seen as part leisure, where the leisure component need not be paid.

Empirical applications of the theory of compensating differentials by labor economists have focused on testing whether *physical* disamenities are associated with higher wages. In principle, however, the theory applies to nonphysical amenities or disamenities as well. For example, if the marginal worker likes authority, jobs with authority should pay less than jobs not requiring authority, other things equal. But if the marginal worker dislikes authority, jobs with authority should pay a wage premium. Similarly, if exercising a particular kind of skill is a disamenity to the marginal worker, jobs requiring this skill should pay more. The theory is particularly difficult to test because workers vary in their tastes regarding job characteristics. Thus, even when we can comfortably assume, based on commonsense knowledge, that the average person dislikes a job characteristic, we still cannot be sure whether the marginal worker likes or dislikes the characteristic. This makes a theory-based prediction of whether a given job characteristic should have a positive or negative effect on wages difficult to make. Hence, the theory of compensating differentials is less falsifiable than most theories. Given this, it is hard to evaluate the extent to which evidence supports the theory.

My reading of available studies is that they provide only sketchy support for the theory of compensating differentials. Robert Smith (1979) reviews such studies and notes that not even a majority show the predicted positive effects on wages for alleged disamenities such as physical work, repetitiveness, lack of freedom, and job insecurity. One study found that jobs involving physical discomfort and hazards paid compensating differentials (i.e., higher wages) to male but not to female production workers (Barry 1985). However, another study found little evidence of a compensating differential for hazardous work for either women or men, black or white (Kilbourne et al. 1990; Kilbourne 1991). Positive compensating differentials have been found fairly consistently for jobs involving a risk of death (R. Smith 1979; Olson 1981; Duncan and Holmlund 1983), but findings for other physical disamenities are very mixed (Brown 1980). The studies referred to above generally used national probability samples, and thus cast doubt on the theory of compensating differentials for the economy as a whole, most of which is made up of the private sector. Jacobs and Steinberg (1990a, 1990b) review findings from a number of job evaluation studies done in the public sector. In general, these studies find a net *negative* return for onerous physical working conditions they presume to be disamenities to workers, such as hazards and demands for physical effort. If these job characteristics are really disamenities to the marginal worker, we would expect them to have net positive returns if the theory of compensating differentials is true.

Usually the notion of compensating differentials refers to wage premiums or penalties that compensate for *nonpecuniary* aspects of work. But if we allow the notion to apply across both pecuniary and non-pecuniary costs and benefits of a job, then even the theory of human capital is subsumed within the theory of compensating differentials (Rosen 1986). In human capital theory, the reason jobs requiring more skill pay more is to "compensate" for the disamenity (mainly the opportunity cost of forgone earnings) required to attain the necessary skill. Such disamenities that one "pays" before taking the job are investments. Other compensating differentials refer to nonpecuniary disamenities endured in an ongoing way as the job is performed; these are compensated by the wages in a "pay as you go" fashion. Despite this difference in when the worker gets paid for the disamenity, and whether it is pecuniary, the principle of equalization at the margin remains the same in both views.

If female jobs pay less than male jobs, net of human capital requirements, a neoclassical view suggests that the male jobs have disamenities (as perceived by the marginal worker) that are being compensated for by the higher wage (Killingsworth 1984, 1985, 1986, 1990; Filer 1985, 1989, 1990a). One study has found the effect of sex composition on wages to disappear under controls for job characteristics intended to measure compensating differentials (Filer 1989). (See Jacobs and Steinberg 1990a, 1990b for a criticism of the study and Filer 1990a for a reply.) However, most studies controlling for multiple job characteristics find that female jobs have lower wages even *net* of these characteristics (Jacobs and Steinberg 1990a; England et al. 1988; Kilbourne et al. 1990). Thus, most studies suggest that compensating differentials do not *entirely* explain the pay gap between female and male jobs. (Chapter 3 contains my own empirical analysis of compensating differentials and comparable worth.)

Crowding. The crowding hypothesis is one view of the origins of the lower pay of predominantly female occupations. Bergmann's (1974, 1986) version of the crowding thesis invokes hiring discrimination. (Bergmann's model builds on an idea advanced by Edgeworth in 1922.) It contrasts with other neoclassical explanations of occupational pay discussed above, none of which involve discrimination. Although it uses neoclassical reasoning about the *consequences* of hiring discrimination, the crowding model's assumption of such discrimination is in a tension with neoclassical claims that discrimination cannot persist in competitive markets.

In Bergmann's (1974, 1986) crowding model, employers prefer not to hire women for some jobs. Some women manage to get hired in these jobs anyway by working for a lower wage than men. But many women take female jobs because there is less or no discriminatory resistance to their entry into these jobs. Female jobs will thus have an artificially high supply of labor. The large supply is artificial in the sense that, for any given wage, the amount of labor supplied to female jobs is greater than it would have been in the absence of the discrimination against women in male jobs. This amounts to saying that the exclusion of women from male jobs shifts the labor supply curve facing female jobs outward (i.e., downward and to the right in Figure 2.1). This lowers the market wage in female jobs below what it would be in the absence of discrimination in the male jobs. As noted above, in neoclassical views, discrimination in hiring and discrimination in wages arises from a single source. But, via crowding, this discrimination within male jobs will affect women's wages in female jobs, even when employers are neutral regarding hiring women or men into these female jobs.

Bergmann's (1974, 1986) crowding model posits a devaluation of female labor when employers are hiring for male jobs, a devaluation that leads them to refuse to hire women or to hire them only at a lower wage than paid to men. But the model ignores the possibility of an analogous devaluation of the work in female jobs, leading to a lower wage for female jobs. Rather, her crowding model posits that the lower wages in female jobs occur entirely because devaluation of females when they seek male jobs leads to "excess" supplies of labor to female jobs.

A kind of crowding can also arise without discrimination. Increases in female labor force participation for reasons other than rising wages will produce an outward shift of supply curves to female occupations if most women select traditionally female jobs. This outward shift in the supply curve will lower the wage in female occupations, although it is not artificial as in the discriminatory case above.

Effects of Comparable Worth Policies.   Many economists are skeptical of comparable worth policies because neoclassical theory implies that raising the wages in female jobs will disemploy women,[5] the very group the policy is designed to help (Oi 1986; Roback 1986; Killingsworth 1990). Some of them believe there is little sex discrimination in labor markets. Others subscribe to Bergmann's (1974, 1986) version of the crowding thesis, yet reject comparable worth wage policies that would force employers to raise the relative pay of female jobs. These economists generally favor prohibiting hiring and wage discrimination in male jobs. According to the crowding thesis, this would eventually lead to higher pay in female jobs as the artificially high supply of labor to these jobs was thereby decreased.

Why do economists believe that raising wages in female jobs will disemploy people? Recall that the downward slope of demand curves indicates that the number of workers that employers will choose to employ in a job (the "quantity demanded") is negatively related to the wage they must pay. Thus, faced with a requirement that they pay a higher wage than previously in female jobs, neoclassical theory says that employers will either lay off workers or hire fewer workers than they otherwise would have hired in these jobs. This would be depicted in Figure 2.1 as an upward and leftward movement along an unchanging demand curve. Thus, persons who would otherwise have been in these female jobs may end up either unemployed or out of the labor force because their next-best job offer is undesirable enough that they decide against employment.[6] Either outcome is referred to as *disemployment.* Since comparable worth makes labor in female jobs more expensive relative to capital than previously, one mechanism of disemployment is that employers may now choose to automate processes done in female jobs, substituting capital for labor. At the same time that a mandated higher wage in female jobs is decreasing the quantity of labor demanded, the existence of higher wages in female jobs will increase the quantity of female labor supplied by bringing more women into the labor force to look for jobs, deterring some women from leaving the labor force, and encouraging both men and women who would otherwise have sought male jobs to seek female jobs (Nakamura and Nakamura 1989). This increase in the quantity of labor supplied would be depicted in Figure 2.1 as an upward and rightward movement along an unchanging supply curve. Thus, following neoclassical theory, we would expect comparable worth to create an imbalance between the amount of labor demanded and supplied to female jobs, thus creating disemployment. The argument is similar to economists' arguments about the disemployment caused by minimum wage laws.

If employers' *overall* wage bill is increased by comparable worth policies, i.e., if the raises in female jobs are not compensated for by reductions in wages in male jobs, then we would expect some disemployment to result, as described above. If the overall wage bill is increased, we would also expect increases in the prices of goods and services produced by firms covered by the policy (Killingsworth 1985). However, in the longer run, money spent on comparable worth adjustments might result in smaller raises in male jobs than would otherwise have been awarded. To the extent that this is true, the effect on the total wage bill and hence the *amounts* of theoretically predicted disemployment and price increases are smaller.

Why would neoclassical theory predict that the disemployment resulting from comparable worth policies would fall largely on women? It is female jobs in which the mandated pay raises should lead to a quantity of labor supplied that exceeds the quantity demanded. We would expect it to be largely women who are laid off from the female jobs, or who apply but are not hired in female jobs. However, women might respond to potential disemployment by seeking male jobs (Kahn 1986). Thus disemployment will fall less disproportionately on women to the extent that women seek male jobs and are not met with hiring discrimination in these jobs (Kahn 1986).

Killingsworth (1990) provides estimates of disemployment effects of several implementations of comparable worth. (For earlier studies see Gregory and Duncan 1981; Kahn 1986; Ehrenberg and Smith 1987; and Gregory, Anstie, Daly, and Ho 1989.) In the United States, there is no national policy of comparable worth covering either the private or public sector. As discussed in Chapter 5, some lawsuits have attempted to persuade federal courts to interpret the major federal antidiscrimination law, Title VII of the Civil Rights Act of 1964, to require that employers use wage-setting principles of comparable worth. However, most of these cases have been unsuccessful. Comparable worth policies in the United States have been limited to states and localities passing legislation demanding comparable worth wage setting in their own public sector employment. Thus, Killingsworth uses one state, Minnesota, and one locality, San Jose, California, as two of his cases. His third case is

Australia, where minimum wages for specific jobs are set by a national board affecting private and public sector employers. This board had long explicitly discriminated against women's jobs in wage setting, but adopted comparable worth–like policies in the 1970s, although it has since backed away from them.

Estimating the magnitude of disemployment effects is made difficult by the need to hold other factors affecting employment levels constant except change induced by the comparable worth adjustments. Killingsworth (1990) uses a two-step process: First he estimates how employment levels respond to changes in wages by using data on variation in wages and employment levels across time and occupation within each of his three cases. This step assesses the wage elasticity of demand. In the second step, he estimates the magnitude of wage increases in female jobs from the pay adjustments. Then the wage elasticities of demand are applied to the wage increases to estimate disemployment.

Using this method, Killingsworth estimates that in San Jose the amount of female employment growth typical for one year was lost due to comparable worth pay increases. However, a study by Kahn (1986) of the San Jose case found no disemployment in targeted female jobs. (For a discussion of differences in the two studies' methods, see Ehrenberg 1989.) In Minnesota, Killingsworth estimates that the amount of female employment growth typical for three years was lost. However, another analysis of the Minnesota case, using somewhat different methods, found substantially less disemployment than this (Sorensen 1991a, 1991b). Whether one views such effects as small or large is a matter of judgment. Killingsworth points out that in neither of these cases was pay in women's jobs raised all the way to the pay of the male jobs to which the job evaluation studies showed them comparable. Thus, he concludes that under a more stringent comparable worth policy, the disemployment effects might be substantially larger. In Australia there were larger disemployment effects initially, but virtually no disemployment effects after the policy had been in force several years. (For a criticism of Killingsworth's analysis of the Australian case, see Sorensen 1991a.) The small effects after several years must, however, be weighed against the fact that there was no net improvement in wages in women's compared to men's jobs several years later when this later assessment of disemployment was made. Overall, then, Killingsworth (1990) provides some evidence of a disemployment effect of comparable worth, although there is debate about its magnitude.

Some neoclassical economists have suggested that, in addition to causing disemployment, comparable worth policies could lower some women's wages, quite the opposite of the intent of the policy (Oi 1986; Smith 1988). This is a possible prediction from neoclassical theory *if* the

policy covers some firms but not others. Suppose, for example, that
small firms were exempted or, as a practical matter, that the law was
seldom enforced against them even though it applied. Such firms would
become an uncovered sector absorbing the overflow labor disemployed
from the covered sector. With the existence of such an uncovered sector,
workers disemployed from the covered sector would not all become
unemployed or leave the labor force, as would be more likely if all
sectors were covered by the policies. Rather, some workers disemployed
from the covered sector would crowd into the uncovered sector, and the
crowding would lower wages. To the extent that those ending up in the
uncovered sector were disproportionately women, the sex gap in wages
could increase. At the least, the amount that the sex gap in pay decreased as a direct result of the comparable worth policies would be
reduced. Since comparable worth has not been adopted on a large scale
anywhere but Australia, we do not yet have evidence of what the economywide effects would be on women's earnings.

III.   The New Neoclassical Institutionalism

A new development within economics purports to explain various
anomalies to neoclassical theory, but to remain within the neoclassical
tradition. This development is called *the new institutionalism*. It includes
models of implicit contracts and agency (or bonding) models (Baily 1974;
Azariadis 1975; Akerlof and Miyazaki 1980; Lazear 1981), the transactions cost economics of Oliver Williamson (1975, 1981, 1985, 1988), and
efficiency wage models (Akerlof and Yellen 1986; Katz 1986; Dickens and
Katz 1987; Krueger and Summers 1988). These ideas provide possible
explanations for otherwise theoretically anomalous realities such as unemployment, interindustry wage differentials between workers with
equal human capital in the same occupation, golden parachutes for early
retirement, and wage trajectories that do not equal marginal revenue
product in each time period.

A.   Implicit Contracts, Specific Capital, Agency,
and Transaction Costs

The term *implicit contract* refers to a situation in which there is no
formal, legally binding, written contract, yet things are structured in
such a way as to create incentives for employers and employees each to
engage in behavior in which the other party has an interest. Sometimes
the term has been used to describe a narrower subset of economic mod-

els that are distinct from models of specific capital, bonding, and trans-actions costs. I will use the term here in a broader sense that encom-passes all these developments.

The notion of implicit contracts, broadly construed, was fore-shadowed by Becker's (1962) discussion of firm-specific human capital (often referred to as simply specific capital), discussed previously. What are the costs and benefits of this training to the employer and employee? Costs may include expenses for materials or teachers. But even when the training is informal and the costs less visible, there are still costs. An example is the opportunity cost of forgone productivity while an experi-enced worker teaches a new worker. Gains include higher productivity that results from the training and higher wages. Hashimoto (1981, p. 475) summarizes the standard analysis this way:

> (T)he worker invests in specific human capital by accepting a wage lower than his *(sic)* alternative wage, and receives a return on his *(sic)* investment during the post-investment periods in the form of a wage higher than his *(sic)* alternative wage. The employer invests in specific capital by paying the worker a wage larger than the value of his *(sic)* marginal product, and receives a return on the investment in subsequent periods by paying a wage smaller than the value of his *(sic)* marginal product.

Although at the end of a worker's career with the firm, s/he is earning less than MRP, this is nonetheless more than the worker could make elsewhere since we are discussing training with applicability only to this firm. So, compared to a worker's alternatives elsewhere, wages are lower initially but higher later in the firm providing the specific training. Although Hashimoto (1981) does not use the term *implicit contract*, he describes what is, in essence, an implicit contract between employer and employee. The wage trajectory, which makes employees pay their share of training costs initially, gives the employee an incentive to stay with the firm, which the employer wants in order to avoid the costs of train-ing a new worker. The fact that the employee makes less than MRP late in the career gives the employer an incentive not to fire the worker. Thus the wage trajectory creates incentives for both parties to act as if they were honoring a contract to keep the relationship intact. We can think of this as an implicit contract.

But would it not be better for both parties to write a legal, binding contract stating that the employer will provide training and a specified wage trajectory and that the employee will stay long enough for the employer to recoup search and training costs? In a sense, in proposing the implicit rather than such an explicit contract, Becker (1962) was foreshadowing the transactions cost models introduced by Williamson

(1975, 1981, 1985, 1988). One of the insights of transactions cost models is relevant to labor markets: In the presence of both a joint investment (the training) and prohibitive costs of transacting an explicit contract, implicit contracts are often the solution.

In jobs with specific training, both employer and employee have invested in an asset, firm-specific human capital, that benefits both parties most if the employee continues to work at this firm. It benefits the employer in that the worker is more productive than workers who might be newly hired, since they would not have this specific training. It benefits the employee in that s/he is more productive here than at firms for which s/he has not received specific training, and thus will get paid more here than elsewhere. Williamson (1988) calls this a situation of "asset specificity." It leads both employer and employee to want a contract to guard their specific asset. But why not a formal, written, legally binding contract that spells out each party's rights and obligations under all contingencies? This is what economists call a *perfect contingent-claims contract*.

What would either party want such a contract to cover? Employees would want such contracts to promise future wage increases, promotion chances, pensions, and layoff protection. Employers would wish such contractual promises to be contingent upon both the employee's performance and the economic conditions confronting the firm. For example, if the firm experienced an unexpected increase in the cost of raw materials, or a decline in the price it receives for its product, the employer would want these facts to condition whether s/he had to give raises, or could lay off workers. Employers would also want a promise from employees to stay with the firm to safeguard the firm's investment in on-the-job training, or to compensate the employer for the cost of the training if the employee quit before a specified amount of time had passed. Employees would wish any such agreement to be contingent upon the offers available to the employee in other firms, and upon the inflation rate.

Perfect contingent-claims contracts would have to cover a myriad of contingencies. While explicit contracts exist in unionized jobs and some others, contracts as detailed as those described above are unheard of. Such detailed contracts are impractical because of their excessive transactions costs (Williamson, Wachter, and Harris 1975; Wachter and Williamson 1978). Transactions costs include the time it takes to bargain over the contract, the costs of obtaining information about whether the contingencies of the contract have been met (e.g., whether the employee's performance has been adequate), and the costs of enforcement of the contract (perhaps including lawyers' fees). These costs are quite high relative to the benefits of such contracts. As a consequence of these transactions costs, elaborate contingent-claims contracts are rare. Yet something like a contract arises in at least some jobs. According to the new institutionalists, in the presence of both transactions costs and the asset specificity constituted by specific capital, the real-world outcome is often implicit contracts (Williamson et al. 1975; Wachter and Williamson 1978; Nalebuff and Zeckhauser 1981; Okun 1981; England and Farkas 1986, Chapter 6; Rebitzer 1989). What these contracts include varies, but they may include raises, promotions, protection from layoffs, seniority-based callbacks from layoffs, and pensions, depending on the richness of the contract involved.

The term *implicit contract* also has a narrower use, as I said above. Here it refers to models that do not add the complications of firm-specific human capital, although it is clear that the desire for such a contract by either party would be greater in the presence of specific capital. The narrower use refers to models I will call "insurance" models of implicit contracts. These models see implicit contracts as providing a kind of insurance scheme to protect workers from unwanted layoffs or wage reductions and to protect employers from unwanted quits. Orthodox theory predicts that reductions in the demand for a firm's product will lower MRP and lead to layoffs or, if conditions are better elsewhere, quits that anticipate such layoffs. If the reduction of MRP is economywide, then the market wage will fall.

This class of implicit contract models posits that firms offer "contracts" that amount to a kind of insurance that risk-averse workers "buy" from their employers in the form of a lower but predictable wage. The insurance protects them against later layoffs in the event of reductions in demand for the firm's product (Baily 1974; Gordon 1974; Azariadis 1975; Azariadis and Stiglitz 1983). In essence, employers have entered the insurance business and the employee is paying a small insurance premium deducted from every paycheck. Such contracts are seen to function in the aggregate to improve matches between workers and firms.

Another "insurance-based" implicit contract model posits insurance against unemployment and wage reductions as well, but only after some seniority is built up (Azariadis and Stiglitz 1983). Here, the implicit contract states that any layoffs undertaken will be seniority-based, with seniority-based callbacks, but that wages will not be reduced (Okun 1981) or will only be reduced temporarily, while conditions facing the firm are bad (Hall and Lilien 1979; Grossman and Hart 1981; Grossman, Hart, and Maskin 1983).

Because implicit contracts have no explicit mechanisms of enforcement, Okun (1981) has referred to them as the "invisible handshake." What protects employees from employers who renege? If the employer lays off workers after the worker has paid for insurance in the form of a lower wage, or lowers wages when the contract promises this will not be done, there is little the employee can do about it. Indeed, such events occur. However, there is one long-term incentive for employers not to renege on the contract. This incentive stems from the fact that the firm's reputation as an employer who treats employees well affects whether good workers will sign on with the firm, and affects the turnover rate among its recently trained workers (Lazear 1981; Azariadis and Stiglitz 1983; Bull 1983; Yellen 1984).

Those contracts in which the implicit promise is that wages will not be lowered and that any layoffs when times are bad will be seniority-based have an additional protection for the worker from the employer reneging. The "moral hazard" problem that would otherwise result from asymmetric information (i.e., the fact that employers observe decreases in product demand, but workers do not) is avoided in such arrangements.[7] This is because employers may have an incentive *at any time* to lie and declare that times are bad for the firm so they can lower the wage, but they do not have an incentive to lay workers off except when times are really bad for the firm. Thus, layoffs, combined with seniority rights of protection from them, are less likely to be seen by workers as a violation of the contract than are wage reductions (Okun 1981). Alternatively, an implicit contract might permit temporary wage reductions but only when in conjunction with layoffs. Here again, since the firm has no incentive to lay people off except when demand for their product is falling, moral hazard is avoided (Hall and Lilien 1979; Grossman and Hart 1981; Grossman et al. 1983).

What is to prevent employees from reneging on the implicit contract? If an employee takes a job with a lower wage as insurance against bad times, but times are good later and a higher wage could be earned at another firm without such insurance premiums, what keeps the employee from quitting? Reputation effects are one possibility, but they seem a less plausible answer for employees than for employers (Azariadis and Stiglitz 1983; Holmstrom 1983). After all, it is much more feasible that each employee checks on the reputation of the few firms s/he is thinking about joining than that an employer checks out the reputation of every prospective employee with respect to quit record. This led to the idea that perhaps the "insurance payment" is "front loaded," i.e., paid mostly in the early period of employment (Azariadis and Stiglitz 1983; Holmstrom 1983). This gives employees an incentive to stay with the firm since it is only in the later period that they may be able to make more in this firm than in alternative firms. Another way to think of the same arrangement is that the employee puts up a "bond" (paid in the form of a lower starting wage) to be repaid later in the form of higher wages and/or protection from layoffs. This assures the employer that the employee has a motivation to stay with the firm.

Such front-loaded versions of the insurance implicit contract model feature wage profiles like those in the specific capital model in that both models see workers as initially earning less than their alternative wage in other firms. In the case of the specific capital model, workers were paying for part of their training in this period, while in front-loaded implicit contract models, workers pay their insurance premium in this early period rather than spread out across the life cycle. In the specific capital model the later wage is higher than the worker's alternative elsewhere because the training has increased the worker's productivity in this firm but not in others, although the later wage is still less than MRP (Hashimoto 1981). In front-loaded versions of insurance implicit contract models, later wages are often higher than either MRP or what the worker could make elsewhere. This part of the contract is what motivates the employee to stay through the initial period of low wages (Azariadis and Stiglitz 1983; Holmstrom 1983; Bull 1983). Thus both models feature a steep wage trajectory in which wages are not equal to MRP at each time point, although they do equal expected MRP across the entire life course. A model that includes *both* firm-specific human capital *and* insurance implicit contracts should have an even *steeper* trajectory with even lower starting wages and even higher later wages. To the extent that there is a competitive market in jobs with implicit contracts, it is a market for long-term contracts and an expected lifetime wage. Market forces have to work exclusively at the point of entry to the firm.

So far the implicit contract models that have been considered are all motivated, from the employer's side, by a concern that workers not quit. Some of these models have led to a wage trajectory that pays less than MRP or the worker's alternative wage in the early period and provides greater benefits of one form or another in the later period. Lazear (1979, 1981) proposes a model in which employers offer a similar wage trajectory based, not on concerns about quits, as above, but on concerns about the level of effort put forth by employees. His model is commonly referred to as an "agency" model. The name refers to the fact that employers (the "principals") are trying to use wage profiles to get workers to act faithfully as their "agents" in the sense of putting forth effort and not engaging in malfeasance. Lazear (1979, 1981) suggests that workers can be motivated to put forth more effort by making initial wages lower than MRP and later wages higher than MRP. This way they have to perform well enough not to get fired in order to reach the period where rewards are higher than what they could make elsewhere. Thus, in

Lazear's agency model, as in some other implicit contract models, expected lifetime wages equal expected lifetime MRP, but the shape of the
trajectory is changed to lower initial wages and raise later wages. The
incentive system created by the wage trajectory makes workers act as if
they are honoring a contract to put forth diligent effort. Although he
does not label this an implicit contract model, his model features the
same wage trajectory as the front-loaded implicit contract models discussed above, and involves arrangements that create incentives in place
of an explicit contract. Thus, under the broader definition I am using
here, it can be considered an implicit contract model.

How can we apply the notion of implicit contracts to illuminate gender differentiation in labor markets? From those implicit contract models
that feature a low starting wage and steep wage trajectory one can
derive a supply-side explanation of occupational segregation that has
the same predictions as the human capital theory of sex segregation
explained above. Indeed, if the implicit contract model in question is the
specific capital model, the explanations are the same. In this view, wom-
en planning intermittent employment are well advised to avoid jobs
with implicit contracts since these jobs have lower starting wages. One
who plans only a short spell of employment will maximize earnings by
choosing a job with higher starting wages, despite its less steep trajectory, since a short spell of employment affords one little of the gain from
the steep wage trajectory. However, the evidence does not support this
explanation of segregation, since women's jobs do not have higher starting wages than male jobs of the same skill level (Greenberger and Steinberg 1983; England 1984; England et al. 1988).

A second possible application of implicit contract theory would emphasize demand-side statistical or error discrimination. If women have
higher or more variable quit rates than men, this may lead employers to
discriminate against women in jobs offering substantial amounts of on-
the-job training or to organize jobs already filled by women to exclude
such training. Since implicit contracts are particularly likely in jobs with
provision of firm-specific training, it would seem at first glance that this
could explain the fact that women are typically not in jobs with steep
wage trajectories (England et al. 1988). However, this explanation would
only make sense within a neoclassical model if women's turnover rates
are higher or more variable than men's, and the evidence reviewed in
Chapter 1 casts doubt on this commonly made assumption.

While the models of implicit contracts featuring low starting wages
and steep trajectories propose reasons why women's wage trajectories
have a less steep *slope* than men's, they do not provide an obvious
explanation for the lower wage *levels* of women and of female jobs *across
the entire life cycle.* I want to suggest one rather unorthodox application of

implicit contract theory that I believe *can* illuminate the slow erosion of discrimination in labor markets, and thus the lower wages of women and of female jobs over the entire life cycle (England et al. 1988). I should be clear, however, on the fact that this has *not* been suggested by economists writing in the literature on implicit contracts. Many implicit contract models amount to giving experienced workers more privileges than less-experienced workers, by providing them with raises and promotions, and by protecting them from wage decreases or layoffs. These strategies discourage the replacement of experienced men by cheaper women. But such replacement would speed the arbitrage process discussed above, which neoclassical theorists believe erodes discrimination in competitive markets (England et al. 1988; Jacobs 1989b). Thus, in jobs with implicit contracts, most of the competitive forces that should otherwise erode discriminatory wage differentials are reduced to operating at the discrete time points of each worker's entry to the firm. It is at this point that employers offering greater lifetime earnings will be motivated to choose the cheapest available workers with the greatest productive potential without discrimination. Because this "precontract" point is affected by competitive forces, economists generally presume that the usual conclusions about erosion of discriminatory wage differentials still hold in a model including implicit contracts. Despite the fact that the new neoclassical institutionalism can be given this conservative reading, it also has implications consistent with a notion of demand-side discrimination and segmentation in labor markets. When the competitive forces of labor markets impinge primarily on the initial moment in an individual's career with a firm, as is implied by implicit contract theory, their effects are much less swift and powerful than the orthodox neoclassical view suggests (England et al. 1988). Although many economists still resist these implications, I believe they provide one possible explanation for the failure of discrimination to erode in competitive markets.

B. *Efficiency Wage Models*

Efficiency wage models provide one possible explanation for wages being higher in some jobs than others in a way that is "uncompensated" by either nonpecuniary disamenities or demands for human capital. The key insight of efficiency wage models is that paying higher wages may induce behavior in workers (or prospective workers) that increases rather than decreases profits. The behavior desired by employers may be working hard (in the shirking or gift exchange model), staying with the firm (in the turnover model), joining the firm if one is of high quality (in the adverse-selection model), not unionizing (in the union threat model), or applying for or accepting a job with the firm (in the recruiting model). Efficiency wage models differ from orthodox neoclassical models in asserting that such worker behavior is endogenous rather than exogenous to the wage. In such a situation, it may be profit maximizing for employers to raise wages above the market-clearing level implied by the usual supply-demand model. Wages will be raised as long as they lead to revenue increases greater than the cost of the wage increase.

Below I review several efficiency wage models. Each proposes a different rationale for why, within some range, profits might be a positive function of the wage offered to workers of equivalent human capital. Each model suggests different hypotheses about the types of firms, industries, or occupations in which above–market efficiency wages are most likely to be present. (For an overview, see Katz 1986.) Then the models are examined to see whether they can illuminate gender inequality in labor markets.

One efficiency wage model is the *shirking* or *effort elicitation* model (Bulow and Summers 1986; Shapiro and Stiglitz 1984; Bowles 1985). Here the focus is on potential costs of workers' engaging in malfeasance (such as sabotaging equipment) or putting forth low levels of effort, and on the costs of detecting such shirking. Even with minimal surveillance, workers know that there is some probability of losing their jobs for shirking. If they are paid more than they could make at other firms, they will have a motivation to avoid shirking so as to avoid the wage drop they would experience if they were caught and fired, and had to procure a job at a firm not paying above–market efficiency wages. In some situations it may be cheaper to reduce shirking through raising the wage above the market level than to spend extra money on technology or personnel for more thorough surveillance. The model predicts that above–market efficiency wages are more likely where the elasticity of effort with respect to the wage is greater, and this elasticity may be greater where monitoring costs are higher.

A second efficiency wage model focuses on *turnover* (Stiglitz 1987). Here above-market wages lower turnover. This reduces the costs that firms expend in screening and training new employees. This model suggests that above–market efficiency wages will be found in occupations, industries, or firms where hiring and training costs are larger.

A third efficiency wage model is the *adverse-selection* model. Firms that pay higher wages are more likely to have their offers accepted by applicants of higher quality on dimensions that are not possible to observe and screen. This is true if workers who are better on such unobservables have higher reservation wages. A worker's reservation wage is the smallest wage below which s/he will turn down the job. Higher reservation wages among better workers might occur for two reasons. If "good" workers are also better, on average, at either homemaking or self-employment, then they will have higher reservation wages since their alternative to taking the job is more valuable (Weiss 1980). If we introduce imperfect information and search costs, there is a second reason why workers who are better on qualities that are unobservable at hire might have higher reservation wages. This is because such workers know that if they get a high-wage job (an "efficiency wage" job) they are unlikely to be fired for malfeasance, and thus it is more worth the continued search costs for them to hold out for a high-wage job than is true for other workers.

A fourth efficiency wage model is the *union threat* model (Dickens 1986). In this model nonunionized firms that face a threat of unionization pay union or near-union wages to avoid unionization. We would expect this model to apply where unionization is a more likely threat.

A fifth efficiency wage model is a *recruiting* model (Lang 1991; Montgomery 1991; Weitzman 1989). Here the focus is on the costs to firms of an insufficient number of applicants or of workers turning down their offers. Such costs include the costs of screening and processing applications of additional workers, and costs of physical capital that goes unused while positions are empty. By having an above-market wage that is publicized, firms can get more applicants and have more of them accept their offers. Where the costs avoided exceed the extra wage paid, profit-maximizing firms will adopt this strategy. We would expect such a strategy to be especially likely in jobs where employees work with much physical capital. This is because the capital increases workers' productivity, and thus increases the forgone costs of the position being vacant.

A final efficiency wage model is the *gift exchange* model (Akerlof 1982, 1984). In this model, a wage above the market-clearing level is perceived by workers as a gift and as compliance by the employer with norms of fairness. This increases workers' morale and hence their effort, also offered as a gift and as compliance with norms of fairness. Akerloff's efficiency wage theory departs form neoclassical orthodoxy in a way that the other efficiency wage models do not in not assuming entirely selfish actors, but assuming some altruism among both employers and employees. Each offers an altruistic gift—one a higher-than-market wage, the other a higher-than-minimal effort. Perhaps for this reason, economist Akerlof (1982, 1984) refers to this gift exchange model as "sociological," because the mechanism linking wages and productivity involves norms of altruism and fairness affecting group morale.

If employers in all sectors benefited from gift exchange efficiency wages to an equal extent, the notion would have little relevance to the explanation of why some jobs pay more than others. But workers' norms of fairness may include the notion that firms should pay higher wages when they have a greater "ability to pay," i.e., when they have higher profit levels. If so, then firms with higher profit levels will gain more in workers' morale and productivity from paying above-market wages than will other firms (Katz 1986). Thus, the gift exchange model offers one explanation of why industries' profit rates affect wages (Seidman 1979), a finding that is otherwise an anomaly for neoclassical theory. Orthodox theory implies that investment in less-profitable sectors will eventually cease and the sectors will disappear unless their return on investments equals other sectors, and thus that economic profit rates between industries should not differ in the long run.

Overall, efficiency wage theory provides possible explanations for two common findings that have been regarded as anomalies for orthodox neoclassical theory. One is the presence in the economy of unemployed workers willing to work for less than the wage of employed workers of equal productivity, but unable to get jobs by offering themselves for this lower wage. Efficiency wage theory explains this by the dual role being paid by the wage. The same wage cannot clear the market for new hires (which implies paying as little as competition allows, and thus predicts wage decreases rather than unemployment during recessions), while simultaneously altering the behavior of current employees or applicants in the direction employers wish to alter it. Efficiency wage theory and implicit contract theory are alternative, competing explanations of why wages do not fall sufficiently during recessions to allow the economy to absorb unemployed workers, as orthodox theory would predict.

Efficiency wage theory also provides one possible explanation for persistent interoccupational, interfirm, and interindustry wage differentials that cannot be explained by differences in workers' human capital or by compensating differentials. Efficiency wage theory challenges the orthodox contention that, through competition and attendant mobility, interjob wage differences will disappear, except those needed to compensate for human capital investment or nonpecuniary disamenities of jobs. In this sense, efficiency wage models are a greater departure from neoclassical orthodoxy than are implicit contract models. Implicit contract models maintain the notion of a lifetime wage that is just that needed to compensate for human capital investment and nonpecuniary disamenities, but allow the timing of pay increases to deviate from the time path of MRP. In efficiency wage theory even the lifetime wage is decoupled from MRP. This is because wages cannot simultaneously play the market-clearing function of equalizing differentials between sectors accorded them in orthodox theory, while still staying high enough to affect workers' behavior in the efficiency-producing ways specified by the theory. Since individual profit-maximizing employers have more stake in the latter, the "invisible hand" of competition does not produce the former.

One critique of efficiency wage theory asks why employers cannot motivate the desired behavior with the implicit contract scheme discussed above, in which early low wages and high later wages motivate the behavior efficiency wages are supposed to accomplish (Carmichael 1985, 1990). This is called the "bonding" critique, and applies to three of the efficiency wage models, the shirking, turnover, and adverse-selection models (Katz 1986). Would not the higher-than-market wages in the later portions of the career that are featured in some of the implicit contract models provide as effective an incentive against shirking and turnover? Would not wage profiles with lower starting wages and rewards later serve to self-select better workers (since they know they are unlikely to be found wanting enough to be fired)? If so, why would neoclassical theorists prefer an efficiency wage model that makes the wage above market for the entire career, rather than a competitive market lifetime wage that is sequenced so that bonding (a lower wage) is present in the early period but the wage is higher than MRP later? Clearly the former is a greater departure from neoclassical orthodoxy. Efficiency wage theorists choose the model with a lifetime wage above the competitive wage because of their belief that, as a practical matter, employers cannot set starting wages low enough to pay for the later above–market efficiency wages (Katz 1986, pp. 243–246). In the extreme, this might require a negative starting wage! Minimum wage laws and imperfect capital markets on which workers could borrow this bond may explain why such a solution is impractical. Thus, all efficiency wage models retain a greater anomaly for orthodox theory than do either Lazear's (1981) agency model or other implicit contract models. The anomaly is interjob lifetime wage differentials between workers in various industries, firms, or occupations that cannot be explained by human capital or compensating differentials.

Can efficiency wage models help us to understand gender differences in wages? It is hard to think of a supply-side reason that women would avoid jobs with efficiency wages. Do the models suggest any reason that employers would be more likely to discriminate against women seeking to enter jobs with efficiency wages, and/or be less likely to pay efficiency wages in predominantly female occupations?

In the shirking model, some firms find it cheaper to reduce shirking by increasing the wage than by increased surveillance. However, if women have higher quit rates, then the cost to women of losing the job would be less than the cost to men, since the women would forgo the above-market wage for only the limited time period they intended to stay. Thus, a high efficiency wage would do less to deter women's than men's shirking (Bulow and Summers 1986; Aldrich and Buchele 1989). Put another way, it would take a higher wage increment to deter women's than men's shirking. Given this, if women have higher quit rates than men, the model predicts statistical discrimination against women in jobs with high monitoring costs and efficiency wages (Goldin 1986). As discussed in Chapter 1, the evidence is not clear on whether women's quit rates are higher than men's beyond what can be explained by job placements that result from discrimination (other than merely statistical discrimination). Thus, the relevance of this model to explaining segregation and the sex gap in pay remains questionable.

In the turnover model, above-market-clearing wages exist to deter turnover. Since firms that pay such wages are those in which turnover is especially expensive, they may also not want to hire women if women have higher turnover. If employers are risk-averse, then they may avoid hiring women because female turnover is more variable than men's, even if it is not higher. Thus, this model also suggests that in hiring for jobs with efficiency wages there will be statistical discrimination against women based on beliefs in sex differences in turnover (Aldrich and Buchele 1989). However, if women's turnover rates are *more* sensitive to their wage than are men's, this might be a mitigating factor throwing the rationality of statistical discrimination against women in such jobs in doubt even if women's turnover is higher or more variable. Two studies have shown a greater wage elasticity of women's than men's quits (Kahn and Griesinger 1989; Blau and Kahn 1981). Thus, it is not clear that it *is* rational for employers to discriminate against women in jobs where they are trying to deter turnover.

The adverse-selection model says that efficiency wages designed to attract better workers (presumed to be those with higher reservation wages) are most likely in jobs where it is particularly difficult to observe worker quality in advance of hire. Presumably this strategy would work to attract either male or female workers of high quality, and hence should have no implications for discrimination. But Aldrich and Buchele (1989) claim that the very screening costs that lead firms to adopt efficiency wages under the adverse-selection model also lead to statistical discrimination based on women's higher turnover rates. An objection to this is parallel to the objection I have raised about applications of all the models to gender differences via statistical discrimination: Based on the evidence reviewed in Chapter 1, it is not clear that women have turnover rates that are higher than men's for reasons exogenous to discriminatory practices.

The union threat model suggests that efficiency wages are less likely in female jobs *if* such jobs do not exhibit as realistic a threat of unionization as male jobs. It is often assumed that women are harder to organize than men, presumably because they plan to stay in their jobs less long. However, little evidence is ever presented that women are harder to organize, and, as argued above, the alleged difference in exogenous turnover rates is not firmly established.

The recruiting model suggests efficiency wages are most likely in capital-intensive jobs because the opportunity cost of letting a position go vacant is greater in such jobs. It is not obvious from the model why firms using this strategy would be any more or less likely to discriminate against women than other firms.

In sum, it seems that none of the efficiency wage models reviewed above is very helpful in explaining why employers with efficiency wages would be particularly motivated to engage in sex discrimination. Where such implications have been suggested, they hinge on assuming that women have higher turnover rates. Yet Chapter 1 showed that we lack compelling evidence that women have higher turnover rates that are exogenous to discriminatory treatment by employers.

The gift exchange efficiency wage model has more promise in explaining gender-relevant differences, although this application was not discussed by Akerlof (1982, 1984). The model says that group norms will affect wage differentials because workers put forth more effort when they see that employers are following the norms. It follows, then, that if prevailing norms are sexist in that they devalue traditionally female jobs and skills, the model predicts lower wages for female jobs. However, this would only be true if women as well as men hold sexist norms, or to the extent that efficiency wages in male but not female jobs increased men's productivity more than it lowered women's.

IV. Framing Models

Psychologists and social psychologists (whether within the discipline of sociology or psychology) have long used laboratory experiments to test theory. In recent years some psychologists and economists have begun to use the method of laboratory experiments to test assumptions of and predictions from neoclassical theory. This enterprise is referred to as *behavioral* or *experimental economics.* Some of the experimental results support neoclassical theory. However, one body of this experimental research finds what can be interpreted as violations of the rationality assumption in the form of "framing effects" (Kahneman and Tversky 1979; Tversky and Kahneman 1987; Kahnamen and Thaler 1991). A *frame* refers to features of the situation surrounding a decision that affect what an option is compared to, and thus affect how the option is valued.

Whether a choice looks good or bad depends on what it is compared to, on what else is in the frame. The frame seldom contains all the available options, thereby leading to something other than a rational decision. Framing effects involve something more than *random* errors in cognition, which would pose little threat to neoclassical theory. Rather, frames affect decisions in *systematic* ways that distort rationality. Framing models also suggest endogenous tastes, a violation of neoclassical assumptions.

How might framing effects apply to comparable worth? They suggest that employers may use present wage levels as a frame for deciding appropriate future wage levels. This will perpetuate any initially erroneous estimates of the relative MRP of jobs, and perpetuate effects of any past discrimination in the pay of female jobs, whether it was based on cognitive error or other factors, such as tastes or collective action. Studies by experimental social psychologists have shown that, in assessing the fairness of their pay, people generally compare their pay to that of those in the same or a similar occupation and to those of the same sex (Major and Forcey 1985; Hegtvedt 1989; Major 1989). Also, one's own past pay tends to frame an evaluation of one's current pay (Hegtvedt 1989; Major 1989). Since women are often segregated in low-paying jobs, these framing effects mitigate against employees' (male or female) or employers' ability to see the pay as discriminatory.

Major (1989), a social psychologist, emphasizes that what is in the frame for comparison affects norms of entitlement as well as one's cognitive evaluation of alternatives. Since norms can be thought of as tastes, we can regard these findings as challenging economists' notion that tastes are exogenous to economic processes. This leads to a paradox that social psychologists concerned with norms of distributive justice have noted: Distinctions between what is, what one expects, and what is seen as fair tend to blur over time (Jackson 1989; Major 1989). Existing arrangements come to be expected and seen as fair. Thus the low pay of female occupations comes to be expected and seen as fair over time, regardless of how overtly discriminatory the origin of the differentials. While even the victims of the discrimination themselves internalize this belief, I suspect that they generally hold it with more ambivalence and doubt than those who gain from the discrimination.

So far, the implications of framing models I have discussed have been quite pessimistic about the possibility of achieving comparable worth reforms voluntarily, highlighting how the status quo perpetuates itself through providing the frame. However, framing models have more optimistic implications about how people would respond to the reform once instituted. If employers are required to make wage adjustments based on principles of comparable worth, these adjusted wage levels will become part of the frame for future wage setting, thus making comparable worth wages seem more reasonable to both employers and employees.

Another aspect of how evaluations and decisions are framed, called loss aversion (Tversky and Kahneman 1987), has implications for comparable worth. This refers to the fact that the negative response to a loss (relative to what one now has or expects to have) is more extreme than the positive response to a gain of the same amount. That is, people behave in ways that imply that they perceive the displeasure of losing a sum of money to exceed the pleasure of gaining the same amount. This principle of asymmetry is observed in experiments in discrepancies between the amount of money people say they are willing to pay for something and the larger amount they would require to give it up if they already have the good. The asymmetry in the perception of losses and gains implies that opportunity costs and out-of-pocket costs are not treated alike, as assumed by neoclassical theory. In a similar vein, experimental social psychologists have found that affective or behavioral responses to a punishment (defined as losing a benefit one already had) are much greater than to a reward of the same size (Gray and Tallman 1987; Molm 1991).

As suggested in Chapter 1, this asymmetry principle provides a hypothesis about why women's employment would rise when men's wages go down, but women's levels of employment would not fall when some or all of these male wage losses are regained. I also used the asymmetry principle to explain why increasing inequality in husbands' incomes may increase wives' employment, as the income losses of men at the bottom create more women's employment than the gains of men at the top do to reduce it.

This same principle of asymmetry in perceptions of and responses to losses and gains of the same objective size also provides predictions of probable responses to comparable worth. It suggests that wage losses by men will be fought with more intensity than will forgone gains. Thus, achieving gender equity in part through slower raises in male jobs than would otherwise ensue will entail less resistance than will lowering wages in male jobs.

V. Marxist Views

I start with an overview of Marxism, discuss how orthodox and revisionist Marxists have approached questions of gender discrimination, and end by considering how Marxist perspectives can illuminate comparable worth. In Marxist literature the distinction between sociology and economics is scarcely relevant, since Marxists in both disciplines are following a common, though not monolithic, paradigm. (See Marx [1844] 1975; [1852] 1963; [1867] 1967; [1885] 1967; [1894] 1967; Tucker 1978; Burawoy 1990.)

A. Basic Concepts of Orthodox Marxism

Fundamental to a Marxist analysis of modern capitalist societies is the notion of a conflict of interest between two classes, capitalists and workers. This conflict is seen as inherent to a capitalist society. Classes are defined by their relationship to the means of production. Those who own capital (i.e., factories, equipment, or other nonhuman infrastructure necessary to production) are able to reap profits and to have managerial authority over workers. Workers must make a living by selling their labor. Thus, capitalists earn profits even if they do not work, while workers must work for wages.

Marx saw work (i.e., transforming nature into something of use) as what is most essentially human. His labor theory of value contended that everything of value is created by work.[8] In this view, capitalists' profits are inherently exploitative because they are not a result of work but are taken from value created by workers' labor.

Marxists see change as the result of conflicts of interest. Change comes from the resistance that capitalism's oppressions engender in workers. Workers resist capitalism because they would prefer that profits not be taken from their wages. Yet financial exploitation is not the only reason that workers resist capitalism, in a Marxist view. The hierarchical division of labor is alienating to workers because decision-making authority over many work processes is given to managers rather than workers, and because workers cannot see the whole product they produce.

Marxists assert that struggle ensues within capitalism when workers gain "class consciousness." This means they come to see that their interests are distinct from those of capitalists, that capitalism is exploitative, and that collective action is the appropriate response.

The elusive concept of dialectics is important to Marxist theory. A dialectical view is one in which the same features of the system that encourage one outcome also encourage the opposite effect. Let us take the power of capitalists as an illustrative example. In one sense, the more their power, the more stable the system of capitalism is, because with more power capitalists are better equipped to defeat workers' acts of resistance through such actions as strike breaking, hiring lobbyists, and transferring production abroad. Yet in another sense, the greater

capitalists' power the more oppressive the system will become for workers, and the more resistance is developed, thus raising the likelihood of
change. The notion that capitalists' power has these two contradictory
effects is an example of dialectical thinking.

The dialectic posits contradictions that resolve into some synthesis,
which itself may embody new contradictions. Since each of the two
contradictory elements is simultaneously affecting the other before the
synthesis emerges, a dialectical relationship also implies something
other than one-way causation. In mature capitalism, the *social relations of
production* are seen by Marxists to be in a contradictory relationship with
the *forces of production*. The social relations of production refer to the
hierarchical division of labor and the fact that some make profits while
others sell their labor. The forces of production include both the infrastructure of machinery, called capital, and human capacities and
skills, called labor power. The idea is that the social relations of capitalism hold back the development of the full potential for productivity
inherent in the forces of production. For example, Marxists claim that
private ownership of capital and a hierarchical division of labor make an
industrial economy less productive than it would be under a true socialism, which most North American and Western European Marxists do
not believe has ever existed anywhere in the world.

Marx's vision was not entirely dialectical in that he believed that, with
the coming of communism, all significant exploitation and conflict
would end. This vision (unlike that followed by the Soviets, for instance)
entailed nonhierarchical social relations in work. It also entailed an end
to the private ownership of the means of production and, hence, an end
to private profits.

Marxist theory is materialist in asserting the causal primacy of the
mode of production (which includes the social relations of production)
in influencing other features in society. Marx distinguished between the
material base and the superstructure of a society. The base refers to the
mode of production, for example, industrial capitalism. The superstructure refers to other institutions of society such as the state, churches,
and schools. The superstructure also includes the realm of ideas—
culture, ideology, and religion. In general, Marxists believe that institutions of the superstructure will serve the interests of capital, although
they will also be a locus of struggle between capital and labor. Materialism also implies that the ideas that predominate in an era are more
determined by the mode of production than vice versa. In this view, a
religion or ideology could hardly change the world. Rather, those re-
ligions or other belief systems that make current arrangements of economic power seem legitimate are the ideas that those in power will allow
to survive. In short, to Marxists, materialism means that the mode of

production has causal primacy over other institutions and over ideas.

However, developments in the post–World War II period have "softened" the materialism or "economism" of Marxist theory. For example, the critical theorists who are intellectual descendants of the Frankfurt School (Held 1980; Benhabib 1986) reject the traditional base/superstructure model, not only in seeing greater causal weight for the latter than Marxists traditionally have, but also in seeing culture as a material force in its own right. They see the confrontation of cultural and personal forms of domination as a necessary part of any progressive struggle, rather than something that contradictions in the material relations of productions will automatically bring about.

Other lines of Marxist thought have also deepened this emphasis on the role of ideas. Gramsci (1971) developed the idea of domination through "hegemony," referring to the way in which the ideas that come to be taken for granted reproduce the domination of capitalism. Althusser (1970, 1971) extended this, arguing that internalized ideology, propagated by the "ideological state apparatus," has an important causal role in perpetuating domination, although he retained the belief that the economic base is determinative "in the last instance." Poulantzas (1974, 1978) furthered this development by collapsing the base/superstructure distinction, so that ideology, the state and the "economic base" are seen as one complex unity. Poststructuralist Marxists, such as LaClau and Mouffe (1985), reject even the "in-the-last-instance" version of materialism. Overall, these developments have increased the importance given to ideas and noneconomic institutions by contemporary Marxists (Bergesen 1988).

B. The Hierarchical Division of Labor and Class Categories in the Modern Occupational Structure

Marglin (1978) argues that the hierarchical division of labor in early capitalism arose out of efforts to control work processes and markets rather than to achieve technical efficiency. (See also Gorz 1978.) Marglin contrasts a worker's role in the division of labor of a factory or office to the role of an artisan who buys materials, makes a product, and markets it. In an economy of self-employed artisans, there is no capitalist controlling the labor process and extracting surplus value; every artisan is an independent producer. Marglin concedes that the modern factory is a more technically efficient form of production than decentralized artisanship, in the sense that more product can be produced for the same dollar inputs of capital, labor, and raw products. Nonetheless, Marglin (1978) argues that the usual rendering of economic history in which the hierarchical division of labor arose because this greater technical efficiency could increase profits is false. Rather, he argues that the hierarchical aspect of the process developed first, within the system of putting-out, before the efficiencies of the factory were developed. While still using the system of putting-out, large capitalists increasingly divided the tasks entailed in making a product between different self-employed "workers" who got materials from capitalists and performed production at home. Allocating the tasks needed to make a single product to various workers was begun, according to Marglin, so that the large capitalists would have a necessary role and thus be positioned to take profits. In the short run, control was a higher priority than maximizing profits.

Marxists deemphasize the way that jobs within a hierarchical division of labor differ in skill. Rather, they see a long-term trend to deskill all jobs, thus producing increased homogeneity in the working class (Braverman 1974). They also argue that the modern bureaucratic division of jobs into graduated authority and status levels serves to divide and conquer workers by leading them to focus on status competition with each other rather than on unified class consciousness and action (Edwards et al. 1975).

Some Marxists also see occupational differences in authority as indicating contradictory class location. For example, Wright (1978) argued that one's class is determined by whether or not one (1) owns the means of production, (2) has control over the production process, (3) has control over the labor power of others via supervision, and (4) has control over one's own labor power via autonomy. This leads to two clear class locations (capitalists and nonsupervisory workers) and a contradictory class location for managers and supervisors. Capitalists have all four advantages. Workers without supervisory or managerial functions have none. However, managers and supervisors are a contradictory class location in that they do not own companies (though some high-level managers have stock options as part of their compensation) but often have substantial amounts of the other three types of control.

The relatively high earnings of managers and supervisors is interpreted by Wright, Costello, and Sprague (1982) as a result of this class position, rather than as a result of managerial skill. The most pronounced difference that Wright et al. (1982) found between women and men's placement across these categories is that women are much less likely than men to be managers or supervisors. Recall from Chapter 1 that this is a finding common to researchers within and outside the Marxist tradition. This difference, which Wright et al. (1982) interpret as differential class location, explains a portion of the sex gap in pay. But how do women and men come to be differentially distributed across job categories, whether the categories differ in class location or not? One possibility is discrimination, so it is important to see how Marxists have interpreted such discrimination.

C. Discrimination as a Capitalist Strategy to Divide and Conquer Workers

Here I examine contemporary applications of Marxist ideas to under-standing labor market discrimination and comparable worth. However, it is important to recognize that Marxist theory sees the structured in-equalities between workers and capitalists as much more central than inequalities between groups of workers such as men and women. The relevance of discrimination to orthodox Marxist theory is that it is in-terpreted as a divide-and-conquer strategy by capitalists to weaken working class solidarity.

In this view, employers discriminate by race or sex to create divisions or hostilities between groups of workers that will prevent workers from organizing cohesively enough to threaten profit levels by unionization, strikes, or more radical political action (Gordon, 1972, pp. 71–78; Ed-wards et al. 1975, pp. xiii–xiv; Bonacich 1976; Bowles and Gintis 1976, p. 174; Humphries 1976; Reich 1978, 1981; Stevenson 1988). Capitalists, as a class, have a material interest in preventing such solidarity of workers.

As discussed above, through neoclassical lenses, the problem with this view is why free riding employers do not subvert the class "monop-oly" to lower their individual wage bill by hiring women in jobs for which other employers are paying more for men. It is at least plausible that individual capitalists could lower their overall wage bill more effec-tively by hiring women (or whatever group is discriminated against) at their lower market wage in all the jobs generally reserved for the favored group than by the divide-and-conquer strategy. But free rider behavior that advantages the individual capitalist will undercut the strategy of the capitalist class to keep workers divided. The fact that Marxists have had little to say about this makes clear that most Marxists implicitly assume *collectively* self-interested action by a class. In contrast, neoclassical theo-ry posits that each capitalist acts to maximize *individual* self-interest. (The relatively new analytic Marxism, by contrast, assumes individual self-interest. See Roemer 1979, 1988.)

While it is difficult to document whether divide and conquer is the *motive* for most employers' discrimination, one can investigate whether discrimination has the *effect* of impeding working-class gains. Reich (1978, 1981) provides some evidence in favor of the divide-and-conquer thesis; he shows that states in which black/white relative income is lower also have more disadvantaged white working classes, net of other factors. (See Szymanski 1976 for related evidence.) Another study did not support the thesis; Beck's (1980) time series analysis did not find unionism to be negatively related to blacks' relative income. But if the subordination of blacks serves to divide and thereby weaken the power of the working class, Marxist theory predicts a negative relationship between blacks' relative status and union power. These studies provide conflicting findings about whether racism subverts progress for the working class. A Marxist perspective on comparable worth would suggest that discriminatory segregation and discriminatory wages in female jobs are part of a strategy to divide and conquer workers. Whether these mechanisms of sexism serve to divide and conquer the working class has not been well studied.

D. Socialist-Feminist Views

Socialist feminists accept the broad contours of a Marxist analysis of class relations, but reject the tendency of orthodox Marxists to see sexism as merely a by-product of capitalist class relations. The view of sex discrimination described above, which sees sexism as part of capitalists' strategy to divide and conquer the working class, is an example of seeing sex inequality as a derivative of class relations. Socialist feminists argue that without preexisting sexism, capitalists could not get workers to see gender as a salient enough issue to be able to engage in a strategy of divide and conquer.

Socialist feminists see patriarchy to be as important a form of women's oppression as capitalism. One difference between the two types of oppression is that with patriarchy the beneficiaries of oppression are men of all classes (though perhaps some more than others), whereas with capitalism, the beneficiaries are the much smaller number of (male or female) capitalists. Some socialist feminists see "capitalist patriarchy" as merged into one system. Other socialist feminists espouse a view that sees capitalism and patriarchy as analytically distinct, coexisting systems of oppression. Some socialist feminists see capitalism and patriarchy as mutually reinforcing while others see them as contradictory. (These positions are reviewed in Walby 1986; Shelton and Agger forthcoming.)

In what institutions do socialist feminists believe that patriarchy operates? Shelton and Agger (forthcoming) note the tendency of some socialist feminists (e.g., Delphy 1984) to see class relations as relevant to wage labor and patriarchy as relevant only to sexuality and the household. In contrast, Hartmann (1976, 1981) is a socialist feminist who sees *both* capitalism and patriarchy as structuring the family *and* the realm of wage labor. Thus the analytical distinction Hartmann makes between capitalism and patriarchy does not mean that there is a separate institutionalized sphere in which each operates. Patriarchy in the household is exemplified by men's ability to control women's labor and sexuality, to get women to do onerous childrearing and household work, and to meet men's sexual needs regardless of their own needs. Hartmann (1976) documents how patriarchal organization is also present in the paid workplace; male workers have been active in efforts to keep women in lower-paying, segregated jobs. One can also see male workers' resistance to comparable worth, and their ignoring and minimizing of the skills involved in women's jobs, as part of patriarchy.

In the socialist-feminist view, discrimination against women in labor markets may occur because of either a class-based divide-and-conquer strategy, the collective patriarchal efforts of men, or both. In addition, many socialist feminists acknowledge the Marxist-feminist argument that women are disadvantaged in competing in labor markets because capitalists have encouraged a system in which women perform reproductive labor in the home without pay. Such reproductive labor is generally taken to include the emotional services wives perform for husbands, which makes them able to perform another day of alienated labor, as well as the socialization of children, who are the next generation to provide wage labor. This arrangement frees capitalists of having to pay as much as they otherwise would need to for the reproduction of the labor force upon which they rely (Shelton and Agger forthcoming).[9] Capitalists may encourage the arrangement in many ways, including paying low enough wages to women that they need husbands, and encouraging patriarchal ideologies. All these may contribute to women's disadvantage, in the socialist-feminist view.

In sum, while socialist feminists share with orthodox Marxists a belief that women's disadvantage may sometimes stem from the divide-and-conquer strategies of capitalists, and share with Marxist feminists the belief that women's disadvantage in labor markets may sometimes arise from capitalists' interests in women doing reproductive labor in the home, they depart from these views in insisting that there is also an independent causal role for patriarchy in explaining women's oppression. At least for some socialist feminists such as Hartmann (1976, 1981), this causal role of patriarchy is at work in the labor market as well as in the home.

VI. Other Sociological and Institutional Views

In this section I relate gender inequality and comparable worth to three somewhat overlapping theoretical positions within sociology:

functionalism, conflict theory, and social structural views. I also include a discussion of a nonneoclassical institutionalist tradition within economics because of its closer connection with sociological than neoclassical views.

It is more difficult to write an overview of theories of labor markets for sociology than economics because there is less consensus within sociology. Economics has a paradigm, and most economists agree upon many of its implications. Fifteen years ago, most sociologists saw the two major competing sociological theories to be functionalism (associated with Talcott Parsons) and conflict theory (in either a Marxist or Weberian variety), the two traditions to be discussed below. Some would have included symbolic interactionism as a third competing tradition. Today, sociology is much more fragmented. Few identify themselves as functionalists, though there is some interest in what Alexander (1985) calls "neofunctionalism." As I see it, conflict theory has won out in that it is widely acknowledged that functionalism underemphasized power and overemphasized consensus as a basis for order. There is also increasing agreement that arrangements cannot be explained simply because of their functionality for some "whole," but have to be constructed by specific social groups with both the power and motivation to do so. But the version of conflict theory that has won out in the mainstream of the profession is not orthodox Marxism with its rather specific predictions and prescriptions about the contradictions of capitalism. Indeed, even the Marxist tradition has become increasingly fragmented, as discussed above. The relative importance of the base and the superstructure are under debate, the new analytic Marxists have questioned whether capitalists may not free ride on class interests, and socialist feminists insist that women's oppression derives from patriarchy as well as class relations. Thus conflict theorists today agree on only the most general propositions. What results is a view in which the possible bases of power are multiple, and the possible outcomes of inequalities are not determinant in a way easily summarized by a theory. Another way to describe the situation is that the distinction between functionalism and conflict theory has blurred. Alexander (1985) comments that neofunctionalist theories are often about conflict. Marxist writers now talk about ideological hegemony, acknowledging that subordinated groups often hold beliefs that support their oppression. Given this increased blurring, the debate between functionalism and conflict is no longer at the forefront of the discipline. Because of this, other debates, such as those about the relationship between "micro" and "macro," and between the individual and the structural, have received increased attention. Thus, structuralist views are also discussed below.

A. Functionalism

The functionalist theory of stratification (Davis and Moore 1945) posits that, in order to adapt and survive, societies must give higher rewards to occupational positions that are most functionally important. The incentives provided by higher rewards are seen as necessary to ensure that the positions are filled, and filled with sufficiently qualified persons. Being more "functionally important" is not precisely the same thing as contributing more to marginal revenue product (MRP) in neoclassical theory, since the functionality is to the entire society, whereas MRP refers to the contribution to profit of individual firms. However, Parsons's version of functionalism saw what is functional for each institution in society contributing to the functionality of the whole, and neoclassical economists, following Adam Smith, believe that an economy made up of selfish profit maximizers leads, via the invisible hand, to growth for all. Given this, the functionalist claim is similar to the neoclassical claim. One difference is that in functionalism the mechanism is consensus on internalized values. In contrast, in the neoclassical case it is the invisible hand of competition that generally creates efficient outcomes despite each individual's self-interested behavior.

How does this view compare with the implicit view of reward systems in the literature on comparable worth? Job evaluation as a method of achieving comparable worth, discussed in Chapter 4, shares basic assumptions with functionalism. It is a method that purports to determine the relative value of jobs to organizations. Both functionalism and job evaluation posit that average rewards in a job depend most directly upon the characteristics of a position that determine its functional importance, and only indirectly upon individual characteristics. Thus, both functionalism and job evaluation focus on the position as the fundamental unit of analysis. In that limited sense, they are both structural views. This point is sometimes obscured (e.g., in Horan 1978) when status attainment research (e.g., Blau and Duncan 1967; Treiman and Terrell 1975a; Featherman and Hauser 1978) is taken as the main exemplar of functionalist research, because the focus of status attainment research is on how individual characteristics affect access to highly rewarded occupations. However, functionalist theory also contains a structuralist claim about how the functional contribution of *positions* affects their reward levels.

Despite these links, research on comparable worth also undermines some functionalist assumptions. Research shows that women's jobs are generally paid less (relative to men's jobs) than is commensurate with their value to the organization, as assessed by job evaluation (Remick 1984; Rothchild 1984; Steinberg et al. 1986; Acker 1987; Orazem and Mattila 1989). (Of course, critics of comparable worth would dispute that job evaluations measure value to the organization.) Studies using national data, reviewed in Chapter 1, generally reach the same conclusion. Such research disputes the claim that a functionalist theory tells the whole story of how jobs are paid. If the factors used in job evaluation are proxies for functional worth to an organization, it is clear from such studies that functional factors explain much of interjob variance in pay, but equally clear that women's jobs are relatively underpaid in a way that functionalism cannot explain.

Functionalists would have to strain to come up with a functional explanation for such pay differences between male and female jobs. Parsons's writings on gender differentiation described a gender-based division of labor, with husbands emphasizing the "instrumental" realm through their jobs, while wives emphasize what he called the "expressive" realm of childrearing and creating emotional solidarity in the family (Parsons 1954, 1966; Parsons and Bales 1955). The nonemployment of women was seen as functional because it created a differentiated and specialized role for socialization and familial solidarity, and because it reduced solidarity-threatening competition between husbands and wives. In the more recent context where a majority of married women are employed, functionalists see sex segregation of jobs with women in different and lower-paying jobs to be functional to reduce competition between husbands and wives (Gross 1968). (See Oppenheimer 1982 for a critical discussion.)

However, functionalism also posits that it is adaptive for societies, in an evolutionary sense, to become increasingly universalistic. Universalism refers to using a consistent set of criteria to make decisions about people. This implies nondiscrimination by sex in hiring and in setting the wages for jobs. In this sense, sex discrimination is an anomaly for functionalism as it is for neoclassical economics. Thus, it would seem more consistent with a functionalist view to posit that women self-select out of jobs that could be construed as competing with their husbands, rather than to posit discrimination by employers. Little research has tested whether women do this as a conscious strategy, although Oppenheimer (1982) interprets some results this way. But even if this is true, it would lead to the question of why functionalism does not predict eventual universalism in role assignment in the family as well as the labor market. (For a defense of functionalism by a feminist, see Johnson 1989, forthcoming.)

B. Institutionalist Economics

The institutionalist school of economics traces its origins to turn-of-the-century writers such as Thorstein Veblen, John Commons, and John

Dewey, as well as midcentury writers such as Clarence Ayres. The school still has adherents today, although institutionalism, like Marxism, is marginal in American economics. (For an overview of contemporary institutionalism, see Tool 1988.)

The views of institutionalists share much with those of functionalist sociologists. Both views emphasize consensual cultural values and the distinction between instrumental and expressive or ceremonial behaviors. This may surprise sociologists who have noted a similarity between functionalist sociology and neoclassical economics (Horan 1978) in their conservative political overtones, as well as a similarity between institutionalists among economists and nonfunctionalist sociologists in their left-leaning politics. As an example of the divergence of institutionalist from neoclassical views, the 1984 special issue of the institutionalist journal, *Journal of Economic Issues,* was devoted to comparable worth, and was made up entirely of articles sympathetic to the notion that there is institutionalized sex discrimination in labor markets. As discussed above, for most neoclassical economists, persistent discrimination (with the exception of statistical discrimination) is a theoretical anomaly. The acceptance by institutionalists of the notion of sex discrimination also points out a difference between institutionalism and functionalism. To institutionalists, norms are often dysfunctional, irrational traditions from *formerly* functional institutional practices. The idea that culture and institutions lag behind what is functional is less accepted in sociological functionalism.

Central to institutionalist thought is the dichotomy between *instrumental* and *ceremonial* aspects of behavior and institutions. The instrumental side of life involves knowledge, skills, and technology. It is the tendency to evaluate things in terms of their consequences. Instrumentalism is seen as the source of economic progress in a society because it is adaptive to the environment. Because of this emphasis, institutionalism is sometimes called evolutionary economics.

Institutionalists implicitly ascribe greater value to the instrumental than the ceremonial aspects of institutions. This valuation is in the same spirit as the implicit valuing of optimizing and efficiency by neoclassical economics. Institutionalists differ from neoclassical economists, however, in recognizing a more ritualistic, habitual, and inertial aspect to institutions that is often denied in neoclassical theory. In a neoclassical view, what institutionalists call the ceremonial realm is relegated to the realm of tastes, and is seen as more relevant in consumption than in production. This is because firms are generally assumed to be profit maximizers. The neoclassical view that tastes for discrimination cannot persist indefinitely in competitive labor markets is an example of this view. Thus, while institutionalists share with both neoclassical economists and functionalists a privileging of instrumentality, institutionalist thought nonetheless differs from the neoclassical view in its emphasis on the inertial drag of institutions.

The institutionalist view suggests that habits are a result of instrumental values but then become ceremonial when they no longer serve their original purpose but remain institutionalized. A similar view of habits is found among some sociologists (Camic 1986). In an institutionalist view, habits of discrimination are seen as a ceremonial lag in the system. Thus, institutionalist theory is consistent with what appear to be anomalies in neoclassical labor market analysis (Greenwood 1984).

C. Conflict Theory

Modern conflict theory has varied strands, but all emphasize the non-consensus and conflict of interests between societal groups. The domination of some groups over others is seen as the force holding society together, as well as the source of change through the conflict it engenders (Collins 1975; Kerbo 1983, Chapters 4 and 5). What functionalists consider to be common values are, in the eyes of conflict theorists, the values of those with power. If subordinate groups do internalize these values, this may reflect the power of elites to control the institutions of socialization. Marxist versions of conflict theory, discussed above, see power as based primarily on the ownership and control of property. Here I discuss a more eclectic conflict view. This view sees a multidimensional set of possibilities for bases of conflict, does not assume that material relations always have primacy, and has a less clear view of the destination toward which processes of change point than is present in most Marxist views.

Thus, in such a view, gender becomes one among many possible vectors for conflicting interests and collective action (Folbre forthcoming). Men's collective efforts to keep women out of male jobs and to keep male jobs evaluated as more worthy is thus consistent with conflict theory. Notions of discrimination reviewed above based on taste or group monopoly are also consistent with conflict theory. Sociological conflict theory does not explain the origins of the subordination of women, but it provides one framework for understanding the processes by which women have been kept out of some jobs, and work performed by women has been devalued and assigned a lower wage. However, the emphasis on devaluation is a relatively new development within conflict theory.

Another literature within conflict theory that can be appropriated for its relevance to gender inequality is Bordieu's theory of cultural capital (Bourdieu 1977; Bourdieu and Passeron 1977; DiMaggio 1979). The theory is about one mechanism through which class advantage is reproduced intergenerationally. It suggests that cultural capital—certain skills, knowledge, tastes, and life-styles—is passed on intergenerationally within a class through socialization. Elites make holding such capital a prerequisite of rewards even when such capital does not contribute to the "bottom line" of production and profit. In doing this, elites engage in a symbolic struggle to impose the definition of the social world most in conformity with their collective class interests.

Bordieu does not discuss how this might apply to gender inequality. However, extending this idea to gender inequality in labor markets, one could see skills and interests that men are encouraged to develop as a form of cultural capital that is reproduced among men and arbitrarily rewarded in labor markets. This could be applied to understanding gender differences in access to occupations as well as comparable worth. With respect to access to positions, it is in men's interest that those qualifications that men typically have more of be weighted more heavily in deciding whom to hire. For example, consider the fact that experience managing a home or in voluntary organizations often counts less than military experience in getting a job. This could be interpreted as valuing men's cultural capital over that of women in a way that cannot always be justified by differential relevance to skills needed in the job. Requiring years of experience for promotions might be explained as differentially valuing forms of capital men have more of, rather than in terms of the relevance of learning on the job the ability to handle the new position. I know of no empirical research that has tried to assess whether cultural capital or necessary skills explain job requirements that favor men. Such research would be relevant to what in the law is called discrimination on the basis of disparate impact. Here a criterion is applied neutrally to men and women. However, this "neutral" application favors men since they have more of this type of capital. If the type of capital is shown not to be relevant to performing the job well, discrimination has been found under the doctrine of disparate impact. Otherwise, the differential is not seen as discriminatory. (See Chapter 5 for a discussion of disparate impact proofs of sex discrimination in employment.)

Feminist critics of current job evaluation practices charge that the choice of factors and weights is biased in favor of men (Shepala and Viviano 1984; Hartmann, Roos, and Treiman 1985; Acker 1987; Steinberg and Haignere 1987). This criticism can be viewed as harmonious with theories of cultural capital. (See England and Dunn 1988 for an interpretation of studies by Barrett 1980; Phillips and Taylor 1980; Dex 1985; Acker 1987; and Reskin 1988 in this vein.) The contention is that the skills or tasks that typify female jobs will receive lower positive or even negative returns (weights) in comparison to skills and tasks typical to men's jobs. For example, physical strength, supervisory or managerial power, and mathematical skills may be highly valued because men are often in jobs requiring these. On the other hand, finger dexterity, verbal skills, and skills in nurturant human relations may receive low or negative returns precisely because female jobs are more likely to require them. Using the vocabulary of cultural capital, we could say that jobs that require typically male cultural capital are rewarded more than jobs that require typically female cultural capital, even if the female jobs contribute as much to firms' profits.

Kilbourne et al. (1990; Kilbourne 1991) draw from both cultural-feminist theory and the cultural capital view to make a similar argument. (Cultural-feminist theory is discussed more fully in Chapter 6.) The argument is that male power and biases in the culture lead to a devaluation not only of women, but also of all work done by women, and of the skills and activities typically performed by women. This would give rise to women's disadvantage in labor markets in ways that will often not appear to be overt discrimination simply because the criteria themselves are stacked in the interests of men. They show, for example, that there is a negative return to working in a job requiring nurturing social skills, even when cognitive and physical skills are held constant (Kilbourne et al. 1990, Kilbourne 1991).

However, even with the biases built into job evaluation systems, most of them find women's jobs underpaid, as discussed in Chapter 4. This finding, too, would be seen by conflict theorists as evidence of the exercise of male and/or employers' power. Conflict theory suggests that women's groups will have to organize and struggle to persuade employers and governments to raise the relative pay of female jobs. Establishing pay equity is not merely a matter of finding a technocratic way to measure job worth "objectively." The opposition being waged against pay equity initiatives by groups such as the U.S. Chamber of Commerce and the Eagle Forum (an organization of the new religious right) illustrates this point.

One unresolved debate within conflict theory is germane to comparable worth. This is the question of who benefits from sex discrimination: male workers, employers (generally capitalists, but sometimes governments), or both? Bonacich's (1972, 1976) theory of split labor markets discusses ethnic stratification with principles that might be generalized to gender stratification. She argues that the dominant group of workers benefits and capitalists lose from keeping minorities out of desirable jobs. Applying this logic to gender stratification suggests that men gain from segregating women into lower-paying jobs and from assigning low wages to women's occupations because employers who devalue women or the work they do can pay more to men. Some socialist feminists also hold this view. An alternative Marxist view, discussed above, sees sex discrimination increasing profits by a divide-and-conquer strategy that makes women's wages lower than men's, but *both* men's and women's wages lower than they would be in the absence of discrimination against women. In this view, what men would otherwise gain from discrimination is more than offset by the effects of discrimination on worker solidarity leading to lower wages for all workers. That is, if there were no discrimination, men would see that their interests are united with those of women, since both groups are workers, and through collective class organization, both men and women could gain wages higher than under discrimination. In this view, only capitalists gain from discrimination; it increases the rate of profit. As indicated in the discussion of Marxist views above, this is an important but empirically unresolved question within conflict views of discrimination.

D. *Structuralist Views*

In this section I combine two sociological views that have a structural focus in that they emphasize the causal effects of *positions* on individuals' outcomes. Unfortunately, the term *structuralism* now has so many meanings that it no longer carries much information about theoretical positions. (For a discussion of the various meanings of the term *structural* within sociology, see Wilson 1983, pp. 40–62.) Some see a structural analysis as one in which all concepts must be properties of systems (e.g., societies, organizations) rather than of their parts (e.g., occupational positions or their individual incumbents). Others do not see an analysis as structural unless all the concepts are defined relationally (as in some forms of network analysis, or as in a Marxist as opposed to a continuous view of class). Some see a structural analysis as one in which characteristics of positions held by individuals have causal effects on their behavior and rewards, even *net* of the characteristics of these individuals before they entered the positions. Here, I will use this latter definition. I will draw upon two distinct traditions that are structural in this sense, applying each to gender and labor markets. The first, the "new structuralism" in stratification research, deals with how job characteristics affect wages net of the race, sex, and human capital of the individuals in the positions. I then link this to a discussion of the "social structure and personality" school of social psychology, which emphasizes how structural positions, such as jobs, affect individuals' habits, preferences, and behavior. When we combine these two structural views and apply them to questions of gender inequality, they suggest a pattern of feedback effects between gender inequality in jobs and in households that helps explain the perpetuation of discrimination and its effects.

The new structuralism in stratification research arose as a reaction against the exclusive focus of status attainment research on individual and familial characteristics, and its neglect of how structural positions within labor markets affect rewards. The status attainment tradition (Blau and Duncan 1967; Featherman and Hauser 1978) showed how the socioeconomic status (education and occupational status) of one's father as well as one's own education affects one's occupational attainment and earnings. Variations on the model included other social-psychological characteristics that might be picked up in the home or neighborhood.

Initially, new structuralists borrowed heavily from theories of economic (Averitt 1968) and labor market (Doeringer and Piore 1971) segmentation being developed by institutionalist and radical economists. The literature on economic segmentation is often called the *dual economy* thesis. The notion is that the economy is divided into two sectors, often called *core* and *periphery*. The core contains large (sometimes multinational), unionized, oligopolistic firms with capital-intensive production, high profit rates, and high wages. These firms have internal labor markets that make promotions and wage increases with seniority likely. Firms that manufacture durable goods are mostly in the core. The periphery contains smaller firms with less unionization, more competition in product markets (i.e., many firms selling the same product), labor-intensive production, low profit rates, low wages, and dead-end jobs for many workers. (For reviews of the theory by sociologists see Beck, Horan, and Tolbert 1978; Wallace and Kalleberg 1981; Althauser and Kalleberg 1981; Hodson and Kaufman 1982; Farkas, England, and Barton 1988.)

As work in this tradition developed, it became clear that a unidimensional dualism is an inadequate representation of the segmentation at issue (Zucker and Rosenstein 1981; Coverdill 1988; Tigges 1988). That is, not all the proposed indicators of whether industries are marginal are highly correlated, not all have effects on earnings, and the cutting point between core and periphery is somewhat arbitrary. Thus, recent research has generally used multiple continuous indicators of sectoral marginality and advantage (Baron and Bielby 1980; Hodson 1984; Kalleberg, Wallace, and Althauser 1981).

To oversimplify and ignore many debates about how concepts should be operationalized, new structuralist research has shown that wages are generally higher in firms that are larger, more capital intensive, unionized, and more profitable (Beck et al. 1978; Tolbert, Horan, and Beck 1980; Kalleberg et al. 1981). The contention of the theory that *rates of return* to human capital are greater in more advantaged sectors has been supported much less consistently (Zucker and Rosenstein 1981; Hauser 1980).

Applications of this view to gender inequality have shown that part (most estimates are between 5 and 15%) of the sex gap in pay arises from women's concentration in marginal industries (Beck et al. 1980; Hodson and England 1986; Coverdill 1988). Yet women's concentration in marginal industries is much less important to the wage gap than is occupational sex segregation, segregation that exists in firms in all sectors.

How is the new structuralist view related to the literature on comparable worth? On the one hand, the focus is very different: Comparable worth addresses intraorganizational pay differences, while the new structuralism focuses on interindustry and interfirm variations in pay. The part of the gender gap in pay that new structuralist research has explained by men's and women's differential placement across industries cannot be reached by intrafirm job evaluations of the sort proposed by pay equity proponents. Yet the fact that sex *composition* is a characteristic of positions rather than of individuals renders comparable worth a structural issue. In addition, comparable worth shares with the new structuralism the contention that some structural positions have lower pay that is "uncompensated" (Farkas et al. 1988), i.e., not balanced by lower requirements for human capital or for working conditions requiring compensating differentials. That is, they share a claim that the neoclassical doctrine of "equalization at the margin" does not hold. Thus, in this more abstract sense, claims of comparable worth discrimination are very much in the spirit of the new structuralist view in their challenge to the neoclassical view and in their emphasis on effects of characteristics of positions. The literature on comparable worth also shares with the new structuralism an emphasis on pay differences for which there is no obvious explanation in functionalist theory.

This structural view of labor markets can be combined with a social-psychological view of the sort advanced by the "social structure and personality" school (e.g., Kohn and Schooler 1983; Kanter 1977). The labor market contains structural positions characterized by different kinds of work and by uncompensated advantages and disadvantages. Once sex discrimination gets started, effects of women's and men's structural positions in labor markets on their job and household behavior helps perpetuate the concentration of women in disadvantaged jobs. This combined view differs from the neoclassical view by insisting that institutional inertia and feedback effects between supply and demand sides of labor markets allow discrimination and its effects to persist indefinitely, despite market forces operating to erode discrimination (England and Farkas 1986).

Feedback effects are social-psychological consequences of discrimination that create new discrimination, or perpetuate groups' disadvantages that resulted originally from discrimination. Table 2.2 presents a

Table 2.2. A Typology of Feedback Effects from Discrimination

	Effects on	
Effects on	A. Employees' Behavior That Affects Rewards	B. Employers' Propensity to Discriminate
I. Effects of Discrimination on Current Adults		
1. Rational responses	I.A.1	I.B.1
2. Skills	I.A.2	I.B.2[2]
3. Habits, tastes, or cognitions	I.A.3[1]	I.B.3[1,2]
II. Effects of Discrimination on Next Generation		
1. Rational responses	II.A.1	II.B.1[2]
2. Skills	II.A.2	II.B.2[2]
3. Habits, tastes, or cognitions	II.A.3[1]	II.B.3[1,2]

Notes:
[1] Violates assumptions of neoclassical economic theory. "Habits" imply nonrationality, a violation of the rationality assumption. The notion that discrimination alters tastes violates the assumptions that tastes are unchanging and exogenous to economic models. The notion that cognitions are other than correct challenges the rationality assumption.
[2] Violates usual neoclassical conclusion that discrimination will eventually disappear from competitive market forces alone.

typology of such effects. The structuralist contention is that the *position* (in this case, job) one holds molds one's rational responses, as well as one's skills, habits, tastes, and cognitions. The last three of these five types of effects are incompatible with neoclassical theory.

Let us consider first the effects of discrimination on employees who are the victims of the discrimination (cells I.A.1–I.A.3 of Table 2.2). These effects of discrimination on jobs and earnings endure even if discrimination has declined. They involve alterations in employees' behavior caused by the demands and expectations of the jobs they hold. One such effect, rational responses to constraints (cell I.A.1 of Table 2.2.), is entirely compatible with neoclassical theory. For example, if discrimination steers women into jobs with little reward for seniority, frequent turnover is a rational response. The resultant lack of seniority will adversely affect later earnings, even if discrimination lessens. Similarly, sex discrimination makes it more rational for couples to emphasize the man's career and assign domestic responsibilities to the wife. This, in turn, limits the woman's later career prospects.

Discrimination may also affect the training and skills one attains on the job, and this affects future earnings (cell I.A.2 of Table 2.2.) Examples of this kind of effect abound. Women are concentrated in jobs offering less on-the-job training and such training has large effects on future earnings (Corcoran and Duncan 1979). When placement into the initial job is discriminatory, this sequence is a feedback effect from discrimination. Thus the common distinction between portions of group differences in earnings due to discrimination and portions due to human capital investment is blurred when discriminatory employers decide whose human capital to develop. Even when the "training" aspects of jobs are invisible, sociologists have shown that jobs with greater cognitive demands increase the intellectual abilities of jobholders, while jobs with less demands erode such abilities, and that this affects future job attainment (Kohn and Schooler 1983). Such effects undoubtedly exist for other kinds of skills as well.

This structuralist view of social psychology also posits that discrimination may affect the habits, tastes, or cognitions of current employees (cell I.A.3 of Table 2.2.) By "habits" I refer to behavioral patterns that are learned, perhaps initially because of their adaptive advantage, but that persist when they are no longer helpful and are even harmful. Habits have been emphasized by nonneoclassical institutionalist economists as well, as noted previously. The notion of habits that are harmful to an actor's own interests contradicts the neoclassical rationality assumption but is consistent with institutionalism in economics. The notion of "tastes" here is like that of economists; they refer to the preferences for experiences that give one "utility" (i.e., satisfaction or happiness). However, the notion that experiences in labor markets can affect workers' tastes is inconsistent with the usual neoclassical assumption that tastes are unchanging and exogenous to economic models (Lang and Dickens 1988). It is, however, consistent with framing models, discussed above. These models assert that one's cognitive evaluation as well as how much satisfaction one gets from a particular reward level is framed and thus affected by one's past rewards, themselves a function of one's structural position. Thus, the structuralist version of social psychology is incompatible with neoclassical economics in arguing that one's *position* can affect habits, cognitions, and tastes.

How might such effects of position on tastes and habits work to perpetuate effects of discriminatory job placements? If women are discriminatorily assigned to jobs demanding the social skills of nurturing rather than authoritative managing, this may cultivate women's preferences and habits toward nurturing work and men's toward managerial work (Kanter 1977).

Feedback from discrimination may also involve *intergenerational* effects such that the children of current employees are disadvantaged when they reach employment age because of consequences of discrimination against the previous generation of their race or sex group (cells II.A.1–

II.A.3 of Table 2.2). These intergenerational effects may involve rational responses, skills, tastes, cognitions, or habits. Developing any cognitions other than the "correct view" violates the rationality assumption. The possibility of habits the actor herself would define as "bad" violates the neoclassical rationality assumption. The idea that parents' jobs affect their children's tastes is inconsistent with the neoclassical assumptions of exogenous tastes, unless the family sphere in which the changes in tastes occur is considered exogenous to economic models (England and Kilbourne 1990a, p. 165).

So far we have examined feedback effects acting upon current or next-generation employees (cells I.A.1–I.A.3 and II.A.1–II.A.3 of Table 2.2). These involve perpetuation of the *disadvantage* that arises from discrimination rather than the perpetuation of discrimination itself. They are an example of what Feagin and Feagin (1978) call effects of past discrimination in the present. But since none of them involve the perpetuation or creation of discrimination itself, none of the effects in the A column of Table 2.2 challenge the neoclassical view that discrimination will erode in competitive markets. It is the effects involving employers (cells I.B.1–I.B.3 and II.B.1–II.B.3 of Table 2.2) that challenge this view.

When employers discriminate they create differences in the skills and habits of groups of employees, as discussed above. This in turn creates the conditions for statistical discrimination as a rational response (cell I.B.1 of Table 2.2). Further, if employers or their managers discriminate long enough, their "skills" in selecting applicants on the basis of merit may fail to develop or may atrophy, making continued discrimination likely (cell I.B.2 of Table 2.2.). In addition, the practice of discrimination may be self-perpetuating through inculcating discriminatory habits and tastes and through providing a frame for cognitions and tastes that make discrimination appear to be the right course of action (cell I.B.3 of Table 2.2). For example, consider the practice of discriminatory placement, which encourages occupational sex segregation. Such segregation may create a sufficient "taste" of male solidarity that male managers decide to collude with male workers rather than being the "free-riding arbitrageurs" who would contribute to the erosion of discrimination. All these effects may be intergenerational as well, such that the next generation of employers and managers grows up with reasons to engage in statistical discrimination, and the skills, tastes, cognitions, and habits compatible with other types of discrimination (cells II.B.1–II.B.3 of Table 2.2).

In sum, using Table 2.2, I have explored the implications of the social-structural view that sees positions as affecting the individuals who hold them, and have applied this view to the perpetuation of women's disadvantage. I began with a discussion of the causal cycle with discrimination. This does not mean that I believe that the demand side is always the "prime mover" in gender inequality. Rather, my goal was to show that a structural view implies that discrimination can beget both future disadvantage for women and future discrimination, even in competitive markets. Many of the mechanisms implied by this view are denied by neoclassical theory. These feedback effects between gender inequality in households and in labor markets are one key implication of a sociological view (England and Farkas 1986).

VII. Adjudicating Between Theories

In this section I identify and try to resolve five issues upon which the theories discussed above disagree. The issues are (a) whether deviations from rationality are random or are systematic in theoretically specified directions, (b) whether actors follow the interest of groups to which they belong even when it violates selfish interests, (c) whether preferences are exogenous or endogenous to economic outcomes, (d) whether the sort of discrimination at issue in comparable worth is merely a result of hiring discrimination, and whether any discrimination can persist in competitive markets, and (e) the probable effects on women's well-being if comparable worth policies were to be instituted. For each of these issues, I discuss how the issue is dealt with by those theories for which it is relevant, and then present my own view.

A. Rationality

The theories reviewed in this chapter differ in the degree of rationality they assume of actors in labor markets. The aspect of rationality at issue here is the process of making calculations and inferences regarding which means will best meet one's ends. Neoclassical theory assumes strict rationality. Employers are presumed to know how much the marginal worker in each job is contributing to the firm's profit. Workers are presumed to know the earnings trajectories in various occupations and the returns to various levels and types of human capital. While the costs of collecting data to make such computations are acknowledged by the new information economics, such costs are generally seen to lead to *random* rather than *systematic* errors.

Other theories posit systematic rather than merely random distortions in perceptions and calculations, biases that are a violation of strict rationality. Experimental work in behavioral economics and social psychology has shown systematic effects on decisions of how the options are framed. One's perception of benefits or costs of a choice are influenced by the context in which the decision occurs. These findings of systematic departures from rationality are relevant to comparable worth in several ways. First, because information on those who are socially similar to oneself enters the frame of wage comparisons particularly strongly, comparisons are likely to be made with others of the same sex and in a similar occupation, making devaluation of female occupations hard for anyone to see. Second, since past earnings are in the frame for evaluating current earnings, past wages in women's and men's jobs influence what is seen as an appropriate present wage by employers and employees. Both of these implications are examples of how, once discrimination starts, powerful forces of cognitive distortion by both workers and employers operate to keep it from being corrected.

Conflict theories, including Marxism, assume a basic tendency toward rationality, with two caveats: First, they posit collective rather than individual rationality, a point to which I return in discussing selfishness versus group self-interest below. Second, conflict theorists focus on power differentials, believing that those with greater resources will utilize those resources in part to disseminate communications that favor their positions. For example, since the U.S. Chamber of Commerce has more resources with which to disseminate its position on comparable worth than does the women's movement, this skews the information available to the public.

The social-psychological portion of the structuralist sociological view sketched above challenges the rationality assumption in yet another way. This view posits that one's structural position affects habits. For example, job roles can engender habits that make job mobility unlikely, even when such mobility is desired. The notion of a habit assumes a lack of reflection that allows one to persist in self-defeating behavior. In such cases, habits are irrational.

While all theories reviewed assume a basic orientation toward rationality among actors, all except the neoclassical theory specify circumstances under which cognition is systematically distorted. But relaxing the rationality assumption makes theories less able to generate determinate predictions than is possible from neoclassical theory. In my view, actors generally intend rationality, but often have their perceptions and calculations biased in systematic rather than merely random ways. The exceptions to rationality posited by behavioral economics, social psychologists, conflict theory, and the structuralist view of social psychology have important implications for comparable worth. They all suggest that discrimination and its effects are harder to root out than is suggested by the neoclassical view, in which market forces driven by rational actors are sufficient to reduce discrimination.

B. Selfishness versus Group Self-Interest

If rationality entails calculating the most efficient means to one's goals, a theory using rationality to generate predictions must also specify whether goals are set "selfishly." Alternatively, actors may see their interests in a collective fashion, and rationally pursue what is in the interest of the group, even when it conflicts with selfish individual interests. In those cases where collective and selfish interests diverge, a collective orientation amounts to selective altruism toward members of one's group. Such altruism in no way implies lack of rationality, but rather a different unit (the group rather than the individual) to which rationality is applied. The theories reviewed above differ in their assumption on this issue.

In a formal sense, neoclassical theory assumes self-interest, not selfishness, and self-interest does not necessarily preclude altruism (Friedman and Diem 1990). However, when economists discuss behavior in markets they generally presume interest to be pursued at the individual level (England forthcoming). This is sometimes made explicit by assuming that actors' utilities are not interdependent (Folbre forthcoming). This amounts to an individual selfishness assumption. (Yet, curiously, economists often see these same actors to be altruistic within the family.)

Sociologists who are functionalists often see elites as altruistic, leading to the apt criticism of functionalism that it does not recognize self-interested exercises of power.

Conflict theory, including its Marxist variety, presumes the eventual development of group consciousness and often ignores conflicts of interest between individuals within groups. For Marxists the relevant group is a class. Once class consciousness is achieved, members of classes are seen to operate in the interest of the class. For example, discrimination pursued by capitalists is seen as a divide-and-conquer strategy. But neoclassical theory points out the individual interest each capitalist has in being a free-riding arbitrageur on this collusive arrangement. A free rider would secretly sabotage fellow capitalists by hiring women in men's jobs for bargain wages made available by the colluders. If all capitalists acted as free riders, there would be no collusion from which to have benefits. Although this is seldom made explicit by Marxists, their notion of class consciousness presumes self-interest at the group level *and* selective altruism by individuals toward members of their class. Individuals are seen as altruistic enough to other members of their class to cooperate with them and resist a selfish free-rider stance. Yet they are self-interested enough on behalf of the class as a whole to lack any altruism or solidarity toward those outside the class.

This assumption of altruism toward in-group members but self-interest on behalf of one's group is implicit in non-Marxist varieties of conflict theory as well. However, in these theories, groups other than classes may be the collective on behalf of which one is assumed to renounce both individual selfishness vis-à-vis in-group members *and* any altruism felt toward out-group members. Non-Marxist conflict theorists see many potential groups other than classes as possible bases of collective action. These include gender, racial, cultural, or ethnic groups. I find this a more realistic view than the Marxist view that effectively sees classes as the only collectives whose members subordinate individual selfishness to group self-interest. However, one indeterminacy of such non-Marxist conflict theories is a difficulty predicting which of the various groups to which each individual belongs will engage her or him in collective action.

I believe that both selfishness and altruism abound in labor market institutions, and it is extremely difficult to make broad a priori assertions about which will prevail when. I find the neoclassical view that individual selfishness always overrides collective interests in market behavior to be implausible. But I am also unconvinced by the particular mix of selfishness and selective altruism assumed by Marxists and some other conflict theorists. Sometimes individuals are selfish in a way that undercuts their class or group, and sometimes they are moved by altruism for those outside their class or group. Neither of these two possibilities is recognized by conflict theorists, and the second is generally assumed out of existence by neoclassical economists. I believe that there are conflicting pulls toward both individual self-interest and group consciousness with which theories must contend (Elster 1979). For example, when do men transcend class or race barriers to engage in collective action that disadvantages women? This indeterminism makes generating predictions very difficult.

C. Preferences

What is the source of the preferences of actors in labor markets? Neoclassical theorists refer to preferences as tastes, and would include what sociologists call values or norms in this category as well. Neoclassical theory sees tastes as exogenous to economic models. That is, none of the variables in economic models are seen to affect tastes. Thus, the outcome of market processes (e.g., what job and wage one gets) cannot affect tastes, in this view. Efficiency wage models (part of the new neoclassical institutionalism) depart from orthodox theory in seeing em-

ployees' productivity as endogenous to their wage. For example, the
shirking model sees how hard one works as affected by one's wage in
comparison to the market wage that could be earned in another firm.
However, even here, *tastes* are not made endogenous to the wage; it is
not the *taste* for shirking that is altered by the wage in the model, but
rather the opportunity cost and thereby the probability of shirking.
Thus, efficiency wage models do not break with the neoclassical assumption that tastes are exogenous; this is true of other parts of the new
neoclassical institutionalism as well.

Other theories see tastes as affected by economic processes and outcomes. Behavioral economics can be interpreted as seeing tastes to be
framed just as cognitions are. For example, models of loss aversion posit
that decreases of a reward are seen to be worth more than increases of
the same amount. One's valuation of a reward, which is a taste, is
framed by one's current resource level.

The Marxist notion of false consciousness refers, at least in part, to
what in neoclassical terminology would be called endogenous tastes. For
example, Marxists would see the taste or gender group loyalty involved
in sex discrimination by male coworkers as false consciousness induced
by employers' efforts to divide and conquer the working class.

Sociological functionalism sees values as endogenous to the social
structures of the society. On this functionalists agree with conflict theorists, including Marxists. However, functionalism differs from conflict
theory in seeing prevailing values as functional for the whole society
rather than in the narrower interest of powerful groups. Here functionalists ignore the fact that power is often used in a self-interested
way, while conflict theorists ignore the possibility of altruistic behavior
on the part of elites toward nonelites.

Institutionalists among economists discuss how institutional practices
that were once functional become ceremonial tastes that have inertia
even when they are no longer rational. Thus, institutionalists also see
the possibility of endogenous tastes.

While some structuralist sociological views seek to make tastes entirely irrelevant, the view of structuralism I presented sees tastes as
affected by the structural role one holds.

In my view, tastes are often affected by economic processes and outcomes in ways described by each of the models other than the neoclassical model. This is relevant for comparable worth in two ways. First,
it explains how a discriminatory environment perpetuates itself, in part,
through creating tastes in women and men, and in employers and employees, that perpetuate segregation, the low pay of female jobs, and
discrimination. It also suggests that if comparable worth policies are
instituted, they will affect what wages employers and employees come

to think of as fair. Through changed values, this will create effects of the policy that are more salutary for women and that last longer than would be predicted by neoclassical theory.

D. The Nature and Persistence of Discrimination

The theories reviewed in this chapter differ in their notions about the nature and persistence of discrimination. Of particular interest here is the nature of the discrimination at issue in comparable worth. Neoclassical writing insists that if wages in predominantly female jobs are discriminatorily low, this must be because there are discriminatory barriers keeping women from entering male jobs, and this in turn leads to an artificially high supply of labor to female jobs, thus driving their wages down. Other views of the discrimination at issue in comparable worth, particularly in sociological and feminist writing, see a devaluation of jobs because they are filled by women and/or because they require skills traditionally seen as feminine. This is seen to lower the wages in female jobs relative to male jobs, irrespective of whether there is an artificially high supply of labor to female jobs.

I believe that there is an inconsistency in the neoclassical view that crowding is the sole source of discriminatory wages in women's jobs. In this view, employers devalue female *labor* for certain jobs such that they will not hire women unless they work for a lower wage than would be offered men. The devaluation of female labor is generally seen as motivated by tastes, statistical generalization, or group collusion. Yet, in seeing this as the sole discriminatory source of low wages in women's jobs, neoclassical writers implicitly reject the possibility that employers devalue certain jobs or job characteristics because of their present or historic association with women. But surely if the first devaluation is plausible, the second is as well. If employers tend to underestimate the value of women's labor for a given job in the hiring process, surely it is likely that they also tend to underestimate the contribution of the work done in women's jobs to the organization's productivity. Much of the radical/cultural-feminist view to be discussed in Chapter 6 centers on the fact that spheres of human endeavor associated with women have been systematically deprecated in Western thought and institutions. This devaluation is consistent with a cultural capital version of sociological conflict theory as well. I believe that both the devaluation of female labor for particular jobs (acknowledged by neoclassical theorists) *and* the devaluation of particular jobs or job characteristics because they are done by women or are seen as feminine (denied by neoclassical theorists) occur in labor markets.

These disagreements about the nature of sex discrimination have implications for the appropriateness of comparable worth policies. In a neoclassical view, comparable worth wages do nothing to eradicate what is seen as the underlying discrimination against women seeking entry to male jobs. Hence, they also do nothing about the crowding in female jobs. The view of discrimination I have advocated also recognizes the devaluation of jobs and job characteristics because they are presently done by women or traditionally associated with women. In this view, mandating higher relative wages in female jobs is precisely germane to the nature of the discrimination.

A second issue on which theories disagree regards whether discrimination can persist in a market economy. Most neoclassical theorists see the persistence of discrimination as an anomaly. The anomaly arises because market forces should erode discrimination as employers with a lesser propensity to discriminate take over more of product and labor markets because of their lower wage bill and higher profits. Neoclassical economists concede that statistical discrimination can persist in competitive markets, but do not believe that other kinds of discrimination can persist. Goldberg (1982) adds the caveat that taste discrimination could persist, *if* it involved the promale altruism of paying men more than MRP. But most neoclassical economists ignore this because they assume selfishness in market behavior.

I suggested that implicit contract theory (part of the new neoclassical institutionalism) can be used to explain how the process of the erosion of discrimination is slower where there are implicit contracts and internal labor markets. This is because in such settings competitive market forces operate only at moments of entry to firms, rather than throughout employees' life cycles. However, most neoclassical implicit contract theorists have ignored this implication of their theory.

Marxist models assume that discrimination will persist as long as capitalism does since it is rational for the capitalist class to divide and conquer workers. In my view, orthodox Marxists exaggerate the extent to which all sex discrimination is derivative of class relations.

Models from behavioral economics and structuralism in sociology offer discussions of how one's current position affects tastes, cognitions, and habits. Some of these claims are at odds with neoclassical assumptions of exogenous tastes and rationality, and thus help explain the persistence of discrimination and its effects.

Taken together, nonneoclassical perspectives provide ample theoretical reason to believe that discrimination is as self-reinforcing as it is self-destroying. Neoclassical theory sees only the latter. I believe that the arbitragelike market forces operating against discrimination posited in neoclassical theory *are* present. However, given the other effects discussed, they are usually not decisive. Thus, discrimination, including the sort at issue in comparable worth, is unlikely to disappear without governmental or other collective action.

E. Trade-offs between Gains and Losses from Comparable Worth Policies

Comparable worth policies are designed to remedy the wage inequality resulting from discriminatorily low wages for women's jobs. Would such policies do this? What would be the side effects? The theories reviewed above differ in the answers they suggest to these questions.

Neoclassical theory implies that wage gains some women make through comparable worth will lead to either disemployment or wage losses for others, and these others will be disproportionately female. I believe that this possibility of disemployment or crowding into uncovered sectors should not be ignored. However, the magnitude of the effect is an empirical question.

Other theories discuss effects that the elevated wages in female occupations would have that are ignored by neoclassical theory, effects that increase the benefits of comparable worth policies. Framing models suggest that higher wages in female occupations would start to remedy cognitive errors, norms, or tastes that devalue jobs held by women, and would start to create perceptions that higher relative wages for female/male occupations are fair. This would affect future wage setting practices even in the absence of continual enforcement efforts. These salutary effects should not be ignored in considering the benefits of such a policy, but they are ignored in neoclassical theory. On a more pessimistic note, conflict theorists remind us that the powerful groups behind discrimination will not change their practices without a serious struggle, a struggle for which they have disproportionate resources.

VIII. Conclusion: An Interdisciplinary View

I conclude this chapter by presenting an interdisciplinary view of labor markets, gender differentials, and comparable worth that draws upon those portions of the theories reviewed that I find most defensible. I certainly do not settle all points of disagreement between theories here, but focus on what a viable theory of labor markets would say about those questions most relevant to comparable worth: causes of occupational sex segregation and the sex gap in pay.

First, let us consider the question of what factors affect sex differences in the occupations in which men and women work. While the neoclassical theory of human capital does have some explanatory power explaining individuals' allocation to occupations (e.g., that education affects the job one obtains), it is of little use in explaining occupational *sex* segregation. Women and men in the labor market scarcely differ in average years of education, and at entry level they do not differ in experience, yet typically they are employed in very different jobs. Those applications of human capital theory that see differences in occupational choice hinging upon differences in *expected* experience have not generated predictions consistent with the data; women's occupations offer neither higher starting wages nor lower wage drops during time out of the labor force.

I believe that two factors explain occupational sex segregation, and they reinforce each other. Discrimination is the relevant demand-side factor. Employers prefer to hire men in some jobs and women in others. This type of discrimination may arise from indulging male workers' desires to exclude women. It may be based upon believing that it is improper for women to do some jobs, and men others. Or discrimination may be based on erroneous beliefs about women's abilities or turnover propensities. It may be based on women's larger variance on turnover. It may be based on divide-and-conquer attempts by employers. I do not have a strong view as to the relative contribution of these types of discrimination.

Neoclassical theorists argue that discrimination should not be able to persist in competitive markets. These arguments are ultimately unconvincing. The market forces specified by neoclassical theory do exist but are seldom decisive against forces articulated by other theoretical perspectives. For example, if discrimination is based on employers' taste for selective in-group "altruism" toward men, Goldberg (1982) has shown that it will not erode in competitive markets. Another reason that discrimination may not erode in competitive markets is because competitive forces impinge only upon hiring in entry-level jobs in firms with implicit contracts and internal labor markets. It may not erode because of institutional inertia via habits, or because discrimination has caused employers' skills for nondiscriminatory selection to atrophy.

A second factor in explaining men's and women's different occupational positions is sex role socialization. This is a supply-side factor, but relatively unrelated to the usual derivations from human capital theory. One could put sex role socialization into the language of human capital theory and say that women invest in different kinds of human capital than men, leading to different kinds of jobs. Girls may take secretarial courses while boys take "shop" and learn welding. College women major in nursing while men major in chemistry. But these are not issues of women investing in *less* human capital than men. Rather, they are issues of different kinds of investments reflecting the different interests or aspirations into which men and women have been steered by the socialization process. Women may often not realize the adverse implications on their future earnings of the decisions they are making, because information about earnings in jobs is often scarce. Although sex role socialization is a supply-side factor, to use the language of economics, it would be incorrect to see socialized job preferences as what economists would call exogenous tastes. Social-psychological research has shown that what one observes is often converted into what one thinks is morally proper. Thus, the distribution of women and men across occupations is an important input into the socialization of the next generation's values and tastes. This renders these tastes endogenous to economic outcomes at the system level. Socialization should also be seen as a lifelong process. If a woman enters a male job and is ridiculed and isolated by the men in the job, this may change her tastes to "preferring" a female job.

In sum, occupational sex segregation is established and perpetuated through the two processes of discrimination and sex role socialization.

What about the sex gap in pay? How is this explained? Three main factors are relevant: First, women, on average, have fewer years of seniority and labor force experience than men, and this explains somewhere between one quarter and one half of the sex gap in pay. This part of the explanation is consistent with human capital theory. The educational dimension of human capital is not very relevant, because men and women average approximately equal years of education.

What of the portion of the sex gap in pay not explained by human capital? It results mainly from the different jobs men and women hold. But what about these jobs leads women's jobs to pay less? Part of this may be that women are concentrated in jobs that are low on some of the skills or disamenities that neoclassical theories predict to affect wages. Another portion of the gap comes from the wage discrimination at issue in comparable worth. Jobs are discriminatorily assigned low wages when they are filled by women. This results in part from employers' sense of the propriety of paying men more. One could think of this as a taste, selective altruism toward male employees, or collusion with them. Second, the discriminatorily low pay in female jobs results from systematic cognitive errors in assessing the contribution that the work done in female occupations makes to organizations' profits or other goals. Neoclassical theorists reject both of these explanations, arguing that if discrimination is relevant at all, it must operate through barriers to women's entry into male jobs, which indirectly depress the wages in female occupations via crowding. I accept that crowding may occur, but as I have argued above, I think it inconsistent to believe that employers devalue women's *labor* when they engage in hiring decisions but do not also systematically devalue women's *jobs*. I believe that the *persistence* of this wage discrimination becomes plausible when we think about framing effects (discussed by social-psychologists and behavioral economists). This helps us to understand how errors in cognition about the value of women's jobs might persist, since present pay is in the frame used to assess the appropriateness of future pay. This also helps us to realize why it is difficult for women to develop a sense of injustice that might lead them to change jobs or to engage in collective action in favor of comparable worth.

All theorists agree that comparable worth policies would raise the relative wages of women in covered jobs. However, several of the theories other than neoclassical economics provide reasons to think that the policy, once instituted, would have long-term effects in this direction even in the absence of its continued enforcement—through its effects on the frame within which people evaluate the appropriateness of the wages of jobs and through institutional inertia. I suspect that the disemployment effects economic theory predicts would and do occur. While they will not affect only women, they will disproportionately affect women. Thus, the net assessments of benefit to women of the policy should take this possibility into account. Because changes in frames and institutional inertia make the potential benefits of such policies larger than would otherwise be the case, I make a more optimistic assessment than most neoclassical theorists of the potential gains for women of comparable worth. This is not to minimize the political difficulty of obtaining comparable worth wage adjustments of a nontrivial magnitude (see Steinberg forthcoming; Blum 1991; Acker 1989). It is rather to say that if these political hurdles can be overcome, the potential benefits to women are great.

One major conclusion of this chapter is that there is theoretical warrant for believing that the sort of discriminatory devaluation of women's jobs at issue in comparable worth is a salient and persistent feature of labor markets. I turn in Chapter 3 to a more detailed empirical analysis that provides evidence for this assertion.

Notes

1.   Technically speaking, the labor demand curve is equivalent to only the *downward-sloping* portion of the MRP curve, i.e., the portion in the range after marginal returns begin diminishing. Also, note that I use the term MRP rather

than the traditional marginal product (MP) or value of marginal product (VMP) because the latter two terms are appropriate only where product markets are competitive. In this case they equal MRP. However, MRP is the more general case; even where labor markets are competitive but product markets are not, the labor demand curve equals the downward-sloping portion of the MRP curve.

2.   This statement presumes, for expositional simplicity, that we can hold the supply and demand in one job constant while varying them in another job. In reality, supply and demand in each job are affected by the wage in the other job. For example, if one job becomes more lucrative, the number of people supplied to the other job at any given wage may be reduced, i.e., the location of the other job's supply curve shifts inward and upward. Also for simplicity, I have ignored the fact that supply or demand curves may differ in slope or elasticity as well as in level.

3.   The observation that predominantly female occupations have flatter wage trajectories *and* lower starting wages is possible to reconcile with neoclassical theory if (1) lack of on-the-job human capital investment explains the lower trajectories, which, other things equal, we would expect to be accompanied by higher starting wages, while (2) compensating differentials explains the lower starting wages. However, in one analysis that introduced a large number of job characteristics to control for compensating differentials, female jobs were still found to have lower starting wages (England et al. 1988). Another possible reconciliation is suggested by Kuhn (1991).

4.   However, we should not leap to the conclusion that all sex discrimination is statistical. In their analysis of 1960s and 1970s data from approximately 300 businesses in California, Bielby and Baron (1986) found that many employers openly stated that they reserved some jobs for one sex or the other. In many such jobs, the skills required were *not* skills on which there are commonly known sex differences in average attainment (as might be argued, for example, for upper body strength). Thus, the thrust of Bielby and Baron's argument is to minimize the importance of statistical discrimination based on real group differences in means. Rather, they stress that segregation derives mainly from other forms of discrimination, such as what I call taste or error discrimination. They also stress that these forms of discrimination may perpetuate stereotypes, leading to further discrimination, and sometimes becoming self-fulfilling prophecies leading to later statistical discrimination.

5.   There is one exception to the statement that neoclassical theory predicts comparable worth policies to cause disemployment. If a monopsony model of discrimination is assumed, disemployment will not necessarily result (Kahn 1986; Ehrenberg and Smith 1987). Competitive employers can hire all the labor they want at the market wage, and none at a lower wage. By contrast, a monopsonistic employer faces the entire market's labor supply curve, and thus has to pay *all* workers hired a higher wage in order to increase the quantity employed. Put another way, since a monopsonist is the entire demand side of the labor market, s/he can only hire more workers by increasing the wage paid to all workers. Thus, for monopsonists, the cost of the marginal worker is more than his or her wage. As a consequence, many monopsonists employ fewer workers than they would prefer at the existing wage, and thus would cut back fewer workers than would a competitive employer in the face of a required increase in the wage in female jobs.

6.   U.S. government statistics distinguish between those who are unemployed and those who are out of the labor force. The unemployed are those who

do not have a job but are actively looking for one. Those not looking for a job are instead counted as out of the labor force. This includes homemakers, retirees, students, and those who have become discouraged and given up looking for work. A mandated wage increase in female jobs might add people to both categories. The term *disemployment* is used by economists to refer to increases in either category.

7. *Moral hazard* is a term used by economists to refer to incentive systems, particularly those involving insurance of any sort, that reduce the incentives for "good" behavior. For example, from the point of view of insurance companies, the moral hazard problem about auto insurance is that once the insurance is bought, people's individual self-interest-based incentive to drive carefully is reduced.

8. The "new analytical Marxism" rejects the labor theory of value, but retains the conclusion that workers are exploited under capitalism (Roemer 1988). In this view, the basis of exploitation is unequal initial endowments of property; those with little or no property are exploited whether those who own more property hire them as workers or whether they rent the property owners' capital to engage in self-employment. Under the orthodox labor theory of value, the latter would not entail exploitation.

9. In a Marxist-feminist view, homemakers perform reproductive labor, which benefits capitalists in re-creating the current generation of workers and producing the next generation. This labor contributes to surplus value formation. Thus, the innovation of Marxist feminists was to deviate from the orthodox Marxist contention that homemakers are not, technically speaking, exploited by capitalists, because surplus value is not extracted from their labor. Most socialist feminists agree with the Marxist-feminist contention that homemakers are exploited by capitalists. However, because they recognize patriarchy as an independent system, socialist feminists also see homemakers as oppressed by the men they live with. Thus, the difference between socialist feminists and Marxist feminists on questions of domestic labor is parallel to the difference between socialist feminists and orthodox Marxists on questions of sex discrimination in paid labor. In each case, socialist feminists refuse to accept the contention that women's disadvantage is *simply* a derivative of capitalist class relations. In each case, socialist feminists argue that it is at least partly a result of patriarchy. See Chapter 6 for further discussion of the issue.

3

Pay in Female and Male Occupations:
Findings from National Data

I. Introduction

Across the national economy, female jobs (i.e., jobs filled primarily with women) usually pay less than male jobs. What explains this lower pay in female jobs? In particular, how important a factor is the sort of wage discrimination at issue in comparable worth? What other factors are operative in explaining why some occupations pay more than others, and, more specifically, in explaining why female occupations pay less than male occupations? This chapter explores these questions, using 1980 census data. I will not be concerned here with explanations of why men and women get into the occupations they hold, nor with lack of equal pay for men and women in the same job, topics discussed in earlier chapters. Here I narrow the focus to an empirical analysis directly relevant to comparable worth: whether an occupation pays less if it is "women's work."

Among full-time year-round workers in the United States, the 1980 census showed a sex gap in pay of \$3.39/hour, with men averaging \$8.59/hour compared to women's \$5.20/hour. This overall gap is not the same as the pay gap between female and male occupations, since not all women are in female occupations, nor are all men in male occupations, and since there is also a sex gap in pay within occupations. However, a portion of this overall sex gap in pay *is* due to female jobs paying less than male jobs. In general, the higher the percentage of females in an occupation, the less the job pays either men or women. For example, in the census data used in this chapter, when summarized as a linear relationship, pay and sex composition are related such that those in occupations that are virtually all male earn approximately \$1.00/hour more than those in occupations that are virtually all female. This relationship holds both for men and women, so that men as well as women have lower wages if they work in a predominantly female occupation.[1] This relationship between sex composition and earnings contributes to the sex gap in pay. My interest here is to determine how much of the overall sex gap in pay, and of the pay gap between male and female occupations, can be explained by the sort of between-occupation wage discrimination at issue in comparable worth. This requires a statistical analysis that controls for characteristics of occupations that influence their wages for reasons other than gender bias.

What are the major explanations of why female occupations pay less than male occupations? Thinking about logical possibilities will suggest what variables need to be included as controls in the analysis, and what variables' effects will index gender-based wage discrimination. Several possibilities must be considered:

1. Women may be concentrated in occupations that require less cognitive, social, or physical skills. The idea that the skill level required by a job affects its wage is consistent with the functionalist theory of stratification as well as with human capital theory in economics (both discussed in Chapter 2).

2. A lower proportion of women than men may be in jobs involving supervisory social skills. Marxist theory (discussed in Chapter 2) predicts that jobs involving managerial or supervisory authority pay more, not due to their skill requirements, but due to their class location.

3. Men may be concentrated in occupations with less pleasant or more onerous working conditions (such as danger, dirt, or stress); and employers may have to pay a wage premium to fill jobs with greater nonpecuniary disamenities or less nonpecuniary amenities. Economists' theory of compensating differentials, discussed in Chapter 2, predicts this.

4. Women may be concentrated in jobs that require less effort. If expending effort is onerous to workers, then the theory of compensating differentials would predict effort to affect wages positively.

5. Female occupations may be concentrated in industries or firms that have lower wage scales for some reason other than the fact that women work in them. Theories of efficiency wages proposed by economists as well as the new structuralism in sociological stratification research suggest the importance of such factors in wage determination. (See Chapter 2.)

The discussion so far suggests that an analysis to detect wage discrimination against female occupations in the economy at large must adjust out of any estimates of such discrimination differences in pay due to skill demands, working conditions that tap required effort and other amenities and disamenities, and industrial and firm characteristics.

6. In addition, women's occupations may have lower wages because they are crowded. This will result if hiring discrimination keeps women out of male occupations, and this creates an artificially large supply of labor to the jobs in which employers will hire women. This oversupply or crowding of female jobs may then explain their lower wages, according to economist Bergmann's (1974, 1986) crowding thesis, discussed in Chapter 2. Unfortunately, I know of no way to disentangle this portion of the wage gap from the estimate of direct wage discrimination against female occupations.

7. Female occupations may have their wages lowered by the direct sort of wage discrimination at issue in comparable worth. What I term direct gender bias occurs when employers respond to an occupation's sex composition in setting its wage level. If an occupation is filled largely by women (for whatever reasons, discriminatory or not), employers may discriminate in wage setting by offering lower wages to (both male and female) workers in the occupation. This direct gender bias will be assessed by estimating the effect of occupations' percentage female on the wages they offer, net of control variables designed to capture effects involved in other explanations.

8. Women's occupations may require kinds of skills, such as nurturant social skills, that have lower or negative rates of return compared to the skills typically required by men's jobs. This indirect sort of gender bias in occupational wage determination is also part of what is at issue in comparable worth. It will be assessed by comparing the returns to nurturant social skills, the one clear example of a type of skill associated with women's traditional sphere, to returns for other skills (such as physical, cognitive, or supervisory skills) more commonly required by male occupations. Both direct and indirect gender bias in occupational wage setting are plausible predictions from those conflict theories in sociology that deal with gender, including Marxist and feminist views. (See Chapter 2.)

9. Women's jobs may also employ more racial or ethnic minorities, and this may depress the wages in such jobs as a result of racial or ethnic bias in wage setting. Just as there could be a devaluation of a job leading to lower wages because the occupation is predominantly female, such bias in wage setting could exist for jobs with concentrations of African Americans and Mexican Americans as well. Various conflict theories in sociology suggest that both the race and sex composition of jobs may affect their earnings.

II. Data and Variables

A. *Units of Analysis*

The analysis to follow uses a dataset in which 1980 census detailed (three-digit) occupations are the units of analysis. All jobs have been categorized by the Census Bureau into 503 occupational categories. There are 403 of these occupations that do not have missing values on any of the variables. All regressions, means, and decompositions presented in this chapter are based on these 403 occupations.[2]

The Census Bureau's detailed occupational classification is used because it provides the most detailed categories for which national data on earnings are available. However, these categories are less detailed than the job titles used within many firms. Thus, some of the sex gap in pay *within* these occupational categories may arise from sex segregation of more detailed job categories. This portion of the pay gap will not get counted in the estimates I provide of how much of the overall sex gap in pay is explained by gender bias in occupational wage settings. Thus, estimates provided here could be underestimates of direct gender bias in wage setting.

B. *Description of Variables*

Variables used in the regression analyses reported in this chapter are described below. I first describe the variables in groups discussed together for conceptual reasons. In the next section, I discuss the data sources for the variables. All variables used in any of the regression models to be presented are listed in Table 3.1, which also gives the data source for each variable. As the discussion proceeds, I will identify each variable with a short, descriptive name, given in capital letters.

The independent variables are included as measures of factors that may affect the earnings that occupations offer. I am particularly interested in the effect of sex composition on earnings. Other variables that are correlated with sex composition may also provide partial explanations for why male occupations generally pay more than female occupations.

In dividing variables into groups, I distinguish between indicators of skill demands and indicators of amenities or disamenities. The former are relevant to predictions from human capital theory. The theory suggests that, insofar as any kind of skill has costs (even opportunity costs) of acquisition, occupations requiring more of it will pay more, controlling for other factors. Measures of amenities and disamenities are

Table 3.1. Description of Variables Used in Regression Analyses[1]

Variable	Description	Source	N^2
Sex composition			
% FEMALE	% Female of all FTYR wkrs in occ	U.S. Census 1980	503
Race composition			
% BLACK	% Black of all wkrs in occ	Census P.U.M.S.	503
% MEXICAN	% Mexican of all wkrs in occ	Census P.U.M.S.	503
Cognitive skill and training demands			
COMPLEXITY W/ DATA	Complexity of task w/ data	DOT	495
GEN'L EDUC	General education (schooling)	DOT	495
INTELLIGENCE	Intelligence	DOT	495
NUMERICAL APTITUDE	Numerical aptitude	DOT	495
VERBAL APTITUDE	Verbal aptitude	DOT	495
FEM EDUC	Mean education in years of women in occ	Census P.U.M.S.	502
MALE EDUC	Mean education in years of men in occ	Census P.U.M.S.	503
FEM PERCENT COLLEGE	% Women w/ 4 or more years college	Census P.U.M.S.	502
MALE PERCENT COLLEGE	% Men w/ 4 or more years college	Census P.U.M.S.	503
VOC OR OJT TRAINING	Vocational or OJT time, in months	DOT	495
LEARN NEW THINGS	Need to learn new things on the job	Filer, QES	432
COGNITIVE FACTOR	Factor created with above 11 variables; principal-components factor analysis	Created by author	430
FEM EXPER	Mean estimated wk experience of women in occ	Filer, NLS, Census	431
Social skill demands			
AUTHORITY	Dummy variable for whether occ involves supr or mgr authority over other wkrs	Coded by author	503
NURTURANCE	Dummy variable for whether occ involves nurturance toward clients or customers	Coded by author	503
COMPLEXITY W/ PEOPLE	Complexity of task in relation to people	DOT	495
DEAL W/ PEOPLE	% Wkrs req to deal w/ people beyond give/take instructions	DOT	495

(continued)

Table 3.1. (Continued)

Variable	Description	Source	N^2
SOCIAL COMPLEXITY SCALE	Variable created by averaging Z scores of 2 variables above	Created by author	495
INFLUENCE	% Wkrs req to influence people in opinions, judgments	DOT	495
Physical skill demands			
COMPLEXITY W/ THINGS	Complexity of task in relation to things	DOT	495
EYE-HAND-FOOT COORD	Eye-hand-foot coordination req	DOT	495
SPATIAL APT	Spatial aptitude req	DOT	495
MOTOR COORD	Motor coordination req	DOT	495
MANUAL DEXTERITY	Manual dexterity req	DOT	495
STRENGTH	Physical strength req	DOT	495
CLERICAL PERCEPTION	Clerical perception req	DOT	495
MEASUREMENT	% Wkrs req to make judgments based on measurement	DOT	495
PRECISION	% Wkrs req to meet precise technical standards	DOT	495
Amenities			
SOCIETAL CONTRIB	Extent to which wkrs place imp on making contrib to society	Filer, FPC	432
EFFECT ON OTHERS	Extent to which wkrs see performance in job to affect others	Filer, QES	432
PRESTIGE	% Wkrs involved in activ resulting in prestige	DOT	495
CREATIVE	% Wkrs involved in abstract and creative activ	DOT	495
SELF-DETER WORK SPEED	Wkr report of self-determination of work speed on job	Filer, QES	432
ADEQ TIME FOR JOB	Wkr report of adequate time to perform job	Filer, QES	432
SELF-DETER HAPPENINGS	Wkr report of self-determination of happenings on job	Filer, QES	432
% MEDICAL INSUR	% Wkrs w/ medical insurance	Filer, Census P.U.M.S.	432
POWER	Extent to which wkrs place importance on power	Filer, FPC	432
CONTROL	% Wkrs w/ responsibility for direction, control, planning	DOT	495

130

Disamenities

EMERGENCY STRESS	% Wkrs req to peform under stress in emergency, etc.	DOT	495
REPETITION	% Wkrs performing repetitive work	DOT	495
AGAINST CONSCIENCE	Extent to which wkrs report performing tasks against conscience on job	Filer, QES	432
FUMES	Atmospheric conditions, esp fumes	DOT	495
COLD	% Wkrs working in extreme cold	DOT	495
HAZARDS	% Wkrs facing physical hazards	DOT	495
HEAT	% Wkrs working in extreme heat	DOT	495·
OUTDOORS	% Wkrs working outdoors	DOT	495
WET	% Wkrs working in wet or humid conditions	DOT	495
ATTACK HAZARD	Wkrs report of danger of attack by people or animals	Filer, QES	432
STOOP	% Wkrs req to stoop, kneel, crouch, or crawl	DOT	495
CLIMB	% Wkrs req to climb or balance	DOT	495
REACH/HANDLE	% Wkrs req to reach or handle	DOT	495
NOISE	% Wkrs experiencing noise or vibrations	DOT	495

Effort

EFFORT REL TO TV	Wkrs report of effort on job relative to effort to watch TV	Filer, D&S	432
EFFORT	Wkrs report of effort required	Filer, QES	432
EXTRA EFFORT	Wkrs report of extra effort expended	Filer, QES	432
FAMILY IMPORTANCE	Extent to which wkrs in occ report importance of family to them	Filer, FPC	432
% FEM MARRIED	% Females in occ who are married	Filer, Census P.U.M.S.	439

Industrial and organizational characteristics

% GOVT	% Wkrs in occ work for fed, state, or local government	Census P.U.M.S.	502
% SELF-EMPLOYED	% Wkrs in occ who are self-employed	Census P.U.M.S.	502
% UNION	% Wkrs in occ in a union	Filer, KLK	432
INDUS CAP INTENS	Occ mn of industries' assets per employee	Hodson	497
INDUS OLIGOPOLY	Occ mn of industries' % of sales by top 8 firms	Hodson	473

(continued)

131

Table 3.1. (Continued)

Variable	Description	Source	N^2
INDUS FOR DIVIDENDS	Occ mn of industries' mn $ of dividends from foreign subsid per firm	Hodson	497
INDUS SALES TO GOVT	Occ mn of industries' $ of sales to government	Hodson	497
INDUS SALES PER WKR	Occ mn of industries' $ of sales per employee	Hodson	473
INDUS PROFITS	Occ mn of industries' net income per $ value of assets	Hodson	473
INDUS SALES PER FIRM	Occ mn of industries' mean sales per firm	Hodson	475
INDUS EARNINGS	Occ mn of industries' median earnings	U.S. Census 1980	502
Earnings			
FEMALE HOURLY EARNINGS	Mn hourly earnings of women in ECLF who worked FTYR in 1979	U.S. Census 1980	503
MALE HOURLY EARNINGS	Mn hourly earnings of men in ECLF who worked FTYR in 1979	U.S. Census 1980	503
Weights			
NUMBER WOMEN, FTYR	Number women working in occ FTYR, 1979	U.S. Census 1980	503
NUMBER MEN, FTYR	Number men working in occ FTYR, 1979	U.S. Census 1980	503

Key to sources (see text for further details):
Census P.U.M.S., U.S. Census, 1980, Public-Use Microdata Sample.
D&S, measure from Duncan and Stafford (1980).
DOT, *Dictionary of Occupational Titles,* 4th edition.
Filer, data provided by Randall Filer (1989).
FPC, data from Filer Psychological Consultants (Filer 1989).
Hodson, data on industrial characteristics provided by Hodson.
KLK, measure from Kokkelenberg and Sockell (1985).
NLS, *National Longitudinal Survey.*
QES, *Quality of Employment Survey.*
U.S. Census 1980, published volumes from 1980 census.

[1] Abbreviations used: activ, activities; apt, aptitude; contrib, contribution; ECLF, experienced civilian labor force; esp, especially; exp, experience; fem, female; FTYR, full-time year-round; imp, importance; mgr, manager; mn, mean; occ, occupation; OJT, on-the-job training; rel, relative; req, required; subsid, subsidiaries; supr, supervisor; voc, vocational; w/, with; wk, work; wkr, worker.
[2] Number of nonmissing values for this variable.

132

relevant to testing for compensating differentials. However, we really cannot make a clear distinction between skills and amenities/ disamenities. In particular, skill demands can also be thought of as amenities or disamenities that the market may price via compensating differentials. That is, if the marginal worker does not like exercising a certain skill, having to do so is a disamenity, and jobs requiring this skill may have to pay more to be filled than jobs requiring skills that the marginal worker enjoys exercising. If the marginal workers enjoys exercising a particular skill, then the neoclassical view admits the possibility that the negative effect of this on wages could partially, fully, or even more than offset the wage premium required for acquiring the skill.

I began with a list of all variables available to me that might plausibly have effects on occupations' pay. This list was shortened somewhat to avoid multicollinearity; I dropped variables so that no pair had correlations over 0.75.[3] In most cases where a variable was dropped, another indicator of the same concept was retained.

Three variables were dropped because they generated implausible coefficients in the full regression model. These variables measured the average time traveled to work, the percentage of time at work spent not working, and the percentage of time at work spent "goofing off" by those in the occupation. Average time it takes to travel to work among people in the occupation was classified as a disamenity, predicted to have a positive effect on earnings. A positive effect was found, but it was so large as to be implausible. For men, each extra minute of travel was associated with 14 cents per hour, and for women, with 8 cents per hour. This means, for example, that for one occupation that had an average travel time of 20 minutes more than another, we would expect average earnings for men to be $2.80/hour higher. Given these large coefficients, the small difference between the male and female means of 2 minutes explained 5 or 8% of the sex gap in pay. In the case of percentage of time at work spent not working, the coefficients were even more implausible. Each extra one percentage point *not* working *increased* men's earnings by 67 cents per hour and women's by 9 cents per hour. Here both sexes' means were within one percentage point of 17%. In the case of percentage of time goofing off, men's mean was 6%, while women's was 5%. Again, the coefficients were implausible. Each extra 1% of average time spent goofing off was associated with a 39 cents/hour *increase* in wages for men. (The 7 cents/hour decrease for women is more plausible.) My judgment is that these measures are tapping something other than what they ostensibly measure. One criticism I have of Filer's (1989) analysis is his inclusion of these variables.

Some of the variables were originally coded in a counterintuitive manner, so that a higher score indicated less of the characteristic for which the variable is named. To make interpretation of results simpler, all these codings were reversed before an analysis was undertaken. Thus in all tables and discussions in this chapter, one can assume that variables are coded so that a higher score indicates more of the named characteristic, and thus a positive coefficient in an earnings regression indicates that occupations with more of the characteristic pay more, net of the other factors controlled. All variables described as percentages are expressed in percentage points (0–100) rather than as proportions.

Sex Composition. An independent variable of major interest is % FEMALE, the percentage female of those who were employed full-time year-round in the occupation in 1980. In theory, occupations can range from 0 to 100% female, although there are no values quite this extreme. The occupation with the highest % FEMALE was secretary, of which 98.8% were women. Typists, child care workers, and dental assistants were also over 97% female. There were 18 occupations containing over 99% males in 1980. They include architects, firefighters, auto mechanics, plumbers, and supervisors in a number of blue-collar trades. As in previous chapters, I will sometimes refer to male or female occupations in discussing the analysis. However, the reader should remember that all analyses reported in the tables of this chapter treat occupations' sex composition as a continuum from 0 to 100% female.

One limitation of the ability of the analysis to measure the extent of wage discrimination against female jobs should be noted. I cannot directly measure crowding, since there is no way to measure oversupply of labor to an occupation. The data tell us the number of people employed in each occupation, but we cannot infer that the larger the number is, the higher the supply, since a large number employed may also indicate more demand. Nor can we measure oversupply by the unemployment rate among people formerly employed in that occupation, since unemployment may be affected by whether employment in this occupation is sensitive to the business cycle, as well as by crowding. Thus, net effects of sex composition on wages may indicate some combination of crowding in women's occupations due to discriminatory exclusion of women from male jobs, and the devaluation of occupations because they are filled largely with women.

Race Composition. The analysis also includes variables measuring the percentage of blacks (% BLACK) and Mexicans (% MEXICAN) among workers in each occupation. Mexican workers include both Mexican Americans and Mexican nationals.

Cognitive Skill and Training Demands. The amount of cognitive skill and training required by occupations is a concept for which many detailed measures are available. As Table 3.1 shows, measures were available for how much the occupation was judged by experts to require complexity dealing with data (COMPLEXITY W/ DATA), education of the sort obtained in school (GEN'L EDUC), INTELLIGENCE, NUMERICAL APTITUDE, and VERBAL APTITUDE, and by how much respondents in a national survey reported that their job requires learning new things (LEARN NEW THINGS). A measure was also available for the mean education of women (FEM EDUC) and of men (MALE EDUC) in each occupation, as well as for the percentage of women with at least four years of college (FEM PERCENT COLLEGE) and of men (MALE PERCENT COLLEGE). Vocational and on-the-job training (VOC OR OTJ TRAINING) measures the number of months of training that it is standard for those in the occupation to receive in vocational education, in high school or college courses that are directly relevant to the job, or in on-the-job training. All these measures of cognitive skill and training are highly intercorrelated. Thus, attempts to net out their separate effects on earnings would be hampered by multicollinearity, a statistical problem produced when independent variables are so highly correlated that attempts to isolate their individual effects produce coefficients that are highly unstable from sample to sample. In such cases, it is not advisable to enter such variables in the same regression equation. Thus, these measures of cognitive skill and training were combined into one measure through a factor analysis of this list of items. Although each of the variables is listed separately in Table 3.1, the regression analyses reported in this chapter always use what I term the COGNITIVE FACTOR in place of these variables. The principal-component analysis yielded only one factor with an eigenvalue above 1. Table 3.2 shows how each of these variables loaded on the COGNITIVE FACTOR.

Table 3.2. Factor Loadings on the Cognitive Factor

Variables	Loadings
COMPLEXITY W/ DATA	0.30
VOC OR OJT TRAINING	0.27
LEARN NEW THINGS	0.25
GEN'L EDUC	0.32
INTELLIGENCE	0.32
VERBAL APTITUDE	0.32
NUMERICAL APTITUDE	0.29
FEM EDUC	0.31
MALE EDUC	0.31
FEM PERCENT COLLEGE	0.30
MALE PERCENT COLLEGE	0.30

Social Skill Demands. I used four measures of social skills. The first, SOCIAL COMPLEXITY SCALE, is a scale made by combining two measures that were too highly correlated to allow estimation of their separate effects. The two variables measured the complexity of the task in relation to people (COMPLEXITY W/ PEOPLE) and the percentage of works required to deal with people beyond giving and taking instructions (DEAL W/ PEOPLE). To make the scale, both were converted to standardized scores so they would have the same metric (a mean of 0 and a standard deviation of 1). Then an unweighted average of the two was taken for each occupation. This average is the SOCIAL COMPLEX-ITY SCALE.

Three other measures of social skill were included to distinguish between different types or applications of social skill. One type is managerial or supervisory skill, where one wields authority over other workers. This was measured with a dummy variable called AUTHORITY, which I coded 1 if the job involved management or supervision of other workers and 0 otherwise. Basically, these were all occupations with the word *manager* or *supervisor* in the title. They included lower, middle, and upper levels of management in both the public, private, and not-for-profit sectors, as well as foremen and other supervisors of blue-collar workers. A second judge coded occupations as to which involve authority over other workers as well. A zero-order correlation of 0.76 showed a fairly high degree of interjudge reliability. My codings were used in the analysis. Table 3.3 provides a list of all occupations coded 1 on AUTHORITY.

One can also exercise nurturant skill (NURTURANCE), an application of social skills to activities providing a service to customers or clients. This was measured by a dummy variable that I coded 1 if, in my judgment, the job involves providing a service to an individual or small group with whom the worker has a face-to-face relationship. This service providing need not be the only task involved in the job, but it must be one of the major activities on which people working in the occupation spend time. The service must be provided to clients or customers, not coworkers or managers. A second judge also coded occupations on this variable, using the criteria stated above. A zero-order correlation of 0.70 showed a fairly high degree of interjudge reliability. My codings were used in the analysis. Table 3.4 lists all the occupations coded as involving nurturant skill.

A final measure of social skill is INFLUENCE, which measures the extent to which members of the occupation are called upon to influence people's opinions or attitudes. These might be workers, clients, customers, or others. Some occupations that score high on this variable are also coded as nurturant occupations, since the service that is performed involves influencing. Examples are clergy, teachers, and sales workers.

Table 3.3. Occupations That Were Coded 1 As Involving Authority

Title	Census Code
Chief executives and general administrators, public administration	004
Administrators and officials, public administration	005
Administrators, protective services	006
Financial managers	007
Personnel and labor relations managers	008
Purchasing managers	009
Managers, marketing, advertising, and public relations	013
Administrators, education and related fields	014
Managers, medicine and health	015
Managers, properties and real estate	016
Postmasters and mail superintendents	017
Funeral directors	018
Managers and administrators, not elsewhere classified	019
Supervisors and proprietors, sales occupations	243
Supervisors, general office	303
Supervisors, computer operators	304
Supervisors, financial records processing	305
Chief communications operators	306
Supervisors, distribution, scheduling, and adjusting clerks	307
Supervisors, firefighting and fire prevention occupations	413
Supervisors, police and detectives	414
Supervisors, guards	415
Supervisors, food preparation and service occupations	433
Supervisors, cleaning and building service workers	448
Supervisors, personal service occupations	456
Managers, farms, except horticultural	475
Managers, horticultural specialty farms	476
Supervisors, farm workers	477
Supervisors, related agricultural occupations	485
Supervisors, forestry and logging workers	494
Captains and other officers, fishing vessels	497
Supervisors, mechanics and repairers	503
Supervisors, brickmasons, stonemasons, and tile setters	553
Supervisors, carpenters and related workers	554
Supervisors, electricians and power transmission installers	555
Supervisors, painters, paperhangers, and plasterers	556
Supervisors, plumbers, pipefitters, and steamfitters	557
Supervisors, construction, not elsewhere classified	558
Supervisors, motor vehicle operators	803
Ship captains and mates, except fishing boats	828
Supervisors, material moving equipment operators	843
Supervisors, handlers, equipment cleaners, and laborers, not elsewhere classified	863

Table 3.4. Occupations That Were Coded 1 As Involving Nurturance

Title	Census Code
Physicians	084
Dentists	085
Optometrists	087
Podiatrists	088
Health diagnosing practitioners, not elsewhere classified	089
Registered nurses	095
Inhalation therapists	098
Occupational therapists	099
Physical therapists	103
Speech therapists	104
Therapists, not elsewhere classified	105
Physicians' assistants	106
Prekindergarten and kindergarten teachers	155
Elementary school teachers	156
Secondary school teachers	157
Special education teachers	158
Teachers, not elsewhere classfied	159
Educational and vocational counselors	163
Librarians	164
Social workers	174
Recreation workers	175
Clergy	176
Religious workers	177
Licensed practical nurses	207
Motor vehicles and boats sales workers	263
Apparel sales workers	264
Shoe sales workers	265
Furniture and home furnishing sales workers	266
Radio, television, hi-fi, and appliances sales workers	267
Hardware and building supplies sales workers	268
Parts sales workers	269
Other commodities sales workers	274
Sales counter clerks	275
Cashiers	276
Hotel clerks	317
Transportation ticket and reservation agents	318
Receptionists	319
Information clerks, not elsewhere classified	323
Bank tellers	383
Teachers' aides	387
Child care workers, private household	406
Bartenders	434
Waiters and waitresses	435
Dental assistants	445
Health aides, except nursing	446

(continued)

Table 3.4. (*Continued*)

Title	Census Code
Elevator operators	454
Barbers	457
Hairdressers and cosmetologists	458
Attendants, amusement and recreation facilities	459
Guides	463
Usher	464
Public transportation attendants	465
Baggage porters and bellhops	466
Welfare service aides	467
Child care workers, except private household	468
Personal service occupations, not elsewhere classfied	469
Taxicab drivers and chauffeurs	809
Parking lot attendants	813

Yet other nurturant occupations, such as waitresses, score low on IN-FLUENCE. Some nonnurturant occupations, such as bill collectors and lawyers, score high on INFLUENCE.

Physical Skill Demands. The measures of physical skills used in the analyses include the demands of the occupation for eye-hand-foot coordination (EYE-HAND-FOOT COORD), spatial aptitude (SPATIAL APT), motor coordination (MOTOR COORD), MANUAL DEXTERITY, STRENGTH, CLERICAL PERCEPTION (e.g., maintaining visual concentration to read across rows), and basing decisions on measurable criteria (MEASUREMENT) or precise limits (PRECISION) (e.g., such as the limit that boards must be cut to within $\frac{1}{32}$ inch of the right length). Another measure included in this group is complexity with things (COMPLEXITY W/ THINGS), a measure of the complexity with which workers in the occupation must deal with inanimate objects. Successive levels of complexity are indicated by the categories of handling, feeding or offbearing, tending, manipulating, driving, controlling, precision working, and setting up.

Some of these variables measure the extent to which cognitive skill is involved as one performs a physical operation. For example, complexity with things, precise limits, and measurable criteria fall in this category. Others are measures of physical dexterity, coordination, or strength. Of course, even these more physical skills are somewhat cognitive; the dichotomous way that mind and body have been conceptualized in Western thought (discussed in Chapter 6) notwithstanding, the "body" is never used without the "mind" being involved, and vice versa.

Amenities. Workers do not evaluate jobs only on the basis of their pay. Jobs also have fringe benefits. In addition, they have nonpecuniary characteristics that are intrinsic to the process of performing the job, at least given the way the job is currently physically and socially organized. The analysis includes a number of measures of such characteristics, which I have classified into amenities (things I believe most workers would prefer) and disamenities (things I believe most workers prefer to avoid). One amenity is % MEDICAL INSUR, measuring the percentage among those in the occupation who are covered by employer-subsidized medical insurance.

Several measures of amenities were based on occupational averages for individuals' responses to one of the statements below (coded strongly disagree, disagree, agree, or strongly agree). The first two were tapped by responses to "I have a lot of say about what happens on my job" (SELF-DETER HAPPENINGS) and "I determine the speed at which I work" (SELF-DETER WORK SPEED). These two items were presumed to be amenities because past research shows that job autonomy increases satisfaction (Gruneberg 1979, pp. 45–46; Sheppard and Herrick 1972; Bonjean, Brown, Grandjean, and Macken 1982). Two other amenities were occupational averages for degree of agreement with the statements. "I have enough time to get the job done" (ADEQ TIME FOR JOB) and "A lot of people can be affected by how well I do my work" (EFFECT ON OTHERS). These were considered amenities on the assumption that people derive satisfaction from a sense of efficacy.

Other measures were also considered amenities because they index autonomy or efficacy. One such measure was the occupational average for workers' self-report of the importance of power (POWER) to them. I reasoned that occupations in which more people said they consider power important are likely to be those that offer more autonomy and efficacy. Similarly, I consider a measure of the average for each occupation of workers' self-report of the importance of making a contribution (SOCIETAL CONTRIB) as an amenity, based on the assumption that jobs containing more people who claim such a contribution is important to them are those in which workers see themselves as more able to make such a contribution. A measure of how much the job allows direction, control, and planning (CONTROL) was also seen as an amenity on the assumption that this measure relates to both autonomy and efficacy. A measure of how much the job involves CREATIVE or abstract activities was also seen as an amenity, based on the reasoning that being able to be creative in one's work will make work less alienating and provide greater autonomy.

A measure of the percentage of workers involved in activities typically resulting in PRESTIGE was also considered an amenity on the assumption that individuals prefer to be esteemed by others.

Disamenities. Having to do tasks against one's conscience (AGAINST CONSCIENCE) was presumed a disamenity. This was measured by the occupational average for respondents' responses (strongly disagree, disagree, agree, or strongly agree) to the statement "On my job, I have to do some things that really go against my conscience." A measure of the extent to which people in the occupation reported that being attacked by people or animals is a problem on their job was also presumed a disamenity (ATTACK HAZARD). Other characteristics presumed to be disamenities included measures of having to perform under stress when confronted with an emergency or a dangerous situation (EMERGENCY STRESS), demands for repetitive work (REPETITION), having to work OUTDOORS or in COLD, HEAT, or WET conditions, having to STOOP, CLIMB, reach or handle (REACH/HANDLE), to work in NOISE, or be exposed to HAZARDS or FUMES.

Effort. Several measures of the effort required in a job were also included. Measures of effort are conceptualized here in two ways. We could think of them as nonpecuniary disamenities of jobs that, like the disamenities discussed above, would require employers to offer higher wages if the theory of compensating differentials is correct. This formulation hinges on the assumption that workers (at least "at the margin") prefer not to expend effort, an unflattering and perhaps inaccurate assumption about workers. However, even if we reject this assumption, there is still a good common sense basis for believing that social norms may lead employers to be willing to pay more and workers to require more in an occupation requiring more effort. Thus, the best strategy seemed to be to include these variables. Since all of these measures were formed by creating occupational averages from workers' own reports about their effort on the job, we can view these variables either as a characteristic of the job (how much effort it requires) or as a compositional measure of what kind of people (with respect to proclivity to expend effort) the job attracts. Either way, an effect on average earnings in the job is plausible.

One item, which I call EFFORT, is based on the average score given by survey respondents in each occupation to a questionnaire item asking, "Altogether, how much effort, either physical or mental, does your job require—a lot, some, only a little, or none?" An item I will call EXTRA EFFORT was based on occupational averages in responses to this question: "And how much effort do you put into your job beyond what is required—a lot, some only a little, or none?" A final measure of effort involved computing, for each respondent, a score that "anchored" the respondent's reported work effort to his or her report of the effort required to watch television. Respondents were asked to rate, on a 0–10 scale, the amount of energy and effort put into "a typical hour of time spent watching TV." Then, on the same scale, they were asked to rate the amount of energy and effort put into "a typical hour of time at work." A variable was then formed by subtracting the answer given for an hour of TV from the answer given for an hour or work. The measure was normed by dividing this difference by 10 minus the number given for TV. Finally, the natural logarithm was taken of this quotient. This measure is referred to as EFFORT REL TO TV.

Occupational averages for respondents' assessment of the importance of family (FAMILY IMPORTANCE) to them is taken to index priority given to one's family, which might detract from effort expended at work.

Industrial and Organizational Characteristics. Literatures on the new structuralism, the dual economy, and efficiency wages (discussed in Chapter 2) all suggest that some organizations and some entire industries pay more than others to equivalent workers. This could affect occupational earnings to the extent that some occupations are concentrated in particular industries or types of organizations. Thus, the analyses presented here include measures of the characteristics of the organizations and industries in which incumbents in each occupation are likely to work. The distinction between an occupation and industry is that an occupation defines the function one performs, while an industry is defined by the product (good or service) that firms in the industry sell. (An exception to this definition occurs for governmental or nonprofit service organizations, which are represented in census industrial categories but often provide rather than sell their "outputs.") Thus the secretary and car assembler working for General Motors are in different occupations but the same industry. Janitors who work for IBM, for a city, and for a store are in the same occupation but different industries. Some occupations, however, are concentrated in certain industries. For example, teachers are concentrated in the public sector, retail sales clerks work exclusively in retail sales industries, and assemblers are virtually all in manufacturing industries.

The organizational context in which work is done is affected by whether one is self-employed, works for government, or works in the private sector. Measures of the percentage of an occupation's workers who worked for government (% GOVT) and were self-employed (% SELF-EMPLOYED) were included. To avoid multicollinearity, the percentage of workers in private industry was not included because it is highly negatively correlated with the percentage working in government. Thus, roughly speaking, coefficients for % GOVT can be interpreted as the effects of working for government compared to working in the private sector.

Another determinant of wages is whether workers are unionized. I included a measure of the percentage of workers in the occupation who are unionized (% UNION), averaged over a three-year period centered upon 1980.

The most direct way to measure whether some industries have higher wage scales is to take the average wage of workers in each industry, and then compute a weighted mean on this variable for each occupation, with the weights based on what percentage of the workers in the occupation are employed in each industry. This measure, INDUS EARNINGS, indexes the extent to which workers in a particular occupation are likely to work in high-wage industries. The two-digit level of detail, providing 87 industrial categories, was used to create the industry means.

Occupational averages for several other industrial characteristics that have been hypothesized to affect wages were also included. These are not entirely redundant with the measure of industry wage discussed above because a greater level of detail of industrial categories (231 three-digit detailed categories) was used for the industrial means on these variable than for the earnings in industries. These variables measured the capital intensity (INDUS CAP INTENS) of production, measured by the average assets of firms in the industry per employee; INDUS OLIGOPOLY, what percentage of all sales in the industry go to the top eight firms; INDUS FOR DIVIDENDS, average dollar dividends from foreign subsidiaries per firm; INDUS SALES TO GOVT, the percentage of sales (in dollars) going to the government among firms in the industry; INDUS SALES PER WKR, dollars of sales per employee; INDUS PROFITS, net income per dollar value of assets; and INDUS SALES PER FIRM, the average dollars of sales per firm. A measure of each of these variables for each industry was converted into an occupational average according to the likelihood of members of the occupation working in each industry. More details on this procedure are provided in the next section with the discussion of data sources.

These industrial measures tell us the tendency of those in an occupation to be in industries with characteristics predicting high or low wages for reasons affecting the industry as a whole. Thus, for example, for the variable measuring averaging dollars of sales per firm in an industry, the occupational average would tell us the dollars of sales per firm of the industry the "average" person in a given occupation was in.

Miscellaneous Variables. Two items are included as controls in some regression analyses predicting women's earnings. These are the percentage of women married (% FEM MARRIED) in the occupation and an estimate of average labor force experience (FEM EXPER) for the women in the occupation. For women, marriage could be seen to interfere with occupational effort. The number of years of experience has been shown by human capital studies reviewed in Chapter 1 to affect earnings at the

individual level. Thus, we might expect women's wages to be higher in
occupations in which the average woman is single and has more years of
labor force experience.

Another two variables are used to weight the regression analyses.
These are measures of the number of men (NUMBER MEN, FTYR) and
number of women (NUMBER WOMEN, FTYR) among the full-time
year-round workers in each occupation. The rationale for weighting is
presented below in the discussion of statistical models.

Dependent Variables: Earnings.   The two dependent variables are average female and average male hourly earnings of full-time year-round
workers in the occupation in 1980. Individuals are classified as full-time
in census data if they currently work at least 35 hours/week. They are
classified as year-round workers if they were employed the entire year
before the census. Thus, the average female hourly earnings for each
occupation was computed on only those women who were employed
full-time when the 1980 census was taken and had been employed the
entire year before. The same applies to the measure of male earnings. By
using data pertaining only to full-time year-round workers, I prevent the
analysis from erroneously attributing to sex composition any effects on
wages that may actually stem from the greater propensity of women and
men in female occupations to work part-time. This would be a danger
because part-time workers are often paid less per hour than full-time
workers in the same occupation.

C. Sources of Data

Census Data.   Some measures were taken from published or machine-
readable sources provided by the U.S. Bureau of the Census. The measures of the number of men and women who work full-time year-round
in each occupation (used to weight the regression analyses) and the
average hourly earnings of full-time year-round men and women were
taken from a publication from the 1980 census (U.S. Bureau of Census
1984a, Table 1). The measure of sex composition, the percentage female
among full-time year-round workers, was also computed from this census publication. The data on average annual earnings among all workers
in each two-digit industry were taken from another 1980 census publication (U.S. Bureau of Census 1984b, Table 2). The measures of the percentage of workers in each occupation who were Mexican and black as
well as the percentage self-employed and employed by government
were computed from the Public-Use Micro-data Sample (P.U.M.S.) from
the 1980 census (documented in U.S. Bureau of Census 1983a). Four
measures, the percentage of men and women having four years or more

of college, and mean education in each occupation for men and women, which were used in the COGNITIVE FACTOR, were also taken from this source.[4]

Dictionary of Occupational Titles. The best available indicators of the demands for skill, training, and working conditions of occupations that can be used on a national data set are provided by the *Dictionary of Occupational Titles* (DOT) in its most recent fourth edition (U.S. Department of Labor 1977). (For a discussion of properties of these data, see Miller, Treiman, Cain, and Roos 1980; Cain and Treiman 1980). The DOT contains data on 12,099 occupations, much more detailed categories than the 503 detailed 1980 census occupational categories. Each of the occupational titles in the DOT has been rated on a large number of variables describing the demands of the occupation. These ratings were done by observers from the Department of Labor who visited various employment sites to watch the tasks being done, spoke to workers, and spoke to supervisors. While the variables undoubtedly contain measurement error, they are the best available for my purposes.

When developing scores for the fourth edition DOT, a deliberate attempt was made to redress sex bias that had been in the third edition DOT. In particular, the third edition assessed many predominantly female jobs to involve no significant relationship with things, when arguably comparable male jobs were assessed as having more complexity in their relationship with things (Cain and Treiman 1981). For example, in the earlier edition, the relationship clerical workers have to typewriters was given little or no credit.

Many of the measures of skill, amenities, and disamenities used in the analysis in this chapter are from the DOT. Table 3.1 indicates which of the variables described above came from the DOT. For this analysis, fourth edition DOT variables were coded to 1980 census occupational categories using the process described below. (For a description of the dataset containing occupational averages for all DOT variables created for this analysis, now publicly available through the Interuniversity Consortium of Political and Social Research at University of Michigan, see England and Kilbourne 1989.)

The starting point was a data file of over 50,000 individuals from the 1970 census on which each individual's occupation was coded with both the 1970 and 1980 detailed census occupational codes.[5] An earlier analysis (National Academy of Science 1981) had calculated the average score on each DOT variable for each 1970 detailed occupational category (using the most recent fourth edition DOT). These NAS DOT variable scores were merged onto this individual file according to the individual's 1970 occupational code.[6] Then, since individuals were also classified by their 1980 occupational code, it was possible to compute a mean score on each DOT variable for each 1980 occupational code. These occupational means became the DOT scores on the file being created for this analysis, where 1980 occupational codes are the cases.

Variables from Filer Dataset. Another group of variables was provided by Randall Filer.[7] These include a number of the measures of amenities and disamenities, all the measures of effort, the measure of unionization, and one variable in the cognitive factor. Table 3.1 notes which variables were obtained from Filer. Below I explain the original sources of each of the variables from Filer's dataset that I utilized. (These variables are described briefly in Filer 1989.)

Several of the variables measuring effort, amenities, and disamenities are from the 1977 Quality of Employment Survey (QES) conducted by the University of Michigan's Institute for Survey Research. (The QES is described in Quin and Staines 1979.) The QES is based upon a national probability sample of individuals collected in 1977. The measures from the QES are indicated in Table 3.1. They include ADEQ TIME FOR JOB, EFFECT ON OTHERS, SELF-DETER HAPPENINGS, SELF-DETER WORK SPEED, AGAINST CONSCIENCE, ATTACK HAZARD, EFFORT, and EXTRA EFFORT. One variable included in the cognitive factor, LEARN NEW THINGS, is also from the QES. Filer also used those variables from the QES measuring effort expended on the job and on watching television, using the algorithm discussed above, developed by Duncan and Stafford (1980), to create EFFORT REL TO TV.

Filer also provided three measures from a proprietary dataset from Filer Psychological Consultants. These items result from surveys of workers in companies that were clients of the consulting firm. Respondents were asked about the importance to them of a number of things. Filer computed averages for each occupation. The measures from this source are FAMILY IMPORTANCE, POWER, and SOCIETAL CONTRIB.

For all of those measures provided by Filer that were discussed above, he computed an average for each occupation from the responses of those in the survey in the occupation. The measures used here (and in Filer 1989) are these occupational averages.

Filer also provided measures of the percentage of women in each occupation who are married, computed from the 1980 census (U.S. Bureau of Census 1983a). In addition, he provided an estimate of average years of labor force experience of women in each occupation. The estimate was obtained from a two-step process. The first step utilized data from all years in the National Longitudinal Survey of Young Woman and National Longitudinal Survey of Mature Women datasets (described in

Center for Human Resources Research 1983). These datasets were pooled such that a person at a given year was the unit of analysis. A regression was run predicting years of labor force experience from education, age, year of observation, race, and marital status. Separate regressions were run for each occupation. The second step was to give each occupation a predicted experience score based on its means on these independent variables in 1980 census data and the coefficients from the regressions described above. (For details, see Filer 1990b.)

Filer took a measure of unionization from Kokkelenberg and Sockell (1985), who computed the proportion of persons in each occupation who were union members during the three-year period centered on 1980 using May Current Population Surveys conducted by the Census Bureau.

Industrial and Organizational Characteristics. To create occupational averages for the industrial characteristics, I began with variables describing industries developed by Randy Hodson.[8] One advantage of this dataset over other similar sets is that it is not limited to manufacturing, but includes the service sector as well. Variables were included that were believed to affect average wage levels offered in the industry. Table 3.1 shows which variables were taken from Hodson's data set. (The original sources for these variables are described in Hodson 1983 and Hodson and England 1986.) For each variable, where measures were not available for the detailed 1970 census industrial categories, average measures for broader industrial categories were assigned to each of the constituent detailed census codes.

As a first step, this dataset was converted to 1980 census industrial categories. The conversion made use of the dataset containing over 50,000 individuals from the 1970 census mentioned above. This dataset coded individuals by both their 1970 and 1980 detailed census industrial category. Since industrial categories changed much less than occupational categories between the 1970 and 1980 censuses, for the majority of industrial categories, there was a noncontroversial one-to-one mapping of 1970 to 1980 categories. If a 1970 category contained at least 85% of the people in one 1980 code, and no second 1970 code contained more than 5% of those in the 1980 category, it was considered a one-to-one match. However, wherever a second 1970 code contained more than 5% of those in the 1980 code, a weighted average was created. The resulting file had 1980 census industrial categories as cases, with selected variables from Hodson's dataset on it.

The next task was to create occupational averages for each industrial variable. Creating these averages required using a matrix of detailed 1980 occupational by detailed 1980 industrial categories. Such a machine-readable matrix, with the numbers of men and women in each occupation-industry cell, is available from the Census Bureau (documented in U.S. Bureau of Census 1985). Variables from the file described in the paragraph above were merged onto this matrix, according to 1980 industry categories.[9] Also, the measures of mean female and male earnings in the industry were merged onto the matrix. Published census documents do not provide a measure of earnings for each of the 231 detailed (three-digit) 1980 industrial categories, but have such a measure for each of the 87 two-digit categories. Thus, average earnings for a given two-digit category were assigned to each three-digit category that is a subset of the two-digit category.

Finally, for each industrial variable, weighted occupational averages were computed for each 1980 detailed occupational category and output to the occupational file used in the analysis to follow. The resulting industrial variables for each occupation are measures of the average characteristics of the industries in which people in a given occupation work. Thus, for example, an occupation's score on the variable INDUS FOR DIVIDENDS tells us the average dollars of dividends from foreign subsidiaries per firm for the "average" industry for which people in this occupation work.

III. Statistical Models

The analysis uses ordinary-least-squares (OLS) multiple regression. The units of analysis are occupations.[10] Separate regressions are run for men and women. Thus the dependent variable in male regressions is mean hourly earnings among men employed full-time year-round, while the dependent variable in the female regressions is the mean hourly earnings among women employed full-time year-round. Separate regressions for women and men are necessary to assess the effect of the sex composition of occupations on their earnings. Without separate regressions (i.e., if mean earnings of all persons in the occupation was the dependent variable and only one regression was used), the coefficient for sex composition would be affected by the extent of within-occupation sex differences in earnings. A hypothetical example helps clarify why this is true. Suppose that there were 100 occupations, each occupation had the same average earnings, and in each occupation males averaged $10.00/hour while females averaged $6.00/hour. If occupations differed in their % FEMALE, occupations with a higher % FEMALE would have lower average earnings. This would result entirely from the within-occupation differences in earnings. Yet a female in a predominantly female occupation would not be any worse off than a female in a predominantly male occupation, nor would a male in a pre-dominantly female occupation be any worse off than a male in a pre-dominantly male occupation. If all that is driving the sex gap in pay is men and women earning different amounts within occupations, then the claim of comparable worth proponents that occupational tasks are devalued because they are done primarily by women is not correct. To put it another way, we need to control for sex while testing for an effect of occupations' sex composition on earnings. In this way, we only claim an effect of sex composition if both men and women have lower earn-ings when they are in predominantly female occupations. In this analy-sis, this is achieved by using separate regressions for women and men.[11]

The male and female equations are both based on the same set of 403 detailed 1980 census occupations, but the male and female analyses differ in two respects: First, the male equation has mean male hourly earnings as its dependent variable while the female equation has mean female hourly earnings as its dependent variable. Second, the regression analyses are weighted differently. The male equation is weighted by the number of males in each occupation, while the female equation is weighted by the number of females in each occupation. In each case the numbers refer to full-time year-round workers. This is a simple demo-graphic weighting such that large occupations "count" more in the re-sults.

The regression analyses yield, for each sex, a coefficient (slope) for each independent variable. How do these results illuminate whether and to what extent there is discrimination in wages against predomi-nantly female occupations? I will emphasize the coefficient for occupa-tions' % FEMALE. This coefficient will be interpreted as indicative of the most direct sort of discrimination at issue in comparable worth: paying men and women in predominantly female occupations less because the typical worker is a woman. (Recall, however, the caveat that this esti-mate could contain effects of crowding as well.) The coefficient for % FEMALE indicates whether and how much occupations containing a higher percentage of women pay less than occupations that contain a lower percentage of women but that are "comparable," where compara-ble means net of or controlling for other variables in the equation. Thus, we can interpret the coefficient for the variable measuring an occupa-tion's % FEMALE in this way: Suppose that for each occupation we compute a predicted earnings score based on all the variables in the equation besides % FEMALE. The extent to which each variable "counts" or is weighted in determining predicted earnings is deter-mined empirically. Comparable occupations are those with the same predicted earnings scores based on variables other than sex composition. A negative effect of occupations' % FEMALE reveals the extent to which, on average, jobs with a higher % FEMALE pay less than comparable jobs that have a lower % FEMALE.[12]

If the coefficient on % FEMALE is significant and negative in both male and female equations, I take this as evidence of the most direct kind of discrimination at issue in comparable worth. This conclusion is suspect to the extent that there are unmeasured characteristics of occupations or their incumbents that are determinants of earnings *and* are correlated with the sex composition of occupations. This is the familiar statistical problem of "omitted variable bias" or "spurious correlation." In the case where the omitted variable is a characteristic of the average incumbent in the occupation, this problem takes the form of "selection bias"; it is a matter of whether those who chose or were selected by employers into the occupations high on % FEMALE have individual characteristics predictive of low or high wages. The analysis here deals with these problems in two ways: First, I have included a large number of occupational characteristics that may affect wages in the regression analyses to minimize the chance of omitted variables that cause such bias in measuring the effect of sex composition. Second, by performing separate equations for men and women I avoid some of the selection bias problem. Sex-specific regressions control for any systematic differences between men and women that might affect differences in earnings between predominantly male and female occupations. With separate equations for men and women, we are only comparing the wages of women in female occupations to those of women in male occupations, and the wages of men in female occupations to those of men in male occupations. Thus, if there is a selection bias problem it must be of the type that women who are in male occupations are systematically different than women in female occupations (or men are different in the two types of occupations) along dimensions that are not covered in the control variables.

Are coefficients on variables *other* than % FEMALE relevant to the assessment of the wage discrimination at issue in comparable worth? For the most part, no. Other variables are included as controls to ensure an accurate assessment of the net effect of occupations' sex composition on wages. However, one other coefficient is of particular interest for what it reveals about a more indirect kind of sex bias in wage determination, the bias resulting from a devaluation of types of skills or activities traditionally associated with women. Consider nurturance, one type of social skill. We traditionally associate nurturance with women. If being in an occupation exercising nurturance has a net negative return, I will interpret this as an indirect form of sex bias. This indirect sex bias exists where types of skills traditionally exercised by women receive a lower or negative return *whether they occur in male or female occupations.* This latter proviso is invoked by including % FEMALE in the equation. It corrects the slopes on other variables, including NURTURANCE, for bias due to their current association with sex composition. As an illustration, suppose that female jobs are more likely than male jobs to require verbal skill but there are some male jobs that require some amount of it. If we do not include % FEMALE in the equation, some of the low weight for verbal skills may result because jobs requiring much of it are female jobs and female jobs pay less due to direct sex bias in occupational wage setting. Putting % FEMALE in the regression makes us confident that a low positive or negative return to a variable is not merely because occupations requiring more of this characteristic have their wages lowered by direct gender bias. However, adding % FEMALE to the equation will not remove the bias that comes from a factor having a low return in either male or female jobs because of its *historic* or *traditional* association with women or female spheres of activity (Kilbourne et al. 1990). I refer to this as indirect gender bias.

The possibility of interaction effects is considered in this analysis in two ways. The first is achieved by running separate regressions for men and women. Interactions of independent variables with sex are indicated whenever coefficients are significantly different for men and women. These interactions tell us whether men or women receive larger returns (or penalties) to various occupational characteristics.

I also assess a second type of interaction. These are interactions between the sex composition of occupations and each other independent variable. To do this, an interaction term is computed for each independent variable (other than % FEMALE) by multiplying this variable by % FEMALE. Then, supplementary regressions are run that include all these interaction terms. A significant interaction term in these equations implies that the (positive or negative) returns to the occupational characteristic differ in size depending upon the sex composition of the occupation.

It is important to realize what *different returns* for male and female occupations means. The phrase should not be used in cases where the occupational characteristic and sex composition each have additive effects; it should only be used to refer to cases where the *coefficient* for effects of a given occupational characteristic changes significantly as we move across occupations that vary in sex composition. In this case, the interaction terms discussed above will be significant in the regression including them. Let me illustrate the distinction between the additive and interactive case with some examples that simplify the discussion by treating occupational sex composition as if it were a dichotomy—male and female occupations. My examples will further simplify things by assuming that the same interaction effects are significant in the male and female regressions.

First, let us look at a hypothetical example where effects are additive, not interactive. Average years of schooling of those in the occupation will be used as the variable in question. Suppose that computations from the regression equation show that female occupations requiring 12 years of education pay $6/hour, those requiring 13 years pay $7/hour, and those requiring 14 years pay $8/hour; and that male occupations requiring 12 years pay $10/hour, those requiring 13 years pay $11/hour, and those requiring 14 years pay $12/hour. Here, the effects of education and sex composition are additive, not interactive. For any level of education, female occupations pay $4/hour less; and for both levels of occupational sex composition, the return to each year of education required is $1/hour. Because the returns to each year of education are the same at both levels of sex composition, and the penalty for being in a female occupation is the same at every level of education, the effects of the two variables are additive, not interactive. Here the interaction term would be zero in the regression that included it.

Now let us consider an example where the effects of education and sex composition interact. Suppose that female occupations requiring 10 years of education pay $7/hour, those requiring 12 years pay $8/hour, and those requiring 14 years pay $9/hour; while male occupations requiring 10 years pay $6/hour, those requiring 12 years pay $10/hour, and those requiring 14 years pay $14/hour. Here the returns to education are not the same in male and female occupations; in the male occupations, each year of education yields an additional $2/hour, whereas in the female occupations it yields only 50 cents/hour. Here we also see that the penalty for being in a female occupation varies with the level of education; the penalty is $5/hour at 14 years of education but diminishes to $2/hour at 12 years of education, and at 10 years of education female occupations actually pay more.

Is it advantageous or disadvantageous to work in occupations with lower returns to education or any other characteristic? At first glance, one might think that female occupations are victims of wage discrimination if they receive lower positive returns to some variable, such as education. But upon closer examination, this is not so clear. In the example above, female occupations have lower returns, yet the lines summarizing average returns to education for male and female occupations cross at some point, and below that level of education female occupations actually have higher earnings than do male occupations. Thus if there are occupations to the left of this point of intersection, there is a range in which female occupations are advantaged. Even if the lines did not cross, the fact that female occupations receive a low return to some characteristic, which sounds like a disadvantage, also means that they receive a lower penalty for not having a higher level of the characteristic, which could be construed as advantageous. Thus, I do not believe that interactions have an unambiguous interpretation as regards either disadvantage or discrimination. Although they are assessed and reported below, they are not emphasized in the substantive discussion regarding wage discrimination. Most of the discussion focuses on the additive models, which, in cases of significant interactions, give us the *average* effect of each independent variable across the range of occupational sex composition.

How do we interpret the difference between the intercept (constant) in the male and female equations? As with differences in slope coefficients, the answer to this question is importantly affected by the fact that our dependent variable is mean earnings. (This conclusion would also follow if it were median earnings.) The difference between intercepts in this analysis is affected by differences in pay between the occupations men and women are concentrated in, as well as differences in pay between men and women within occupations. Thus, we cannot use the difference between the two intercepts as a measure of wage discrimination against female jobs.[13]

I will also use the regression equations to decompose the overall sex difference in pay. A common technique is to decompose group differences (here between men and women) in a dependent variable (here mean earnings) into portions due to differences in means on the independent variables, different slopes, different intercepts, and an interaction between slopes and intercepts. However, it is only possible to distinguish between the part of the earnings gap due to sex differences in slopes and that part of the earnings gap due to sex differences in intercepts, where all independent variables have a nonarbitrary zero point (Jones and Kelley 1984; Aldrich and Buchele 1986). Unfortunately, this is not true for the DOT variables and some other variables used here. Moreover, differences between the male and female equations in either their slopes or intercepts are affected by within-occupation differences in this analysis. Therefore, we do not want to include them as part of a measure of comparable worth discrimination. Thus, my focus here will be on how differences between men and women in the average characteristics of the occupations in which they work explain differences in their earnings. Put another way, I will focus upon how sex differences in mean occupational characteristics contribute to the sex difference in pay. Male and female means will be computed for each variable by taking the mean across all occupations, using the male and female weights, respectively. To compute the effect on the pay gap of sex differences in means for any one independent variable, one multiplies the differences between the male and female mean on an independent variable times the coefficient for that variable. To do this, we face the problem of whether to use the male or female coefficients. I will provide both estimates, as well as a weighted average of the two, where the weight is determined by the number of men and women working full-time year-round in the labor force in 1980. (This method is recommended by Jones and Kelley 1984, Note 13.)

IV. Empirical Findings

A. Introduction

Using the data described above, this section discusses results from regression analyses and decompositions of the sex gap in pay.

Before discussing the findings from regression analyses, let us review the predictions made about each group of variables. I predict that all kinds of skill demands—cognitive, social, and physical—will enhance occupations' earnings. This would be predicted by functionalist theory, human capital theory, and neoclassical theory more generally. The one exception to this is my prediction that nurturant social skill will have a small or even negative return, as a form of indirect gender bias, because of its association with traditionally female activities. The bias is called indirect because it is net of the current sex composition of the occupation. This is predicted from feminist theory, particularly the variety of cultural-feminist theory to be discussed in Chapter 6. Authority (over other workers) is predicted to affect earnings positively. Authority can be viewed as a social skill and hence predicted to have positive effects on earnings because of the skill required. However, it is also predicted to enhance earnings from Marxist theories that see managers and supervisors as in contradictory class locations less "fully" working-class than that of other workers. The theory of compensating differentials predicts that amenities will have negative effects on earnings while disamenities will have positive effects. As discussed in Chapter 2, this prediction is an implication of the theory only on the assumption that I have correctly classified variables as amenities or disamenities to the marginal worker. Various of the industrial and organizational characteristics are predicted to have effects by new structuralist theories of economic segmentation as well as efficiency wage theories. All the variables included are predicted to have positive total effects on earnings, with the exception of the percentage of workers in the occupation who are self-employed or government workers. Such workers are predicted to make less than those who work for private sector firms. Race composition is predicted to affect earnings such that occupations with a higher percentage Mexican or black have lower earnings, all else equal. This would be predicted by conflict theory to result from a devaluation analogous to the devaluation leading to negative effects for the percentage female in an occupation. Here I am choosing the predictions from conflict theory in sociology over the prediction that would be made by neoclassical economics of no effect of race or sex composition. The negative effect of occupations' percentage female is predicted by conflict theories dealing with gender as well as cultural-feminist theory.

Three regression models provide the results presented in Table 3.5. Each model is run separately for men and women. The only differences between the male and female model are the weights (each occupation weighted by number of men for the male model and number of women for the female model) and the dependent variables (mean female hourly earnings versus mean male hourly earnings). The first model I label the "full model." This full model contains 56 variables, and thus is cumbersome to interpret, although multicollinearity diagnostics show no problems. However, for comparison and simplicity, I also consider findings from two other models. The second model eliminated all variables that were not statistically significant in the full model for at least one of the two sexes (at the .05 level, using a two-tailed test). The third model eliminated all variables that were not statistically significant in the full model for the sex to which the model applies. Thus, the third model contains a different set of variables in the male and female regressions. The choice between the three models presented is rather arbitrary; thus I will put most stock in substantive conclusions that are consistently found across all three models.

Although I report tests of statistical significance, such significance should be less a prerequisite for taking effects seriously in this compared to some other analyses. In many analyses the units of analysis are individuals who are a probability sample from a population, and statistical significance tests are how we allow for random sampling error. In this analysis, the underlying data on which information on earnings and some of the compositional variables, such as education, sex composition, and race composition, were based is the 1980 census of population, which includes thousands of individuals even in the public-use sample data. Other variables, such as those taken from Filer (discussed above), were computed from surveys based on probability samples, where the number of occupations here is less than the number of people in these surveys. Thus, when I use statistical significance here, it should be seen as a rough way to discipline ourselves to focus on differences and effects

Table 3.5. Regression Results from Three Models[1]

Dependent Variable	Female Hourly Earnings			Male Hourly Earnings		
Independent Variables — Model:	Full Model	Only Variables Significant[2] for at Least One Sex	Only Variables Significant for Women	Full Model	Only Variables Significant[2] for at Least One Sex	Only Variables Significant for Men[3]
Sex composition						
% FEMALE	-0.004 (2.14)	-0.005 (3.95)	-0.006 (4.05)	-0.005 (0.82)	-0.009 (2.18)	-0.010 (2.87)
Race composition						
% BLACK	-0.010 (1.22)	—	—	-0.019 (0.79)	—	—
% MEXICAN	-0.042 (1.89)	-0.029 (1.63)	—	-0.132 (2.64)	-0.105 (2.88)	-0.117 (3.35)
Cognitive skill and training demands						
COGNITIVE FACTOR	0.466 (12.98)	0.493 (21.81)	0.512 (24.21)	0.774 (10.35)	0.821 (15.63)	0.792 (16.89)
Social skill demands						
AUTHORITY	0.376 (3.61)	0.448 (4.75)	0.457 (5.19)	1.292 (4.81)	1.367 (5.89)	1.190 (5.40)
NURTURANCE	-0.441 (4.08)	-0.257 (3.33)	-0.236 (3.24)	-1.707 (4.61)	-1.388 (4.58)	-1.247 (4.37)
SOCIAL COMPLEXITY SCALE	-0.021 (0.56)	—	—	0.043 (0.29)	—	—
INFLUENCE	-0.003 (1.71)	—	—	0.001 (0.23)	—	—
Physical skill demands						
COMPLEXITY W/ THINGS	-0.17 (0.52)	—	—	-0.095 (1.04)	—	—

156

	(1)	(2)	(3)	(4)	(5)	(6)
EYE-HAND-FOOT COORD	0.217 (1.93)	—	—	0.005 (0.02)	—	—
SPATIAL APT	0.158 (1.56)	—	—	0.048 (0.20)	—	—
MOTOR COORD	0.441 (4.44)	0.243 (4.76)	0.254 (5.06)	0.315 (0.87)	0.263 (1.29)	—
MANUAL DEXTERITY	-0.226 (1.54)	—	—	0.628 (1.70)	—	—
STRENGTH	0.213 (2.29)	0.378 (6.20)	0.380 (6.63)	-0.042 (0.16)	0.365 (2.14)	—
CLERICAL PERCEPTION	-0.172 (1.74)	—	—	-0.081 (0.28)	—	—
MEASUREMENT	0.002 (1.08)	—	—	0.001 (0.29)	—	—
PRECISION	-0.001 (0.57)	—	—	-0.006 (1.09)	—	—
Amenities						
SOCIETAL CONTRIB	0.096 (2.63)	0.113 (4.02)	0.109 (3.91)	0.092 (0.89)	0.178 (2.00)	—
EFFECT ON OTHERS	0.155 (1.43)	—	—	0.302 (1.01)	—	—
PRESTIGE	0.003 (1.14)	0.001 (0.33)	—	0.014 (2.19)	0.016 (4.12)	0.012 (4.06)
CREATIVE	-0.001 (0.45)	0.002 (0.82)	—	-0.029 (4.10)	-0.027 (5.40)	-0.026 (5.91)
SELF-DETER WORK SPEED	-0.299 (2.44)	-0.341 (3.42)	-0.334 (3.52)	-1.015 (3.58)	-1.203 (5.12)	-1.127 (4.91)
ADEQ TIME FOR JOB	0.054 (0.39)	—	—	-0.016 (0.05)	—	—
SELF-DETER HAPPENINGS	-0.030 (0.31)	—	—	0.115 (0.48)	—	—

(*continued*)

157

Table 3.5. (Continued)

Independent Variables	Dependent Variable	Female Hourly Earnings			Male Hourly Earnings		
	Model:	Full Model	Only Variables Significant[2] for at Least One Sex	Only Variables Significant for Women	Full Model	Only Variables Significant[2] for at Least One Sex	Only Variables Significant for Men[3]
% MEDICAL INSUR		-0.006 (3.16)	-0.004 (2.56)	-0.005 (2.88)	-0.019 (3.92)	-0.017 (4.14)	-0.020 (5.67)
POWER		0.024 (0.52)	—	—	-0.204 (1.60)	—	—
CONTROL		-0.005 (2.22)	-0.001 (0.62)	-0.001 (0.96)	-0.005 (0.94)	-0.005 (1.26)	—
Disamenities							
EMERGENCY STRESS		0.003 (1.41)	—	—	0.001 (0.20)	—	—
REPETITION		0.007 (4.33)	0.008 (6.34)	0.008 (6.85)	0.014 (2.53)	0.012 (3.45)	0.015 (4.49)
AGAINST CONSCIENCE		0.305 (2.54)	0.221 (2.77)	0.186 (2.38)	0.243 (0.88)	0.391 (1.87)	—
FUMES		-0.002 (0.60)	—	—	-0.000 (0.01)	—	—
COLD		0.008 (1.15)	—	—	0.021 (1.83)	—	—
HAZARDS		-0.005 (2.20)	-0.001 (0.87)	-0.001 (0.78)	-0.006 (1.09)	-0.005 (1.60)	—
HEAT		0.005 (0.91)	—	—	0.007 (0.74)	—	—
OUTDOORS		-0.004 (0.75)	—	—	0.007 (1.10)	—	—

158

	(1)	(2)	(3)	(4)	(5)	(6)
WET	0.002	—	—	0.004	—	—
	(0.49)			(0.40)		
ATTACK HAZARD	-0.099	—	—	-0.855	—	—
	(0.40)			(1.60)		
STOOP	0.003	—	—	0.005	—	—
	(1.42)			(0.97)		
CLIMB	0.002	—	—	-0.001	—	—
	(0.53)			(0.13)		
REACH/HANDLE	-0.003	—	—	0.003	—	—
	(1.28)			(0.46)		
NOISE	-0.004	—	—	-0.003	—	—
	(1.66)			(0.80)		
Effort						
EFFORT REL TO TV	2.134	1.472	1.158	6.703	6.553	6.260
	(3.05)	(2.42)	(2.00)	(4.53)	(5.62)	(5.73)
EFFORT	0.141	—	—	-0.108	—	—
	(0.61)			(0.17)		
EXTRA EFFORT	0.065	—	—	-0.209	—	—
	(0.34)			(0.48)		
FAMILY IMPORTANCE	-0.118	-0.148	-0.134	-0.224	-0.294	—
	(2.08)	(3.36)	(3.09)	(1.56)	(2.50)	
Industrial and organizational characteristics						
% GOVT	-0.002	-0.004	—	-0.021	-0.020	-0.021
	(0.69)	(1.79)		(3.59)	(4.27)	(5.37)
% SELF-EMPLOYED	-0.022	-0.018	-0.014	0.008	0.015	—
	(3.94)	(3.51)	(3.36)	(0.72)	(1.43)	
% UNION	0.001	0.001	—	0.018	0.015	0.019
	(0.35)	(0.28)		(2.10)	(2.10)	(3.22)
INDUS CAP INTENS	-0.155	-0.144	-0.148	0.190	0.136	—
	(3.45)	(3.52)	(3.77)	(1.53)	(1.25)	

(continued)

159

Table 3.5. (Continued)

Independent Variables	Female Hourly Earnings			Male Hourly Earnings		
Model:	Full Model	Only Variables Significant[2] for at Least One Sex	Only Variables Significant for Women	Full Model	Only Variables Significant[2] for at Least One Sex	Only Variables Significant for Men[3]
INDUS OLIGOPOLY	-0.009 (1.45)	—	—	-0.025 (1.75)	—	—
INDUS FOR DIVIDENDS	0.011 (2.34)	0.005 (1.38)	0.008 (2.88)	0.003 (0.31)	0.003 (0.45)	—
INDUS SALES TO GOVT	-0.052 (4.28)	-0.045 (4.64)	-0.055 (6.34)	-0.006 (0.29)	-0.027 (1.47)	—
INDUS SALES PER WKR	-0.155 (0.55)	—	—	-0.591 (1.05)	—	—
INDUS PROFITS	-8.639 (3.27)	-11.221 (4.76)	-11.796 (5.23)	2.605 (0.52)	-3.485 (0.83)	—
INDUS SALES PER FIRM	0.001 (0.87)	—	—	0.002 (0.71)	—	—
INDUS EARNINGS	0.0003 (7.27)	0.0003 (9.09)	0.0003 (10.36)	0.0004 (4.29)	0.0004 (4.45)	0.0003 (4.47)
Intercept	1.712	2.832	3.029	1.632	5.400	7.903
R^2	0.90	0.89	0.89	0.83	0.83	0.82
N	403	403	403	403	403	403

Notes:

[1] Absolute value of t-statistics in parentheses.

[2] Statistically significant at the .05 level, two-tailed test, in the full model.

[3] % FEMALE was not dropped despite its nonsignificance in the male full model because screening its effect was of primary interest.

that are sizable relative to their standard errors, rather than as a way to avoid sampling error in a precise sense.

The reader should bear in mind that the magnitude of coefficients generally cannot be compared across variables since they differ in metric. Magnitudes of slopes for the *same* variable *can* be compared across the three models, and across the same model for men and women, however. Some variables have an intuitively meaningful metric. For example, all variables with "%" in their title are on a scale from 0 to 100, where a one-unit change is one percentage point. Thus, for example, since the dependent variable is expressed in dollars, the coefficient of −0.004 at the upper left of Table 3.5 means that in this model (after adjusting for other variables) each 1% female in a woman's occupation reduces her earnings by 0.004 dollars, which equals four tenths of a cent. Although this is statistically significant (as assessed by the *t*-statistic), the magnitude sounds tiny upon first glance. However, it sounds larger when we realize that this implies that if one were to move between two occupations comparable on other variables, but one occupation was all male whereas the other was all female[14], this would make a difference of 40 cents per/hour (0.0040 × 100 = 0.40). Given that the average full-time year-round woman in these 1980 data earned $5.20/hour, this move would provide a raise of over 8%—hardly trivial. The COGNITIVE FACTOR and the SOCIAL COMPLEXITY SCALE are in standardized scores such that one unit is a standard deviation. Many other variables have no intuitive metric.

Table 3.5 presents the coefficients from all three models for both the male and female regression. Effects of variables are discussed below, divided into broad groups of variables: sex composition, race composition, cognitive skill and training demands, social skills demands, physical skill demands, amenities, disamenities, effort, and industrial and organizational characteristics.

B. Effects of Occupational Variables on Earnings: Regression Results

Direct Gender Bias: Effects of Sex Composition on Earnings. Do occupations that have a higher % FEMALE pay lower wages, even when they are comparable on the other occupational characteristics controlled in the model? The results from the three models show that this is definitely true for women. In all three models, the net effect of occupational % FEMALE is negative and significant. Moving from an all male to an all female occupation, holding constant all other occupational characteristics, would lead to a wage drop of between 40 cents/hour and 60 cents/hour, depending upon which one of the models we use. If we add the variables measuring percentage married and estimated average labor force experience of women in the occupation to these three models (results not shown in Table 3.5), the % FEMALE coefficients stay statistically significant and are approximately the same size (ranging from -0.004 to -0.005 in the three models).

The negative effect of the % FEMALE in one's occupation is found for men as well. The magnitude of the effect is larger for men than women; for men, moving from an all-male to an all-female occupation (holding constant other occupational characteristics) leads to a drop in pay of between 50 cents/hour and \$1.00/hour. However, in one of the three models the effect is not statistically significant. Given that statistical significance does not have the same precise interpretation here as it does where data are a sample, and given that the effect does attain significance when other nonsignificant variables are dropped, I think the safest conclusion is that being in a more heavily female occupation depresses earnings for men as well as women.

Effects of Race Composition on Earnings.   As discussed in Chapter 1, the discussion of comparable worth here is focused on *gender bias.* When we take comparable worth as a gender issue and focus on direct bias in wage setting, we ask whether jobs that are comparable in their skill, effort, amenities, etc., pay less simply because more of their incumbents are women. There is an analogous issue of comparable worth related to direct race or ethnic bias in occupational wage setting. While this issue is not my focus here, I have included variables measuring the % BLACK and % MEXICAN in occupations to assess this, as well as to control for these variables in assessing direct gender bias. Table 3.5 shows that the effect of % BLACK has a negative sign but does not achieve statistical significance for either sex. This may mean that race discrimination is more likely to take the form of refusal to hire blacks for demanding jobs rather than taking the form of wage discrimination against occupations employing more blacks. Given that the proportion of the work force that is black is much smaller than the proportion that is female, there are virtually no jobs that have a percentage black even as high as 50%, whereas there are a number of jobs that are over 90% female. Thus, at least on a national basis, it is fairly unheard of for a job to take on a label of a "black job." In only 19 out of all 403 occupations are over 20% of workers black. Only 7 of all 403 occupations contain more than 30% black workers. By contrast, there are occupations that are predominantly female in virtually every locality and organization (e.g., secretaries or nurses). However, in particular localities or organizations, certain jobs are predominantly black. Thus, it is possible that this sort of race bias in wage setting may exist at a local or organizational level but not be revealed by a national analysis such as this.

In contrast, the % MEXICAN in an occupation does have a significant negative effect on pay for men. The effect is negative but smaller in magnitude and not statistically significant for women. The coefficients in Table 3.5 indicate that if a job moved from being 0 to 10% Mexican, hourly earnings would decrease by between 29 and 42 cents/hour for women, and between $1.05 and $1.32/hour for men, other occupational demands controlled. Several things caution us against a "comparable worth" interpretation of the negative coefficient on % MEXICAN. First, this coefficient may be affected by within-occupation pay differences between Mexicans and others since we do not have separate equations and dependent variables by ethnicity. Second, these results are heavily affected by the low earnings of agricultural occupations, which have the highest representation of Mexican workers. Rerunning the full regression model with % MEXICAN transformed into several dummy variables shows that the effect is not linear and the negative effects begin only above 10% for men and 15% for women. There are only 7 occupations out of the 403 that contain more than 10% Mexican workers, and none that contain over 20%. This nonlinear specification does not change other coefficients substantially, so the linear specification seems adequate for purposes of using % MEXICAN as a control here. (See Jacobs and Steinberg 1990a, note 12, for citations to single-employer public sector comparable worth studies testing whether racial composition affects wages. The studies have had mixed results.)

Effects of Cognitive Skill Demands on Earnings. Table 3.5 shows that occupations requiring more cognitive skill pay both men and women more, although the returns are higher for men than for women. A one standard deviation increase in the cognitive factor leads to an increase in wages of between 47 and 51 cents/hour for women and between 77 and 82 cents/hour for men.

Indirect Gender Bias: Effects of Social Skill Demands on Earnings. The findings with respect to social skills are a way of testing for indirect gender bias in wage systems. Four variables measuring social skills are included in the analysis, measuring the complexity of the social skill, the influence required (on coworkers, clients, or others), whether the job involves nurturance, and whether it involves authority. The effect of the SOCIAL COMPLEXITY SCALE, although always positive, is not significant in most models, and its magnitude is trivial. One standard deviation on the scale is associated with increments of less than 5 cents/hour. In large part, this scale is measuring the degree of intellectual complexity involved as the social skill is exercised. Thus, it is not surprising that its effects are not seen when the COGNITIVE FACTOR is controlled. INFLUENCE does not have significant effects for either women or men.

What is dramatic is the comparison between the effects of NUR-TURANCE and AUTHORITY. Being in a job involving authority over other workers has a significant positive effect on wages for both men and women, although it is much larger for men. For women, being in a job involving authority over coworkers adds 38 to 46 cents/hour to pay, depending on which model is chosen. For men, the estimates range from $1.19 to $1.37/hour. Since the measure of authority is crude, classi-fying all positions involving supervision or management together with a score of 1, the lower returns for women may indicate that women are in lower levels of the authority pyramid in organizations. In contrast to the positive returns to authority, being in a job exercising another kind of social skill, NURTURANCE, lowers wages significantly for both men and women. Just as the reward for authority was greater for men, the penalty for being in an occupation involving nurturance is greater for men as well. Women lose between 24 and 44 cents/hour for holding a nurturant job, while the estimates of men's loss vary between $1.25 and $1.71/hour. It is important to realize that this penalty does not result from nurturant jobs requiring less cognitive skill, being concentrated in lower-paying industries, or having other nonpecuniary amenities, since these variables are included in the models and thus are held con-stant in assessing this effect. Nor does it result from a wage penalty for female jobs since the sex composition of jobs is also controlled as this effect is assessed. Economists might argue that the contrast in how these two kinds of social skill—nurturance and authority—are re-warded is to be explained by compensating differentials. However, this interpretation is only viable if we assume that the marginal worker con-siders practicing nurturance to be an amenity and wielding authority to be a disamenity. My preferred interpretation of this effect is that it is a form of indirect gender bias. Types of skills traditionally associated with women are devalued. Thus they fail to add—and even take away from—wages, regardless of the current sex composition of the occupa-tion.

Effects of Physical Skill Demands on Earnings. The findings with respect to physical skills are confusing. There is no variable that has significant effects for both men and women in all three models. Nor is there a consistent tendency for variables to have positive signs; each sex shows some coefficients with positive and some with negative signs. MOTOR COORDINATION and STRENGTH are the only two measures of phys-ical skills that have positive and significant effects for women; STRENGTH has a significant positive effect for men in one model. Over-all, we see that many of the physical skills are neither rewarded nor penalized in our economy.

Effects of Amenities on Earnings. The theory of compensating differentials predicts that job characteristics that are amenities will lead to lower earnings, ceteris paribus, as the nonpecuniary amenity substitutes for part of the wage that would otherwise have been required to fill the job. Of course, to test the theory, we must make an assumption about what characteristics are considered an amenity by the marginal worker. I assumed, for this analysis, that the marginal worker would prefer, other things equal, to be in a job with all the characteristics listed as amenities in Table 3.5. A look at the results shows that, where effects were significant, they were negative, with two exceptions, PRESTIGE, and SOCIETAL CONTRIB. Jobs offering more prestige pay more to men; jobs in which more workers say that making a social contribution is important increases women's wages significantly in all three models and men's in one. Jobs allowing workers to be CREATIVE pay significantly less to men, though this is not found for women. Jobs on which more workers reported self-determination of work speed have significantly lower wages for both men and women, other things equal. Jobs providing medical insurance also had significantly lower wages for both men and women, other things being equal. It should be remembered that this finding does not contradict the well-known fact that most well-paying jobs offer insurance, whereas many low-wage jobs do not. These negative effects are *net* of other independent variables in the model. If we compare occupations with similar industrial distributions and requiring a similar amount of cognitive and other skills, occupations in which more employers offer health insurance can be filled with lower wages than where health insurance is not offered. Other variables do not show significant effects. With the exception of PRESTIGE and SOCIETAL CONTRIB, those effects that are significant are all in the negative direction predicted by the theory of compensating differentials.

Effects of Disamenities on Earnings. The theory of compensating differentials predicts that nonpecuniary disamenities—characteristics about jobs that people do not like—will have net positive effects on earnings because a higher wage will have to be paid to lure people into jobs with such characteristics. I made the assumption that those job characteristics listed as disamenities in Table 3.5 are seen by the marginal worker as disamenities. Most of the effects are not significant for either men or women. Occupations involving repetition pay more to both women and men (with the effects larger for men). Having to engage in tasks against one's conscience adds earnings for women; the effects are also positive for men but not significant. But none of the other variables show significant positive effects. It is striking that none of the measures of physical danger or discomfort (FUMES, COLD, HAZARDS, HOT, OUTDOORS,

WET, ATTACK HAZARD, STOOP, CLIMB, REACH/HANDLE, or NOISE) have significant positive effects. HAZARDS has a significant negative effect for women in one model. In sum, while there is some support for compensating differentials for repetition or going against one's conscience, there is *no* evidence that physically dangerous or unpleasant work is rewarded. (One possible exception to this conclusion is the positive effect on women's earnings of being in a job requiring physical strength, which I treated as a skill rather than disamenity.)

Effects of Effort on Earnings. The three measures of effort adopted from Filer (1989) were predicted to have positive effects on earnings. The anchored measure of EFFORT REL TO TV shows the expected positive effects on earnings, significant for both sexes in all three models. The other measures of effort do not show significant effects. FAMILY IMPORTANCE, entered as a variable that might tap the extent to which workers gave less attention to their job because of placing more importance on their family role, was thereby predicted to have negative effects. Consistent with this prediction, it has significant negative effects on earnings for women in all models and for men in one model.

Effects of Industrial and Organizational Characteristics on Earnings. Occupations containing more government workers have lower earnings, although these effects are significant only for men. Net of other factors, each percentage point increase in % GOVT WKR yields a decrease of about 2 cents/hour for men. Occupations containing more self-employed workers pay less for women; each percentage point increase in % SELF-EMP yields a decrease of between 1 and 2 cents/hour for women. The effect is positive but nonsignificant for men.

Some of the industrial variables are hypothesized to have their total causal effects via intervening variables included in the model. The coefficients in Table 3.5 are direct effects. They are not total effects for those variables that we might expect to have their effects through other variables in the model. Thus, predictions about total causal effects for these variables require a reduced-form model to be tested. The variables INDUS CAP INTENS, INDUS OLIGOPOLY, INDUS FOR DIVIDENDS, INDUS SALES TO GOVT, INDUS SALES PER WKR, and INDUS SALES PER FIRM may well have their effects through the intervening variables of INDUS PROFITS, % UNION, and INDUS EARNINGS. Thus, in regression results not detailed in the tables, I removed INDUS PROFITS, % UNION, and INDUS EARNINGS from the male and female full models in order to assess the total effects of the causally prior variables mentioned above. These reduced-form models revealed that INDUS CAP INTENS, INDUS OLIGOPOLY, INDUS SALES TO GOVT, INDUS SALES PER WORKER, and INDUS SALES PER FIRM do not have significant total effects on pay for either women or men. (Thus the significant negative effect of INDUS CAP INTENS in the female full model with all variables entered should not be interpreted to indicate a total negative effect.) These reduced-form models found INDUS FOR DIVIDENDS to have positive effects on both men's and women's earnings. I ran two additional reduced-form models that removed INDUS EARNINGS in order to assess the total effects of INDUS PROFITS and % UNION. INDUS PROFITS was found to have a significant negative effect on women's pay and no significant effect on men's. The proportion of the occupation that is unionized (% UNION) has a positive effect on both men's and women's pay. Table 3.5 shows that, net of all the other industrial and organizational characteristics, occupations in which the average worker is in an industry with higher average wage levels (INDUS EARNINGS) have higher earnings for both women and men. The lack of effects of many of the other industrial variables, even in the reduced-form models, seems surprising at first glance, since other research has found effects of many of these variables. However, it is important to remember that what are entered here are occupational averages for industrial characteristics. We might expect such effects to be much weaker. However, the importance of including them lies in controlling for those factors that may be correlated with sex composition or other occupational characteristics whose effects this analysis assesses.

Models with Interaction Effects. The regression models in Table 3.5 allow interactions between occupational characteristics, sex, and earnings by running separate regression models for men and women. I have mentioned differences in male and female coefficients in passing in discussing the findings above, without saying much about their appropriate interpretation. Glancing at Table 3.5, one notices that, on many variables, men have larger coefficients than women, whether the coefficients have a positive or negative sign. This means that, compared to women, men experience higher rewards for being in occupations with characteristics with positive returns, but also higher penalties for being in occupations with negative returns. Examples of the latter are the fact that men suffer larger penalties than do women for being in occupations that are high on % MEXICAN, NURTURANCE, self-determination of work speed (SELF DETER WORK SPEED), % MEDICAL INSUR, and being a government worker. Indeed, even the negative effects of % FEMALE are larger in magnitude for men than women (although they have smaller t-statistics). These larger negative coefficients for men do not mean that men in occupations high on these characteristics make less than women in occupations high on these characteristics. Rather, they mean that the extent to which men in occupations high on these variables make less money than men in occupations low on the characteristics is greater than the extent to which women in the first group of occupations earn less than women in the second. Examples of characteristics with positive returns for both sexes, where men's returns are larger, include the cognitive complexity of the job (COGNITIVE FACTOR), AUTHORITY, PRESTIGE, REPETITION, % UNION, and EFFORT REL TO TV. (For all these cases of differences in slopes, the effect is significant for at least one of the sexes and has the same sign for both.) I have not done formal tests of the significance of the differences between men's and women's coefficients since I am not interested in detailed substantive interpretations of each effect. My point here is that the general *pattern* is for effects—either positive or negative—to be larger for men.

What explains the larger positive and negative coefficients for men? I believe that the most likely explanation is that the distribution of men's mean earnings across occupations has a higher variance than does women's. The standard deviation of mean male earnings is $2.67/hour across the 403 occupations on which the analysis is based; the standard deviation of mean female earnings is $1.14/hour. (These, like the regressions, are computed across occupations weighted, respectively, by the number of men and women they contain.) This seems a more compelling interpretation of the differences in slopes than to see them as evidence of discrimination. It is hard to see the fact that men suffer larger penalties for devalued characteristics than women as clearly advantageous. Even men's larger returns for positively rewarded characteristics are not unambiguously an advantage since this also means that the penalties for being in occupations low on these characteristics are greater for men.

I have also tested for a second type of interaction. The male and female full models were estimated with interaction effects included for % FEMALE interacted with each of the 55 other independent variables. (These regression results are not shown in the tables.) A significant interaction in these regressions means that the return to a given characteristic varies with the sex composition of the occupation. Out of a total of 55 interaction effects in each model, I found that 18 were statistically significant for women and 13 for men. There were only four variables for which the same interaction effect was significant and had the same sign for both men and women. These were a positive effect of the interaction of % FEMALE with CREATIVE, and a negative effect of the interaction of % FEMALE with % SELF-EMPLOYED, MANUAL DEXTERITY, and INDUS SALES TO GOVT.

A positive interaction effect can be interpreted two ways. First, it tells us that the effect of the variable with which % FEMALE was interacted is more positive (or less negative) in occupations with high % FEMALE.

Thus, the positive interaction effect of % FEMALE and CREATIVE tells us that being in a highly creative or abstract job (which was, on average, negative for men and nonsignificant for women) is less negative the more women are in the occupation. The second interpretation of a positive interaction effect is that the effect of % FEMALE is less negative (or more positive) at higher levels of the variable that % FEMALE was interacted with. Thus, using this interpretation, the positive interaction of % Female and CREATIVE tells us that, among occupations entailing a higher level of creative and abstract work, the penalty for each increment of % FEMALE is less severe.

A negative interaction with % FEMALE can also be interpreted two ways. It implies that the higher the % FEMALE in the occupation, the less the positive or the more the negative effect of the other variable involved in the interaction. Thus, the effects of SELF-EMPLOYED, MANUAL DEXTERITY, and INDUS SALES TO GOVT (which were negative or nonsignificant in the additive model) are more strongly negative the higher the % FEMALE of the occupation. A negative interaction can also be interpreted a second way. It implies that the higher the other variable, the less the negative effect of % FEMALE. Thus, the negative interactions of % FEMALE with % SELF-EMPLOYED, INDUS SALES TO GOVT, and MANUAL DEXTERITY tell us that the penalty for each increment of the % FEMALE in one's occupation is less when these variables are higher.

Since there is no obvious pattern to the interaction results, I have relied upon the additive model for the major substantive interpretations. The additive model gives us the effects of each variable averaged across levels of % FEMALE. I also rely upon the additive models to compute the decompositions, to which I now turn.

C. Decomposition of the Sex Gap in Pay

The discussions above explored which characteristics of occupations affect their pay. However, the findings that a variable affects earnings does not necessarily imply that it affects the sex gap in earnings. A variable will affect the sex gap in earnings to the extent that it affects earnings positively *and* women have a lower mean than men on the variable, or to the extent that the variable affects earnings negatively *and* women have a higher mean than men on the variable. As discussed above, I am confining the decomposition of sex differences in mean earnings to those components due to sex differences in means on independent variables. I will ignore the components due to sex differences in intercepts and slopes because they cannot be distinguished in these data.

Table 3.6. Male and Female Means on All Variables

Variable	Male Mean	Female Mean	t-Statistic	Difference (Male Minus Female)
Sex composition				
% FEMALE	18.97	62.77	−24.60	−43.80***
Race composition				
% BLACK	8.08	9.92	−4.44	−1.84***
% MEXICAN	3.15	2.81	2.77	0.34**
Cognitive skill and training demands				
COMPLEXITY W/ DATA	3.09	2.81	10.04	0.28***
GEN'L EDUC	3.78	3.72	1.07	0.06
INTELLIGENCE	2.3	2.33	−0.70	−0.03
NUMERICAL APTITUDE	2.88	2.84	0.94	0.04
VERBAL APTITUDE	3.10	3.21	−2.33	−0.11*
FEM EDUC	14.35	14.44	−0.87	−0.09
MALE EDUC	14.67	15.07	−3.19	−0.40**
FEM PERCENT COLLEGE	15.51	12.78	2.27	2.73*
MALE PERCENT COLLEGE	21.46	24.18	−1.76	−2.72
VOC OR OJT TRAINING	29.17	20.42	6.76	8.75***
LEARN NEW THINGS	4.10	4.02	1.80	0.08
COGNITIVE FACTOR	0.29	0.18	0.58	0.11
Social skill demands				
AUTHORITY	0.20	0.12	3.09	0.08**
NURTURANCE	0.07	0.18	−4.76	−0.11***
COMPLEXITY W/ PEOPLE	2.05	1.94	−1.04	−0.11
DEAL W/ PEOPLE	42.24	58.32	−5.87	−16.08***
SOCIAL COMPLEXITY SCALE	0.04	0.34	−2.53	−0.30*
INFLUENCE	12.31	8.66	2.40	3.65*
Physical skill demands				
COMPLEXITY W/ THINGS	2.67	2.79	−0.91	−0.12
EYE-HAND-FOOT COORD	1.55	1.28	8.17	0.27***
SPATIAL APT	2.78	2.35	11.81	0.43***
MOTOR COORD	2.55	2.76	−6.00	−0.21***
MANUAL DEXTERITY	2.74	2.69	1.63	0.05
STRENGTH	2.39	1.89	9.78	0.50***
CLERICAL PERCEPTION	2.54	2.97	−9.09	−0.43***
MEASUREMENT	47.91	26.80	9.65	21.11***
PRECISION	47.94	56.36	−3.32	−8.42***
Amenities				
SOCIETAL CONTRIB	5.60	5.91	−5.21	−0.31***
EFFECT ON OTHERS	4.17	4.19	−0.87	−0.02
PRESTIGE	23.52	15.27	4.31	8.25***
CREATIVE	4.46	2.69	1.84	1.77
SELF-DETER WORK SPEED	3.82	3.79	1.35	0.03
ADEQ TIME FOR JOB	2.97	3.04	−3.65	−0.07***
SELF-DETER HAPPENINGS	3.46	3.21	6.00	0.25***
% MEDICAL INSUR	69.77	71.54	−1.26	−1.77

(continued)

Table 3.6. *(Continued)*

Variable	Male Mean	Female Mean	t-Statistic	Difference (Male Minus Female)
POWER	7.22	7.26	−0.85	−0.04
CONTROL	28.00	18.67	4.41	9.33***
Disamenities				
EMERGENCY STRESS	3.24	9.33	−4.44	−6.09***
REPETITION	20.73	21.29	−0.28	−0.56
AGAINST CONSCIENCE	2.79	2.81	−0.98	−0.02
FUMES	10.25	5.67	4.11	4.58***
COLD	1.26	0.41	2.46	0.85*
HAZARDS	18.97	7.15	13.88	11.82***
HEAT	3.33	1.63	2.78	1.70**
OUTDOORS	6.35	1.67	6.33	4.68***
WET	4.77	2.77	3.11	2.00**
ATTACK HAZARD	0.22	0.18	3.64	0.04***
STOOP	33.55	14.08	9.68	19.47***
CLIMB	17.35	4.39	9.02	12.96***
REACH/HANDLE	73.68	79.90	−3.04	−6.22**
NOISE	25.59	7.90	10.88	17.69***
Effort				
EFFORT REL TO TV	0.56	0.56	0	0.00
EFFORT	3.70	3.68	1.82	0.02
EXTRA EFFORT	3.44	3.48	−2.60	−0.04**
FAMILY IMPORTANCE	6.17	6.03	3.93	0.14***
Industrial and organizational characteristics				
% GOVT	12.00	18.05	−5.11	−6.05***
% SELF-EMPLOYED	6.96	4.09	5.29	2.87***
% UNION	24.41	15.70	6.74	8.71***
INDUS CAP INTENS	0.52	0.65	−2.59	−0.13**
INDUS OLIGOPOLY	20.11	19.12	1.71	0.99
INDUS FOR DIVIDENDS	17.09	12.49	4.93	4.60***
INDUS SALES TO GOVT	6.96	6.62	1.16	0.34
INDUS SALES PER WKR	0.41	0.40	1.00	0.01
INDUS PROFITS	0.06	0.06	0.00	0.00
INDUS SALES PER FIRM	48.42	48.02	0.18	0.40
INDUS EARNINGS	8402.78	8190.80	2.36	211.98*

Note: These means were computecd on the 403 occupations that had nonmissing values for all variables in the full regression model presented in Table 3.5.

* $p < .05$, two-tailed test. Indicates mean difference is statistically significant at the .05 level.

** $p < .01$, two-tailed test.

*** $p < .001$, two-tailed test.

The presentation of results of the decomposition is organized as follows. First, Table 3.6 shows the male and female mean on each variable and indicates whether this difference is statistically significant. Both male and female means were computed across the same 403 occupations used in the regression analyses because they did not have missing values on any variable in the full model. A given occupation contributes the same score to the calculation of either the male or female mean. However, since occupations are weighted by their number of women to compute the female mean and by their number of men for the male mean, sex differences in means on the independent variables arise only from men's and women's differential distribution across occupations.

Tables 3.7 and 3.8 present the results from the decomposition of the sex gap in pay using the first two regression models in Table 3.5, respectively. (The third model in Table 3.5 cannot be used for decomposition since it does not contain the same variables for the male and female regressions.) Tables 3.7 and 3.8 show, for each variable, the sex difference in means, the slope (i.e., coefficient) from the male and from the female regression, and then two estimates of the dollar portion of the sex gap in pay explained by the sex difference in means on this variable. The first estimate is the mean difference times the male slope. This tells us how many dollars per hour men would lose if they had the female mean on this variable instead of their own mean, but retained the return for this characteristic that the regression analysis shows men to experience. A positive number here means that men have the advantageous mean (i.e., a higher mean on a variable where they have a positive slope, or a lower mean on a variable where they have a negative slope). A negative number means that women have an advantageous mean on this variable (i.e., a higher mean on a variable where men have a positive slope, or a smaller mean on a variable where men have a negative slope); thus, if men moved to the female mean but retained their own slope they would gain earnings. The second estimate is the sex difference in means on the variable times the female slope. This tell us how many dollars per hour women would gain if they had the male mean on this variable instead of their own mean, but retained the return for this characteristic that the regression analysis shows women to experience. Positive and negative numbers have meanings as above, except that women's slopes have been used.

Finally, Table 3.9 adds these estimates of the dollar proportion of the sex gap in pay explained by sex differences in means on each variable into totals for each group of variables, then converts this total to a percentage of the overall sex gap in pay. The conversion is done by dividing the total dollar contribution for a group of variables by the dollar amount of the sex gap in pay in the 403 occupations used for the

Table 3.7. Decomposition of Sex Gap in Pay into Portions (in Dollars) Explained by Mean Differences, Using Full Regression Model

Variable	Difference: Male Minus Female Mean	Male Slope	Female Slope	Diff. Times Male Slope	Diff. Times Female Slope
Sex composition					
% FEMALE	−43.80*	−.005	−.004*	.20	.17
Race composition					
% BLACK	−1.84*	−0.019	−0.010	0.04	0.02
% MEXICAN	0.34*	−0.132*	−0.042	−0.05	−0.01
Total for group				−0.01	0.01
Cognitive skill and training demands					
COGNITIVE FACTOR	0.11	0.774*	0.466*	0.08	0.05
Social skill demands					
AUTHORITY	0.08*	1.292*	0.376*	0.10	0.03
NURTURANCE	−0.11*	−1.707*	−0.441*	0.20	0.05
SOCIAL COMPLEXITY SCALE	−0.30*	0.043	−0.021	−0.01	0.01
INFLUENCE	3.65*	0.001	−0.003	0.01	−0.01
Total for group				0.30	0.08
Physical skill demands					
COMPLEXITY W/ THINGS	−0.12	−0.095	−0.017	0.01	0.00
EYE-HAND-FOOT COORD	0.27*	0.005	0.217	0.00	0.06
SPATIAL APT	0.43*	0.048	0.158	0.02	0.07
MOTOR COORD	−0.21*	0.315	0.441*	−0.06	−0.09
MANUAL DEXTERITY	0.05	0.628	−0.226	0.03	−0.01
STRENGTH	0.50*	−0.042	0.213*	−0.02	0.11
CLERICAL PERCEPTION	−0.43*	−0.081	−0.172	0.04	0.08
MEASUREMENT	21.11*	0.001	0.002	0.03	0.04
PRECISION	−8.42*	−0.006	−0.001	0.05	0.01
Total for group				0.10	0.27
Amenities					
SOCIETAL CONTRIB	−0.31*	0.092	0.096*	−0.03	−0.03
EFFECT ON OTHERS	−0.02	0.302	0.155	−0.01	−0.00
PRESTIGE	8.25*	0.014*	0.003	0.12	0.02
CREATIVE	1.77	−0.029*	−0.001	−0.05	−0.00
SELF-DETER WORK SPEED	0.03	−1.015*	−0.299*	−0.03	−0.01
ADEQ TIME FOR JOB	−0.07*	−0.016	0.054	0.00	−0.00
SELF-DETER HAPPENINGS	0.25*	0.115	−0.030	0.03	−0.01
% MEDICAL INSUR	−1.77	−0.019*	−0.006*	0.03	0.01
POWER	−0.04	−0.204	0.024	0.01	−0.00
CONTROL	9.33*	−0.005	−0.005*	−0.04	−0.05
Total for group				0.03	−0.07
Disamenities					
EMERGENCY STRESS	−6.09*	0.001	0.003	−0.01	−0.02
REPETITION	−0.56	0.014*	0.007*	−0.01	−0.00
AGAINST CONSCIENCE	−0.02	0.243	0.305*	−0.01	−0.01

(continued)

Table 3.7.   (Continued)

Variable	Difference: Male Minus Female Mean	Male Slope	Female Slope	Diff. Times Male Slope	Diff. Times Female Slope
FUMES	4.58*	−0.000	−0.002	−0.00	−0.01
COLD	0.85*	0.021	0.008	0.02	0.01
HAZARDS	11.82*	−0.006	−0.005*	−0.08	−0.06
HEAT	1.70*	0.007	0.005	0.01	0.01
OUTDOORS	4.68*	0.007	−0.004	0.04	−0.02
WET	2.00*	0.004	0.002	0.01	0.00
ATTACK HAZARD	0.04*	−0.855	−0.099	−0.04	−0.00
STOOP	19.47*	0.005	0.003	0.09	0.06
CLIMB	12.96*	−0.001	0.002	−0.01	0.02
REACH/HANDLE	−6.22*	0.003	−0.003	−0.02	0.02
NOISE	17.69*	−0.003	−0.004	−0.06	−0.07
Total for group				−0.07	−0.07
Effort					
EFFORT REL TO TV	−0.00	6.703*	2.134*	−0.02	−0.01
EFFORT	0.02	−0.108	0.141	−0.00	0.00
EXTRA EFFORT	−0.04*	−0.209	0.065	0.01	−0.00
FAMILY IMPORTANCE	0.14*	−0.224	−0.118*	−0.03	−0.02
Total for group				−0.04	−0.03
Industrial and organizational characteristics					
% GOVT WKR	−6.05*	−0.021*	−0.002	0.13	0.01
% SELF-EMPLOYED	2.87*	0.008	−0.022*	0.02	−0.06
% UNION	8.71*	0.018*	0.001	0.16	0.01
INDUS CAP INTENS	−0.13*	0.190	−0.155*	−0.03	0.02
INDUS OLIGOPOLY	0.99	−0.025	−0.009	−0.03	−0.01
INDUS FOR DIVIDENDS	4.60*	0.003	0.011*	0.01	0.05
INDUS SALES TO GOVT	0.34	−0.006	−0.052*	−0.00	−0.02
INDUS SALES PER WKR	0.01	−0.591	−0.155	−0.01	−0.00
INDUS PROFITS	0.00	2.605	−8.639*	0.00	−0.00
INDUS SALES PER FIRM	0.40	0.002	0.001	0.00	0.00
INDUS EARNINGS	211.98*	0.0004*	0.0003*	0.09	0.07
Total for group				0.34	0.07

Note:
* Indicates that the coefficient or the sex difference in means is statistically significant at the .05 level, using a two-tailed test.

regression analyses, \$3.50/hour, to get a percentage. This yields, for each group of variables in each of the first two models in Table 3.5, two estimates of the percentage of the gap explained, one using the male slopes and one using the female slopes. Table 3.9 also presents a weighted average of these two estimates for each group of variables and for each of the two models. For each variable group, the estimate using the male slope is weighted by 0.66, the proportion of the 1980 full-time year-round labor force in the 403 occupations in the analyses that were men.

Table 3.8. Decomposition of Sex Gap in Pay into Portions (in Dollars) Explained by Mean Differences, Using Regression Model Containing Only Variables Significant for at Least One Sex

Variable	Difference: Male Minus Female Mean	Male Slope	Female Slope	Diff. Times Male Slope	Diff. Times Female Slope
Sex composition					
% FEMALE	−43.80*	−0.009*	−0.005*	0.38	0.24
Race composition					
% MEXICAN	0.34*	−0.105*	−0.029	−0.04	−0.01
Cognitive skill and training demands					
COGNITIVE FACTOR	0.11	0.821*	0.493*	0.09	0.05
Social skill demands					
AUTHORITY	0.08*	1.367*	0.448*	0.11	0.04
NURTURANCE	−0.11*	−1.388*	−0.257*	0.17	0.03
Total for group				0.28	0.07
Physical skill demands					
MOTOR COORD	−0.21*	0.263	0.243*	−0.05	−0.05
STRENGTH	0.50*	0.365*	0.378*	0.18	0.19
Total for group				0.13	0.14
Amenities					
SOCIETAL CONTRIB	−0.31*	0.178*	0.113*	−0.06	−0.04
PRESTIGE	8.25*	0.016*	0.001	0.13	0.01
CREATIVE	1.77	−0.027*	0.002	−0.05	−0.00
SELF-DETER WORK SPEED	0.03	−1.203*	−0.341*	−0.03	−0.01
% MEDICAL INSUR	−1.77	−0.017*	−0.004*	0.03	0.01
CONTROL	9.33*	−0.005	−0.001	−0.04	−0.01
Total for group				−0.02	−0.04
Disamenities					
REPETITION	−0.56	0.012*	0.008*	−0.01	−0.00
AGAINST CONSCIENCE	−0.02	0.391	0.221*	−0.01	−0.01
HAZARDS	11.82*	−0.005	−0.001	−0.06	−0.02
Total for group				−0.08	−0.03
Effort					
EFFORT REL TO TV	−0.00	6.553*	1.472*	−0.02	−0.00
FAMILY IMPORTANCE	0.14*	−0.294*	−0.148*	−0.04	−0.02
Total for group				−0.06	−0.02
Industrial and organizational characteristics					
% UNION	8.71*	0.015*	0.001	0.13	0.01
% GOVT WKR	−6.05*	−0.020*	−0.004	0.12	0.02
% SELF-EMPLOYED	2.87*	0.015	−0.018*	0.04	−0.05
INDUS CAP INTENS	−0.13*	0.136	−0.144*	−0.02	0.02
INDUS FOR DIVIDENDS	4.60*	0.003	0.005	0.01	0.02
INDUS SALES TO GOVT	0.34	−0.027	−0.045	−0.01	−0.02
INDUS PROFITS	0.00	−3.485	−11.221*	−0.00	−0.00
INDUS EARNINGS	211.98*	0.0004*	0.0003*	0.08	0.07
Total for group				0.35	0.07

Note:
* Indicates that the coefficient or the sex difference in means is statistically significant at the .05 level, using a two-tailed test.

Table 3.9. Summary of Decomposition Results: Percentage of Sex Gap in Pay Explained by Mean Differences in Groups of Independent Variables in Two Models

Model:	Full Model			Only Variables Significant for at Least One Sex		
Independent Variable Groups	Using Male Slopes[1]	Using Female Slopes[2]	Using Weighted Average[3]	Using Male Slopes	Using Female Slopes	Using Weighted Average
Sex composition	5.7	4.9	5.4	10.9	6.9	9.5
Race composition	−0.3	0.3	−0.1	−1.1	−0.3	−0.9
Cognitive skill and training demands	2.3	1.4	2.0	2.6	1.4	2.2
Social skill demands	8.6	2.3	6.5	8.0	2.0	6.0
Physical skill demands	2.9	7.7	4.5	3.7	4.0	3.8
Amenities	0.9	−2.0	−0.1	−0.6	−1.1	−0.8
Disamenities	−2.0	−2.0	−2.0	−2.3	−0.9	−1.8
Effort	−1.2	−0.9	−1.1	−1.7	−0.6	−1.3
Industrial and organizational characteristics	9.7	2.0	7.1	10.0	2.0	7.3

Notes:
[1] This is calculated, based on information in Table 3.7 or 3.8, as follows:

$$\frac{[\Sigma(\bar{X}_m - \bar{X}_f)b_m] \times 100}{3.50}$$

where m = male, f = female, b = slope, summation is across all the independent variables, and \$3.50 = the sex gap in pay in the 403 occupations upon which all regression analyses were based.

[2] This is calculated as follows:

$$\frac{[\Sigma(\bar{X}_m - \bar{X}_f)b_f] \times 100}{3.50}$$

where notation is as in note 1.

[3] This is calculated as follows:

$$\frac{([\Sigma(\bar{X}_m - \bar{X}_f)b_m] \times 0.66 + [\Sigma(\bar{X}_m - \bar{X}_f)b_f] \times 0.34) \times 100}{3.50}$$

where notation is as in note 1, and 0.66 and 0.34 are weights reflecting the proportion of the full-time year-round labor force that was male and female, respectively.

The estimate using the female slope receives a weight of 0.34 because women were 34% of this labor force. This weighted-average estimate is a sensible estimate of what would happen to the sex gap in pay if men and women came to have the same mean on some group of occupational variables if we assume that the implied convergence of men's and women's occupational distributions would lead men to move toward women's slopes and vice versa.